International Agricultural Development

THE JOHNS HOPKINS STUDIES IN DEVELOPMENT

Vernon W. Ruttan and T. Paul Schultz, *Consulting Editors*

International Agricultural Development

THIRD EDITION

Edited by

Carl K. Eicher and John M. Staatz

THE JOHNS HOPKINS UNIVERSITY PRESS

Baltimore and London

The Johns Hopkins University Press
2715 North Charles Street, Baltimore, Maryland 21218-4363
The Johns Hopkins Press Ltd., London
www.jhu.press.edu

Library of Congress Cataloging-in-Publication Data will be
found at the end of this book.
A catalog record for this book is available from
the British Library.

ISBN 0-8018-5878-X
ISBN 0-8018-5879-8 (pbk.)

Contents

PART V
LESSONS FROM ECONOMIES IN TRANSITION

Preface

In 1990, when the second edition of this book was published, the Cold War was winding down, the role of the state in development was being redefined, and nongovernmental organizations were struggling to make the transition from relief organizations to development agencies. The decade of the nineties has turned out to be a period of revolutionary change in thinking about the role of the state, institutions, and markets in development. State companies in Africa, Latin America, Asia, and the former Soviet Union and Central and Eastern Europe have been put on the auction block like items in a gigantic "white elephant" sale. Economic growth has exploded in many countries in Asia; China, the world's most populous nation, has doubled its per capita income in a decade.

The sweeping political and economic changes of the nineties have ushered in a more global and more market-driven view of development and have called into question the simplicity of the term "Third World," which encompasses countries that have become increasingly diverse since the 1970s. Grouping Singapore with Chad, or Brazil with Bangladesh now confuses more than it enlightens. The development of institutions adapted to individual settings is now at the core of development thinking, and prepackaged institutional models such as T&V (training and visit) extension are being rapidly replaced by more pluralistic and demand-driven models that are less dependent on the whims and pressure of donors. Today mainstream debates about development in poor countries are centered on globalization of economies, policies, and institutions; and on issues such as privatization and sustainability. Because of these changes, we replaced "Third World" in the title of this edition with a more global title: *International Agricultural Development.* The geographical scope of this new edition encompasses low- and middle-income countries throughout the world.

Despite substantial economic growth in many developing countries during the 1990s, rural poverty, malnutrition, and food insecurity remain urgent problems that demand attention. Various Food and Agriculture Organization and World Bank reports estimate that there are 800 million to 1.3 billion poor in the world. Half to three-fourths of the poor live in rural areas and depend on increasing agricultural productivity and off-farm employment for their livelihood. The focus of this edition is on improving our understanding of how to promote sustainable agricultural growth and rural economic development in low- and middle-income countries throughout the world in the context of an increasingly global economy.

This book is a product of the vast agricultural and rural development litera-

ix

ture that has been produced since the 1950s. It includes twenty-four new chapters, while retaining eleven key contributions from the first and second editions. Ten of the twenty-four new chapters are original essays commissioned to fill gaps in the literature. The thirty-five essays address three basic questions about agricultural development in low- and middle-income countries: What are the strategic roles of agriculture in national development strategies? How can the agrarian transformation be accelerated? How can rural economic development be promoted to generate jobs and reduce poverty in rural areas? Our selection of articles and papers was guided by three convictions. First, we believe that agricultural and rural economic development should be viewed as a long-term historical process. Second, analysts and policy makers need to understand the growing interdependence between agriculture and the rest of the economy, the growing convergence of rural and urban issues, and the increasing globalization of the world economy. Third, although agricultural development issues are often best understood in an open-economy, general equilibrium framework, we believe that that framework needs to be built upon a firm microeconomic data base. Careful empirical studies are needed of farmer, merchant, and consumer behavior, and of the institutional arrangements that influence that behavior, in order to understand how rural economies function, how they are likely to react to new policies, and how they interact with other sectors of the national and global economies. The contribution of empirical research to policy analysis is a major theme of this book.

Guided by favorable feedback from teachers and students, we have retained the five hallmarks of the first and second editions: (1) an introductory chapter that provides a framework for the book and traces the evolution of the field of agricultural development from the 1950s through the 1990s, (2) introductory comments for each section to highlight the key issues in each chapter and the common themes in each section and to serve as a guide to the broader literature, (3) a treatment of both the theory and the practice of agricultural development, (4) analysis of both macro- and microeconomic aspects of the agricultural sector and the food system, and (5) country studies of food systems in transition to provide broader insights into the interaction between policies, technology, and institutions in the development process.

This new edition has been extensively revised to reflect the new directions in development thought and policy. It is designed to assist teachers and students by examining what has been learned theoretically and empirically about agricultural and rural economic development since the 1950s. It concentrates on core problems: market failures, food insecurity, rural poverty, environmental degradation, income and asset inequality, fiscally unsustainable organizations, the changing roles of the public and private sectors in research, input delivery systems and marketing, and the low rates of agricultural growth in much of sub-Saharan Africa.

This book is designed to be used as a text in courses in international agricultural development and as a supplementary text in economic development courses.

Space constraints explain the lack of chapters devoted exclusively to important topics such as agricultural marketing, rural labor markets, nutrition, and biotechnology. We have, however, included in chapter 1 and in the introduction to each part extensive references to the vast literature on agricultural development.

We wish to thank numerous colleagues and students at Michigan State University and other universities, foundations, and international development agencies for their counsel on this edition. Our task in compiling the new edition has been immensely facilitated by the hard work of Pat Eisele and Roxie Damer.

I

The Challenge

Introduction

The three chapters in part I provide a historical overview of the evolution of thinking about agricultural development, analyze the controversy over the world food outlook to year 2025, and examine the reasons for the sharp decline in foreign aid for agricultural development over the past decade. In chapter 1 we discuss the evolution of thinking about the role of agriculture, the state, and the market from the 1950s through the 1990s. The authors highlight the dominance of the agricultural sector in the initial stages of development in poor countries, the need to generate and capture some of the agricultural surplus for reinvestment in other sectors without destroying incentives to farmers and traders, the concurrent need to reinvest some of the agricultural surplus back into the agricultural sector, and the need to maintain the natural resource base for future generations. The authors also discuss the changing development approaches of donors and how difficult it is to get donors to take the long view and invest in helping low- and middle-income countries[1] build a *system* of fiscally sustainable development institutions. Chapter 1 concludes by noting that, although much has been learned about the agricultural development process over the past five decades, an emerging set of issues demands research attention by social and technical scientists. A central issue to be worked out is the evolving redefinition of the roles of the state, the private sector, and civil society in development and in agricultural policy. How countries resolve this issue critically determines how they address such problems as rural poverty, market failures, marketing, food safety, natural resource management, the role of NGOs, and the financing of research and farmer support services. Chapter 1's extensive bibliography highlights the growing number of empirical studies about the complexities of agricultural development.

In chapter 2 Alex McCalla discusses the disagreement among food experts over the world food outlook to year 2025. In considering McCalla's analysis, much can be learned from similar disagreements in the 1970s over the world food outlook to year 2000. After the world food crisis of 1972 to 1974, several research teams carried out in-depth studies of the world food outlook to the year 2000. A decade later, Fox and Ruttan (1983) reviewed these major studies of food balance projections and concluded that almost without exception the studies forecast rising food deficits and increasing real food prices in developing countries in the 1980s and 1990s. The spread of the Green Revolution, however, undermined the food pessimism of the seventies, and by the early eighties grain supplies in Asia had sharply increased.[2] By the mid-eighties, real world rice prices had reached an all-time low. Fox and Ruttan concluded their assessment by noting that most food projection studies devoted too much attention to the short-run events, such as weather and oil shocks, occurring at the time the assessments were made.

Triggered by volatile grain prices in world markets, unfavorable weather in the United States (1995–96), and China's sharp increase in food imports in the early 1990s, a number of analysts initiated studies of the long-term food outlook. A Food and Agriculture Organization (FAO) team looked ahead to 2010, while analysts from the International Food Policy Research Institute (IFPRI) selected 2020 and a World Bank team selected the year 2025. In chapter 2, McCalla reviews these studies and addresses an important question surrounding the world food outlook in year 2025: Why is there so much agreement on the demand side and so little agreement on the supply side of the world food outlook? McCalla notes that most demographers agree that the world's population will exceed 8 billion by 2025 and that food demand will likely double by 2025 because of the increase in population, urbanization, and per capita incomes.[3] The demographic projections imply that around 80 million people will be added every year to the world population over the coming twenty-five years (United Nations 1996). Most food and nutrition experts also agree that there will be wide regional variations in the supply and demand prospects of food staples and in the severity of malnutrition and hunger. Most food analysts also agree that sub-Saharan Africa and South Asia will face particularly difficult food insecurity problems because of poverty and the lack of effective demand (Pinstrup-Andersen and Pandya-Lorch 1997a).

McCalla examines why there are such sharp differences in the world food outlook by analysts in the World Bank, the World Watch Institute, the FAO, and IFPRI. The 1990s debate over the world food outlook was kicked off in 1993 when two World Bank economists, Mitchell and Ingco, circulated a draft paper that concluded that there was no world food crisis, that "Malthus must wait," and that China's sharp increase in food demand could easily be met with higher productivity and a modest increase in grain imports. This paper was subsequently updated by Mitchell, Ingco, and Duncan and published as the *World Food Outlook* in 1997. In 1994 Lester Brown and Hal Kane presented a pessimistic view of the world food outlook in *Full House,* followed a year later by Brown's controversial book *Who Will Feed China?: Wake-up Call for a Small Planet* (Brown 1995). Brown's book on feeding China served as a lightning rod for debate, having been written at a time when bad weather in the United States, China's increasing food imports, and China's 8.3 percent per capita GNP growth rate (the second highest in the world from 1985 to 1995) led to fears of much higher world grain prices in the coming decade.[4]

Between these poles of food optimism and food pessimism are more conventional views by analysts for the FAO (Alexandratos 1995) and IFPRI (Rosegrant and Agcaoili 1994), who believe that the challenge of feeding a growing world population is indeed serious but can be met if investments in agricultural research increase and donors reverse the decline in support for agriculture. There are many questionable assumptions in each of the major studies and many regional issues that require more in-depth treatment.

McCalla's synthesis of the four views of the world food outlook concludes that regardless of who is correct "the productivity-food production challenge for the globe is very substantial." In 1997 approximately 840 million people in the world were chronically malnourished, and even with moderate increases in food production, the number of malnourished children in the world is likely to fall by only about 17 percent between 1990 and 2020 (Pinstrup-Andersen and Pandyra-Lorch 1997b). In India, the poorest 30 percent of the population (roughly 285 million) has seen practically no improvement in their low cereal and nutrient intakes over the past twenty-five years (Rao and Radhakrishna 1997).

Although McCalla focuses on the supply side debates, there are also some important demand side issues that require intensive analysis in world food projections. The first is quantifying and figuring out how to meet the rising global demand for feedgrains that will accompany increased consumption of livestock products as consumers' incomes move through the range of $500 to $5,000 per year. The second is the need to compute the investments needed in the entire food marketing system (not just farm-level production) as countries become more urbanized and consumers demand more marketing services. The third is meeting the growth in the demand for food if current policy and institutional reforms lead to higher rates of growth and a reduction of poverty in Africa and South Asia.

On the supply side, the following issues require ongoing analysis and debate: biotechnology, environmental degradation, water resources, sustainability, international agricultural trade, and the industrialization of the global food system. As D. Gale Johnson (1997, 11) points out, access to knowledge is likely to be more important than access to land in determining future food supplies because "agricultural land now accounts for no more than 1.5 percent of the resources of industrial nations . . . and . . . the major factors that limit the growth of food production in developing countries are knowledge and research, availability of nonfarm inputs and reasonable prices and the government policies that affect incentives."

In chapter 3 John Mellor addresses foreign aid and agriculture by chronicling the history of foreign aid and development, calling attention to the success of foreign aid in general and food aid in particular. He highlights the success of foreign aid in helping solve Asia's first-generation problem—food production—and why this success unexpectedly contributed to a subsequent decline in donor aid to agriculture. Mellor and many other agricultural scientists are distressed that agriculture has been downgraded in the portfolio of many development agencies and that the number of agriculturalists in most agencies has fallen. He points out that global bilateral aid to agriculture was cut by one-fourth and multilateral aid to agriculture was cut by one-third from 1990 to 1993.

Turning to Africa, Mellor raises a fundamental point by noting that donors have failed to apply in Africa what they had learned about helping solve the first-generation food production problem in Asia. In the sixties and seventies, donors helped build research, infrastructure, and human capital and stayed the course until Asia's critical food bottleneck was overcome in the early to middle 1980s. But instead of donors helping solve Africa's first-generation food production problems, Mellor observes, donors became captivated with second-generation problems, such as rural poverty, environmental degradation, and the neglect of women. In the 1990s, donors reduced their support for national agricultural research and extension projects in many countries in Africa. Mellor calls for increased and sustained donor support for training and institution building in Africa.

NOTES

1. The World Bank's 1997 *World Development Report* classified 107 countries (with populations of more than a million and having an adequate data base) as being either low- or middle-income economies (World Bank 1997).

2. The increase of grain supplies in Asia did not mean that hunger was banished. Although the proportion of the Asian population that was hungry fell, many still lacked the income to gain access to the increased food supplies.

3. See Cohen (1995) and Dyson (1996) for a discussion of population growth rates.

4. Brown's book has subsequently been discredited by many specialists on Chinese agriculture, including Justin Lin (see Lin 1998).

REFERENCES

Alexandratos, Nikos, ed. 1995. *World Agriculture: Towards 2010 (An FAO Study).* Rome and Chichester: U.N. Food and Agriculture Organization and John Wiley.

Brown, Lester. 1995. *Who Will Feed China? Wake-up Call for a Small Planet.* New York: W. W. Norton.

Brown, Lester R., and Hal Kane. 1994. *Full House: Reassessing the Earth's Population Carrying Capacity.* New York: W. W. Norton.

Cohen, Joel. 1995. *How Many People Can the Earth Support?* New York: Norton.

Dyson, Tim. 1996. *Population and Food: Global Trends and Future Prospects.* London: Routledge.

Fox, Glenn, and Vernon Ruttan. 1983. "A Guide to LDC Food Balance Projections." *European Review of Agricultural Economics* 10:325–56.

Johnson, D. Gale. 1997. "Agriculture and the Wealth of Nations." *American Economic Review* 87 (2): 1–11.

Lin, Justin. 1998. "How Did China Feed Itself in the Past? How Will China Feed Itself in the Future?" (Second Distinguished Economist Lecture) Mexico, D.F.: CIMMYT.

Mitchell, Donald O., Merlinda D. Ingco, and Ronald C. Duncan. 1997. *The World Food Outlook.* Cambridge: Cambridge University Press.

Pinstrup-Andersen, Per, and Rajul Pandya-Lorch. 1997a. "Can Everybody Be Well Fed by Year 2020 without Damaging Natural Resources?" CIMMYT Economics Program. First Distinguished Economist Lecture. 14 February. Mexico, D.F., CIMMYT.

———. 1997b. "Food Security: A Global Perspective." Plenary paper presented at 23rd International Conference of Agricultural Economists, August 10–16, Sacramento, Calif. Washington, D.C.: International Food Policy Institute.

Rao, C. H. Hanumantha, and R. Radhakrishna. 1997. "National Food Security: A Policy Perspective for India." Plenary paper presented at 23rd International Conference of Agricultural Economists, August 10–16, Sacramento, Calif.

Rosegrant, Mark W., and Mercedita Agcaoili. 1994. "Global and Regional Food Demand, Supply and Trade Prospects to 2010." (Paper presented at roundtable meeting, Population and Food in the Early Twenty-first Century: Meeting Future Food Needs of an Increasing World Population, February 14–16, Washington, D.C.) Washington, D.C.: International Food Policy Research Institute.

United Nations. 1996. *World Population Prospects: The 1996 Revision.* New York: United Nations.

World Bank. 1997. *World Development Report, 1997.* Washington, D.C.: World Bank.

1

Agricultural Development Ideas in Historical Perspective

JOHN M. STAATZ AND CARL K. EICHER

 Economists have grappled with issues of growth and development since at least the time of the mercantilists in the seventeenth century. Yet modern development economics, as a field of study of "less developed" countries, emerged as a separate branch of study only following World War II.[1] The past half-century has witnessed remarkable economic and agricultural growth in many developing countries, in spite of rapid population growth. The FAO estimates that over the period 1969–71 to 1990–92, the proportion of food-insecure people in developing countries fell from 35 percent to 20 percent, despite an increase in world population of 57 percent, almost all of which (86 percent) occurred in developing countries (Alexandratos 1995). Between 1972 and 1995, the rate of infant mortality in these countries fell by half, and life expectancy increased by ten years (World Bank 1996, 1). Over the same period, a number of countries, particularly in Southeast Asia, witnessed rapid increases in per capita incomes and industrialization of their economies.

Yet despite this formidable progress, development economists still face major conceptual and practical challenges. In a world where capital and technology are extremely mobile, why do roughly 1.3 billion people, most in South Asia, East Asia and sub-Saharan Africa, still remain mired in poverty (Pinstrup-Andersen and Pandya-Lorch 1997)? Why, in spite of a 20 percent increase in per capita world food production between 1961–63 and 1996 do roughly 840 million people still suffer chronic malnutrition (1)? What explains the rocky road to market and policy reform in many countries, particularly in sub-Saharan Africa and parts of Eastern Europe and the former Soviet Union? Is it, as Mancur Olson (1982) and Joseph Stiglitz (chapter 6 in this volume) suggest, mainly a question of the institutions that different countries adopt to govern their economies? Or is it, as Spencer and Badiane (1995) argue, that the Green Revolution strategy that sparked growth in much of Asia during the 1960s and 1970s is unsuited to the

JOHN M. STAATZ is professor of agricultural economics and CARL K. EICHER is University Distinguished Professor in the Department of Agricultural Economics and African Studies at Michigan State University.

ecological and infrastructural conditions in lagging areas? What practical steps can economists suggest to break the shackles of poverty that still grip many countries? What role should agriculture and rural development play in a poverty alleviation and growth strategy? Will the technologies and strategies that fueled rapid growth in Asia and parts of Latin America be sustainable in the face of rising population pressure and increased demands for food and other natural resources? These are the major questions addressed by this book. We begin in this chapter by laying out what has been learned over the past half-century, both theoretically and empirically, about the role of agriculture in economic development. This background sets the stage for the chapters that follow, which address the specific challenges in designing agricultural development and poverty alleviation strategies for the twenty-first century.

The history of the field of agricultural development can be divided roughly into three periods. During the economic-growth-and-modernization era of the 1950s and 1960s, development was defined largely in terms of growth in average per capita output. In the 1970s, Western development economists stressed the concept of growth with equity, broadening their focus to include income distribution, employment, and nutrition, and greatly expanding the amount of empirical research on the rural economy. The 1980s and 1990s have been a period of macroeconomic and economic policy reform, momentous institutional restructuring, and heightened emphasis on food security and environmental sustainability. The prevailing view of agriculture's role in development changed profoundly during these periods. This chapter examines the changing view of agriculture in economic development during each of these three periods and concludes by outlining some of the development challenges for the early decades of the twenty-first century.

THE ROLE OF AGRICULTURE IN DEVELOPMENT ECONOMICS, 1950–69

WESTERN DEVELOPMENT ECONOMISTS' PERSPECTIVES ON AGRICULTURE

Most Western development economists of the 1950s did not view agriculture as an important contributor to economic growth.[2] As I. M. D. Little comments in his survey of development economics, "It is fairly obvious from reading their works that the leading development economists of the 1950s knew little about tropical agriculture or rural life. They had no time for rural rides and there was no considerable body of empirical grassroots literature on which they could draw" (Little 1982, 106). Development was often equated with the structural transformation of the economy, that is, with the decline in agriculture's relative share of the national product and of the labor force. The role of development economics was seen as facilitating that transformation by discovering ways to transfer resources, especially labor, from traditional agriculture to industry, the presumed engine of growth. Agriculture itself was often treated as a "black box from which people, and food to feed them, and perhaps capital could be released" (105).

Development economics throughout the 1950s and 1960s was strongly influenced by W. Arthur Lewis's 1954 article "Economic Development with Unlimited Supplies of Labor." Lewis presented a model of expansion in an economy with two sectors—a modern capitalist exchange sector and an indigenous non-capitalist sector, which was dominated by subsistence farming. Lewis's model focused on how the transfer of labor from the subsistence sector (where the marginal productivity of a laborer approached zero as a limiting case) to the capitalist sector facilitated economic growth through reinvestment of profits. The labor supply facing the capitalist sector was "'unlimited' in the sense that when the capitalist sector offers additional employment opportunities at the existing wage rate, the numbers willing to work at the existing wage rate will be greater than the demand; the supply curve of labor is infinitely elastic at the ruling wage" (Meier 1976, 158). In Lewis's model, expansion in the capitalist sector continued until earnings in the two sectors were equated, at which point a dual-sector model was no longer relevant; growth proceeded as in a one-sector neoclassical model. Lewis's analysis was later extended by Ranis and Fei (1961) and Jorgenson (1961).

Most economists equated Lewis's capitalist sector with industry and the non-capitalist sector with traditional agriculture and argued that "surplus" labor and other resources should be transferred from agriculture to industry in order to promote growth. Many analysts concluded that since economic growth facilitated the structural transformation of the economy in the *long run,* the rapid transfer of resources (especially "surplus" labor) from agriculture to industry was an appropriate *short-run* economic development strategy.[3] But Johnston observed that "this preoccupation with 'surplus labor' often seems to have encouraged neglect of the agricultural sector as well as a tendency to assume too readily that a surplus can and should be extracted from agriculture, while neglecting the difficult requirements that must be met if agriculture is to play a positive role in facilitating overall economic growth" (1970, 378).

The relative neglect of agriculture in the 1950s was reinforced by two other developments. In 1949, Raul Prebisch and Hans Singer independently formulated the thesis that over time the terms of trade would turn against countries that export primary products and import manufactures.[4] From this they concluded that the scope for growth through agricultural and other primary exports was very limited. Prebisch and his colleagues at the United Nations Economic Commission for Latin America (ECLA) therefore advocated a development strategy based upon import substitution of manufactured goods rather than promotion of agricultural exports.[5] The "secular-decline hypothesis" became an article of faith for some development economists and planners, reinforcing the tendency to downplay agriculture's potential role in development.

Albert Hirschman's book *The Strategy of Economic Development* (1958) also strongly influenced development thinking in the fifties. Hirschman introduced the concept of *linkages* as a tool for investigating how investment in one type of activity induced subsequent investment in other income-generating activities. Hirschman asserted, "Agriculture certainly stands convicted on the count of its lack of direct stimulus to the setting up of new activities through linkage effects—the superiority of manufacturing in this respect is crushing" (1958, 109–10). Therefore, Hirschman argued, investment in industry would generally lead to more rapid and more broadly based economic growth than would investment in agriculture. Hirschman's analysis reinforced ECLA's policy recommendation that priority be given to import substitution of manufactures.

Many agricultural economists were distressed by the lack of attention to agriculture. In a seminal article entitled "The Role of Agriculture in Economic Development" (1961), Johnston and Mellor drew on insights from the Lewis model to stress the importance of agriculture in economic growth. They argued that far from playing a passive role in development, agriculture could make five important contributions to the structural transformation of developing countries: it could provide labor, capital, foreign exchange, and food to a growing industrial sector and could supply a market for domestically produced industrial goods. William H. Nicholls's article "The Place of Agriculture in Economic Development" (1964) was also instrumental in encouraging economists to view agriculture as a potentially positive force in development, and it stimulated debate on the interdependence of agricultural and industrial growth. This in turn led to a growing interest in the empirical measurement of intersectoral resource transfers during the course of development.[6] During the 1960s many agricultural economists also stressed the importance of understanding the process of agricultural growth per se if agriculture's potential contribution to overall economic development was to be exploited.

THE INFLUENCE OF THE AGRICULTURAL DEVELOPMENT EXPERIENCE OF THE 1950S AND 1960S ON DEVELOPMENT ECONOMICS

An important characteristic of the literature on agricultural development since the 1950s has been its movement from a priori theorizing towards empirical research. During the 1950s European and North American agricultural economists viewed development through the lens of the historical experiences of their own countries. For example, most Western agricultural economists working on problems of agriculture in developing countries during this period believed that the problem of rural surplus labor could be resolved by transferring "excess" rural workers to urban industry. It was also assumed that Western agricultural advisers could directly transfer agricultural technology and models of agricultural extension from high-income to low-income countries, that community development programs could help rural people overcome the shackles of poverty and inequitable land tenure systems, and that food aid could serve humanitarian needs and provide jobs for the rural poor. The implicit model of development for many economists was the Marshall Plan, in which large transfers of physical capital and technology from the United States quickly rebuilt postwar Western Europe.

Agricultural development programs of the 1950s therefore placed heavy emphasis on the American model of agricultural extension and the "diffusion model" of agricultural development, which assumed that farmers could substantially increase their agricultural productivity by allocating existing resources more efficiently and by adopting agricultural practices and technologies from the industrial countries. Also during the 1950s, community development programs were promoted by Western donors as a nonrevolutionary approach to rural change. Community development advocates assumed that villagers, meeting with community development specialists, would express their "felt needs" and unite to design and implement self-help programs aimed at promoting rural development (Holdcroft 1984).[7]

The failure of many agricultural extension programs to achieve rapid increases in agricultural output and the inability of community development projects to solve the basic food problem in many countries (particularly India in the mid-1950s) led to a reevaluation of the diffusion model of agricultural development. Two elements were critical in this reappraisal. First, it became apparent that in many countries there were important structural barriers to rural development, such as highly concentrated political power and asset ownership. Second, T. W. Schultz's influential book *Transforming Traditional Agriculture* (1964) argued that farmers and herders, far from being irrational and fatalistic, were calculating economic agents who carefully weighed the marginal costs and benefits associated with different agricultural techniques. Through a long process of experimentation, these farmers had learned how to allocate efficiently the factors of production available to them, given existing technology. This implied that "no appreciable increase in agricultural production is to be had by reallocating the factors at the disposal of farmers who are bound by traditional agriculture. . . . An outside expert, however skilled . . . will not discover any major inefficiency in the allocation of factors" (39).

Schultz argued that major increases in per capita agricultural output in developing countries would come about only if farmers gained access to new, more productive factors of production (that is, new agricultural technologies) and the new skills needed to exploit them. Given their existing technologies, these farmers were "efficient but poor." The cause of rural poverty, in other words, lay in the lack of profitable technical packages for farmers and the lack of investment in human capital needed to cope with changing agricultural technologies. Schultz later attributed the low levels of investment in agricultural research and rural education in most countries to policies that taxed and undervalued agriculture (Schultz 1978, 1981).

Transforming Traditional Agriculture called for a major shift from agricultural extension towards investment in agricultural research and human capital. The book, which appeared five years after the establishment of the International Rice Research Institute (IRRI) in the Philippines and one year after the establishment of the International Maize and Wheat Improvement Center (CIMMYT) in Mexico, reinforced the increasing emphasis being given to agricultural research by the Rockefeller and Ford foundations and other organizations in the 1960s. As a result of IRRI's and CIMMYT's success in developing high-yielding varieties of rice and wheat, which were rapidly adopted in Asia during the 1960s and 1970s, the "Green Revolution," or high-payoff input, model replaced the diffusion/community development model as the dominant agricultural development model (see Ruttan, chapter 9 in this volume).

The Green Revolution had important effects on the theory as well as the practice of agricultural development. Several authors noted that the new technologies, based on fertilizer-responsive grain cultivars, were divisible and scale-neutral, allowing them to be incorporated into existing systems of small-scale agriculture. Therefore, these authors argued, intensification of agricultural production based on high-yielding cereal varieties offered the opportunity to provide productive employment for the rapidly growing rural labor force while at the same time it produced the wage goods needed for an expanding industrial labor force. The high-yielding varieties, it was argued, made it possible to achieve both employment and output objectives (Johnston and Kilby 1975). The early enthusiasm for the Green Revolution had a number of critics who argued that the new varieties often benefited mainly landlords and larger farmers in ecologically favored areas, while they frequently impoverished small farmers and tenants, particularly those in upland areas, by inducing lower grain prices and evictions from the land, as landlords found it profitable to farm the land themselves using mechanization.

Although some authors, such as Lester Brown (1970), oversold the accomplishments of the Green Revolution, the impact of the new varieties was substantial in Asia. Lipton and Longhurst (1989) pointed out that Green Revolution varieties were adding 40 to 50 million tons of additional grain each year in the late 1980s, which significantly reduced the real price of food to the poor and reduced the need to cultivate environmentally fragile areas. One of the important lessons of the past decades is that, with rising population pressure on land, technological change must be included as a central component in both the theory and the practice of agricultural and rural development.

During the 1960s and the 1970s, food and agricultural policy focused on increasing food production to solve the Ricardian food bottleneck, especially in Asia. But agriculture was taxed heavily in most developing countries during this period, both directly through mechanisms such as export taxes and indirectly through industrial protection and overvalued exchange rates. Many countries imposed such taxation because of the conventional wisdom that agriculture was unresponsive to price incentives, agricultural taxes were easy to administer and agriculture was subject to declining terms of trade. In many countries agricultural tax revenues were used to finance the expansion of highly visible social services and state-led industrialization. In some countries, the revenues financed the expansion of govenment employment—a means of distributing political patronage.

RADICAL POLITICAL ECONOMY AND DEPENDENCY PERSPECTIVES ON AGRICULTURE

Beginning in the 1950s, Western neoclassical development economics was challenged by the emergence of radical political economy and dependency models of development and underdevelopment. The radical political economy models have their roots in the writings of Lenin on imperialism and Kautsky on agriculture and in the post–World War II writings of Paul Baran and other Marxist economists. Baran, in an important article entitled "On the Political Economy of Backwardness" (1952), argued that in most low-income countries it would be impossible to bring about broad-based capitalist development without violent changes in social and political institutions. Although Baran was clearly ahead of his time in identifying institutional and structural barriers to development and the need to put effective demand at the center of development programs, he tended, as did many of the Western development economists he was criticizing, to see small-scale agriculture as incapable of making major contributions to economic growth. For example, Baran accepted the view that the marginal product of labor often approached zero in agriculture and that therefore "there is no way of employing [labor] usefully in agriculture." Farmers can "only be provided with opportunities for productive work by transfer to industry." Baran, like many economists of the time, believed that "very few improvements that would be necessary in order to increase productivity" could be "carried out within the narrow confines of small-peasant holdings" and that therefore farm consolidation was necessary.

Marxist analysis of agricultural and rural development was further advanced in the 1950s and 1960s by several Latin American and French scholars, who often blended Marxian analyses with dependency theory. The dependency interpretation of underdevelopment was first proposed in the 1950s by the Economic Commission for Latin America, under the leadership of Raul Prebisch. The basic hypothesis of this perspective is that underdevelopment is not a stage of development but the result of the expansion of the world capitalist system. Underdevelopment, in other words, is not simply the lack of development; it is a condition of impoverishment brought about by the integration of low-income economies into the world capitalist system. Although a number of different views of dependency have been put forward by scholars, such as Sunkel (1973), Furtado (1973), Frank (1966), and Galtung (1971), Dos Santos's definition of dependency has been widely cited: "By dependency we mean a situation in which the economy of certain countries is conditioned by the development and expansion of another economy to which the former is subjected" (1970, 231). Dependency theorists argued that trade was often a zero-sum game—that low-income countries ("the periphery") were pauperized through both a process of unequal exchange with the industrialized world ("the center") and repatriation of profits from foreign-owned businesses.[8]

In the 1960s, dependency theory was imported into Africa from Latin America. Samir Amin provided leadership in developing a Marxist version of dependency theory. In *Accumulation on a World Scale* (1974) and *Unequal Development* (1976) Amin presents an analytical framework of underdevelopment in Africa based on surplus extraction and the domination of the world capitalist system.

Radical scholars made several important contributions to agriculture and rural development thought. First, they helped demolish the myth of "a typical underdeveloped country" by stressing that each country's economic development had to be understood in the context of that country's historical experience. For example, they argued that Schultz's concept of "traditional agriculture"—a situation in which farmers have settled into a low-level equilibrium after years of facing static technology and factor prices—ignored the historical process of integration of individual economies into the world economy and therefore was not a very useful analytical concept. Second, in arguing that rural poverty in developing countries resulted from the functioning of the global capitalist economy, the radical writers focused attention on the relationships between villagers and the wider economic system. Unlike Schultz, who attributed rural poverty to the lack of productive agricultural technologies and human capital, radical scholars stressed the importance of the linkages and exchange arrangements that tied villages to the global economy. This concern about how structural conditions in the economy affect who can participate in a market economy, and under what terms, has attracted more attention by mainstream orthodox economists in the 1990s in the wake of mixed results from structural adjustment programs in many countries. Third, the radical economists directly attacked what Hirschman (1981, 3) has called the "mutual benefit claim" of development economics—the assertion that economic relations between high- and low-income countries (and among groups within low-income countries) can be shaped in a way to yield benefits for all. In disputing this claim, the radical scholars stressed that economic development was more than just a technocratic matter of determining how best to raise per capita GNP. Development involved restructuring institutional and political relationships, and these authors urged neoclassical economists to include these considerations explicitly in their analyses. In de Janvry's words, "Economic policy without political economy is a useless and utopian exercise" (1981, 263).

The radical analyses and the Western dual-sector models of the 1960s suffered from some of the same shortcomings—abstract theorizing, inadequate attention to the need for technical change in agriculture, lack of attention to the biological and location-specific nature of agricultural production processes, and lack of a solid micro foundation based on empirical research at the farm and village level. Recognition of some of these shortcomings was important in leading to a reevaluation of the goals and approaches of development economics and of the role of agriculture in reaching those goals in the period following 1970.

THE GROWTH-WITH-EQUITY ERA OF THE 1970S

Around 1970, mainstream Western development economics began to give greater attention to employment and the distribution of real income, broadly defined. This shift in emphasis came about for at least three reasons. The first was ideological, a response to the radical critique of Western development economics, especially the critique of the belief that economic growth was mutually beneficial for everyone. The goal of economic growth was seriously questioned by this critique, leading some development economists to redefine the goals of development more broadly, in order to preserve the legitimacy of the subdiscipline.

Second, from the 1960s onwards it became apparent that rapid economic growth in some countries, such as Pakistan, Nigeria, and Iran, was accompanied by deleterious, and in some cases disastrous, side effects such as civil wars and social turmoil. Hirschman (1981, 20–21) argues that development economists were forced to reevaluate the goals of their profession, because "when it turned out . . . that the promotion of economic growth entailed not infrequently a sequence of events involving serious retrogression in . . . other areas, including the wholesale loss of civil and human rights, the easy self-confidence that our subdiscipline exuded in its early stages was impaired."

Third, there was a growing awareness among development economists that even in countries where rapid economic growth had not contributed to social turmoil, the benefits of economic growth often were not trickling down to the poor and that frequently the income gap between rich and poor was widening. Even where the incomes of the poor were rising, often they were rising so slowly that the poor would not be able to afford decent diets or housing for at least another generation.

Rather than simply waiting for increases in average per capita incomes to "solve" the problems of poverty and malnutrition, economists, political leaders in the developing countries, and the leaders of major donor agencies argued in the early 1970s that greater explicit attention needed to be paid to employment, income distribution, and "basic needs," such as nutrition and housing. For example, Robert McNamara, then president of the World Bank, called on the Bank to redirect its activities towards helping people in the bottom 40 percent of the income distribution in low-income countries (McNamara 1973).

INTEGRATED RURAL DEVELOPMENT AND BASIC NEEDS

As a result of these concerns, many donors and governments endorsed integrated rural development (IRD) and basic needs projects. IRD projects focused on simultaneously increasing agricultural production and improving health, education, sanitation, and a variety of other social services. However, many IRD projects expanded social services faster than the economic base needed to support them, and the projects often proved to be extraordinarily complex and difficult to implement and replicate over broader areas (Lele 1975; World Bank 1988; Uphoff, Esman, and Krishna 1998). By 1980 many donors had retreated from IRD projects or had redesigned these projects to give greater emphasis to agricultural production (Food and Agriculture Organization 1988). The rise and decline of IRD was in some ways very similar to the fate of community development in the 1950s. (See Binswanger, chapter 17 in this volume.)

In the mid-1970s the basic needs approach was also popularized by the International Labour Office (ILO) (1976) and subsequently spearheaded by the World Bank. The premise of the approach is that development projects should give priority to increasing the welfare of the poor directly, through projects to improve nutrition, education, housing, and so on, rather than focus mainly on increasing aggregate growth rates.[9] The basic needs advocates supported their case by citing impressive gains in life span, literacy, and nutrition in Cuba, Sri Lanka, and China, countries that had emphasized basic needs. They also cited empirical studies that revealed that increases in average per capita income did not always lead to improved nutrition and that at times malnutrition actually increased with growing incomes (Reutlinger and Selowsky 1976). Therefore, many analysts argued that nutrition projects, targeted to the poor and malnourished, were needed to supplement other development activities.

Although investments in health, nutrition, education, and housing contribute importantly to improving the welfare of the poor in the short run, it soon became obvious that it was impossible to achieve a decent living standard for the bulk of the rapidly growing populations simply by redistributing existing assets. In the early 1980s, this recognition led donors away from basic needs towards a more growth-oriented strategy.

The increased concern in the 1970s about income distribution as well as growth implied a much greater role for agriculture in development programs. Because the majority of the poor in most developing countries were living in rural areas and because food prices are a major determinant of the real income of both the rural and the urban poor, the low productivity of agriculture was seen as a major cause of poverty. Furthermore, because urban industry had generally provided few jobs for the rapidly growing labor force, development planners concentrated on ways to create productive employment in rural areas, if only as a holding action until the rate of population growth declined and urban industry could create more jobs. (Nonetheless, investment policies in many countries continued to favor urban areas [Lipton 1977].) The need to create productive rural employment was underlined by a growing awareness of the increasing landlessness in many parts of developing countries, particularly South Asia and Latin America.

RESEARCH FINDINGS OF THE 1970s

These growth-with-equity concerns stimulated several important theoretical and policy debates, which led to new research. The debates focused on (1) how economic growth and alternative patterns of agricultural development affected income distribution, and vice-versa; (2) employment generation and the possibility of employment-output trade-offs in agriculture and industry; (3) the performance of output markets; and (4) ways of improving the productivity of agricultural research. It soon became apparent that, in order to address these concerns, policy makers needed a more detailed understanding of rural economies than that provided by the simple two-sector models of the 1950s and early 1960s. There was therefore a rapid expansion of micro-level research on the rural economy.

Relationship between Growth and Income Distribution

The debate on how growth patterns affected income distribution focused on what percentage of the population received what proportion of a country's income or assets. It also dealt with the distribution of income between men and women and among various social groups and owners of different factors of production, and with how this distribution was affected by different growth strategies. For example, greater attention was given to the impact of economic growth on small farmers (Stevens 1977; Fei, Ranis, and Kuo 1979) and on women (Boserup 1970; Tinker and Bramsen 1976).

One important question in the growth-distribution debate is what determines patterns of agricultural technology development (e.g., whether a country develops labor-intensive or capital-intensive technology). Hayami and Ruttan's induced innovation model (outlined in chapter 10) was a major step in understanding this issue. Hayami and Ruttan argued that there are multiple technological paths to agricultural growth, each embodying a different mix of factors of production, and that changes in relative factor prices can guide a country's researchers to select the most "efficient" path. This implied that countries with different factor endowments would have different efficient growth paths and that the wholesale importation of agricultural technology from industrialized to developing countries could lead to highly inefficient patterns of growth (e.g., displacing abundant workers with expensive imported machinery). Hayami and Ruttan argued that relative factor prices not only affected technological development but also often played an important role in guiding the design of social institutions.

Several authors, particularly Mellor (1966, 1976), Johnston and Kilby (1975), and Tomich, Kilby, and Johnston (1995), examined how alternative strategies of agricultural development affected overall economic growth rates and distribution of income. Mellor argued that it was possible to design employment-oriented strategies of development based on the potential growth linkages inherent in the new high-yielding grain varieties.[10] He emphasized how the new varieties could raise the incomes of foodgrain producers, thereby generating increased effective demand for a wide variety of labor-intensive products. Indeed, Mellor saw most of the potential growth in employment that could result from the new varieties as lying outside the foodgrain sector itself, in sectors producing labor-intensive goods such as dairy products, fruit, other consumer products, and agricultural inputs. This expanded employment was made possible by the simultaneous increase in effective demand for these products and the increased supply of inexpensive wage goods in the form of foodgrains. Mellor analyzed the types of agricultural and industrial policies needed to exploit the growth linkages of the new grain varieties. Johnston and Kilby showed that broad-based agricultural growth by smallholders was more effective than plantation production in stimulating the demand for industrial products and hence speeding the structural transformation of the economy. Tomich, Kilby, and Johnston's analysis strongly supported the view that concentrating agricultural development efforts on the mass of small farmers in low-income countries, rather than promoting a bimodal structure of small and large farms, would lead to faster growth rates of both aggregate economic output and employment.

Employment Generation, Factor Markets, and Choice of Technique

By 1970 it had become apparent that urban industry in most countries could not expand quickly enough in the short run to provide employment for the expanding rural labor force. Policy makers quickly quit worrying about how to transfer surplus labor from agriculture to urban industry and focused instead on how to generate more jobs in rural areas, to help slow down the flood of rural immigrants to the cities. Concern about creating new jobs stimulated research in three areas: (1) employment generation and the possible existence of employment-output trade-offs in industry and agriculture; (2) the functioning of labor markets, including how they affected rural-urban migration; and (3) the impact of policies in other factor markets on job creation.

The need to create more jobs raised questions in both agriculture and industry about the relative output and employment-generation capacities of large and small enterprises. In agriculture, debate centered on how much emphasis should be given to improving small farms as opposed to creating larger and more capital-intensive farms, ranches, and plantations. Empirical evidence from the late 1960s and early 1970s revealed that the economies of size in tropical agriculture were more limited than had previously been believed and that small farms often achieved greater output *and* employment per hectare than did large-scale farming. Several scholars argued that in many countries land reform would stimulate economic growth because small-scale farms had higher potential employment and land productivity than did large estates. The higher land productivity was due largely to greater use of labor (mainly family labor) per unit of land. Although there was widespread agreement among these scholars that land reform was an attractive policy instrument for raising farm output, increasing rural employment, and improving the equality of income distribution, political support for land reform waned during the 1970s.

In industry, the small-versus-large debate led to a number of empirical studies of rural small-scale enterprises. In both agriculture and industry the concern with possible employment-output trade-offs also stimulated research on the choice of appropriate techniques in agricultural production and processing. This work focused on how poorly functioning markets for other factors of production, such as capital, led to displacement of workers. Overvalued exchange rates and subsidized credit, for example, often encouraged excessive substitution of capital for labor in low-wage economies. Concern about the impact of such factor-price distortions on output and employment in both agriculture and industry also stimulated research on the functioning of rural financial markets. Chapters 23–25 and 30 in this volume summarize the major findings on these issues.

Concern for creating jobs also stimulated research on how well rural labor markets functioned. Many studies during the 1970s evaluated the performance of labor markets in low-income countries and generally found that at peak periods of the agricultural cycle there was little unemployment in rural areas, while at other periods of the year there were labor surpluses. The studies also documented that earlier researchers had frequently overestimated the size of the surplus because they had failed to take account of the considerable time devoted to rural nonfarm enterprises and to walking to and from fields. Studies also confirmed that labor markets in most countries were generally competitive, with wage rates, particularly in rural areas, following seasonal patterns of labor demand (Berry and Sabot 1978).

Labor-market research also investigated why rural people often moved to the cities even when urban unemployment levels were high. Much of the research built on a model first introduced by Todaro (1969; Harris and Todaro, 1970). The model posited that a potential migrant was motivated to move to the city primarily by the difference between his or her *expected* (rather than actual) income and the prevailing rural wage. The model implied that attempts to reduce urban unemployment by creating more urban jobs could paradoxically result in *more* urban unemployment. By leading potential migrants to believe that their chances of getting an urban job had increased, urban employment programs could induce greater migration to the cities. Consequently, these researchers argued, urban unemployment could often be addressed best through reducing the incentives to move to the cities by raising rural incomes via a broad range of agricultural and rural development programs.

Product Market Performance

During the 1960s and 1970s, economists evaluated the performance of agricultural product markets and found little support for allegations of widespread collusion and extraction of monopoly profits by private merchants in low-income countries.[11] They did, however, document how insufficient infrastructure, the lack of reliable public information systems and other public goods, and corruption and arbitrary regulation often reduced market efficiency and lowered farmers' incentives to specialize in market-oriented production. The studies were often critical of state monopolies in the domestic food trade, citing the frequent high costs of state marketing agencies. The studies identified important roles for the state in providing public goods (such as better information systems and standardized weights and measures) to facilitate private trading, price stabilization, and regulation of international trade. These studies provided important intellectual justification for many of the market reform programs adopted in the 1980s.

Farming Systems Research and Farmer Decision Making

During the late 1960s and the 1970s economists and biological scientists sought to improve the productivity of agricultural research systems through better understanding of the factors that influenced farmers' decisions concerning whether to adopt new varieties and farming practices. This work eventually led to the development of farming systems research. Farming systems research attempts to incorporate farmers' constraints and objectives into agricultural research by involving farmers in problem identification, on-farm agronomic trials, and extension.

Interest in farming systems research and the new household economics also led to efforts to model the farm household as both a production and a consumption unit. Inspired in part by Chayanov's work on the behavior of Russian peasants in the early 1900s, the farm household models stressed the need to understand how government policies could simultaneously affect both the production and the consumption decisions of smallholders.[12]

These various strands of microeconomic research during the 1970s contributed to an accumulation of knowledge about (1) the behavior of farmers; (2) the constraints on the expansion of farm and nonfarm production, income, and employment; (3) the linkages between agricultural research and extension organizations; and (4) the complexity and location-specific nature of the agricultural development process. One of the major accomplishments was a large increase in knowledge about agricultural development in sub-Saharan Africa (see Eicher and Baker 1992). But because research was increasingly oriented towards the micro level, relatively less attention was being paid to research on food policy, links between agriculture and the macroeconomy, and the role that agriculture can play in national development.

DEVELOPMENT THEMES IN THE 1980S AND 1990S: MACROECONOMIC AND INSTITUTIONAL REFORM, FOOD SECURITY, AND SUSTAINABLE AGRICULTURAL GROWTH

The 1980s and 1990s have been an era of unprecedented macroeconomic reform, globalization of the world economy, an end to the Cold War, and institutional restructuring of economies throughout the world. These changes unleashed rapid economic growth in some countries, particularly in Southeast Asia. At the same time, roughly a billion people, mainly in South Asia and sub-Saharan Africa, were being left behind in poverty, unable to reap many benefits from the growing market economies. Political vacuums created by the end of the Cold War stimulated increased internal and regional conflicts (e.g., in ex-Yugoslavia, Rwanda, Somalia, and Armenia), which redirected donor efforts from development to emergency relief. And even where economic growth was proceeding rapidly, many raised concerns about whether it was environmentally sustainable.

MACROECONOMIC REFORM AND RESTRUCTURING

The international debt crisis of the early eighties triggered a wave of policy reforms in Latin America, Africa, and Asia (Ranis 1997). With the support of the World Bank, the International Monetary Fund, and bilateral donors, many developing countries carried out policy reforms under the umbrella of structural adjustment programs (SAPs). These programs typically had two phases. The stabilization phase attempted to reestablish macroeconomic balance by reducing government budget deficits (by cutting government spending and increasing revenues) and lowering balance-of-payments deficits (typically via currency devaluation and export promotion). The restructuring phase tried to re-ignite economic growth by aligning domestic prices more closely with world prices (which represent the opportunity cost of resources for most countries) and through greater reliance on the private sector for allocation of resources. This second phase of the SAPs typically involved the selling off of state enterprises ("privatization") and broadening the scope of activities in which the private sector was allowed to participate ("liberalization"). This section focuses on the macroeconomic reforms, while the following section discusses institutional restructuring, but in most countries the two were closely intertwined.

Turkey was one of the first countries to adopt an SAP (in 1980); it was followed by many countries in Latin America. In Latin America, the adoption of the "free market–free trade paradigm" represented a dramatic change from the import-substitution-based strategy of industrialization of the previous decades (de Janvry, Key, and Sadoulet 1997). In Africa, macro policy reform was strongly advocated in the World Bank's report *Accelerated Development in Sub-Saharan Africa* (1981). The first structural adjustment program in sub-Saharan Africa was launched in Ghana in 1983. By 1989, adjustment programs were under way in thirty-two of the forty-five countries in sub-Saharan Africa. As part of these programs, many countries scaled back subsidies on staple foods, agricultural credit, fertilizer, and water, as such programs became financially unsustainable (Heisey and Mwangi 1997; Smith 1995; and Jayne et al. 1997a).

In Asia, structural adjustment programs, new technology, and institutional reforms helped increase agricultural growth in the 1980s and 1990s (David and Otsuka 1994). India achieved self-sufficiency in grain production in the mid-1980s, and macroeconomic and institutional reforms led to increased foreign investment in other sectors of the Indian economy (Rao 1994). Yet, in spite of the impressive growth, Rao and Radhakrishna (1997) report that there was hardly any improvement in the cereal and nutrient intake of the poorest 30 percent of the population between 1972–73 and 1987–88.[13] In 1984, Indonesia, formerly the largest rice importer in the world, achieved rice self-sufficiency, which helped fuel growth in the rest of the economy. In China agricultural policy reforms were launched in 1978 and agricultural production expanded rapidly, spurring faster growth throughout the economy (Lin, Cai, and Li 1996). And in much of Southeast Asia (e.g., Thailand, Vietnam), policy reforms and more outward-oriented strategies stimulated rapid agricultural and agribusiness growth. World trade has expanded dramatically during the 1980s and 1990s, particularly in manufactured goods, with lower-income Asian countries stressing labor-intensive manufacturing such as textiles and electronics.

The more outward looking orientation of developing countries was driven in part by international negotiations aimed at reducing regional and global trade barriers. The new trade arrangements included expansion of the European Union to include lower-income European countries such as Greece and Portugal (which threatened the market share of other low- and middle-income countries exporting to Europe), the creation of the North American Free Trade Agreement (NAFTA) and the Association of Southeast Asian Nations (ASEAN), and results of the Uruguay Round of GATT negotiations.[14] The Uruguay Round negotiations (1986–94), although initially driven by the concerns of high-income countries, eventually involved 125 nations and led to commitments to remove most nontariff barriers to trade and greatly reduce tariff barriers and agricultural subsidization. The negotiations also created the World Trade Organization (WTO) to promote world trade, handle trade disputes, and serve as a forum for future trade negotiations. While the Uruguay Round provided some temporary exemptions for lowest-income countries, it became clear that in the future developing countries will be dealing with a much more open world trading regime.

The increased integration of domestic and international markets eroded the power of domestic agricultural policies to influence agricultural incomes and rural development independent of world market conditions. In increasingly open economies, it has become very costly for countries to try to isolate their agricultural sectors from world markets. Yet, exposure to international markets also carries risk. If foreign investors lose confidence in the economy—with the result being capital flight, collapse of the exchange rate, and weakening of financial organizations, as occurred in much of Southeast Asia in the late 1990s—economies can fall into severe recession. Thus, developing clear rules and policies, particularly to govern financial markets, is essential for sustainable growth. Given the importance of trade and international capital flows, macroeconomic policies often have more impact on rural incomes than do agricultural policies. The increased influence of world trade in dictating domestic agricultural policies has led to concerns about whether countries can provide safety nets for the poor and national environmental policies without violating WTO rules.

The emphasis on macroeconomic and policy reform was stimulated by, and in turn stimulated, a large amount of conceptual and empirical research on the impact of macroeconomic reforms on food system performance. G. Edward Schuh (1968, 1990) was a leader among agricultural economists in arguing that domestic food and agricultural policies needed to be analyzed in an open-economy framework that took account of how domestic agriculture was linked to global product and financial markets. This shift in orientation was influenced by several studies that concluded that countries which adopted outward-oriented trade strategies achieved higher rates of economic growth than nations that had pursued import-substituting industrialization (Krueger 1978). Research by D. Gale Johnson, Schuh, Krueger, and Schiff and Valdés (1992) on trade and capital markets helped broaden the scope of agricultural policy in poor countries from a primary concern over food self-sufficiency to one that focused on developing food and agricultural trade policy in an international context (Staatz and Wohl, 1991).

On the conceptual side, *food policy analysis* was a major analytical advance of the early 1980s. Timmer, Falcon, and Pearson wrote an influential book *Food Policy Analysis* (1983). The food policy approach helped resolve the conflict between the production incentives school, led by T. W. Schultz, and the basic needs school, which was popularized in *Food First,* by Lappé and Collins (1977). The production incentives school emphasized the need to "get prices right" (which usually meant raising agricultural prices), in order to increase farmers' incentives to produce. The basic needs approach stressed the need to keep food prices low, in order to ensure that the poor could afford an adequate diet. The food policy approach recognized that the production concerns of the production incentives school and the consumption concerns of the basic needs school were both legitimate, and it showed how they were linked through food prices. Food policy analysis hence formed a bridge between the two approaches. Also, the food policy approach recognized, more explicitly than had earlier agricultural policy work, that policy formation takes place in an open economy where the financial and commodity markets are increasingly integrated. Therefore, in an open-economy framework there is a need to link food and agricultural policy with macro policies, such as the exchange rate and interest rates.

On the empirical side, numerous scholars have attempted to measure the impact of structural adjustment programs on agricultural development and economic growth. Many analysts have focused on factors that facilitated or hindered supply response to the reforms (Meerman 1997; Valdés 1986; Husain 1995; Martin, Larivière, and Staatz 1995; de Janvry, Key, and Sadoulet 1997; Jayne et al. 1997b), while others have focused on the income-distributional impacts of the reforms, particularly the impact on the poor (Oxfam 1993; Cornia and Helleiner 1994; Rao 1994). A frequently voiced concern by these latter authors is that the poor might be especially hurt by the reduction in government spending on social services, such as health, and on subsidies on basic staples. Others have voiced the concern that the severe cuts in government spending that were part of the stabilization phase of structural adjustment programs would slash vital support services to agriculture, such as research, extension, and infrastructure development, thereby limiting supply response (Staatz and Ba 1996).

The performance of agriculture in low- and middle-income economies varied widely during the 1980s and 1990s. Massive currency devaluations and other structural reforms allowed agriculture to play a leading role in the economic growth of a number of Latin American countries during this period. But de Janvry, Key, and Sadoulet (1997), Valdés (1986), and the FAO (1988) point out that some of these countries were blessed with favorable domestic and international demand (e.g., Chile's fruit and vegetable exports to the United States), available technology, and responsive agricultural institutions to induce the required supply response. By contrast, many African countries, such as the Côte d'Ivoire, faced sluggish world demand for cocoa and cotton, while others, such as Zaire, Senegal, and Tanzania, were unable to break structural constraints on the supply side, such as lack of technology, roads and vehicles, and poor systems of public administration (Lipumba 1994). The differing responses to structural adjustment between African and some of the Latin American countries can be illuminated by referring to Timmer's four stages of the agricultural transformation outlined in chapter 7 of this volume. Most African economies are in the first stage of that transformation, where massive investments are needed in training and rural infrastructure development, while most Latin American countries passed through this stage twenty-five to fifty years ago.[15]

Without question, the pursuit of structural adjustment and open markets has redefined the relationship between agricultural policy and macroeconomic and social policy. However, there is growing concern that, with the ascendancy of the market liberalization paradigm, agricultural policy is being "dictated by macroeconomic policy, with often little explicit concern for agriculture, rural development or poverty" (de Janvry, Key, and Sadoulet 1997, 3).

INSTITUTIONAL RESTRUCTURING

The 1980s and 1990s also witnessed widespread institutional reforms that fundamentally redefined the role of the government, the private sector, and civil society (e.g., nongovernmental organizations) in countries throughout the world. These changes came about for several reasons: the globalization of the world economy and the information revolution, which weakened the control of individual governments over their economies and populations; the structural adjustment programs described above; and the collapse of the Soviet bloc and the end of the Cold War. The institutional reforms included changes in the rules under which the economies operated and fundamental political restructuring, such as the redrawing of international borders, decentralization, and in many countries, democratization. Large firms in industrialized countries also restructured, shifting towards greater reliance on various forms of contracting to produce the goods and services they needed rather than producing all their inputs themselves (Reich 1992). This opened greater opportunities for local firms and farmers in developing countries to subcontract with overseas firms. As a result of all these changes, countries as diverse as Chad and the Czech Republic struggled to redefine how they organized their economies and, in the new institutional context, to revise strategies for agricultural and rural development. Part V of this book presents case studies of how countries throughout the world have dealt with the profound macroeconomic and institutional transitions of the 1980s and 1990s.

The massive institutional restructuring led to greatly increased interest among economists in the role of institutional change in economic performance. By "institutions" we mean the rules under which the economy operates. The burgeoning of work on institutional economics in the 1980s and 1990s drew on insights from economic historians such as Fogel (1994) and North (1990), the "old" institutionalism of authors such as Commons (1924, 1950) and Veblen (1912, 1927), and the neoclassically based "new" institutional economics that has roots in the writings of Coase (1937, 1960) and Stiglitz (1988). Indeed, a major characteristic of development writings of the 1980s and 1990s has been the incorporation of institutional analysis into the examination of land tenure, labor and financial markets, risk management strategies, international trade, policy reform, and a host of other development issues. Many of the contributions to this volume reflect this new approach.

Two features of the institutional analysis are particularly striking. The first is the recognition that history matters, a point stressed by many economic historians as well as the dependency theorists of the 1950s. The concept of path dependency, which argues that a country's or firm's current options depend critically on its past decisions, was incorporated increasingly into policy analyses in the 1990s. The implication of path dependency is that the "one-size-fits-all" approach to policy reform advocated in the early 1980s is unlikely to be successful; reform programs need to be tailored to an individual country's circumstances. For example, after a twenty-year investigation of the growth and development experience of twenty-three countries over the period 1850 to 1914, Morris and Adelman (1988) reported that no single theory of causation could account for the many directions economic development followed in those countries. Contrary to neoclassical theory, for instance, comparable resources and export opportunities did not assure countries similar patterns and paces of growth. In fact, the authors found that "diversity in growth patterns, diversity in institutions and diversity in applicable theories" were the hallmarks of the development process during the nineteenth century (Morris and Adelman 1988).

A second characteristic of the new institutionalist approach is its emphasis on the importance of information and transaction costs in influencing the way economic activities are organized. Building on the work of authors such as Williamson (1985), analysts showed that many institutions previously viewed as exploitative or economically inefficient (such as sharecropping and linked sales between input and output markets) had marked advantages in terms of reducing risk and transaction costs (Bardhan 1989; Hayami and Otsuka 1993; Nabli and Nugent 1989; Hoff, Braverman, and Stiglitz 1993). Other authors focused on how government regulations often discouraged investment and prevented emerging firms from entering the formal sector, by creating large transaction costs (de Soto 1989), and how high transaction costs in rural markets reduced farmers' incomes and food security by reducing incentives for specialization and trade (Bromley and Chavas 1989; de Janvry, Fafchamps, and Sadoulet 1991; Jayne 1994).

One of the challenges of this period was institutional design: helping develop organizations and rules of the game that would permit smallholders and the rural poor to capture the benefits of the more open, market-driven economies even though certain activities in these markets are characterized by economies of scale. Experience showed, for example, that the degree to which the market reforms led to concentration of land holding depended on the institutional setting within which new agricultural technologies and policies were introduced. With inputs provided and the social barriers to producing cash crops like coffee and tea removed, smallholders in Kenya increased their share of national production from 4 percent in 1965 to 49 percent in 1985 (Lele and Agarwal 1989). Similarly, smallholders' market share of cotton and maize production in Zimbabwe rose dramatically following independence in 1980. In other countries and regions, however, such as the Sudan and the Punjab and other states in India, access to modern inputs has been biased towards owners of large farms, as a result of which an increasing share of land has been cultivated by those farms.

The end of the Cold War and the recognition of the importance of institutions led Western donors to place greater emphasis on the need for good governance, to create an environment conducive to broad-based economic development.[16] Good governance was typically defined as having transparent rules governing the economy and civil rights, nonarbitrary enforcement of laws and contracts, and some degree of democracy. Throughout the 1990s, more donors and lenders (including the IMF) have begun to make their programs contingent on progress in the area of governance. Historical analyses (e.g., North and Weingast 1989) show the importance of the rule of law for economic growth, but the links between democracy per se and rapid growth are less clear.

The decentralization and democratization in many countries during the 1980s and 1990s also led to greater interest in the role for civil society, such as independent farmer and trader organizations and trade unions, in the development process. In some countries, these organizations have become major players in the articulation of development goals and the mobilization of resources to help achieve them. Such movements were seen most dramatically in Eastern Europe, with the rise of independent labor unions during and after the fall of communism in the 1980s and 1990s, but they were also increasingly important in Latin America and parts of Asia and Africa (Leftwich 1996; Bingen 1998).

Nongovernmental organizations (NGOs), both local and international, also began playing a larger role in agricultural and rural development activities during the 1980s and 1990s. In countries where political reforms gave greater scope for civil society in the development process, local NGOs often quickly emerged. At the other extreme, where central governments completely broke down (such as in Somalia in the early 1990s) or were considered unreliable by donors, international and local NGOs played an increasing role, especially in administering disaster relief. Many donors favored working through NGOs, because they believed NGOs had better grassroots connections to the local populations than did the government and were more efficient and less venal. In the 1990s, however, many international NGOs' greatest area of expertise lay in the logistics of relief operations; these organizations faced the challenge of strengthening their skills in development work as more resources flowed towards them.

The preference for NGOs led some observers to argue that donors were trying to substitute NGOs for effective local government. Tendler (1997) criticizes the mainstream donor community's advice about downsizing governments and replacing local government bureaucracies with NGOs. She contends that this antigovernment view has emerged from studies of poor government performance. Tendler draws on her long-term research in northeastern Brazil and presents four case studies of "good" government, including a study of front-line extension workers, to challenge the decisions of donors to downsize government bureaucracies. Tendler makes a plea to avoid simplistic views on public and private roles in development and argues that good governments have important but highly circumscribed roles to play in development.

The redefinition of the role of the state during the 1990s has involved redesigning ways in which support services to agriculture are provided, such as agricultural research, extension, and credit. In many countries, new models have been tried, often involving greater financial and administrative autonomy for research and extension services and increased involvement of the private sector and NGOs. The debate over appropriate extension models that are fiscally sustainable in low- and middle-income countries has been especially intense in the 1990s. Many countries in Asia have moved beyond the training and visit (T&V) model and have introduced more demand-driven, pluralistic models that have lower recurrent costs.[17]

By the beginning of the 1990s, institutional economics had become mainstreamed into development economics, with much of the focus turning to how rules affect incentives in both the public and private sectors.[18] In 1997 the World Bank embraced many of the basic concepts of institutional economics and devoted its 1997 *World Development Report* to the role of the state in a changing world. The central message of the report is that in the promotion of development, effective institutions matter as much as sensible policies (see also Binswanger and Deininger 1997). It remains to be seen how the World Bank will operationalize its belated conviction that effective institutions are critical in development. In Africa this is a particularly vexing problem because of the rapid build up of project aid during the seventies and eighties: for example, ten major donors were funding 180 different projects in the agricultural sector in Zambia in 1997.

FOOD INSECURITY AND POVERTY

While the 1980s and 1990s witnessed rapid economic growth in some parts of Southeast Asia and Latin America, the period was marked by famine, war, and huge flows of refugees in other areas, particularly Africa (Ethiopia in 1985, Somalia in the early 1990s, and Rwanda in the mid-1990s), North Korea, and parts of Europe (Bosnia) and the former Soviet Union. These disasters drew the public's attention to the challenges of designing relief for short-term food crises. At the same time, there was growing recognition that, in addition to the people facing short-term crises due to war and famine, between 800 million and 1 billion people, mostly in South Asia and sub-Saharan Africa, remained chronically poor and malnourished (U.S. Department of Agriculture 1996; Tweeten and McClelland 1997). Despite the achievement of national food self-sufficiency in several major Asian countries (e.g., India and Indonesia), it was apparent that a large percentage of people neither had the access to resources (e.g., land, credit) nor the purchasing power to secure their food needs. Thus, the pioneering work of Reutlinger and Selowsky (1976), followed by Sen's *Poverty and Famines*

(1981), set the stage for moving beyond the belief that national food self-sufficiency could solve problems of famine and malnutrition. Both these works, as well as many that followed them, stressed that food security involved assuring both an adequate supply of food (through a country's own production and trade) and access by the population to that supply. The poor could gain access to the food by producing it themselves, by earning sufficient income to purchase food in the market, or through grants, such as free rations or food stamps. Research and empirical experience during the 1980s and 1990s demonstrated that working on only one side of the "food security equation" (i.e., either the supply side or the access side) failed to alleviate food insecurity. In addition, researchers pointed to the need for complementary investments in health facilities and clean water to assure that the hungry could utilize the food available to them.

Food security can be analyzed at several levels: international, regional, national, subnational (as in provinces and districts), household, and individual. In the early 1980s, researchers focused on international food security issues, such as international grain reserves and, later, regional grain reserves (e.g., in the Sahel and in Southern Africa); but in the mid-1980s, researchers shifted to national and household food security issues and also began paying more attention to factors affecting the distribution of food within households (Strauss and Beegle 1996).

Beginning in the mid-1980s numerous studies of national food security were carried out to help answer the following key policy question: What combination of policies, technological changes, and institutional reforms is required to achieve food availability and access to food for nations and for families?[19] The need for primary data to further food security policy analysis was particularly acute in the case of Africa. For example, in the 1980s, many policy makers, scholars, and donors commonly assumed (on the basis of secondary data) that most African farm households were net food sellers and that increasing official farm-level prices would lead to higher food output and improved rural welfare. But research results revealed that from 15 to 73 percent of the rural households in the major grain-producing areas of Mali, Somalia, Senegal, Rwanda, and Zimbabwe were net buyers of staple grains and only 22 to 48 percent were net sellers of these grains in recent years (Weber et al. 1988, 1046). Hence, raising grain prices in these countries would hurt, at least in the short run, a large number of rural households. From this new evidence it follows that policies to improve food security must correspondingly be tailored to local food security profiles.

In the wake of the World Food Summit in 1996, poverty alleviation reemerged as a central concern of major donor agencies and lenders, such as the World Bank (World Bank 1996). Consequently, generation of rural income and employment continued as an important theme, for three reasons. First, the achievement of national food self-sufficiency in many countries, such as India (Rao and Radhakrishna 1997), was unable to ensure that all families could secure their food needs. Second, because of high urban unemployment rates, most of the new entrants to the rural labor force would have to find employment in farming and rural nonfarm activities. Third, while such countries as Sri Lanka, China, and Brazil had reaped short-term benefits from food subsidies and food transfer programs, it became apparent that most countries could not finance such measures over the long term. Hence, there was a long-term need to help the rural poor increase production and/or the income to secure their own food needs. Much attention focused on ways of using small nonfarm enterprises, often financed by micro-credit, to reach the poor, particularly women. Chapters 21, 23, 24, and 25 in this book review the experience of these efforts.

ENVIRONMENTAL SUSTAINABILITY

Acid rain, pollution, environmental degradation, and sustainable agriculture also emerged as central issues in the 1980s and 1990s, especially following the release of the influential Bruntland Report, *Our Common Future* (World Commission on Environment and Development 1987) and the U.N. Conference on the Environment and Development (the "Earth Summit") in Rio de Janeiro in 1992. Concerns about sustainability were raised at several levels: local, subnational, national, and global (see chapters 26–29). At the local level, increasing population pressure on fragile upland (rainfed) environments had led to worries that existing farming systems in many parts of the world were no longer sustainable, that is, that continuing current practices would lead to falling agricultural productivity, major food crises, and more rural poverty. But Pingali, Hossain, and Gerpacio report in *Asian Rice Bowls* (1997) that the fertile lowland rice paddies in Asia are as susceptible to environmental degradation as the fragile uplands. (Also see chapter 29, by Pingali, in this volume.) At the subnational level, analysts and activists raised concerns about the externalities generated by modern agricultural practices—for example, the impact of pesticide runoff and siltation from dams on local fisheries, and the destruction of wildlife habitat caused by agricultural expansion. At the national level, additional concerns were raised about the economic capacity of many countries to afford high-input agriculture given their shortages of foreign exchange, as well as the impact of macroeconomic adjustments on farmers' incentives to conserve natural resources (Spencer and Badiane 1995; Diagana and Kelly 1996). At the global level, the 1980s and 1990s have seen increasing consternation about the "greenhouse effect"—the increase in global temperature associated with the build-up of carbon dioxide and other gases in the atmosphere—as well as concerns about acid rain and worldwide pesticide contamination. Since the cutting and burning of tropical rainforests for conversion into agricultural land is believed to be a major contributor to global warming, there were increasing calls for the development and adoption of less destructive farming systems.

The 1990s have seen the increasing recognition (as noted by Reardon in chapter 27) that environmental and agricultural development agendas need to be addressed jointly, for most natural resources in developing countries are managed by farmers and herders trying to make a living from them. One of the key areas of research by economists and political scientists was the investigation of institutional arrangements designed to allow such natural resources to be managed locally by farmers, herders, and others in an environmentally sustainable way (Ostrom 1990).

LOOKING FORWARD: DEVELOPMENT CHALLENGES OF THE TWENTY-FIRST CENTURY

By the end of the 1990s, development thinking had come nearly full circle. In the 1950s and 1960s, many development economists analyzed how the agricultural and nonagricultural sectors interacted during the process of economic growth, using simple two-sector models. This abstract theorizing was sharply criticized by dependency theorists, among others, who argued that such work abstracted from the institutional and structural barriers to broad-based growth in most low-income countries. During the 1970s and 1980s, the focus of research shifted to developing a more detailed theoretical and empirical understanding of the rural economy. But the emphasis on structural adjustment in the 1980s forced reexamination of agriculture's relationship to the macroeconomy. By the late 1990s, economists were again focusing on how the rural economy was linked to the broader world market, but they demonstrated a renewed recognition of how important institutions are in determining a country's pattern of growth and the distribution of the benefits of growth. A key difference between the 1950s and the late 1990s is the level of disaggregation of the analysis. In the fifties, intersectoral relations were analyzed using simple, two-sector models, and the institutional constraints were discussed in terms of development approaches writ large—capitalism versus socialism, center versus periphery. In the 1990s, the analysis of both intersectoral relationships and institutional arrangements is much finer, with an emphasis on understanding the details of the various relationships and with a recognition that multiple paths of development are possible. One implication of this recognition is that empirical analysis is an essential input into the formulation of alternative development strategies.

As John Mellor states in chapter 3 (p. 65), "much has been learned about agricultural development, and many of the essential institutions are at least partly built." A key lesson from the agricultural development experience of the 1980s and 1990s is that macroeconomic policies can be powerful stimuli to agricultural growth and to the national economy. But, as shown by part V's case studies of economies in transition, for macroeconomic and agricultural policies to succeed in stimulating both growth and poverty alleviation, there must be sufficient domestic and international effective demand, public investments in research and rural infrastructure, and an institutional environment conducive to mobilizing the energy and capability of the *majority* of rural people. While political stability and macroeconomic reform alone can produce impressive rates of agricultural growth for a minority of commercial farmers, the evidence is clear that the success of policies to deal with rural poverty and food insecurity will be "a function of the extent to which 'countervailing power' is available to the poor through the presence of social action groups and politically viable opposition parties" (Bhagwati

1984). The growth of the role of civil society in many countries during the 1990s held promise of such progress.

One of the clearest lessons of experience is that agricultural and rural development require well-trained individuals and strong local organizations to carry out research, provide services to farmers and traders, and represent their interests. International research centers and expatriate advisers are at best complements to, not substitutes for, these national organizations and this local policy analysis capability.

NOTES

1. Development economics emerged as a subdiscipline of economics in the post–World War II period with the work of Nurkse, Mandelbaum, Rosenstein-Rodan, Singer, Prebisch, and others. The first major text on economic development was W. Arthur Lewis's influential *Theory of Economic Growth* (1955). Lewis's emphasis on economic growth set the tone for work in development economics during the "growth era" of the 1950s and 1960s.

2. This section draws heavily on Johnston 1970, an excellent review of the literature on the role of agriculture in economic development, and on Stern 1989. For a survey of the agricultural development literature from 1950 to 1992 see also Martin 1992; Eicher and Baker 1992; Mellor and Mudahar 1992; and Schuh, Salazar, and Brandâo 1992.

3. Nicholls (1964) was one of the first critics of the rapid transfer of surplus labor as a short-run strategy. See also Mellor 1984.

4. For a summary of this thesis see Prebisch 1959.

5. Prebisch later modified his views about import substitution (1981).

6. See Mellor 1984.

7. Community development's emphasis on providing social services presaged the basic needs approach to development of the late 1970s.

8. For other critiques of the dependency school of thought in Latin America see Cardoso and Faletto 1979 and de Janvry 1981.

9. The basic needs approach is not simply a call for increased social welfare spending, however. It is also based on recognition of the importance to economic growth of investment in human capital and of the synergy of nutrition, health, and family planning decisions.

10. Mellor's views are articulated in *The New Economics of Growth: A Strategy for India and the Developing World* (1976). See also Mellor and Lele 1973.

11. See reviews by Lele (1977) and Riley and Staatz (1981).

12. For a summary of the literature on farm-household modeling see Singh, Squire, and Strauss 1986; Moock 1986; and Tripp 1991.

13. Rao and Radhakrishna (1997, 1) attribute this lack of improvement in nutrient intake to the slow growth of GDP and the consequent sluggish growth in employment, the failure of land reforms to provide land to the rural landless poor, ineffective implementation of poverty alleviation programs, and the lack of targeting in public distribution of foodgrains.

14. See Hertel, Masters, and Gehlhar (1997) for a discussion of how regional trade agreements, such as the European Union, can lead to trade diversion, hurting countries from outside the agreement that formerly exported to the region.

15. See Mosher 1966 for insights into the policy actions required for countries at an early stage of development (Timmer's stage 1).

16. The end of the Cold War reduced industrialized countries' perceived need to allocate aid purely on a strategic basis.

17. See chapter 22 in this volume. For a summary of recent debates over agricultural extension in Africa, see Picciotto and Anderson 1997 and Bindlish and Evenson 1997. For a discussion of public, private, and NGO extension models, see Umali-Deininger 1997.

18. See the following literature on institutions and development: Williamson 1985; North 1990; Lin and Nugent 1995; Fafchamps, de Janvry, and Sadoulet 1995; Drobak and Nye 1997; Hayami 1997; and Clague 1997.

19. A rich set of empirical research on food security in Africa was carried out during the 1980s and 1990s by scholars at Michigan State University. Summaries of their key findings as well as extensive links to food security research by others can be found at the Michigan State's food security website (http://www.aec.msu.edu/agecon/fs2/index.htm).

REFERENCES

Alexandratos, Nikos, ed. 1995. *World Agriculture: Towards 2010, An FAO Study.* New York: John Wiley and Sons for the Food and Agriculture Organization.

Amin, Samir. 1974. *Accumulation on a World Scale: A Critique of the Theory of Underdevelopment.* New York: Monthly Review Press.

———. 1976. *Unequal Development: An Essay on the Social Formations of Peripheral Capitalism.* New York: Monthly Review Press.

Baran, Paul A. 1952. "On the Political Economy of Backwardness." *Manchester School of Economic and Social Studies* 20:66–84.

Bardhan, Pranab, ed. 1989. *The Economic Theory of Agrarian Institutions.* Oxford: Clarendon Press.

Berry, A., and R. H. Sabot. 1978. "Labor Market Performance in Developing Countries: A Survey" *World Development* 6:1199–1242.

Bhagwati, Jagdish. 1984. "Development Economics: What Have We Learned?" *Asian Development Review* 2(1): 23–38.

Bindlish, Vishva, and Robert E. Evenson. 1997. "The Impact of T&V Extension in Africa: The Experience of Kenya and Burkina Faso." *World Bank Research Observer* 12, no. 2 (August): 182–201.

Bingen, R. James. 1998. "Cotton, Democracy, and Development in Mali." *Journal of Modern African Studies* 36 (2).

Binswanger, Hans P., and Klaus Deininger. 1997. "Explaining Agricultural and Agrarain Policies in Developing Countries." *Journal of Economic Literature* 35 (4): 1958–2005.

Boserup, Ester. 1970. *Women's Role in Economic Development.* New York: St. Martin's Press.

Bromley, Daniel W., and Jean-Paul Chavas. 1989. "On Risk, Transactions, and Development in the Semiarid Tropics." *Economic Development and Cultural Change* 37, no. 4 (July): 719–36.

Brown, Lester R. 1970. *Seeds of Change.* New York: Praeger.

Cardoso, E. H., and E. Faletto. 1979. *Dependency and Development in Latin America.* Berkeley: University of California Press.

Clague, Christopher, ed. 1997. *Institutions and Economic Development: Growth and Governance in Less-Developed and Post-Socialist Countries.* Baltimore: Johns Hopkins University Press.

Coase, Ronald H. 1937. "The Nature of the Firm." *Economica* 4:386–405.

———. 1960. "The Problem of Social Cost." *Journal of Law and Economics* 3 (October): 1–44.

Commons, John R. 1924. *Legal Foundations of Capitalism.* New York: Macmillan.

———. 1950. *The Economics of Collective Action.* New York: Macmillan.

Cornia, G. Andrea, and G. Helleiner, eds. 1994. *From Adjustment to Development in Africa: Conflict, Controversy, Convergence, and Consensus?* New York: Macmillan.

David, Cristina C., and Keijiro Otsuka. 1994. "Modern Rice Technology: Emerging Views and Policy Implications." In *Modern Rice Technology and Income Distribution in Asia,* edited by Cristina C. David and Keijiro Otsuka. Boulder, Colo.: Lynne Rienner.

de Janvry, Alain. 1981. *The Agrarian Question and Reformism in Latin America.* Baltimore: Johns Hopkins University Press.

de Janvry, Alain, Marcel Fafchamps, and Elisabeth Sadoulet. 1991. "Peasant Household Behaviour with Missing Markets: Some Paradoxes Explained." *The Economic Journal* 101 (November):1400–1417.

de Janvry, Alain, Nigel Key, and Elisabeth Sadoulet. 1997. "Agricultural and Rural Development Policy in Latin America: New Directions and New Challenges." Working Paper no. 815, Department of Agricultural and Resource Economics, University of California, Berkeley.

de Soto, Hernando. 1989. *The Other Path: The Invisible Revolution in the Third World.* New York: Harper and Row.

Diagana, Bocar, and Valerie Kelly. 1996. *Will the CFA Franc Devaluation Enhance Sustainable Agricultural Intensification in the Senegalese Peanut Basin?* MSU Policy Synthesis no. 9, Department of Agricultural Economics, Michigan State University, East Lansing.

Dos Santos, T. 1970. "The Structure of Dependence." *American Economic Review* 40 (2): 231–36.

Drobak, John N., and John V. C. Nye, eds. 1997. *The Frontiers of the New Institutional Economics.* San Diego: Academic Press.

Eicher, Carl K., and Doyle C. Baker. 1992. "Agricultural Development in Sub-Saharan Africa: A Critical Survey." In *A Survey of Agricultural Economics Literature.* Vol. 4, *Agriculture in Economic Development, 1940s to 1990s,* edited by Lee R. Martin, 3–328. Minneapolis: University of Minnesota Press.

Fafchamps, Marcel, Alain de Janvry, and Elisabeth Sadoulet. 1995. "Transaction Costs, Market Failures, Competitiveness and the State." In *Agricultural Competitiveness: Market Forces and Policy Choice. Proceedings of the Twenty-Second International Conference of Agricultural Economists, Harare, Zimbabwe, 22–29 August 1994,* edited by G. H. Peters and Douglas D. Hedley, 343–54. Aldershot, U.K.: Dartmouth Publishing.

Fei, John C. H., Gustav Ranis, and Shirley W. Y. Kuo. 1979. *Growth with Equity: The Taiwan Case.* New York: Oxford University Press for the World Bank.

Fogel, Robert W. 1994. "Economic Growth, Population Theory, and Physiology: The Bearing of Long-Term Processes on the Making of Economic Policy." *American Economic Review* 84 (3): 364–95.

Food and Agriculture Organization. 1988. *Potentials for Agricultural and Rural Development in Latin America and the Caribbean: Main Report.* Rome: Food and Agriculture Organization of the United Nations.

Frank, A. G. 1966. "The Development of Underdevelopment." *Monthly Review* 18 (4): 17–31.

Furtado, Celso. 1973. "The Concept of External Dependence in the Study of Underdevelopment." In *The Political Economy of Development and Underdevelopment,* edited by Charles Wilbur, 118–27. New York: Random House.

Galtung, J. 1971. "A Structural Theory of Imperialism." *Journal of Peace Research* 2:81–116.

Harris, John R., and Michael P. Todaro. 1970. "Migration, Unemployment, and Development: A Two Sector Analysis." *American Economic Review* 60 (1): 126–42.

Hayami, Yujiro. 1997. *Development Economics: From the Poverty to the Wealth of Nations.* London: Oxford University Press.

Hayami, Y., and K. Otsuka. 1993. *The Economy of Contract Choice.* Oxford: Clarendon Press.

Heisey, Paul W., and Wilfred Mwangi. 1997. "Fertilizer Use and Maize Production." In *Africa's Emerging Maize Revolution,* edited by Derek Byerlee and Carl K. Eicher, 193–212. Boulder, Colo.: Lynne Rienner Publishers.

Hertel, Thomas W., William A. Masters, and Mark J. Gehlhar. 1997. "Regionalism in World Food Markets: Implications for Trade and Welfare." Plenary paper presented at the 23rd International Conference of Agricultural Economists, Sacramento, Calif., August 10–16.

Hirschman, Albert O. 1958. *The Strategy of Economic Development.* New Haven: Yale University Press.

———. 1981. "The Rise and Decline of Development Economics." In *Essays in Trespassing: Economics to Politics and Beyond.* New York: Cambridge University Press.

Hoff, Karla, Avishay Braverman, and Joseph E. Stiglitz, eds. 1993. *The Economics of Rural Organization: Theory, Practice, and Policy.* New York: Oxford University Press.

Holdcroft, Lane E. 1984. "The Rise and Fall of Community Development, 1950–65: A Critical Assessment." In *Agricultural Development in the Third World,* edited by Carl K. Eicher and John M. Staatz, 46–58. Baltimore: Johns Hopkins University Press.

Husain, Ishrat. 1995. "The Macroeconomics of Adjustment in Sub-Saharan Countries: Results and Lessons." In *Agricultural Competitiveness: Market Forces and Policy Choice. Proceedings of the Twenty-Second International Conference of Agricultural Economists, Harare, Zimbabwe, 22–29 August 1994,* edited by G. H. Peters and Douglas D. Hedley, 227–42. Aldershot, U.K.: Dartmouth Publishing.

International Labor Office. 1976. *Employment, Growth and Basic Needs: A One-World Problem.* Geneva: ILO.

Jayne, Thomas S. 1994. "Do High Food Marketing Costs Constrain Cash Crop Production? Evidence from Zimbabwe." *Economic Development and Cultural Change* 42, no. 2 (January): 387–402.

Jayne, Thomas S., Stephen Jones, Mulinge Mukumbu, and Share Jiriyengwa. 1997a. "Maize Marketing and Pricing Policy in Eastern and Southern Africa." In *Africa's Emerging Maize Revolution,* edited by Derek Byerlee and Carl K. Eicher, 213–43. Boulder, Colo.: Lynne Rienner Publishers.

Jayne, Thomas S., John M. Staatz, Michael T. Weber, Stephen Jones, and Eric W. Crawford. 1997b. "Agricultural Policy Reform and Productivity Change in Africa." Paper presented at the 23rd International Conference of Agricultural Economists, Sacramento, Calif., August 10–16. Department of Agricultural Economics Staff Paper no. 97-34, Michigan State University, East Lansing.

Johnston, Bruce E. 1970. "Agriculture and Structural Transformation in Developing Countries: A Survey of Research." *Journal of Economic Literature* 3(2): 369–404.

Johnston, Bruce E., and Peter Kilby. 1975. *Agriculture and Structural Transformation: Economic Strategies in Late-Developing Countries.* New York: Oxford University Press.

Johnston, Bruce E., and John W. Mellor. 1961. "The Role of Agriculture in Economic Development." *American Economic Review* 51 (4): 566–93.

Jorgenson, D. W. 1961. "The Development of a Dual Economy." *Economic Journal* 72 (June): 309–34.

Krueger, Anne O. 1978. *Liberalization Attempts and Consequences.* Lexington, Mass.: Ballinger.

Lappé, Frances Moore, and Joseph Collins. 1977. *Food First: Beyond the Myth of Scarcity.* Boston: Houghton-Mifflin.

Leftwich, Adrian, ed. 1996. *Democracy and Development: Theory and Practice.* Cambridge, U.K.: Polity Press.

Lele, Uma. 1975. *The Design of Rural Development: Lessons from Africa.* Baltimore: Johns Hopkins University Press for the World Bank.

———. 1977. "Considerations Related to Optimum Pricing and Marketing Strategies in Rural Development." In *Decision Making and Agriculture,* edited by T. Dams and K. Hunt. Lincoln: University of Nebraska Press.

Lele, Uma, and M. Agarwal. 1989. *Smallholder and Large-Scale Agriculture in Africa: Are There Trade-Offs between Growth and Equity?* MADIA Project, Washington, D.C.: World Bank.

Lewis, W. Arthur. 1954. "Economic Development with Unlimited Supplies of Labor." *Manchester School of Economic and Social Studies* 22 (2): 139–91.

———. 1955. *The Theory of Economic Growth.* London: George Allen and Unwin.

Lin, Justin Yifu, Fang Cai, and Zhou Li. 1996. *The China Miracle: Development Strategy and Economic Reform.* Hong Kong: Chinese University Press.

Lin, Justin Yifu, and Jeffrey B. Nugent. 1995. "Institutions and Economic Development." In *Handbook of Development Economics,* edited by Jere Behrman and T. N. Srinivasan, 3A:2302–70. Amsterdam: Elsevier.

Lipton, Michael. 1977. *Why Poor People Stay Poor: A Study of Urban Bias in World Development.* London: Temple-Smith.

Lipton, Michael, with Richard Longhurst. 1989. *New Seeds and Poor People.* Baltimore: Johns Hopkins University Press.

Lipumba, Nguyuru H., 1994. *Africa Beyond Adjustment.* Washington, D.C.: Overseas Development Council.

Little, I. M. D. 1982. *Economic Development: Theory, Policy, and International Relations.* New York: Basic Books.

Martin, Frédéric, Sylvain Larivière, and John M. Staatz. 1995. "Success Stories of Adjustment: Results and Lessons from Africa and Latin America." In *Agricultural Competitiveness: Market Forces and Policy Choice. Proceedings of the Twenty-Second International Conference of Agricultural Economists, Harare, Zimbabwe, 22–29 August 1994,* edited by G. H. Peters and Douglas D. Hedley, 208–26. Aldershot, U.K.: Dartmouth Publishing.

Martin, Lee R., ed. 1992. *A Survey of Agricultural Economics Literature.* Vol. 4, *Agriculture in Economic Development, 1940s to 1990s.* Minneapolis: University of Minnesota Press.

McNamara, Robert S. 1973. *Address to the Board of Governors, Nairobi, Kenya, September 24, 1972.* Washington, D.C.: International Bank for Reconstruction and Development.

Meerman, Jacob. 1997. *Reforming Agriculture: The World Bank Goes to Market.* A World Bank Operations Evaluation Study. Washington, D.C.: World Bank.

Meier, Gerald. 1976. *Leading Issues in Economic Development.* 3rd ed. New York: Oxford University Press.

Mellor, John W. 1966. *The Economics of Agricultural Development.* Ithaca: Cornell University Press.

———. 1976. *The New Economics of Growth: A Strategy for India and the Developing World.* Ithaca: Cornell University Press.

———. 1984. "Agricultural Development and the Intersectoral Transfer of Resources." In *Agricultural Development in the Third World,* edited by Carl K. Eicher and John M. Staatz, 136–46. Baltimore: Johns Hopkins University Press.

Mellor, John W., and Uma Lele. 1973. "Growth Linkages of the New Foodgrain Technologies." *Indian Journal of Agricultural Economics* 28 (1): 35–55.

Mellor, John W., and Mohinder S. Mudahar. 1992. "Agriculture in Economic Development: Theories, Findings, and Challenges in an Asian Context." In *A Survey of Agricultural Economics Literature.* Vol. 4, *Agriculture in Economic Development, 1940s to 1990s,* edited by Lee R. Martin, 331–544. Minneapolis: University of Minnesota Press.

Moock, Joyce, ed. 1986. *Understanding Africa's Rural Households and Farming Systems.* Boulder, Colo.: Westview Press.

Morris, Cynthia Taft, and Irma Adelman. 1988. *Comparative Patterns of Economic Development 1850–1914.* Baltimore: Johns Hopkins University Press.

Mosher, Arthur. 1966. *Getting Agriculture Moving: Essentials for Development and Modernization.* New York: Praeger.

Nabli, M. K., and B. Nugent, eds. 1989. *The New Institutional Economics and Development: Theory and Applications to Tunisia.* New York: North Holland.

Nicholls, William H. 1964. "The Place of Agriculture in Economic Development." In *Agriculture in Economic Development,* edited by Carl K. Eicher and Lawrence W. Witt, 11–44. New York: McGraw-Hill.

North, Douglass C. 1990. *Institutions, Institutional Change, and Economic Performance.* New York: Cambridge University Press.

North, Douglass C., and Barry R. Weingast. 1989. "Constitutions and Commitment: The Evolution of Institutions Governing Public Choice in Seventeenth-Century England." *Journal of Economic History* 49, no. 4 (December): 803–32.

Olson, Mancur. 1982. *The Rise and Decline of Nations: Economic Growth, Stagflation, and Social Rigidities.* New Haven: Yale University Press.

Ostrom, Elinor. 1990. *Governing the Commons: The Evolution of Institutions for Collective Action.* New York: Cambridge University Press.

Oxfam. 1993. *Africa, Make or Break: Action for Recovery.* Oxford: Oxfam.

Picciotto, Robert, and Jock R. Anderson. 1997. "Reconsidering Agricultural Extension." *World Bank Research Observer* 12, no. 2 (August): 249–59.

Pingali, Prabhu L., M. Hossain, and R. V. Gerpacio. 1997. *Asian Rice Bowls: The Returning Crisis?* Wallingford, U.K.: CAB International.

Pinstrup-Andersen, Per, and Rajul Pandya-Lorch. 1997. "Food Security: A Global Perspective." Plenary paper presented at the 23rd International Conference of Agricultural Economists, Sacramento, Calif., August 10–16. Washington, D.C.: International Food Policy Research Institute.

Prebisch, Raul. 1959. "Commercial Policy in the Underdeveloped Countries." *American Economic Review* 64 (May): 251–73.

———. 1981. "The Latin American Periphery in the Global System of Capitalism." *CEPAL Review* (April): 143–50. Reprinted in *International Economic Policies and Their Theoretical Foundations: A Source Book,* edited by John M. Letiche. New York: Academic Press, 1982.

Ranis, Gustav. 1997. "Successes and Failures of Development Experience since the 1980s." In *Economic and Social Development into the Twenty-first Century,* edited by Louis Emmerij, 81–98. Washington, D.C.: Inter-American Development Bank.

Ranis, Gustav, and John C. H. Fei. 1961. "A Theory of Economic Development." *American Economic Review* 51 (4): 533–65.

Rao, C. H. Hanumantha. 1994. *Agricultural Growth, Rural Poverty, and Environmental Degradation in India.* Delhi: Oxford University Press.

Rao, C. H. Hanumantha, and R. Radhakrishna. 1997. "National Food Security: A Policy Perspective for India." Plenary paper presented at the 23rd International Conference of Agricultural Economists, Sacramento, Calif., August 10–16.

Reich, Robert B. 1992. *The Work of Nations: Preparing Ourselves for the Twenty-first Century.* New York: Random House.

Reutlinger, Shlomo, and Marcelo Selowsky. 1976. *Malnutrition and Poverty: Magnitude and Policy Options.* World Bank Staff Occasional Paper no. 23. Baltimore: Johns Hopkins University Press for the World Bank.

Riley, Harold, and John M. Staatz. 1981. "Food System Organization Problems in Developing Countries." *A/D/C Report* no. 23. New York: Agricultural Development Council.

Schiff, Maurice, and Alberto Valdés. 1992. *The Political Economy of Agricultural Pricing Policy: A Synthesis of the Economics in Developing Countries.* Baltimore: Johns Hopkins University Press.

Schuh, G. Edward. 1968. "Effects of Some General Economic Development Policies on Agricultural Development." *American Journal of Agricultural Economics* 50:1283–93.

———. 1990. "The New Macroeconomics of Food and Agricultural Policy." In *Agricultural Development in the Third World,* 2nd ed., edited by Carl K. Eicher and John M. Staatz, 140–53. Baltimore: Johns Hopkins University Press.

Schuh, G. Edward, Antonio Salazar, and P. Brandâo. 1992. "The Theory, Empirical Evidence, and Debates on Agricultural Development Issues in Latin America: A Selected Survey." In *A Survey of Agricultural Economics Literature.* Vol. 4, *Agriculture in Economic Development, 1940s to 1990s,* edited by Lee R. Martin, 545–967. Minneapolis: University of Minnesota Press.

Schultz, Theodore W. 1964. *Transforming Traditional Agriculture.* New Haven: Yale University Press.

———. 1978. "On the Economics and Politics of Agriculture." In *Distortions of Agricultural Incentives,* edited by Theodore W. Schultz, 3–23. Bloomington: Indiana University Press.

———. 1981. *Investing in People: The Economics of Population Quality.* Berkeley: University of California Press.

Sen, Amartya. 1981. *Poverty and Famines.* Oxford: Clarendon Press.

Singh, I. J., L. Squire, and J. Strauss, eds. 1986. *Agricultural Household Models: Extensions, Applications, and Policy.* Washington, D.C.: World Bank.

Smith, Lawrence D. 1995. "Malawi: Reforming the State's Role in Agricultural Marketing." *Food Policy* 20 (6): 561–71.

Spencer, Dunstan S. C., and Ousmane Badiane. 1995. "Agriculture and Economic Recovery in African Countries." In *Agricultural Competitiveness: Market Forces and Policy Choice. Proceedings of the Twenty-Second International Conference of Agricultural Economists, Harare, Zimbabwe, 22–29 August 1994,* edited by G. H. Peters and Douglas D. Hedley, 61–78. Aldershot, U.K.: Dartmouth Publishing.

Staatz, John M., and Moussa Ba. 1996. *Fostering Agricultural and Food System Transformation in Africa.* MSU Policy Synthesis no. 13. East Lansing: Michigan State University.

Staatz, John M., and Jennifer B. Wohl. 1991. "The Evolution of Food Self-Sufficiency Policies in West Africa." In *National and Regional Self-Sufficiency Goals: Implications for International*

Agriculture, edited by Fred Ruppel and Earl Kellogg, 65–87. Boulder, Colo.: Lynne Rienner Publishers.

Stern, Nicholas. 1989. "The Economics of Development: A Survey." *Economic Journal* 99 (September): 597–685.

Stevens, Robert D., ed. 1977. *Tradition and Dynamics in Small-Farm Agriculture.* Ames: Iowa State University Press.

Stiglitz, Joseph E. 1988. "Economic Organization, Information, and Development." In *Handbook of Development Economics,* edited by H. Chenery and T. N. Srinivasan, 1:93–160. New York: North Holland.

Strauss, John, and Kathleen Beegle. 1996. *Intrahousehold Allocations: A Review of Theories, Empirical Evidence, and Policy Issues.* MSU International Development Working Paper no. 63, Departments of Agricultural Economics and Economics, Michigan State University, East Lansing.

Sunkel, O. 1973. "Transnational Capitalism and National Disintegration in Latin America." *Social and Economic Studies* 22:132–76.

Tendler, Judith. 1997. *Good Government in the Tropics.* Baltimore: Johns Hopkins University Press.

Timmer, C. Peter, Walter P. Falcon, and Scott R. Pearson. 1983. *Food Policy Analysis.* Baltimore: Johns Hopkins University Press.

Tinker, Irene, and Michele Bo Bramsen, eds. 1976. *Women and World Development.* Washington, D.C.: Overseas Development Council.

Todaro, M. P. 1969. "A Model of Labor Migration and Urban Unemployment in Less Developed Countries." *American Economic Review* 59:138–48.

Tomich, Thomas P., Peter Kilby, and Bruce F. Johnston. 1995. *Transforming Agrarian Economies: Opportunities Seized, Opportunities Missed.* Ithaca: Cornell University Press.

Tripp, Robert, ed. 1991. *Planned Change in Farming Systems: Progress in On-Farm Research.* Chichester, U.K.: John Wiley.

Tweeten, Luther G., and Donald G. McClelland, 1997. *Promoting Third-World Development and Food Security.* New York: Praeger.

Umali-Deininger, Dina. 1997. "Public and Private Agricultural Extension: Partners or Rivals?" *World Bank Research Observer* 12, no. 2 (August): 203–24.

Uphoff, Norman, Milton J. Esman, and Anirudh Krishna. 1998. *Reasons for Success: Learning from Instructive Experiences in Rural Development.* West Hartford, Conn.: Kumarian Press.

U.S. Department of Agriculture. 1996. *The U.S. Contribution to World Food Security: The U.S. Position Paper Prepared for the World Food Summit.* Washington, D.C.: U.S. Department of Agriculture.

Valdés, Alberto. 1986. "Impact of Trade and Macroeconomic Policies on Agricultural Growth: The South American Experience." In *Economic and Social Progress in Latin America: 1986 Report,* 161–83. Washington, D.C.: Inter-American Development Bank.

Veblen, Thorstein. 1912. *The Theory of the Leisure Class: An Economic Study of Institutions.* New York: Macmillan.

———. 1927. *The Theory of Business Enterprise.* New York: Scribner.

Weber, Michael, John M. Staatz, John S. Holtzman, Eric W. Crawford, and Richard H. Bernsten. 1988. "Informing Food Security Decisions in Africa: Empirical Analysis and Policy Dialogue." *American Journal of Agricultural Economics* 70, no. 5 (December): 1045–54.

Williamson, Oliver. 1985. *The Economic Institutions of Capitalism.* New York: Free Press.

World Bank. 1981. *Accelerated Development in Sub-Saharan Africa: An Agenda for Action.* Washington, D.C.: World Bank.

———. 1988. *Rural Development: World Bank Experience, 1965–86.* Washington, D.C.: World Bank.

———. 1996. "Poverty Reduction: The Most Urgent Task." World Bank Brief. Washington, D.C.: World Bank (available at http://www.worldbank.org/html/extdr/pov.htm).

———. 1997. *World Development Report, 1997.* Washington, D.C.: Oxford University Press.

World Commission on Environment and Development. 1987. *Our Common Future.* Oxford: Oxford University Press.

2

Agriculture and Food Needs to 2025

ALEX F. McCALLA

INTRODUCTION

Everyone agrees that the world's population will exceed 8 billion people by 2025, an increase of over 2½ billion in the next thirty years. Everyone agrees that most of the increase will occur in the cities of developing countries. The world's urban population is expected to rise from 1 billion in 1985 to 4 billion in 2025. Most everyone agrees that developing countries' food needs could nearly double by 2025, because of expected increases in income and urbanization in addition to population growth.

Given this widespread agreement on the needs, or demand, side of the equation, and its magnitude—the greatest growth in human numbers in history and the corresponding increase in food production that will be required—why is there so little agreement on the ease or difficulty of generating the supply to meet that demand? The spectrum of views ranges from one extreme—"there is no problem"—to the other—"the imminent arrival of the Malthusian nightmare, unless effective population control is implemented immediately." By far the predominance of views is toward the "no problem" end and can only be characterized as bordering on complacency.

Therefore, the puzzle addressed in this lecture is the following: how can intelligent students of the international food economy agree so closely on the demand side and disagree so wildly on the capacity of the world to provide the supply to meet that demand? The objective of this lecture is to critically appraise the competing viewpoints and to show that, regardless of which view you prefer, the productivity improvement challenge facing world agriculture is enormous. From initiation to implementation in farmers' fields, agricultural research takes ten to twenty years to have an impact. Twenty years from now there will be at least 1.8 billion more people in the world to feed. Research and technolo-

ALEX F. McCALLA is director of the Rural Development Department of the World Bank.

This is a slightly revised version of the Tenth Annual Sir John Crawford Lecture, International Centers Week, CGIAR, Washington, D.C., October 27, 1994. Published by permission of the CGIAR, the World Bank, and the author.

gy development, if it is to contribute to the needed production, must start today. Every day spent on further debate about whether "Malthus must wait" or "Malthus is finally right" is "fiddling while Rome burns."

Specifically I will do five things. First, I will review briefly the past history of "food crises" debates. Second, I will quickly summarize the demand side upon which most people agree. Third, I will summarize four different viewpoints on the supply side of the world food equation, running the gamut from the "no problem" view, as exemplified by Donald O. Mitchell, Merlinda D. Ingco, and Ronald C. Duncan in their book entitled *The World Food Outlook* (1997) to the ominous predictions of Lester R. Brown and Hal Kane in *Full House: Reassessing the Earth's Population Carrying Capacity* (1994). Fourth, I will critically appraise the consequences of each of these scenarios for agricultural development and technology generation. Finally, I will focus on the consequences of not recognizing the urgency of the productivity challenge.

PAST DEBATES

The sufficiency of future food supplies has been a recurrent issue in international debate during most of the post–World War II period. The debate is most frequently driven by supply side considerations. Since Thomas Malthus wrote his "Essay on the Principle of Population as It Affects the Future Improvement of Society" in 1798, the debate has focused on the race between supply (seen to grow linearly) and population (seen to grow exponentially). New lands, new technology, and capital investment in irrigation have delayed the "Malthusian cross" (i.e., when population growth exceeds the rate of increase in food supply) for most of the world; but the debate over the question "For how long?" has raged for years.

Immediately after World War II, there were concerns about imminent food shortages. These quickly gave way to food production surges and rising stocks in the 1950s and early 1960s. Two bad monsoons in South Asia during 1965–66 led to resurgent concerns about imminent famine. In 1967 William and Paul Paddock wrote a best-seller called *Famine, 1975!*, which predicted famine by 1975. In the late 1960s and early 1970s, Malthus was kept at bay again by expanded output. The years 1972–74 saw a coincidence of events—production shortfalls in several locations simultaneously and rapid demand expansion, particularly from the Soviet Union, which caused agricultural prices to skyrocket. Grain prices tripled over an eight-month period. Global food shortages were predicted. Then U.S. secretary of agriculture Earl Butz exhorted farmers to "plant fencerow to fencerow."

Food stocks were rebuilt in the early 1980s. The United States instituted its most comprehensive and expensive supply control program, Payment in Kind (PIK), in 1983 as stocks soared. The 1988 drought brought a brief return of the issue of possible shortages, but concerns about excess supplies soon cooled the debate, at least in developed countries. Mitchell, Ingco, and Duncan reviewed food shortages in historical perspective and concluded that technological pessimists have always been wrong.

Currently, the food production versus population growth issue is the subject of some increased debate caused by recent (1995–96) increases in international grain prices, but the issue is still not viewed as critical, even though there are widely divergent views on the world's capacity to increase production sufficiently to feed more than 8 billion people.

WORLD FOOD NEEDS TO 2025: THE CONVERGENT VIEW

World population will double in the next forty years. By 2025, the median variant of projections by the United Nations suggests a global population approaching 8.5 billion people. A larger share of that population will live in developing countries than have in the past. In 1985, 75 percent of the world's population lived in developing countries; in 2025 more than 83 percent will live there. At present, approximately 31 percent of the population of developing countries live in cities, although there are strong regional differences. It is estimated that by 2025, 57 percent of the population in developing countries will live in cities. The number of people living in cities will more than triple, from 1 billion to over 3 billion. Regionally, compared to 1985, the population in Asia will nearly double, to over 4 billion, while that in sub-Saharan Africa will more than triple, from 420 million to nearly 1.3 billion in 2025 (table 1). The number of malnourished will rise from the current level of 750 million to more than 1 billion.

Like population growth, income growth increases the demand for food. Even with modest income growth in developing countries, their demand for food in

TABLE 1
GLOBAL POPULATION DISTRIBUTION PATTERNS

	World	Developed Countries	Developing Countries	Sub-Saharan Africa	Latin America	Asia and the Pacific	West Asia, North Africa
			Population (millions)				
1960	3,019	964	2,055	209	218	1,505	123
1985	4,855	1,210	3,645	421	404	2,575	245
2010	7,195	1,365	5,826	916	631	3,810	469
2025	8,467	1,422	7,045	1,296	761	4,379	609
			Distribution (percentage)				
1960	100.0	31.9	68.1	6.9	7.2	49.8	4.1
1985	100.0	24.9	75.1	8.7	8.3	53.0	5.0
2010	100.0	19.0	81.0	12.7	8.8	53.0	6.5
2025	100.0	16.8	83.2	15.3	9.0	51.7	7.2

SOURCE: CGIAR 1990.

2025 could be nearly double their current levels of production. Further, urbanization, in conjunction with income growth, will cause the character of diets to shift away from roots and tubers and lower quality staple grains to higher quality cereals, such as rice and wheat, then to livestock products and vegetables.

The large projected increases in urban population in developing countries perhaps has not received the attention it deserves in the demand debate. Further, much of this urbanization will occur in Asia, where rapid growth in incomes, particularly in the Pacific Rim, are also occurring. The combination of these factors will cause significant changes in the composition, form, and location of food demand. For example, very rapid increases in the demand for meat and fruits and vegetables are occurring in China and have already occurred in other fast growing countries of the Pacific Rim. The increase in meat consumption is predominantly of poultry and to a lesser extent pork. The production of both requires an expanded use of feedgrains.

Different and more complex forms of processing are required to satisfy urban needs. Fruits and vegetables are perishable and expensive to transport. This explains why they are grown on the urban fringes. Further, urbanites are typically wage workers who require food that can be prepared more conveniently.

While it is relatively easy to multiply projected population by estimates of per capita cereal consumption, it is much more difficult to project the quantitative amounts of demand for the components of a more complex diet. The International Food Policy Research Institute (IFPRI) projects significant shifts in the composition of diets because of urbanization and income growth. Therefore, we should temper our statement that everyone agrees on the demand side. It is perhaps more appropriate to say that there is wide agreement on the aggregate magnitude of future cereal demands.

With massive urbanization will come increased need for basic infrastructure, as well as urban-oriented food security policies. With these changes will come the need for increased investment in "the beyond the farmgate marketing system" to accommodate a very large increase in the demand for marketing services. At least five factors will contribute to the increase in this demand: (1) expanded use of purchased inputs in intensified farming systems; (2) a more than doubling of the volume of food moving from farms to towns and cities; (3) the income-induced increase in demand for perishable products (fruits, vegetables, and animal products); (4) increased demand, with rising incomes, for additional services (e.g., packaging, portion control, and location) to be incorporated into food; and (5) the possibility of expanded nontraditional exports to industrial countries.

If, as is often the case, more than 50 percent of the value added to agricultural products is done by the marketing system, then increasing the productivity of the off-farm segments of the food system may be as critical to reducing real food prices to consumers as on-farm productivity growth. It is unlikely that the development of this market infrastructure will be done solely by the private sector. Significant public investment will also be needed in the food system beyond the farmgate. Finally, most observers also agree that there will be wide regional differences in the severity of hunger and malnutrition. All agree that sub-Saharan Africa and South Asia will face particularly difficult problems. Let us recall that by 2025 these two regions will have a population of around 4 billion people.

THE SUPPLY SIDE: THE DIVERGENT VIEWS

Perceptions of the capacity of the world to meet the above challenges vary widely. On the optimistic side are analysts who use global projection models based on past trends, which basically conclude that on a global basis the world can feed itself until at least 2010. The clearest and most comprehensive presentation of this view is Mitchell, Ingco, and Duncan 1997. At the opposite end of the spectrum is Brown and Kane 1994. These two works present such vastly contrasting views that one wonders whether they are talking about the same planet.

Between these two poles are two other views. One, which I call the "conventional scenario," argues that the challenge is serious indeed, requiring that developing countries increase significantly their capacity to feed themselves and in a sustainable fashion. The perception is that the job can be done, but that if current investments in agricultural development and productivity improvement are not maintained or increased the world will spin toward the Brown-Kane model. A fourth scenario is often put forward by developed country exporters, namely that "the North will feed the South." One characteristic of this approach is a hypothesis presented by Ian Carruthers under the title "Going, Going, Gone! Tropical Agriculture As We Knew It" (1993), which argues that developing countries will not be able to meet their growing urban cereal demands and that the developed countries must fill the gap with greatly expanded trade.

I begin by presenting the conventional view and then turn to the other three scenarios.

SCENARIO 1: THE CONVENTIONAL VIEW

The challenge facing world agriculture is enormous. Developing country food production could be required to double. Until the middle of the twentieth century, expansion of cultivated area roughly kept pace with population growth. In the past forty years, the doubling of cereal output came from three sources—expansion of land under cultivation, increased intensity of cultivation (mainly through expanded irrigation), and yield increases. While irrigated area more than doubled from 1950 and 1980, its rate of growth has since slowed substantially, as has expansion of cultivated acreage in rainfed areas. The current view is that the next doubling of food production must come primarily from increased productivity (i.e., yield). Already an increase in productivity in many developing countries is putting stress on the natural resource base—in some countries as much land is lost to erosion and salinization as is brought into production through irrigation or area expansion.

Therefore, the difficult challenge facing world agriculture is to double production on the same land base while maintaining or, hopefully, improving the natural resource base. These are the twin challenges of creating environmentally sustainable production systems—productivity improvement and improved management of natural resources.

The aggregate challenge is staggering enough, but when we begin to disaggregate food demand, the task is more complicated. As noted, rising incomes and increased urbanization alter the composition of food demand. Consumers demand more diverse and higher-quality diets, and they need foods that can be transported and stored. While yields of some cereals, such as wheat and rice, have doubled in the last thirty years, yields of crops such as maize, cassava, sorghum, millet, beans, and edible legumes have shown less rapid increases. To double again the wheat and rice yields and to more than double the yields of other basic food products will be problematic without increased research and development efforts. While biotechnology holds the promise for significant genetic improvements, the flow of new technology is proving to be slower than expected.

This scenario implicitly views the food supply problem as basically a nationalistic one (i.e., countries are responsible for their own food security). This is generally translated to mean that they are responsible for their own food production. Trade enters the scenario in a limited way. If food demands double, grain consumption—of wheat, rice, and maize—will need to increase from today's 1.9 billion metric tons to 3.8 billion metric tons. International grain trade is now around 200 million metric tons, or approximately 10 percent of the supply, and is not likely to grow as a percentage. If developing countries are to grow their own food, and if their populations increase at 2 percent per year, then their food production must also rise by 2 percent per year.

Scenario 2: The Optimists

Analysts have been projecting world food supply and demand balances for decades. In the simplest form of these projections, rates of population growth are added to rates of income growth, modified by the income elasticity of the demand for food, and result in a rate of growth in food needs (i.e., demand). This rate is then compared to rates of growth in productivity (i.e., production), usually made up of an estimate of new land availability plus projected yield increases. These models, therefore, are basically projections of two compounding growth rates. Any deviation between these rates leads to either food gaps or food surpluses, and the difference increases the further the projection. If the model has endogenous prices, then real prices either rise or fall. Over a twenty-five-year time horizon a .1 percent difference leads to substantial divergence. In reality, of course, food gaps or food surpluses do not occur, because prices in the marketplace equilibrate quantity supplied to quantity demanded, thus the strong focus on the direction of real prices of food over future periods.

One such model deserves our attention here. In Mitchell, Ingco, and Duncan's controversial book *The World Food Outlook,* after reviewing predictions of global food shortages from the past several decades, the authors conclude that the world has really done quite well. Using three indicators—real food prices, calories available to consumers, and per capita food production—they conclude that, overall, the world is better fed in 1990 than it was in 1960. Real food prices, except for a blip from 1972 to 1974, have continued their century-long decline. "Per capita calorie supplies in developing countries have risen by 27 percent since the early 1960s" (Mitchell, Ingco, and Duncan 1997, 1) and overall per capita food supplies "have increased steadily since 1961" (25).

Mitchell, Ingco, and Duncan pose the basic question, What can we expect in 2010? Their model is based on two critical assumptions. The first is that the global population growth rate will decline from 1.74 percent in 1994 to 1.4 percent in 2010. The second is that the world grain production will grow at 2 percent per annum from now until 2010. The results of their baseline simulation model is that global increases in food production will more than keep pace with increases in demand. Grain imports by developing countries are expected to more than double between 1990 and 2010, but these will easily be provided by expanded exports from developed countries and reduced net imports by formerly centrally planned economies (120–21).

The conclusions of the study by Mitchell, Ingco, and Duncan are:

1. The simulation results strongly suggest that the outlook for the world food situation is good, despite regional problems. (120)
2. It should become increasingly easy to meet the world's demand for grain if past trends in production and consumption continue. (145)
3. The most important conclusion to come from our analysis is that the world food system has many options to meet future demand. (146)

Mitchell, Ingco, and Duncan's overall conclusion is as follows:

The world food situation has improved dramatically during the past thirty years and the prospects are very good that the twenty-year period from 1990 to 2010 will see further gains. However, these gains depend on continued increases in food production along the trends of the past. *This will not occur automatically, rather it will require continued investments in research to increase crop yields and in other factors of production.* If past crop yield trends continue and if population growth rates slow as projected, then the gains in the world food situation seen during the past thirty years should continue. If Malthus is ultimately to be correct in his warning that population will outstrip food production, then at least we can say: *Malthus Must Wait.* (16, emphasis added)

Other studies, such as *Agriculture: Towards 2010,* by the Food and Agriculture Organization of the United Nations (FAO), and an IFPRI paper by Mark W. Rosegrant and Mercedita Agcaoili entitled "Global and Regional Food Demand, Supply, and Trade Prospects to 2010" (1994), reach similar, though not identical, conclusions. The FAO study uses the same population growth rate for 2010—1.4 percent—but a slightly lower rate of global production increase—1.8 percent. The study concludes that per capita calorie supplies will rise and the absolute numbers of people suffering chronic undernutrition will decline. Production increases for grains are projected to be 2.2 percent per annum, made up of a 1.4 percent per annum increase in yield and a .8 percent per annum increase in area harvested.

Rosegrant and Agcaoili use an IFPRI simulation model to project to 2010. Aggregate simulation results suggest declining or constant real prices of major food commodities, which suggest optimism for future aggregate food supplies. As with the studies by Mitchell, Ingco, and Duncan and the FAO, the IFPRI study also points to potential regional problems, particularly in sub-Saharan Africa, but in general it is upbeat.

The conclusion of the IFPRI study is:

> If governments and the international community maintain (or renew) their commitment to agricultural growth through policy reform and sustained, cost-effective investment in agricultural research, extension, irrigation and water development, human capital, and rural infrastructure, there will be no overwhelming pressure on aggregate world food supplies from rising population and incomes. Projected per capita availability of food will increase and real world food prices will be stable or declining for key food crops. However, these aggregate price trends conceal emerging problems at the regional and country level, which show that there will continue to be problems in getting food to those who need it most. (Rosegrant and Agcaoili 1994, 40–41)

Thus, these models project that growth in global production will keep pace with global demand. In fact, they argue that production could grow faster than 2 percent if land currently held out of production in developed countries is returned to production. The conclusion is that supply will continue to press on demand, leading to a continuation of the decline in real grain prices that has persisted with few exceptions for the last hundred years. They conclude that there will be no global world food problem, as aggregate supply will be equal to or greater than aggregate demand at constant or lower real prices. Finally, none of the studies sees resource degradation as a critical issue. In fact Mitchell, Ingco, and Duncan suggest that less land will be needed to feed the world in year 2010.

They do, however, admit that there will be problems in some areas, such as sub-Saharan Africa and South Asia, where there is severe malnutrition. The problems, they predict, will be ones of access to food, which is a poverty problem not a food problem. If pressed, the supporters of these models will admit that a 1.8 percent to 2 percent output growth assumption is critical and that there will, therefore, be a role for research and technology development, but they do not foresee a global food crisis in the next decade or two. They are generally silent about the longer term.

SCENARIO 3: THE PESSIMISTS

At the opposite end of the spectrum we find Brown and Kane in *Full House: Reassessing the Earth's Population Carrying Capacity*. This book is in stark contrast to the Mitchell, Ingco, and Duncan analysis. The basic premise is that the decade of the 1990s marks the beginning of a new era during which it will be much more difficult to expand food output:

Many knew that this time would eventually come, that at some point the limits of the earth's natural systems, the cumulative effects of environmental degradation on cropland productivity, and the shrinking backlog of yield-raising technologies would slow the record growth in food production in recent decades. But because no one knew exactly when or how this would happen, the food prospect was widely debated. Now we can see that several constraints are emerging simultaneously to slow the growth in food production. (1994, 22)

The "facts" according to Brown and Kane are different from those used by Mitchell, Ingco, and Duncan. Brown and Kane say grain production expanded at 3 percent per year from 1950 to 1984 but that the rate of growth dropped to scarcely 1 percent annually during the period 1984–93. Recall that Mitchell, Ingco, and Duncan projected a continuation of the 2 percent per year growth in production that occurred in the 1980s. Further, Brown and Kane argue that production of fish has reached its biological limit and the carrying capacity of rangelands has been exceeded, requiring future food needs to be met only by the cropland food system, whereas before it was met by all three—fish, livestock, and crops.

Therefore, Brown and Kane argue, future supply trends will be subject to six new constraints:

1. the shrinking backlog of unused agricultural technology,
2. the growing human demands that are pressing against the limits of what fisheries and rangelands can contribute to increase food needs,
3. the demands for water that are pressing against hydrologic limits,
4. the declining response of crops in many countries to additional fertilizer application,
5. the substantial losses of cropland to industrialization and urbanization, and
6. The "social disintegration, often fed by rapid population growth and environment degradation [that] is undermining many national governments and their efforts to expand food production." (24)

Full House presents quantitative information to back up these basic propositions. Food production increases have slowed perceptibly in the past ten years and may slow even more in the future. Per capita grain production has fallen from a peak of 346 kilograms per capita in 1984 to 303 kilograms per capita in 1993. World grain stocks, as a percentage of production, are at an all-time low. Relatively little land is currently being held out of production in the United States and the European Union, and what is out is of low productivity. Bringing all this land back into production would "expand the world grain area by only 1.6 percent, not half enough to get it back to the historical high reached in 1981" (99).

Further, China is losing nearly 1 million hectares, or 1 percent of its cropland, per year to industrialization. Brown and Kane predict that China will follow a path similar to those of Japan, South Korea, and Taiwan, where their combined grain areas decreased from 8 million hectares to 4 million hectares from 1950–90. Thus, in their scenario, China will experience a 66 million-metric-ton *reduction* in grain production between 1990 and 2030 and an increase of 210 million metric tons in imports—more than the total world trade in grain in the 1990s.

In a more recent book, *Who Will Feed China?*, Brown expands his analysis and produces two scenarios that could have China importing between 207 and 369 million metric tons by 2030. While many forecasters project increases in Chinese imports, to the range of 30–50 million metric tons, none approaches Brown's level. In fact, Rozelle, Huang, and Rosegrant analytically show that only under the most extreme assumptions about land degradation and declining research expenditures can they generate imports that approach Brown's lower limit.

These facts plus others—declining fertilizer use, a fall off in yield increases in recent years in many countries (world grain yields increased 2.3 percent per year from 1950 to 1984 but only 1 percent per year 1984 to 1993), declining investments in agricultural research, and increasing environmental pressures—lead Brown and Kane to conclude that the world is close to exceeding its carrying capacity. Their analysis suggests that by 2030 world grain import needs will "exceed exportable supplies by 526 million tons, an amount approaching the current grain consumption in the United States and China combined" (188). Their bottom line is that the growing imbalance between food and people can only be redressed by frontally attacking the population issue. In sum, if Brown and Kane were to paraphrase Mitchell, Ingco, and Duncan's concluding sentence it would read "Malthus is here."

SCENARIO 4: THE DEVELOPED COUNTRIES FILL THE GAP

A scenario gaining favor in the developed world has the North feeding the South. One example of this scenario is the one put forward by the late Ian Carruthers in "Going, Going, Gone! Tropical Agriculture As We Knew It." Carruthers's view is that our traditional model wherein developed (i.e., rich) countries supply the world with manufactured goods and financial services while the developing (i.e., poor) countries provide primary products—such as food, natural resource–based products, and minerals—is not sustainable. This view says that in the long run developing countries will produce manufactured goods and trade them for food from developed countries. Carruthers' argument, in simplified terms, runs as follows:

1. The tropical nations are incapable of producing enough basic foodstuffs for the burgeoning cities in the developing world, where population is estimated to reach 4 billion by 2025. Their fragile tropical and subtropical environments will be lucky to support the remaining 50 percent that will still subsist from the land.
2. The trend has already started that developed countries—the United States, Canada, Europe, and Australia—export food to developing countries and increasingly import labor intensive manufactured goods.
3. Production increase potentials are greater in the temperate zone nations, be-

cause they have better technology and significant areas of idle land. Therefore, developed countries can provide increased food supplies through
trade.

4. If, as the scenario suggests, developing countries export manufactured
goods (i.e., from labor abundance), urbanites in developing countries will
have enough income to import basic foods (i.e., grains).

The implications of this kind of scenario are enormous. If the additional 2+
billion urban dwellers are to be fed by trade, international grain trade in the next
thirty years will have to increase at least three times, from 200 million metric
tons to over 600 million metric tons per year, assuming minimum consumption
of 200 kilograms per capita. This is—physically, biologically, and economically—a huge task. If trade does not expand this rapidly, the impact on food prices
could be substantial, causing greater increases in malnutrition in poor countries.
However, since Carruthers's paper does not contain any numbers, he is unable
to address the issue of the feasibility of the required increase in grain production
in developed countries. The United States currently provides about half of world
grain exports. To maintain that share U.S. grain production would have to almost
triple by 2030.

SOME COMPARISONS OF THE SCENARIOS

The four scenarios presented look at the same "facts" and reach vastly different conclusions. The reasons for the differences, despite all the rhetoric, reside
basically in four projection parameters:

1. the rate of increase in biological cereal yields to be expected over the next
fifteen to thirty years,
2. the amount of new land to be added to or lost from agricultural production,
3. the amount of land subject to increased intensification of cultivation, primarily through irrigation, and
4. the impact of environmental degradation on food production capacity.

Mitchell, Ingco, and Duncan assume a continuation of the rate of increase in
grain production seen during the past several decades, with 90 percent of that increase coming from yield increases. In their terms, yield is output per unit of
land, which includes the impact of both biological yield increases and intensification. Presumably the rate of growth in both biological yield and irrigation is
assumed to be the same as during 1960–90. Therefore, the assumption with respect to increased land area appears to be close to zero. They minimize any significant negative impact on production of resource degradation.

On the other extreme, Brown and Kane argue that growth in biological yield
has slowed to about 1 percent per year during the past decade and may decline
further. Herein lies the major difference—a 1 percent difference in a compound
growth rate over thirty years makes an enormous difference at the end of the pro-

jection period. Further, Brown and Kane argue that land lost from agricultural production coupled with increased urban competition for water leads to a projected decline in irrigated acreage. Environmental degradation will further constrain production increases. Carruthers makes no explicit presumptions about any of these parameters but must implicitly be assuming low yield growth in developing countries, very high rates of yield growth plus expansion of cultivated area in developed countries, and environmental constraints mainly in the tropics and subtropics.

The conventional scenario argues that biological yields must increase to about 2 percent per annum to replace the contributions made by area expansion and intensification in the last three decades. These yield increases must be accomplished without degrading the environment further.

All scenarios recognize the need for sustained or increased investments in research and technology development.

One must be somewhat cautious in assuming that it will be easy to achieve future biological yield increases. Research by the International Rice Research Institute (IRRI) and the International Maize and Wheat Improvement Center (CIMMYT) has found a significant slowing in the rate of yield increases of rice and wheat in intensified production systems (Pingali and Heisey 1996). Nor should we be blasé about area or irrigation expansion. While the area of potentially useable arable land seems large, its potential for production has been seriously questioned in a recent study by Feder and Keck (1994).

The trade implications of the four scenarios are also widely different. The North will feed the South scenario appears to be arguing that, given population increases in developing countries, exports from developed countries would need to accomplish an increase of more than 300 percent to possibly 600–700 million metric tons by 2025. Brown and Kane have export requirements that appear to exceed 700 million metric tons. The Mitchell-Ingco-Duncan model sees a doubling of developing country imports by 2010 and, presumably, if the models were projected further, developing country imports could double again by 2025. This would imply a tripling of cereal trade. Finally, the conventional scenario would imply a doubling of cereal trade.

All scenarios but the conventional one raise two critical issues: first the capacity of the developed countries, and possibly the formerly centrally planned economies, to achieve the required rate of increase in output, particularly given environmental concerns and resource limits; second, the physical capacity of developing country infrastructure to handle the volume of trade projected. These three models are very cavalier about assuming that these two barriers can be overcome. A third issue is, of course, the substantial investment required in post-farmgate markets and infrastructure. The authors of these models do not address this issue.

Of course, no one knows who will be right. Projections thirty years ahead, particularly those by economists, are invariably wrong. This is partly because of questionable assumptions, limited models, and poor information, but also because a dynamic world economy is self-adjusting, since it does not tolerate disequilibrium easily.

THE CONSEQUENCES FOR THE FUTURE

While my own views tend to be more consistent with the conventional view than with any of the others, this is not crucially important. Regardless of who is correct, the productivity–food production challenge for the globe is very substantial. Given the agreement on the demand side, all scenarios "require" 1.8 to 2.0 percent per year increases in global food production. However, each scenario would have a different distribution of required relative increases. At one extreme, the North feeds the South scenario places almost the entire burden of production increases on developed countries. Mitchell, Ingco, and Duncan clearly imply a larger rate of yield increase in developed countries. The conventional view places more of the burden on developing countries and implies that virtually all of these increases must come from biological yield increases. Brown and Kane are skeptical about the possibility of feeding the expanding population. Under all scenarios, the biological yield increases accomplished over the last thirty years must be at least maintained, or better yet, increased.

Several other points need to be made:

1. The global requirement that production systems be nondegrading to the environment (i.e., sustainable production systems) increases an already enormous research and development challenge. Few systems have sustained increases of over 2 percent per year, and these have often been at the expense of resource degradation.
2. Sources of new rainfed land are limited and the rate of increase of irrigated land has slowed considerably because of rising costs and the threat of long-term salinization. Therefore, production increases must come from yield increases. How difficult will it be to get 250 bushes per acre of corn or to increase the average irrigated rice yields in developing countries from 3.5 tons to 7 tons per hectare? Doubling sorghum yields in the Sahel from 500 kilograms to 1 metric ton per hectare is not going to help much in meeting global food security needs no matter how important it is to the Sahel.
3. Even increasing production does not solve the malnutrition problem, which will surely grow. It is a problem of access and income.
4. The mix of crops will need to change, to produce more tradable surpluses that are transportable and storable. Further, the increased foreign exchange earnings required by developing countries for imports require a much more open trading system than we now have.

The recently concluded GATT/WTO Agreement has brought agricultural trade under the rules of GATT for the first time but resulted in little immediate reduction in trade distortions. The impact of the agreement on the level of world prices over the life of the agreement is likely to be small, and in the long run the agreement should decrease the amplitude of fluctuations in world prices. However, internal price instability could increase in individual countries as quantitative barriers are converted to tariffs. The run up in international prices in the mid-1990s was caused by weather and policy-related changes. These resulted in a substantial reduction in harvested area in the United States, the European Union, and the former Soviet Union. The accompanying run down in stocks has probably contributed to price instability and reduced availability of food aid. However, it is inappropriate to link these events to the GATT Agreement. Overall the GATT Agreement should increase the efficiency of global production (which should decrease prices) and increase price stability in world markets as more and more countries adjust to changes in price.

Finally, we must recognize that the agricultural productivity issue is not just an issue of food supplies or even biological food security. Let me make three quick but very important, points in this regard.

First, in the poorest countries of the world, the agricultural sector remains the most important, in terms of both employment and income generation. Increased productivity in subsistence and smallholder agriculture is a powerful engine of labor-intensive growth, income improvement, and better access to food. It is a major contributor to poverty alleviation and equity improvement.

Second, more of the poorest of the poor and the malnourished currently live in low-potential areas than in high-potential areas, and rural numbers will far exceed urban numbers well into the next century (Pinstrup-Andersen and Pandya-Lorch 1994b). Thus, improvement in productivity in agriculture in both low- and high-potential areas has the multiple impact of increasing production, reducing poverty, reducing malnutrition, and generating growth, thereby improving food security broadly defined. Agricultural development is not just about increasing cereal yields. Further, for the growing number of urban poor, ever-declining real food prices are a positive contribution to reducing malnutrition and poverty.

Third, increased yield per unit of land, particularly biological yield increases, reduces pressure on fragile environments. Feder and Keck (1994) argue that "every 0.1 percent of yield increase in the period 2010 to 2025 'substitutes' for about 25 million hectares of rainfed cropland" (22). Further, given that agricultural production systems are dominant users of the arable landscape, attention to environmental issues in the development of sustainable production systems is an indispensable component of any successful future strategy.

CONCLUDING COMMENTS

The frightening part of this story is that, while the challenge just outlined is, in my view, critical and immediate, funds to support agricultural development and productivity improvement are being reduced in developed countries, and aid agencies and international development institutions are reducing the share of resources going towards agriculture. This trend is made worse by the overall decline in development assistance. Even the interest of developing country governments in agricultural development appears to be in steep decline. There is at least a twenty-year lag between initiating strategic research and any resulting significant increases in production in farmers' fields. Twenty years from now there will be at least 1.8 billion more people to feed and most of them will be in developing country cities. Not to recognize the challenge and increase efforts is bad enough, but to allow existing research capacity to erode is much worse.

Explanations for the apparent neglect of a critical problem abound: the short attention span of politicians; perceptions of over production and surpluses in rich countries; protectionist domestic agricultural policies that reduce incentive prices in developing countries; aid fatigue; fiscal crises in countries of the Organization for Economic Co-operation and Development; the end of the Cold War, which reduced the urgency for development assistance; and on and on. Regardless of the reason, not addressing these issues now will clearly have serious future consequences. Unfortunately, extremely pessimistic or optimistic scenarios, both of which must be questioned, detract us from serious debate on this critical issue. The effort of IFPRI, through their 2020 Vision for Food, Agriculture, and the Environment Initiative, has moved some way in that direction, but there still remain wide divergences in view.

REFERENCES

Alexandratos, Nicholas, and Hartwig de Haen. 1995. "World Consumption of Cereals: Will It Double by 2025?" *Food Policy* 20 (4): 359–66.

Brown, Lester R. 1995. *Who Will Feed China? Wake-up Call for a Small Planet.* New York: W. W. Norton.

Brown, Lester R. and Hal Kane. 1994. *Full House: Reassessing the Earth's Population Carrying Capacity.* New York: W. W. Norton.

Carruthers, Ian. 1993. "Going, Going, Gone! Tropical Agriculture As We Knew It." *Tropical Agriculture Association Newsletter* (U.K.) 13 (3): 1–5.

CGIAR, Technical Advisory Committee. 1990. "A Possible Expansion of the CGIAR." Paper AGR/TAC: IAR/90/24. Rome: TAC Secretariat, Food and Agriculture Organization of the United Nations.

Feder, Gershon, and Andrew Keck. 1994. "Increasing Competition for Land and Water Resources: A Global Perspective." Paper presented at workshop, Social Science Methods in Agricultural Systems: Coping with Increasing Resource Competition in Asia, May 2–4, Chiang Mai, Thailand. Washington, D.C.: Agriculture and Natural Resources Department, World Bank.

Food and Agriculture Organization of the United Nations. 1993. "Agriculture: Towards 2010." Conference paper C-93/24. Rome: FAO.

IFPRI. 1995. *A 2020 Vision for Food, Agriculture, and the Environment: The Vision, Challenge, and Recommended Action.* Washington, D.C.: International Food Policy Research Institute.

Mitchell, Donald O., Merlinda D. Ingco, and Ronald C. Duncan, 1997. *The World Food Outlook.* New York: Cambridge University Press.

Paddock, William, and Paul Paddock. 1967. *Famine, 1975! America's Decision: Who Will Survive?* Boston: Little, Brown.

Pingali, Prabhu L., and Paul W. Heisey. 1996. "Cereal Crop Productivity in Developing Countries: Past Trends and Future Prospects." Paper presented at Global Agricultural Science Policy for the 21st Century Conference, Melbourne, Australia, 26–28 August.

Pinstrup-Andersen, Per, and Rajul Pandya-Lorch. 1994a. "Alleviating Poverty, Intensifying Agriculture, and Effectively Managing Natural Resources." Food, Agriculture, and the Environment Discussion Paper no. 1. Washington, D.C.: International Food Policy Research Institute.

————. 1994b. "Poverty, Agricultural Intensification, and the Environment." Paper prepared for the 10th Annual General Meeting of the Pakistan Society of Development Economists, Islamabad, April 2–5. Washington, D.C.: International Food Policy Research Institute.

Rosegrant, Mark W., and Mercedita Agcaoili. 1994. "Global and Regional Food Demand, Supply and Trade Prospects to 2010." Paper presented at roundtable meeting, Population and Food in the Early Twenty-first Century: Meeting Future Food Needs of an Increasing World Population, February 14–16. Washington, D.C.: International Food Policy Research Institute.

Rozelle, Scott, Jikun Huang, and Mark Rosegrant. 1996. "Why China Will Not Starve the World." *Choices* (first quarter): 18–25.

3

Foreign Aid and Agriculture-Led Development

JOHN W. MELLOR

BACKGROUND

Foreign aid tends implicitly to be judged by how well it gets countries onto a sustainable growth path—towards graduating from receiving foreign aid. The basic logic of foreign aid in assisting growth derives from the potential for latecomers to grow rapidly by drawing on the experience and capital of the front runners. Foreign aid makes that capital and experience available to others. The basics of achieving sustainable growth have included the following elements: a policy environment that fosters competitive private firms and markets, infrastructure development, broad participation in education, and getting agriculture moving on a broad base.

By the standard of graduation, foreign aid has been important in accelerating the development of low-income countries, primarily in Asia and Latin America. The rate and aggregate impact of Asian growth is now immense and widely recognized. Foreign aid, with an emphasis on agriculture, has played a major role in Asian growth, first in Taiwan, then in Southeast Asia, and now in South Asia. But the extent to which agricultural growth is associated with success in achieving other objectives (e.g., poverty reduction, improved status of women, improved maternal and child health, and democratization), has not been generally recognized. Perhaps this lack of understanding accounts for some of the unpopularity of foreign aid. It is unfortunate that agriculture's share of foreign assistance has declined over the past decade. This is especially true in the case of the United States, because of its comparative advantage in helping build the basic institutions of agricultural growth.

Particularly in agriculture, foreign aid has taken the form of capital flows, commodities, and technical and institution-building assistance. At times, foreign aid has been used to support major policy changes. At the apogee of U.S. foreign aid, in the early 1960s in Asia and Latin America, physical infrastructure and institutional development for agriculture were emphasized. In more recent

JOHN W. MELLOR is president of John W. Mellor Associates, Inc., Washington, D.C.

years, direct action on poverty reduction, environmental improvement, and participation of women have increased in relative importance, and the number of agricultural staff in the U.S. Agency for International Development (USAID) has declined sharply.

This chapter devotes special attention to the United States and the World Bank, despite the sharp decline in U.S. contributions to aid, because these are still the two most influential donors. Japan, the largest national donor by far, contributes relatively more than the United States to the multilateral agencies, does not emphasize policy as overtly as the United States, and gives relatively more emphasis to physical infrastructure.

TRENDS IN FOREIGN AID LEVELS AND ALLOCATION

In the early days of foreign aid, in the 1950s, it was almost entirely bilateral, largely from the United States. By the mid-1960s, the share of assistance contributed by the United States had declined to about half of total official development flows, and by the early 1990s to less than one-third. In 1995, the United States ranked fourth in total foreign assistance and last in percent of GDP among all twenty-one Development Assistance Committee reporting countries (OECD various years). Less than 1 percent of the U.S. federal budget is currently allocated to foreign assistance, equivalent to $34 per tax-paying family. Total U.S. development assistance is less than half that of Japan. However, because the United States has always decentralized its foreign aid to country missions, USAID has had a disproportionately large influence on country development policy relative to its financial flows. The World Bank, in the mid-1990s, increased its staff at the country level, in emulation of the United States.

Over time, the United States has increased the concentration of aid on a few countries. In 1960–61 Brazil and India, the two top recipients, received just short of 20 percent of all U.S. official development assistance. By the mid-1980s Israel and Egypt received nearly 40 percent. This reflects the growing use of U.S. foreign aid to pursue military and national security interests (Ruttan 1996). And with more direct concern for environmental and poverty issues, it is not surprising that attention to agriculture has dropped sharply. Other bilateral donors also concentrate their assistance on a few countries, but not nearly to the extent the United States does. Greater stability on the part of the multilateral donors has partly mitigated this unfavorable feature (Mellor and Masters 1991).

HISTORICAL EVOLUTION OF FOREIGN AID POLICY

U.S. foreign aid started with the Marshall Plan, delivering postwar assistance to Europe, to bring about recovery in nations that had been on approximate economic par with the United States before World War II. The amount of aid was massive, representing, annually, over 5 percent of the U.S. GDP. That is about twenty-five times greater than present levels of U.S. foreign assistance, as a percent of GDP.

The Marshall Plan supported the rebuilding of infrastructure, but its corner-stones were food aid to solve a temporary food shortage, management training in all sectors, institution building, and enhancement of agricultural productivity. The institutional, management, and personnel improvements in agriculture played a role in helping Europe shift from a cereal importer to an exporter. The effect of the European takeoff, which was much accelerated by foreign assis-tance, was trade-induced prosperity in the United States in the 1960s. That is analogous to the current trade-related prosperity associated with the present ex-traordinary growth rates in Asia.

U.S. foreign assistance to developing countries started in the mid-1950s, as the success of the Marshall Plan in Europe was becoming apparent. The em-phasis was on physical infrastructure, institution building, and professional edu-cation to staff these institutions. Agriculture and food aid received particular at-tention. The justification for each element of the assistance package was simple: How could a country obtain the economies of specialization without efficient, productive transport? How could productivity be increased without effective sup-porting institutions and the people to operate them? How could the mass of peo-ple eat well without more food? And if the United States had ample supplies of food, and people were hungry in developing countries, why not share the sur-plus with those that had too little (Ruttan 1996).

THE EVOLUTION OF FOREIGN AID'S ATTENTION TO AGRICULTURE

Foreign aid has evolved over time in light of experience and the changing po-litical pressures and fashions of donors. We shall examine how these changing fashions have affected the priority of agriculture in aid programs.

THE EARLY YEARS

In the 1950s most foreign aid specialists had a simplistic view of agricultural development—build extension systems and community structures to absorb American technology, particularly new crop varieties and practices. Both the U.S. aid program and the Ford Foundation gave primary emphasis to extension and community development, while the Rockefeller Foundation emphasized re-search, in its program in Mexico.

However, it soon became apparent that this technology was not transferable without some adaptive research. By the 1960s, the importance of technological change in agriculture was beginning to be recognized. Several foundations fo-cused on building agricultural research systems, which were seen as critical to the development of technology for smallholder agriculture. These efforts in-cluded Rockefeller's work in Mexico and later in India, culminating in the joint Ford/Rockefeller effort to launch the International Rice Research Institute in the Philippines. The early success of IRRI in developing high-yielding rice varieties sparked an effort to create a set of international agricultural research centers.

Concurrently with the emphasis on building research capacity to develop new technology, the Ford Foundation developed a package program for agricultural development in India that emphasized improvements in technology and fertilizer and water control in areas that already had adequate roads and market outlets. That effort, with its tight sense of priority and direction, created a favorable environment for the improved rice and wheat varieties when they came on the scene in Asia in the mid-1960s.

The improved varieties were stunningly successful, and food production accelerated in Asia in the late 1960s and 1970s. The success of the Green Revolution is attributed to the short, fertilizer-responsive wheat and rice varieties, to irrigation, and to improvements in national agricultural institutions and an increase in the number of trained agriculturalists. The high-yielding seeds in Asia were made available along with technical assistance and support for basic agricultural institutions.

The success of the Green Revolution also required political support and a favorable macroeconomic policy environment. Foreign aid was helpful in this regard. In the sixties, the governments of most developing countries were largely urban oriented. Agriculture was seen as a holding ground, while the "real investment" in development was thought to take place in the urban, large-scale industrial sector. Foreign aid drew attention to the critical importance of production agriculture in improving the welfare of society. Foreign aid also strengthened the hands of national leaders, who recognized the critical importance of agriculture and of solving the food bottleneck in Asia.

SECOND-GENERATION PROBLEMS AND THE DECLINE
OF AID TO AGRICULTURE

The success of the Green Revolution in Asia in the 1970s led to a concern with "second-generation problems," such as the impact the Green Revolution was having on the poor, resource-poor farmers, nutrition, and women. While the claim that the Green Revolution enriched the rich at the expense of the poor was patently incorrect, it was true that special institutional modifications were needed to help the poor capture the benefits of the Green Revolution (Mellor and Desai 1985). It was also clear that, while the initial environmental impact of the Green Revolution was favorable, several critical environmental problems have emerged in the rice bowl of Asia where three crops of rice are grown each year.

Without question, the food production success story in Asia over the 1965–85 period was followed by a decline in foreign aid for agriculture. For example, Alex (1996) reports that USAID support for national agricultural research systems (including universities) declined by 73 percent, or from $205 million annually in 1984–86 to $56 million in 1994–96. Between 1990 and 1993 global bilateral aid to agriculture dropped by nearly one-fourth and multilateral aid by nearly one-third.[1]

Buoyed by the success of the Green Revolution, USAID reduced the number of its agricultural specialists starting in the late 1970s and early 1980s. Part of this decline is attributed to the inability of agriculturalists to justify their role in a rapidly changing foreign aid environment. Also, many donors simply overlooked the time required to train people and build agricultural institutions. Many American aid officials failed to grasp that the U.S. land grant system came to be considered a success only in the 1920s, nearly fifty years after the passage of the Morrill Act in 1862.

For Africa, the shift in donor attention away from first-generation food production problems to second-generation problems has been a disaster, because most countries in Africa are currently at an earlier stage of scientific and human capital development than their Asian counterparts were in the mid-sixties, on the eve of the Green Revolution (Eicher 1990). In Africa, instead of focusing on food production and the building the basic institutions for a modern agriculture over a period of decades, donors jettisoned much of what had been learned about the agricultural development experience in Asia and in the seventies introduced new programs, such as a diffused provision of services targeted to the poor, integrated rural development, programs targeted to women, and an attack on environmental problems. These programs overlooked the critical need to address concurrently agricultural productivity and sustainability issues.

The changing fashions of foreign aid in the 1980s and 1990s have been prejudicial to agriculture and to Africa. Given agriculture's central role in the initial stages of the developmental process, this decline was also prejudicial to participatory development in general. Small-scale farms require support from public institutions, at least initially, while private institutions are being developed. Farmers and traders may require some state participation in agricultural marketing, particularly if poor infrastructure is responsible for high marketing costs. Asian countries, in general, did not lose in this shift of donor priorities away from agriculture, because they already had the basic institutions of agricultural development and lobbies of farmers who could protect those institutions. But Africa has suffered by the shift of foreign aid away from agriculture over the past decade.

One final point should be made about the declining foreign aid emphasis on agriculture. There has been an explosive growth of knowledge about agricultural development over the past four decades (Martin 1992). Development professionals have reached substantial agreement on the priorities for agricultural development, including the critical role of technology, human capital, and institutions. There is even a consensus about the appropriate priorities at each stage of development and the sequencing over time. However, this expanded knowledge base is only partially reflected in current foreign assistance programs for agriculture, especially in Africa.

In the 1990s, U.S. foreign aid has been driven by the objectives of environmental enhancement, broad-based development, and democratization. In poor countries, these are all basically rural issues. They all require rising rural incomes to succeed, and that in turn requires agricultural growth. But, there is little technical capacity left within USAID to pursue an agricultural strategy.

POLICY REFORM

Policy reform was a major foreign aid thrust in the 1980s and 1990s. Support for policy reform came from noting that, in general, the front runners in growth had more open, liberal economies that gave relatively free rein to the private sector and let market forces operate freely to allocate resources. To address policy distortions, foreign assistance put increasing weight on using aid to reward or punish policy behavior that the donor favored or wished to discourage. The United States and the World Bank led the way in urging poor countries to carry out policy reforms. The reforms they promoted were salutary for agriculture in many countries, because agriculture had suffered from a range of polices that depressed relative agricultural prices. These reforms helped increase high-value agricultural exports. In some countries, however, agriculture suffered from oversimplified policy reforms, such as across-the-board cutting of government expenditures. In numerous cases these reforms led to a reduction in support for key agricultural institutions. Also, public suppliers of services to farmers were sometimes eliminated before private firms could step in.

To summarize, foreign aid in Asia initially focused on building agricultural institutions, increasing food production, and promoting agricultural growth; then it moved on to a wider range of second-generation problems. In Africa, however, foreign aid agencies focused on the second-generation problems starting in the early seventies before the first-generation food production problem had been solved.

In the period of ascendancy of U.S. foreign aid to agricultural development, the cornerstone of the effort was the system of land-grant colleges and universities. They held the best talents on agricultural research, extension, and policy. They worked closely with a large core of highly professional USAID employees. However, over the past ten to fifteen years the number of professional staff within USAID has contracted sharply; there has been a sharp reduction in support for agricultural education and training. Also the recruitment of technical assistance has shifted from the land-grant colleges and universities towards consulting firms, and contract offices in foreign aid agencies have increased their influence in the selection of consultants, in a drive to minimize expenditure and perceived risk.

The reduction in the number and seniority of agricultural professionals within AID reduced its capacity to tell good from mediocre work, and consulting firms naturally turned to whatever it took to get contracts. Contract offices simply identified firms that could perform at a minimum level, so that they could choose the cheapest one with the most substantial track record. The latter reduced risk, always the bane of the bureaucrat. The contract system essentially gave little weight to capability. And with rapidly shifting aid fashions, the land-grant institutions also tried to conform to those fashions, which caused a loss of professionalism on their side as well. Such problems are innately compounding.

THE ROLE OF FOREIGN AID IN FOSTERING
AGRICULTURE-LED DEVELOPMENT

AGRICULTURE AND ECONOMIC GROWTH

Most developing countries exited colonialism under the guidance of urban elites who were influenced by Fabian socialism. Foreign aid has a natural tendency to encourage urban elites and urban-oriented processes because it comes from countries that are largely urbanized. However, in the early years of foreign aid in Asia in the 1950s, this urban bias was overcome, because senior agriculturalists in the foreign assistance establishment, having participated in building the critical institutions of agricultural development in industrial countries, recognized the importance of agriculture to growth.

In the 1950s, the development literature started with the assumption that agriculture was critical to overall development. Economists such as W. Arthur Lewis, Nicholas Kaldor, and Simon Kuznets provided a strong intellectual basis on which more technical agriculturalists could ply their trade. Also, at that time it was not difficult to get foreign aid administrators to allocate personnel budgets and resources to agriculture. In that context, the head of agricultural operations for the World Bank reported directly to the president. Today the highest-ranking agricultural operations person has to report through several levels of bureaucracy to get to the President.

Today agriculture has largely disappeared from USAID. In the nontechnical atmosphere in USAID, there is currently little opposition to the false claims that agricultural growth is not reaching the poor, that women are not benefiting, and that agricultural growth is bad for the environment. And, even with a recognition that rural people were important, an implicit belief has emerged that they could be lifted up without getting agriculture moving. The current emphasis on microenterprise fails to recognize that essentially all rural enterprise depends on agricultural incomes for effective demand. Further, if agriculture is neglected, rural infrastructure languishes and trade between rural and urban areas is restricted to narrow bands around the major cities.

Also unlike the 1950s, most general economists in foreign aid agencies today are not calling attention to the critical importance of agriculture, because they believe that sectoral balance, input balance, and institutional development will all respond to price signals. Thus, one does not have to give special emphasis to a particular sector, because the market is assumed to be efficient.

Throughout the past forty years, agricultural economists have assembled evidence to support the importance of agriculture in promoting economic growth and the role of small-scale farms in diffusing the benefits of growth throughout the countryside (Mellor 1995). Increasing empirical evidence supports this view. Perhaps most striking, given the current poverty orientation of many donors, is a recent study in India showing that urban growth brought some benefits to the urban poor but had no impact on rural poverty (Ravallion and Datt 1996). The Indian data also show that rural consumption growth reduces poverty in both rural and urban areas. A succession of unpublished studies by Ravallion and his associates for other countries corroborate the Indian results. Similar evidence of strong agricultural multipliers on employment, and the widespread increase in real wages in the face of rapid agricultural growth all argue for a major effort on agricultural growth (Mellor 1995). The World Bank reports that the rapid agricultural growth in China following the reforms of the late seventies and early eighties has lifted 200 million people above the poverty line (World Bank 1996).

All this evidence about agriculture's role in promoting growth and reducing poverty has meant nothing to urban-oriented governments and urban-dominated foreign assistance agencies. The declining emphasis on agriculture in foreign aid reinforces the urban orientation in most developing countries and results in the following: (1) urbanization is concentrated in a few major cities, (2) the breadth of participation in growth is poor, (3) environmental destruction accelerates in rural areas, (4) women tend to be left out of the development process except as short-term factory laborers, and (5) poverty fails to decline.

The decline of attention to agriculture in foreign aid has the greatest impact on countries that are lagging developmentally, currently the bulk of Africa and a few Asian countries. The front runners in development have already benefited from the period when agriculture was uppermost in technical assistance. In Asia, for example, agriculture is moving, and now rapid industrial growth is providing a demand pull to agriculture. The laggard countries are still largely agricultural, with weak institutional structures for agricultural growth and limited human resources.

IMPROVED TECHNOLOGY

Once it was recognized, in the late 1950s, that Western agricultural biological technology required adaptive research before it could be applied elsewhere, foreign aid responded with a wide range of technology development programs at the national and international levels. In the 1950s and the 1960s, a large number of expatriate scientists were used to generate new technology and build national research capacity. The Rockefeller Program in India was a hands-on effort by expatriates, and building national capacity was essentially a process of learning by doing—national scientists working along with expatriates. The first international research centers, such as IRRI and CIMMYT, were also very much hands-on operations. These centers provided striking results in terms of new crop varieties and cropping practices. They had clear objectives and were well financed, well directed, and well managed.

But the first stage of the Green Revolution generated a lot of negative publicity. As a result, donors pressed both the international research centers and the national research and extension systems to address a wider range of concerns—that is, the second generation problems. This has caused a premature loss of focus and contributed to ineffective national systems. It is widely believed that building agricultural research institutions in Asia has been more successful than in Africa, but the technical problems are more difficult in Africa. In the final analysis, the critical ingredient lacking in Africa may have been patience, particularly on the part of donors.

INFRASTRUCTURE

Physical infrastructure was strongly emphasized in the early aid efforts, in the 1950s and 1960s. That may have been in part a hangover from the physical reconstruction of Europe. It must also have been a reflection of the commonsense approach in those early days of foreign aid—how could a country develop without infrastructure? Whatever the reason, the emphasis on central infrastructure created the essential trunk systems onto which rural infrastructure could be grafted. Also, the intellectual and bureaucratic environment for arguing for rural infrastructure was favorable. Food aid was helpful and important in mobilizing rural labor to build rural roads. Since most of the income from such work was spent on food, food aid helped constrain food prices.

MARKETING AND PRODUCT DEVELOPMENT

In the early days of foreign assistance to agriculture, the emphasis was largely on increasing the production of cereals. Although the development literature recognized the long-term growth potential for high-value agricultural commodities, capitalizing on high-income elasticities and rising incomes, the domestic demand and the less-open trade regimes limited the market in the short run. With rapidly rising global incomes and increasingly open trade regimes, the demand opportunities burgeoned, and marketing problems became paramount. This shift in focus from cereal production to marketing was complemented by the shift towards the private sector, particularly in foreign markets. The single most important change in agricultural development potentials between the 1960s and the 1980s was the increase in emphasis towards high-value commodities. Aid provided technical assistance in diagnosing markets and the means for meeting those market needs. The U.S. aid program was a leader in this shift, but the multilateral banks and the other bilateral donors also quickly expanded their support for marketing.

FOOD AID

Food aid has always been an important part of foreign assistance, because of the availability of surpluses in the developed countries and because of its role in humanitarian programs. In general, food aid has been used to build infrastructure, to generate employment more rapidly than local food supplies would allow, and to provide foreign exchange by substituting food aid for commercial imports. The rules of the food aid donors, particularly the United States, were not supposed to allow food aid to substitute for commercial markets, but that was often allowed (Singer and Maxwell 1983).

Despite the surface logic, two powerful arguments have been made against food aid, making it a contentious issue in policy circles today. First, it is argued that food aid increases domestic food supplies and reduces domestic prices and hence the incentives for farmers to increase production. However, this argument ignored two keys features of the food market in developing countries: (1) domestic food demand can be increased roughly commensurately with food aid quantities by ensuring that food aid is used in increasing rural employment programs; (2) infrastructure and technology are generally more important than higher farm prices in increasing food production in food aid receiving countries (Mellor and Pandya-Lorch 1992).

A second argument against food aid is that since developing country governments were urban and industry oriented, they were eager to use food aid as a means of continuing policies that exploited agriculture. In that context, food aid donors needed to put pressure on developing agriculture to see to it that food aid was used in a manner that expanded food demand roughly in proportion to the expanded supply. In any case, in the 1950s and 1960s, unlike in the 1990s, the key donors kept constant, focused pressure on developing countries to pursue the core institutional developments that are the key to moving the agricultural sector.

There is very little empirical evidence of a negative impact of food aid on the domestic food economy. Indeed, some former food aid importers have increased their domestic production of food concurrently with rapidly increasing their demand for commercial imports (Srinivasan 1989). In recent years, food aid has declined because of the decline in food surpluses in developed countries and the disincentive argument.

LOOKING AHEAD

If past trends in foreign assistance continue, U.S. aid will likely decline in total expenditure, diffusing that expenditure over more and more broadly defined activities, with less and less sectoral activity. Fortunately, some donors are maintaining their overall aid levels, but most donors have followed the United States in reducing their support for agriculture and the number of agriculturalists on their staffs. The effect of the decline of foreign assistance in Asia has not been particularly deleterious, except in a small number of latecomer nations, such as Nepal. However, one of the tragedies of foreign aid is that the United States has not learned how to deal with the success stories in Asia. The United States should develop new models, such as shifting the foreign assistance effort in newly emerging middle-income countries to the State Department and focusing it on Fulbright-like programs for education and scientific interchange.

The future for much of Africa is bleak. The gradual decline in overall U.S. assistance should be checked. Debate is needed on how to make aid to Africa more effective. Should there be stiff standards in terms of government commitment? Should weak governments face a few simple aid priorities to get agriculture moving? The first step in revitalizing aid in support of agricultural development in Africa should be a return to the basics. Getting back to basics would provide more emphasis on training and institution building (Agency for International Development 1985). The institution building would be for a purpose—economic growth. Food aid would be revived and would have an emphasis on generating rural employment in the face of lagging food production. Food aid should be conditioned by good agricultural growth policy and be tied to building rural infrastructure and rural education (Lele 1992).

To achieve the essential Green Revolution for Africa is not as daunting as it appears after several decades of inefficient effort. Much has been learned about agricultural development, and many essential institutions are at least partly built (Mellor, Delgado, and Blackie 1987). Donors to Africa need to recognize that development takes time. Europe rebuilt itself in fifteen years. Countries such as Taiwan only took a decade and a half or so to take off. But countries in South Asia, with their harsh colonial heritage, are beginning to take off only now, more than forty years after the aid process got under way. Judging by the experience of South Asia, foreign aid in Africa has at least twenty years to go before rapid self-sustaining growth starts to occur.

Africa today has three major advantages over Asia in the 1950s. First, the knowledge base about development is larger (Martin 1992). Second, the availability of international capital is greater than in the 1950s or 1960s (Mellor and Masters 1991). Thus, we can assume that capital for private investment is not limiting to growth. Third, the trade potentials are greater now than they were forty years ago. For example, in agriculture, we can give far more attention to exports of high-value agricultural commodities, with their potential for 6–8 percent growth rates, than to the underlying cereals, at 3 percent.

CONCLUSION

Over the past fifty years, we have seen the rise and decline of foreign aid for agricultural development. It started with Marshall Plan assistance to Europe—a quick and immediate success. It went on to Asia and achieved slow and continuing success. Perhaps it would be realistic to say that development in Asia would have occurred without foreign aid, but ten to twenty years were probably saved by its presence.

We are left with uncompleted business in Africa. The inappropriateness of many of the types of foreign aid that have been used in Africa has resulted in wasted time and resources. Another thirty years of lost time would leave Africa with a population of close to a billion people and Asian-style population densities. Our inability to slow rural to urban migration should give us pause, quite aside from the environmental and human costs of such neglect. The Asian lessons regarding concentration, focus, priority, physical infrastructure, agriculture, and agricultural institutions are relevant to Africa today. Focusing on the first-generation problem of getting agriculture moving is needed to solve an immense food problem. We know that if the food problem is solved by concentrated effort, poverty will decline drastically, environmental degradation will be reduced, and the condition of women will be greatly improved.

NOTE

1. The share of investment in the rural sectors of developing countries that has been funded by official development finance increased from around US$12 billion in the early 1980s to nearly US$16 billion in 1988 and then declined to US$10 billion in 1994 (FAO 1996, 32).

REFERENCES

Agency for International Development. 1985. *Plan for Supporting Agricultural Research and Faculties of Agriculture in Africa.* Washington, D.C.: AID.

Alex, Gary. 1996. "USAID and Agricultural Research: Review of USAID Support for Agricultural Research." Office of Agriculture and Food Security. Washington, D.C.: USAID.

Eicher, Carl K. 1990. "Building African Scientific Capacity for Agricultural Development." *Agricultural Economics* 4 (2): 117–43.

Food and Agriculture Organization. 1996. *World Food Summit: Synthesis of the Technical Background Documents.* Rome: FAO.

Lele, Uma, ed. 1992. *Aid to African Agriculture: Lessons from Two Decades of Donor Experience.* Baltimore: Johns Hopkins University Press.

Martin, Lee R., ed. 1992. *A Survey of Agricultural Economics Literature.* Vol. 4, *Agriculture in Economic Development, 1940s to 1990s.* Minneapolis: University of Minnesota Press.

Mellor, John W., ed. 1995. *Agriculture on the Road to Industrialization.* Baltimore: Johns Hopkins University Press.

Mellor, John W., Christopher L. Delgado, and Malcolm J. Blackie, eds. 1987. *Accelerating Food Production Growth in Sub-Saharan Africa.* Baltimore: Johns Hopkins University Press.

Mellor, John W., and Gunvant M. Desai, eds. 1985. *Agricultural Change and Rural Poverty: Variations on a Theme by Dharm Narain.* Baltimore: Johns Hopkins University Press.

Mellor, John W., and W. A. Masters. 1991. "The Changing Roles of Multilateral and Bilateral Foreign Assistance." In *Transitions in Development: The Role of Aid and Commercial Flows,* edited by Uma Lele and Ijaz Nabi. San Francisco, Calif.: ICS Press.

Mellor, John W., and Rajul Pandya-Lorch. 1992. "Food Aid and Development in the MADIA Countries." In *Aid to African Agriculture: Lessons from Two Decades of Donor Experience,* edited by Uma Lele. Baltimore: Johns Hopkins University Press.

Organization for Economic Co-operation and Development. Various years (annual). *Development Cooperation.* Paris: OECD.

Oehmke, James F., and Eric W. Crawford. 1996. "The Impact of Agricultural Technology in Sub-Saharan Africa." *Journal of African Economies* 5 (2): 271–92.

Ravallion, Martin, and Gaurav Datt. 1996. "How Important to India's Poor is the Sectoral Composition of Economic Growth?" *World Bank Economic Review* 10 (1): 1–25.

Ruttan, Vernon W., ed. 1993. *Why Food Aid?* Baltimore: Johns Hopkins University Press.

———. 1996. *United States Development Assistance Policy: The Domestic Politics of Foreign Economic Aid.* Baltimore: Johns Hopkins University Press.

Singer, H. W., with S. J. Maxwell. 1983. "Development through Food Aid: Twenty Years' Experience." *Report of the World Food Programme,* 31–46. The Hague: Government of the Netherlands.

Srinivasan, T. N. 1989. "Food Aid: A Cause of Development Failure or an Instrument for Success." *World Bank Economic Review* 3 (1): 39–65.

World Bank. 1996. *World Development Report, 1996.* New York: Oxford University Press.

II

Historical and Theoretical
Perspectives

Introduction

There are many definitions of economic growth, economic development, agricultural development, and agricultural transformation. Arthur Lewis narrowly defined economic growth as an increase in per capita income (Lewis 1955). Irma Adelman and Cynthia Taft Morris define economic development as "widely shared, sustainable economic growth accompanied by significant structural change in production patterns and in economic and political institutions and by generalized improvements in living standards" (Adelman and Morris 1997, 831). The seven chapters in part II present historical and theoretical perspectives on economic development as a process by which a predominantly agricultural economy is transformed into a primarily urban, industrial, and service-oriented economy. The essays analyze the growth of markets, market failures, the crucial role of institutions in facilitating the development of market economies, the stages of the agricultural transformation, and models of agricultural development.

In chapter 4, Nobel laureate Douglass C. North discusses the limitations of the neoclassical economics paradigm in studying development and asserts, "There is no mystery why the field of development has failed to develop during the five decades since the end of World War II. Neoclassical theory is simply an inappropriate tool for analyzing and prescribing policies that will induce development. . . . it contained two erroneous assumptions: (1) that institutions do not matter and (2) that time does not matter."

In North's approach, "institutions" refers to the *rules* under which an economy operates, not to organizations, such as research institutes, universities, banks, and extension services. Hence, an institutional approach emphasizes how changing the basic rules of the game affects economic performance, including both the rate of growth and who benefits from that growth. The rules affect how organizations such as research institutes operate, but the essential focus of an institutional analysis is on understanding how the basic rules of the economy (including the definition of property rights) affect economic performance.

During the 1950s and 1960s economic historians such as Simon Kuznets, Alexander Gerschenkron, Henry Rosovsky, and Douglass North devoted considerable attention to the evolution of institutions in development and to understanding development as a historical, cultural, political, and technological process. But this intense interest in economic history and institutions was not sustained in the 1960s, because mainstream development economists became captivated by an array of dual-sector models, and then in the seventies by agricultural sector modeling. But while dual-sector models gave some insight into intersectoral relationships, they were not disaggregated enough to provide much understanding of how to accelerate agricultural growth in poor countries.

In the early eighties there was a revival of interest in the role of institutions in development. The new institutional economics emerged by drawing on the work of Coase (1937), who made the crucial connections between institutions, transactions costs, and neoclassical theory. The work of Coase "laid the intellectual foundation for a transaction cost analysis of economic institutions" (North and Wallis 1994, 611). Academics and members of international and donor agencies have thus come full circle, acknowledging, as they had in the 1950s, that the ideas of economic historians have much to contribute to development economics. The current need is for pilot studies and action research on how to build relevant institutions and organizations for small-scale farmers, how to sequence public and private investments over time, and how to build fiscally sustainable scientific and organizational capacity in low- and middle-income countries.[1]

One of the big challenges is integrating technology development and institutional change in field research. In a recent article, North and Wallis (1994) addressed the vexing problems of integrating institutional and technical change. They point out that in practice one cannot assume that technology is given, but that institutions and technologies are interdependent and need to evolve simultaneously. Hayami and Ruttan (1985, 429–32) provide insights into this interplay between technology and institutions in their study of how technological advances and institutional innovations transformed Danish agriculture from a grain exporter to an exporter of bacon and dairy products from 1875 to 1900. More recently, the financial crisis in Southeast Asia during the late 1990s has illustrated the dangers that arise when institutions governing financial markets are not adapted to the increased mobility of international capital flows.[2]

In chapter 5 of this volume Yujiro Hayami examines the role of traditional village institutions and the government in agricultural and rural economic development. Too often, Hayami notes, central governments have condemned money lenders and traders as usurious and have held peasants and their village and community institutions in disdain, seeing peasants as tradition bound and traditional village and community institutions as "feudal yokes." For example, based on a conviction that peasants and smallholders were tradition bound, that middle farmers (Kulaks) were exploitative and the market system was unreliable, Stalin set up state and collective farms in the USSR during the early 1930s and Chairman Mao implemented communal farms from 1958 to 1978. These anti-peasant, anti-market, and anti-community beliefs also explain Nigeria's ill-fated decision to import Israeli settlement schemes in the early sixties and Nyerere's blunder in ordering the police in Tanzania to round up smallholders and move them into Ujamaa villages in the seventies. The rationale for these command-directed agricultural development models is based on two convictions: tradition-bound peasants and smallholders cannot be trusted to produce a reliable agricultural surplus, and market forces cannot be relied upon to transfer the surplus to feeding the urban labor force and the military.

Hayami criticizes the anti-market, anti-peasant, and anti-community views and argues that rural economies in developing countries cannot grow and prosper without judicious government policies that guide market forces, correct market failures, protect property rights, and mobilize the participation and voice of rural people and their communities in designing and implementing development programs.

In chapter 6, Joseph Stiglitz addresses the puzzle of the continuing differences in the levels of income and rates of growth between the developed and developing countries over the past fifty years.[3] Stiglitz observes that "the prediction of the standard neoclassical growth model of a convergence of growth rates in per capita income, with permanent differences in per capita consumption being explained by differences in savings rates and reproduction rates, does not seem to be born out."

Stiglitz advances the thesis that the differences between poor and rich countries lie largely in matters of economic organization (i.e., institutions) and that understanding market failures is central to understanding the gap between rich and poor countries. He argues that market failures are pervasive in poor countries, that more research is needed on microeconomic issues, and that there is a need to develop a theory of rural organization. He then illustrates three examples of imperfect markets: learning, capital markets, and product markets.[4]

Following the discussion in chapters 4–6 of institutional issues in overall economic development, the remaining chapters in part II focus on the role of the agricultural sector in the development process. In the early 1960s, Johnston and Mellor (1961) and several other agricultural economists stressed the fundamental role that agriculture could potentially play in economic development and the importance of understanding the process of agricultural growth per se if that potential was to be exploited.

In chapter 7, Peter Timmer describes the agricultural transformation as "a remarkably uniform process" that is characterized by a decline in agriculture's share in a country's labor force and total output as per capita incomes increase. Timmer depicts the agricultural transformation as moving through four stages, with different policy approaches associated with each stage:

1. The first stage of development, characterized by a high percentage (70 to 90 percent) of the labor force in agriculture. Major policy emphasis is on "getting agriculture moving" (Mosher 1966). Public investment is needed in research and infrastructure to lay the foundation for agriculture to become a key contributor to economic growth.

2. During the second stage, agriculture begins to make major contributions to the growth of other sectors of the economy (Johnston and Mellor 1961). The growth strategy emphasizes new technology to generate an agricultural surplus and the development of improved factor markets, institutions,

and policies to mobilize the agricultural surplus for industrial development without destroying incentives to farmers.

3. In the third stage, agriculture is gradually integrated into the rest of the economy through the development of more efficient input and output markets to link the rural and urban economies.
4. In the fourth stage, the share of the labor force in agriculture falls below 20 percent, the share of food in urban expenditures drops to 20–30 percent, and subsidies become common vehicles for maintaining a farm production structure characterized by political influence and overproduction. Although the percentage of the population and GNP based in agriculture is low in this stage, the process of specialization proceeds to the point where only 10–15 percent of the value added in food in many industrial countries originates on the farm. The bulk of the food system at this stage is located off the farm, and food policy becomes much broader than farm policy.

Timmer contends that agriculture's declining share of national output during the agricultural transformation is partially responsible for the widespread misunderstanding in many countries that agriculture is unimportant and does not require public investment and a favorable policy environment. But he shows that the combination of agricultural growth and relative decline is not a paradox but a normal and desirable process and that continuing public and private investments in agriculture are essential to completing the transformation process.

Agriculture's relative decline in a nation's structural transformation is caused by two well-documented but not widely understood mechanisms. First, Engels' law holds that as incomes rise demand for the products of the agricultural sector will rise, but more slowly than income. Second, technical change in agriculture leads to growing agricultural productivity, measured in terms of output per laborer or per hectare, which in turn leads to increased supply of farm products. The combination of slow growth in demand for farm products and increased supply leads to falling agricultural prices, which puts pressure on farmers to find jobs in rural nonfarm activities or migrate to the cities. This explains why the proportion of the total population in farming in the United States, for example, declined from 40 percent in 1900 to 17 percent in 1940 and 2 percent in the late 1990s.

One of the most important of the questions that flows from Timmer's analysis concerns the role of population growth in speeding or delaying the agrarian transformation. Many low-income countries are facing the challenge of initiating three crucial transitions simultaneously: the demographic transition, the agrarian transition, and the transition towards an industrial society. Integrating population growth more closely into an analysis of an agricultural transformation is a first step in responding to that challenge. Boserup (1981) argues that demographic pressure has historically been a driving force in inducing technological change and diffusion both in agriculture and in industry.[5]

In chapter 8, John Mellor presents a strategy for broad-based employment and income growth built upon a foundation of agricultural innovation. The engine of growth in this strategy is continuous technological change in agriculture, usually in the basic staples. Mellor argues that such technological change, combined with proper policies, can lead to rapid, employment-oriented growth in both the agricultural and the nonagricultural sectors. A key variable in Mellor's strategy is how the initial adopters of improved agricultural technologies use their increased incomes. If they spend a high proportion of increments to income on labor-intensive agricultural and nonagricultural goods, their purchases will generate increased demand for labor. Higher demand for labor, in turn, leads to higher employment in agriculture, industry, and services (as long as capital is not subsidized to induce inappropriate mechanization). Higher employment, in turn, boosts the demand for food staples, which helps maintain farm prices in the face of the expanded supply. Hence, given appropriate investments in research and policy, the growth of output and employment in the agricultural and nonagricultural sectors can reinforce each other.

In chapter 9, Vernon Ruttan outlines six models of agricultural development that are useful in understanding agricultural change: the frontier or resource exploitation model, the conservation model, the urban-industrial impact model, the diffusion model, the high-payoff input model, and the induced innovation model. The frontier (area expansion) model is still relevant in parts of some land-abundant countries such as Indonesia, Malaysia, Zaire, and Brazil, where public investments in transportation and rural infrastructure rather than yield-increasing innovations have been major sources of agricultural growth. For instance, until the 1980s Thailand's agricultural boom was fueled by investments in roads, tractors, and modest investments in seed and fertilizer technology. Despite the relatively low yield of 1.9 tons of paddy per hectare, Thailand has been a major rice exporter (Siamwalla 1995). But concerns that the pursuit of the frontier strategy has led to the destruction of tropical rainforests and the possible consequence of global warming raise serious questions about whether continued area expansion represents a "cheap" way of expanding agricultural output.[6]

Growing environmental concern has led to revived interest in the conservation model. The conservation model is still relevant in many countries such as Somalia, Botswana, Chad, and Mali where extensive pastoral grazing is practiced with few, if any, external inputs. Many of the elements of the conservation model are incorporated in sustainable agriculture and low-input sustainable agriculture (LISA). Advocates of these models generally eschew the use of external inputs such as pesticides and fertilizer. However, the historical record shows that these low-input models are capable of producing agricultural growth of only around one percent per year. The challenge facing advocates of the conservation and LISA models is to develop technologies that can generate higher rates of agricultural growth, in order to meet the increasing demand for agricultural products resulting from population and income growth.[7] Unfortunately, there is very little hard evidence on the economics of the conservation and LISA models. Low (1993) reports that the LISA model has been found to be simplistic and misleading in crop production in southern Africa.

The diffusion model served as the intellectual justification for the heavy emphasis by foreign aid donors on agricultural extension during the 1950s, and it had a close affinity with the community development (CD) effort of that time.[8] Because the agricultural extension programs and community development efforts of the 1950s often failed to accelerate food production, the diffusion model was de-emphasized during the 1960s, and increasing attention was given to agricultural research.

T. W. Schultz's high-payoff input or Green Revolution model was instrumental in convincing international donors and policy makers in the 1960s to devote more resources to the development of new inputs for poor farmers, such as high-yielding, fertilizer-responsive grain varieties (Schultz 1964). The model stresses agricultural research and human capital formation, and it became the dominant agricultural development model of the 1960s and the 1970s. But the high-payoff input model provides an incomplete explanation of why agricultural growth does or does not occur in a given country. Both technical and institutional change are exogenous to the model. Although technical change is the engine of agricultural growth in the high-payoff input model, the model itself does not predict whether or what types of technical change will occur in a given country.

In chapter 10, Ruttan and Hayami present an induced innovation model of agricultural development, in which technical and institutional change are endogenous.[9] Central to the induced innovation model are the notions that countries can pursue alternative paths of technical change and productivity growth in agriculture and that changes in relative factor prices, reflecting changes in relative factor scarcities, can play a determining role in guiding the search for new agricultural technologies and institutions. For example, because of the differences in relative factor prices, reflecting different worker-land ratios, Japan and the United States followed different technological paths but achieved the same long-term compound rate of agricultural growth of 1.6 percent per year over the 1880–1980 period (Hayami and Ruttan 1985, 166).[10] Ruttan and Hayami note that "the classical problem of resource allocation, which was rejected as an adequate basis for agricultural productivity and output growth in the high-payoff input model, is, in this context, treated as central to the agricultural development process. Under conditions of static technology, improvements in resource allocation represent a weak source of economic growth. The efficient allocation of resources to open up new sources of growth is, however, essential to the agricultural development process" (104).

For the induced innovation mechanism to guide technological change along an efficient path, two key conditions must be met: changes in factor prices must reflect changes in relative factor scarcities, and researchers in both the private and the public sectors must adjust their research programs in response to changes in factor prices. Since Hayami and Ruttan first outlined their induced innovation model in 1970, the model's emphasis on continuous technical change as central to long-term agricultural growth has been reaffirmed by a large number of tests of the model. A strategic implication of the model is that different nations can pursue different technological paths in response to differences or changes in relative resource endowments and factors prices over time. But to do this, the countries need well-functioning product and factor markets to signal resource scarcities and a set of incentives that will induce researchers to respond to those scarcities.

More controversial is Hayami and Ruttan's concept of induced *institutional* innovation, which posits that the evolution of economic institutions, as well as technology, is guided by relative factor prices. The theory states that as relative prices change, incentives are created for certain groups in society to push for institutional changes that would allow the groups to benefit from the changing factor prices. For example, growth in the labor force may lead to pressures to change the institutions governing remuneration of agricultural labor from a fixed share of the harvest to a daily wage. The theory then focuses on the factors affecting the supply of and demand for such institutional innovations (Hayami and Ruttan 1985, 73–114). The view that economic forces determine the structure of economic institutions is not new; Marx argued the same point in the nineteenth century. What is controversial is the view that relative factor prices, themselves a product of the existing institutional environment, can guide society in the design of "efficient" institutions.

During the 1980s and 1990s, the emphasis on structural adjustment shifted much of the focus in agricultural development theory and practice back to the role of agriculture in the broader economy with emphasis on removing policy "distortions." A challenge now is to meld that perspective with the more detailed knowledge of how institutions affect the mechanisms of agricultural growth and rural poverty alleviation. Understanding both the mechanisms of agricultural growth and the links between agriculture and the rest of the economy will be crucial in developing agricultural and rural economic growth strategies as tools for alleviating poverty throughout the economy.

NOTES

1. Elinor Ostrom 1992 and Mandivamba Rukuni 1996 provide insights into the art of crafting demand-driven irrigation and extension systems. See Akhtar Hameed Khan 1996 for a summary of Khan's vast experience in crafting rural and urban development projects for the poor in Bangladesh and Pakistan.

2. The crisis hit several countries severely, including South Korea, Indonesia, Thailand, the Philippines, and Hong Kong. Between October 1997 and January 1998, for example, the Indonesian rupiah lost 80 percent of its value relative to the U.S. dollar.

3. According to Adelman and Morris (1997, 839), only "20 semi-industrialized countries" have emerged in the past generation and "only a half-dozen developing countries have so far been able to graduate to OECD status in the 50 years since the post war development process started."

4. Pursuant to Stiglitz's call for a theory of rural organization, Hoff, Braverman, and Stiglitz (1993) brought together an important volume of empirical studies, *The Economics of Rural Organization*, which examined the impact of information constraints and transaction costs on the development of the rural sector. The book is divided into four parts. Each part examines one area where governments in developing countries have intervened: rural credit markets, land markets, agricultural

taxation, and technology development. Much has been learned in the past twenty years about the problems of incentives and information that give rise to market failures. We shall draw on this expanded knowledge base in part IV, in our analysis of land, labor, and capital markets.

5. Pingali, Bigot, and Binswanger (1987) draw on Boserup's population-led agricultural intensification model in their analysis of the evolution of farming systems in sub-Saharan Africa.

6. That global warming may result from the cutting of rainforests for agricultural expansion represents a classic case of an international externality. Although area expansion may appear to be the cheapest way in the short run of expanding agricultural output for the farmers and countries involved, such actions may impose serious long-run costs on the rest of the world's inhabitants. The problem arises because there are no international institutions in place that align the private and social costs facing these farmers (e.g., a system to tax the rest of the world to compensate the farmers for the higher private costs of production from engaging in less environmentally destructive forms of agriculture).

7. See chapter 27 in this volume for Reardon's discussion of the LISA model.

8. Several ingredients of CD programs—local initiative, participation, matching grants—were common to the integrated rural development (IRD) projects of the 1970s and 1980s. The rise and decline of IRD is discussed by Ruttan (1975), Holdcroft (1984), and by Binswanger in chapter 17 in this volume.

9. For more details on the induced innovation model see Hayami and Ruttan 1985; Binswanger and Ruttan 1978; and Ruttan and Thirtle 1989.

10. In Japan, land being the scarce input, farmers on tiny farms (1–2 hectares) pursued labor intensive rice cultivation. In the United States, where land was abundant, farmers pursued mechanized farming to reduce labor costs.

REFERENCES

Adelman, Irma, and Cynthia Taft Morris. 1997. "Editorial: Development History and Its Implications for Development Theory." *World Development* 25 (6): 831–40.

Binswanger, Hans P., and Vernon W. Ruttan. 1978. *Induced Innovation: Technology, Institutions, and Development.* Baltimore: Johns Hopkins University Press.

Boserup, Ester. 1981. *Population and Technical Change.* Chicago: University of Chicago Press.

Coase, Ronald. 1937. "The Nature of the Firm." *Economica* 4:386–405.

Hayami, Yujiro, and Vernon W. Ruttan. 1985. *Agricultural Development: An International Perspective.* Revised edition. Baltimore: Johns Hopkins University Press.

Hoff, Karla, Avishay Braverman, and Joseph E. Stiglitz, eds. 1993. *The Economics of Rural Organization: Theory, Practice, and Policy.* New York: Oxford University Press.

Holdcroft, Lane. 1984. "The Rise and Fall of Community Development, 1950–65: A Critical Assessment." In *Agricultural Development in the Third World,* Carl K. Eicher and John M. Staatz, eds., 46–58. Baltimore: Johns Hopkins University Press.

Johnston, Bruce F., and John W. Mellor. 1961. "The Role of Agriculture in Economic Development." *American Economic Review* 51 (4): 566–93.

Khan, Akhtar Hameed 1996. *Orangi Pilot Project: Reminiscences and Reflections.* Karachi: Oxford University Press.

Lewis, W. Arthur. 1955. *The Theory of Economic Growth.* London: Allen and Unwin.

Low, Allan R. C. 1993. "The Low-Input, Sustainable Agriculture (LISA) Prescription: A Bitter Pill for Farm-Households in Southern Africa." *Project Appraisal* 8 (2): 97–101.

Mosher, Arthur T. 1966. *Getting Agriculture Moving: Essentials for Development and Modernization.* New York: Praeger.

North, Douglass C., and John J. Wallis. 1994. "Integrating Institutional Change and Technical Change in Economic History: A Transaction Cost Approach." *Journal of Institutional and Theoretical Economics* 150:609–24.

Ostrom, Elinor. 1992. *Crafting Institutions for Self-Governing Irrigation Systems.* San Francisco: ICS Press.

Pingali, Prabhu, Yves Bigot, and Hans P. Binswanger. 1987. *Agricultural Mechanization and the Evolution of Farming Systems in Sub-Saharan Africa.* Baltimore: Johns Hopkins University Press.

Reynolds, Lloyd G., ed. 1975. *Agriculture in Development Theory.* New Haven: Yale University Press.

Rukuni, Mandivamba. 1996. "A Framework for Crafting Demand-Driven National Agricultural Research Institutions in Southern Africa." Staff Paper no. 96-76, Department of Agricultural Economics, Michigan State University, East Lansing.

Ruttan, Vernon W. 1975. "Integrated Rural Development: A Skeptical Perspective." *International Development Review* 4:9–16.

Ruttan, Vernon, and Colin Thirtle. 1989. "Induced Technical and Institutional Change in African Agriculture." *Journal of International Development* 1 (1): 1–45.

Schultz, Theodore W. 1964. *Transforming Traditional Agriculture.* New Haven: Yale University Press.

Siamwalla, Ammar. 1995. "Land Abundant Agricultural Growth and Some of Its Consequences." In *Agriculture on the Road to Industrialization,* edited by John W. Mellor, 150–74. Baltimore: Johns Hopkins University Press.

4

Economic Performance
through Time

DOUGLASS C. NORTH

I

 Economic history is about the performance of economies through time. The objective of research in the field is not only to shed new light on the economic past, but also to contribute to economic theory by providing an analytical framework that will enable us to understand economic change. A theory of economic dynamics comparable in precision to general equilibrium theory would be the ideal tool of analysis. In the absence of such a theory, we can describe the characteristics of past economies, examine the performance of economies at various times, and engage in comparative static analysis, but missing is an analytical understanding of the way economies evolve through time.

A theory of economic dynamics is also crucial for the field of economic development. There is no mystery why the field of development has failed to develop during the five decades since the end of World War II. Neoclassical theory is simply an inappropriate tool for analyzing and prescribing policies that will induce development. It is concerned with the operation of markets, not with how markets develop. How can one prescribe policies when one doesn't understand how economies develop? The very methods employed by neoclassical economists have dictated the subject matter and militated against such a development. That theory in the pristine form that gave it mathematical precision and elegance modeled a frictionless and static world. When applied to economic history and development it focused on technological development, and more recently human-capital investment, but ignored the incentive structure embodied in institutions that determined the extent of societal investment in those factors. In the analysis of economic performance through time it contained two erroneous as-

Douglass C. North is professor of economics, Washington University, St. Louis, Missouri.

This is the lecture Douglass C. North delivered in Stockholm, Sweden, December 9, 1993, when he received the Alfred Nobel Memorial Prize in Economic Sciences. It was published in the *American Economic Review* 84, no. 3 (1994). Text copyright The Nobel Foundation 1993, published by permission of the Nobel Foundation, the American Economic Association, and the author.

sumptions: (1) that institutions do not matter and (2) that time does not matter.

This essay is about institutions and time. It does not provide a theory of economic dynamics comparable to general equilibrium theory. We do not have such a theory.[1] Rather, it provides the initial scaffolding of an analytical framework capable of increasing our understanding of the historical evolution of economies and a necessarily crude guide to policy in the ongoing task of improving the economic performance of economies. The analytical framework is a modification of neoclassical theory. What it retains is the fundamental assumption of scarcity and hence competition and the analytical tools of microeconomic theory. What it modifies is the rationality assumption. What it adds is the dimension of time.

Institutions form the incentive structure of a society, and the political and economic institutions, in consequence, are the underlying determinants of economic performance. Time as it relates to economic and societal change is the dimension in which the learning process of human beings shapes the way institutions evolve. That is, the beliefs that individuals, groups, and societies hold which determine choices are a consequence of learning through time—not just the span of an individual's life or of a generation of a society, but the learning embodied in individuals, groups, and societies that is cumulative through time and passed on intergenerationally by the culture of a society.

The next two sections of this essay summarize the work I and others have done on the nature of institutions and the way they affect economic performance (Section II) and then characterize the nature of institutional change (Section III).[2] The remaining four sections describe a cognitive-science approach to human learning (Section IV), provide an institutional/cognitive approach to economic history (Section V), indicate the implications of this approach for improving our understanding of the past (Section VI), and finally suggest implications for current development policies (Section VII).

II

Institutions are the humanly devised constraints that structure human interaction. They are made up of formal constraints (e.g., rules, laws, constitutions), informal constraints (e.g., norms of behavior, conventions, self-imposed codes of conduct), and their enforcement characteristics. Together they define the incentive structure of societies and specifically economies.

Institutions and the technology employed determine the transaction and transformation costs that add up to the costs of production. It was Ronald Coase (1960) who made the crucial connection among institutions, transaction costs, and neoclassical theory. The neoclassical result of efficient markets only obtains when it is costless to transact. Only under the conditions of costless bargaining will the actors reach the solution that maximizes aggregate income regardless of the institutional arrangements. When it is costly to transact, then institutions matter. And it is costly to transact. John J. Wallis and North (1986) demonstrated in an empirical study that 45 percent of U.S. GNP was devoted to the transaction sector in 1970. Efficient markets are created in the real world when competition is strong enough via arbitrage and efficient information feedback to approximate the Coase zero-transaction-cost conditions and the parties can realize the gains from trade inherent in the neoclassical argument.

But the informational and institutional requirements necessary to achieve such efficient markets are stringent. Players must not only have objectives but know the correct way to achieve them. But how do the players know the correct way to achieve their objectives? The instrumental rationality answer is that, even though the actors may initially have diverse and erroneous models, the informational feedback process and arbitraging actors will correct initially incorrect models, punish deviant behavior, and lead surviving players to correct models.

An even more stringent implicit requirement of the discipline-of-the-competitive-market model is that, when there are significant transaction costs, the consequent institutions of the market will be designed to induce the actors to acquire the essential information that will lead them to correct their models. The implication is not only that institutions are designed to achieve efficient outcomes but that they can be ignored in economic analysis, because they play no independent role in economic performance.

These are stringent requirements that are realized only very exceptionally. Individuals typically act on incomplete information and with subjectively derived models that are frequently erroneous; the information feedback is typically insufficient to correct these subjective models. Institutions are not necessarily or even usually created to be socially efficient: rather they, or at least the formal rules, are created to serve the interests of those with the bargaining power to create new rules. In a world of zero transaction costs, bargaining strength does not affect the efficiency of outcomes; but in a world of positive transaction costs it does.

It is exceptional to find economic markets that approximate the conditions necessary for efficiency. It is impossible to find political markets that do. The reason is straightforward. Transaction costs are the costs of specifying what is being exchanged and of enforcing the consequent agreements. In economic markets, what is being specified (measured) is the valuable attributes—the physical and property-rights dimensions—of goods and services or the performance of agents. While measurement can frequently be costly, there are some standard criteria: the physical dimensions have objective characteristics (size, weight, color, etc.), and the property-rights dimensions are defined in legal terms. Competition also plays a critical role in reducing enforcement costs. The judicial system provides coercive enforcement. Still, economic markets, past and present, are typically imperfect and beset by high transaction costs.

Measuring and enforcing agreements in political markets is far more difficult. What is being exchanged (between constituents and legislators in a democracy) is promises for votes. The voter has little incentive to become informed, because the likelihood that one's vote matters is infinitesimal; further, the complexity of the issues produces genuine uncertainty. Enforcement of political agreements is beset by difficulties. Competition is far less effective than in economic markets.

For a variety of simple, easy-to-measure, and important-to-constituent-well-being policies, constituents may be well informed, but beyond such straightforward policy issues, ideological stereotyping takes over and (as I shall argue below in Section IV) shapes the consequent performance of economies.[3] It is the polity that defines and enforces property rights, and in consequence it is not surprising that efficient economic markets are so exceptional.

III

It is the interaction between institutions and organizations that shapes the institutional evolution of an economy. If institutions are the rules of the game, organizations and their entrepreneurs are the players.

Organizations are made up of groups of individuals bound together by some common purpose to achieve certain objectives. Organizations include political bodies (e.g., political parties, the Senate, a city council, regulatory bodies), economic bodies (e.g., firms, trade unions, family farms, cooperatives), social bodies (e.g., churches, clubs, athletic associations), and educational bodies (e.g., schools, universities, vocational training centers).

The organizations that come into existence will reflect the opportunities provided by the institutional matrix. That is, if the institutional framework rewards piracy then piratical organizations will come into existence, and if the institutional framework rewards productive activities then organizations—firms—will come into existence to engage in productive activities.

Economic change is a ubiquitous, ongoing, incremental process that is a consequence of the choices individual actors and entrepreneurs of organizations are making every day. While the vast majority of these decisions are routine (Richard Nelson and Sidney G. Winter 1982), some involve altering existing "contracts" between individuals and organizations. Sometimes that recontracting can be accomplished within the existing structure of property rights and political rules, but sometimes new contracting forms require an alteration in the rules. Equally, norms of behavior that guide exchanges will gradually be modified or wither away. In both instances, institutions are being altered.

Modifications occur because individuals perceive that they could do better by restructuring exchanges (political or economic). The source of the changed perceptions may be exogenous to the economy—for instance a change in the price or quality of a competitive product in another economy that alters perceptions of entrepreneurs in the given economy about profitable opportunities. But the most fundamental long-run source of change is learning by individuals and entrepreneurs of organizations.

While idle curiosity will result in learning, the rate of learning will reflect the intensity of competition among organizations. Competition, reflecting ubiquitous scarcity, induces organizations to engage in learning to survive. The degree of competition can and does vary. The greater the degree of monopoly power, the lower is the incentive to learn.

The speed of economic change is a function of the rate of learning, but the direction of that change is a function of the expected payoffs to acquiring different kinds of knowledge. The mental models that the players develop shape perceptions about the payoffs.

IV

It is necessary to dismantle the rationality assumption underlying economic theory in order to approach constructively the nature of human learning. History demonstrates that ideas, ideologies, myths, dogmas, and prejudices matter, and an understanding of the way they evolve is necessary for further progress in developing a framework for understanding societal change. The rational-choice framework assumes that individuals know what is in their self-interest and act accordingly. That may be correct for individuals making choices in the highly developed markets of modern economies,[4] but it is patently false under conditions of uncertainty—the conditions that have characterized the political and economic choices that shaped (and continue to shape) historical change.

Herbert Simon (1986, S210–11) has stated the issues succinctly: "If ... we accept the proposition that both the knowledge and the computational power of the decisionmaker are severely limited, then we must distinguish between the real world and the actor's perception of it and reasoning about it. That is to say we must construct a theory (and test it empirically) of the process of decision. Our theory must include not only the reasoning processes but also the processes that generated the actor's subjective representation of the decision problem, his or her frame."

The analytical framework we must build must originate in an understanding of how human learning takes place. We have a way to go before we can construct such a theory, but cognitive science has made immense strides in recent years—enough strides to suggest a tentative approach that can help us understand decision making under uncertainty.[5]

Learning entails developing a structure by which to interpret the varied signals received by the senses. The initial architecture of the structure is genetic, but the subsequent scaffolding is a result of the experiences of the individual. The experiences can be classified into two kinds—those from the physical environment and those from the sociocultural linguistic environment. The structures consist of categories—classifications that gradually evolve from earliest childhood to organize our perceptions and keep track of our memory of analytic results and experiences. Building on these classifications, we form mental models to explain and interpret the environment—typically in ways relevant to some goal. Both the categories and the mental models will evolve, reflecting the feedback derived from new experiences: feedback that sometimes strengthens our initial categories and models or may lead to modifications—in short, learning. Thus, the mental models may be continually redefined with new experiences, including contact with others' ideas.

At this juncture the learning process of human beings diverges from that of other animals (such as the sea slug—a favorite research subject of cognitive scientists) and particularly diverges from the computer analogy that dominated early studies of artificial intelligence. The mind appears to order and reorder the mental models from their special-purpose origins to successively more abstract forms so that they become available to process other information. The term used by Andy Clark and Annette Karmiloff-Smith (1993) is "representational redescription." The capacity to generalize from the particular to the general and to use analogy is a part of this redescription process. It is this capacity that is the source not only of creative thinking, but also of the ideologies and belief systems that underlie the choices humans make.[6]

A common cultural heritage provides a means of reducing the divergence in the mental models that people in a society have and constitutes the means for the intergenerational transfer of unifying perceptions. In premodern societies, cultural learning provided a means of internal communication; it also provided shared explanations for phenomena outside the immediate experiences of the members of society in the form of religions, myths, and dogmas. Such belief structures are not, however, confined to primitive societies but are an essential part of modern societies as well.

Belief structures get transformed into societal and economic structures by institutions—both formal rules and informal norms of behavior. The relationship between mental models and institutions is an intimate one. Mental models are the internal representations that individual cognitive systems create to interpret the environment; institutions are the external (to the mind) mechanisms individuals create to structure and order the environment.

V

There is no guarantee that the beliefs and institutions that evolve through time will produce economic growth. Let me pose the issue that time presents us by a brief institutional/cognitive story of long-run economic/political change.

As tribes evolved in different physical environments, they developed different languages and, with different experiences, different mental models to explain the world around them. The languages and mental models formed the informal constraints that defined the institutional framework of the tribe and were passed down intergenerationally as customs, taboos, and myths that provided cultural continuity.[7]

With growing specialization and division of labor, the tribes evolved into polities and economies; the diversity of experience and learning produced increasingly different societies and civilizations with different degrees of success in solving the fundamental economic problems of scarcity. The reason is that as the complexity of the environment increased as human beings became increasingly interdependent, more complex institutional structures were necessary to capture the potential gains from trade. Such evolution requires that the society develop institutions that will permit anonymous, impersonal exchange across time and space. To the extent that the culture and local experiences had produced diverse institutions and belief systems with respect to the gains from such cooperation, the likelihood of creating the necessary institutions to capture the gains from trade of more complex contracting varied. In fact, most societies throughout history got "stuck" in an institutional matrix that did not evolve into the impersonal exchange essential to capturing the productivity gains that came from the specialization and division of labor that have produced the Wealth of Nations.

The key to the foregoing story is the kind of learning that the individuals in a society acquired through time. Time in this context entails not only current experiences and learning but also the cumulative experience of past generations that is embodied in culture. Collective learning—a term used by Friedrich A. Hayek—consists of those experiences that have passed the slow test of time and are embodied in our language, institutions, technology, and ways of doing things. It is "the transmission in time of our accumulated stock of knowledge" (Hayek 1960, 27). It is culture that provides the key to "path dependence"—a term used to describe the powerful influence of the past on the present and future. The current learning of any generation takes place within the context of the perceptions derived from collective learning. Learning then is an incremental process filtered by the culture of a society which determines the perceived payoffs, but there is no guarantee that the cumulative past experience of a society will necessarily prepare it to solve new problems. Societies that get "stuck" embody belief systems and institutions that fail to confront and solve new problems of societal complexity.

We need to understand a great deal more about the cumulative learning of a society. The learning process appears to be a function of (1) the way in which a given belief structure filters the information derived from experiences and (2) the different experiences confronting individuals and societies at different times. The perceived rate of return (private) may be high to military technology (in medieval Europe), to the pursuit and refinement of religious dogma (Rome during and after Constantine), or to the research for an accurate chronometer to determine longitude at sea (for which a substantial reward was offered during the Age of Exploration).

The incentives to acquire pure knowledge, the essential underpinning of modern economic growth, are affected by monetary rewards and punishments; they are also fundamentally influenced by a society's tolerance of creative developments, as a long list of creative individuals from Galileo to Darwin could attest. While there is a substantial literature on the origins and development of science, very little of it deals with the links between institutional structure, belief systems, and the incentives and disincentives to acquire pure knowledge. A major factor in the development of Western Europe was the gradual perception of the utility of research in pure science.

Incentives embodied in belief systems as expressed in institutions determine economic performance through time, and however we wish to define economic performance the historical record is clear. Throughout most of history and for most societies in the past and present, economic performance has been anything but satisfactory. Human beings have, by trial and error, learned how to make economies perform better; but not only has this learning taken ten millennia (since the first economic revolution), it has still escaped the grasp of almost half of the world's population. Moreover, the radical improvement in economic performance, even when narrowly defined as material well-being, is a modern phenomenon of the last few centuries and confined, until the last few decades, to a small part of the world. Explaining the pace and direction of economic change throughout history presents a major puzzle.

Let us represent the human experience to date as a 24-hour clock in which the beginning consists of the time (apparently in Africa between 4 and 5 million years ago) when humans became separate from other primates. Then the beginning of so-called civilization occurs with the development of agriculture and permanent settlement in about 8000 B.C. in the Fertile Crescent—in the last three or four minutes of the clock. For the other 23 hours and 56 or 57 minutes, humans remained hunters and gatherers; and, while population grew, it did so at a very slow pace.

Now if we make a new 24-hour clock for the time of civilization—the 10,000 years from development of agriculture to the present—the pace of change appears to be very slow for the first 12 hours, although our archeological knowledge is very limited. Historical demographers speculate that the rate of population growth may have doubled as compared to the previous era but still was very slow. The pace of change accelerates in the past 5,000 years with the rise and then decline of economies and civilizations. Population may have grown from about 300 million at the time of Christ to about 800 million by 1750—a substantial acceleration as compared to earlier rates of growth. The last 250 years—just 35 minutes on our new 24-hour clock—are the era of modern economic growth, accompanied by a population explosion that now puts world population in excess of 5 billion.

If we focus now on the last 250 years, we see that growth was largely restricted to Western Europe and the overseas extensions of Britain for 200 of those 250 years.

Not only has the pace varied over the ages; the change has not been unidirectional. That is not simply a consequence of the decline of individual civilizations; there have been periods of apparent secular stagnation—the most recent being the long hiatus between the end of the Roman Empire in the West and the revival of Western Europe approximately 500 years later.

VI

What can an institutional/cognitive approach contribute to improving our understanding of the economic past? First of all it should make sense out of the very uneven pattern of economic performance described in the previous section.

There is nothing automatic about the evolving of conditions that will permit low-cost transacting in the impersonal markets that are essential to productive economies. Game theory characterizes the issue. Individuals will usually find it worthwhile to cooperate with others in exchange when the play is repeated, when they possess complete information about the other players' past performance, and when there are small numbers of players. Cooperation is difficult to sustain when the game is not repeated (or there is an endgame), when information about the other players is lacking, and when there are large numbers of players. Creating the institutions that will alter the benefit-cost ratios in favor of cooperation in impersonal exchange is a complex process, because it not only entails the creation of economic institutions but requires that they be undergirded by appropriate political institutions.

We are just beginning to explore the nature of this historical process. The remarkable development of Western Europe from relative backwardness in the tenth century to world economic hegemony by the eighteenth century is a story of a gradually evolving belief system in the context of competition among fragmented political/economic units producing economic institutions and political structure that produced modern economic growth.[8] And even within Western Europe there were successes (the Netherlands and England) and failures (Spain and Portugal) reflecting diverse external environmental experiences.[9]

Second, institutional/cognitive analysis should explain path dependence, one of the remarkable regularities of history. Why do economies once on a path of growth or stagnation tend to persist? Pioneering work on this subject is beginning to give us insights into the sources of path dependence (Brian Arthur 1989, Paul A. David 1985). But there is much that we still do not know. The rationality assumption of neoclassical theory would suggest that political entrepreneurs of stagnating economies could simply alter the rules and change the direction of failed economies. It is not that rulers have been unaware of poor performance. Rather, the difficulty of turning economies around is a function of the nature of political markets and, underlying that, the belief systems of the actors. The long decline of Spain, for example, from the glories of the Hapsburg Empire of the sixteenth century to its sorry state under Francisco Franco in the twentieth century was characterized by endless self-appraisals and frequently bizarre proposed solutions.[10]

Third, this approach will contribute to our understanding of the complex interplay among institutions, technology, and demography in the overall process of economic change. A complete theory of economic performance would entail such an integrated approach to economic history. We certainly have not put all the pieces together yet. For example, Robert W. Fogel's path-breaking work on demographic theory (1994) and its historical implications for reevaluating past economic performance have yet to be integrated fully with institutional analysis. The same is true for technological change. The important contributions of Nathan Rosenberg (1976) and Joel Mokyr (1990) exploring the impetus for and consequences of technological change have ongoing implications which need to be integrated with institutional analysis. An essay by Wallis and North (1986) is a beginning at integrating technological and institutional analysis. But a major task of economic history is to integrate these separate strands of research.

VII

We cannot account for the rise and decline of the Soviet Union and world communism with the tools of neoclassical analysis, but we should with an institutional/cognitive approach to contemporary problems of development. To do so— and to provide an analytical framework for understanding economic change—we must take into account the following implications of this approach:

1. It is the admixture of formal rules, informal norms, and enforcement characteristics that shapes economic performance. While the rules may be changed overnight, the informal norms usually change only gradually. Since it is the norms that provide "legitimacy" to a set of rules, revolutionary change is never as revolutionary as its supporters desire, and performance will be different than anticipated. And economies that adopt the formal rules of another economy will have very different performance characteristics than the first economy because of different informal norms and enforcement. The implication is that transferring the formal political and economic rules of successful Western market economies to Third World and Eastern European economies is not a sufficient condition for good economic performance. Privatization is not a panacea for solving poor economic performance.
2. Polities significantly shape economic performance because they define and enforce the economic rules. Therefore, an essential part of development policy is the creation of polities that will create and enforce efficient property rights. However, we know very little about how to create such polities, because the new political economy (the new institutional economics applied to politics) has been largely focused on the United States and developed polities. A pressing research need is to model Third World and Eastern European polities. However, the foregoing analysis does have some implications: (a) Political institutions will be stable only if undergirded by organizations with a stake in their perpetuation. (b) Both institutions and belief systems must change for successful reform, since it is the mental models of the actors that will shape choices. (c) Developing norms of behavior that will support and legitimize new rules is a lengthy process, and in the absence of such reinforcing mechanisms, polities will tend to be unstable. (d) While economic growth can occur in the short run with autocratic regimes, long-run economic growth entails the development of the rule of law. (e) Informal constraints (norms, conventions, and codes of conduct) favorable to growth can sometimes produce economic growth even with unstable or adverse political rules. The key is the degree to which such adverse rules are enforced.

3. It is adaptive rather than allocative efficiency which is the key to long-run growth. Successful political/economic systems have evolved flexible institutional structures that can survive the shocks and changes that are a part of successful evolution. But these systems have been a product of long gestation. We do not know how to create adaptive efficiency in the short run.

We have just set out on the long road to achieving an understanding of economic performance through time. The ongoing research embodying new hypotheses confronting historical evidence will not only create an analytical framework enabling us to understand economic change through time; in the process it will enrich economic theory, enabling it to deal effectively with a wide range of contemporary issues currently beyond its ken. The promise is there. The recognition of that promise by the Nobel Committee should be the essential spur to move us on down that road.

NOTES

I am indebted to Robert Bates, Lee and Alexandra Benham, Avner Greif, Margaret Levi, Randy Nielsen, John Nye, Jean-Laurent Rosenthal, Norma Schofield, and Barry Weingast for their comments on an earlier draft and to Elisabeth Case for editing this essay.

1. In fact such a theory is unlikely. I refer the reader to Frank Hahn's prediction about the future of economic theory (Hahn 1991).

2. These two sections briefly summarize material contained in North (1990a).

3. See the author's "A Transaction Cost Theory of Politics" for a transaction-cost approach to the relative inefficiency of political markets (North 1990b).

4. However, see the anomalies even here in the studies by Amos Tversky and Daniel Kahneman (1986) and others (Robin M. Hogarth and Melvin W. Reder 1986).

5. See John H. Holland et al. (1986) for an excellent introduction to the cognitive-science literature.

6. Ideologies are shared frameworks of mental models that groups of individuals possess that provide both an interpretation of the environment and a prescription as to how that environment should be ordered.

7. Ronald Heiner (1983), in a path-breaking article, not only made the connection between the mental capacities of human and the external environment, but suggested the implications for arresting economic progress.

8. See North and Robert P. Thomas (1973), E. L. Jones (1981), and Nathan Rosenberg and L. E. Birdzell (1986) for accounts of this growth.

9. See part 3 of North (1990a) for a brief discussion of the contrasting paths of the Netherlands and England on the one hand and Spain on the other.

10. DeVries (1976, 28) has a description of the bizarre remedies proposed by a royal commission to reverse Spain's decline.

REFERENCES

Arthur, Brian. 1989. "Competing Technologies, Increasing Returns, and Lock-In by Historical Events." *Economic Journal* 99(394):116–31.

Clark, Andy, and Annette Karmiloff-Smith. 1993. "The Cognizer's Innards: A Psychological and Philosophical Perspective on the Development of Thought." *Mind and Language* 8(4):487–519.

Coase, Ronald. 1960. "The Problem of Social Cost." *Journal of Law and Economics* 3(1):1–44.

David, Paul A. 1985. "Clio and the Economics of QWERTY." *American Economic Review* 75(2):32–37.

DeVries, Jan. 1976. *The Economy of Europe in an Age of Crises, 1600–1750.* Cambridge: Cambridge University Press.

Fogel, Robert W. 1994. "Economic Growth, Population Theory, and Physiology: The Bearing of Long-Term Processes on the Making of Economic Policy." *American Economic Review* 84(3):369–95.

Hahn, Frank. 1991. "The Next Hundred Years." *Economic Journal* 101(404):47–50.

Hayek, Friedrich A. 1960. *The Constitution of Liberty.* Chicago: University of Chicago Press.

Heiner, Ronald. 1983. "The Origin of Predictable Behavior." *American Economic Review* 73(4): 560–95.

Hogarth, Robin M., and Melvin W. Reder, eds. 1986. *Rational Choice: The Contrast between Economics and Psychology.* Chicago: University of Chicago Press.

Holland, John H., et al. 1986. *Induction: Processes of Inference, Learning, and Discovery.* Cambridge: MIT Press.

Jones, E. L. 1981. *The European Miracle.* Cambridge: Cambridge University Press.

Mokyr, Joel. 1990. *The Lever of Riches.* New York: Oxford University Press.

Nelson, Richard, and Sidney G. Winter. 1982. *An Evolutionary Theory of Economic Change.* Cambridge: Harvard University Press.

North, Douglass C. 1990a. *Institutions, Institutional Change, and Economic Performance.* New York: Cambridge University Press.

———. 1990b. "A Transactions Cost Theory of Politics." *Journal of Theoretical Politics* 2(4): 355–67.

North, Douglass C., and Robert P. Thomas. 1973. *The Rise of the Western World: A New Economic History.* Cambridge: Cambridge University Press.

Rosenberg, Nathan. 1976. *Perspectives on Technology.* Cambridge: Cambridge University Press.

Rosenberg, Nathan, and L. E. Birdzell. 1986. *How the West Grew Rich: The Economic Transformation of the Industrial World.* New York: Basic Books.

Simon, Herbert. 1986. "Rationality in Psychology and Economics." In *Rational Choice: The Contrast Between Economics and Psychology,* edited by Robin M. Hogarth and Melvin W. Reder, 25–40. Chicago: University of Chicago Press.

Tversky, Amos, and Daniel Kahneman. 1986. "Rational Choice and the Framing of Decisions." In *Rational Choice: The Contrast between Economics and Psychology,* edited by Robin M. Hogarth and Melvin W. Reder, 67–94. Chicago: University of Chicago Press.

Wallis, John J., and Douglass C. North. 1986. "Measuring the Transaction Sector in the American Economy." In *Long-Term Factors in American Economic Growth,* edited by Stanley L. Engerman and Robert E. Gallman, 95–148. Chicago: University of Chicago Press.

5

Community, Market, and State

This essay discusses the interrelationship among market systems, rural community institutions, and government activities in agricultural and economic development, with a focus on developing economies. As a pedestrian agricultural economist I know little about preferences and decision rules of politicians, bureaucrats, and business executives in the metropolis. Rather, I am familiar with the work and life of peasants and petty traders and their petty politics at the level of a village microcosm in the monsoon areas of Asia. Inevitably the perspective presented here is circumscribed by my narrow observations from Asian paddy fields.

RIVAL VIEWS ON COMMUNITY AND MARKET

Since the eve of modern economic growth, two rival views have contested the relationship between community and market. One view, which may be called the "community-yoke" thesis, considers traditional institutions in precapitalist and preindustrial communities to be the feudal yokes preventing realization of not only the economic but also the moral potential of mankind. In this view, the market is efficient in resource allocation and also provides the "rules of justice" that emancipate people from the yokes of traditional community ties and the arbitrary command of despotism, thereby enabling them to develop virtues such as industriousness, frugality and probity. This view has been asserted by great thinkers from early enlightenment philosophers like Montesquieu and Adam Smith to contemporaries such as Friedrich A. Hayek and Milton Friedman.[1] In this view the "Protestant ethic" identified by Max Weber as underlying modern industrial development is seen to be acquired through market exchange (Rosenberg 1964).

YUJIRO HAYAMI is professor of agricultural economics in the School of International Politics, Economics, and Business, Aoyama Gakuin University, Tokyo.

Previously published in *Agriculture and Government in an Interdependent World,* edited by A. Maunder and A. Valdés. (Proceedings of the Twentieth International Conference of Agricultural Economists, Buenos Aires, Argentina, 24–31 August 1988.) Aldershot, U.K.: Dartmouth Publishing. Published with minor editorial revisions by permission of the International Association of Agricultural Economists and the author.

Diametrically opposite to the community-yoke thesis is the view that we may call the "evil-market" thesis. In this view, the morals that are considered necessary for the efficient functioning of a market economy based on contracts among free individuals, such as honesty, trust, and restraint, are not something to be learned from commerce and market but are virtues nurtured through social interactions in precapitalist communities bound by common religion and mutual love. Since those traditional virtues are undermined by market forces based on the unrestricted release of self-interest and material greed, the capitalist market system is demoralizing, and hence, self-destructive (Hirsch 1976).

The community-yoke thesis asserts that the transition from precapitalist communities, which are bound by hierarchical status, traditional customs, and personal ties, to modern market economies is beneficial to a majority of the poor, as it emancipates them from the inferior occupations to which they are consigned by their low status at birth; the evil-market thesis argues the contrary. Indeed, a deep-rooted popular belief is that the destruction of traditional community relations, such as mutual help and income sharing, due to commercialization results in greater inequality and misery for the poor. Since the time of Sir Thomas More, who in his *Utopia* lamented the misery of peasants whose lands were enclosed into a large pasture for commercial wool production in sixteenth-century England, this view has been expressed repeatedly, by Russian *Narodniks,* U.S. populists, and the followers of Mahatma Gandhi in India. Karl Marx recognized the role of the market in emancipating the poor from the yoke of feudal regulations, but the freedom gained by a majority of the emancipated peasants meant to him nothing but the freedom for them to join the industrial reserve army of the lumpenproletariat (Marx 1909).

The battle between the community-yoke and the evil-market theses resounded again in a recent debate between the so-called moral economy and political economy approaches to peasant communities.[2] The former approach, advocated by James C. Scott (1976), Migdal (1974), and Wolf (1966), assumes that social relations in precapitalist peasant communities are geared to secure minimum subsistence for all community members. Normally, peasants eke out their living at a near-subsistence level. They are exposed to the constant danger that their income may decline below the subsistence minimum, because of external variations such as weather or internal incidents such as the sickness of family members. The compelling demand of the peasants to avoid subsistence crises is said to have resulted in a "subsistence ethic," under which social arrangements designed to insure against these crises are considered fair and legitimate.

In the view of moral economists, common features of village communities such as the exchange of labor, the use of communal property for the livelihood of the orphaned or the widowed, rent reductions in a year of crop failure are institutionalized patterns developed under this ethic. The basic principle "claims that all should have a place, a living, not that all should be equal" (Scott 1976, 40). To the extent that a landlord protects the poor members in the community (tenants) against ruin in bad years, he is considered a legitimate patron.

Thus, moral economists assume a pervasive tendency in village communities to set informal social controls on the better-off members to redistribute wealth or to impose specific obligations to provide for the minimum needs of the poor. With the intrusion of the market economy, the moral principle of securing minimum subsistence is replaced by the hard economic calculation of maximizing profit. The well-to-do members of the community tend to rely more on external legal means to protect their property. They become more concerned about increasing their incomes in order to purchase modern goods from outside than about buying goodwill among their fellow villagers. Mutual-help and patron-client relationships are weakened, and the poor are exposed to the risk of subsistence crises. Some of the small landholders are compelled to sell their land and become landless workers selling their labor in the labor market, while others accumulate land to become market-orientated farmers. Peasants stripped of the protection of traditional village institutions and patron-client bonds and faced with subsistence crises feel ill-treated and may eventually rise in revolt. Thus, moral economists view peasant uprisings as the desperate efforts of peasants to restore traditional rights destroyed by capitalism.

The moral economy view has been challenged by Samuel Popkin (1979) among others. In his political economy approach, Popkin denies that the pre-capitalist peasant community is morally oriented to protecting the poor. He insists that traditional village institutions and patron-client relationships have been neither motivated by nor effective in guaranteeing the subsistence need of community members. It is his essential contention that even in the traditional peasant community, people are predominantly motivated to seek personal gain rather than group interests; that peasants rely on their families or groups smaller than the village community for their subsistence guarantees because the village-wide scheme to insure against risk is bound to be ineffective, because everyone tries to be a free rider or to claim profit from group action without bearing the cost; and that elites exploit such village institutions as community property for their own profit rather than to protect the poor. As a result, village procedures reinforce, rather than level, differences in income and wealth. In this view the market system is beneficial to a majority of peasants to the extent that it emancipates them from the control of village elites and enables them to engage in transactions based on their own economic calculations.[3]

MARKET FAILURE AND COMMUNITY CORRECTION

While the perspectives of the community-yoke and the evil-market theses are diametrically opposite, they both regard community and market as rival institutions in terms of both growth and equity.[4] My basic doubt is whether they are absolute rivals or whether they are complementary to a significant extent, at least in the early stage of economic development. In my view the conditions of production and exchange faced by semisubsistent peasants are such that the market pervasively fails in achieving the efficient allocation of resources. Community relations are often relied upon to correct market failures.

One major source of market failure in agrarian communities in developing economies (such communities will hereafter be referred to as villages) is pervasive externalities. By nature, agricultural production activities are strongly interdependent, due to the ecological interdependence of biological processes. Overgrazing in a mountain pasture may increase the incidence of flooding in nearby crop fields. Diversion of irrigation water upstream may result in a water shortage for downstream farms. An individual peasant is usually too small a production unit to internalize such production externalities. It becomes imperative for the village to coordinate and reduce conflicts over the use of such resources.

Because production externalities are pervasive, and because possible conflicts are numerous and variable, customs or accumulated precedents tend to be a more effective means of settling conflicts than the stipulations of formal laws. Because village property, in the form of standing crops and grazing animals, is often physically unprotected in open fields, morals and taboos can be the most effective means of policing. Thus, the institutions that govern the use of resources efficiently in the village are customary rules and moral principles rather than formal laws and explicit contracts.

Those customary rules and moral principles are enforced through intensive social interactions in the small village community, where everyone is watching everyone and where gossip about one's misconduct is circulated by word of mouth faster than via modern communication means.[5] In such an environment, violation of time-honored village rules usually entails a significant cost. Even if an individual expects large material gains from violating the rules, he may not dare to do so because of the risk of social opprobrium and perhaps ostracism.

The close social interactions that reduce opportunism, cheating, and shirking, helping to prevent free riders in the provision of public goods, are also instrumental in enforcing contracts on the transaction of private goods and services. In the economic environment of rural villages in developing countries, transaction costs among anonymous agents in the market tend to be high. ("Market" is here defined rather narrowly, referring to the concept conventionally used in both the neoclassical and the Marxian economics texts.) First of all, the marketable agricultural surplus of semisubsistent peasants is usually small in volume and variable in quality. A market tends to be inefficient or vanish altogether because of high transaction costs.[6]

The problem of quality uncertainty is even more serious in labor markets. In urban industries characterized by the machine process, work is highly standardized and relatively easy to monitor. The biological process of agricultural production, however, is subject to infinite variations in ecological conditions. Very different treatments for a crop or an animal are required in response to slight differences in temperature and soil moisture. It matters a great deal whether a laborer performs his work with careful attention and adjustment to variations in plants, animals, and ecology. Such work quality is extremely difficult to monitor. The scattering of agricultural operations over a wide space adds to the difficulty of monitoring. If an employment relationship is limited to a spot exchange among anonymous agents in the marketplace, it is difficult to avoid hiring workers who are dishonest or shirkers in terms of the quality of their physical work. Market transaction by hierarchical internal organizations such as firms is limited, partly because of the small market size and partly because of production uncertainty and the difficulty of delineating and standardizing production operations in the biological process.[7]

The presence of severe quality uncertainty, coupled with the small market size makes it unprofitable for specialized agents to engage in the marketing of various goods and services separately. Consequently, a strong tendency emerges in the village economy for various transactions to be interlinked in a highly personalized relationship. A typical arrangement is a sharecropping tenancy. Usually a landlord does not simply receive a share rent for his contribution of land but also bears a part of production cost and advances credit. Moreover, he often patronizes his tenant in such ways as giving gifts at the birth of a child or the death of a father and using his connections and influence to solve a tenant's problems with other villages or with outsiders. The tenant reciprocates with loyal service and support to the landlord.

In such a patron-client relationship, exchanges are multistranded and the balance is cleared in the long run. Multiple transactions between the same parties permit the saving of transaction costs, because much of the cost of information collection and contract enforcement is common to all transactions.[8] Moreover, once the patron-client relationship is established, the client will be morally obliged to conform to the implicit terms of contract and will risk penalty for the commitment of moral hazards, since the loss of the patron's protection would mean a very high cost in economies with developed insurance and credit markets. On the other hand, if the patron fails to provide sufficient protection or pay legitimate remuneration, he will face cheating, shirking, and stealing and be penalized by social opprobrium.

I share Samuel Popkin's political economy perspective that peasants in the precaptialist society are as egoistic as any hard-calculating capitalists in seeking personal gains. However, the fact that the peasants are egoists does not necessarily conflict with their apparently altruistic behavior as observed by moral economists like James Scott. If a village community is characterized by a high degree of social interaction, a well-to-do villager may try to simulate the behavior of a benevolent patron in terms of traditional norms, if he is a wise egoist. Likewise, a poor villager may simulate the behavior of a conscientious and faithful client.

To the extent that opportunism and moral hazards are suppressed by such community mechanisms, market failures due to pervasive production externalities and high transaction costs are reduced. Thus, strong social interactions and shared traditional customs and moral principles can enable community members to arrive at and maintain agreements of mutual advantage and to avoid the mutual distrust that causes the "prisoner's dilemma" (mutual distrust).[9]

Such a role of community relations is not limited to preindustrial society but is also important in industrial and/or postindustrial societies. As the work required for modern times has shifted from that based on muscles to that based on brain, it has become increasingly difficult to enforce work rules through a hierarchical command system. It has become necessary to design the forms of contract that incorporate incentives to improve unobservable work efforts by improving morale (Mirrlees 1974; Nalebuff and Stiglitz 1983). One possible direction is to establish relations of a community type within a firm. A typical example along this line is the Japanese-management system. In the Japanese system, employment is life-long with no explicit contract, but both management and employees are assumed to follow the customary rules of the company; a boss is supposed to develop a patron-client relationship with workers under him, so that a section or a division or even a whole company simulates a family or a village. Such a system, which was once regarded as premodern, feudalistic, and hence inefficient, is now considered to underlie the high efficiency of Japanese industries, as it minimizes the X-inefficiency arising from the prisoner's dilemma situation (Leibenstein 1987).

COMMUNITY FAILURE AND MARKET CORRECTION

Of course, in the real world no community is perfect in eliminating opportunism, cheating, and shirking. The community with zero transaction cost, completely free from the prisoner's dilemma problem, is as much an abstraction as a perfectly competitive market.[10]

First of all, the traditional customs and the moral principles that govern the village community are, by nature, slow to change. These community rules and institutions might have promoted efficient resource use when they were created, but they often become its fetters, because institutional adjustments tend to lag behind changes in resource endowments, technology, and market conditions.[11] For example, overgrazing of common pasture in a village may be explained by a lag in the shift from the traditional rule of free access to the village property to a system that facilitates resource conservation, such as private property rights.

Second, the community mechanism of rule enforcement based on common belief and intensive social interactions is bound to be limited to a small community. While the community system may be effective in coordinating resource use within a village, it is largely incapable of solving conflicts between this village and other villages or the outside world in general. The prisoner's dilemma tends to emerge among villages or tribes, especially when they belong to different ethnic groups. One village alone may be able to develop and enforce rules to regulate the number of animals in a grazing land. But, this village may not dare to do so, for fear that other villages will react by increasing their own stock to take

advantage of the first village's conservation effort. Indeed, I have often encountered cases in which an irrigation system covering the area of one village
is efficiently administered, while another nearby system covering several villages is very poorly maintained and the abuse of water in upstream villages results in shortages in downstream villages. This general tendency for a village
community to allow or even encourage the exercise of opportunism by its members against outsiders is also a serious constraint on the development of a market over a wide area. The need for setting and enforcing common rules to prevent the intercommunity opportunism is considered one of the major factors
underlying the emergence of the state endowed with coercive power over a wide
area.

Third, although the community mechanism may be effective in reducing transaction costs within a village, it does not guarantee efficient resource allocation
in the sense of a Pareto optimum. Because potential participants in the patron-
client contracts are few in a small community, the implicit contracts to be reached
through subtle bargaining tend to be similar to those of bilateral monopoly. If
land and capital are concentrated in the hands of the few elites, resource allocation will be close to that of pure monopoly or monopsony in the interlinked-fac-
tor and product markets, especially where it is easy for the landed elite to col-
lude through intensive social interactions. Penetration of the market system, or
exposure of landless villagers to wide market opportunities, will strengthen their
bargaining position, and hence bring equilibrium closer to that of perfect competition. In such a case, the development of the market will have the effect of
increasing both efficiency and equity.

Further, if a community is artificially segregated from market competition, the
likelihood is high that the community principles, such as mutual help and reci-
procity, may lead to mutual shirking. This evolution may explain, in part, the
relative inefficiency in collective or state farms in socialist economies as well as
in Japanese agricultural cooperatives operating under strong government protection (Hayami 1988). Japan's incorporation of a community relations structure
into the internal organization of firms does not sufficiently explain the efficiency of Japanese industries. That explanation lies in management's developing a
community morale among employees that causes them to work hard without
costly supervision for the sake of survival of their company under fierce market
competition.[12]

ANTI-COMMUNITY AND ANTI-MARKET POLICIES

The structure of a community and the structure of its markets play critically
important roles in coordinating rural people for the efficient use of scarce resources. Of course, no system is perfect. The community-yoke and evil-market
theses have concentrated on condemning the failings of each system, on entirely different grounds, without due consideration of their complementarity. Under
the influence of these rival views, governments in developing countries have of-

ten tried to suppress the mechanisms of community and market and, in the process, have destroyed their positive functions.

On the basis of the community-yoke thesis, it has been considered necessary to suppress the "feudal and exploitative" rules and institutions of traditional village communities. A typical example is the prohibition of sharecropping tenancy stipulated in the land reform laws of many developing countries. Share tenancy has been considered both exploitative and inefficient because landlords derive an unfair share of the product of tenants' efforts and hence reduce the tenants' incentive to apply labor and other inputs below optimum levels.[13] However, recent empirical as well as theoretical studies tend to support the hypothesis that the share contract can achieve the same degree of efficiency as the fixed-rent contract and owner farming and that share tenancy can be more beneficial for tenants because of its features of risk sharing and utilization of the landlord's credit. Furthermore, prohibition of share tenancy reduces the possibility for landless laborers to climb up the agricultural ladder via sharecropping to lease holding and eventually to owning a farm.[14] An emerging consensus is that the artificial limitations on the choice of contracts, such as the prohibition of share tenancy, reduces both efficiency and equity.

On the other hand, the market system has also been condemned by the popular image that middlemen and money lenders exploit peasants through the practice of monopoly or monopsony pricing and usury. This evil-market perspective has often underlain pervasive government interventions into the market in developing countries, ranging from controls on farm product prices, interest, and land rent, to government monopolies in marketing agricultural production, distributing inputs, and providing credit.

However, accumulated empirical evidence has been largely inconsistent with the hypothesis of monopoly and monopsony exploitation by middlemen and moneylenders. Rather, private marketing in developing countries has been found to be fairly competitive and efficient.[15] Government regulations of markets have often proved not only detrimental to efficient resource allocation but also inequitable. For example, the prohibition of usury has increased the effective rate of interest to the poor by the amount of expected penalty risk to moneylenders; rent control reduced landowners' incentive to rent out their land, thereby reducing the opportunity of landless laborers to become tenant farmers; and controls on food prices have benefited relatively rich urban dwellers at the expense of peasant producers.[16]

More wasteful has been the substitution of governmental agencies, such as marketing boards and parastatal organizations, for private marketing channels. This has resulted in the substitution of high opportunity-cost resources, such as modern equipment and educated manpower, for low opportunity-cost local resources, especially labor in the off-farm season. We need not mention increases in X-inefficiency due to a shift from private to governmental monopoly firms. It is well known that those governmental agencies have been used as a means to procure food from peasants at lower-than-market prices for delivery to urban dwellers. Also, the governmental monopoly of credit and input supplies has been used by politicians to reward their supporters selectively and centralize power and resources in their hands (Bates 1981; Lipton 1977).

Government interventions and regulations in indigenous community and market relations have created large institutional rents for bureaucrats and local elites. The other side of the coin is that interventions and regulations have multiplied as the result of bureaucratic and political rent-seeking activities (Buchanan, Tollison, and Tullock 1980; Tollison 1984; Collander 1984). When politicians in developing countries calculate the probability of their staying in office, the support from bureaucrats, rural elites, urban business, and organized labor, weighs more heavily than the support from unorganized peasants and laborers in rural areas.

Because the group of bureaucrats and local elites consists of a small number of educated, resourceful people, it is relatively easy for them to lobby for the rules and institutions that are expected to yield them institutional rents. The peasants and laborers, though large in number, are weak politically because they are poorly organized. In general, as the theory of Mancur Olson (1965) predicts, the large group is more difficult to organize because of the difficulty of preventing free riders. Moreover, peasants and agricultural laborers in developing economies are mostly uneducated and distributed over a wide area that has poor communications and transportation infrastructure. It is, therefore, too costly for them to organize themselves for countervailing group action against a political campaign by the elites (Olson 1985). Inefficient and inequitable institutions and policies are the product of political forces.[17] This is the basic source of government failure in achieving socially efficient resource allocation. It is important to recognize that ideologies in such forms as the community-yoke and the evil-market theses have been highly useful to politicians and rent-seekers, providing a rationale for suppressing opposition to their anti-community and anti-market policies.[18]

TOWARDS COMMUNITY AND MARKET DEVELOPMENTS

My argument does not imply that governments should reduce their rural development efforts. On the contrary, governments should expand their efforts in the spheres in which both community and market fail to achieve socially efficient resource allocation. In this endeavor, governments should try to supplement rather than replace indigenous community and market systems.

As discussed, individual village communities are often incapable of building large public infrastructures covering several villages. For these, the government should take the responsibility. In this case, too, efforts are needed to mobilize the collaboration and the participation of local communities to the greatest possible extent. For example, while major dams and canals for large-scale irrigation need to be built and maintained by governmental agencies, collaboration with local communities must be deliberately designed for the operation and maintenance of subsidiary canals and farm ditches. A critical role of government in reducing community failure is to enhance collaboration, or at least to reduce antagonism and distrust among small local communities, educating and persuading communities of the need for cooperation in the efficient use of a large infrastructure.

Also, plenty of room exists for government to improve the efficiency of local markets. Marketing margins for agricultural products are large in developing countries, because of high transportation costs and the cost of collecting the agricultural surplus in small lots from small producers. In isolated villages a collection monopoly typically emerges, because the agricultural surplus is so small (relative to the cost of transportation) that no more than one middleman can profitably operate. When this is the case, the way to improve marketing efficiency is for the government to invest in transportation and communication infrastructure, as well as in agricultural research and extension for increasing agricultural output, productivity, and marketable surplus.

The supply of credit, especially from outside a village, is often constrained by the absence of adequate institutions to stipulate and enforce collateral. In such a case, government efforts to improve the registry of real assets and the procedures of civil courts to enforce collateral contracts will contribute greatly to reducing credit costs. In general, the stipulation and enforcement of private property rights by the government are the basis for efficient functioning of the market.

A paramount danger is to overemphasize the failures of existing community and market systems while ignoring the possibility of government failure. Such arguments have been used to justify the displacement of indigenous community and market institutions by "modern" institutions heavily loaded with bureaucracy. The imposition of institutions imported from developed countries or founded on ideological preconceptions that do not consider the traditional norms and organizational principles is bound to meet with widespread noncompliance or sabotage by local people, as evidenced by the repeated failures of institutional credit programs and the rapid deterioration of some modern large-scale irrigation systems.

Self-sustaining growth of the rural economy in developing countries cannot be expected without a policy that makes positive use of indigenous community relations and local market organizations as a basis for modern rural development institutions. The search for an appropriate policy design should begin with serious investigations into the reality of the grassroots in each developing country.

NOTES

1. For contesting views on the role of market and its relationship with community, see Hirschman 1982 and Inoki 1987.

2. Also see Hayami and Kikuchi 1982.

3. For further debates between the moral and the political economy approaches, see the proceedings of a symposium on this subject in the *Journal of Asian Studies*, August 1983.

4. Also see Hayami and Kikuchi 1982.

5. Following Becker 1974, the term "social interactions" is defined here in terms of the utility function of a person to include other persons' reactions to his action. For example, A's welfare depends not only on his own personal consumption but also on how B looks at A's income and consumption levels. If A enjoys B's goodwill or fears his envy, A may transfer a part of his income to B up to a point where A's marginal loss of utility from the income transfer to B equals the marginal gain in A's utility due to the improvement in B's evaluation of A.

6. For the theory of market failure due to quality uncertainty, see Akerlof 1970. For an application to agricultural marketing in developing economies, see Siamwalla 1978.

7. For the role of hierarchical internal organization in reducing transaction costs, see Coase 1937 and Williamson 1975. See Brewster 1950 for a discussion of the difficulties in applying a hierarchical command system to the management of agricultural production relative to industrial production.

8. This is considered a major factor underlying the emergence of interlocked factor markets (see Bardham 1980).

9. The prisoner's dilemma is a solution of mutual disadvantage for two persons engaged in a noncooperative game under a situation in which each person fears that the other person may pursue a strategy to benefit himself at the expense of the other. The setting of traditional village communities is opposite to the prisoner's dilemma game. Rather it is considered to approximate the "super game," in which all villagers (players) expect transactions (games) among them to be repeated endlessly, so that everybody knows opportunism does not pay because it will sooner or later meet retaliation from others. See Luce and Raiffa 1957.

10. For example, the general absence of a draft animal rental market is considered as evidence of the difficulty of preventing careless treatment and overwork of animals by borrowers, even in a village community. For the causes of inefficiency or absence of some markets in the rural economy in developing countries, see Binswanger and Rosenzweig 1986.

11. This problem is inherent in any institutional change, as pointed out by Karl Marx in the famous preface to his *Contribution to the Critique of Political Economy,* but it is considered especially severe in the case of traditional community institutions.

12. For the mode of competition and cooperation among Japanese firms, see Abegglen and Stalk 1985.

13. Until recently this view had been common among modern economists, too, based on a misunderstanding of Alfred Marshall's theory. For a review of the literature, see Otsuka and Hayami 1988.

14. This problem has become serious under land reform in the Philippines. See Hayami, Quisumbing, and Adrians 1987.

15. Also see Ruttan 1969, Lele 1971, and Scott 1995.

16. The inefficiency resulting from agricultural price distortions was emphasized by Schultz (1978).

17. For a political economy model of agricultural policies, see Hayami 1988. For a general economic theory of politics, see Downs 1957.

18. This role of ideology or, more broadly, cultural endowments as instruments for politicians is emphasized by North (1981), and Hayami and Ruttan (1985).

REFERENCES

Abegglen, James C., and George Stalk, Jr. 1985. *Kaisha: The Japanese Corporation.* New York: Basic Books.

Akerlof, George A. 1970. "The Market for 'Lemons': Quality Uncertainty and the Market Mechanism." *Quarterly Journal of Economics* 84:488–500.

Bardhan, Pranab K. 1980. "Interlocking Factor Markets and Agrarian Development: A Review of Literature." *Oxford Economic Papers* 32:82–98.

Bates, Robert H. 1981. *Markets and States in Tropical Africa.* Berkeley: University of California Press.

Becker, Gary S. 1974. "A Theory of Social Interactions." *Journal of Political Economy* 82:1063–93.
Binswanger, Hans P., and Mark R. Rosenzweig. 1986. "Behavioural and Material Determinants of Production Relations in Agriculture." *Journal of Development Studies* 22:503–39.
Brewster, John M. 1950. "The Machine Process in Agriculture and Industry." *Journal of Farm Economics* 32:69–81.
Buchanan, James M., Robert D. Tollison, and Gordon Tullock, eds. 1980. *Towards a General Theory of the Rent-Seeking Society.* College Station: Texas A&M University Press.
Coase, Ronald H. 1937. "The Nature of the Firm." *Economica* 4: 386–405.
Collander, David C., ed. 1984. *Neoclassical Political Economy.* Cambridge, Mass.: Ballinger.
Downs, Anthony. 1957. *Economic Theory of Democracy.* New York: Harper and Row.
Hayami, Yujiro. 1988. *Japanese Agriculture under Siege: The Political Economy of Agricultural Policies.* London: Macmillan.
Hayami, Yujiro, and Masao Kikuchi. 1982. *Asian Village Economy at the Crossroads.* Baltimore: Johns Hopkins University Press.
Hayami, Yujiro, Agnes R. Quisumbing, and Lourdes F. Adrians. 1987. *In Search of a Land Reform Design for the Philippines.* Los Baños: University of the Philippines.
Hayami, Yujiro, and Vernon W. Ruttan. 1985. *Agricultural Development: An International Perspective.* Revised edition. Baltimore: Johns Hopkins University Press.
Hirsch, Fred. 1976. *Social Limits to Growth.* Cambridge: Harvard University Press.
Hirschman, Albert O. 1982. "Rival Interpretations of Market Society: Civilizing, Destructive, or Feeble?" *Journal of Economic Literature* 20:1463–84.
Inoki, Takenori. 1987. *Keizai Shiso* (Economic Thoughts). Tokyo: Iwanami-Shoten.
Lele, Uma. 1971. *Food Grain Marketing in India.* Ithaca: Cornell University Press.
Leibenstein, Harvey. 1987. *Inside the Firm: The Inefficiency of Hierarchy.* Cambridge: Harvard University Press.
Lipton, Michael. 1977. *Why Poor People Stay Poor: Urban Bias in Development.* Cambridge: Harvard University Press.
Luce, Duncan R., and Howard Raiffa. 1957. *Games and Decisions.* New York: Wiley.
Marx, Karl. 1909. *Capital.* Vol. 1. Chicago: Kerr. (Originally published 1867).
Migdal, Joel S. 1974. *Peasants, Politics, and Revolution.* Princeton: Princeton University Press.
Mirrlees, James. 1974. "Notes on Welfare Economics, Information, and Uncertainty." In *Essays on Economic Behavior under Uncertainty,* edited by M. Balch et al. Amsterdam: North-Holland.
Nalebuff, B. J., and J. E. Stiglitz. 1983. "Prizes and Incentives: Towards a General Theory of Compensation and Competition." *Bell Journal of Economics* 14:21–43.
North, Douglass C. 1981. *Structure and Change in Economic History.* New York: Norton.
Olson, Mancur. 1965. *The Logic of Collective Action.* Cambridge: Harvard University Press.
———. 1985. "Space, Agriculture, and Organization." *American Journal of Agricultural Economics* 67:928–37.
Otsuka, Keijiro, and Yujiro Hayami. 1988. "Theories of Share Tenancy: A Critical Survey." *Economic Development and Cultural Change* 37 (1): 31–68.
Popkin, Samuel L. 1979. *The Rational Peasant.* Berkeley: University of California Press.
Rosenberg, Nathan. 1964. "Neglected Dimensions in the Analysis of Economic Change." *Oxford Bulletin of Economics and Statistics* 26:59–77.
Ruttan, Vernon W. 1969. "Agricultural Product and Factor Markets in Southeast Asia." *Economic Development and Cultural Change* 17 (4): 501–19.
Schultz, Theodore, ed. 1978. *Distortions of Agricultural Incentives.* Bloomington: Indiana University Press.
Scott, Gregory C. 1995. *Prices, Products, and People: Analyzing Agricultural Markets in Developing Countries.* Boulder, Colo.: Lynne Rienner Publishers.
Scott, James C. 1976. *The Moral Economy of the Peasant.* New Haven: Yale University Press.

Siamwalla, Ammar. 1978. "Farmers and Middlemen: Aspects of Agricultural Marketing in Thailand."
    Economic Bulletin for Asia and Far East (UN-ESCAP) 29:38–50.
Tollison, Robert D. 1984. "Rent Seeking: A Survey." *Kyklos* 35:575–602.
Williamson, Oliver M. 1975. *Market and Hierarchies.* New York: Free Press.
Wolf, Eric. 1966. *Peasants.* Englewood Cliffs, N.J.: Prentice-Hall.

6

Markets, Market Failures, and Development

JOSEPH E. STIGLITZ

A central question in development economics is, how can we account for differences in the levels of income and the rates of growth between the developed and less developed economies? In the 1950s and 1960s, there was a standard answer to this question: the poor are just like the rich, except they are poorer—they have less human and nonhuman capital. There was an immediate prescription for this diagnosis: increase the resources of LDCs, either by transferring capital to them (either direct aid or education) or by encouraging them to save more.

Today, these answers seem less convincing than they did two decades ago. If the problem were primarily a shortage of physical capital, the return to capital should be much higher in LDCs than in developed countries, and the natural avarice of capitalists would lead to a flow of capital from the more developed to the less developed economies (see Pack 1984 and Stiglitz 1988). If the problem were primarily a shortage of human capital, then the educated in LDCs should receive a higher (absolute as well as relative) income than the educated in more developed economies. How then can we account for high levels of unemployment among the educated and the migration of the educated from LDCs to more developed economies?

Moreover, the predictions of the standard neoclassical growth model, of a convergence of growth rates in per capita income, with permanent differences in per capita consumption being explained by differences in savings rates and reproduction rates, do not seem to have been borne out.

These observations suggest that the LDCs differ from the developed countries in at least some other important respects, and this view is corroborated by those studies which have looked at the productivity of similar plants operating in developed and less developed economies. (See Pack 1984, 1987.)

The difference can be attributed, perhaps tautologically, to differences in eco-

JOSEPH E. STIGLITZ is chief economist, World Bank, Washington, D.C.

Previously published in the *American Economic Review* 79, no. 1 (1989): 197–210. Published with minor editorial revisions by permission of the American Economic Association and the author.

nomic organization, to how individuals (factors of production) interact, and to the institutions which mediate those interactions. Among the most important of these "institutions" are markets.

It is by now well recognized that there are many instances of market failures in more developed economies (see Greenwald and Stiglitz 1986). In some cases, market failures may be ameliorated by nonmarket institutions. If, for instance, capital markets do not function well ("perfectly"), if only because of costly and imperfect information, nonmarket institutions (internal capital markets within large conglomerates) may develop.[1] Market failure is more prevalent in LDCs, and the nonmarket institutions that ameliorate its consequences are, at least in many instances, less successful in doing so. The objective of this paper is to explore the causes and consequences of these market failures and the failure of private nonmarket solutions and to suggest possible roles for government intervention.

In this discussion, I focus on three examples of central importance to LDCs: learning, capital markets, and product markets. In each instance, I shall identify why markets do not work in the way hypothesized by neoclassical theory.

LEARNING AND INFORMATION

Among the "commodities" for which markets are most imperfect are those associated with knowledge and information (for instance, see Stiglitz 1987b). In many respects, knowledge is like a public good. Firms may have a difficult time appropriating their returns to knowledge, resulting in an undersupply; and to the extent that they are successful in appropriating, underutilization results (since they will have to charge for its use.) This has several consequences for the development process.

LEARNING BY DOING

Some recent studies (Lucas 1988, Stiglitz 1987a, Romer 1986) have argued that a major difference between the more and less developed countries arises from learning by doing (Arrow 1962) and limits on the ability to transfer what learning occurs across international boundaries. The less developed countries, finding it impossible to acquire the learning of the more developed countries, find it optimal (given their initial disadvantage) to specialize in technologies or products with lower learning potentials. While undoubtedly the learning phenomenon is related to development processes, the relationship is more subtle than a simple analysis might suggest.

Price effects. In the case where goods are competitively produced and there is free trade, price adjustments may partially (fully, or more than fully) offset differentials in increases in (physical) productivity: with unitary price elasticities, countries producing commodities with lower growth rates of productivity will experience fully offsetting increases in relative prices (Skeath 1988).

Imperfect competition. When spillovers of knowledge within a country (as one surely would expect) are less than perfect, then markets will never be perfectly competitive. The first entrant in a market will enjoy monopoly rents (Dasgupta and Stiglitz 1988). These monopoly rents may account for the persistence of income differences, and changes in the pace of innovation would then account for a widening of income differentials.

Localized learning. Moreover, to the extent that technological change (learning) is localized (Atkinson and Stiglitz 1969), productivity increases for the kinds of production processes used in more developed economies will have limited spillovers for the less developed countries. Again, an increase in the degree of "localization" (an increase in the disparity between the kinds of technologies used in LDCs and those used in more developed economies) will result in an increase in the gap between the two.

Learning to learn. Finally, my earlier paper (1987a) suggested that the ability to learn is itself learned,[2] and that learning abilities may themselves be localized.

Low-level equilibria. Among the several implications of "learning to learn" and localized learning abilities is the possibility of a low-level equilibrium trap: a country may not only find itself in a steady-state equilibrium with a low level of capital, using a technology with a low rate of technological change and a low ability to learn, but it may find it optimal (given high enough discount rates) to remain there.

Consider a simple life-cycle model, in which individuals live for two periods, working in the first only, where savings during the first period finance consumption during retirement, and where savings rates are an increasing function of the rate of growth in income per capita and a decreasing function of the rate of interest. We assume technological change is labor augmenting, that the steady-state rate of labor-augmenting technological progress associated with technology k is $n(k)$, where k is the capital-effective labor ratio, and that more capital-intensive technologies have higher steady-state learning functions ($n' > 0$). For simplicity, it is assumed that population is constant. Then in steady-state equilibrium, the rate of growth of capital (K) must equal the rate of growth of the effective labor supply, that is,

$$d \ln K/dt = sQ/K = s(k)q(k) = n(k),$$

where Q is total output and $q(k)$ is the output capital ratio for technique k; q is a declining function of k. Under these assumptions, the savings rate, s, is simply a function of k; if s increases rapidly enough with k (either because of growth or interest rate effects), there can clearly exist more than one solution to the above equation, as figure 1 illustrates, with the equilibria at higher values of k being associated with higher rates of growth of productivity. Alternative formulations with infinitely lived individuals yield similar results.

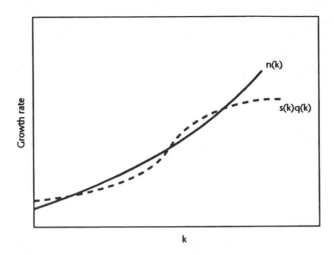

Fig. 1. Multiple Equilibria with Localized Learning

History matters (hysteresis). Which of the multiple equilibria characterizes a particular country depends on history. Indeed, in models of learning, especially with localized learning, particular events (wars, plagues, depressions, etc.) have permanent effects. (In contrast, in the Solow neoclassical growth model, the steady-state equilibrium to which the economy converges is independent of initial conditions and historical occurrences.)

Dynamic comparative advantage. Learning itself, and the fact that learning (and learning to learn) is localized, means that it will not be optimal to pursue myopic policies; one cannot use current comparative advantages as the only basis for judgments of how to allocate resources. Moreover, it may be optimal to initially incur a loss; the imperfections of capital markets (which I discuss in the next section) thus may impose a more serious impediment on LDCs taking advantage of potentials for learning.

Learning externalities. The experience of Silicon Valley suggests that there are important externalities in the learning and R&D process. The intellectual ferment undoubtedly contributes to innovative activity. There are always unappropriated spillovers of knowledge. These nonmarket externalities are *diffuse,* which is why it is difficult for any single firm to internalize them (for example, by mergers.)

Risk and entry. Karla Hoff (1988) has explored one important class of such externalities. The process of development involves entrepreneurs taking risks: are the resources of the country well suited to the production of a particular commodity? The success or failure of an entrepreneur conveys information to other entrepreneurs, the return to which cannot be easily appropriated. Hoff has shown that as a result there may be too little entry into new industries.

Externalities and multiple equilibria. These nonmarket externalities, too, can give rise to multiple equilibria. There are positive feedbacks: the high level of expenditures on R&D by firm *i* has sufficiently high spillovers that it may increase the marginal return to research by firm *j*. (See Sah and Stiglitz 1989.)

There are other *positive* feedbacks that may give rise to multiple equilibria. Assume that there are two groups within the population: innovators and inventors. Inventors generate new ideas; innovators turn them into profitable businesses. Innovators search among inventors for good ideas. The more inventors there are, the more it pays to be an innovator; and the more innovators there are, the greater the returns to invention.[3] Having more educated individuals in a society may serve to increase the returns to education.[4]

Income effects also give rise to multiplicity of equilibria. If all other sectors of the economy are growing rapidly, demand for my products will be growing rapidly. It will pay me to produce more and to expand my production rapidly, leading to rapid learning. (This effect is obviously less important for internationally traded goods.)

Differences between developed and less developed countries. The problems I have discussed arise in developed economies as well as LDCs, but they have particular force within LDCs for two reasons. First, the large scale of more developed economies, and the enterprises within them, allow them to reap sufficient benefits from undertaking what in many instances can be viewed as "overhead information acquisition activities," thus reducing welfare losses from the failure to appropriate all of the returns. Thus, AT&T found it profitable to support basic research leading to the development of the laser and transistor; the private gains from their undertaking this research were sufficiently large to warrant the expenditures, even though they were clearly lower than the social gains.

Second, to a large extent, the problem of development, and particularly industrialization, is that of the acquisition of information about technology, of ascertaining what products can and should be produced, how they should be produced, and how the technology should be acquired.

CAPITAL MARKETS

Problems of adverse selection, moral hazard, and contract enforcement imply that even in developed economies, capital markets do not look like the (old) textbook models of perfect capital markets. Even competitive markets may be characterized by credit rationing (see Stiglitz and Weiss 1981) and what Bruce Greenwald and I call "equity rationing" (1988b): new share issues result in sufficiently large decreases in firm's market value that few firms resort to new equity issues as a way of raising capital.

Equity rationing implies that firms cannot divest themselves of the risks which they face. They will, accordingly, act in a more risk-averse manner. Shocks to the economy, resulting for instance from an instability in the international market at which exports are sold, may have strong adverse effects both on their willingness to invest in capacity expansion and on their willingness to produce. (Of course, even with well-organized internal equity markets, firms would not be able to divest themselves of the political risks that may impose major impediments to investment.)

The greater riskiness of the environment in which they live and the poorer performance of their markets in allowing entrepreneurs to divest themselves of these risks have further repercussions on the rate of growth of productivity, so long as productivity is a result either of investment in R&D or of learning by doing (see Greenwald and Stiglitz 1988b). Again, multiple equilibria may result.

The greater prevalence of credit rationing means, further, that firms may rely more on internal financing for their capacity expansion. Capital is less effectively reallocated.

In more developed economies, large firms have developed internal capital markets that lead to reallocation of funds among units that are the size of many firms in LDCs. The LDCs are thus at a double disadvantage: not only are there informational imperfections, leading to credit and equity rationing; not only are these informational imperfections likely to be more important within LDCs, because the process of change itself leads to greater informational problems; but more importantly, the institutional framework for dealing with these capital market imperfections is probably less effective, because of the small scale of firms within LDCs and because the institutions for collecting, evaluating, and disseminating information are likely to be less well developed.

Moreover, as noted in the previous section, learning implies the optimality of nonmyopic policies, entailing firms' borrowing; thus borrowing constraints have a greater impact on countries in earlier parts of their learning curves.

PRODUCT MARKETS

Informational imperfections affect producers directly, and indirectly, through their effect on consumers. Imperfect information is one of the reasons that most firms in the industrialized sector of developed countries as well as LDCs face downward-sloping demand curves for their products, as opposed to the perfectly elastic demand postulated in neoclassical theory.

For the LDCs, this has two implications. First, lowering exchange rates may not have large immediate effects on sales. Second, there appear to be important externality effects across producers with regard to quality. Consumers may lump together goods produced by different firms within the same country; a shoddy good produced by one firm may lead consumers to think it more likely that other firms from the same country produce shoddy goods. There may be good Bayesian reasons for these inferences: if quality is partly related to the nature of the economic environment in which the goods are produced, for example, the quality of inputs, of labor, or the weather. (See Hoff for a similar Bayesian formulation, in a somewhat different context.) If this is the case, then there will be an underproduction of high-quality commodities.

Imperfect information impedes entry into markets for two reasons. First, because consumers may be concerned about the quality of the good produced, new entrants may have difficulty in establishing themselves in new markets. And firms in LDCs may face great uncertainties about their ability to produce and market new goods.

There are, furthermore, important externalities. For instance, the information acquired by a firm that explores the market potential for its product is not fully appropriable; other firms may see where the firm has been successful, and try to enter.

Some earlier literature stressed the importance of the absence of complementary products: if consumers only like tea with sugar, it would not pay to develop tea in the absence of sugar, and conversely. The need for coordination has to be put forward as grounds for government planning. In the example just given, there is good reason to believe that the externality could be internalized; it is only in the case of the *diffuse externalities* discussed earlier that such internalization appears to be difficult.

MARKET FAILURE AND GOVERNMENT INTERVENTION

In this paper, I have illustrated the thesis that market failures, particularly those related to imperfect and costly information, may provide insights into why the LDCs have a lower level of income and why so many find it difficult to maintain existing current differentials, let alone to catch up. What is at stake is more than just differences in endowments of factors, but basic aspects of the organization of the economy, including the functioning of markets. I have also argued that some of the ways by which developed countries ameliorate these market failures through nonmarket institutions (such as large firms) may be less effective in LDCs.

The kinds of market failures with which I have been concerned are markedly different from those that were the focus of attention some two decades ago. There, the concern was with the ability of the market to provide good signals for investment. Planning, or at the very least indicative planning, was the prescription. That view was wrong on three accounts. First, it underestimated the extent of planning that firms undertake. When firms make an investment decision, they make forecasts concerning future prices of inputs and outputs. Second, it overestimated the importance of the general equilibrium problem, particularly for small open economies, for whom material balance equations (for particular products) do not have to hold. It probably also overestimated the ability of general equilibrium models to improve significantly on forecasts made in less sophisticated ways. Third, it underestimated the importance of micromanagement. It may be less important to know what sector to expand than to find some niche within a particular sector. The success of a project is likely to be highly dependent on finding good managers and providing good incentive structures. These are the problems associated with the market imperfections, in the capital, product, and labor market, with which I have been concerned in this paper. National planning simply does not address these issues.

Indeed, if, as I suggested in the introduction to this paper, the differences between LDCs and the more developed countries lies largely in matters of economic organization, then the first item on the research agenda should be a better understanding of the *microeconomics* of LDCs. What is needed is a theory of rural organization, as well as a theory of industrial organization, focusing on the special characteristics of LDCs.

While the market failures with which I have been concerned do provide a rationale for a variety of types of government intervention, governments face information and incentive problems no less than does the private market. It may be foolhardy for the government to go where the private market fears to tread: credit rationing in private capital markets does not necessarily suggest a role for government providing credit. It may, indeed, be at a disadvantageous position in both screening applicants and monitoring loans (ignoring the obvious political economy problems to which government loan programs can give rise, particularly in highly inflationary situations).

In some instances, such as the imperfect capital market, I suspect that there may be little scope for government intervention. (I say this in spite of the results of Greenwald and Stiglitz 1986 and Stiglitz and Weiss 1981 showing that, in principle, there are Pareto-improving welfare interventions.) In these cases, the question facing the government is, Are there government policies that can ameliorate some of the adverse effects of these market imperfections? Commodity price stabilization schemes, for instance, may, if properly designed, reduce the risks facing producers, leading to higher levels of production and investment. Eliminating tax policies that exacerbate the risks facing firms (limited loss offset provisions) provides another example. In other cases, there is a more positive potential role for the government, in taxes and subsidies (to offset some of the informational externalities I have identified) and in institutional development (for example, in forming export-marketing cooperatives, possibly with compulsory membership, to avoid free-rider problems). These examples also provide a cautionary note on government intervention: in some cases, special interests have diverted price stabilization schemes and export-marketing cooperatives to serve their narrow interests. But the fact that government policies have sometimes been used in this way does not mean that government interventions are necessarily bad. Government intervention has played a critical role in successful development efforts.

Markets are an important set of institutions in the organization of modern economies. We need to remember that much of production in more developed economies is not, however, mediated through markets, but occurs within large corporations, each of which is the size of at least the smaller of the LDCs.

Market failures are particularly pervasive in LDCs. Good policy requires identifying them, asking which can be directly attacked by making markets work more effectively (and in particular, reducing government imposed barriers to the effective working of markets) and which cannot. We need to identify which market failures can be ameliorated through nonmarket institutions (with perhaps the government taking an instrumental role in establishing these nonmarket institutions). We need to recognize both the limits and strengths of markets, as well as the strengths, and limits, of government interventions aimed at correcting market failures.

NOTES

Financial support from the Olin Foundation, the Hoover Institution, and the National Science Foundation are gratefully acknowledged. I am indebted to Karla Hoff, Susan Skeath, Partha Dasgupta, Raaj Sah, and Edwin Lai for helpful discussions.

1. Nonmarket institutions may not fully ameliorate the inefficiencies arising from market failure, and they may actually exacerbate the market failure. (See Arnott and Stiglitz 1988.)

2. That is, if we postulate a learning function of the form, say, $Lnc_t - lnc_{t+1} = a + blnQ_t$, then learning to learn means that there may be changes in the parameter b. Localized learning-to-learn means that changes in the parameter b for one technology leave the parameter b unaffected for other technologies.

3. In other contexts, Peter Diamond (1982) has shown that search models can give rise to multiple equilibria, while Dale Mortenson (1982) and Greenwald and I (1988a) have shown that search equilibria are, in general, Pareto inefficient.

4. There are also socioeconomic interactions that give rise to multiple equilibria: a society with more innovators at time t is likely to produce more innovative individuals at later dates; innovation breeds on itself. By the same token, bureaucratic environments reward bureaucratic behavior.

REFERENCES

Arnott, R., and J. E. Stiglitz. 1988. "Dysfunctional Non-Market Institutions and the Market." NBER Working Paper no. 2666.

Arrow, K. J. 1962. "The Economic Implications of Learning by Doing." *Review of Economic Studies* 29:155–73.

Atkinson, A., and J. E. Stiglitz. 1969. "A New View of Technological Change." *Economic Journal* 79:46–49.

Dasgupta, P., and J. E. Stiglitz. 1988. "Learning-by-Doing, Market Structure and Industrial and Trade Policies." *Oxford Economic Papers* 40:246–68.

Diamond, P. 1982. "Aggregate Demand Management in Search Equilibrium." *Journal of Political Economy* 90:881–94.

Greenwald, B., and J. E. Stiglitz. 1986. "Externalities in Economies with Imperfect Information and Incomplete Markets." *Quarterly Journal of Economics* 101:229–64.

———. 1988a. "Pareto Inefficiency of Market Economies: Search and Efficiency Wage Models." *American Economic Review Proceedings* 78:351–55.

———. 1988b. "Financial Market Imperfections and Productivity Growth." Paper given at Stockholm conference, June.

Hoff, Karla. 1988. "Essays in the Theory of Trade and Taxation under Incomplete Risk Markets." Ph.D. diss. Princeton University.

Lucas, R. E., Jr. 1988. "On the Mechanics of Economic Development." *Journal of Monetary Economics* 22:3–42.

Mortenson, D. 1982. "Property Rights and Efficiency in Mating, Racing, and Related Games." *American Economic Review* 72:968–79.

Pack, Howard. 1984. "Total Factor Productivity: Some International Comparisons." In *Comparative Development Perspectives: Essays in Honor of Lloyd Reynolds,* edited by G. Ranis & R. West. Boulder: Westview Press.

———. 1987. *Productivity, Technology, and Industrial Development.* Oxford: Oxford University Press.

Romer, P. 1986. "Increasing Returns and Long-Run Growth." *Journal of Political Economy* 94:1002–38.

Sah, R. K., and J. E. Stiglitz. 1989. "Debt Stabilization and Development." In *Essays in Memory of Carlos Diaz-Alejandro,* edited by G. Calvo et al. London: Basil Blackwell.

Skeath, S. 1988. "Learning, Price Effects, and Income Growth." Mimeo. Princeton University.

Stiglitz, J. E. 1987a. "Learning to Learn. Localized Learning and Technological Progress." In *Economic Policy and Technological Performance,* edited by P. Dasgupta and P. Stoneman. Centre for Economic Policy Research, Cambridge University Press.

———. 1987b. "On the Microeconomics of Technical Progress." In *Technology Generation in Latin American Manufacturing Industries,* edited by Jorge M. Katz. London: Macmillan.

———. 1988. "Economic Organization, Information, and Development." In *Handbook of Development Economics,* edited by H. Chenery and T. N. Srinivasan, vol. 1. Amsterdam: Elsevier.

Stiglitz, J. E., and A. Weiss. 1981. "Credit Rationing in Markets with Imperfect Information." *American Economic Review* 71:393–410.

7

The Agricultural Transformation

The agricultural transformation has been a remarkably uniform process when viewed from outside the agricultural sector itself. As documented by Clark (1940), Kuznets (1966), Chenery and Syrquin (1975), the share of agriculture in a country's labor force and total output declines in both cross-section and time-series samples as incomes per capita increase. The declining importance of agriculture is uniform and pervasive, a tendency obviously driven by powerful forces inherent in the development process, whether in socialist or capitalist countries, Asian, Latin American, or African, currently developed or still poor.

It is at least slightly puzzling, then, that a second uniform and pervasive aspect of the development process also involves agriculture—the apparent requirement that rapid agricultural growth accompany or precede general economic growth. The logic of the classical model of economic growth requires it:

> Now if the capitalist sector produces no food, its expansion increases the demand for food, raises the price of food in terms of capitalist products, and so reduces profits. This is one of the senses in which industrialization is dependent upon agricultural improvement; it is not profitable to produce a growing volume of manufactures unless agricultural production is growing simultaneously. This is also why industrial and agrarian revolutions *always* go together, and why economies in which agriculture is stagnant do not show industrial development (Lewis 1954, 433, emphasis added).

The historical record to which Lewis alludes supports the strong link between agricultural and industrial growth, at least in market-oriented economies. The English model is often held up as the case in point:

> Consider what happened in the original home of industrial development, in England in the eighteenth century. Everyone knows that the spectacular industrial revolution would not have been possible without the agricultural revolution that preceded it. And what was this agricultural revolution? It was based on the introduction of the turnip. The lowly

C. PETER TIMMER is Dean of the Graduate School of International Relations and Pacific Studies at the University of California, San Diego.

Reprinted from *Handbook of Development Economics*, volume 1, edited by H. Chenery and T. N. Srinivasan. Copyright © 1988 by Elsevier Science Publishers B. V., Amsterdam. Reprinted with omissions and minor editorial revisions by permission of Elsevier Science Publishers B. V. and the author.

turnip made possible a change in crop rotation which did not require much capital, but which brought about a tremendous rise in agricultural productivity. As a result, more food could be grown with much less manpower. Manpower was released for capital construction. The growth of industry would not have been possible without the turnip and other improvements in agriculture (Nurkse 1953, 52–53).

Despite a significantly different view in the current literature about the impact of the English agricultural revolution on labor productivity, the key importance of the increase in agricultural output has not been challenged (Timmer 1969; Hayami and Ruttan 1985). Nor is this importance restricted to the lessons from the currently developed countries. In surveying the statistical link between agricultural and overall economic growth in currently less developed countries, the World Bank reached the following conclusions:

> The continuing importance of agriculture in the economies of the developing countries is reflected in the association between the growth of agriculture and of the economy as a whole. Among countries where the agricultural share of GDP was greater than 20 percent in 1970, agricultural growth in the 1970s exceeded 3 percent a year in 17 of the 23 countries whose GDP growth was above 5 percent a year. During the same period, 11 of the 17 countries with GDP growth below 3 percent a year managed agricultural growth of only 1 percent or less. Agricultural and GDP growth differed by less than two percentage points in 11 of 15 countries experiencing moderate growth. There have been exceptions, of course, but they prove the rule: fast GDP growth and sluggish agriculture was a feature of some of the oil- or mineral-based economies such as Algeria, Ecuador, Morocco, and Nigeria.
>   The parallels between agricultural and GDP growth suggest that the factors which affect agricultural performance may be linked to economy-wide social and economic policies. . . . Expanding agricultural production through technological change and trade creates important demands for the ouputs of other sectors, notably fertilizer, transportation, commercial services, and construction. At the same time, agricultural households are often the basic market for a wide range of consumer goods that loom large in the early stages of industrial development—textiles and clothing, processed foods, kerosene and vegetable oils, aluminum holloware, radios, bicycles, and construction materials for home improvements (World Bank 1982, 44–45).

The need for rapid agricultural growth and for the decline in the agricultural sector's share of output and the labor force are not contradictory, of course, but the apparent paradox gave rise to a widespread misperception that agriculture is unimportant—that it does not require resources or a favorable policy environment—*because* its relative share of the economy declines.

So long as market forces provide the primary direction to the sectoral allocation of resources, how academics perceive this process is irrelevant to the process itself. When government planners intercede, however, they do so within a framework of objectives and constraints, and this framework is ultimately conditioned by the prevailing academic understanding of how economic growth proceeds. The mainstream paradigm of the 1950s suggested that agriculture could and should be squeezed on behalf of the more dynamic sectors of the economy. This strategy could be successful if agriculture was already growing rapidly (as in Western Europe and Japan) or if it started with a large surplus relative to the subsistence needs of the rural population (as in the USSR). But if the agricultural sector started with traditional technology and yields and living standards near subsistence, the "squeeze agriculture" paradigm created economic stagnation, not growth. In those cases, major attention was needed to induce an agricultural transformation if the industrial revolution was to have any real hope of success.

Upon closer examination, it is not paradoxical that agricultural growth leads to agricultural decline. At least two mechanisms, now relatively well understood and documented, account for this process of structural transformation.[1] Engel's Law alone, in a closed economy with constant prices, explains a declining share for agriculture (and low farm incomes unless some farmers leave agriculture), no matter how fast the sector grows. Because growth is led by demand patterns in market economies, a less-than-unitary income elasticity for the products of the agricultural sector guarantees that gross value of sales by farmers will grow less rapidly than gross domestic product. As Lewis implies in the previous quotation, if agricultural output fails to grow rapidly enough, rising prices might actually garner farmers a higher share of consumers' expenditures. But this reflects *lower* real incomes, not the result of economic growth.

If the terms of trade are not to rise in favor of agriculture, farm productivity must rise—an agricultural revolution is needed. The second factor that explains the joint agricultural growth and relative decline is seen in the rapid growth in agricultural productivity, measured by output per laborer or output per hectare, in all the successfully developed countries. Technical change in agriculture in all of the OECD (Organization for Economic Cooperation and Development) countries proceeded at such a pace that the long-run terms of trade declined for farm products. Lower prices thus exacerbated the sluggish demand growth due to low income elasticities; the combination put pressure on agricultural resources to move out of farming and into the more rapidly growing sectors of the economy. Such intersectoral movements of resources have been painful in all societies that have undergone successful structural transformation, and all societies have found mechanisms to cushion the adjustment process.

The paradox over the agricultural transformation occurs at this point. Just as countries learn how to institutionalize the process of rapid technical change in agriculture, its product no longer has high social value. The resulting low incomes for farmers create powerful political pressures to slow the process of structural change, and the seemingly inevitable result is massive distortion of the price structure (Johnson 1973; Anderson and Hayami 1986; World Bank 1986). Nearly all rich countries protect their agricultural sectors from international competition, and countries no farther along in the development process than Malaysia, Indonesia, Zimbabwe, and Mexico protect key food-producing sectors during periods of depressed world prices.

THE PROCESS OF AGRICULTURAL TRANSFORMATION

From both historical and contemporary cross-section perspectives, the agricultural transformation seems to evolve through at least four phases that are roughly definable. The process starts when agricultural productivity per worker rises. This increased productivity creates a surplus, which in the second phase can be tapped directly, through taxation and factor flows, or indirectly, through government intervention into the rural-urban terms of trade. This surplus can be utilized to develop the nonagricultural sector, and this phase has been the focus of most dual economy models of development. For resources to flow out of agriculture, rural factor and product markets must become better integrated with those in the rest of the economy. The progressive integration of the agricultural sector into the macro economy, via improved infrastructure and market-equilibrium linkages, represents a third phase in agricultural development. When this phase is successful, the fourth phase is barely noticeable; the role of agriculture in industrialized economies is little different from the role of the steel, housing, or insurance sectors. But when the integration is not successfully accomplished—and most countries have found it extremely difficult for political reasons—governments encounter serious problems of resource allocation and even problems beyond their borders because of pervasive attempts by high-income countries to protect their farmers from foreign competition. Managing agricultural protection and its impact on world commodity markets thus provides a continuing focus for agricultural policy makers even when the agricultural transformation is "complete."

Evolving Stages

The four phases in the agricultural transformation call for different policy approaches, as shown in figure 1. In the earliest stage of development the concern must be for "getting agriculture moving," to use Arthur Mosher's vivid phrase (Mosher 1966). A significant share of a country's investable resources may well be extracted from agriculture at this stage, but this is because the rest of the economy is so small. Direct or indirect taxation of agriculture is the only significant source of government revenue.

Building a dynamic agriculture requires that some of these resources be devoted to the agricultural sector itself. As the section on agricultural development policy at the end of this chapter explains, these resources need to be allocated to public investment in research and infrastructure as well as to favorable price incentives to farmers to adopt new technology as it becomes available. As these investments *in* agriculture begin to pay off, the second phase emerges in which the agricultural sector becomes a key contributor to the overall growth process through a combination of factors outlined by Johnston and Mellor (1961).

As the empirical literature on structural patterns of growth emphasizes, there is a substantial disequilibrium between agriculture and industry at this early stage of the development process (Kuznets 1966; Chenery and Taylor 1968; Chenery and Syrquin 1975). Indeed, differences in labor productivity and measured income (as

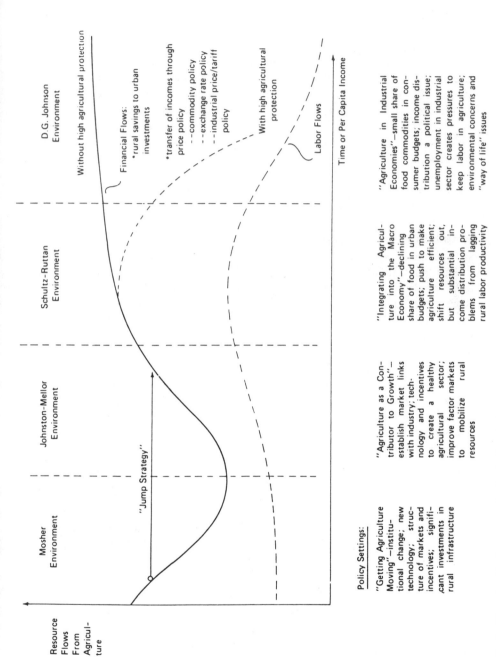

Fig.1. Changing Environments for Agriculture's Contribution to Economic Growth

opposed to psychic income) between the rural and urban sectors persist to the present in rich countries, although the gap is narrowing and now depends on agricultural prices for any given year.[2]

The process of narrowing the gap gives rise to the third environment for agriculture, in which is it integrated into the rest of the economy through the development of more efficient labor and credit markets that link the urban and rural economies. This integration is a component of the contribution process; the improved functioning of factor markets merely speeds the process of extracting labor and capital from those uses in agriculture with low returns for those in industry or services with higher productivity. The improved markets have welfare consequences as well, because they lessen the burden on individuals trapped in low-income occupations. The gain has costs, however. As agriculture is integrated into the macro economy, it becomes much more vulnerable to fluctuations in macro prices and level of aggregate activity and trade (Schuh 1976) and much less susceptible to management by traditional instruments for the agricultural sector, such as extension activities and specific programs for commodity development and marketing.

This vulnerability and complexity create the fourth phase in the agricultural transformation, the treatment of agriculture in industrialized economies. As the share of the labor force in agriculture falls below about 20 percent and the share of food expenditures in urban household budgets drops to about 30 percent, low-cost food is not as important to the overall economy nor is it as expensive in relative terms to increase in price (Anderson 1983). A host of political problems arise if low farm incomes, induced by rapid technical change and low farm-gate prices, are allowed to push resources out of agriculture. Farmers do not want to leave, especially if they must sell their farms under duress at low prices; and urban-based unions do not want to see them coming to the cities in search of industrial jobs. A nostalgic memory of farming as a "way of life" leads many second- and third-generation farm migrants living in cities to lend political support to higher incomes for agriculture, even at the expense of higher grocery bills (which may be barely noticeable). By this stage of the process, the share of the farm-gate price of the commodity in the consumer's market basket is small, because of processing and marketing costs. Commodity price supports become the primary vehicle for supporting farm incomes, and the subsidies have devastating effects on resource allocation. Farmers invest heavily in land and machinery when farm prices are high, only to produce surpluses that are impossible to sell profitably (Johnson 1985; Cochrane 1979). Eventually, the budgetary and distortionary costs of this approach become so high that even the European Community, Japan, or the United States must face choices over how to rationalize agricultural returns with their social profitability.

The economic environments for agriculture created by these four phases are shown schematically in figure 1. The financial and labor resource flows out of agriculture over time (or as incomes increase in a cross-section sample) are impressionistic. Whether the trough between the "Mosher environment" and the "Johnston-Mellor environment" in figure 1 drops into negative ground or always remains positive presumably depends on alternative sources of financial resources at this stage in development. Urban or overseas remittances, petroleum revenues, or foreign assistance might temporarily fill the gap left by a declining relative contribution from agriculture.[3] But as agricultural productivity begins to rise, labor and financial flows to the rest of the economy increase. The "Schultz-Ruttan environment" begins as the absolute population in agriculture starts to decline, and the "D. G. Johnson environment" begins as the agricultural labor force drops to a fairly small proportion of the overall labor force. Whether financial resources continue to flow out of agriculture at this stage in the process depends almost entirely on government price policy and its resulting impact on farm investment. Policies to cushion the impact on farmers of successful structural change need not inevitably rely on price interventions that impede the adjustment process, but price supports have been the most popular in the United States, Western Europe, and Japan, for plausible political reasons (Anderson and Hayami 1986).

AGRICULTURE AND ECONOMIC DEVELOPMENT

This overview of the agricultural transformation raises two basic issues to be discussed in this chapter: the contribution or role of agriculture in economic development and the conditions or factors that lead to the modernization of the agricultural sector itself. Obviously, many other important topics are not treated here. One is the changing control over resources in the rural sector, which determines who gains and who loses during the agricultural transformation. Only the structuralist and radical political economy literature deals directly with the distribution of income and power in rural areas as an integral component of agricultural development. A major theme of "neo-neoclassical analysis" since the mid-1970s, however, has been the incorporation of such issues into rational actor models of rural household decision making. While much of the dynamic and macroeconomic perspective of the radical models is lost in the household models, much is gained in the form of testable hypotheses about the impact of new technology or pricing policies on the structure of rural markets and distribution of output in the short run.

The historical record after the Second World War suggests that many countries saw an opportunity to pursue a "jump strategy" and move directly from the early stages of the Mosher environment (see figure 1) to the later stages of the Johnston-Mellor environment, thus bypassing the necessity to invest in agricultural development.

Bairoch describes some of the difficulties inherent in a jump strategy as follows:

. . . the most significant comparison . . . is that between the levels of productivity in the under-developed countries and the western countries at the period when the latter began to industrialize. . . . The present average level of agricultural productivity in African and Asian countries (between them representing four-fifths of the Third World population) is 45 percent below that reached by the developed countries at the start of the industrial revolution. In fact it is at the same level as that of the European countries before their agricultural revolution.

Now, most under-developed countries wish, consciously or unconsciously, to by-pass this stage just when other structural conditions of development are making a "take off" more difficult than it was when most European countries and the United States were imitating England's example. What makes the failure to admit or even to recognize this problem all the more serious is that the problem itself is intractable. Leaving aside mental attitudes, landownership and political considerations, it cannot be stressed too forcibly that an increase in the area cultivated per agricultural worker is one of the essential conditions of an increase in productivity. But in view of the population explosion it is impossible to assume, even on most hopeful assumption, that the reduction in cultivated area per worker will be anything but slight (Bairoch 1975, 42).

A jump strategy sees the extraction of resources from agriculture for economic development as being in conflict with the investment of public and private resources in its modernization. This has been especially true in countries with systems of planned resource allocations designed to force the pace of economic development. As more and more countries adopted the paradigm of central planning to direct these resource allocations, the separate issues of contribution and modernization became key analytical issues as well. Unfortunately, the economics profession was ill-equipped to address them because all previous examples of agricultural modernization had taken place within more or less market-oriented settings (except in the Soviet Union, where agricultural modernization remains quite incomplete). The behavior of backward agricultural systems under the new planning context became a topic of much theorizing and debate, but only in the 1960s and 1970s did the empirical record become both long and varied enough to draw reasonably firm conclusions.

It is worth summarizing briefly what the empirical record showed by 1960 when the results of Kuznets's decade-long study of the quantitative aspects of modern economic growth started to be widely available. The historical record began as early as the late eighteenth century in the United Kingdom and in 1839 in the United States and as late as 1880 in Japan and 1925 in the USSR. For all countries for all time periods observed, the share of agriculture in the total labor force declined, sometimes sharply, as in Sweden, the United States, and Japan, and sometimes more gradually, as in the United Kingdom, Belgium, Italy, and Australia. The share of agriculture in national output showed slightly more mixed patterns than those of the labor force. The share was nearly stable or even rose slightly over some periods in the United Kingdom, France, the United States, and Australia. The more general tendency of the share in output to decline is clear, but the share of the labor force always declined more rapidly. The obvious result was that labor productivity in agriculture rose more rapidly than in the economy as a whole when measured over the long periods of time required for sustained economic growth to cause substantial changes in the structure of an economy. Although agricultural productivity per worker was nearly always less than the level of national productivity, its faster rise meant that the gap tended to narrow.

Three clear exceptions to this trend in Kuznets's data are Italy, Japan, and the USSR, all of which are latecomers to the process of sustained growth and are countries in which state intervention into the industrialization process was much more active than in the early developers. The failure of agricultural productivity per worker to rise as fast as national productivity in these three countries might thus be seen as an early signal that the patterns in the less developed countries seeking to start down the path of modern economic growth might be significantly different from the historical path followed by the Western countries and documented by Kuznets. Hayami (1986) shows that the recent productivity record for the rapidly growing East Asian economies confirms a strongly different pattern from that in North America and Western Europe. Even the more slowing growing developing countries (Philippines and India) have a mild reversal of the "traditional" pattern in which growth in labor productivity in agriculture exceeds that of labor productivity in manufacturing.

This "premature" growth in manufacturing productivity (or, alternatively, the neglect of efforts needed to raise agricultural productivity) is especially troubling in historical perspective, as the quote from Bairoch indicated. Table 1 reproduces Bairoch's historical comparisons of "net agricultural production by male labor employed in agriculture expressed in 'direct' calories." Only Italy in 1840 had a lower productivity level than that of Africa and Asia in modern times. The gap in agricultural productivity on average between European countries beginning their in-

TABLE 1
COMPARISONS BETWEEN LEVELS OF AGRICULTURAL PRODUCTIVITY

Country and Stage of Development	Period	Index Number of Agricultural Productivity
Developed Countries		
Recent position		
France	1968/72	100.0
United States	1968/72	330.0
Position before or during "take-off"		
France	1810	7.0
Great Britain	1810	14.0
Sweden	1810	6.5
Belgium	1840	10.0
Germany	1840	7.5
Italy	1840	4.0
Russia	1840	7.0
Switzerland	1840	8.0
United States	1840	21.5
Spain	1860	11.0
Less Developed Countries		
Recent position		
Africa	1960/64–1968/72	4.7
Latin America[a]	1960/64–1968/72	9.8
Asia	1960/64–1968/72	4.8
Middle East	1960/64–1968/72	8.6
Total for all less developed countries	1960/64–1968/72	5.5

SOURCE: Bairoch 1975.
[a]Excluding Argentina.

dustrial revolutions and Africa and Asia is, as Bairoch already noted, about 45 percent. "A gap of about 45 percent is sufficiently wide for us to be able to assert that agricultural conditions in the currently developed countries before the beginning of the industrial revolution must have been very different from those of the underdeveloped countries of Asia and Africa today" (Bairoch 1975, 40–41).

The Role of the Agricultural Sector

The debate over the role of agriculture in the process of economic development extends at least as far back as the physiocrats in the eighteenth century. The biblical advice to store during seven good years to be ready for seven lean years certainly reflects a concern for agricultural planning. Clark (1940) and Kuznets (1966) provided the general facts about the role of agriculture during the growth process available to economists and planners at the beginning of the drive for economic growth in the less developed countries. These facts formed the basis for the prevailing neoclassical view that agriculture was a declining sector, a "black box" in Little's phrase (1982), which contributed labor, food, and perhaps capital to the essential modernization efforts in industry. No policy efforts on behalf of agriculture's own modernization were needed because the sector declined naturally. Most interpretations of the Lewis model (1954), especially the Fei-Ranis versions (1964), which became the main teaching paradigms, ignored the factors needed to modernize traditional agricultural sectors so that they could play positive contributory roles in the development of the rest of the economy. The structuralist views of Prebisch (1950) about declining terms of trade for traditional products and the importance Hirschman (1958) attached to linkages to "modern" economic activities further diminished any apparent rationale for actively investing in the modernization of agriculture itself. As Hirschman wrote in 1958, "agriculture certainly stands convicted on the count of its lack of direct stimulus to the setting up of new activities through linkage effects—the superiority of manufacturing in this respect is crushing" (Hirschman 1958, 109–10).

A final reason for the neglect of agriculture has recently been clarified by Sah and Stiglitz (1984). The Soviet debate in the early 1920s over industrialization policy revolved around whether turning the terms of trade against agriculture (the "price scissors") would speed the rate of accumulation for investment by the state. Preobrazhensky (1965) argued successfully that it could. Sah and Stiglitz show the precise conditions under which he was right and the welfare consequences that flowed from implementing such a policy. Although the conditions that must hold for their analysis to be valid are very stringent, a robust result is that the agricultural terms of trade should be lowered only if the state has a low rate of time discount, that is, it favors investment over current consumption. Forced-pace industrialization campaigns in such circumstances then rely on the state's capacity to extract surpluses from agriculture even in the face of stagnant or falling agricultural production.

It is easy to see why agriculture was neglected as a source of growth in early strategies of economic development. The historical record shows that it always declines in relative importance in growing economies. It is the home of traditional people, ways, and living standards—the antithesis of what nation builders in developing countries envisioned for their societies. Moreover, agriculture was thought to provide the only source of productivity that could be tapped to fuel the drive for modernization. Surplus labor, surplus savings, and surplus expenditures to buy the products of urban industry, and even surplus foreign exchange to buy the machines to make them, could be had from an uncomplaining agricultural sector. Nothing more was needed to generate these resources than the promise of jobs in the cities and a shared nationalistic pride in the growing power of the state. Despite how simplistic these promises sound today, the success of the Soviet approach caused them to be very appealing when first uttered by such charismatic leaders of the developing world as Sukarno, Nkrumah, Nasser, and Nehru. The unique features of agriculture as a sector were simply not widely understood in the 1950s. Nor was it accepted that the development of a modern agriculture was necessary as a concomitant to development of the rest of the economy.

Some of these factors began to be recognized by the 1960s, and a more positive emphasis was placed on "role" rather than the more forced concept of "contribution" of agriculture. The classic article by Johnston and Mellor (1961) listed five roles for agriculture in economic development:

1. increase the supply of food for domestic consumption;
2. release labor for industrial employment;
3. enlarge the size of the market for industrial output;
4. increase the supply of domestic savings; and
5. earn foreign exchange.

Although the second, fourth, and fifth roles are certainly consistent with the earlier "extractive" views of agriculture, Johnston and Mellor insisted that all five roles are equally important. Agriculture in the process of development is to provide increased food supplies and higher rural incomes to enlarge markets for urban output, as well as to provide resources to expand that urban ouput.

> It is our contention that "balanced growth" is needed in the sense of simultaneous efforts to promote agricultural and industrial development. We recognize that there are severe limitations on the capacity of an underdeveloped country to do everything at once. But it is precisely this consideration which underscores the importance of developing agriculture in such a way as to both minimize its demand on resources most needed for industrial development and maximize its net contribution required for general growth (Johnston and Mellor 1961, 590–91).

Others, especially Nicholls (1963), Schultz (1953), and Jorgenson (1961), also emphasized this interdependence between a country's agriculture and its industry. Myint (1975) stressed a curious inconsistency between the "closed economy" model implicit in this domestic interdependence and the fifth role, earning foreign exchange, which obviously implies the country is open to international trade. This trade perspective returns in the 1970s and 1980s to dominate thinking about appropriate development strategies, but it was largely ignored in the 1960s, perhaps because of the dominance of the "Indian model" in development thinking, in which sheer size keeps the importance of foreign trade quite small, even apart from the "inward looking" strategy being pursued.

Despite the early insistence by agricultural economists that the agricultural sector must be viewed as part of the overall economy and that the emphasis be placed on the sector's interdependence with the industrial and service sectors rather than on its forced contributions to them, the notion of agriculture as a resource reservoir has persisted in general development models. Reynolds emphasized an important but usually overlooked distinction between static and dynamic views of the resource transfers:

> In most development models, modern industry is the cutting edge of economic growth, while agriculture plays the role of a resource reservoir which can be drawn on for supplies of food, labor, and finance to fuel the growth or urban activities. It is argued that this is both a logical necessity and a matter of historical experience, illustrated by the case of Japan.
>
> In commenting on this view, I must emphasize a distinction that is often not clearly drawn: (1) It is one thing to assert that, in an economy where agricultural output is not rising, the agricultural sector contains potential surpluses of labor time, food output, and saving capacity requiring only appropriate public policies for their release. This we may term the static view of resource transfer. (2) It is quite a different thing to assert that, in an economy where agricultural output is being raised by a combination of investment and technical progress, part of the increment in farm output and income is available for transfer to non-agriculture. This we may term the dynamic view of resource transfer. The model-building implications of this approach are different, and its policy implications are decidedly different (Reynolds 1975, 14–15).

The welfare consequences of the two views are also sharply different. Forced extraction of resources from a stagnant agricultural sector almost always creates widespread rural poverty, sometimes famine. Market linkages that connect a dynamic agricultural sector to rapidly growing industrial and service sectors offer an opportunity for rural inhabitants to choose in which sector they wish to participate. There are certainly losers in this process: high-cost producers in unfavorable ecological settings who cannot compete with low-cost producers in favored locales who have access to new technology; or newly landless laborers who have lost their tenancy access to land when commercial relationships replace patron-client relationships. But new technology and market linkages create more opportunities than they destroy if both the agricultural and nonagricultural sectors are growing. An emphasis on finding the policy environment that creates such mutual growth is needed. For agriculture, that environment must call forth rapid technical change. Experience since the mid-1960s has demonstrated how to do that, but the key has been to understand why the agricultural sector is different from the industrial and service sectors (Hayami and Ruttan 1985; Timmer, Falcon, and Pearson 1983).

WHY AGRICULTURE IS DIFFERENT

The early purposeful neglect of agriculture can in part be attributed to development economists who were remote from any real understanding of what makes the agricultural sector quite different from either manufacturing or services (Little 1982). In developing countries, the agricultural sector is different from other productive sectors of an economy, particularly in its large contribution to national income and the large numbers of participants in the sector. Both the agricultural transformation itself and the contribution of agriculture to the rest of the economy depend on three important features discussed here: the peculiarities of the agricultural production function, the importance of home consumption of output for the sector, and the role of the agricultural sector as a resource reservoir. These features are more evident in traditional societies, and their distinctiveness erodes during the process of economic modernization. The design of agricultural policy, in both poor and rich countries, is complicated by these features, but a recognition of them is essential to a full understanding of the contribution agriculture might realistically be asked to make to a country's development effort.[4]

DECISION MAKING IN AGRICULTURE

In both private and collective agricultures, decision making is conditioned primarily by the nature of incentives to work rather than by the pace and design of the work itself, and these incentives are difficult to structure in an efficient manner unless the cultivator owns the land. In situations where ownership and operation are separate, a host of complicated contractual arrangements that strive for second-best efficiency outcomes have evolved in different settings.

Farming is an undertaking that involves many decisions. What crops to plant, what inputs to use, when to plow, to seed, to cultivate, to irrigate, to harvest, how much to keep for home consumption, how much to sell and how much to store for later sale are the farming decisions that occupy the daily routine of most agricultural producers. What is unique about agriculture is that literally millions of individuals and households are making these decisions themselves. Changing agricultural production decisions to increase food output is an entirely different process from changing decisions about how much steel or cement to produce. In most countries a dozen or so individuals could take direct action which would lead to a 10 percent increase in steel output in a year or so, and their decisions would be decisive.

Nowhere, not even in socialist countries, can a similar small group of individuals decide to raise food production by 10 percent. A small group of planners, or the president and the cabinet, can decide they *want* food production to rise by 10 percent. They can tell the food logistics agency, the ministry of agriculture, the newspapers, and agricultural extension agents that they want food production to rise by 10 percent. But they cannot increase food production 10 percent by themselves. They must also convince the millions of farmers in their country to want to increase food production by 10 percent and make it in their self-interest to do so.

The vast number of agricultural decision makers implies that there are simply too many to reach directly with either pleas for cooperation or police power. Farmers must see the benefits of higher output for themselves because there are too many opportunities to let high yields slip beneath the hoe or in a late fertilizer application, even under the watchful eyes of a guardian. Farming is a subtle combination of skilled craft and brute force. The brute force alone will not achieve high yields.

CHARACTERISTICS OF AGRICULTURAL PRODUCTION FUNCTIONS

Several unique features of agricultural production functions contribute to the decision-intensity of farming, to the productivity of the family farm, and to the search for reasonably efficient substitutes for direct landownership where the family farm is not prevalent. Seasonality and geographical dispersion are important.

Seasonality

Two features of seasonality are important in designing agricultural policy. First, seasonal aspects of agricultural production frequently constrain yields because of input bottlenecks. Labor (and its supervision) is most often the constraining factor, but fertilizer, seeds, credit, or irrigation water supplies must also be available in highly specific time periods. When fertilizer reaches the village godown a month after the proper application time, it might as well not have arrived at all. Government authorities responsible for the management of agricultural input supply distribution are frequently unaware of or insensitive to the extreme importance of timely input availability. Suppliers whose incomes depend on providing inputs to farmers when and where needed are much more responsive to shifts in weather, cropping patterns, and new technologies than are agencies trying to allocate inputs within the guidelines of five-year plans and supplies available from a planned industrial sector. Modern agriculture that uses industrial inputs as the basis for high yields is a dynamic enterprise quite unlike factories. Input and output markets must function efficiently, reacting to weather changes, alterations in cropping patterns, and technical change if production is to grow rapidly. Centrally planned allocations of industrial products to the agricultural sector are almost never in the right place at the right time, nor are they even the right products.

Second, there are often very high private economic returns to eliminating seasonal bottlenecks in production. When these private returns are at least partly generated by higher and more stable yields of agricultural products, society is also likely to gain. But if the private gains come from displacing hired labor that has few alternative production opportunities, the social gains might be small or even negative. The seasonal dimensions to agricultural production complicate the planning process considerably. Most agricultural data are published on an annual basis, and there is an inevitable tendency to think about the sector in terms of the same annual growth performance criteria that are used to evaluate the steel or cotton textile industries. Such an annual approach hides two important roles for government analysis and intervention: in the appropriate provision of inputs when and where they are needed, and in the full analysis of the social impact on agricultural production of private investments to reduce seasonal bottlenecks.

Geographical Dispersion

Agriculture is the only major sector that uses the land surface as an essential input into its production function. In combination, seasonality and geographical dispersion create the need for a marketing system that can store the product from a short harvest period to the much longer period of desired consumption and can move the commodity from the farm where it was grown to the many households where it will be consumed. Both of these functions require that the commodity change hands and that exchange of ownership take place. This transaction can happen only when both parties agree on the terms of the exchange or the price for the commodity at the point of sale. In socialist economies the terms of exchange are often set by the state. But all other marketing services must still be provided if the food grown by farmers is to be eaten by consumers. This necessary growth of marketing services is an often overlooked component of the agricultural transformation.

THE FARM HOUSEHOLD AS PRODUCER AND CONSUMER

Most farm households still retain some or most of their farm production for home consumption, and this role of home consumption is a further distinguishing feature of the agricultural sector. Few steelworkers or even textile workers take their products home for household use. Only under highly restrictive and unrealistic assumptions about the completeness of markets and access of all farm households to them can production and consumption decisions be analyzed separately (Singh, Squire, and Strauss 1986). In rural areas of developing countries, the need to make connected production and consumption decisions within a single household obviously complicates life for the farm household; the value of additional time spent in food preparation or tending the children must be balanced against the productivity of an additional hour weeding the rice, driving the ducks, or tending the home garden. Where it exists, the opportunity to spend some of that time working for cash on a neighbor's farm or in a rural wage-labor market places a lower bound on the value of household-farm time, and the value of leisure ultimately places a limit on the willingness to work, especially at low-productivity tasks. For households with inadequate land to grow surplus crops for sale and with limited outside employment opportunities, however, the marginal value of leisure time might be low indeed, possibly near zero. Even tiny increments to output can be valuable for very poor households.

WHAT DIFFERENCE DOES THE DIFFERENCE MAKE?

Two important implications flow from the distinctive characteristics of agriculture relative to industry, and both are treated extensively in sections that follow.

First, if agricultural decision making is in fact based on rational assessments of highly heterogeneous environments, substantial knowledge of micro environments is necessary to understand the impact of policy interventions or technical change on the agricultural sector. Designing new technology and fostering its widespread adoption is primarily a public sector activity because of the relatively small scale of individual farmers, but the success of any given technical innovation depends on the private decisions of those same multitudinous farmers. Understanding the source, dynamics, and impact of technical change in agriculture is thus a major part of understanding the agricultural transformation, a process vastly complicated by the smallness of scale, geographic dispersion, and heterogeneity of the environment, both economic and ecological, that is characteristic of agriculture in developing countries.

The second important implication of agriculture's distinctiveness is how it conditions the role of public policy, particularly that other than the design and implementation of research leading to technical change. The vision dies hard of agriculture as a resource reservoir to be tapped indiscriminately, without reinvestment or adverse consequences for growth, on behalf of the urban economy. Although a few countries have a record of sustained progress in agriculture and concomitant overall economic growth, the list is short. Only eight countries listed in the *World Development Report 1986* have growth rates for agricultural GDP of 3 percent per year or greater for both the 1965–73 and 1973–84 periods, along with growth rates for total GDP of 4 percent per year or greater for the same two periods: Kenya, Pakistan, Indonesia, the Ivory Coast, the Philippines, Thailand, Brazil, and Mexico. Sri Lanka and Turkey came close; Malaysia would probably have been included had data been available for the earlier period. Because population growth in several of these countries is near or more than 3 percent per year, even these excellent aggregate performances leave the rate of growth per capita at levels that permit a doubling of incomes in a quarter of a century at best.

It has obviously been difficult to find the right mix of policies to sustain agricultural growth. Much of the reason traces to a failure of policy makers to understand the characteristics of agriculture that make policy design so complicated. They face yet another paradox: the essentially private-sector nature of agricultural decision making at the same time that the environment for that decision making is heavily dependent on sound government interventions into agricultural research, rural infrastructure, and market relationships. The distinctive characteristics of agriculture argue that governments intervene into agricultural decision making at great risk, for they can easily cause farmers to withdraw from making investments and producing for the market, which are essential to mobilizing resources for overall economic growth. And yet, intervene they must. The environment for transforming agriculture is a public good created by wise but active public intervention.

It is easy to get the mix wrong, even to have the elements backward. Some governments have tried to dictate farm-level decisions on inputs and outputs while totally ignoring both the investments in research and infrastructure needed to create a healthy agriculture and the pricing environment that will mobilize peasants on behalf of higher productivity.

AGRICULTURAL DEVELOPMENT STRATEGY

ALTERNATIVE STRATEGIES FOR MAINTAINING THE TRANSFORMATION PROCESS

Several lessons have been learned since the mid-1960s about the functioning of the agricultural sector and its potential role in the development process. The agricultural sector has been seen in a general-equilibrium perspective, and the importance of macroeconomic policy for agricultural performance has been recognized. Rapid economic growth has been considered necessary to deal with the human welfare concerns that stem from poverty and hunger, and such growth is feasible because of the potential for technical change. Market-oriented systems with private incentives have shown superior performance in achieving this growth. Policy analysis has tended to concentrate on one of three dimensions of government intervention into the agricultural growth process: (1) stimulating traditional agriculture into growth; (2) maintaining the transformation process and the contribution of agriculture to overall economic growth; and protecting the welfare of farmers from their own high productivity during the final and painful stages of structural change in industrialized societies. Here we discuss the second of these dimensions, maintaining the transformation process.

The agricultural sector is a means to an end—not an end in itself. Three sharply different paths for appropriate policies toward agriculture are open if the goal is to speed the overall process of development. The first path has parallels to the philosophy of the 1950s, in which benign neglect of agricultural policy was thought to be sufficient for stimulating the process of economic growth. This perspective grows out of the recognition of the role of well-functioning markets and decision makers operating in a world of "rational expectations." In this view, most policy is irrelevant to farmers in more than a very transitory sense, and this is especially true of price policy:

> One lesson that we should be able to learn from observation of the world is that the absolute incomes earned by farm families in various countries have no relationship to farm prices. Even stronger, the relative incomes of farm families have no relationship to farm prices, except as benefits of higher prices have been capitalized into the value of land and land has been acquired by gift or inheritance (Johnson 1985, 43).

In this world, agricultural incomes are determined by employment opportunities outside agriculture, the agricultural sector *must* decline in proportional output terms and absolutely in the labor force, and the long-run decline in basic agricultural commodity prices due to technical change simply emphasizes that society is best served by getting resources out of agriculture as rapidly as possible. Although the clearest case for this view of the world is in the OECD countries, a host of middle-income countries, and even some quite poor countries, are also facing the problem of declining real incomes in the agricultural sector under the impact of rapid technical change domestically and lower world prices for the resulting output. This perspective is obviously consistent with the view that open economies will show better performance than those with substantial trade barriers.

A sharply different path has been sketched by Mellor and Johnston (1984). Building on their earlier stress on balanced growth (Johnston and Mellor 1961), they call for an "interrelated rural development strategy" that improves nutrition in one dimension while it fosters the broader growth process in the other. The approach calls for a major role of government in strategic design and program implementation, a role that is in marked contrast with the free-market approach sketched out previously:

> We have, therefore, emphasized that improvements in nutrition [one of Mellor and Johnston's key objectives for agricultural development] require a *set of interacting forces:* accelerated growth in agriculture; wage goods production; a strategy of development that structures demand towards high employment content goods and services; increased employment; and increased effective demand for food on the part of the poor. Agricultural growth not only satisfies the need for food to meet nutritional requirements (which is the other side of the wage-goods coin), but fosters a favorable employment-oriented demand structure as well. Agriculture's role in generating a structure of demand, favorable to rapid growth in employment, is central (Mellor and Johnston 1984, 567–68, emphasis added).

Mellor and Johnston go on to summarize their earlier argument that agriculture can play this multiplicity of roles only if a unimodal development strategy is followed, that is, one in which a broad base of smallholders are the central focus of agricultural research and extension services and the recipient of the bulk of receipts from agricultural sales. The authors see the dualism inherent in bimodal strategies—those placing modernization efforts primarily on large, "progressive" farms while neglecting the "backward" smallholders—as the major obstacle to putting their set of interacting forces in motion:

> The most common barrier to the interrelated strategy indicated is pronounced dualism in capital allocations—too much to industry and the unproductive elements of the private sector rather than to agriculture, and to capital-intensive elements within those, as well as to large-scale and therefore capital-intensive allocations within agriculture. The outcome of the strategy will depend upon national-level decisions about macroeconomic policies, exchange rates, interest rates, and investment allocations among sectors and regions, not just within agriculture itself. Indeed, the whole strategy fails if it is viewed simply as the responsibility of agriculture ministries (Mellor and Johnston 1984, 568).

This interrelated strategy must be directed by government planners; there is relatively little concern or role for the private sector, other than small farmers. The analysis leading to the strategy remains heavily influenced by closed economy considerations, and little attention is given to either domestic marketing activities or their relationship to international markets.

Three key elements are suggested as essential to meeting all objectives of agricultural development:

1. massive investment in human capital through nutrition, health, and family planning services in the countryside;
2. creation of the complex rural organizational structures seen in Japan and Taiwan that provide services to small farmers while also serving as a voice for their interests; and
3. investment in rapid technical change appropriate to these small farmers in order to raise agricultural output and rural incomes simultaneously.

Notably missing in this list of key elements is significant concern for the structure of incentives for agriculture relative to industry's or for the country's tradables relative to those of foreign competitors. Although it is realized that the macroeconomic setting is no doubt important to agriculture, it remains outside the scope of appropriate strategy for agricultural development. Not surprisingly, given the argument in Johnston and Clark (1982), the intellectual foundation for this strategy lies in rural development, not in a vision of agriculture linked to the macro economy and world markets by powerful market mechanisms. It is this latter vision which provides the third potential path for agricultural development strategy for the 1990s.

The third approach contrasts with both the "free market" and "interrelated rural development strategy" approaches. It calls for government policy interventions into outcomes in domestic markets but uses markets and the private marketing sector as the vehicle for those policy interventions. This "price and marketing policy" approach recognizes widespread *market failures* in agriculture as well as extensive *government failures* in implementation of direct economic functions. The strategic dilemma is how to cope with segmented rural capital and labor markets, poorly functioning land markets, the welfare consequences of sharp instability of prices in commodity markets, the pervasive lack of information about current and future events in most rural economies, and the sheer absence of many important markets, especially for future contingencies involving yield or price risks.

One powerful lesson emerged from the postwar development record: direct government interventions through state-owned enterprises to correct market failures frequently make matters worse by inhibiting whatever market responses were possible in the initial circumstances, without providing greater output or more efficient utilization of resources. The agricultural sector in particular is vulnerable to well-intended but poorly conceived and managed parastatal organizations that attempt a wide array of direct economic activities, including monopoly control of input supplies, capital-intensive state farms, and mandated control over crop marketing and processing. As Bates (1981) has demonstrated, these direct controls and agencies have a strong political economy rationale for a government that tries to reward its supporters and centralize power and resources in the hands of the state. (See also Lipton 1977.)

The answer to the dilemma over making matters worse, in the "price and market policy" approach, is to gain a much clearer understanding of the necessary interaction between the public and private sectors. Government intervention into agriculture for political reasons has an ancient history. One major claim of monarchs to the throne was their capacity to keep food prices cheap and stable, as Kaplan (1984) made clear and as several modern governments have discovered, to their demise. Political objectives for the performance of agriculture—its capacity to feed the population regularly and cheaply or its ability to provide fair incomes to farmers caught in the painful pressures of successful structural transformation—are inevitable and, in some long-run sense, highly desirable.

The "price and marketing policy" path argues that these objectives are best served by making carefully designed interventions into the prices determined in markets, not by leaving markets alone or by striving to reach the objectives through direct activities by the government (Timmer 1986). If the "free market" approach incurs heavy political costs as markets relentlessly redistribute incomes to the winners in the course of economic development, and the "interrelated rural development strategy" incurs heavy managerial and administrative costs as the government plays an active and direct economic role, the "price and marketing policy" approach incurs heavy analytical costs.

These analytical costs come from the need to understand each country's path of structural change, the workings of factor and commodity markets, and the potential impact of macro and commodity price interventions on these markets and ultimately on the structural path itself. It requires that government intervention be based on an empirical understanding of economic responses to a change in policy and the political repercussions from them. There is an important role for models in illuminating where to look for these responses, but the models themselves cannot provide the answers. This is especially true as attempts are made to build into the models the response of policy itself to changes in the economic environment (see Roe, Shane, and Vo 1986). Such endogenous policy models might reveal some of the historical factors that accounted for policy shifts, but they seldom provide a sense of when the degrees of freedom for policy initiative are about to expand. Frequently, this is in times of crisis. Policy makers often embark on bold experiments in such times, and the payoff would be very high if sufficient analytical understanding already existed in order for them to anticipate the response to a policy change.

All three strategic approaches recognize the importance of government investments in agricultural research and rural infrastructure. Even here, however, there are likely to be significant differences in emphasis. The free-market approach is likely to put a relatively greater share into research, the rural development strategy into human capital investments, and the price and marketing approach into rural infrastructure that lowers marketing costs. Investments in all three areas are obviously desirable. The issue is at the margin: where are scarce resources to be invested? In addition, different countries have different starting points and different needs, so no single strategic approach makes sense for all countries. But it is difficult to see how countries can develop their rural sectors without relatively efficient marketing systems and adequate financial incentives for their farmers. Accordingly, significant elements of the price and marketing approach seem destined to be incorporated into all successful agricultural development strategies, even if they emphasize the free market or rural development approaches in other dimensions.

NOTES

I would like to thank Larry Westphal, Pranab K. Bardhan, David Dapice, and Scott Pearson for serious and critical readings of the first draft. As always, my deepest debt is to my wife and editor, Carol, for her patience and persistence in helping me make my manuscripts readable and for her mastery of the wonderful new technology that permits me to lose half the manuscript with the push of a button and her to get it back after considerable effort and anguish.

1. For a very useful summary of the literature that documents the agricultural transformation process itself and also attempts to explain it in terms of the prevailing models of economic development, see Johnston 1970.

2. The structural rigidities in the economy that give rise to this substantial disequilibrium obviously mean that neoclassical models based solely on perfect markets and rational actors will fail to predict accurately the impact of government interventions. However, purely structural models that assume an absence of market response might be equally far from the mark. A messy amalgam of structural rigidities, imperfect markets, and decision makers interested in their own, though vaguely defined, welfare seems to characterize the actual starting point from which government interventions must be evaluated.

3. It is also important to distinguish subsectors within agriculture. An export crop subsector producing rubber or coffee might continue to provide financial resources to the rest of the economy, some of which could be returned to the foodcrop subsector in order to foster its development. Much of the discussion in this chapter is concerned with modernizing the foodcrop subsector while recognizing the important role played by the other agricultural subsectors.

4. An effort to formalize the impact of agriculture's distinct features, especially the behavioral and material determinants of production relations, is in Binswanger and Rosenzweig 1986.

REFERENCES

Anderson, K. 1983. "Growth of Agricultural Protection in East Asia." *Food Policy* 8:327–36.

Anderson, K., and Y. Hayami, with associates. 1986. *The Political Economy of Agricultural Protection: East Asia in International Perspective.* London: Allen and Unwin.

Bairoch, P. 1975. *The Economic Development of the Third World since 1900.* Berkeley: University of California Press.

Bardhan, P. K. 1984. *Land, Labor, and Rural Poverty.* Cambridge: Cambridge University Press.

Bates, R. H. 1981. *Markets and States in Tropical Africa: The Political Basis of Agricultural Policies.* Berkeley: University of California Press.

Binswanger, H. P., and M. R. Rosenzweig. 1986. "Behavioral and Material Determinants of Production Relations in Agriculture." *The Journal of Development Studies* 22:503–39.

Chenery, H. B., and M. Syrquin. 1975. *Patterns of Development, 1950–1970.* London: Oxford University Press.

Chenery, H. B., and L. Taylor. 1968. "Development Patterns among Countries and Over Time." *Review of Economics and Statistics* 50:391–416.

Clark, C. 1940; 1957. *The Conditions of Economic Progress,* 3rd ed. London: Macmillan.

Cochrane, W. W. 1979. *The Development of American Agriculture: A Historical Analysis.* Minneapolis: University of Minnesota Press.

Fei, J. C. H., and G. Ranis. 1964. *Development of the Labor Surplus Economy: Theory and Policy.* Homewood, Ill.: Irwin.

Hayami, Y. 1986. "Agricultural Protectionism in the Industrialized World: The Case of Japan." Prepared for a conference held at the East-West Center, Honolulu, February 17–21.

Hayami, Y., and V. Ruttan. 1985. *Agricultural Development: An International Perspective,* revised and expanded ed. Baltimore: Johns Hopkins University Press.

Hirschman, A. O. 1958. *The Strategy of Economic Development.* New Haven: Yale University Press.

Johnson, D. G. 1973. *World Agriculture in Disarray.* New York: St. Martin's Press.

Johnson, D. G. 1985. "World Commodity Market Situation and Outlook." In *U.S. Agricultural Policy: The 1985 Farm Legislation,* edited by B. L. Gardner. Washington, D.C.: American Enterprise Institute for Public Policy Research.

Johnston, B. F. 1970. "Agriculture and Structural Transformation in Development Countries: A Survey of Research." *Journal of Economic Literature* 3:369–404.

Johnston, B. F., and W. C. Clark. 1982. *Redesigning Rural Development: A Strategic Perspective.* Baltimore: Johns Hopkins University Press.

Johnston, B. F., and J. W. Mellor. 1961. "The Role of Agriculture in Economic Development." *American Economic Review* 51:566–93.

Jorgenson, D. W. 1961. "The Development of a Dual Economy." *Economic Journal* 71:309–34.

Kaplan, S. L. 1984. *Provisioning Paris: Merchants and Millers in the Grain and Flour Trade during the Eighteenth Century.* Ithaca: Cornell University Press.

Kuznets, S. 1966. *Modern Economic Growth.* New Haven: Yale University Press.

Lewis, W. A. 1954. "Economic Development with Unlimited Supplies of Labor." *Manchester School of Economic and Social Studies* 22:139–91.

Lipton, M. 1977. *Why Poor People Stay Poor: Urban Bias in World Development.* Cambridge: Harvard University Press.

Little, I. M. D. 1982. *Economic Development: Theory, Policy, and International Relations.* New York: Basic Books.

Mellor, J. W., and B. F. Johnston. 1984. "The World Food Equation: Interrelations among Development, Employment, and Food Consumption." *Journal of Economic Literature* 22:531–74.

Mosher, A. T. 1966. *Getting Agriculture Moving: Essentials for Development and Modernization.* New York: Praeger.

Myint, H. 1975. "Agriculture and Economic Development in the Open Economy." In *Agriculture in Development Theory,* edited by L. G. Reynolds. New Haven: Yale University Press.

Nicholls, W. H. 1963. "An 'Agricultural Surplus' as a Factor in Economic Development." *Journal of Political Economy* 71:1–29.

Nurkse, R. 1953. *Problems of Capital Formation in Underdeveloped Countries.* New York: Oxford University Press.

Prebish, R. 1950. *The Economic Development of Latin America and Its Principal Problems.* Lake Success, N.Y.: United Nations Department of Economic Affairs.

Preobrazhensky, E. 1965. *The New Economics.* Oxford: Clarendon Press.

Reynolds, L. G., ed. 1975. *Agriculture in Development Theory.* New Haven: Yale University Press.

Roe, T., M. Shane, and D. H. Vo. 1986. "Price Responsiveness of World Grain Markets: The Influence of Government Intervention on Import Price Elasticity." Technical Bulletin no. 1720. Washington, D.C.: International Economics Division, Economic Research Service, U.S. Department of Agriculture.

Sah, R. K., and J. E. Stiglitz. 1984. "The Economics of Price Scissors." *American Economic Review* 74:125–38.

Schuh, G. E. 1976. "The New Macroeconomics of Agriculture." *American Journal of Agricultural Economics* 58:802–11.

Schultz, T. W. 1953. *The Economic Organization of Agriculture.* New York: McGraw-Hill.

Singh, I. J., L. Squire, and J. Strauss. 1986. *Agricultural Household Models: Extensions, Applications, and Policy.* Baltimore: Johns Hopkins University Press for the World Bank.

Timmer, C. P. 1969. "The Turnip, the New Husbandry, and the English Agricultural Revolution." *The Quarterly Jounal of Economics* 83:375–95.

———. 1986. *Getting Prices Right: The Scope and Limits of Agricultural Price Policy.* Ithaca: Cornell University Press.

Timmer, C. P., W. P. Falcon, and S. R. Pearson. 1983. *Food Policy Analysis.* Baltimore: Johns Hopkins University Press for the World Bank.

World Bank. 1982. *World Development Report 1982.* New York: Oxford University Press.

———. 1986. *World Development Report 1986.* New York: Oxford University Press.

8

Agriculture on the Road to Industrialization

JOHN W. MELLOR

 Economic development is a process by which an economy is transformed from one that is dominantly rural and agricultural to one that is dominantly urban, industrial, and service-oriented in composition. The objectives of the process can be usefully categorized as increased societal wealth, equity, and stability. But because these objectives require a diversification of the economy away from agriculture (no high-income, equitable, stable nations have agriculture as their dominant activity), the process is one of major structural transformation.

If economic development is a process of transforming an economy from producing mainly agricultural to producing mainly industrial and service outputs, what is the nature of a constructive role for the initially dominant agricultural sector? What is the scope for synthesizing an agricultural role into the mainstream of development thought? More specifically, what is the dynamic relation between agriculture and industry in an optimal growth strategy?

Given agriculture's initial importance, it is not surprising that it has received the explicit attention of eminent economists and has been the subject of intensive analysis by generalists and specialists alike. Yet, in view of the contemporary expansion of knowledge about how to develop agriculture, it is surprising that the principal, broad conceptualizations in development economics have not articulated a central place for agriculture. This has held true through wide-ranging shifts in development-strategy styles—from emphasis on direct allocation of resources to growth in the capital stock, to import displacement, to basic human needs, to export-led growth. In fact, each of these development fashions has had its own strong arguments for not emphasizing agriculture in either capital allocations or public policy. For countries following these mainstream strategies, occasional

JOHN W. MELLOR is president of John Mellor Associates, Inc., Washington, D.C.

Reprinted from *Development Strategies Reconsidered,* edited by John P. Lewis and Valeriana Kallab, Transaction Books, New Brunswick, N.J., for the Overseas Development Council. Copyright © 1986 by the Overseas Development Council, Washington, D.C. Published by permission of the Overseas Development Council and the author.

crises of domestic food supplies, foreign-exchange constraints in association with sudden, large food imports, or threatened cutoffs in large-scale food aid have prompted flurries of attention for agriculture. But such spurts of concern all too often have generated only such short-term palliatives as higher prices for food producers; they have not produced sustained long-run development efforts that build agriculture as part of a larger strategy.

There are, of course, numerous examples of development *practice* that have indeed given agriculture a central place. Notable are the post-Meiji restoration period in Japan as well as the developmental thrusts in Taiwan, Thailand, Ivory Coast, Malaysia, the Punjabs of India and Pakistan, and to some extent other parts of South Asia. It is ironic that, perhaps because of the critical importance of trade expansion in an agriculture-based strategy, several of these successes are perceived as examples of export-led growth rather than as a successful agriculture-based strategy.

The intellectual neglect of agriculture's role in development no doubt is rooted in an underlying view of agriculture as initially backward; development promoters have wanted to move directly to building those sectors that carry the image of modernization. An urban-based intelligentsia (including development economists), a related caste-like separation of largely micro-oriented agricultural economists and largely macro-oriented development economists, and urban-based political systems all combine to provide an intellectual basis and political pressure for directing resources to the urban sector.

In decrying this neglect, however, it is important to recognize that there is an intellectual case for downplaying agriculture in the development process. To make the contrary case, three substantial questions must be answered affirmatively:

1. Can agricultural production be increased by means of advances in resource productivity?
2. Can effective demand for agricultural commodities expand apace with accelerated agricultural growth?
3. Can a dynamic agriculture provide an effective demand "pull" for growth in other sectors?

The following discussion will show why these are the vital questions, why it is not unreasonable to think that the answer to each may be "no," and what the contrary bases are for the affirmative answer that in turn defines a central role for agriculture in a dynamic process of economic transformation and growth. This exploration will make clear the essential connection between agricultural growth and employment growth—and hence the need always to speak of an agriculture- and employment-based strategy, not of one or the other independently.

The strategy described here has two key distinguishing features aside from the emphases on agriculture and employment. First, continuous, institutionalized technological change provides the basic engine of cumulative growth. Second, growth in domestic demand provides the basic markets both for the increasing agricultural output and for the activities that create rapid growth in employment. Trade is important—but mainly to serve the purpose of restraining growth in capital-intensiveness.

Before discussing the main elements of an agriculture- and employment-based strategy, common failings of alternative strategies will be noted briefly, as well as which of those failings an agriculture-based strategy might or might not meet. A sketch of the debate as to the efficacy of agricultural and nonagriculture-based strategies follows.

DEVELOPMENT FAILINGS AND AGRICULTURE'S POTENTIAL

Robert McNamara's presidential address to the 1973 World Bank annual meeting epitomized a widespread and growing view that the ascendant development strategies of the 1950s and 1960s had an unacceptably small impact on poverty. That the expression of such concern had subsided so much by the late 1970s owed less to a diminution of the reality of the problem and more to the realization that the various direct attacks on poverty meanwhile ventured were no more successful than earlier efforts in mitigating the problem.

Failure to make a dent in the poverty problem was associated with four related phenomena:

1. Food supplies per capita rose little or not at all, and hence the diets, nutritional status, and related well-being of the poor could not be enhanced.
2. Employment growth rates seemed to lag even behind population growth rates, so that the poor could not obtain income to command more food or other basic wants.
3. Growth and basic services were often available only in a small number of immense urban concentrations, with high overhead costs and little impact on the population dispersed over the rest of the country.
4. Overall growth rates were themselves much slower and less well sustained than expected.

The first three are directly related to the lack of poverty abatement. The last, even if it was not a direct cause, certainly reinforced equity-related failings. Clearly, an agricultural emphasis strikes at one of the root causes of poverty: inadequate food supplies. Accelerated agricultural growth also provides a substantial direct increase in employment, because of the large aggregate size of the sector and the nature of its technology. An agriculture, as a broadly diffused activity, spreads economic activity and employment beyond the megalopolis.

One should be clear, however, as to what accelerated agricultural growth cannot do *directly*. First, it cannot provide high overall growth rates in output or employment. For the staple foods sector, growth of 3–4 percent is considered very rapid, and 4–5 percent for the agricultural sector as a whole is extraordinarily rapid.[1] The constraint of limited land area, the biological nature of agricultural production, and the dispersed, variable production system explain the common experience of such low ceilings on growth rates. Similarly, it is doing well indeed to experience a 0.6 percent growth rate in agricultural employment for each percentage point in the output growth rate.[2] Thus the agricultural sector can at best provide employment for its own population growth, and it is likely to fall far short of that. And agricultural growth alone obviously cannot supply the broadening of consumption patterns beyond food that all people desire.

These limitations explain why an agriculture-based strategy must have major *indirect* effects on growth and employment in other sectors if it is to be seen as central to development strategy. These indirect effects must come from the expenditure of increased agricultural income on nonagricultural goods and services, in turn creating not only additional output in those sectors but also additional employment. To be consistent with an agriculture- and employment-oriented strategy, one must ask of those activities that they be large in aggregate, employment-intensive, and broadly distributed geographically.

From these foundations, we can skip ahead of the story to outline what a development strategy must look like if agriculture and employment are to play a central role. First, the agricultural production growth rate must be accelerated; this must normally derive from technological change. Second, the expenditure pattern from the net additions to income arising from the accelerated growth must create demand for a wide range of goods and services with a high employment content, much of the production of which must be broadly diffused in rural areas (e.g., in major market towns). Third, increased food marketing will somewhat depress food prices,[3] thereby encouraging employment in other sectors by making labor somewhat cheaper relative to the goods and services it produces.

HISTORICAL SKETCH OF THE AGRICULTURE VERSUS INDUSTRY DEBATE

INDUSTRIAL ORIENTATION

With G. S. Fel'dman's writing as the theoretical base, the Soviet Union's practice in the 1920s was to equate industrialization with modernization. The arguments constantly recurred in subsequent development literature. Capital and labor were believed to be more productive in industry. Industry was seen as having major economies of scale and external economies, while agriculture was subject to diminishing returns. Industrial "externalities," including industry's modernizing force, promoting new modes of economic behavior and new forms of social organization, were all seen as supportive of growth. Given the diminishing returns in agriculture, if underemployed labor could be mobilized out of agriculture with no loss of production, the argument for industry was compelling. In this context, it is fitting that Paul Rosenstein-Rodan's piece on economic development, published in 1943, was entitled "Problems of Industrialization of Eastern and South-Eastern Europe."[4]

A major force in the development literature of the 1950s and 1960s and in the practice of both India and China[5] grew out of the conceptualization by Fel'dman, as further developed by P. C. Mahalanobis, and related to the concepts of Roy Harrod and Evsey Domar.[6] Increase in the capital stock was the source of growth. It followed, in the view of Fel'dman and Mahalanobis, that this resource should be directly allocated to capital-goods production, and not to consumer-goods, including agricultural production. In practice, industrialization became highly capital-intensive, with little employment growth and consequently little growth in demand for food; hence there was little upward pressure on food prices, even though agriculture was doing poorly. The strategy, since it was inward-looking, spawned a whole generation of closed-economy growth models showing how capital should be deployed among subsectors. The push was always on industry.

A substantial ancillary literature dealt with the balance of growth and the issue of whether or not capital intensity could be reduced by choice of technology. The answer, in the confines of an inward-looking strategy, was that it could not. A. K. Sen provided the definitive rationalization of that conclusion, basing it on the inevitable need for more food to underpin the increased wages from employment growth and diminishing returns (increasing capital intensity) in agriculture.[7] The proponents of this capital-intensive strategy realized that equity and poverty abatement would be postponed by the strategy, although they hoped that relatively inexpensive efforts in agriculture and cottage industries (e.g., community development in India) would mitigate the problem.

The import-substitution strategy popularized for Latin America by Raul Prebisch[8] was driven by the view that primary-commodity prices, particularly including those of agricultural commodities, would inevitably trend downward relative to the prices of manufactured goods. It followed that a developing country should shift out of agriculture and into industry as quickly as possible. The market would come from displacement of previously imported goods. In practice, however, as implementation of the strategy progressed, more and more capital-intensive imports were displaced by domestic production. Thus as expansion proceeded, capital intensity increased, employment growth slowed, income distribution became more skewed, and the growth rate decelerated.

By the mid-1960s, concern was growing that development was moving too slowly, and the poor were not participating significantly in such growth as was occurring. At the same time, agricultural research was demonstrating the capacity to provide major new technology to increase agricultural productivity—the Green Revolution. Why did the concurrence of these breakthroughs and the concern for poverty reduction of that time not bring a sharp swing in development strategy toward an agriculture- and employment-based strategy of growth?

The Green Revolution is based on new technology and rapid growth in fertilizer use, increased commercialization of agriculture, and a complex set of national-level institutions run by a large and rapidly growing number of highly trained people. The sharp rise in energy prices led to a wish to deemphasize the use of fertilizer and even of irrigation based on energy-using pumps. Western environmental concerns also were on the ascent and did not favor fertilizer. Mounting attention to equity problems strengthened interest in dependency theorists, who in turn also had a negative view of fertilizer as an instrument of Western multinationals. Concurrently, anti-elitism favored primary over higher education, turning foreign aid away from advanced training of the scientists and technicians essential to the success of the Green Revolution. Concern with poverty reduction, energy depletion, environment, dependency, and elitism all seemed associated with each other. All this was reinforced by a literature decrying the then reputed negative effect of the Green Revolution in further skewing the rural income distribution; it was said (incorrectly, it is now clear) that only the larger farmers benefited from the new technology[9] and that they would use their new wealth to buy out small farmers and tenants.

The combined impact of these forces retarded response to the essential requirements of the Green Revolution and spawned a "basic human needs" approach that emphasized social welfare functions and agricultural production only in highly complex regional projects. The integrated rural development projects that resulted not only were not integrated into national support structures for agricultural growth; they tended to raid the latter for personnel. Almost universally, the integrated rural development projects failed due to excessive complexity and a lack of central support services.[10] (Local institutions are, of course, central to the Green Revolution, but they are effective only when serviced by national-level support structures, including research.) The basic-needs approach had a major influence on foreign assistance in the 1970s, particularly in the least developed countries, which include the bulk of Africa and a few Asian countries, such as Nepal.

Asian countries that had benefited from earlier foreign assistance emphasizing large-scale, high-level technical training and well-developed agricultural research systems were able to pursue the Green Revolution effectively and even to restrain foreign aid from single-minded pursuit of the new directions of the 1970s. In that context, the basic-needs strategy could be used to deal with "second-generation" problems in the context of the other requisites of a successful Green Revolution. It is notable, however, that where—as in India and the Philippines—the Green Revolution was not associated with an employment orientation; it served substantially to displace food imports and build food stocks rather than as the base for a new development strategy. The basic-needs strategists, while often vigorously and specifically attacking the Green Revolution, were generally silent about strategies giving priority to capital-intensive industry and import-substitution. There was urgent need to change those strategies to provide the essential employment complement to the Green Revolution.

The failings of the capital-intensive strategies, dependent as they were on market interference, also prompted a trend quite separate from the equity-oriented basic-needs strategy: a renewed interest in a market-oriented strategy commonly emphasizing export promotion. With the gradual demise of the basic-needs orientation in the early 1980s, the strategy of export-led growth or export promotion became the new fashion. Of all the post–World War II strategies, this was the one least deleterious to agriculture. It argued against overvalued currencies, which discriminate so strongly against agriculture. It argued generally for prices favorable to agriculture, supported commercialization of agriculture (including import of key inputs), and fostered better domestic markets for agricultural output by favoring employment-intensive industries—with beneficial effects on employment for the poor and hence greater expenditure on food. In practice, however, the export-promotion strategy looks explicitly to markets abroad—rather than to the broad-based domestic markets that accelerated agricultural growth can provide. This, combined with an anti-governmental bias, works against support for large public investments in the key areas of research, education, rural roads, and rural electrification that are so critical to an agriculture- and employment-based growth strategy. In practice, the export-promotion strategy also emphasizes trade to allow economies of scale, thereby favoring more capital-intensive industries relative to relying more on vigorous domestic markets.[11]

AGRICULTURAL ORIENTATION

Although a clear agriculture- and employment-based strategy has not been ascendant, agriculture has never lacked for a good word from an eminent economist. During the postwar renaissance of concern for the macroeconomics of growth, Nicholas Kaldor stated:

> Economic development will, of course, invariably involve industrialization . . . this can be expected to follow, almost automatically, upon the growth of the food surpluses of the agricultural sector. . . . Once this is recognized, the efforts of under-developed countries could be concentrated—far more than they are at present—in tackling the problem of how to raise productivity on the land, as a prior condition of economic development.[12]

It is, however, clear from succeeding lines in Kaldor's piece that he had little grasp of what was involved in the modernization of agriculture and least of all as to what was required to provide a stream of land-augmenting technological changes—although his intuition as to the importance of agriculture and the importance of education to agricultural growth were both correct. Perhaps Kaldor was also facile in his perception of the near-automaticity of agriculture's growth converting into industrial growth. Our knowledge of these processes has improved immensely since 1954, although its scant diffusion to macroeconomists still prejudices thought about development.

Paralleling the broad orientation of development economics away from agriculture was an evolution of knowledge about how to develop agriculture. Farmers were presented as economically rational responders to prices and technology;[13] understanding of the need for radically improved technology was articulated in economic terms,[14] and the nature of a range of complementary agricultural growth requirements was set forth.[15] Myriad empirically based analyses have filled in the picture. More important, the scientific groundwork for the Green Revolution was laid by the activities of the Rockefeller Foundation in Mexico and India and by the

Ford and Rockefeller foundations in establishing the International Rice Research Institute, the precursor of and role model for the Consultative Group on International Agricultural Research. The result was the bursting of the Green Revolution in Asia in the late 1960s and a clear appreciation of the requisites of accelerated agricultural growth.

Compared with the immense gains in our understanding of the agricultural development process per se, the relationships between agriculture and the rest of a developing economy remain less fully explored. While there have been many contributions on the subject, the empirical data underlying the relationships asserted are much less complete than is the case with the microeconomics of agriculture— and hence the policies implied remain more speculative.

Nevertheless, four major threads of the analysis can be defined. First, the critical role of food as a wage good (the object of consumption from the increased income of employment) was elegantly defined in W. Arthur Lewis's classic paper.[16] Second, the need for productivity increase in agriculture and the role of technology was laid out by Johnston and Mellor.[17] Third, the resource transfers from agriculture that so facilitate growth of the nonagricultural sector were delineated from the Japanese experience by Kazushi Ohkawa, Bruce Johnston, and S. Ishikawa,[18] and meticulously documented for Taiwan by T. H. Lee.[19] Fourth, the critical role of agriculture in stimulating growth in the non-agricultural sector has been explored with respect to both consumption goods[20] and producer goods.[21]

AN AGRICULTURE- AND EMPLOYMENT-BASED STRATEGY OF ECONOMIC GROWTH

An agriculture- and employment-based strategy of economic growth has three basic elements. First, the pace of agricultural growth must be accelerated despite the limitations of fixed land area. Technological change solves a major, special problem of agricultural growth and allows low-income countries to use the most powerful element of growth. Second, domestic demand for agricultural output must grow rapidly despite inelastic demand. This can occur only through accelerated growth in employment (more precisely, increased demand for labor), which is facilitated by the indirect effects of agricultural growth itself. Third, the demand for goods and services produced by low capital-intensity processes must increase. This, too, is facilitated by the technology-based increase in agricultural income. As we proceed, we will see that these three elements continually interact in the strategy.

TECHNOLOGICAL CHANGE IN AGRICULTURE

One of the most important theoretical and empirical findings in analysis of Western economic growth is the identification of technological change as a major source of growth. Hence it is initially surprising that in the various ascendant macroeconomic theories of economic growth for developing countries, technological change has not been assigned a central role.

On a second thought, however, the neglect is understandable: These ascendant theories have been preoccupied with growth in the initially minuscule industrial sector, where the first concern necessarily has been to expand the capital stock as the basis of growth. Only if the dominant agricultural sector is to be central to growth can technological change play an immediate, major role. It happens that, because of Ricardian diminishing returns, technological change is in any case essential to agricultural growth. The land area for agriculture being generally limited, increased output is traditionally obtained via declining increments in output per unit of input as input intensity increases. The result is rising costs, which must be offset by rising prices if incentives are to prevail. It is apparent that cumulatively increasing relative food prices are not socially acceptable. Thus it is essential that the incentive to produce more in the face of constantly rising costs be met by technological change rather than by price increases. Continuous, cumulative technological change is the proven effect of institutionalized agricultural research systems.

The rudiments of getting agriculture moving through technological change have been fully understood for a long time.[22] Development of a technology system (including research) and technically competent extension are primary. The nature of agricultural technology is such that rapid growth of sophisticated input delivery systems is essential. For this latter, and for effective multipliers of other sectors, a highly developed infrastructure of roads is required. Underlying the total process is rapid growth in the number of highly trained people and of the institutional structure within which they can work effectively.

In all of these elements, the public sector must play a key role in physical investment and institution building. The essential financial and organizational requirements of governments are so immense that every effort must be made to maximize activities in the private sector and to concentrate public-sector attention on only those essential agricultural support activities not taken up by the private sector. Agriculture, with its small-scale orientation, is more in need of public-sector support than industry. The sharp turn-around in Asian agriculture—resulting in a 30 percent increase in growth rates in basic food-staple production from the 1960s to the 1970s—impressively demonstrates the results of turning the public sector's attention to the requisites of technological change in agriculture.

The urgency of moving the agricultural sector is underlined by its role as a supplier of food as essential backing to employment growth. It is generally understood that developing countries have a large pool of extremely low-productivity if not idle labor. In effect, this provides a highly elastic labor supply. If jobs become available, labor is ready to march into them. What has not been fully recognized is that the supply of labor is a function of two independent markets: a labor market and a food market.[23] Increased employment provides the labor class with added income, 60 to 80 percent of which is spent on food. If the food supply is not expanded, increased employment will cause the price of food to rise, squeezing the real incomes of laborers back nearly to the previous level, reducing the incentive to work, placing upward pressures on wages, and reducing employment. Thus, accelerated growth in employment must be accompanied by accelerated growth in food supplies.[24] Three arguments have been used against the need to emphasize domestic food production in this context.

First, the labor-surplus arguments take the position that labor is already maintained and idle in the rural sector; hence, until there is a "turning point" at which labor is fully absorbed, food supply is available for labor transferred to other occupations.[25] This argument neglects the theoretically and empirically verifiable fact that increased employment, even in the face of surplus agricultural labor, results in increased wage payments in the hands of people with high marginal propensity to spend on food. A related argument is that employment can grow only very slowly, because of the capital constraint. The striking contrary evidence is that developing countries that have done well in agriculture expand employment rapidly enough to have to increase food imports.[26] We will, however, return to this argument later.

Second, there is a widespread belief that the aggregate supply of food is elastic with respect to price. If such is the case, higher food prices induced by increased purchasing power in the hands of the poor will readily bring forth the needed increased supply of food. The theoretical and empirical evidence is clear on this point: Under essentially all conditions, the aggregate supply of food is only slightly responsive to price.[27] Most simply, this is due to Ricardian diminishing returns. It is possible to accelerate the growth rate of food production sharply, but only through the processes of technological change. With existing technology, the aggregate supply response to higher prices is comparatively limited.

Third, it is believed that the supply of food from imports is highly elastic. Up to a point, this assumption is probably correct. Certainly Singapore and Hong Kong have been able to expand employment rapidly and to meet the consequent increased demand for food with imports. It is less certain that supplies would be adequate if the bulk of the developing countries succeeded in a rapid employment growth strategy without increasing domestic food production. But the possibility of importing food to meet the demands of increased employment strengthens the argument that generating demand and resources for growth of other sectors must be an important part of the argument for an emphasis on agriculture.

ADEQUATE EFFECTIVE DEMAND FOR FOOD

There is an important theoretical problem in realizing the full potential of accelerated technological change in agriculture. The demand for food tends to be inelastic. If food production increases rapidly without increased employment, prices will tend to fall sharply and eventually cause reduced production. The way to deal with the problem is through accelerated growth in employment, which under the low-income conditions of developing countries is efficiently translated into increased demand for food. The correct response to increased food production is no more through constantly decreasing prices than the way to meet the need for increased production is through constantly increasing prices. The correct response to the former is employment; to the latter, it is technological change.

Prices, it must be emphasized, are not so much problems as indicators of problems. If food prices are rising, this indicates that the supply is not being increased rapidly enough through technological change. One should, in such circumstances, redouble efforts in the technological change arena. While waiting for those re-doubled efforts to succeed, food would have to be imported, to prevent employment being held back by rapidly rising food prices.

Conversely, declining food prices mean that the success in technological change is moving ahead of the employment strategy. Governments may come under substantial pressure from organized farm interests to maintain agricultural prices as technology moves ahead, even though demand is not keeping pace. The result will be either subsidized exports or, more likely, rapid growth in domestic stocks. India's record in the early and mid-1980s has been a prime example: stocks were built up to four times the level that would be justified by optimal stocking policies. This is an example of a country achieving modest success in technological change and doing badly on employment growth. One should in those circumstances examine the allocation of capital and of demand structures to see what can be done on the employment side.

Just as the preceding discussion emphasized the need to meet food requirements by domestic production, so this discussion stresses growth in domestic income, not exports, for generating effective demand for growing supplies of food. If one is exporting staple foods, this means that one has a more-than-adequate supply of food to provide for the growth in demand from the existing rate of growth of employment. In a low-income, low-employment economy, one should obviously be striving for policies that increase domestic employment as a way of fully taking up food supplies.

DEMAND STIMULUS TO NONAGRICULTURAL EMPLOYMENT

The role of agriculture in providing effective demand for production from the nonagricultural sector has received little emphasis in the literature and has been poorly understood. In the most extreme phase of its evolution, this view was: "Agriculture stands convicted on the count of its lack of direct stimulus to the setting up of new activities through linkage effects—the superiority of manufacturing in this respect is crushing."[28] This position overlooked that technological change in agriculture can increase net national income and thereby generate added demand for consumer goods. The neglect of this aspect was reinforced by capital-centered growth theory, which tended to view consumption and the production of consumption goods as antithetical to growth. This bias was aggravated by excessive emphasis on "modern" consumer and capital goods to the neglect of services and more traditionally produced consumer goods. A more careful review of early Western development history, despite the weak technological base of its agricultural growth, would have helped avoid this misreading.[29]

A central problem of contemporary development practice is illuminated by a quote from Sir John Hicks that has roots in a long history of his own work: "That it is possible for a 'developing country,' by choice of techniques that are too capital-intensive, to expand employment in its modern sector less rapidly than it might have done is nowadays familiar."[30]

The failures in economic development to which Hicks refers have been associated with a poor record in agricultural growth and failure to connect success in agriculture to driving the rest of the economy. These failures have been associated with a marked dualism in capital investment—a small portion of the labor force operating with high capital intensity and a large portion with low capital intensity. The result, as Hicks would lead one to expect, is generally low productivity of both capital and labor. That dualism exhibits itself partly in low allocations of capital to agriculture, occasional instances of investment in state farms and other capital-intensive elements within agriculture, and a widespread tendency to place the bulk of additional capital in large-scale, capital-intensive industries with few additional employees, leaving little capital for the dominant remainder of the labor force.[31]

Agricultural development offers a potential for rapid growth in domestic demand for labor-intensive goods and services. Incremental consumption patterns of peasant farmers have a large rural-services component, and a large share of other goods consumed is also produced relatively labor-intensively.

It is essential to note two needs if the favorable demand effects of agricultural growth are to be achieved. First, the increments to demand must come from volume-increasing and unit-cost–decreasing technological change. Raising prices is not likely to help. Although the income transfer from urban to rural people arising from higher agricultural prices may provide some modest, net restructuring of demand favorable to employment, only a major, continuous increase in net national income from new technology can be expected to provide a continuous aggregate effect. Second, the infrastructure of communications essential to growth of rural industry and services must be in place. Highly developed infrastructure is essential to agricultural production growth, favorable consumption incentives, and to the complex, interactive system of region-based urban centers that are so essential to a high-employment content in an agriculture-based growth strategy.

Capital stock must grow rapidly if employment is to do the same. In an agriculture-led strategy, however, market mechanisms should work well to raise the savings rate. Much of the capital needed for agricultural growth can be generated in agriculture itself in response to technology-induced high rates of return. The non-agricultural supply response to increased demand may well be highly elastic. If capital proves to be a constraint, higher prices will result, transferring resources from newly prospering agriculture to those activities. The critical investment bottlenecks are more likely to be in the public sector, with government at the local or national level not gathering or allocating adequate resources for the massive rural infrastructure that is essential to agricultural and employment growth. The 20 to 30 percent savings rates that characterize so many contemporary developing countries are inadequate to the task only because the capital intensity of many productive processes is excessive and because too small a share of the savings is invested in infrastructure. Agricultural linkages can contribute to reducing that intensity and to spreading capital more thinly.

POLICY ISSUES

Pursuit of an agriculture- and employment-based strategy of growth requires quite different public-sector policies than those comprising alternative strategies. Discussion of key policy requirements serves to bring out distinguishing characteristics of the strategy as well as to indicate what policy shifts are needed if it is to succeed.

TRADE

An agriculture- and employment-based development strategy requires an open trading regime. That point must be made explicitly because of the emphasis on meeting the demand for wage goods arising from employment growth from domestic food production and on providing domestic demand for the increased food production. Those inward-looking emphases are a product of comparative advantage, reinforced by the high transfer costs typical of developing countries, and do not require protection.

The high employment-growth leg of the strategy requires that capital be spread thinly over a rapidly growing labor force. There is little scope to restrain rising capital-labor ratios in a closed economy. Although particular goods and services may have low capital-labor ratios, they always seem to have component parts that have very high capital-labor ratios (e.g., fertilizer for agriculture, and steel, aluminum, and petrochemicals for otherwise labor-intensive manufactured goods). Thus, while agricultural growth generates direct demand for a final product that is efficiently produced by labor-intensive processes, there must be rapid growth in imports of capital-intensive intermediate goods and services. Clearly, accelerated growth of such imports must be matched by accelerated growth of exports. The latter should be goods and services with relatively high employment content. This fits obviously with standard trade theory. The need to foster such exports will further restrain increases in aggregate capital-labor ratios. The rapid growth in domestic markets for labor-intensive manufactures would itself be favorable to low-cost production and therefore to their external competitiveness. Taiwan's rapid success in exports in the late 1950s was based on prior development of domestic demand.[32] A somewhat undervalued exchange rate facilitates full pricing of agricultural commodities; encourages restraint in using inputs that are capital-intensively produced, because they will be imported and thus more highly priced; and provides some additional incentive to export the more labor-intensive commodities, helping to overcome the various institutional hurdles to exports that inevitably exist in developing countries. This is, of course, the opposite of the exchange-rate policy that is consistent with the capital-intensive approaches.

If employment does move ahead of the capacity to produce domestic food staples, one should obviously take advantage of that opportunity and import food to support the more rapid growth rate of employment. If, on the other hand, food is being exported, one should examine carefully whether trade policies are restraining the imports of capital-intensive goods and services and the export of labor-intensive goods and services, or whether infrastructure investment is inadequate for rapid growth in domestic employment.

POVERTY REDUCTION

The agriculture-employment strategy is innately favorable to reducing poverty. Thus, it is important to mobilize resources for its vigorous pursuit. The strategy increases the supply of less expensive food and increases the demand for labor. These are the two essentials for removing poverty through growth. Wherever poverty is massive, a shift to such a strategy of growth should be the first priority of poverty alleviation. In the context of such a strategy, special attention is properly given to removing frictions that are especially deleterious to the poor. Thus, attention may be needed to provide infrastructure for remote areas; credit for small, labor-intensive processes; and technical assistance in production and marketing of vegetables and other less capital-intensive, small-scale activities.

In the longer run, the new agriculture- and employment-based strategy does bring a problem of regional disparities. Agriculture will move more rapidly in some regions than others simply because of the accident of technological breakthrough. Even over the long term, there may be some regions with physical resources for which it will be impossible to come up with improved technologies. The first-round effect of widening regional disparities through differential progress in agriculture will be strongly reinforced by the favorable local multiplier effects of accelerated agriculture growth. Historically, migration has proved the most common means of dealing with this problem. With potential for migration, it makes little sense to invest in technology at low rates of return in areas that have very little capacity for its development while at the same time starving areas that could provide faster growth of such an equity-oriented type. On the other hand, the social problems of migration need to be recognized and alternative measures sought.

There is also, of course, a residual problem of equity for persons who are handicapped by their circumstances. Income transfers are necessary for meeting such a problem. Far more pervasive is the problem of poverty during the transition while an agriculture-employment growth strategy is getting under way. Since shifting to such a strategy is so very favorable to poverty reduction, dealing with the interim and transitional problems by redistribution of resources is apt to be costly to later reductions in poverty. Large-scale rural public works may be redistributive and assist the growth strategy itself. Urban food subsidies may serve to stabilize the urban labor force. If nonfungible foreign food aid is used to support such efforts, the cost in terms of less growth and reduction of poverty in the future may be close to nil.

THE ROLE OF GOVERNMENT

The role of government is critical to an agriculture- and employment-oriented strategy. Because agriculture is a small-scale sector, there has to be substantial public-sector investment in the support for that sector in the form of, for example, transportation, power, communication, research, education, and input supply systems. Because these burdens are so heavy, government needs constantly to seek ways of transferring these activities to the private sector. Thus, activities such as marketing, which the private sector performs fairly well, should remain as much as possible in that sector. Input distribution should be moved into the private sector as quickly as the latter can take it up.

Since agricultural development is diffused over a wide geographic area, the infrastructure requirements are massive. And since the process is one of rural modernization, development of small- and medium-scale industry, and upgrading of consumption patterns, the needs for rural electrification and communications are critical. Thus, while a heavy-industry–oriented strategy requires large-scale, public-sector investment in major urban areas, a more rural-oriented strategy still requires considerable investment of this type of service market towns. This will sorely strain the capacity of government to raise capital resources; there will be a tension between the needs for private incentives and the need for public revenues. Governments will need to make tough budgetary choices that will allow scope for little beyond the investments in infrastructure, education, and technological change in agriculture that are the centerpieces of the strategy. The agriculture-employment strategy founders because governments do not recognize its large resource requirements and, therefore, the need to drop activities that may be appropriate only for alternative strategies. This explains why, for example, India and the Philippines have combined success in agriculture so inefficiently with employment growth, as compared with, for example, Taiwan or Thailand.

PRICE POLICY AND TECHNOLOGICAL CHANGE

As pointed out earlier, prices are indicators of, not solutions for, the problems of agricultural production and employment. The answer to the problem of agricultural production is technological change. When the latter has been inadequate, rising prices will indicate a problem and, one hopes, induce corrections. However, because the processes of technological change entail substantial lags between investment and results, prices are an extremely inefficient way to send signals. It is much better to analyze the need, as has been done here, and to act before the price changes indicate a problem. Of course, grossly overvalued exchange rates or other interventions may provide price relations unfavorable even to a technologically dynamic agriculture. However, such policies are probably an essential element of an alternative strategy and will change only as that whole strategy, particularly its capital allocations, changes.

A more serious price problem may arise from a highly dynamic agriculture. Technology may increase agricultural production in specific subregions much more rapidly than effective demand can be created in those regions, which in turn may be isolated by poor infrastructure. In such circumstances, it may be desirable for government to serve as buyer of last resort, build stocks, and transport basic agricultural staples to other regions. Governments must be very careful, however, not to spend massively on building stocks of food, as has been happening in India in recent years, instead of spending to accelerate technological change in agriculture and to provide the infrastructure that is so essential to increasing employment.

The role of agriculture as a stimulator of nonagricultural growth probably means that some of the benefits of lower costs of production in agriculture will be used to stimulate production in other sectors by a swing in the terms of trade in favor of the nonagricultural sector. Indeed, some market-induced depression of agricultural prices in response to lower costs seems an inevitable part of the process.[33]

FOREIGN ASSISTANCE

The critical role of foreign trade in supporting an agriculture-employment–based strategy of development requires that the industrial countries keep their markets open for relatively labor-intensive goods and services from developing countries—so that those countries will have the foreign exchange for purchasing the capital-intensive goods and services they need for a high-employment strategy.

In initiating the strategy, foreign aid has a tremendously important role to play in accelerating the growth of education—particularly higher education, which is so essential to the agriculture- and employment-based growth strategy. Vast numbers of trained people are critical to developing and running agricultural research systems, extension systems, and input supply systems. The details of public policy for an agriculture-employment strategy require constant development and analysis of data, and fine adjustments, which in turn require trained people. Decades of effort can be saved by major commitments of developed countries to expand education through foreign training and technical assistance.

It should also be noted that, although Japan and Taiwan moved into technological change in agriculture after they had already built a very substantial infrastructure in irrigation and transport systems, present-day developing countries may have to make these investments concurrently. Foreign assistance can help with these heavy investments.

Foreign assistance also can contribute to financing imports of capital-intensive goods and services during the early stages of the strategy, when exports may still lag; and food aid can help provide infrastructure, facilitating a stable political environment through food for work and food subsidies.

Foreign assistance may have a powerful role to play in aiding the transition from an inappropriate capital-oriented strategy or an import-displacement one into the more appropriate agriculture- and employment-based strategy. There will be substantial equity problems in the transition. Because the alternative strategies are so inequitable in the short run, they are usually accompanied by food subsidies and other elements to redress the inequities. Foreign assistance can help with the sorting out of these matters, but it must take care to do so in a way that facilitates a genuine transition to the new strategy instead of delaying it.

Today, Africa faces special problems substantially because of unusually inappropriate national and foreign assistance strategies applied in the 1970s. African countries are particularly short of the trained personnel for an agriculture- and employment-oriented strategy of development. They have traditionally had some of the worst infrastructure situations of any of the developing countries, and they suffer from a high degree of instability in principal export commodities. Comparatively massive foreign assistance is needed in the realms of training, investment in infrastructure, and stabilization of export earnings.

Looking Ahead

In most Asian countries, the Green Revolution has demonstrated both the potential and the basic requisites of accelerated growth in agriculture. Unfortunately, the role of investment in rural infrastructure has been inadequately understood, slowing the selective spread of technology to new areas to maintain high growth rates. Similarly, the dynamics of agricultural growth, calling for gradual diversification beyond initially dominant cereals, has not been sufficiently understood to favor continued expansion of research capacities and the dynamic development of complex marketing systems for perishables. Far more important, however, has been the very laggard response of employment growth in countries such as India and the Philippines compared with that in Taiwan and Thailand. The employment record in India and the Philippines, both of which have done moderately well in agriculture, is puzzling. The answer probably lies with a strong import displacement and a capital-intensive development strategy that has left both economies poorly structured to benefit from accelerated growth in agriculture. That problem requires considerable attention. Major past, inappropriate investments may have to be written off and a new start made.

In Africa, the situation is at once conceptually simpler and in practice more difficult. The basic act of moving the agricultural sector has not yet been put together. Training, national institution building, and giving development priority to the needs of the most responsive regions and commodities must be pursued vigorously. A complete reorientation of foreign assistance as well as of national policies is needed.[34] Given the gross inadequacies of trained personnel, institutions, and rural infrastructure, the task will be difficult and lengthy. Obviously, complex political compromises will be needed, but an urgent effort must be mobilized if measurable progress is to be made.

Once an economy gets moving, the nonagricultural sectors will rapidly increase in relative importance and take on a life of their own. Institutions must be developed to foster technological improvement in those activities. As the economy diversifies, so must the capacity to support and foster that diversification. The demands for trained personnel and institutional capacity will burgeon. But these longer-term needs must not be allowed to diminish the here-and-now priorities for agriculture and employment growth upon which the economy's postagricultural prospects so largely depend. Africa, in particular, has suffered from such a lack of priority on the part of national policies and donor-country assistance alike.

NOTES

1. For calculations of a high potential, see John W. Mellor, *The New Economics of Growth: A Strategy for India and the Developing World* (Ithaca: Cornell University Press, 1976).

2. See, for example, C. H. Hanumantha Rao, *Technological Change and Distribution of Gains in Indian Agriculture* (Delhi: Macmillan Company of India, 1975).

3. Uma Lele and John W. Mellor, "Technological Change, Distributive Bias and Labor Transfer in a Two Sector Economy," *Oxford Economic Papers,* vol. 33, no. 3 (November 1981): 426–41.

4. Paul N. Rosenstein-Rodan, "Problems of Industrialization of Eastern and South-Eastern Europe," *Economic Journal* 53 (June–September, 1943).

5. P. C. Mahalanobis, "Some Observations on the Process of Growth of National Income," *Sankhya* (Calcutta: September 1953): 307–12; and Anthony M. Tang and Bruce Stone, *Food Production in the Peoples Republic of China* (Washington, D.C.: International Food Policy Research Institute, Research Report no. 15, 1980).

6. A review of these concepts in the context of agricultural growth is found in John W. Mellor, "Models of Economic Growth and Land-Augmenting Technological Change in Foodgrain Production," in *Agricultural Policy in Developing Countries,* ed. Nural Islam (London: Macmillan, 1974), 3–30.

7. Amartya K. Sen, *Choices of Technique: An Aspect of the Theory of Planned Development* (New York: Augustus M. Kelly, 1968).

8. Raul Prebisch, *The Economic Development of Latin America and Its Principal Problems* (New York: United Nations Economic Commission for Latin America, 1950).

9. For this view, see Keith Griffith, *The Political Economy of Agrarian Change* (London: Macmillan, 1979); and for the contrary evidence, see John W. Mellor and Gunvant M. Desai, eds., *Agricultural Change and Rural Poverty: Variations on a Theme by Dharm Narain* (Baltimore: Johns Hopkins University Press, 1985).

10. Uma Lele, *The Design of Rural Development: Lessons from Africa* (Baltimore: Johns Hopkins University Press, 1975, 1979).

11. Bela Balassa, "The Policy Experience of Twelve Less Developed Countries, 1973–1979," in *Comparative Development Perspectives,* ed. Gustav Ranis. (Boulder, Colo.: Westview Press, 1984).

12. Nicholas Kaldor, *Essays on Economic Growth and Stability* (London: Duckworth, 1960), p. 242.

13. T. W. Schultz, *Transforming Traditional Agriculture* (New Haven: Yale University Press, 1964).

14. John W. Mellor and Robert W. Herdt, "The Contrasting Response of Rice to Nitrogen: India and the United States," *Journal of Farm Economics* 46, no. 1 (February 1964): 150–60.

15. Bruce F. Johnston and John W. Mellor, "The Role of Agriculture in Economic Development," *American Economic Review* 51, no. 4 (September 1961): 566–93.

16. W. Arthur Lewis, "Economic Development with Unlimited Supplies," *The Manchester School,* vol. 2 (May 1954).

17. Johnston and Mellor, "The Role of Agriculture in Economic Development"; and John W. Mellor, *The Economics of Agricultural Development* (Ithaca: Cornell University Press, 1966).

18. Kazushi Ohkawa, *Differential Structure and Agriculture: Essays on Dualistic Growth* (Tokyo: Institute of Economic Research, Hitotsubashi University, 1972); Bruce F. Johnston, "Agricultural Productivity and Economic Development in Japan," *Journal of Political Economy* 59 (December 1951): 498–513; Shigeru Ishikawa, *Conditions for Agricultural Development in Developing Asian Countries* (Tokyo: Committee for the Translation of Economic Studies, 1964).

19. T. H. Lee, *Intersectoral Capital Flows in the Economic Development of Taiwan, 1895–1960* (Ithaca: Cornell University Press, 1971).

20. John W. Mellor and Uma Lele, "Growth Linkages of the New Foodgrain Technologies," *Indian Journal of Agricultural Economics* 28, no. 1 (January–March 1973): 35–55.

21. Bruce F. Johnston and Peter Kilby, *Agriculture and Structural Transformation: Economic Strategies in Late-Developing Countries* (New York: Oxford University Press, 1975).

22. John W. Mellor, *The Economics of Agricultural Development* (Ithaca: Cornell University Press, 1966).

23. Lele and Mellor, "Technological Change," 426–41.

24. Ibid.

25. Gustav Ranis and John C. H. Fei, "A Theory of Economic Development," *American Economic Review* 51, no. 4 (September 1961): 533–46.

26. Kenneth L. Bachman and Leonardo Paulino, *Rapid Food Production, Growth in Selected De-*

veloping Countries: A Comparative Analysis of Underlying Trends, 1961–76, IFPRI Research Report no. 11 (Washington, D.C.: International Food Policy Research Institute, 1979).

27. For a careful example of a difficult genre, see Robert Herdt, "A Disaggregate Approach to Aggregate Supply," *American Journal of Agricultural Economics* 52, no. 4 (November 1970): 512–20.

28. Albert O. Hirschman, *The Strategy of Economic Development* (New Haven: Yale University Press, 1958).

29. Mancur Olson, *The Rise and Decline of Nations: Economic Growth, Stagflation and Social Rigidities* (New Haven: Yale University Press, 1984).

30. John Hicks, *Economic Perspectives: Further Essays on Money and Growth* (Oxford: Clarendon Press, 1977).

31. See Mellor, "New Economics of Growth," for data on potential job losses in India due to increasing capital intensity.

32. Kou-shu Liang and T. H. Lee, "Process and Pattern of Economic Development," mimeograph (Taipei, Taiwan: Joint Committee on Rural Reconstruction, 1972).

33. Lele and Mellor, "Technological Change," 426–41.

34. John W. Mellor, Christopher Delgado, and Malcolm J. Blackie, eds., *Accelerating Food Production Growth in Sub-Saharan Africa* (Baltimore: Johns Hopkins University Press, 1987).

9

Models of Agricultural Development

VERNON W. RUTTAN

Prior to this century, almost all increase in food production was obtained by bringing new land into production. There were only a few exceptions to this generalization—in limited areas of East Asia, in the Middle East, and in Western Europe. By the end of this century almost all of the increase in world food production must come from higher yields—from increased output per hectare. In most of the world the transition from a resource-based to a science-based system of agriculture is occurring within a single century. In a few countries this transition began in the nineteenth century. In most of the presently developed countries it did not begin until the first half of this century. Most of the countries of the developing world have been caught up in the transition only since mid-century. The technology associated with this transition, particularly the new seed-fertilizer technology, has been referred to as the "Green Revolution."

During the remaining years of the twentieth century, it is imperative that the poor countries design and implement more effective agricultural development strategies than in the past. A useful first step in this effort is to review the approaches to agricultural development that have been employed in the past and will remain part of our intellectual equipment. The literature on agricultural development can be characterized according to the following models: (1) the frontier, (2) the conservation, (3) the urban-industrial impact, (4) the diffusion, (5) the high-payoff input, and (6) the induced innovation.

FRONTIER MODEL

Throughout most of history, expansion of the area cultivated or grazed has represented the dominant source of increase in agricultural production. The most

VERNON W. RUTTAN is Regents Professor in the Department of Applied Economics, University of Minnesota.

Originally titled "How the World Feeds Itself." Published by permission of Transaction Publishers, from *Society* 17, no 6. Copyright © 1980 by Transaction Publishers. Published with omissions and minor editorial revisions and with the permission of the author.

dramatic example in Western history was the opening up of the new continents—North and South America and Australia—to European settlement during the eighteenth and nineteenth centuries. With the advent of cheap transport during the latter half of the nineteenth century, the countries of the new continents became increasingly important sources of food and agricultural raw materials for the metropolitan countries of Western Europe.

Similar processes had occurred earlier, though at a less dramatic pace, in the peasant and village economies of Europe, Asia, and Africa. The first millennium A.D. saw the agricultural colonization of Europe north of the Alps, the Chinese settlement of the lands south of the Yangtze, and the Bantu occupation of Africa south of the tropical forest belts. Intensification of land use in existing villages was followed by pioneer settlement, the establishment of new villages, and the opening up of forest or jungle land to cultivation. In Western Europe there was a series of successive changes from neolithic forest fallow to systems of shifting cultivation of bush and grass land followed first by short fallow systems and later by annual cropping.

Where soil conditions were favorable, as in the great river basins and plains, the new villages gradually intensified their system of cultivation. Where soil resources were poor, as in many of the hill and upland regions, new areas were opened up to shifting cultivation or nomadic grazing. Under conditions of rapid population growth, the limits to the frontier model were often quickly realized. Crop yields were typically low—measured in terms of output per unit of seed rather than per unit of crop area. Output per hectare and per man-hour tended to decline—except in delta areas, such as Egypt and South Asia, and the wet rice areas of East Asia. In many areas the result was increasing immiserization of the peasantry.

There are relatively few remaining areas of the world where development along the lines of the frontier model will represent an efficient source of growth during the last two decades of the twentieth century. The 1960s saw the "closing of the frontier" in most areas of Southeast Asia. In Latin America and Africa the opening up of new lands awaits development of technologies for the control of pests and diseases (such as the tsetse fly in Africa) or for the release and maintenance of productivity of problem soils.

CONSERVATION MODEL

The conservation model of agricultural development evolved from the advances in crop and livestock husbandry associated with the English agricultural revolution and the notions of soil exhaustion suggested by the early German chemists and soil scientists. It was reinforced by the application to land of the concept, developed in the English classical school of economics, of diminishing returns to labor and capital. The conservation model emphasized the evolution of a sequence of increasingly complex land- and labor-intensive cropping systems, the production and use of organic manures, and labor-intensive capital formation in the form of drainage, irrigation, and other physical facilities to more effectively utilize land and water resources.

Until well into the twentieth century the conservation model of agricultural development was the only approach to intensification of agricultural production available to most of the world's farmers. Its application is effectively illustrated by development of the wet-rice culture systems that emerged in East and Southeast Asia and by the labor- and land-intensive systems of integrated crop-livestock husbandry which increasingly characterized European agriculture during the eighteenth and nineteenth centuries.

During the English agricultural revolution more intensive crop-rotation systems replaced the open-three-field system in which arable land was allocated between permanent crop land and permanent pasture. This involved the introduction and more intensive use of new forage and green manure crops and an increase in the availability and use of animal manures. This "new husbandry" permitted the intensification of crop-livestock production through the recycling of plant nutrients, in the form of animal manures, to maintain soil fertility. The inputs used in this conservation system of farming—the plant nutrients, animal power, land improvements, physical capital, and agricultural labor force—were largely produced or supplied by the agricultural sector itself.

Agricultural development, within the framework of the conservation model, clearly was capable in many parts of the world of sustaining rates of growth in agricultural production in the range of 1.0 percent per year over relatively long periods of time. The most serious recent effort to develop agriculture within this framework was made by the People's Republic of China in the late 1950s and early 1960s. It became readily apparent, however, that the feasible growth rates, even with a rigorous recycling effort, were not compatible with modern rates of growth in the demand for agricultural output—which typically fall in the 3–5 percent range in the less developed countries (LDCs). The conservation model remains an important source of productivity growth in most poor countries and an inspiration to agrarian fundamentalists and the organic farming movement in the developed countries.

URBAN-INDUSTRIAL IMPACT MODEL

In the conservation model, locational variations in agricultural development are related primarily to differences in environmental factors. It stands in sharp contrast to models that interpret geographic differences in the level and rate of economic development primarily in terms of the level and rate of urban-industrial development.

Initially, the urban-industrial impact model was formulated in Germany by J. H. von Thunen to explain geographic variations in the intensity of farming systems and the productivity of labor in an industrializing society. In the United States it was extended to explain the more effective performance of the input and product markets linking the agricultural and nonagricultural sectors in regions characterized by rapid urban-industrial development than in regions where the urban economy had not made a transition to the industrial stage. In the 1950s, interest in the urban-industrial impact model reflected concern with the failure of agricultural resource development and price policies, adopted in the 1930s, to remove the persistent regional disparities in agricultural productivity and rural incomes in the United States.

The rationale for this model was developed in terms of more effective input and product markets in areas of rapid urban-industrial development. Industrial development stimulated agricultural development by expanding the demand for farm products, supplying the industrial inputs needed to improve agricultural productivity, and drawing away surplus labor from agriculture. The empirical tests of the urban-industrial impact model have repeatedly confirmed that a strong nonfarm labor market is an essential prerequisite for labor productivity in agriculture and improved incomes for rural people.

The policy implications of the urban-industrial impact model appear to be most relevant for less developed regions of highly industrialized countries or lagging regions of the more rapidly growing LDCs. Agricultural development policies based on this model appear to be particularly inappropriate in those countries where the "pathological" growth of urban centers is a result of population pressures in rural areas running ahead of employment growth in urban areas.

DIFFUSION MODEL

The diffusion of better husbandry practices was a major source of productivity growth even in premodern societies. The diffusion of crops and animals from the new world to the old—potatoes, maize, cassava, rubber—and from the old world to the new—sugar, wheat, and domestic livestock—was an important by-product of the voyages of discovery and trade from the fifteenth to the nineteenth centuries. The diffusion approach rests on the empirical observation of substantial differences in land and labor productivity among farmers and regions. The route to agricultural development, in this view, is through more effective dissemination of technical knowledge and a narrowing of the productivity differences among farmers and among regions.

The diffusion model has provided the major intellectual foundation of much of the research and extension effort in farm management and production economics since the emergence, in the latter years of the nineteenth century, of agricultural economics and rural sociology as separate subdisciplines linking the agricultural and the social sciences. Developments leading to establishment of active programs of farm management research and extension occurred at a time when experiment station research was making only a modest contribution to agricultural productivity growth. A further contribution to the effective diffusion of known technology was provided by rural sociologists' research on the diffusion process. Models were developed emphasizing the relationship between diffusion rates and the personality characteristics and educational accomplishments of farm operators.

Insights into the dynamics of the diffusion process, when coupled with the observation of wide agricultural productivity gaps among developed and less developed countries and a presumption of inefficient resource allocation among ''irrational tradition-bound'' peasants, produced an extension or diffusion bias in the choice of agricultural development strategy in many LDCs during the 1950s. During the 1960s the limitations of the diffusion model as a foundation for the design of agricultural development policies became increasingly apparent as technical assistance and rural development programs, based explicitly or implicitly on this model, failed to generate either rapid modernization of traditional farms and communities or rapid growth in agricultural output.

HIGH-PAYOFF INPUT MODEL

The inadequacy of policies based on the conservation, urban-industrial impact, and diffusion models led, in the 1960s, to a new perspective—the key to transforming a traditional agricultural sector into a productive source of economic growth was investment designed to make modern, high-payoff inputs available to farmers in poor countries. Peasants in traditional agricultural systems were viewed as rational, efficient resource allocators. This iconoclastic view was developed most vigorously by T. W. Schultz in his controversial book *Transforming Traditional Agriculture.* He insisted that peasants in traditional societies remained poor because, in most poor countries, there were only limited technical and economic opportunities to which they could respond. The new, high-payoff inputs were classified according to three categories: (1) the capacity of public and private sector research institutions to produce new technical knowledge; (2) the capacity of the industrial sector to develop, produce, and market new technical inputs; and (3) the capacity of farmers to acquire new knowledge and use new inputs effectively.

The enthusiasm with which the high-payoff input model has been accepted and translated into economic doctrine has been due in part to the proliferation of studies reporting high rates of return to public investment in agricultural research. It was also due to the success of efforts to develop new, high-productivity grain varieties suitable for the tropics. New high-yielding wheat varieties were developed in Mexico beginning in the 1950s, and new high-yielding rice varieties were developed in the Philippines in the 1960s. These varieties were highly responsive to industrial inputs, such as fertilizer and other chemicals, and to more effective soil and water management. The high returns associated with the adoption of the new varieties and the associated technical inputs and management practices have led to rapid diffusion of the new varieties among farmers in a number of countries in Asia, Africa, and Latin America.

INDUCED INNOVATION MODEL

The high-payoff input model remains incomplete as a theory of agricultural development. Typically, education and research are public goods not traded through the marketplace. The mechanism by which resources are allocated among education, research, and other public and private sector economic activities was not fully incorporated into the model. It does not explain how economic conditions induce the development and adoption of an efficient set of technologies for a particular society. Nor does it attempt to specify the processes by which input and product price relationships induce investment in research in a direction consistent with a nation's particular resource endowments.

These limitations in the high-payoff input model led to efforts by Yujiro Hayami and myself to develop a model of agricultural development in which technical change is treated as endogenous to the development process, rather than as an exogenous factor operating independently of other development processes. The induced innovation perspective was stimulated by historical evidence that different countries had followed alternative paths of technical change in the process of agricultural development.[1]

Technical Innovation

The levels achieved in each productivity grouping by farmers in the most advanced countries can be viewed as arranged along a productivity frontier. This frontier reflects the level of technical progress achieved by the most advanced countries in each resource endowment classification. These productivity levels are not immediately available to farmers in most low-productivity countries. They can only be made available by undertaking investment in the agricultural research capacity needed to develop technologies appropriate to the countries' natural and institutional environments and investment in the physical and institutional infrastructure needed to realize the new production potential opened up by technological advances.

There is clear historical evidence that technology has been developed to facilitate the substitution of relatively abundant (hence cheap) factors for relatively scarce (hence expensive) factors of production. The constraints imposed on agricultural development by an inelastic supply of land have, in economies such as Japan and Taiwan, been offset by the development of high-yielding crop varieties designed to facilitate the substitution of fertilizer for land. The constraints imposed by an inelastic supply of labor, in countries such as the United States, Canada, and Australia, have been offset by technical advances leading to the substitution of animal and mechanical power for manpower. In some cases the new technologies—embodied in new crop varieties, new equipment, or new production practices—may not always be substitutes per se for land or labor. Rather, they are catalysts which facilitate the substitution of relatively abundant factors (such as fertilizer or mineral fuels) for relatively scarce factors.

INSTITUTIONAL INNOVATION

A developing country which fails to evolve a capacity for technical and institutional innovation in agriculture consistent with its resource and cultural endowments suffers two major constraints on its development of productive agriculture. It is unable to take advantage of advances in biological and chemical technologies suited to labor-intensive agricultural systems. And the mechanical technology it does import from more developed countries will be productive only under conditions of large-scale agricultural organization. It will contribute to the emergence of a "bimodal" rather than a "unimodal" organization structure.

During the last two decades a number of developing countries have begun to establish the institutional capacity to generate technical changes adapted to national and regional resource endowments. More recently these emerging national systems have been buttressed by a new system of international crop and animal research institutes. These new institutes have become both important sources of new knowledge and technology and increasingly effective communication links among the developing national research systems.

The lag in shifting from a natural-resource-based to a science-based system of agriculture continues to be a source of national differences in land and labor productivity. Lags in the development and application of knowledge are also important sources of regional productivity differences within countries. In countries such as Mexico and India differential rates of technical change have been an important source of the widening disparities in the rate of growth of total agricultural output, in labor and land productivity, and in incomes and wage rates among regions.

Productivity differences in agriculture are increasingly a function of investments in scientific and industrial capacity and in the education of rural people rather than of natural resource endowments. The effects of education on productivity are particularly important during periods in which a nation's agricultural research system begins to introduce new technology. In an agricultural system characterized by static technology there are few gains to be realized from education in rural areas. Rural people who have lived for generations with essentially the same resources and the same technology have learned from long experience what their efforts can get out of the resources available to them. Children acquire from their parents the skills that are worthwhile. Formal schooling has little economic value in agricultural production.

As soon as new technical opportunities become available, this situation changes. Technical change requires the acquisition of new husbandry skills; acquisition from nontraditional sources of additional resources such as new seeds, new chemicals, and new equipment; and development of new skills in dealing with both natural resources and input and product market institutions linking agriculture with the nonagricultural sector.

The processes by which new knowledge can be applied to alter the rate and direction of technical change in agriculture, are, however, substantially greater than our knowledge of the processes by which resources are brought to bear on the process of institutional innovation and transfer. Yet the need for viable institutions capable of supporting more rapid agricultural growth and rural development is even more compelling today than a decade ago.

NOTE

1. For more details on the induced innovation model see chapter 10.—ED.

10

Induced Innovation Model of Agricultural Development

VERNON W. RUTTAN AND YUJIRO HAYAMI

During the 1960s a new consensus emerged to the effect that agricultural growth is critical (if not a precondition) for industrialization and general economic growth. Nevertheless, the process of agricultural growth itself has remained outside the concern of most development economists. Both technical change and institutional evolution have been treated as exogenous to their systems.

In this paper we elaborate the concept of induced technical and institutional innovation which we have employed in our own research on the agricultural development process, and we discuss the implications of the induced innovation perspective for the design of national and regional strategies for agricultural development.

AN INDUCED DEVELOPMENT MODEL

An attempt to develop a model of agricultural development in which technical change is treated as endogenous to the development process, rather than as an exogenous factor that operates independently of other development processes, must start with the recognition that there are multiple paths of technological development.

ALTERNATIVE PATHS OF TECHNOLOGICAL DEVELOPMENT

There is clear evidence that technology can be developed to facilitate the substitution of relatively abundant (hence cheap) factors for relatively scarce (hence expensive) factors in the economy. The constraints imposed on agri-

VERNON W. RUTTAN is Regents Professor in the Department of Applied Economics, University of Minnesota. YUJIRO HAYAMI is professor of economics, Aoyama Gakuin University, Tokyo.

Originally titled "Strategies for Agricultural Development." Reprinted from *Food Research Institute Studies in Agricultural Economics, Trade and Development* 9, no. 2 (1972): 129–48, with omissions and minor editorial revisions, by permission of the Food Research Institute, Stanford University, and the authors.

cultural development by an inelastic supply of land have, in economies such as those of Japan and Taiwan, been offset by the development of high-yielding crop varieties designed to facilitate the substitution of fertilizer for land. The constraints imposed by an inelastic supply of labor, in countries such as the United States, Canada, and Australia, have been offset by technical advances leading to the substitution of animal and mechanical power for labor. In both cases the new technology, embodied in new crop varieties, new equipment, or new production practices, may not always be a substitute by itself for land or labor; rather it may serve as a catalyst to facilitate the substitution of the relatively abundant factors (such as fertilizer or mineral fuels) for the relatively scarce factors. It seems reasonable, following Hicks, to call techniques designed to facilitate the substitution of other inputs for labor "labor-saving" and those designed to facilitate the substitution of other inputs for land "land-saving." In agriculture, two kinds of technology generally correspond to this taxonomy: mechanical technology to "labor-saving" and biological and chemical technology to "land-saving."[1] The former is designed to facilitate the substitution of power and machinery for labor. Typically this involves the substitution of land for labor, because higher output per worker through mechanization usually requires a larger land area cultivated per worker. The latter, which we will hereafter identify as biological technology, is designed to facilitate the substitution of labor and/or industrial inputs for land. This may occur through increased recycling of soil fertility by more labor-intensive conservation systems; through use of chemical fertilizers; and through husbandry practices, management systems, and inputs (that is, insecticides) which permit an optimum yield response.

Historically there has been a close association between advances in output per unit of land area and advances in biological technology and between advances in output per worker and advances in mechanical technology. The construction of an induced development model involves an explanation of the mechanism by which a society chooses an optimum path of technological change in agriculture.

INDUCED INNOVATION IN THE PRIVATE SECTOR

There is a substantial body of literature on the "theory of induced innovation."[2] Much of this literature focuses on the choice of available technology by the individual firm. There is also a substantial body of literature on how changes in factor prices over time or differences in factor prices among countries influence the nature of invention. This discussion has been conducted entirely within the framework of the theory of the firm. A major controversy has centered around the issue of the existence of a mechanism by which changes or differences in factor prices affect the inventive activity or the innovative behavior of firms.

It had generally been accepted, at least since the publication of *The Theory of Wages* by J. R. Hicks (1932, 124–25), that changes or differences in the relative prices of factors of production could influence the direction of invention or innovation.[3] There have also been arguments raised by W. E. G. Salter (1960, 43–44) and others (Ahmad 1966; Fellner 1961; Kennedy 1964; Samuelson 1965) against Hicks's theory of induced innovation. The arguments run somewhat as follows: firms are motivated to save total cost for a given output; at competitive equilibrium, each factor is being paid its marginal value product; therefore, all factors are equally expensive to firms; hence, there is no incentive for competitive firms to search for techniques to save a particular factor.

The difference between our perspective and Salter's is partly due to a difference in the definition of the production function. Salter defined the production function to embrace all possible designs conceivable by existing scientific knowledge and called the choice among these designs "factor substitution" instead of "technical change" (1960, 14–16). Salter admits, however, that "relative factor prices are in the nature of signposts representing broad influences that determine the way technological knowledge is applied to production" (ibid., 16). If we accept Salter's definition, the allocation of resources to the development of high-yielding and fertilizer-responsive rice varieties adaptable to the ecological conditions of South and Southeast Asia, which are comparable to the improved varieties developed earlier in Japan and Taiwan, cannot be considered as a technical change. Rather, it is viewed as an application of existing technological knowledge (breeding techniques, plant-type concepts, and so on) to production.

Although we do not deny the case for Salter's definition, it is clearly not very useful in attempting to understand the process by which new technical alternatives become available. We regard technical change as any change in production coefficients resulting from purposeful resource-using activity directed to the development of new knowledge embodied in designs, materials, or organizations. In terms of this definition, it is entirely rational for competitive firms to allocate funds to develop a technology that facilitates the substitution of increasingly less expensive factors for more expensive factors. Using the above definition, Syed Ahmad (1960) has shown that the Hicksian theory of market-induced innovation can be defended with a rather reasonable assumption on the possibility of alternative innovations.[4]

We illustrate Ahmad's argument with the aid of figure 1. Suppose that at a point in time a firm is operating at a competitive equilibrium, A or B, depending on the prevailing factor-price ratio, p or m, for an isoquant, u_0, producing a given output; and this firm perceives multiple alternative innovations represented by isoquants, u_1, u_1', . . . , producing the same output in such a way as to be enveloped by U, a concave innovation possibility curve or meta-production function which can be developed by the same amount of research expenditure. In order to minimize total cost for given output and given research expenditure, innovative efforts of this firm will be directed towards developing Y-saving technology (u_1) or X-saving technology (u_1'), depending on the prevailing factor-price ratio, p (parallel to PP) or m (parallel to MM and MM'). If a firm facing a price ratio m develops an X-saving technology (u_1'), it can obtain an additional

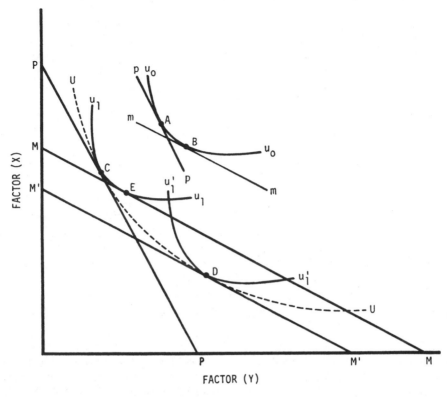

FACTOR (Y)

Fig.1. Factor Prices and Induced Technical Change

gain represented by the distance between M and M' compared with the case that develops a Y-saving technology (u_1). In this framework it is clear that if X becomes more expensive relative to Y over time, in any economy the innovative efforts of entrepreneurs will be directed towards developing a more X-saving and Y-using technology compared with the contrary case. Also, in a country in which X is more expensive relative to Y than in another country, innovative efforts in the country will be more directed towards X-saving and Y-using than in the other country. In this formulation the expectation of relative price change, which is central to William Fellner's theory of induced innovation, is not necessary, although expectations may work as a powerful reinforcing agent in directing technical effort.[5]

The role of changing relative factor prices in inducing a continuous sequence of non-neutral biological and mechanical innovations along the iso-product surface of a meta-production function is further illustrated in figure 2. U represents the land-labor isoquant of the meta-production function, which is the envelope of less elastic isoquants such as u_0 and u_1, corresponding to different types of

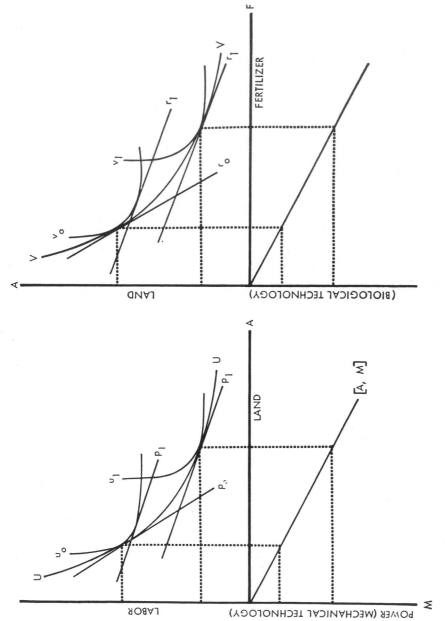

Fig.2. Factor Prices and Induced Mechanical and Biological Innovation

machinery or technology. A certain technology represented by u_0 (for example, a reaper) is created when a price ratio, p_0, prevails a certain length of time. When the price ratio changes from p_0 to p_1, another technology, represented by u_1 (for example, a combine), is induced in the long run, which gives the minimum cost of production for p_1.

The new technology represented by u_1, which enables enlargement of the area operated per worker, generally corresponds to higher intensity of power per worker. This implies the complementary relationship between land and power, which may be drawn as a line representing a certain combination of land and power, $[A, M]$. In this simplified presentation, mechanical innovation is conceived as the substitution of a combination of land and power, $[A, M]$, for labor (L) in response to a change in wage relative to an index of labor and machinery prices, although, of course, in actual practice land and power are substitutable to some extent.

In the same context, the relation between the fertilizer-land price ratio and biological innovations represented by the development of crop varieties that are more responsive to application of fertilizers is illustrated in figure 2. V represents the land-fertilizer isoquant of the meta-production function, which is the envelope of less elastic isoquants such as v_0 and v_1, corresponding to varieties of different fertilizer responsiveness. A decline in the price of fertilizer relative to the price of land from r_0 to r_1 creates an incentive for farmers to adopt crop varieties described by isoquants to the right of v_0 and for private seed companies and public research institutions to develop and market such new fertilizer-responsive varieties.

INDUCED INNOVATION IN THE PUBLIC SECTOR

Innovative behavior in the public sector has largely been ignored in the literature on induced innovation. There is no theory of induced innovation in the public sector.[6] This is a particularly critical limitation in attempting to understand the process of scientific and technical innovation in agricultural development. In most countries that have been successful in achieving rapid rates of technical progress in agriculture, "socialization" of agricultural research has been deliberately employed as an instrument of modernization in agriculture.

Our view of the mechanism of "induced innovation" in the public sector agricultural research is similar to the Hicksian theory of induced innovation in the private sector. A major extension of the traditional argument is that we base the innovation inducement mechanism not only on the response to changes in the market prices of profit maximizing firms but also on the response of research scientists and administrators in public institutions to resource endowments and economic change.

We hypothesize that technical change is guided along an efficient path by price signals in the market, provided that the prices efficiently reflect changes in the demand and supply of products and factors and that there exists effective interaction among farmers, public research institutions, and private agricultural supply firms. If the demand for agricultural products increases, due to the growth in population and income, prices of the inputs for which the supply is inelastic will be raised relative to the prices of inputs for which the supply is elastic. Likewise, if the supply of particular inputs shifts to the right faster than that of others, the prices of these inputs will decline relative to the prices of other factors of production.

In consequence, technical innovations that save the factors characterized by an inelastic supply, or by slower shifts in supply, become relatively more profitable for agricultural producers. Farmers are induced by shifts in relative prices to search for technical alternatives that save the increasingly scarce factors of production. They press the public research institutions to develop the new technology and demand that agricultural supply firms supply modern technical inputs that substitute for the more scarce factors. Perceptive scientists and science administrators respond by making available new technical possibilities and new inputs that enable farmers profitably to substitute the increasingly abundant factors for increasingly scarce factors, thereby guiding the demand of farmers for unit cost reduction in a socially optimum direction.

The dialectic interaction among farmers and research scientists and administrators is likely to be most effective when farmers are organized into politically effective local and regional farm "bureaus" or farmers' associations. The response of the public sector research and extension programs to farmers' demand is likely to be greatest when the agricultural research system is highly decentralized, as in the United States. In the United States, for example, each of the state agricultural experiment stations has tended to view its function, at least in part, as to maintain the competitive position of agriculture in its state relative to agriculture in other states. Similarly, national policy makers may regard investment in agricultural research as an investment designed to maintain the country's competitive position in world markets or to improve the economic viability of the agricultural sector producing import substitutes. Given effective farmer organizations and a mission- or client-oriented experiment station system, the competitive model of firm behavior illustrated in figures 1 and 2 can be usefully extended to explain the response of experiment station administrators and research scientists to economic opportunities.

In this public-sector-induced innovation model, the response of research scientists and administrators represents the critical link in the inducement mechanism. The model does not imply that it is necessary for individual scientists or research administrators in public institutions to respond consciously to market prices, or directly to farmers' demands for research results, in the selection of research objectives. They may, in fact, be motivated primarily by a drive for professional achievement and recognition (Niskanen 1968). Or they may, in the Rosenberg terminology, view themselves as responding to an "obvious and compelling need" to remove the constraints on growth of production or on factor supplies.[7] It is only necessary that there exist an effective incentive mechanism to reward the scientists or administrators, materially or by prestige, for their contributions to the solution of significant problems in the society.[8] Under these conditions, it seems reasonable to hypothesize that the scientists and administrators of public sector research programs do respond to the needs of society in an attempt to direct the results of their activity to public purpose. Furthermore, we hypothesize that secular changes in relative factor and product prices convey much of the information regarding the relative priorities that society places on the goals of research.

The response in the public research sector is not limited to the field of applied science. Scientists trying to solve practical problems often consult with or ask cooperation of those working in more basic fields. If the basic scientists respond to the requests of the applied researchers, they are in effect responding to the needs of society. It is not uncommon that major breakthroughs in basic science are created through the process of solving the problems raised by research workers in the more applied fields.[9] It appears reasonable, therefore, to hypothesize as a result of the interactions among the basic and applied sciences and the process by which public funds are allocated to research that basic research tends to be directed also towards easing the limitations on agricultural production imposed by relatively scarce factors.

We do not argue, however, that technical change in agriculture is wholly of an induced character. There is a supply (exogenous) dimension to the process as well as a demand (endogenous) dimension. Technical change in agriculture reflects, in addition to the effects of resource endowments and growth in demand, the progress of general science and technology. Progress in general science (or scientific innovation) that lowers the "cost" of technical and entrepreneurial innovations may have influences on technical change in agriculture unrelated to changes in factor proportions and product demand (Nelson 1959; Schmookler 1966). Similarly, advances in science and technology in the developed countries, in response to their own resource endowments, may result in a bias in the innovation possibility curves facing the developing countries. Even in these cases, the rate of adoption and the impact on productivity of autonomous or exogenous changes in technology will be strongly influenced by the conditions of resource supply and product demand, as these forces are reflected through factor and product markets.

Thus, the classical problem of resource allocation, which was rejected as an adequate basis for agricultural productivity and output growth in the high-payoff input model,[10] in this context is treated as central to the agricultural development process. Under conditions of static technology, improvements in resource allocation represent a weak source of economic growth. The efficient allocation of resources to open up new sources of growth is, however, essential to the agricultural development process.

INSTITUTIONAL INNOVATION

Extension of the theory of "induced innovation" to explain the behavior of public research institutions represents an essential link in the construction of a theory of induced development. In the induced development model, advances in mechanical and biological technology respond to changing relative prices of factors and to changes in the prices of factors relative to products to ease the constraints on growth imposed by inelastic supplies of land or labor. Neither this process nor its impact is confined to the agricultural sector. Changes in relative prices in any sector of the economy act to induce innovative activity, not only by private producers but also by scientists in public institutions, in order to reduce the constraints imposed by those factors of production that are relatively scarce.

We further hypothesize that the institutions that govern the use of technology or the "mode" of production can also be induced to change in order to enable both individuals and society to take fuller advantage of new technical opportunities under favorable market conditions.[11] The Second Enclosure Movement in England represents a classical illustration. The issuance of the Enclosure Bill facilitated the conversion of communal pasture and farmland into single, private farm units, thus encouraging the introduction of an integrated crop-livestock "new husbandry" system. The Enclosure Acts can be viewed as an institutional innovation designed to exploit the new technical opportunities opened up by innovations in crop rotation, utilizing the new fodder crops (turnip and clover), in response to the rising food prices.

A major source of institutional change has been an effort by society to internalize the benefits of innovative activity to provide economic incentives for productivity increase. In some cases, institutional innovations have involved the reorganization of property rights in order to internalize the higher income streams resulting from the innovations. The modernization of land tenure relationships, involving a shift from share tenure to lease tenure and owner-operator systems of cultivation in much of Western agriculture, can be explained, in part, as a shift in property rights designed to internalize the gains of entrepreneurial innovation by individual farmers.[12]

Where internalization of the gains of innovative activity are more difficult to achieve, institutional innovations involving public sector activity become essential. The socialization of much of agricultural research, particularly the research leading to advances in biological technology, represents an example of a public sector institutional innovation designed to realize for society the potential gains from advances in agricultural technology. This institutional innovation originated in Germany and was transplanted and applied on a larger scale in the United States and Japan.

Both Schultz (1968) and Kazushi Ohkawa (1969) have argued that institutional reform is appropriately viewed as a response to the new opportunities for the productive use of resources opened up by advances in technology.[13] Our view, and the view of Ohkawa and Schultz, reduces to the hypothesis that institutional innovations occur because it appears profitable for individuals or groups in society to undertake the costs. It is unlikely that institutional change will prove viable unless the benefits to society exceed the cost. Changes in market prices and technological opportunities introduce disequilibrium in existing institutional arrangements by creating profitable new opportunities for the institutional innovations.

Profitable opportunities, however, do not necessarily lead to immediate institutional innovations. Usually the gains and losses from technical and institutional change are not distributed neutrally. There are, typically, vested interests that stand to lose and that oppose change. There are limits on the extent to which group behavior can be mobilized to achieve common or group interests (Olson 1968). The process of transforming institutions in response to technical and economic opportunities generally involves time lags, social and political stress, and in some cases disruption of social and political order. Economic growth ultimately depends on the flexibility and efficiency of society in transforming itself in response to technical and economic opportunities.

AGRICULTURAL DEVELOPMENT STRATEGY

The induced innovation model outlined above does not possess formal elegance. It is partial in that it is primarily concerned with production and productivity. Yet it has added significantly to our power to interpret the process of agricultural development.

Research that we have reported elsewhere indicates that the enormous changes in factor proportions that have occurred in the process of agricultural growth in the United States and Japan are explainable very largely in terms of changes in factor-price ratios (Hayami and Ruttan 1970, 1971). When we relate the results of the statistical analysis to historical knowledge of advances in agricultural technology, we conclude that the observed changes in input mixes have occurred as the result of a process of dynamic factor substitution along a meta-production function, associated with changes in the production surface, induced primarily by changes in relative factor prices. Preliminary results of the analysis of historical patterns of technical change in German agriculture (by Adolph Weber); in Denmark, Great Britain, and France (by William Wade); and in Argentina (by Alain de Janvry) add additional support to the utility of the induced innovation model in interpreting historical patterns of technological change and agricultural development.

The question remains, however, as to whether the induced development model represents a useful guide to modern agricultural development strategy. In responding to this concern two issues seem particularly relevant.

First, we would like to make it perfectly clear that in our view the induced development model, in which technical change and institutional change are treated as endogenous to the development process, does not imply that agricultural development can be left to an "invisible hand" that directs either technology or the total development process along an "efficient" path determined by "original" resource endowments.

We do argue that the policies that a country adopts with respect to the allocation of resources to technical and institutional innovation, to the capacity to produce technical inputs for agriculture, to the linkages between the agricultural and industrial sectors in factor and product markets, and to the organization of the crop and livestock production sectors must be consistent with national (or regional) resource endowments if they are to lead to an "efficient" growth path. Conversely, failure to achieve such consistency can sharply increase the real costs, or abort the possibility, of achieving sustained economic growth in the agricultural sector.

If the induced development model is valid—if alternative paths of technical change and productivity growth are available to developing countries—the issue of how to organize and manage the development and allocation of scientific and technical resources becomes the single most critical factor in the agricultural development process. It is not sufficient simply to build new agricultural research stations. In many developing countries existing research facilities are not employed at full capacity because they are staffed with research workers with limited scientific and technical training; because of inadequate financial, logistical, and administrative support; because of isolation from the main currents of scientific and technical innovation; and because of failure to develop a research strategy that relates research activity to the potential economic value of the new knowledge it is designed to generate.

The appropriate allocation of effort between the public and private sectors also becomes of major significance in view of the extension of the induced development model to incorporate innovative activity in the public sector. It is clear that during the early stages of development the socialization of much of biological research in agriculture is essential if the potential gains from biological technology are to be realized. The potential gains from public sector investment in other areas of the institutional infrastructure characterized by substantial spillover effects are also large. One of the most important of these areas for public investment is the modernization of the marketing system through the establishment of the information and communication linkages necessary for the efficient functioning of factor and product markets.[14]

In most developing countries the market systems are relatively underdeveloped, both technically and institutionally. A major challenge facing these countries in their planning is the development of a well-articulated marketing system capable of accurately reflecting the effects of changes in supply, demand, and production relationships. An important element in the development of a more efficient marketing system is the removal of the rigidities and distortions resulting from government policy itself—including the maintenance of overvalued currencies, artificially low rates of interest, and unfavorable factor and product price policies for agriculture (Myint 1968).

The criteria specified above for public sector investment or intervention also imply a continuous reallocation of functions among public and private sector institutions. As institutions capable of internalizing a large share of the gains of innovative activity are developed, it may become possible to transfer activities— the production of new crop varieties, for example—to the private sector and to reallocate public resources to other high-payoff areas. Many governments are presently devoting substantial resources to areas of relatively low productivity— in efforts to reform the organization of credit and product markets, for example—while failing to invest the resources necessary to produce accurate and timely market information, establish meaningful market grades and standards, and establish the physical infrastructure necessary to induce technical and logistical efficiency in the performance of marketing functions (Ruttan 1969).

A second issue is whether, under modern conditions, the forces associated with the international transfer of agricultural technology are so dominant as to vitiate the induced development model as a guide to agricultural development strategy. It might be argued, for example, that the dominance of the developed countries in science and technology raises the cost of, or even precludes the possibility of the invention of, location-specific biological and mechanical technologies adapted to the resource endowments of a particular country or region.

This argument has been made primarily with reference to diffusion of mechanical technology from the developed to the developing countries. It is argued that the pattern of organization of agricultural production adopted by the more developed countries—dominated by large-scale mechanized systems of production in both the socialist and nonsocialist economies—precludes an effective role for an agricultural system based on small-scale commercial or semicommercial farm production units (Owen 1969, 1971).[15]

We find this argument unconvincing. Rapid diffusion of imported mechanical technology in areas characterized by small farms and low wages in agriculture tends to be induced by inefficient price, exchange rate, and credit policies which substantially distort the relative costs of mechanical power relative to labor and other material inputs. Nural Islam reports, for example, that as a result of such policies, the real cost of tractors in West Pakistan was substantially below the cost in the United States (1971). The preliminary findings of work by John Sanders in Latin America also stress the role of market distortions in inducing mechanization.

We are also impressed by the history of agricultural mechanization in Japan and more recently in Taiwan. Both countries have been relatively successful in following a strategy of mechanical innovation designed to adapt the size of the tractor and other farm machinery rather than to modify the size of the agricultural production unit to make it compatible with the size of imported machinery.[16]

We do insist that failure to effectively institutionalize public sector agricultural research can result in serious distortion of the pattern of technological change and resource use. The homogeneity of agricultural products and the relatively small size of the farm firm, even in the Western and socialist economies, make it difficult for the individual agricultural producer to either bear the research costs or capture a significant share of the gains from scientific or technological innovation. Mechanical technology, however, has been much more responsive than biological technology to the inducement mechanism as it operates in the private sector. In biological technology, typified by the breeding of new plant varieties or the improvement of cultural practices, it is difficult for the innovating firm to capture more than a small share of the increased income stream resulting from the innovation.

Failure to balance the effectiveness of the private sector in responding to inducements for advances in mechanical technology, and in those areas of biological technology in which advances in knowledge can be embodied in proprietary products, with institutional innovation capable of providing an equally effective response to inducements for advances in biological technology leads to a bias in the productivity growth path that is inconsistent with relative factor endowments. It seems reasonable to hypothesize that failure to invest in public sector experiment station capacity is one of the factors responsible in some developing countries for the unbalanced adoption of mechanical, relative to biological, technology. Failure to develop adequate public sector research institutions has also been partially responsible, in some countries, for the almost exclusive concentration of research expenditures on the plantation crops and for concentration on the production of certain export crops—such as sugar and bananas—in the plantation sector.

The perspective outlined in this paper can be summarized as follows: an essential condition for success in achieving sustained growth in agricultural productivity is the capacity to generate an ecologically adapted and economically viable agricultural technology in each country or development region. Successful achievement of continued productivity growth over time involves a dynamic process of adjustment to original resource endowments and to resource accumulation during the process of historical development. It also involves an adaptive response on the part of cultural, political, and economic institutions in order to realize the growth potential opened up by new technical alternatives. The "induced development model" attempts to make more explicit the process by which technical and institutional changes are induced through the responses of farmers, agribusiness entrepreneurs, scientists, and public administrators to resource endowments and to changes in the supply and demand of factors and products.

NOTES

1. The distinction made here between "mechanical" and "biological" technology has also been employed by Heady (1949). It is similar to the distinction between "laboresque" and "landesque" capital employed by Sen (1959). In a more recent article Kaneda employs the terms "mechanical-engineering" and "biological-chemical" (1969).

2. The term "innovation" employed here embraces the entire range of processes resulting in the emergence of novelty in science, technology, industrial management, and economic organization rather than the narrow Schumpeterian definition. Schumpeter insisted that innovation was economically and sociologically distinct from invention and scientific discovery. He rejected the idea that innovation is dependent on invention or advances in science. This distinction has become increasingly artificial. See, for example, Solo 1951; Ruttan 1959; and Hohenberg 1967. Our view is similar to that of Hohenberg. He defines technical effort as the product of purposive resource-using activity directed to the production of economically useful knowledge: "Technical effort is a necessary part of any firm activity, and is only in part separable from production itself. Traditionally it is part of the entrepreneur's job to provide knowledge to organize the factors of production in an optimum way, to adjust to market changes, and to seek improved methods. Technical effort is thus subsumed under entrepreneurship" (1967, 61).

3. See also the review of thought on this issue in Ahmad 1966.

4. See also discussions by Fellner (1967) and Ahmad (1967a), and by Kennedy (1967) and Ahmad (1967b).

5. The above theory is based on the restrictive assumption that there exists a concave innovation possibility curve (U) that can be perceived by entrepreneurs. This is not as strong a restrictive assumption as it may at first appear. The innovation possibility curve does not need to be of a smooth, well-behaved shape, as drawn in figure 1. The whole argument holds equally well for the case of two distinct alternatives. It seems reasonable to hypothesize that entrepreneurs can perceive alternative innovation possibilities for a given research and development expenditure through consultation with staff scientists and engineers or through the suggestions of inventors.

6. There is a growing literature on public research policy (see Nelson, Peck, and Kalachek 1967). These authors view public sector research activities as having risen from three considerations: (*a*) fields where the public interest is believed to transcend private incentives (as in health and aviation); (*b*) industries where the individual firm is too small to capture benefits from research (agriculture and housing); and (*c*) broad support for basic research and science education (pp. 151–211). For a review of thought with respect to resource allocation in agriculture see Fishel 1971.

7. Rosenberg has suggested a theory of induced technical change based on "obvious and compelling need" to overcome the constraints on growth instead of relative factor scarcity and factor relative prices (1969). The Rosenberg model is consistent with the model suggested here, since his "obvious and compelling need" is reflected in the market through relative factor prices. C. Peter Timmer has pointed out that in a linear programming sense the constraints that give rise to the "obvious and compelling need" for technical innovation in the Rosenberg model represent the "dual" of the factor prices used in our model (1970). For further discussion of the relationships between Rosenberg's approach and that outlined in this section see Hayami and Ruttan 1973.

8. Incentive is a major issue in many developing economies. In spite of limited scientific and technical manpower, many countries have not succeeded in developing a system of economic and professional rewards that permits them to have access to or make effective use of the resources of scientific and technical manpower that are potentially available.

9. The symbiotic relationship between basic and applied research can be illustrated by the relation between work at the International Rice Research Institute in (*a*) genetics and plant physiology and (*b*) plant breeding. The geneticist and the physiologist are involved in research designed to advance understanding of the physiological processes by which plant nutrients are transformed into grain yield and of the genetic mechanisms or processes involved in the transmission from parents to progenies of the physiological characteristics of the rice plant that affect grain yield. The rice breeders utilize this knowledge from genetics and plant physiology in the design of crosses and the selection of plants with the desired growth characteristics, agronomic traits, and nutritional value. The work in plant physiology and genetics is responsive to the need of the plant breeder for advances in knowledge related to the mission of breeding more productive varieties of rice.

10. For a description of the high-payoff input model see chapter 9 in this volume. —Ed.

11. At this point we share the Marxian perspective on the relationship between technological

change and institutional development, though we do not accept the Marxian perspective regarding the monolithic sequences of evolution based on clear-cut class conflicts. For two recent attempts to develop broad historical generalizations regarding the relationship between insitutions and economic forces see Hicks 1969; and North and Thomas 1970.

12. For additional examples see Davis and North 1970.

13. See also North and Thomas 1970.

14. Hayami and Peterson (1972) show that the return to investment in improvements in market information is comparable to the returns that have been estimated for high-payoff research areas such as hybrid corn and poultry.

15. Owen argues that differentiation of a rural commercial sector from the rural subsistence sector is the first step towards development of relevant agricultural development policies. The "optimum sized commercial farms will comprise the maximum amount of land that can be farmed at a profit by an appropriate set of labor where the latter uses a relatively advanced level of technology for the particular farming area. . . . the optimum sized subsistence farm plot is one that comprises the minimum amount of land that is necessary to assure to the household concerned the minimum acceptable standard of subsistence living'' (1969, 107).

16. This development is reviewed in Hayami and Ruttan 1971.

REFERENCES

Ahmad, Syed. 1966. "On the Theory of Induced Invention." *Economic Journal* 76(302): 344–57.

———. 1967a. "Reply to Professor Fellner." *Economic Journal* 77(307): 664–65.

———. 1967b. "A Rejoinder to Professor Kennedy." *Economic Journal* 77(308): 960–63.

Davis, Lance, and Douglass North. 1970. "Institutional Change and American Economic Growth: A First Step Towards a Theory of Institutional Innovation." *Journal of Economic History* 30(1): 131–49.

Fellner, William. 1961. "Two Propositions in the Theory of Induced Innovations." *Economic Journal* 71(282): 305–8.

———. 1967. "Comment on the Induced Bias." *Economic Journal* 77(307): 662–64.

Fishel, W. L., ed. 1971. *Resource Allocation in Agricultural Development.* Minneapolis.

Hayami, Yujiro, and Willis Peterson. 1972. "Social Returns to Public Information Services: Statistical Reporting of U.S. Farm Commodities." *American Economic Review* 62(1): 119–30.

Hayami, Yujiro, and V. W. Ruttan. 1970. "Factor Prices and Technical Change in Agricultural Development: The United States and Japan, 1880–1960." *Journal of Political Economy* 78(5): 1115–41.

———. 1971. *Agricultural Development: An International Perspective.* Baltimore.

———. 1973. "Professor Rosenberg and the Direction of Technical Change: A Comment." *Economic Development and Cultural Change* 21(2): 352–55.

Heady, E. O. 1949. "Basic Economic and Welfare Aspects of Farm Technological Advance." *Journal of Farm Economics* 31(2): 293–316.

Hicks, J. R. 1932. *The Theory of Wages.* London.

———. 1969. *A Theory of Economic History.* London.

Hohenberg, P. M. 1967. *Chemicals in Western Europe: 1850–1914.* Chicago.

Islam, Nural. 1971. "Agricultural Growth in Pakistan: Problems and Policies." Paper presented at the Conference on Agriculture and Economic Development, Japan Economic Research Center, Tokyo, 6–10 September.

Kaneda, Hiromitsu. 1969. "Economic Implications of the 'Green Revolution' and the Strategy of Agricultural Development in West Pakistan." *Pakistan Development Review* 9(2): 111–43.

Kennedy, Charles. 1964. "Induced Bias in Innovation and the Theory of Distribution." *Economic Journal* 74(295): 541–47.

————. 1967. "On the Theory of Induced Invention—A Reply." *Economic Journal* 77(308): 958–60.

Myint, U. Hla. 1968. "Market Mechanisms and Planning—The Functional Aspect." In *The Structure and Development of Asian Economies*. Tokyo.

Nelson, R. R. 1959. "The Economics of Invention: A Survey of the Literature." *Journal of Business* 33 (April): 101–27.

Nelson, R. R., M. J. Peck, and E. D. Kalachek. 1967. *Technology, Economic Growth and Public Policy*. Washington, D.C.

Niskanen, W. A. 1968. "The Peculiar Economics of Bureaucracy." *American Economic Review* 58(2): 293–305.

North, Douglass C., and R. P. Thomas. 1970. "An Economic Theory of the Growth of the Western World." *Economic History Review*, 2d ser., 23(1): 1–17.

Ohkawa, Kazushi. 1969. "Policy Implications of the Asian Agricultural Survey—Personal Notes." In *Regional Seminar on Agriculture: Paper and Proceedings*. Makati, Philippines.

Olson, Mancur, Jr. 1968. *The Logic of Collective Action: Public Goods and the Theory of Groups*. New York.

Owen, W. F. 1969. "Structural Planning in Densely Populated Countries: An Introduction with Applications to Indonesia." *Malayan Economic Review* 14(1): 97–114.

————. 1971. *Two Rural Sectors: Their Characteristics and Roles in the Development Process*. Indiana University International Developmental Research Center Occasional Paper 1. Bloomington, Ind.

Rosenberg, Nathan. 1969. "The Direction of Technological Change: Inducement Mechanisms and Focusing Devices." *Economic Development and Cultural Change* 18(1, pt. 1): 1–24.

Ruttan, V. W. 1959. "Usher and Schumpeter on Invention, Innovation and Technological Change." *Quarterly Journal of Economics* 73(4): 596–606.

————. 1969. "Agricultural Product and Factor Markets in Southeast Asia." *Economic Development and Cultural Change* 17(4): 501–19.

Salter, W. E. G. 1960. *Productivity and Technical Change*. Cambridge.

Samuelson, P. A. 1965. "A Theory of Induced Innovation along Kennedy, Weisacker [Weizsacker] Lines." *Review of Economics and Statistics* 47(4): 343–56.

Schmookler, Jacob. 1966. *Invention and Economic Growth*. Cambridge, Mass.

Schultz, T. W. 1968. "Institutions and the Rising Economic Value of Man." *American Journal of Agricultural Economics* 50(5): 1113–22.

Sen, A. K. 1959. "The Choice of Agricultural Techniques in Underdeveloped Countries." *Economic Development and Cultural Change* 7(3, pt. 1): 279–85.

Solo, Carolyn Shaw. 1951. "Innovation in the Capitalist Process: A Critique of the Schumpeterian Theory." *Quarterly Journal of Economics* 65(3): 417–28.

Timmer, C. P. 1970. Personal communication, 9 October.

III

Policy Perspectives

Introduction

The five essays in part III provide the political and economic context for developing agricultural policies and strategies for the coming decade. Chapters 11–13, by economists, lay out the new macroeconomic setting in which agricultural development policies are designed, examine the benefits of trade liberalization, and argue that agricultural development and poverty reduction in many low-income countries have been hindered by macro and sectoral policies that systematically discriminate against agriculture and the rural poor. In Chapter 14, Robert Bates, a political scientist, contends that there is a logical political rationale for such policies and that policy analysis needs to take place in a framework that recognizes the political as well as the economic bases of policy. Part III concludes with a selection by Amartya Sen, who asks how the poor's access to food can be assured in countries where food policies are shaped by various economic and political forces.

In Chapter 11, Peter Timmer addresses the complexities of the new macroeconomics of food and agriculture. Building on the influential *Food Policy Analysis* (1983) by Timmer, Falcon, and Pearson and the literature on policy reform, food security, and trade liberalization over the past fifteen years, Timmer focuses on how macroeconomic policy in an open economy affects five prices—often termed "macro prices": wage rates, interest rates, land rental rates, foreign exchange rates, and the rural-urban terms of trade, and how these in turn affect growth of agriculture and the broader food system.

The relationships between agriculture and the macroeconomy run in two directions. A coherent set of macroeconomic policies is necessary for sustained agricultural growth. Equally important, as Timmer states, "a healthy and dynamic food and agricultural economy can contribute in surprisingly important ways to the speed and equity with which the nonagricultural economy grows." Chapter 11 focuses on both sets of relationships. First, Timmer discusses how macroeconomic policies, through their impact on macro prices, affect agricultural growth through a broad array of incentives, ranging from the attractiveness of different types of agricultural technologies to the rewards for savings and investment. Next, he examines how a healthy agricultural and food system contributes to overall growth. Going beyond the contributions stressed by Johnston and Mellor (1961) in their classic article, Timmer explores how food security, in the form of stable, reliable food supplies, induces greater productivity and more effective investment by improving workers' nutrition and reducing risk.

Timmer's analysis implies that there are important spillovers to the rest of the

181

economy from investing in the food and agricultural sector. Yet, such investment will be productive only if it is embedded in a set of broader macro policies that signal appropriate opportunity costs of resources invested in the food system and that facilitate flows of resources across sectors. A relatively open international trade regime is one component of such a policy framework, and Timmer points out how trade can be used as part of a tool to help stabilize food prices. The challenge is to design a trade policy that signals appropriate long-run opportunity costs to farmers, traders, and other business people without necessarily inducing them to over react to short-run fluctuations in world prices.

Developing an appropriate trade policy is thus one key component of an agricultural development strategy. Although global agricultural trade accounts for only 10 to 12 percent of world agricultural production, trade is very important for commodities such as wheat, maize, and soybeans, as well as cotton and traditional beverages, such as coffee and tea. Many of the poorest countries, such as those in Africa, still depend on three or four agricultural exports for much of their foreign exchange earnings (Helleiner 1992; Maizels 1992; Badiane and Delgado 1995). Moreover, in addition to trade in bulk commodities, there has been a burgeoning growth in trade and direct foreign investment in higher value-added components of the world food system, such as processed foods. International food companies are becoming more global in their sourcing of raw materials and in seeking new markets for their products, which opens new opportunities and challenges for developing countries.

In Chapter 12, Rudiger Dornbusch, in the "The Case for Trade Liberalization," examines the advantages to countries of following a trade regime that integrates them more tightly into the world economy. Dornbusch places trade liberalization in historical perspective by calling attention to the deeply embedded protection that contributed to the global depression of the 1930s and how this protection held sway until the late sixties and early seventies. He observes that the swing towards open trade that started in the seventies was a function of four overlapping forces: anti-statism, poor economic performance, better information, and World Bank pressure (Krueger 1997). Dornbusch discusses the gains from liberalization, illustrates these gains with three country studies (Turkey, Korea, and Mexico), and concludes that "liberalized trade has so fundamentally shaken up the production structure that more liberal trade is invariably credited with a good share of the performance." He argues that the case for protection rests on two pillars—externalites and learning-by-doing—but questions whether these conditions are sufficiently strong in most countries to counterbalance the costs of protection. On balance, Dornbusch presents an upbeat message on the gains from liberalization while conceding that unforeseen political events could derail trade liberalization. But he foresees growth in trade liberalization in services and an expansion of regional trade agreements such as NAFTA (de Janvry and Sadoulet 1996).

Nevertheless, the gains from trade liberalization cited by Dornbusch are being challenged by many commentators, in part because of the concern that trade liberalization alone does not address many of the internal political and structural constraints that are major causes of rural poverty. For example, there is growing evidence that higher rates of economic growth are not "making a dent" in rural poverty in Latin America (Huddle 1997). Moreover, in Africa the overall picture of trade liberalization is mixed and the results fall short of those achieved in Asia, in part because of structural constraints, such as poor infrastructure (Lipumba 1994).

Prior to the 1980s, many low- and middle-income countries heavily taxed agriculture, which contributed to slow economic growth and rural poverty (Schultz 1978). In Chapter 13, Maurice Schiff and Alberto Valdés present the results of a pioneering World Bank study of the impact of domestic price policies in eighteen developing countries over the 1960–85 period. In order to measure the impact of price interventions on agricultural performance, they examined both the direct impact through agricultural price controls, export taxes or quotas, and input subsidies or taxes and the indirect impact through macroeconomic policies and industrial protection. The main findings of this eighteen-country study were that agriculture was "milked," with very harmful consequences for overall economic growth:

- Total taxes on agriculture were 30 percent (8 percent direct and 22 percent indirect).
- High rates of taxes on agriculture slowed the growth of agriculture.
- The countries with the highest taxes had zero annual real GDP growth while countries with moderate taxes grew at 2.5 percent annually. (Krueger, Schiff, and Valdés 1988)

If such policies were so obviously counterproductive, one has to ask why they persisted. In chapter 14, Bates argues that there is a political rationale for seemingly inconsistent agricultural policies in many developing countries. He argues that politicians often pursue policies detrimental to overall agricultural growth not out of a misunderstanding of economics but because such policies benefit key groups of rural and urban constituents. Therefore, Bates argues, in analyzing agricultural policies, economists need to move away from a model that assumes that policy makers seek to improve the overall welfare of society and instead recognize that "governments are agencies that seek to stay in power."

The adoption of a political economy approach does not obviate the need for economic analysis of food policies, but it places the analysis in a broader, more realistic context (Lipton 1977; Timmer, Falcon, and Pearson 1983). For example, on the question of agricultural taxation, Mancur Olson (1990) has developed a collective-action perspective on why farmers in rich countries are subsidized while small-scale farms in poor countries are frequently taxed.[1] Olson contends that farmers are more likely to organize to defend their interests when they are few in number, the costs of organizing are low, and when collective benefits from lobbying can be tied to access to individual benefits, such as low-cost insurance. These conditions exist in many high-income countries. In poor countries, however, poor communication and transport systems and (often) repressive political regimes make it difficult and costly for large numbers of small farmers to meet, organize, and make the economic case for smallholders in the national political arena. And without compulsory membership, it is difficult to punish smallholders who act as free riders, reaping the benefits without joining and paying dues.

In Chapter 15 Amartya Sen analyzes how internal domestic policies, the external environment (including world market conditions), and individual characteristics combine to influence an individual's access to food, which Sen terms the person's food entitlement. Sen uses the concept of food entitlement to present the results of his research on famine in Asia and Africa (originally reported in his influential book *Poverty and Famines* [Sen 1981]) and the results of a major study of the political economy of hunger that he carried out in collaboration with Jean Drèze (Drèze and Sen 1990a, 1990b, 1991). Sen's work revolutionized the study of famine by pointing out that famine is often not caused by a sharp decline in food availability, but rather by a decline in entitlements, that is, a fall in the individual's command over food.

Sen's use of the concept of entitlements is a popular way of making the point that food insecurity results primarily from inadequate effective demand for food, not insufficient supply. Nevertheless, Dyson (1996, 74) contends that Sen and others may have contributed to a misleading impression that a sizeable proportion of modern famines do not involve a food availability decline (FAD). A number of recent studies of famine in Ethiopia (Webb, von Braun, and Yohannes 1992) and Bengal show that an FAD can occur over a wide geographical area. For example, half the countries in southern Africa were severely affected by the 1992 drought. If 10 million tons of food aid had not been dispatched to the region, the death toll from famine in southern Africa would have been high.

The vast increase in the number and depth of empirical studies of hunger, malnutrition, and famine over the past twenty years has provided an improved data base for policy makers (Reutliner 1977; Dasgupta 1993; Behrman 1993; Strauss 1990; Pinstrup-Andersen 1993). This expanded knowledge base has helped deepen our understanding that poverty and a lack of entitlements are major causes of household food insecurity. It has also helped shift the policy focus from national food self-sufficiency to food security and from nationwide food subsidies to targeting as a means of improving the fiscal sustainability of food and income transfer programs in the context of more open, market-oriented economies (Staatz et al. 1993; Timmer 1993; Jayne et al. 1994; Tweeten and McClelland 1997).

NOTES

1. Jayne et al. (1997) contend that Bates's and Olson's arguments about smallholders being taxed do not hold for Anglophone Southern and Eastern Africa in the 1980s and early 1990s. They contend that smallholder maize producers received substantial subsidies for both outputs and inputs, which subsequently had to be reduced in the mid-1990s because they proved financially unsustainable (Masters 1993).

REFERENCES

Badiane, Ousmane, and Christopher Delgado. 1995. "A 2020 Vision for Food, Agriculture, and the Environment in Sub-Saharan Africa." Washington, D.C.: International Food Policy Research Institute.

Behrman, J. R. 1993. "The Economic Rationale for Investing in Nutrition in Developing Countries." *World Development* 21 (11): 1749–71.

Dasgupta, Partha. 1993. *An Inquiry into Well-Being and Destitution.* New York: Oxford University Press.

de Janvry, Alain, and Elisabeth Sadoulet. 1996. "NAFTA and Agriculture: An Early Assessment." Berkeley: University of California.

Drèze, Jean, and Amartya Sen, eds. 1990a. *The Political Economy of Hunger.* Vol. 1, *Entitlement and Well-Being.* Oxford: Clarendon Press.

————. 1990b. *The Political Economy of Hunger.* Vol 2, *Famine Prevention.* Oxford: Clarendon Press.

————. 1991. *The Political Economy of Hunger.* Vol. 3, *Endemic Hunger.* Oxford: Clarendon Press.

Dyson, Tim. 1996. *Population and Food: Global Trends and Future Prospects.* London: Routledge.

Helleiner, Gerald K. 1992. "Structural Adjustment and Long-term Development in Sub-Saharan Africa." In *Alternative Development Strategies in Sub-Saharan Africa,* edited by F. Stewart, S. Lall, and S. Wangwe, 48–78. London: Macmillan.

Huddle, Donald L. 1997. "Review Article: Post-1982 Effects of Neoliberalism on Latin American Development and Poverty: Two Conflicting Views." *Economic Development and Cultural Change* 45, no. 4 (July): 881–97.

Jayne, Thomas S., John M. Staatz, Michael T. Weber, Stephen Jones, and Eric W. Crawford. 1997. "Agricultural Policy Reform and Productivity Change in Africa." MSU Agricultural Economics Staff Paper no. 97-43, Department of Agricultural Economics, Michigan State University, East Lansing.

Jayne, Thomas S., D. L. Tschirley, John M. Staatz, James D. Shaffer, Michael T. Weber, Munhamo Chisvo, and Mulinge Mukumbu. 1994. *Market-Oriented Strategies to Improve Household Access to Food: Experience from Sub-Saharan Africa.* MSU International Development Paper no. 15, Department of Agricultural Economics and Department of Economics, Michigan State University, East Lansing.

Johnston, Bruce F., and John W. Mellor. 1961. "The Role of Agriculture in Economic Development." *American Economic Review* 51 (4): 566–93.

Krueger, Anne O. 1997. "Trade Policy and Economic Development: How We Learn." *American Economic Review* 87 (1): 1–22.

Krueger, Anne, Maurice Schiff, and Alberto Valdés. 1988. "Agricultural Incentives in Developing Countries: Measuring the Effect of Sectoral and Economywide Policies." *World Bank Economic Review* 2:255–72.

Lipton, Michael. 1977. *Why Poor People Stay Poor: A Study of Urban Bias in World Development.* London: Temple-Smith.

Lipumba, Nguyuru H. 1994. *Africa Beyond Adjustment.* Washington, D.C.: Overseas Development Council.

Maizels, Alfred. 1992. *Commodities in Crisis: The Commodity Crisis of the 1980s and the Political Economy of International Commodity Policies.* Oxford: Clarendon Press.

Masters, William A. 1993. "The Scope and Sequence of Maize Market Reform in Zimbabwe." *Food Research Institute Studies* 22 (3): 227–51.

Olson, Mancur. 1990. "Agricultural Exploitation and Subsidization: There Is an Explanation." *Choices* (fourth quarter): 8–11.

Pinstrup-Andersen, Per, ed. 1993. *The Political Economy of Food and Nutrition Policies.* Baltimore: Johns Hopkins University Press.

Reutlinger, Shlomo. 1977. "Malnutrition: A Poverty or Food Problem?" *World Development* 5: 715–24.

Schultz, Theodore W., ed. 1978. *Distortions of Agricultural Incentives*. Bloomington: Indiana University Press.

Sen, Amartya. 1981. *Poverty and Famines: An Essay on Entitlement and Deprivation*. Oxford: Clarendon Press.

Staatz, John M., Thomas S. Jayne, David Tschirley, James D. Shaffer, Josué Dioné, James Oehmke, and Michael T. Weber. 1993. "Restructuring Food Systems to Support a Transformation of Agriculture in Sub-Saharan Africa: Experience and Issues." Staff Paper 93-36, Department of Agricultural Economics, Michigan State University, East Lansing.

Strauss, John. 1990. "Households, Communities, and Preschool Children's Nutrition Outcomes: Evidence from Rural Cote d'Ivoire." *Economic Development and Cultural Change* 38: 231–61.

Timmer, C. Peter. 1993. "Food Price Stabilization: The Relevance of the Asian Experience to Africa." In *Policy Options for Agricultural Development in Sub-Saharan Africa*, edited by Nathan C. Russell and Christopher R. Dowswell, 107–27. Mexico, D.F.: CASIN/SAA/Global 2000.

Timmer, C. Peter, Walter P. Falcon, and Scott R. Pearson. 1983. *Food Policy Analysis*. Baltimore: Johns Hopkins University Press.

Tweeten, Luther G., and Donald G. McClelland. 1997. *Promoting Third World Development and Food Security*. New York: Praeger.

Webb, Patrick, Joachim von Braun and Yisehac Yohannes. 1992. *Famine in Ethiopia: Policy Implications of Coping with Failure at National and Household Levels*. Research Report 92. Washington, D.C.: International Food Policy Research Institute.

11

The Macroeconomics of Food and Agriculture

C. PETER TIMMER

Economies are highly complex systems. This complexity characterizes even the economies of poor countries still heavily dependent on agriculture for national income and employment. If a balance between supply and demand for food at reasonably stable prices is to be established, decisions by consumers about food procurement, agricultural production decisions by farmers (who are also consumers), and marketing decisions by traders, wholesalers, processors, and retailers must be coordinated. This balance speaks only to one aspect of an economy: food and agricultural commodities. All the goods and services produced, imported, exported, and consumed in the rest of the economy must also be factored into an overall balance for the macro economy. How this overall balance is achieved and the policies that influence it are topics of great importance. In poor countries, the agricultural sector plays a major and direct role in establishing the balance.

To complicate matters further, static balance in the macro economy, although essential as an analytical base and as a foundation for establishing macro policy, is only the starting point for what really matters: the expanding dynamic balance that is economic growth. The food and agricultural sector is linked to this economic growth in two ways.

First, the food and agricultural sector cannot grow rapidly and efficiently for prolonged periods of time unless a set of macroeconomic policies is in place whose main purpose is to stimulate the rest of the economy to grow rapidly and efficiently. Second, a healthy and dynamic food and agricultural economy can contribute in surprisingly important ways to the speed and equity with which the nonagricultural economy grows. This stimulation of economic growth is a key part of the two-way interaction between agriculture and the macro economy.

This chapter begins by explaining the key macroeconomic variables that determine the pace of economic growth and the mechanisms by which they also influence the food and agricultural sector. The "macro price dilemma" is shown

C. PETER TIMMER is Dean of the Graduate School of International Relations and Pacific Studies at the University of California, San Diego.

to be a generalization of the "food price dilemma" that confronts all poor societies. The food price dilemma arises because high food prices help farmers raise rural productivity and household income, whereas low food prices help poor consumers gain access to adequate amounts of food. Macro policy makers face equally difficult dilemmas over policies toward wage rates and interest rates.

The focus of the chapter then shifts to the positive role that the agricultural sector can play in speeding the process of growth in the entire economy. The limited, but still important, circumstances in which agriculture can be a direct, significant contributor to overall economic growth are discussed in the context of "Lewis linkages" and "Johnston-Mellor linkages," which operate through factor markets and product markets, respectively. In the poorest countries, in which the share of agriculture in GDP remains high, particularly in several formerly socialist countries in Central and East Asia and throughout much of Africa, getting agriculture moving is crucial to achieving satisfactory macroeconomic performance.

In these countries, stimulating the Lewis linkages and the Johnston-Mellor linkages by improving the efficiency of markets will be a major key to maximizing the direct contribution of agriculture to economic growth. Even in these countries, however, macroeconomic policy will be the main determinant of whether agriculture gets moving or not. For middle-income countries, a set of indirect links between agriculture and the rest of the economy remains significant for overall growth, and these links are not well mediated by markets. The direct contribution of agriculture to economic growth, however, is limited by the declining share of agriculture in GDP as incomes rise.

The last part of the chapter examines a more controversial dimension of the relationship between agriculture and economic growth—that is, whether food security and price stability are directly enhanced by performance of the domestic agricultural economy, on the one hand, and stimulate growth in the rest of the economy, on the other. Theoretical models of economic growth and the empirical literature are suggestive on both counts, but the evidence remains tentative. Building further understanding of this interplay between stability and growth is an important topic for research.

THE MACRO ECONOMY

Macro economies can be described in four quite different, and yet ultimately identical, ways: in terms of demand, supply, and income, and in monetary terms. In the demand approach, the total of a nation's economic activity is disaggregated into the major components of final demand—usually consumption, private investment, government expenditures, and any excess of exports over imports. When totaled, these components make up a country's gross domestic product, or GDP. When net income transfers to or from abroad are added, the total is gross national product, or GNP. The composition and overall aggregate of demand has been the centerpiece of macroeconomic theory and policy in market economies since the Keynesian revolution began in the 1930s.

Just as food cannot be consumed unless it is first produced, aggregate demand cannot be met without a supply of goods and services. The supply approach focuses on the structure by sector of production in an economy. When output from agriculture, industry, services, and government is totaled, the result is also GDP, and hence aggregate supply equals aggregate demand. The supply approach to macroeconomics has a long tradition; classical macroeconomic theory directs attention to the dynamics of long-run aggregate supply. This concern for long-run expansion of output has led to new approaches by theorists of economic growth and has obvious relevance to developing countries—a relevance that concern for managing short-run fluctuations in aggregate demand often does not have (Barro and Sala-i-Martin 1995).

The production of goods and services requires the employment of factors of production—labor, capital, land, entrepreneurship, and management—in which income is earned in return for services. These incomes provide the wherewithal to purchase the goods and services that have been produced. Incomes thus provide a third way of tallying up national economic activity. In market economies the total of wages, interest, rent, and profits is spent on the components of aggregate final demand, and so total incomes also equal GDP. Aggregate income and its distribution among the basic claimants in the economy are major subjects of macroeconomic analysis.

Each of these three ways of describing a macro economy—demand, supply, and income—are equally valid even in a traditional subsistence economy where exchange of goods and services takes place only by physical barter. Nearly all economies have found a more efficient mechanism of exchange—the use of money as a medium in which the prices of all goods and services are quoted. Indeed, it is through prices that all the components can be added in a meaningful way. The use of monetary units, however, should not hide the "real" nature of the economy being examined. In particular, the monetary total of economic activity can change because of changes in the general level of prices even when the real level of activity is constant.

A general increase in prices—inflation—is a monetary phenomenon caused by increases in the amount of money in circulation (or the rate at which it changes hands), at rates faster than expansion of output (or of people's willingness to hold increased cash balances). The monetary policies that bring about inflation, however, also involve variables that affect the real economy. A complex and poorly understood relationship exists among the money supply, interest rates, inflation, price expectations, investment, and the distribution of income. Money is more than just a convenient medium of exchange. It is also a significant factor with direct influence on the level of macroeconomic activity.

Most governments try to influence the level and distribution of macroeconomic activity with a variety of policy instruments, nearly all of which have powerful direct or indirect effects on the agricultural system as well as on overall economic performance. Some of these effects are intended, but most are simply accidental fallout. Much of macro policy is designed with little thought to its ultimate impact on such important variables as agricultural production, commodity prices, distribution of food consumption, and volume of food imports.

All macro economies have complicated and frequently simultaneous connections among their various components. Starting the discussion anywhere eventually leads everywhere. There is, however, a certain logic and convenience to organizing the discussion around budget policy because it has direct impact on food and agricultural policy through funding of projects, programs, and rural investments, such as roads and irrigation systems. At the same time, budget policy feeds through an indirect and complicated set of connections to fiscal policy, monetary policy, macro price policy, and ultimately again to food and agricultural policy via international trade policy and the domestic rural-urban terms of trade. This set of connections is illustrated in figure 1, which is reproduced from *Food Policy Analysis* (Timmer, Falcon, and Pearson 1983, 223).

Because total government expenditures often exceed the revenues raised by taxes, budget deficits are common. The deficits must be financed by private savings, foreign borrowing, or by money creation by the central bank (that is, by "monetizing" the debt). A budget surplus, when it occurs, adds government savings to private savings for investment in the economy. The inflation that usually results from deficit financing puts pressure on the foreign exchange rate and influences real levels of wage rates and interest rates. All three rates are components of a government's macro price policy.

The macro price environment, working through trade policy to influence the rural-urban terms of trade, and through choice of technique and financial deepening to influence economic growth and employment creation, creates the commodity price and income context in which agricultural and food policy must be effective. The design and implementation of specific agricultural and food-sector projects and programs, funded directly from the budget, determines the allocation of resources within sectors. Among other things, this allocation affects the adequacy of food intake among various income classes, because of the importance of food subsidies in many countries, as well as the short-run and long-run technological environment in which farmers make their production decisions.

The combination of price policy and the design and efficacy of budget allocations make up a country's short-run food and agricultural policy. The determinants of a country's long-run policy toward the food and agricultural sector are the long-run price policy environment, the payoff from investments funded from the budget and from the private sector, and the rate of economic growth and job creation.

In Western economies, most attention to macroeconomic policy has been given to budget, fiscal, and monetary issues and to the resulting levels of aggregate output and rates of inflation. Relatively little attention has been devoted to the other arena of government macro policy: the formation of prices for factors of production—labor, capital, and land—and the formation of two important

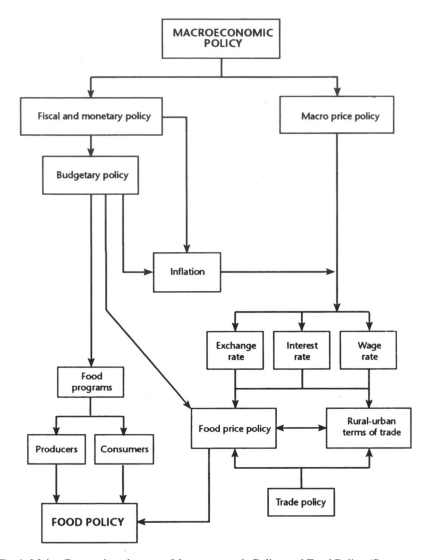

Fig. 1. Major Connections between Macroeconomic Policy and Food Policy (Source: Timmer, Falcon, and Pearson 1983, 223.)

terms of trade—between domestic and international goods and between rural and urban goods. These five prices, often termed "macro prices"—wage rates, interest rates, land rental rates, foreign exchange rates, and the rural-urban terms of trade—are significantly influenced by basic macro economic policy in an economy.

MACRO PRICES

Macro prices reflect the scarcity of factors of production and, consequently, the incomes flowing to each factor. Because most governments wish to affect income distribution in their societies, the temptation to set macro prices directly, rather than to use government policy to influence their determination by market forces, is very great. If wage rates can be set high, labor is no longer cheap, and poverty is eliminated. If interest rates can be set low, capital is not scarce, and a country can quickly have a modern industrial sector. If food prices are kept low, food is abundant, and no one will go hungry. Knowing that macro prices reflect the most basic conditions of a country's economy, a government that directly sets these prices to reflect its urgent desire for a modern, prosperous society is attempting to short-circuit the economic development process. It is no wonder that even countries with well-intentioned policy makers have tried this approach. But a basic price dilemma keeps the approach from working.

At its simplest, the price dilemma is whether to set food prices low, to help poor consumers maintain access to an adequate diet, or set them high, to provide farmers incentives to produce adequate food supplies. At the aggregate level, the price dilemma involves all of the macro prices because of their dual role in providing incomes to important sectors of the economy while simultaneously signaling investors and producers how intensively to use each resource. Thus, high wages provide good incomes for those employees who have jobs but discourage investment in labor-intensive industries that promise jobs for the millions of unemployed. The general macro price dilemma, and specifically the food price dilemma, are central themes of any discussion of the macroeconomics of food and agriculture.

Foreign Exchange Rates

An exchange rate for a nation's currency establishes its value in relation to the currency of another country. For most industrialized countries the price of foreign exchange is determined in international currency markets by the daily, or even hourly, movements in the supply and demand for a country's currency. These movements are established by the country's balance between imports and exports (including services) and by international capital flows, which are often larger than the trade flows.

Similar fundamental economic forces exist in developing countries, but their exchange rates are typically pegged by governments rather than determined solely in markets. Whether a government sets its foreign exchange rate at a level that will more or less clear the market determines whether imports and exports are priced (in domestic currency) at levels that reflect their economic scarcities in relation to domestic goods and services that are not traded internationally.

Overvaluation

The exchange rate reflects the rate at which a country must give up its own currency to obtain foreign currency to import goods and services, and it simultaneously determines the value in domestic currency of goods and services that are exported. Many developing countries choose, explicitly or implicitly, to maintain a rate of exchange that overvalues the domestic currency. Such rates keep the cost of foreign exchange low and hence imports cheap. These rates cannot be maintained with free markets for foreign exchange, however, or there would be excess demand for foreign currency to pay for a flood of imported goods. The low exchange rates can be maintained only by currency controls, import tariffs and barriers, and allocations of foreign exchange to preferred importers or for high-priority uses (often, unfortunately, military hardware rather than fertilizer or essential drugs). The presence of such controls and trade barriers shows that a country's currency is overvalued.

If a country's currency is overvalued, commodities such as food crops that normally are traded internationally either as imports or as exports are undervalued. Farmers receive less for their crops than they would if the price of foreign exchange were market determined. Hence, overvalued domestic currencies act as an implicit tax on agriculture. All consumers of food and other traded goods are thus subsidized indirectly because of the low prices for these items. The government budget is also relieved of part of the direct burden of providing any food subsidies, since these are shifted to food producers through lower prices. Consequently, the tendency toward overvalued domestic currencies has a strong biasing effect on the food and agricultural system, favoring urban food consumers and penalizing rural producers.

Exchange rates that overvalue domestic currencies are a major reason the rural-urban terms of trade are so unfavorable to agricultural producers in many developing countries, and they are a major source of the "urban bias" that, according to Lipton (1977, 1993), leaves poor people poor. This urban bias has strong political roots, the power base of most governments in the developing world being students, industrial workers, members of the military, and civil servants. But overvalued currencies are often not the result of an overt and conscious choice of the government, even though the urban political support is welcome. In many cases, overvalued currencies are generated without specific policy decisions by differential inflation rates and are sustained to some extent by the prevalence of industrial protection.

If a country begins with a fixed exchange rate that correctly prices its currency in relation to foreign currencies, the demand for foreign exchange will be matched by its supply. Domestic inflation (relative to inflation rates in the economies of trading partners), however, places pressure on a country's fixed exchange rate, because import demand will increase in the face of lower relative prices for imported goods, export earnings will decline because of decreased demand for the goods the country sells, and the market for foreign exchange will not clear at the fixed exchange rate without capital inflows.

Many developing countries are able to maintain overvalued currencies because of protective trade policies, often supplemented by exchange controls and restrictions on outflows of capital. Most governments impose tariffs or quantitative restrictions on imports in an attempt to promote more rapid industrialization or to raise government revenues. Taxes on exports also raise government revenues while keeping domestic commodity prices low.

Protection is an instrument of industrial policy and of agricultural policy in many industrialized countries as well as developing countries, although the World Trade Organization is dedicated to reducing the level of protection while making remaining trade barriers more transparent. In addition, however, protection has an important, and often fully intended, impact on exchange rates that is more important for poor countries. Protection raises the domestic market prices of protected goods that are or could be imported. In the absence of such protection the prices of these goods would drop, demand for them would rise, and more would be imported. Bidding for the foreign exchange to pay for these imports would cause the equilibrium value of foreign exchange to rise. When the government maintains protectionist policies, the domestic currency can be overvalued, although supply of and demand for foreign currency is in balance.

Overvalued domestic currencies tend to divert the flow of purchasing power to urban areas, usually widening rural-urban income disparities. The depressed rural incentives cause low growth in output and little gain in rural employment. Low food prices provide general subsidies to food consumers, which may protect the welfare of the poor and raise total food intake; but since domestic food production is depressed and foreign exchange is cheap (for those who can get it), food imports tend to expand considerably. The strong tendency in developing countries toward overvalued currencies thus places heavy burdens on the design of food and agricultural policy.

Devaluation

The remedy for overvaluation is devaluation, which is meant to permit the economy to regain its international competitiveness and bring the market for foreign exchange into balance. A devaluation, by itself, cannot solve the problem. Differential inflation is the cause of the overvaluation. If domestic inflation is permitted to continue at levels exceeding inflation in the major trading partners, devaluation alone will be followed by a rise in the relative price of nontradable goods because of inflation. This rise will offset the initial price change and thwart the switching of demand from tradable to nontradable goods and of supply in the reverse direction. The currency will again become overvalued, albeit at the new exchange rate. To be successful even in the short run, a devaluation must be accompanied by fiscal and monetary policies that reduce inflation by cutting aggregate demand and lowering domestic expenditures. To be successful in the long run, the devaluation must change expectations and generate greater investment by both domestic and foreign firms.

Most governments, however, find it very difficult to adopt more stringent fiscal, monetary, and exchange rate policies—an example of the macro price dilemma. Devaluation is a politically sensitive topic largely because two groups are immediately worse off after a devaluation: owners of firms and workers producing nontradable goods and services or using large quantities of tradable inputs (for example, civil servants and factory workers); and consumers, especially urban residents, who have a high propensity to consume tradable goods. Continued overvaluation subsidizes the real incomes of civil servants and urban residents in the short run and thus is politically popular, but it acts as an implicit tax on agriculture, because part of the cost of food subsidies is transferred from the government budget to food producers. A devaluation usually raises food prices and thus shifts the rural-urban terms of trade in favor of agriculture, resolving the food price dilemma in favor of producers. Many rural dwellers produce tradable goods with the use of nontraded land and labor and few tradable inputs, and they often consume larger proportions of nontradable goods than do urban residents.

A failure to devalue in order to create better incentives for the rural sector lies not with urban-oriented government policy alone, although this factor is important. Many painful adjustments must be made by both producers and consumers in an economy when the domestic currency is devalued. The food consumption adjustments of the very poor can be especially painful, and awareness is needed of the potential benefits from "safety net" programs that attempt to guarantee a certain level of food consumption by the poor. In the face of all these problems, it bears repeating that devaluation offers the long-run prospect, probably the only long-run prospect, of more jobs and faster growth. But the dilemma for both the government and for the poor is how to survive until then.

INTEREST RATES AND FINANCIAL POLICY

Interest rates reflect two fundamental aspects of all economies. First, interest is the "wage" of capital and reflects its productivity in increasing output. Capital has an opportunity cost and can be rented just like labor and land. It must be compensated for its use at a competitive rate if owners of capital are not to withdraw its services. Second, interest rates reflect an essential time dimension, as owners of capital have the choice between consuming their capital in the present or saving it to reap potentially larger, but later, consumption returns. If capital markets were perfect and riskless, the productivity dimension of interest rates would just match the "liquidity," or time dimension, because transactions between different opportunities for productive investments would produce an equilibrium rate of time discount.

In the real world, however, such perfection is seldom achieved. Investments are risky, access to capital markets is highly uneven, and, especially in developing countries, knowledge of actual investment opportunities and payoffs is quite imperfect. Consequently, the marginal productivity of capital—one definition of the interest rate—frequently diverges from the rate at which society values future consumption versus present consumption—the alternative definition of the interest rate. An important goal of financial policy is to make this divergence as small as possible.

Most governments are reasonably effective at setting foreign exchange rates and making them widely applicable, even if they diverge somewhat from equilibrium levels. As the divergence widens, gray and black markets for foreign currency spring up, and eventually the government loses control of the foreign exchange rate. In such cases, most foreign currency will be exchanged for domestic currency through unofficial channels at rates that more closely reflect its opportunity costs to importers and exporters. Furtive foreign exchange markets reflect a breakdown of government policy, but when government policy is generally effective, foreign exchange transactions are handled routinely through the central bank.

Capital markets, where governments attempt to influence interest rates, are structured quite differently. Almost everyone in a monetary economy has the opportunity to be either a borrower or a lender, however small, while the great majority of a country's population seldom sees another country's currency. Each time a borrowing-lending agreement is transacted, a miniature capital market has been established. No matter what the central government may want the interest rate in the society to be, such individual capital transactions can and do go on. Consequently, understanding the functioning of a country's capital markets and the role of government policy in setting interest rates in those capital markets is much more complicated than understanding how foreign exchange rates are set. In turn, understanding wage rate formation is more complicated still and would take the analysis in this chapter beyond its primary focus on macroeconomic issues.

Multiple Tasks

Government policy with respect to capital markets is significantly affected by three related factors: interest rate formation, the development of financial institutions, and the impact of monetary policy as an outgrowth of budgetary and fiscal policy. Because there are two legitimate interpretations of an interest rate, government policy is frequently caught between the scarcity value of capital in increasing production and a desire to make capital available at a rate that reflects the government's valuation of future consumption in relation to current consumption.

Keeping interest rates low reflects a concern for the welfare of future generations. Low interest rates make it cheaper to invest in a capital stock to bequeath to children and grandchildren, and they make the conservation of natural resources and investments in social infrastructure with long expected lives easier to justify economically. Keeping interest rates high, on the other hand, reflects the current scarcity and productivity of capital in production, induces greater savings, and comes closer to matching the rate of time discount of private decision makers in the economy. The first issue for government policy with respect to capital markets is at what level interest rates will be formed in the absence of specific interventions designed to alter those rates.

The second issue concerns the development of major institutions that actually carry out the day-to-day functions in a capital market. In simple economies, households with surplus cash can lend to their neighbors who need a temporary addition to their incomes. But the essence of a modernizing economy is its reliance on an emerging and developing network of financial intermediaries that provide convenient and safe places to save money as well as efficient vehicles for accumulating savings for onward loans to businesses that make real investments to expand the productive capacity of the economy.

In most economies capital markets are better developed in urban centers and wealthier agricultural areas, where there are local financial intermediaries, such as banks, savings and loan companies, and insurance companies that provide indirect financing to firms and other investors. This uneven development of financial institutions is one of the factors that causes segmentation of the capital market and a wide range of interest rates, even for similar risks and transaction costs. The result is that rural credit markets tend to be informal, with very high interest rates.

The third factor affecting government policy on interest rates is not unique to developing countries. The role of monetary policy as it serves to facilitate fiscal policy and the financing of government budget deficits is a topic of great concern in developed countries as well. To avoid inflation, the growth in money supply should not be significantly greater than the growth in real output plus changes in the willingness to hold money, which increases dramatically as an economy becomes monetized. But "tight money" means that a government deficit must be financed from private savings (or from abroad), which tends to drive up interest rates, as private borrowers compete with the government for the available capital. Alternatively, monetizing the government deficit usually leads to inflation, which lowers the value of holding a monetary debt instrument. Lenders understandably insist on higher interest rates to compensate for this decline in value.

Moving in the Right Direction

Capital moves relatively freely internationally, as modern communications and a sophisticated global banking system permit billions of dollars to be moved anywhere in the world at a moment's notice. This mobility of capital further complicates the link between interest rates and monetary policy. High interest rates in a country attract an inflow of international capital; low interest rates tend to cause a capital outflow. These flows of international capital affect the supply of and demand for foreign currency and thus influence the exchange rate. Since the equilibrium exchange rate is significantly affected by differential inflation among trading partners, the connections among monetary policy and inflation, interest rates and exchange rates, and interest rates and monetary policy become obvious, although they are extraordinarily complicated and not well understood. Indeed, these connections sometimes seem so powerful that individual governments appear to have few degrees of freedom to set their macro policies independently of what the global financial market considers prudent. At a minimum, the costs of policy independence in terms of economic growth forgone are higher because of these connections than when they were weaker in the 1960s and 1970s.

Growth-oriented financial policy that would satisfy global investors requires that a government manage its macro policy so that inflation is modest, set its nominal official interest rate at a level higher than the rate of inflation so that the real official interest rate is positive, and avoid the imposition of regulations that would unnecessarily constrain the growth of financial institutions. Such financial policy causes financial deepening as the services of financial institutions become more widespread. Financial deepening in turn results in (and is assisted by) more rapid economic development. Conversely, negative real rates of interest and excessive regulation cause financial repression. The outcome typically is financial disintermediation—a smaller role for financial institutions—and stagnant or even negative economic growth. The rural sector in particular benefits from an expansion of the financial institutions that gradually replace the higher-cost, informal sources of credit. Inversely, financial repression and disintermediation place a heavy burden on development of the rural sector.

MACRO PRICES AND CHOICE OF TECHNOLOGY

An unfavorable macroeconomic environment in general, and distorted macro prices in particular, will ultimately erode plans to develop the food and agricultural sector. A simple example that integrates effects on production, marketing, and consumption illustrates why. Before rice can be eaten, it must first be grown and then processed into the milled rice preferred by consumers. How the milling is done turns out to be very important, because it affects employment, income distribution, the amount of rice available to consumers (or the amount of rice imported or exported), and incentives to producers to grow rice.

The range of technologies available for milling rice varies enormously, from hand-pounding with a pole in a hollowed log to very sophisticated and expensive multiple-pass milling machines integrated with large-scale drying and storage facilities, which provide optimal control over the rice grain from delivery after harvest to packaging for consumers.

Rice milling facilities in between these two extremes range from very small, self-contained mills, which offer labor savings over hand-pounding at modest capital expense, to larger mills, which become progressively more expensive, more labor-saving, and more technically efficient in converting paddy rice into milled rice. The choice is not restricted to the extremes, although either can be appropriate in particular circumstances. The choice is wide. The opportunity exists to find just the right combination of investment cost, use of labor, and technical efficiency to fit a particular local environment.

What is the appropriate choice of technique in rice milling? The more costly techniques in terms of investment per ton of milling capacity are also more technically efficient. For each ton of rough rice input, the more sophisticated facilities produce higher-quality rice with less waste. The smaller and cheaper mills, however, need more labor per ton of capacity and create more jobs than do larger-scale mills. When the private sector is making the investment decision in the context of market prices, the technique that is least costly per ton of output will be installed. (See chapter 30 for a more complete analysis of this decision.)

However, the relevant prices in the rice miller's decision are not set solely by exogenous market forces; they are susceptible to policy influence. The miller's calculations depend on nearly every important macroeconomic variable in a country: foreign exchange rates, interest rates, wage rates, and rice prices. Foreign exchange rates dictate the cost of imported machinery for the rice mill, interest rates dictate the cost of the loan to pay for the machinery and the building, wage rates determine the labor costs of running the establishment after it is operational, and rice prices determine the value of the additional milled rice produced from each ton of paddy input by more technically efficient facilities.

When macro policy alters these important prices from their equilibrium values based on existing institutions and domestic abundance or scarcity of the factors, the impact on choice of technique can be dramatic. When grain prices are kept low to favor consumers, storage and processing facilities that save grain are not so profitable; few investments are made to save grain, and little management effort is exerted to run the available facilities efficiently. When interest rates are heavily subsidized and wage rates for unskilled labor are raised by legislation, large-scale, capital-intensive mills are installed in the midst of widespread unemployment. If foreign exchange is allocated to preferred investors at a cheap price, they will invest heavily in imported machinery, which tends to be labor-displacing, whereas other investors outside the allocation process might not even be able to purchase spare parts for their trucks or small-scale mills. Although the example here uses rice mills, the impact of distorted macro prices extends to nearly every sector and investment decision.

The overwhelming lesson of development experience since the 1960s is that the efficiency with which resources are allocated determines how dynamic the growth path will be. This notion is contrary to early expectations of many economists and planners, who noted that static economic losses to allocative inefficiencies tend to be very small, typically less than two percent of national income even for severe distortions, and hence could easily be dominated by more rapid growth. Just the opposite has happened.

The dynamic efficiency losses are compounded, not eliminated, in the face of macro policy that distorts the allocation of economic factors from their most productive uses. These distortions are the main costs to economic growth, not the lost favor of the international financial community. The distortions usually found—overvalued domestic currencies, subsidized interest rates, minimum wage legislation, depressed agricultural incentives, and low food prices—are often motivated by short-run concerns over economic growth and the distribution of output, the basic price dilemma again. But economic growth, including growth in rural areas, is ultimately inhibited by such a set of macro signals. At the same time, the short-run distributional and welfare concerns remain and, indeed, are exacerbated if attempts are made to bring the macro prices and macro policy into alignment with the underlying scarcity value of resources.

To address these problems, structural adjustment programs have been introduced to change the relationship betwen the public and private sectors and the participation of the public sector in the economy. Typically, the government must be reduced in size and redirected to do different things. And it must do the "right things" well if the economy is to prosper (Bromley 1995).

AGRICULTURE AND ECONOMIC GROWTH

Why would a policy maker in a poor country choose to invest in the agricultural sector? It would seem to be an unwise choice if one were influenced by the labor-surplus model of development, with its (at best) passive role for agriculture, by the persistent decline in the share of agriculture in a growing economy, and by the long-term downward trend in prices of basic foods that has occurred during the second half of the twentieth century. For the poorest countries, in which 40 to 50 percent of GDP, 70 to 80 percent of the work force, and 70 to 90 percent of foreign exchange earnings are accounted for by agriculture, the answer is obvious. For these countries, it is impossible to sustain broad-based economic growth without the active participation of the rural economy.

The answer is less obvious for countries that have already escaped the bottom of the poverty trap, but the influence of performance in the agricultural sector on economic growth remains significant well into the development process. Two broad categories of linkages create this connection. First are the traditional market-mediated linkages that form the core of economic analysis of the role of agriculture in economic development. These are often divided into Lewis linkages, which operate through factor markets that transfer labor and capital from agriculture to industry, and Johnston-Mellor linkages, which operate through product markets. The factor-market linkages between agriculture and industry have been so important to the growth process that they led Lewis to the following observation in his famous article published in 1954, for which he won the Nobel Prize in economics: "Industrialization is dependent upon agricultural improvement; it is not profitable to produce a growing volume of manufactures unless agricultural production is growing simultaneously. This is also why industrial and agrarian revolutions always go together, and why economies in which agriculture is stagnant do not show industrial development" (Lewis 1954, 29). Historically, higher productivity in agriculture has provided labor and capital to the expanding industrial sector, to the mutual benefit of both sectors.

In addition to these factor-market linkages, Johnston and Mellor identified a broader set of linkages between the agricultural sector and economic growth in the nonagricultural sector. Contributions through these linkages include food for the industrial work force (thus avoiding the worsening terms of trade for industry that concerned Lewis), raw materials for agro-processing industries, markets for industrial output, especially for the low-quality goods that cannot compete in export markets but which domestic factories produce as part of a learning process, and export earnings that pay for imported capital equipment and intermediate inputs. The Johnston-Mellor linkages tend to be mediated by product markets that become progressively more efficient during the course of economic development (Johnston and Mellor 1961; Ranis, Stewart, and Angeles-Reyes 1990; Timmer 1992; Delgado et al. 1994).

The role of government in strengthening both the Lewis and Johnston-Mellor linkages is to invest in agricultural development at rates dictated by the profitability of increased commodity output and to make factor and product markets more efficient. These linkages are the most important connections between agriculture and economic growth. These linkages are not discussed further here, for two reasons. First, other chapters in this volume discuss them in more detail. Second, and more important, the policy implications of Lewis linkages and Johnston-Mellor linkages are well understood, even if the policies are not always implemented. A market-based analysis of investments in agricultural development, using standard neoclassical economic principles, when coupled to the physical and institutional development of markets themselves, leads to an optimal development strategy.

Another category of linkages, however, is not well mediated by market forces even when markets are working well. Sensitive interventions by governments into market-determined outcomes are required in these circumstances if agriculture is to play its optimal role in support of the rest of the economy (Timmer 1993a; Barrett and Carter 1994). The rest of this chapter explores the mechanisms that provide nonmarket links between agricultural growth and growth in productivity of the nonagricultural sector.

THE RURAL ECONOMY AND GROWTH IN THE MACRO ECONOMY

The most satisfactory approach to measuring the nonmarket impact of agriculture on economic growth is to begin by augmenting recently developed theories of economic growth, which are summarized in Barro and Sala-i-Martin (1995). Typical empirical specifications of modern growth models control for initial conditions, factor accumulation, and quality improvements in labor and capital and then proceed to search for control variables that affect the overall efficiency of resource allocation. Openness of the economy, size of government, price distortions, and instability in the macro economy all influence this efficiency, but the potential contribution of agricultural growth to economic efficiency has never been directly tested in the new models. Indeed, agriculture is not even mentioned in the volume by Barro and Sala-i-Martin.

Early efforts to correct this omission are reported by Hwa (1988), Dawe (1993), and Chai (1995). Hwa finds that growth in agricultural productivity is more important than inflation or trade orientation in explaining growth in total factor productivity, although all three factors are statistically significant. Chai finds that "good" policy with respect to reversing urban bias raises the rate of economic growth per capita by 1.46 percent per year. Urban bias in government policy contributes roughly one-third of the difference in economic performance between countries that have very rapid growth in income per capita and those that have suffered stagnation or retardation.[1]

This positive relationship between the rate of economic growth and growth in rural economies shows clearly in the historical record. In a sample of seventy developing countries, a highly significant positive relationship existed, from 1960 to 1985, between growth in the agricultural sector and growth in the non-agricultural sector; about 20 percent of the growth rate in agriculture was added to the exogenous growth rate in nonagriculture (Timmer 1995). This direct and positive association between growth in the two sectors does not, of course, show causation. Good macroeconomic policy, for example, could have caused both sectors to grow independently. However, rates of agricultural growth lagged five years were a separate, significant additional factor influencing growth in the nonagricultural economy, and such a lag suggests a more causal relationship.

The linkages that help produce this causal relationship are nebulous and hard to measure, because the market-mediated linkages through Lewis and Johnston-Mellor mechanisms are automatically included at their market values in traditional growth accounting. The additional linkages identified here grow explicitly out of market failures, and, if they are quantitatively important, government interventions are required if the growth process is to proceed as rapidly as possible. These nonmarket linkages stem from several sources, and their impact can also be seen within a growth-accounting framework.

FACTOR ACCUMULATION AND FACTOR PRODUCTIVITY

It has been known since the growth accounting carried out by Abramovitz (1956), Solow (1956), and Denison (1967) that differential rates of economic growth are not explained entirely by different rates of growth in physical measures of labor and capital. An additional element is the productivity of labor and capital. Differences in factor productivity are very substantial when contributions of human capital are considered part of factor productivity.

The rapidly growing countries of East and Southeast Asia are distinguished from the rest of the developing world by two factors: high rates of capital accumulation and the productivity with which capital and labor are used. Factor productivity has been growing rapidly in these countries, but it has fallen in Africa and Latin America (World Bank 1991). If "quality" of capital and labor is included as a component of physical accumulation, most differences in growth of total factor productivity disappear (Young 1995). But this approach simply pushes the search for an explanation of differential rates of economic growth to another level and conceals the policy significance of increases in human capital and the mechanisms that lead to its creation.

Empirically, studies of economic growth have discovered three classes of explanatory variables that account for differences in productivity growth for the entire economy—that is, growth net of contributions from factor accumulation. Broadly stated, they are the positive effects of a competitive cost structure, the negative effects from instability, and the positive effects of growth in agricultural productivity. The third effect is difficult to specify in a statistically satisfactory way. The best approach is to test whether factors within the agricultural sector, such as public infrastructure, private investments, or human capital, make a differential contribution to economic growth when measured in comparison with the same independent variables in aggregate in the growth equation. To date, only the human capital variable has been disaggregated into rural and nonrural components (Chai 1995). The result of this one test, however, is quite powerful. Rural human capital is much more important than nonrural human capital in explaining differential growth rates in income per capita among developing countries (holding constant all of the standard factors in a growth equation). Indeed, an increase of one standard deviation in rural human capital would increase the aggregate rate of economic growth by as much as similar improvements in macroeconomic policy or composition of government expenditures.[2] Increases in urban human capital seem not to increase economic growth at all when the level of rural human capital is held constant, probably because such increases would further increase the degree of urban bias, which has a strongly negative effect on economic growth (Chai 1995).

THE NONMARKET LINKAGE MECHANISMS

It is important to know empirically that the rural economy contributes to aggregate economic growth, after controlling for the contributions through the Lewis and Johnston-Mellor linkages. To provide guidance to policy makers, however, it is necessary to identify the nonmarket mechanisms that translate faster agricultural growth into measurably faster economic growth in aggregate, after controlling for the direct contribution of the agricultural sector to growth in GDP itself. These mechanisms include the efficiency with which rural households allocate the resources at their disposal and the low opportunity cost of much household labor. Making more resources available to these households, in the form of higher incomes or new technologies, raises factor productivity for the entire economy (Timmer 1995).

In addition, one reason for the robust relationship between agricultural growth and improvements in total factor productivity arises because of a statistical artifact. Virtually none of the savings (at the margin) within rural households is captured in national income accounts. Because there are so few financial intermediaries in rural areas, savings by farm households are either held as liquid but nonproductive assets, such as gold or jewelry, or they are invested in nonliquid but productive assets, such as livestock, orchards, land improvement, farm implements, or even education (Morduch 1991).

But what if the rural economy is somehow transformed from one that is extremely risky, with few productive investment opportunities, to one that is stable, dynamic, and attractive as a place for individual households to invest? Higher incomes to rural households can then be channeled directly into productive investments on the farm or in the local economy, even though financial intermediaries are totally absent (Birdsall, Ross, and Sabot 1995; Timmer 1995). Greater output results, and this output *does* show up in national income.

To statisticians attempting to account for this growth it appears to be generated with little or no capital, a very efficient process indeed. Capital is used, of course, and proper accounting would identify and measure it. But such accounting would also involve a fundamental shift in attitudes about the productivity of very small and highly dispersed rural investments, as well as about the marginal savings propensity of rural households—and thus the desirability of allowing them to have higher incomes. Countries that stimulate farm incomes and encourage rural investments reap a statistical reward in addition to the higher rural output itself: the measurement of greater total factor productivity as a contributor to their rapid growth. The general failure of rural financial markets thus contributes to a systematic underutilization of rural resources. Higher (and more stable) prices for marketed output can partially correct for this failure, although the food price dilemma appears yet again, as there are many net food buyers even in rural areas. Their short-run nutrient intake could be threatened by the higher prices that are part of a strategy which aims to provide efficient levels of incentives.

Only in East and Southeast Asia has agriculture had a high priority in national plans because of its importance in feeding people and providing a spur to industrialization. In much of Africa and Latin America, a historically prolonged and deep urban bias is almost certain to have led to a distorted pattern of investment (Lipton 1977; 1993). Too much public and private capital has been invested in urban areas and too little in rural areas. Too much capital has been held as liquid and nonproductive investments that rural households use to manage risk. Too little capital has been invested in raising rural productivity.

This historical record suggests that such distortions have resulted in strikingly different marginal productivities of capital in urban and rural areas. A new growth strategy, such as those pursued in Indonesia after 1966, China after 1978, and Vietnam after 1989, which alters investment priorities in favor of rural growth, should be able to benefit from this disequilibrium in rates of return, at least initially. Such a switch in investment strategy and improved rates of return on capital would increase factor productivity, because of improved efficiency in resource allocation.

FOOD SECURITY, FOOD PRICE STABILITY, AND ECONOMIC GROWTH

An important reason for investing in a country's agricultural sector is the potential to stabilize the domestic food economy and thus enhance food security. This potential is greater in large countries that affect world prices when they import; in rice-based economies, because the world rice market is very thin and unstable; and for cropping systems in which reliance on irrigation makes domestic production less variable than prices in the world market. Food imports may well provide a more reliable base for food security than domestic food production in small countries, in wheat- and corn-based food systems, and in rainfed agriculture. There are many circumstances, however, in which imports of food may not offer greater stability.

For both microeconomic and macroeconomic reasons, no country has ever sustained the process of rapid economic growth without first solving the problem of food security. At the microeconomic level, inadequate and irregular access to food limits labor productivity and reduces investment in human capital (Bliss and Stern 1978; Strauss 1986; Fogel 1994; Williamson 1993). At the macroeconomic level, periodic food crises undermine political and economic stability, reducing both the level and the efficiency of investment (Timmer 1989, 1996a; Dawe 1996). The political importance of food security has not been entirely lost on government leaders (Kaplan 1984; Timmer 1993b), but its connection to economic growth raises the potential of linking the political economy of food security to macroeconomic efficiency.

Agricultural Productivity and Nutritional Status of Workers

In a long-run, dynamic context, rapid economic growth that differentially benefits the poor is the key to achieving food security. One reason is the important link between agricultural productivity and the nutritional status of workers. Fogel (1991), in his work on the factors causing the end of hunger and reductions in mortality in Western Europe, provides strong evidence for the importance of increasing caloric intake in reducing mortality and increasing productivity of the working poor. Using a robust biomedical relationship that links height, body mass, and mortality rates, Fogel calculates that increases in food intake among the British population since the late eighteenth century have contributed substantially to increased productivity and income per capita. "Thus, in combination, bringing the ultrapoor into the labor force and raising the energy available for work by those in the labor force explains about 30 percent of the British growth in per capita incomes over the past two centuries" (63).

Virtually all of the food that permitted this increase in nutrient intake was produced by the agricultural revolution in eighteenth- and early-nineteenth-century Great Britain. This agricultural revolution was not a simple response of private farmers to market signals. It was heavily stimulated by the protection offered by the Corn Laws, which both raised average prices for cereals and stabilized them in relation to prices in world markets (Williamson 1990). Much investment in rural infrastructure, even by private parties, was stimulated by these incentives.

More generally, increases in domestically produced food supplies contribute directly to increases in average caloric intake per capita, after controlling for changes in income per capita, income distribution, and food prices. Countries with rapidly increasing food production have much better records of poverty alleviation, perhaps because of changes in the local economics of access to food, changes that are not captured by aggregate statistics on incomes and prices.[3] Whatever the mechanisms, intensive campaigns to raise domestic food production, especially through rapid technical change, can be expected to have positive spillover effects on nutrient intake among the poor. Through the "Fogel linkages," this increased food security of the poor can contribute substantially to long-run economic growth.

Food security also has short-run dimensions. In the macroeconomic context discussed here, a common operational approach points to reasonable stability in the price of the basic foodstuff, both seasonally and from year to year. Food price stabilization confers several benefits. It is beneficial to food producers because it reduces the risk they face making productive investments. This reduction in risk encourages farmers to make greater investments in new innovations and technologies that increase farm productivity. An important component of these investments goes to rural human capital, which is important in the overall process of economic growth.

Consumers benefit from stable food prices because they do not have to incur the transactions costs from reallocating their budgets frequently, nor face the risk of sudden and sharp deterioration in their real income. This benefit accrues disproportionately to the poor because they spend a larger portion of their budgets on food and they react more sensitively to price changes than do the rich (Timmer 1981). Benefits to consumers from food price stabilization thus have a significant equity dimension, and stabilization plays an important role in the short-run alleviation of poverty.

The Macroeconomic Impact of Stabilizing Food Prices

An important class of benefits from stabilizing food prices is macroeconomic in nature. Price stabilization affects investment and growth throughout the entire economy, not just in the food sector. These effects can be large when food is a large share of the economy and when world grain markets are unstable.

Unstable food prices can increase or decrease the level of savings and investment in an economy. The rationale for a decrease is intuitively clear—greater uncertainty drives investors to brighter horizons. The rationale for an increase in the rate of savings and investment draws on the need for precautionary savings (Deaton 1992). Consumers save to protect themselves against the effects of a possible increase in food prices, whereas farmers save to insure themselves against a sudden drop in the crop price. These precautionary savings are kept in liquid form, to be called upon in the event of a sudden change in food prices, and might not contribute much to economic growth.

Also, the quantity of investment is not the only determinant of growth. The efficiency, or quality, of that investment is equally important. Food price instability can affect the quality of investment in at least two distinct ways. When food prices increase (because of a poor harvest or an increase in world prices), consumer expenditures on food also increase, because demand is price inelastic—that is, the percentage increase in price is greater than the percentage decline in the quantity consumed. The increase in expenditures on food causes expenditures for other commodities to fall, which lowers demand for all other commodities in the economy. The opposite situation occurs in the event of a good harvest, when consumer expenditures on food decrease. This reduction causes demand for other commodities to increase temporarily, putting upward pressure on prices in other sectors. Over time, if food is important in macroeconomic terms, instability in food prices causes instability in all other prices in the economy.

These "spillover" effects from the food economy into other sectors have two separate consequences. First, risk is increased in all sectors, because nonfood prices fluctuate more than if food prices were stable. Second, the price changes that occur throughout the economy contain relatively little information about long-run investment opportunities—a classic example of a "signal extraction" problem (Lucas 1973).

The fundamental role of prices in a market economy is to serve as signals for allocating both consumption and investment resources. If demand curves shift because of sustained growth in incomes or a change in consumer preferences, or supply curves shift because of changes in technology used in the production process, then relative prices should change accordingly. These price changes convey information to investors about fundamental shifts in expected returns on investment opportunities, shifts that should lead to a reallocation of investment. If prices are changing frequently in various sectors throughout the economy because of temporary and unexpected fluctuations in the domestic grain harvest or in the world price of food, however, prices convey less information about attractive opportunities for long-run investment than if food prices were stable. Rapid and variable rates of inflation can slow down the rate of economic growth. When food is a significant share of the economy, highly variable food prices can cause similar problems.

The quality of investment might decline for another reason. If spillovers from the food and agricultural sector increase risk throughout the economy, investment is biased toward more speculative activities and away from fundamentally productive activities, such as investment in machinery and equipment, and away from investments in the long-term development of human capital. Both types of investment are closely associated with higher rates of economic growth (De Long and Summers 1991).

Consequently, instability in the food sector can have three important macro-level effects. It can affect the quantity of investment, through an increase in precautionary savings or a decrease caused by greater uncertainty. It can *decrease* the quality of investment (rate of return), because prices contain less information that is relevant for long-run investment. Finally, because of spillovers creating additional risk throughout the economy, instability can induce a *bias* toward speculative rather than productive investment activities and thereby slow down economic growth. Thus, food security can influence economic growth in two ways: through the impact on labor productivity of the Fogel linkages, and through the quantity and efficiency of investment because of the stability linkages.

An Empirical Example: Stabilizing Rice Prices in Indonesia

The net effect of the stability linkages can be determined only empirically. Dawe (1996) demonstrates that when instability is transmitted to the macro economy from instability in exports, the negative impact on efficiency of investment is substantially larger than the positive impact on precautionary savings. Both are statistically significant. When Dawe's coefficients were applied to the program that stabilizes rice prices in Indonesia, contributions to economic growth of nearly one percentage point per year were recorded in the late 1960s and early 1970s, when rice was a quarter of the Indonesian economy. In the early 1990s, despite highly unstable prices for rice in the world market, the price stabilization program contributed less than 0.2 percentage points of economic growth each year, because the share of rice in the much larger Indonesian economy had declined to about 5 percent. Despite the falling share of rice in the economy, over the twenty-five years of the first long-term development plan (1969–94), stabilizing rice prices raised per capita GDP by about 11 percent (Timmer 1996b).

Because the world rice market historically has been extremely unstable, it is difficult to imagine how Indonesia could have been so successful in stabilizing its domestic rice price over the 1969–94 period without growing most of the rice itself. Even for a country as large as Indonesia, however, a rigid goal of self-sufficiency probably does more to destabilize the food economy than to stabilize it. Imports and exports of rice, at the margin, have kept the cost of the stabilization program under control (Timmer 1996b). But on average since the early 1980s Indonesia has produced nearly all of the rice it consumed. The country was able to do this while demand, spurred by population growth and higher income per capita, especially among the poor, was increasing at a rate of more than 3 percent per year. Food security for Indonesia meant rapid poverty alleviation through rural-oriented economic growth and stable rice prices. The economic growth, its distribution toward the poor, and price stability were possible only with rapid increases in rice production. The country made the necessary rural investments and maintained the favorable macroeconomic environment that made these gains in production and income possible. But the combination of growth, stability, and poverty alleviation is a story of political economy, not simply neoclassical economics (Hill 1995).

THE MACRO PERSPECTIVE REVISITED: THE POLITICAL ECONOMY OF INVESTING IN THE RURAL SECTOR

If the route to rapid economic growth is so obvious—a veritable superhighway leading from rapid increases in agricultural output to food security, and from there through a maze of linkages to a rapidly growing industrial economy—why do so many countries fail to find it? There are three components to the answer: technology, economics, and politics.

It is possible that the technology does not exist to foster rapid growth in agricultural productivity in all environmental settings. In particular, the multistaple, rainfed food systems of sub-Saharan Africa have not seen the technological breakthroughs that provided so much impetus to agricultural investment in the irrigated rice and wheat zones of Asia. Perhaps not as much money and intellectual effort have been invested in solving Africa's problems as was forthcoming in the 1960s and 1970s in producing the Green Revolution for Asia (Eicher 1992). But an "agriculture-led" growth strategy without rapid increases in agricultural productivity must rely solely on higher food prices, and, rather than speed up the development process, high food prices alone probably slow it down.

Although the major components of a successful development strategy can be sketched out in a single chapter, every country will have a unique set of circumstances that require specific adaptations and flexibility in policy making if the macroeconomic environment is to be stable and supportive of long-term investments. Analyzing emerging problems and designing appropriate policy responses remain highly skilled tasks, and the global interactions noted earlier have made the tasks harder, not easier. There may be fewer degrees of freedom in policy choice, thus narrowing the range of options for policy analysis, but the margin for error is much smaller than before. The time before mistakes become visible is much shorter. Well-trained economists who understand this new policy environment and can function effectively in it will continue to earn their keep.

Most obvious to the naked eye, the roadblocks to rapid economic growth are often political. The underlying sources of rapid economic growth are high rates of investment and improved efficiency in using resources. Both require short-run sacrifices for long-run gain, and few political systems reward that choice. Politicians do not necessarily need to be venal and uncaring about the welfare of their people to opt for short-run gains at the expense of future economic growth. Indeed, if they appear to be shortsighted, they often reflect the voting preferences of the population. Finding political systems that are capable of choosing savings and efficiency over consumption and transfers of rents is the modern challenge of development.

NOTES

I have drawn from several works of mine, especially *Food Policy Analysis* (Timmer, Falcon, and Pearson 1983) and from the Hibbard Lecture I gave at the University of Wisconsin (Timmer 1993a). I thank Carol F. Timmer for the editorial insights that help link diverse ideas from separate articles, and the editors for a number of very helpful comments on the first draft. Tom Reardon provided useful suggestions for making the chapter more accessible for classroom use. The first draft of this chapter was prepared while I was a visiting professor in the Masters in Public Policy Programme at the National University of Singapore.

1. These statistical results, and those discussed in the next paragraph, are based on a data set originally developed by Barro and Lee (1994) for their analysis of the impact of educational stocks on economic growth between 1960 and 1985. For a sample of seventy developing countries, including several in Africa, Chai was able to disaggregate the Barro-Lee educational stock levels into separate stocks of urban and rural years of schooling per capita. His growth equations then followed the Barro-Lee specifications by including state variables that control for initial conditions (per capita income, physical capital, and human capital) and "environmental" variables that control for government consumption, the rate of investment, the fertility rate, the black market premium on foreign exchange, and measures of political instability. Chai's innovation was the separate inclusion of rural and urban per capita stock levels of education and, as a measure of urban bias, the ratio of urban stocks to rural stocks of education. This latter specification displayed extremely robust statistical results.

2. The costs of increasing rural human capital by one standard deviation in Chai's sample are not known, and thus they cannot be compared directly with the costs of improving macroeconomic policy or the composition of government expenditures by one standard deviation. The usefulness of the comparison is its historical concreteness. With a normal distribution, there is an equal likelihood that a country would be one standard deviation above or below the mean for each measure. Thus, these are "historically equal" comparisons, but not "equal cost" comparisons.

3. See Barrett and Carter (1994) for the African dimensions of this argument.

REFERENCES

Abramovitz, Moses. 1956. "Resource and Output Trends in the United States since 1870." *American Economic Review* 46 (2): 5–23.

Barrett, Christopher, and Michael Carter. 1994. "Does It Take More Than Market Liberalization? The Economics of Sustainable Agrarian Growth and Transformation." Working Paper Series on Development at a Crossroads: Uncertain Paths to Sustainability, no. 4, Global Studies Research Program, University of Wisconsin, Madison.

Barro, Robert J., and Jong-Hwa Lee. 1994. "Sources of Economic Growth," *Carnegie-Rochester Conference Series on Public Policy*, 1–46. Amsterdam: North-Holland/Elsevier.

Barro, Robert J., and Xavier Sala-i-Martin. 1995. *Economic Growth*. New York: McGraw-Hill.

Birdsall, Nancy, David Ross, and Richard Sabot. 1995. "Inequality and Growth Reconsidered: Lessons from East Asia." *World Bank Economic Review* 9 (3): 477–508.

Bliss, Christopher, and Nicholas Stern. 1978. "Productivity, Wages and Nutrition: Parts I and II." *Journal of Development Economics* 5 (4): 331–98.

Bromley, Daniel W. 1995. "Development Reconsidered: The African Challenge." *Food Policy* 20 (5): 425–38.

Chai, Chuckra P. 1995. *Rural Human Capital and Economic Growth in Developing Countries*. Senior honors thesis, Department of Economics, Harvard University.

Dawe, David. 1993. *The Effects of Export Instability on Investment: The Information Content of Prices and Growth*. Ph.D. diss., Harvard University.

———. 1996. "A New Look at the Effects of Export Instability on Investment and Growth." *World Development* 24, no. 12 (December): 1905–15.

Deaton, Angus S. 1992. *Understanding Consumption*. Oxford: Clarendon Press.

Delgado, Christopher, et al. 1994. *Agricultural Growth Linkages in Sub-Saharan Africa*. Washington, D.C.: United States Agency for International Development.

De Long, J. Bradford, and Lawrence H. Summers. 1991. "Equipment Investment and Economic Growth." *Quarterly Journal of Economics* 106, no. 2:445–502.

Denison, Edward F. 1967. *Why Economic Growth Rates Differ: Postwar Experience in Nine Western Countries*. Washington, D.C.: Brookings Institution.

Eicher, Carl K. 1992. "African Agricultural Development Strategies." In *Alternative Development Strategies in Sub-Saharan Africa*, edited by Frances Stewart, Sanjaya Lall, and Samuel Wangwe, 79–102. London: Macmillan.

Fogel, Robert W. 1991. "The Conquest of High Mortality and Hunger in Europe and America: Timing and Mechanisms." In *Favorites of Fortune: Technology, Growth, and Economic Development since the Industrial Revolution*, edited by Patrice Higonnet, David S. Landes, and Henry Rosovsky, 35–71. Cambridge: Harvard University Press.

———. 1994. "Economic Growth, Population Theory, and Physiology: The Bearing of Long-Term Processes on the Making of Economic Policy." (Nobel Prize speech) *American Economic Review* 84, no. 3 (June): 369–95.

Hill, Hal. 1995. *The Indonesian Economy since 1966: Southeast Asia's Emerging Giant*. Cambridge: Cambridge University Press.

Hwa, Erh-Cheng. 1988. "The Contribution of Agriculture to Economic Growth: Some Empirical Evidence." *World Development* 16 (11): 1329–39.

Johnston, Bruce F., and John W. Mellor. 1961. "The Role of Agriculture in Economic Development." *American Economic Review* 51 (4): 566–93.

Kaplan, Steven Laurence. 1984. *Provisioning Paris: Merchants and Millers in the Grain and Flour Trade during the Eighteenth Century.* Ithaca: Cornell University Press.

Lewis, W. Arthur. 1954. "Economic Development with Unlimited Supplies of Labor." *The Manchester School* 22:3–42.

Lipton, Michael. 1977. *Why Poor People Stay Poor: Urban Bias in World Development.* Cambridge: Harvard University Press.

———. 1993. "Urban Bias: Of Consequences, Classes, and Causality." In *Beyond Urban Bias,* edited by Ashutosh Varshney, 229–58. London: Frank Cass.

Lucas, Robert E. 1973. "Some International Evidence on Output-Inflation Tradeoffs." *American Economic Review* 63:326–34.

Morduch, Jonathan. 1991. *Risk and Welfare in Developing Countries.* Ph.D. diss., Harvard University.

Ranis, Gustav, Frances Stewart, and Edna Angeles-Reyes. 1990. *Linkages in Developing Countries: A Philippine Study.* San Francisco, Calif.: ICS Press for the International Center for Economic Growth.

Solow, Robert M. 1956. "A Contribution to the Theory of Economic Growth." *Quarterly Journal of Economics* 70, no. 1 (February): 65–94.

Strauss, John. 1986. "Does Better Nutrition Raise Farm Productivity?" *Journal of Political Economy* 94, no. 2:297–320.

Timmer, C. Peter. 1981. "Is There 'Curvature' in the Slutsky Matrix?" *Review of Economics and Statistics* 62, no. 3 (August): 395–402.

———. 1989. "Food Price Policy: The Rationale for Government Intervention." *Food Policy* 14, no. 1 (February): 17–42.

———. 1992. "Agriculture and Economic Development Revisited." *Agricultural Systems* 38, no. 5:1–35 (special edition, edited by Paul S. Teng and Fritz W. T. Penning de Vries [Amsterdam: Elsevier]).

———. 1993a. *Why Markets and Politics Undervalue the Role of Agriculture in Economic Development.* Benjamin H. Hibbard Memorial Lecture Series, Department of Agricultural Economics, University of Wisconsin, Madison.

———. 1993b. "Rural Bias in the East and Southeast Asian Rice Economy: Indonesia in Comparative Perspective." In *Beyond Urban Bias,* edited by Ashutosh Varshney, 149–76. London: Frank Cass.

———. 1995. "Getting Agriculture Moving: Do Markets Provide the Right Signals?" *Food Policy* 20, no. 5 (October): 455–72.

———. 1996a. "Food Supplies and Economic Growth in Great Britain, Japan, and Indonesia." Typescript, Harvard Institute for International Development, Harvard University.

———. 1996b. "Does BULOG Stabilize Rice Prices in Indonesia? Should It Try?" *Bulletin of Indonesian Economic Studies* 32, no. 2 (August): 45–74.

Timmer, C. Peter, Walter P. Falcon, and Scott R. Pearson. 1983. *Food Policy Analysis.* Baltimore: Johns Hopkins University Press for the World Bank.

Williamson, Jeffrey G. 1990. "The Impact of the Corn Laws Just Prior to Repeal." *Explorations in Economic History* 27:123–56.

———. 1993. "Human Capital Deepening, Inequality, and Demographic Events along the Asia-Pacific Rim." In *Human Resources in Development along the Asia-Pacific Rim,* edited by Naohiro Ogawa, Gavin W. Jones, and Jeffrey G. Williamson. Singapore: Oxford University Press.

World Bank. 1991. *World Development Report, 1991.* New York: Oxford University Press for the World Bank.

Young, Alwyn. 1995. "The Tyranny of Numbers: Confronting the Statistical Realities of the East Asian Growth Experience." *Quarterly Journal of Economics* 110, no. 3:641–80.

12

The Case for Trade Liberalization

RUDIGER DORNBUSCH

In a broad swing of the pendulum, developing countries have been shifting from severe and destructive protection to free trade fever. Many of the notable examples are in Latin America. Mexico, after a major unilateral trade liberalization, has negotiated a free trade agreement with Canada and the United States; Chile, traditionally a highly protected country, is a leading example of reducing trade barriers; Argentina and Brazil have entered free trade agreements. A free trade area for the Americas is becoming a serious possibility. The enthusiasm for more openness of the economy is not limited to liberalization. There are also cases in Africa—for example Ghana and Botswana—to demonstrate the possibility and the benefits of opening up.

This new enthusiasm for freer trade stems from four overlapping sources.

Anti-statism. In the 1980s, the world has seen a broad intellectual swing away from emphasizing the beneficial role of the state, and protection is seen as one of the manifestations of an overly intrusive state. Of course, a shift to a liberal trade regime has not been the by-product of a more democratic society: Chile under Pinochet or Korea in its liberalizing phase were under authoritarian rule. "Two cheers for the market, but not three," the saying goes; today the market gets at least three cheers, which may be at least one too many.

Poor economic performance. Many developing countries have suffered dismal economic performance and declining macroeconomic policies that engendered debt crises and hyperinflation. Of course, part of the reason was also a very adverse external environment. But since the days of plentiful external credit are gone, attention must shift to productivity gains as the source of growth. Trade may offer part of the solution.

RUDIGER DORNBUSCH is professor of economics at the Massachusetts Institute of Technology, Cambridge, Massachusetts.

Previously published in the *Journal of Economic Perspectives,* Winter 1992:69–85, by the American Economic Association. Published with omissions and minor editorial revisions by permission of the author.

Information. Citizens worldwide are exposed to more information about the opportunities available in other countries. It is no longer possible to conceal that goods in a country cost three or four times the world price or that they are not available. The elite want their BMWs, almost as a civil right; and the poor want cheap food and the low-cost consumer durables that are available in world markets; firms know what technologies and inputs their competitors abroad can use and insist on the same access. It is no longer possible to assert that liberal trade policy must immiserize a country; on the contrary, many economic actors now see access to imports as a way of stretching their buying power.

World Bank pressure and evidence of success. Major research projects under the auspices of the National Bureau of Economic Research (NBER) and the World Bank have documented the problems of inward-looking trade strategies and discerned lessons from successful trade strategies (Balassa 1989; Bhagwati 1978: Bruton 1989; Krueger 1978, 1990; Pack 1988; Michaely, Choksi, and Papageorgiou 1991; Thomas and Nash 1991). The research helped diffuse the black-and-white debate—free trade versus protection—to reach a more differentiated judgment involving the importance of neutral trade regimes as opposed to regimes that are biased against exports. The favorable performance of countries which adopted outward-oriented policies served to make trade liberalization, broadly understood, a central condition for World Bank lending.[1]

This paper next reviews the actual situation of protection in developing countries, to set the stage for a discussion of the prospective gains from liberalization. Three experiences with liberalization are then briefly sketched and the question is raised as to what can go wrong. The paper concludes by taking up two directions in which liberalization is now moving, regional free trade zones and liberalization of trade in services.

PROTECTION IN DEVELOPING COUNTRIES

Protection became the mode for most developing countries during the 1930s. During the Depression, industrial countries adopted restrictive trade policies, and commodity prices—a major source of earnings for developing countries—collapsed. Debt service problems loomed (Eichengreen 1991). The pursuit of a policy of industrialization behind protective walls of tariffs and import quotas took hold first as a means of saving foreign exchange for debt payments and then became viewed as a development strategy. The strategy was predicated on the assumption that primary producing countries would inevitably face a deterioration of the terms of trade; growth in demand for primary commodities was believed to be small because of low income elasticities for commodities and ongoing substitution toward alternative materials. At the same time, high rates of technical progress on the supply side would create a situation of excess supply and declining relative prices.

Trade policy changed little in the period immediately after World War II. Industrial countries continued for some time with highly restrictive trade policies, while many developing countries did not face foreign exchange problems, because they had accumulated foreign exchange reserves during wartime and the subsequent boom in commodity prices during the Korean war. But then commodity prices collapsed again, and developing countries faced stark questions of what were the appropriate trade and exchange policies. As industrial countries moved gradually in the direction of trade liberalization and currency convertibility, should the developing world follow?

The prevailing view, especially in Latin America, was the doctrine from the United Nations Economic Commission for Latin America (ECLA). In this view, developing countries should pursue an import substitution industrialization strategy to avoid the problem of secularly deteriorating terms of trade (Prebisch 1959, 1984). Import substitution is a policy of developing domestic industry behind a high protective barrier of tariffs, quotas, and licences. That policy was pursued vigorously. Direct foreign investment helped industrialization proceed, in some cases with extraordinary success, as in Brazil.

There was an intellectual countercurrent supporting the classical case for free trade, notably in Jacob Viner's (1952) Rio de Janeiro lectures and Gottfried Haberler's (1988) Cairo lectures. The debate carried into the 1960s, when the protection doctrine became the main fare in the newly formed United Nations Conference on Trade and Development (UNCTAD), the intellectual forum in which developing countries shaped their views on trade and development strategy. Interestingly, while major progress was made in trade liberalization among industrialized countries under the General Agreement of Tariffs and Trade, that same GATT allows developing countries substantial leeway in maintaining trade protection (Finger 1991). This seems peculiar today, since poor countries ought to focus on making the best of their resources, but it fit the prevailing ECLA doctrine that protection was a pathway to development.

In the late 1960s and 1970s, protection in developing countries softened in at least one direction. Many countries recognized that protection by tariffs and quotas did keep imports out but that the resulting decline in demand for foreign exchange led to an appreciation of the currency and hence a severe tax on exports of both traditional commodities and emerging industrial goods. Unstable real exchange rates added to the hazards of export activities. Moreover, duties on imported intermediate goods first implied a tax on export activities using these goods, and then helped cause a currency overvaluation, which hurt export competitiveness of these products.

From an industrialization standpoint it made sense to avoid the anti-export ramifications of protectionist rates. The NBER studies mentioned earlier document that countries which adopted outward-oriented policies, at least to the extent of neutralizing anti-export bias, performed better than countries who failed to recognize the adverse effects of restrictions on their export potential.

While it is impossible to find a single representative number characterizing the restrictiveness of a trade regime, it is still possible to get an impression. An at-

TABLE 1
PROTECTION IN A SAMPLE OF FIFTY DEVELOPING COUNTRIES

| | Tariff Rate[a] | | Nontariff Measures[b] |
	All sectors	Manufacturers	
Caribbean	17	20	23
Central America	66	71	100
South America	31	55	60
North Africa	39	45	85
Other Africa	36	37	86
West Asia	5	6	11
Other Asia	25	27	21

SOURCE: Erzan and Kuwahara (1989).
[a]Percent ad valorem tariff.
[b]Percent of tariff positions covered by nontariff barriers.

tempt to measure effective tariff rates, making appropriate adjustments for non-tariff duties, has been made for the mid-1990s by Erzan and Kuwahara (1989). Table 1 presents some of their results. The first two columns show the effective tariff rates for various regions of the world on all sectors and on manufacturers, while the third column shows that nontariff barriers are sometimes responsible for at least half of the protectionism impact. The data reveal that South and Central America and North Africa have had particularly high average tariff rates, and even more so in manufacturing. Within manufacturing, Erzan and Kuwahara also found that machinery and equipment received significantly lower tariff rates than other manufactured goods.

More recently, many developing countries have gone beyond compensation for anti-export bias to more radical reform. Quotas are being turned into tariffs, tariffs are being more tightly focused, and tariff rates are being reduced. Invariably, trade policy reform has also been part of a much broader program of policy reform, including domestic stabilization and deregulation. Readers interested in the diverse experiences of many nations with such reforms might consult Michaely, Papageorgiou, and Choksi 1991; Thomas and Nash 1991; Shepherd and Langoni 1991; Whalley 1989; and World Bank (1987, 1988).

GAINS FROM LIBERALIZATION

Measuring the benefits of trade reform has been a frustrating endeavor. Although the discussions of trade policy at times give the impression that a liberal trade regime can do wonders for a country's economy, and most observers believe firmly that trade reform is beneficial, yet systematic attempts at quantification fail to single out trade policy as a major factor in economic growth. But then, of course, growth accounting has not come up with a satisfactory explanation for the residual, which may be as much as 30 to 50 percent of growth.

The channels through which trade liberalization could bring benefits are broadly these: improved resource allocation in line with social marginal costs and benefits; access to better technologies, inputs, and intermediate goods; an economy better able to take advantage of economies of scale and scope; greater domestic competition; availability of favorable growth externalities, like the transfer of know-how; and a shake-up of industry that may create a Schumpeterian environment especially conducive to growth. This section will comment on each of these factors.

The static gains from improved resource allocation are the classical source of a gain from freer trade. Under perfect competition a small, price-taking country will gain by eliminating tariffs. Consumers are better off because their incomes stretch further, and resources are used more efficiently because they are no longer used to produce goods that could be imported at a lower price. Harberger (1959) estimated the welfare cost of protection in Chile to amount to 2.5 percent of GNP, as opposed to 10 percent for domestic distortions.[2]

While the traditional discussion often focuses on final, homogenous goods, the case for freer trade is enriched by pointing out that trade liberalization increases the variety of goods and increases productivity by providing less expensive or higher quality intermediate goods. This aspect has been explored in some recent models of growth; for example, Romer (1989) emphasizes both the productivity of specialized resources and the limitations given by the size of the market. In a restricted economy, only a narrow range of specialized intermediate goods or capital goods can be profitably produced, and firms therefore cannot effectively exploit the full range of technological possibilities and a potentially broader range of inputs. In this model, having access to a greater variety of inputs does more for production than having a greater quantity of a narrow range of inputs. Thus, access to a variety of foreign inputs at a lower cost shifts the economy-wide production function outward, which illustrates a concrete link between productivity and the trade regime.

The availability of imported intermediate goods and of technology, whether licensed or embodied in imported capital goods, is an important additional source of gain in shedding a restrictive trade system. If foreign exchange restrictions, for example, make it impossible to use a superior process, resources are wasted. They are similarly wasted if duties or prohibitions foreclose the import of key intermediate goods that may be extravagantly expensive or impossible to produce locally. If appropriate intermediate goods can be imported, a country may easily become an exporter of labor-intensive tasks such as assembly services; without such imports, that value-added opportunity is lost, along with the opportunity to graduate over time from assembly to tasks with higher added value.

It is a well-known proposition that reducing certain tariffs, as opposed to eliminating all of them, is a more delicate issue. A partial tariff reduction is a second-best exercise, so welfare need not necessarily improve. However, it will generally be true that an equiproportionate cut in tariff rates will raise welfare. For more complicated situations of partial liberalization, computable general equilibrium models can (at least in principle) offer an answer as to the welfare effects.

Free trade leads to a more economically rational market structure. Gains from liberalization also result from scale economies and economies of scope that arise in wider markets. Moreover, markets in protected economies are narrow, and lack of competitors from the rest of the world fosters oligopoly and inefficiency. Protectionism can create market power for domestic firms in cases where under free trade there would be none.[3] The casual evidence of these effects is striking. For example, when Mexico liberalized, firms put under pressure by import competition rationallized their activities to the point that they became export competitive. In fact, they looked to export markets to achieve a scale that would allow them to be competitive. Particularly in small countries where imports are restricted, quality is exceptionally low and variety falls far short of what is available in the world market. And prices are, of course, far above the world market, the more so the smaller and more protected the country.

An open trading environment is also associated with a transfer of know-how. Much is made, rightly, of the transfer of knowledge virtually by osmosis. Haberler made the point this way: "What J. S. Mill said 100 years ago is still substantially true. 'It is hardly possible to overrate the value in the present low state of human improvement, of placing human beings in contact with persons dissimilar to themselves, and with modes of thought and action unlike those with which they are familiar. Such communication has always been, peculiarly in the present age, one of the primary sources of progress'" (1988, 29).

A similar argument underlies the discussion of the convergence of growth rates among countries in the world economoy, as in Baumol, Blackman, and Wolff 1989 and the literature reviewed in Edwards 1991. However, the force of the argument made by Mill and Haberler is lessened once protectionism is taken into account. Multinationals can bring direct foreign investment, technology, and knowledge, but under the cover of tariffs and quotas they may not do their best. Thus, in Argentina, the 1964 Ford Falcon was produced with the U.S. machinery of that time, without model change, for several decades.

Beyond the general benefit of exposure to an advanced, competitive world market, the act of trade liberalization also carries the potential of dynamic benefits. In their systematic study of industrialization and development, Chenery, Robinson, and Syrquin (1986) focused on the sources of growth in total factor productivity. Their work suggests that periods of trade liberalization also tend to be periods when total factor productivity growth is unusually high. Harrison (1991) and Salvatore and Hatcher (1991) discuss supportive evidence. The 1991 *World Development Report* shows, for a large group of countries, a positive association between trade liberalization and the residual in GDP growth after accounting for the growth in inputs (World Bank 1991, 100). An aggressive trade opening may well qualify as a Schumpeterian change that triggers growth. As Schumpeter wrote in 1934 (1983, 64–66): "Development in our sense is a distinct phenomenon. . . . It is spontaneous and discontinuous change in the channels of the flow, disturbance of equilibrium, which forever alters and displaces the equilibrium state previously existing. . . . Development in our sense then is defined by the carrying out of new combinations."

In Schumpeter's analysis, the discontinuity of events and opportunities is the critical ingredient in promoting a new growth environment, it is *change* that is the source of increased productivity. Such a discontinuity involves, specifically, the introduction of a new good, the introduction of a new method of production, the opening of a new market, the conquest of a new source of supply of raw materials or half-manufactured goods, and the carrying out of the new organization of any industry. Together, deregulation and trade reform can shake an economy out of a slow-growth trap and toward an acceleration of growth that then develops its own dynamics and financing. Of course, there is no basis here for a *sustained* increase in growth. Rather, the model suggests a temporary acceleration of growth that need not be sustained indefinately but will have shifted the economy to a higher growth path.

The Schumpeterian model has substantial theoretical support. For example, firms may well have available better techniques and good ideas, but they are unwilling to implement them except in the favorable setting of economywide, major and irreversible change. Once a program of liberalization is put in place, adaptation must take place, and that is the occasion for implementing major productivity improvements that have been on the shelves. The coordinated response to the change both acts to trigger externalities and assures thereby that a reversal will become far less likely. High rates of investment and the associated increase in productivity are a natural by-product of a successful break away from a trapped slow-growth economy. Trade liberalization also opens up opportunities, because access to cheap inputs creates export opportunities, which carry rents and profits that can be invested in capital goods, which in turn yield further productivity gains. Although case studies of liberalization paint this picture, it is hard to capture in systematic measurements and cross-country comparison.

It would be helpful at this stage to offer summary evidence on the proposition that outward orientation is beneficial, whatever the channels; but even though the case for these productivity gains is highly plausible, it has been hard to document in a clear-cut way. The comprehensive survey by Havrylishyn (1990) does identify systematic evidence in support of the theory, but it is not overwhelming. The most plausible evidence comes from case studies. The other important source of quasi evidence is the more novel work of modeling imperfectly competitive economies in computable general equilibrium models (for example, Norman 1990). These models highlight that, in specific market structures or with specific scale economies, the gains from liberalized trade can be substantial. In fact, in some examples the gains are far larger than the static resource allocation effects and come to more than 10 percent of GNP.

Recently, a number of studies have tried to investigate the link between growth performance and trade regime. The hypothesis, in line with the abovementioned arguments, would suggest that more open economies experience higher growth.

Of course, without a satisfactory single and internationally comparable measure of openness and with so many other critical factors, investigations of this hypothesis start with a major handicap. The difficulty is in standardizing for all the factors impinging on growth performance. Edwards (1991) investigates the link to growth performance of a broad range of indicators of openness proposed in the literature and concludes that the sum of the evidence (though few individual pieces of it) is persuasive of the beneficial effects of an outward trade orientation.

THREE EXAMPLES OF TRADE LIBERALIZATION: TURKEY, KOREA, AND MEXICO

Following an earlier attempt, Turkish liberalization took place in the early 1980s. Compared to Latin America, Turkey's encounter with a debt crisis came early. Growth based on borrowing from abroad had been strong, but when financing disappeared, an adjustment of the economy became necessary (Sareacoglu 1987; Celasun and Rodrik 1989; Michaely, Papageourgiou, and Choksi 1991). In the 1980–84 period, quotas were substantially eliminated, the exchange rate was depreciated, and the foreign exchange regime was liberalized. By the classification of a comparative World Bank study, the Turkish program was "major, strong, and sustained."

The results of Turkish opening (and of accompanying domestic political and economic stabilization and reform) are altogether striking. During the late 1970s, Turkish imports had been growing about 2 percent per year; while exports were declining 1 percent per year. But from 1979 to 1989, although Turkish imports grew by 10.4 percent per year, exports grew by 19.2 percent per year. Since overall growth in GDP was about 3 percent per year, this implies that trade became substantially more important to the Turkish economy. Interestingly, as Turkish imports and exports increased, manufacturing also grew, from 22 percent of GDP in 1980 to 27 percent of GDP in 1989.

A second example is Korea, where trade reform occurred steadily in the 1970s. Here, the trade liberalization was selective. Major sectors of the economy were excluded, but the selection was accomplished in a manner that apparently did not interfere with productivity and growth. Korea made a point, in particular, of allowing capital goods and intermediate goods to be imported. For example, automobile engines were first imported, then produced under license, and now under Korean design. By 1983, of some ten thousand product classes, 19.6 percent still contained import restrictions. By 1989 the fraction had declined to only 5.3 percent, and most of these were primary commodities.

Even though Korea liberalized only selectively, liberalization did take place. Back in 1960, the ratio of non-oil imports to GDP in Korea was less than 10 percent, similar to the figure today in Brazil or Argentina. But since 1973 or so, the figure has been in excess of 25 percent. With the help of a selectively liberal import strategy, Korea has been able to develop a highly competitive manufacturing sector that offers its own brand-names of increasing sophistication, ranging from cars to televisions and now high technology goods. Interestingly, even though trade had been substantially liberalized in the 1980s, of the 12 percent import ratio for finished manufacturing, 1.3 percent was in consumer goods. Thus, liberalization was conspicuously concentrated on capital goods.

A third example of liberalization is Mexico. Until 1985 Mexico was totally protected; tariffs, quotas on top, and licenses in addition just in case. The result was a very poor productivity performance and an extraordinary degree of monopoly, which was strongly reinforced by domestic restrictions on entry and external restrictions on direct investment.

Starting in 1985, the economy was opened. The scheme first envisaged was a gradual opening, but as political pressure for delays and exemptions built up, the Mexican administration reacted by pushing ahead the timetable and opening radically. Although some areas, like chemicals and automobiles, have been substantially exempted so far, a great deal of liberalization has been accomplished. Import penetration increased quickly, from an average of 11.3 percent in 1980–85 to 14.5 in 1986–90. By 1990 import penetration by an offsetting immediate gain in exports gave rise to the free trade agreement with the United States and Canada.

In the three countries considered here, the trade liberalization strategy is not being questioned. Trade liberalization was part of a wider strategy of achieving stability and efficient resource allocation. As such, modernization and growth (and the resulting seeds for improved welfare) cannot be attributed uniquely to the trade strategy. But liberalized trade has so fundamentally shaken up the production structure that more liberal trade is invariably credited with a good share of the performance. In Mexico's case, for example, output growth by 1989–90 was rising to above 4 percent, far exceeding the levels of the previous five years. Even if there is no direct measure of the success of liberalization, indirect support comes from the fact that rolling back trade liberalization is simply not on the economic or political agenda.

WHAT REMAINS OF THE CASE FOR PROTECTION?

The case for protection rests on one of two pillars: externalities or learning effects. Externalities are, of course, the last recourse of scoundrels; they are invariably invoked as the case for intervention even though documenting them (as opposed to modeling them) is notoriously difficult. Externalities associated with a protection strategy would arise if the physical capital formation associated with industrialization or the formation of human capital carried spillover effects, pecuniary or real, that could not be appropriated by the individual firm and industry. Learning-by-doing as an argument for protection, by contrast, does not rely on externalities but rather on capital market imperfections that make firms reluctant to engage in the development of the productivity bonus even though from the social point of view it is warranted. Labor market imperfections may also stand in the way of a warranted industrialization if the training of labor that yields the productivity benefits cannot be captured by the investing firm and cannot be borne (for capital market or information reasons) by the workers who will be vested with the benefits. In either case, it is clear that protection is never the first-best strategy. Targeted subsidies are always better, although considerations of feasibility and political economy will always be brought in favor of protection.

Against the massive evidence that small countries will wither behind protective barriers, there is some evidence that protection can also yield success. Korea, Brazil, and Japan would be the parade cases. These countries were among those with the highest growth rates of GDP and total factor productivity during the 1965–80 period and none of them is a free trader. Brazilian growth averaged 7.7 percent and Korean at 6.7 percent per year over the period; industry grew at 10 and 16 percent per year respectively.

Three essential ingredients of the strong performance were: (1) Exchange rate policy was carefully designed to avoid overvaluation and with it macroeconomic bottlenecks. (2) External credit played a key role, as did foreign investment and foreign technology. (3) The trade regime was sufficiently selective that intermediate goods and capital goods were not excluded. Care was taken in particular not to tax exports implicitly.

Even though we portray the experience as a success, the interpretation might be open to challenge. Brazil did crash in the 1980s and is now seeking trade liberalization as a means to growth. In Korea, the massive investment in the heavy industry was seen in the early 1980s as a major blunder. Today, with lower oil prices, even that judgment is no longer true. While the discussion remains open, the fact is that under the cover of significant (though porous) protection each country developed a world-class manufacturing sector in the 1960s and '70s. It remains to be discerned exactly what makes the difference between an Argentine experience, where protection was a disaster, and these very positive cases.

It is perhaps the experience of Korea and Brazil, where industrialization under the cover of protection led ultimately to highly competitive export industries, that accounts for the interest in the export sector as an engine of growth. One direction is to focus on targeted liberalization that does not interfere with the nurturing of infant industries; infants have to grow up at home. Another is to shift the focus to export strategies. For example, de Melo and Robinson (1990) develop a model of such a process and find that policies that support export externalities yield significant growth effects.[4]

The potential gains from liberalization strategy and the successful nurturing of infant industries by selective protection and subsequent export policies must be qualified in one important dimension. If developing countries as a group open up, there is every reason to believe that their terms of trade will be adversely affected. Flooding the world market with their manufactures while their market access to industrialized countries remains the same cannot fail to reduce the prices at which they will export (Faini, Clavijo, and Senhadji-Semiali 1990). But for the individual country, that is not a reason to shy away from liberalization. Even for developing countries as a group, the benefits from the various sources discussed above are likely to outweigh substantially the costs of worsened terms of trade.

Even when there is a case for protection, as the Korean experience suggests, the strategy works best when used selectively. In this manner the country will not devote resources to accomplishing the impossible and as a result lower productivity economywide. Rather, selective protection (even on a wide basis) serves to capture the learning benefits while minimizing the resource cost. That inevitably involves guessing where the areas of learning and externalities are likely to lie, and it involves the risk of double-guessing markets, and it often fails. But in Korea and a handful of other cases, it has helped improve growth, or at the least it seems to have done no harm to a stellar performance.

WHAT CAN GO WRONG?

One problem for trade reform is political. Too long a phase-in period with too many safeguards for those who might be adversely affected is an invitation to disruption and reversal. The other risk comes from the exchange rate. The elimination of obstacles to trade invariably creates an immediate increase in imports. But although inputs become more readily available and technology improves, the beneficial rise in exports does not happen immediately, even if a real depreciation is undertaken. For example, when Chile first liberalized imports almost fully in the late 1970s (but overvalued its managed exchange rate) import levels exploded and the exchange rate collapsed. Another stabilzation had to be undertaken. Without a real depreciation, exports will scarcely help pay for the higher imports.

Because of balance of payments problems, comprehensive trade reform requires one of two conditions: either the country must be politically in a position to have a major real depreciation of the exchange rate (to help boost exports) or else it must have access to foreign exchange for a substantial period of time. Real depreciation is a problem because it means a fall in real wages unless offset by the improvement in the standard of living that stems from reduced protection. If reserves are not available and depreciation is impractical, the only realistic option for trade policy is to approach liberalization more gradually.

A gradual path to trade liberalization should occur in two steps. In a first round, the country should move from quotas and licenses and other nontariff barriers to a uniform, high tariff of (say) 50 percent. Later, as the economy grows and the external balance can support liberalization without risk of a foreign exchange crisis, tariffs can be taken down to (say) 10 percent. This more moderate policy still opens the economy, because even tariffs at high rates allow competition at the margin, while quotas and licenses are there to prevent it. But at the same time it avoids the grave risk of an exchange crisis.

NEW DIRECTIONS IN TRADE STRATEGY

Most of the discussion of trade liberalization in the past has focused on merchandise trade, and until recently almost no attention and certainly no empirical work has focused on trade in services. Trade in services is a major issue for developed countries who see themselves as exporters, but also for developing countries who expect some export opportunities but recognize the role of services in promoting productivity.

Most of the recent attention has focused on financial services (banking, underwriting, insurance), where there are obvious gains from scale economies and competition. Financial markets in developing countries (and in Europe) operate far less competitively and with far larger spreads and fees than in the United States, hence the case for liberalizing financial service trade. But the interest in service trade liberalization extends to other areas: accounting, consulting, legal services, construction, design, telecommunications, and others. It is clear that the case for liberalized trade in services that have not been much traded in the past draws attention to a stark omission in the traditional assessments of the cost protection.

The second new direction is even more sweeping: developing countries are looking for free trade arrangements with developed countries. Previously, the issue of market access and preferential access to the markets of developed countries had been a chief item on the agenda of UNCTAD. The General System of Preferences, under which industrialized countries gave developing countries privileged market access to a broad range of goods, was a way of implementing that objective. What is new is the willingness to practice free trade as a two-way street. The United States may take the North American Free Trade Agreement as a blueprint to allow other countries to adhere to a conditional most-favored-nation basis. If that turns out to be the case, the Americas may become a free trade area in the next decade or two.

NOTES

I am indebted to Brian Aitken for valuable assistance and to the National Science Foundation for research support. The editors provided abundant, generous, and thoughtful comments.

1. These factors apply even more forcefully to Eastern Europe and the Soviet Union. As these economies shed central planning, a wide-open trade regime is seen as a critical measure. Nothing could more dramatize the belief in the promises of openness than the advice to drop from one day to the next all and any obstacles to international trade (Sachs 1991; Dornbusch 1991). Nor could any policy have a more drastic immediate effect; when East Germany liberalized totally in its union with West Germany, industrial production fell within a year by 50 percent and unemployment skyrocketed.

2. These are the famous "Harberger triangles." See Harberger 1959.

3. See Helpman 1989 and Helpman and Krugman 1989 for a broad analysis of the many issues emerging under imperfect competition. See, too, Baumol and Lee 1991.

4. Going beyond liberalization, de Melo and Robinson conclude: "If there are externalities to be

exploited, policy makers should pursue them aggressively and not worry about getting the instruments just right. . . . [W]hen there are rectangles to gain, an economy can easily afford some triangles along the way" (1990, 30–31).

REFERENCES

Balassa, B. 1989. "Outward Orientation." In *Handbook of Development Economics.* edited by H. Chenery and T. N. Srinivasan, 2:1645–90. New York: North Holland.

Baumol, W., S. A. Batey Blackman, and E. Wolff. 1989. *Productivity and American Leadership: The Long View.* Cambridge, Mass.: MIT Press.

Baumol, W., and L. S. Lee. 1991. "Contestable Markets, Trade and Development." *World Bank Research Observer* 6 (1): 1–18.

Bhagwati, J. 1978. *Foreign Trade Regimes and Economic Development: Anatomy and Consequences of Exchange Control Regimes.* Cambridge, Mass.: Ballinger.

Bruton, H. 1989. "Import Substitution." In *Handbook of Development Economics,* H. Chenery and T. N. Srinivasan, 2:1601–44. New York: North Holland.

Celasun, M., and D. Rodrik. 1989. "Debt, Adjustment, and Growth: Turkey." In *Developing Country Debt and Economic Performance,* edited by J. Sachs and S. Collins, 3:615–808. Chicago: University of Chicago Press.

Chenery, H., S. Robinson, and M. Syrquin. 1986. *Industrialization and Growth.* Oxford: Oxford University Press.

de Melo, J., and S. Robinson. 1990. "Productivity and Externalities. Models of Export-Led Growth." Working Paper Series 387. Washington, D.C.: World Bank.

Dornbusch, R. 1991. "Priorities of Economic Reform in Eastern Europe and the Soviet Union." Policy Paper no. 6., Centre for Economic Policy Research, London.

Edwards, S. 1991. "Trade Orientation, Distortions and Growth in Developing Countries." Mimeograph, University of California, Los Angeles.

Eichengreen, B. 1991. "Historical Research on International Lending and Debt." *Journal of Economic Perspectives* 5, no. 2 (Spring): 149–69.

Erzan, R., and K. Kuwahara. 1989. "The Profile of Protection in Developing Countries." *UNCTAD Review* 1 (1): 29–49.

Faini, R., F. Clavijo, and A. Senhadji-Semiali. 1990. "The Fallacy of Composition Argument: Does Demand Matter for LDC Manufacturing Exports?" Discussion Paper no. 499, Center for Economic Policy Research, London.

Finger, M. 1991. "Development Economics and the General Agreement on Tariffs and Trade." In *Trade Theory and Economic Reform: Essays in Honor of Bela Balassa,* edited by J. de Melo and A. Sapir, 203–23. Cambridge: Basil Blackwell.

Haberler, G. 1988. "International Trade and Economic Development." (The Cairo Lectures, 1959). Reprinted in *International Trade and Economic Development,* 17–54. Washington, D.C.: American Enterprise Institute.

Harberger, A. 1959. "Using Resources at Hand More Effectively." *American Economic Review* 40, no. 1 (May): 134–46.

Harrison, A. 1991. "Openness and Growth: A Time-Series, Cross-Country Analysis of Developing Countries." Washington, D.C.: World Bank.

Havrylishyn, O. 1990. "Trade Policy and Productivity Gains in Developing Countries: A Survey of the Literature." *World Bank Research Observer* 5 (1): 1–24.

Helpman, E. 1989. "The Noncompetitive Theory of International Trade and Trade Policy." *Proceedings of the World Bank Annual Conference on Development Economics,* 193–216. Washington, D.C.: World Bank.

Helpman, E., and P. Krugman. 1989. *Trade Policy and Market Structure.* Cambridge, Mass.: MIT Press.

Krueger, A. 1978. *Foreign Trade Regimes and Economic Development. Liberalization Attempts and Consequences.* Cambridge, Mass.: Ballinger.

―――. 1990. "Comparative Advantage and Development Policy Twenty Years Later." In *Perspectives on Trade and Development,* edited by A. Krueger, 49–70. Chicago: University of Chicago Press.

Michaely, M., D. Papageorgiou, and A. Choksi. 1991. *Liberalizing Foreign Trade: Lessons of Experience in the Developing World.* Cambridge: Basil Blackwell.

Norman, V. 1990. "Assessing Trade and Welfare Effects of Trade Liberalization." *European Economic Review* 34 (4): 725–45.

Pack, H. 1988. "Industrialization and Trade." In *Handbook of Development Economics,* edited by H. Chenery and T. N. Srinivasan, 1:333–80. New York: North Holland.

Prebisch, R. 1959. "Commercial Policy in the Underdeveloped Countries." *American Economic Review* 40:261–64.

―――. 1984. "Five Stages in My Thinking on Development." In *Pioneers in Development,* edited by G. Meier and D. Seers, 175–91. Oxford: Oxford University Press.

Romer, P. 1989. "Capital Accumulation in the Theory of Long Run Growth." In *Modern Business Cycle Theory,* edited by R. Barro, 51–127. Cambridge: Harvard University Press.

Sachs, J. 1991. "Sachs on Poland," *Economist,* January 19.

Salvatore, D., and T. Hatcher. 1991. "Inward Oriented and Outward Oriented Trade Strategies." *Journal of Development Studies* 27 (3): 7–25.

Sareacoglu, R. 1987. "Economic Stabilization and Structural Adjustment: The Case of Turkey." In *Growth-Oriented Adjustment Programs,* edited by V. Corbo, M. Goldstein, and M. Khan, 119–39. Washington, D.C.: International Monetary Fund and World Bank.

Schumpeter, J. 1983 (1934). *The Theory of Economic Development.* New Brunswick, N.J.: Transaction Publishers.

Shepherd, G., and C. Langoni. 1991. *Trade Reform Lessons from Eight Countries.* San Francisco: ICS Press.

Thomas, V., and J. Nash. 1991. "Reform of Trade Policy." *World Bank Research Observer* 6 (2): 153–72.

Viner, J. 1952. *International Trade and Economic Development.* Glencoe, Ill.: Free Press.

Whalley, J. 1989. "Recent Trade Liberalization in the Developing World: What Is Behind It and Where Is It Headed." NBER Working Paper no. 3057, August.

World Bank. 1987. *World Development Report, 1987.* New York: Oxford University Press.

―――. 1988. *Adjustment Lending: An Evaluation of Ten Years of Experience.* Policy and Research Series no. 1, World Bank, Washington, D.C.

―――. 1991. *World Development Report, 1991.* New York: Oxford University Press.

13

The Plundering of Agriculture in Developing Countries

MAURICE SCHIFF AND ALBERTO VALDÉS

 If a country wants to achieve faster agricultural growth, and have fewer poor people, it should stop taxing agriculture relative to other sectors. Industry, long considered the engine of growth, has been the darling of development. Agriculture, by contrast, was believed to be unresponsive to economic incentives and not to lend itself to technical change. Thus, policy makers believed that promoting industry at the expense of agriculture would sacrifice little in output. This was the conventional wisdom in the 1960s and 1970s.

There was a logic to this conventional wisdom. Explicit agricultural taxes, such as export taxes, and implicit taxes, as when marketing boards paid farmers less than market prices, were easy to administer and extremely attractive in countries with a thin tax base. In addition, shifting scarce resources to industry was thought to be justified by agriculture's declining terms of trade (a pound of agricultural exports was buying increasingly less than a pound of industrial imports) and by the rising protection of agriculture in industrial countries. So, policy makers biased incentives against agriculture, directly through sectoral policies and indirectly through industrial protection and other policies.

This conventional wisdom had never been put to a rigorous test. Further, by the 1980s, it was becoming apparent that agriculture was profoundly influenced by events external to the sector—industrial policy and exchange rates—which in turn affected investment, growth, and income in agriculture. It also became apparent that biasing incentives against agriculture was far more harmful to output than had been surmised earlier.

In order to better understand the effects on agriculture of price interventions, a World Bank study looked at eighteen developing countries over the period 1960–85. The study came up with a number of findings that question the conventional wisdom regarding the impact of price interventions on agricultural

MAURICE SCHIFF is principal economist in the International Economics Department of the World Bank.

ALBERTO VALDÉS is an agriculture adviser in the Department of Rural Development in the World Bank.

Previously published in *Finance and Development*, March 1995, 44–47; published with minor changes by permission of the World Bank and the authors.

TABLE 1
DIRECT AND INDIRECT BIAS AGAINST AGRICULTURE

	Period	Indirect Bias (Negative Protection) (avg. %) (1)	Bias Due to Industrial Protection (avg. %) (2)	Direct Bias (avg. %) (3)	Total Bias (avg. %) (4)
Extreme bias	1960–84	28.6	25.7	23.0	51.6
Côte d' Ivoire	1960–82	23.3	23.2	25.7	49.0
Ghana	1958–76	32.6	32.4	26.9	59.5
Zambia	1966–84	29.9	21.4	16.4	46.3
Representative bias	1960–86	24.2	32.8	12.0	36.4
Argentina	1960–84	21.3	39.5	17.8	39.1
Columbia	1960–83	25.2	37.8	4.8	30.0
Dominican Republic	1966–85	21.3	20.8	18.6	39.9
Egypt	1964–84	19.6	27.5	24.8	44.4
Morocco	1963–84	17.4	13.4	15.0	32.4
Pakistan	1960–86	33.1	44.9	6.4	39.5
Philippines	1960–86	23.3	33.0	4.1	27.4
Sri Lanka	1960–85	31.1	40.1	9.0	40.1
Thailand	1962–84	15.0	13.9	25.1	40.1
Turkey	1961–83	37.1	57.4	−5.3	31.8
Mild bias	1960–83	15.7	22.9	0.2	15.8
Brazil	1969–83	18.4	21.4	−10.1	8.3
Chile	1960–83	20.4	37.4	1.2	21.6
Malaysia	1960–83	8.2	9.9	9.4	17.6
Protectors	1960–84	13.6	13.9	−24.0	−10.4
Korea, Republic of	1960–84	25.8	26.7	−39.0	−13.2
Portugal	1960–84	1.3	1.0	−9.0	−7.7
Sample average		22.5	27.9	7.9	30.3

SOURCE: Maurice Schiff and Alberto Valdés, *The Plundering of Agriculture in Developing Countries* (Washington, D.C.: World Bank), 1992.
NOTE: Direct and indirect interventions have depressed agriculture's domestic terms of trade (AGTOT) below the prevailing level in the absence of these interventions. Direct interventions depressed AGTOT by 7.9 percent on average (column 3), indirect interventions depressed AGTOT by 22.5 percent on average (column 1), and total interventions (direct plus indirect) depressed AGTOT by 30.3 percent on average (column 4 = colums 1 and 3). The indirect bias is a weighted average of the effect of the real exchange rate overvaluation and of the effect of industrial protection (shown in column 2).

prices, income transfers, growth, the budget, and income distribution (table 1). These findings provide a solid basis for prescribing agricultural price policies in developing countries. A number of surprises emerged from the study, in particular the size and importance of the effects of industrial protection and exchange rate misalignments on agriculture.

AGRICULTURE WAS TAXED

Governments influence agricultural prices both directly, through agricultural sector policies, and indirectly, through industrial protection and macroeconomic policies. Direct policies are defined as sectoral policies that affect the price level of the agricultural sector relative to the price level of the nonagricultural sector—the domestic terms of trade. Such policies include agricultural price controls, export taxes or quotas, and import subsidies or taxes. Indirect policies are defined as policies originating outside agriculture, such as industrial protection and macroeconomic policies. Indirect interventions depress the prices of agricultural tradables relative to nontradables (through their impact on the real exchange rate) and relative to other tradables (due to industrial protection). These policies affect production incentives by making agriculture less attractive than other sectors of the economy.

What were the effects of such direct and indirect interventions? The indirect effect of industrial protection and real exchange rate overvaluation was to depress agriculture's domestic terms of trade by about 22 percent on average for the eighteen countries over the sample period—nearly three times the direct effect from sectoral pricing policies. The total effect (direct plus indirect) was to depress agricultural domestic terms of trade by over 30 percent (see table). These would have been about 43 percent (30/70 = .43) higher in the absence of total interventions.

Macroeconomic policies caused the appreciation of the real exchange rate, raised the relative cost of nontradable inputs, and reduced the farmers' real purchasing power from the sale of export and import-competing commodities. Moreover, protection for domestic industry hurt agriculture by raising the domestic price of importable agricultural inputs above world prices, by reducing the purchasing power of farm households as consumers of manufactured goods, and by causing further appreciation of the real exchange rate.

Some direct measures benefited agricultural producers. Governments often subsidized the cost of farm credit and important agricultural inputs, such as fertilizer. However, such subsidized credit and fertilizer was often rationed and generally went to the larger, better-connected farmers. Moreover, many developing countries, to increase their food self-sufficiency, protected domestic producers of import-competing food products through quantitative restrictions or tariffs on imported commodities. Also, most countries, responding to the instability of world markets, attempted to stabilize domestic producer prices relative to world prices.

On average, for the eighteen countries examined, direct interventions protected importables (18 percent) and taxed exportables (16 percent). The average reduction of the price of exportables relative to importables was over 30 percent. Direct interventions also led to a significant reduction in price variability—32 percent on average for producer prices and 23 percent for consumer prices. On the other hand, the contribution of indirect interventions to price stability was negligible.

Since 1985, several countries in Africa, Asia, and Latin American have undertaken unilateral liberalization and stabilization programs resulting in relatively lower levels of industrial protection and real exchange rate overvaluation. Thus, both the direct and indirect biases against agriculture have fallen in these countries.

In most industrial countries, the main objective of agricultural price policies is to maintain farm income and employment in the face of declining real world prices for cereals—with massive net income transfers to agriculture. In most developing countries, however, the primary objectives have been food self-sufficiency, domestic price stability, low food prices for urban consumers, and government revenue. This being said, the objectives of developing country agricultural policies have at times been quite contradictory. For instance, food self-sufficiency (implying high producer prices) and low consumer food prices are incompatible with generating government revenue. Fiscal constraints have forced an adjustment via lower producer prices.

On average, during the period 1960–84, the net effect of direct and indirect interventions was an enormous income transfer out of agriculture—averaging 46 percent of agricultural gross domestic product per year. The average net transfer for the countries with a representative bias was 37 percent (see table). Such enormous transfers must have severely depressed private investment in agriculture and agricultural growth. The big winners were government (net revenue gain), urban consumers (lower food prices), and industry (cheap raw materials).

Just as important is what the study did not find. Input subsidies did not compensate, or compensated very little, for the substantial income outflows resulting from interventions in output markets; and in most cases, public investment in agriculture (7 percent of agricultural GDP) did not compensate for the negative effects of price interventions. For the countries with the representative bias, the income transfer through input subsidies was never higher than 1.1 percent of agricultural GDP, and for all eighteen countries, the average for 1960–84 was only 2 percent. Higher investment by government, to compensate for taxing agriculture, was found, to varying degrees, in only five of fifteen cases, with only Egypt and Morocco showing compensation for all agricultural price policy or income variables tested.

THE EFFECT OF TAXATION ON AGRICULTURAL GROWTH

To examine the impact of price policy on annual growth of real agricultural GDP, the study compared the average agricultural growth rate in the group of countries in which the bias was lower with the group in which the bias was higher. This comparison revealed that the group with the lower bias (higher protection rate) had a higher average growth rate. This study provides strong evidence of an association between high total bias (mainly indirect) against agriculture and low rates of agricultural growth. Further statistical tests revealed that the relationship between total bias and agricultural growth was significant: the lower the bias against agriculture, the higher the growth. Higher agricultural prices reduce labor migration from the sector, increase investment, and encourage wider adoption of new techniques—and result in a higher growth rate.

There has long been a presumption that the production of individual agricultural products responds significantly to higher prices—because of shifts between products—but that total agricultural production is unresponsive to incentives. The presumption is wrong. Experience shows that in the long run, the aggregate response can be sizable, though it may require some years to materialize. This highlights the importance of having stable and persistent policies.

As noted above, price interventions in the eighteen countries severely depressed agricultural prices during 1960–84. Without price interventions, agriculture's terms of trade would have been more than 40 percent higher. With such a large price impact from intervention, the effect of price reform on output is likely to be significant. How agricultural production responds to a price reform depends on how severely interventions have depressed prices, how extensive and credible the reform is, how responsive output is to a given price change, and what time period is considered.

THE NET FISCAL IMPACT OF AGRICULTURAL PRICE POLICIES

The fiscal effects of specific agricultural price policies have received much attention and generated intense debate, but there have been few, if any, systematic attempts to quantify the net fiscal impact of price interventions. Consumer food subsidies have frequently been cited as a major drain on government budgets, but while they were a drain for some food-importing countries, this was not the case for most of the countries in the study. Similarly, many countries have a tradition of subsidizing agricultural credit and inputs, conventionally interpreted as compensating producers for the heavy taxation of agricultural production. Yet such subsidies represent only a small part of government expenditure (averaging only about 2 percent over 1960–85), while taxing agricultural exports yields substantial revenue to the government (averaging 10 percent of government expenditure). Indeed, the net effect of direct price interventions in agriculture during the study was a net revenue gain (of output and input policies) to the government of nearly 7 percent over the period 1960–85, and as much as 17 percent during the 1960s.

The government's need for revenue to fund development programs was probably the major impetus behind taxing agricultural exports, and it remains the major constraint to reform of direct interventions. On the other hand, in some countries, the fiscal burden of input and food subsidies escalated so rapidly that it led to macroeconomic imbalances that could be corrected only through policy reform. Changes in agricultural policies in Portugal were dictated chiefly by budget pressures in the early 1980s, when fertilizer and feed subsidies were essentially eliminated. Attempts to reduce food subsidies in Egypt, Morocco, Pakistan, and Zambia also show the link between price policy and the budget.

In most countries, the net budget effect of direct price interventions in agriculture was a gain in revenue, mainly through taxes on agricultural exports, which alone financed as much as 20 percent of government spending in the 1960s. And in three countries—Brazil, Ghana, and Sri Lanka—export tax revenues amounted to 20 percent or more of total government spending over the entire 1960–85 period. Over time, however, the net contribution of the price interventions for this group of countries fell substantially, from 18 percent of government spending in the 1960s to 5 percent in 1980–84. In a few countries, the revenue contribution remains important—and undoubtedly constrains any policy reforms designed to reduce direct agricultural taxation. In those countries, sectoral reforms that would eliminate or reduce agricultural export taxes would need to be accompanied by economywide tax and fiscal reforms.

THE RELATIVE IMPACT OF PRICE INTERVENTIONS ON RURAL VERSUS URBAN AREAS

Contrary to the widely held view that cheap food policies prevail in developing countries, direct price interventions penalized urban consumers in six of fourteen countries for which data were available. In fact, most countries protected the production of agricultural importables, mostly food, and only a few of these countries also reduced consumer food prices through explicit food subsidies. Moreover, despite widespread direct interventions, the impact on the real income of urban households was generally small. However, adding the indirect price interventions revealed that the total income gain for low-income urban consumers ranged from 0.2 percent to 5.3 percent of household incomes in seven of fourteen countries, and was 10 percent or more in three countries—Argentina, Egypt, and Turkey. The effect of the so-called cheap food policies took place mainly through real exchange rate overvaluation rather than through direct price interventions. Over all, direct price interventions have achieved the objective of stabilizing domestic agricultural prices. Hence, a motive underlying food price interventions may have been to prevent sudden large real income losses in years of higher-than-average food prices rather than to raise the standard of living of the urban poor.

For the rural poor, the short-run income effects of price interventions were substantially higher and in the opposite direction from those for urban households in the same country. In most countries, rural households suffered real income losses. And direct interventions had considerably more impact on the real income of larger farms (or wealthier rural households), whether these were positive (as in Korea and Portugal) or negative (as in Egypt and Turkey). Ghana was the exception, with small farmers gaining from direct price interventions, because they produced more rice, which was protected, and larger farmers losing, because they produced more coffee and cocoa, which were heavily taxed.

In the long term, the poor lost disproprotionately in the countries studied. Price interventions seemed to hurt most of the poor in the long run (possibly because the full picture at the household level could not be measured). Taxing agriculture reduces rural demand for labor, so that rural employment and real wages fall. This leads to increased migration to the cities and increased competition for employment, and thus to a fall in income in the informal urban sector as well. Moreover, to the extent that the benefits from food subsidies are captured mainly by urban households—predominantly employees in the government and the formal sector—the cost may be a reduction in the real income of the rural poor and, indirectly, of the urban poor in the informal sector.

In the long run, indirect interventions affect income far more than do direct interventions. Thus, governments should not use direct (sectoral) price interventions to redistribute income, because the distributive benefit is small while the efficiency cost can be very large.

AGRICULTURAL POLICY REFORMS

Since the mid-1980s, there has been a profound change in development strategies—with movements toward more open and outward-oriented economies. Further, there has been a shift in thinking about the role of government in general. This has prompted a number of developing countries to reform policies that affect agriculture.

Economic stabilization and trade liberalization have gradually emerged as centerpieces in the reform of development strategy in several developing countries. This is most clearly the case in Latin America, but this approach is gradually being adopted in other regions as well. A consensus is emerging that the preconditions for restoring economic growth include deep structural reforms that would open up economies and restore the private sector as the principal player. During the late 1980s in Latin America, for example, most countries embarked on a unilateral process of tariffication consisting of converting quantitative restrictions to tariffs, binding the tariffs under GATT, drastically reducing the coverage of nontariff barriers, removing export taxes, and reducing the amount of average import tariffs as well as their dispersion.

These reforms have led to a reduction in industrial protection and to a less distorted level of the exchange rate. Consequently, the indirect bias—the largest component of the total bias on agriculture—has fallen significantly in many countries: Argentina, Chile, Colombia, Ghana, India, Mexico, Morocco, and Turkey. The direct bias has also been reduced in several countries. In Argentina the export tax was eliminated (it had averaged 18 percent during 1960–84). Export taxes were removed in Brazil, Colombia, the Dominican Republic, and many other countries, including ones such as India, where the trade reform has not yet reached the agricultural sector.

Hence, trade liberalization in the manufacturing sector and a reduction of export taxes on agricultural commodities have reversed the strong anti-export bias that prevailed before the mid-1980s in a large number of countries. At the same time, however, there have been new developments that affect incentives for agriculture. One emerging concern has been the evolution of the real exchange rate (RER) in the same countries that have adopted the trade reforms. Largely as a result of increased private capital inflows following stabilization and trade liberalization, several Latin American countries (and this is also becoming an issue in India) have seen their real exchange rate appreciate. A key determinant of the success of trade liberalization is whether the country can maintain a competitive real exchange rate that encourages exports and gives some exchange rate protection to import-competing activities. Effective RER management could be most important for the sustainability of the agricultural trade reform in the near future.

SUMMARY

The findings of the study emphasize the importance of economywide factors on agricultural performance. Several policy recommendations emerge from these findings:

1. If a country wants to prosper, it should not bias incentives against agriculture relative to other sectors or, what amounts to the same thing, it should not use policies to depress agriculture's domestic terms of trade. But to stop this practice, the country must do more than dismantle the sectoral or direct interventions in agricultural prices; it must, in addition, eliminate the indirect bias against agriculture (about three-quarters of the total bias against agriculture in 1960–85), including removing industrial protection and getting the exchange rate in line with its long-run equilibrium value. In other words, reform in the agricultural sector will succeed only if it is part of a general reform of the economy, including stabilization and trade (and domestic market) liberalization.

2. If a country removes the sectoral or direct taxation of agriculture, it must (or at least many countries must) look to other sources of revenue to finance the activities of government. Reducing the indirect bias need not entail revenue losses. Depreciation of the real exchange rate need not affect the budgetary accounts, and trade liberalization usually starts with tariffication of the nontariff barriers, which raises government revenue.

3. If a country wants to reap the large income gains possible from the reform of agriculture, it should stop the direct taxation of exports and the direct protection of imports (so as to put imports and exports on an equal footing), and it should dismantle quotas, licenses, state trading companies (which obscure the real winners and losers from subsidies or taxes), and those internal agricultural marketing regulations that prevent a free flow of goods and services within the country. Nor should governments use social objectives (like protecting the poor) to justify tampering with agricultural prices. The impact on the poor is small in the short run in most countries and impossible to know in the long run. Moreover, agricultural growth—and incomes—will suffer.

4. To reap the full benefit of reforming agricultural prices and agricultural trade, it helps to launch simultaneous reforms outside agriculture—in land, finance, transport, and communication. If a country wants to stabilize prices at a relatively low cost, it should develop efficient hedging instruments, reform other agricultural policy interventions, and stop interest groups from subverting the price stabilization program.

5. A number of reforming countries have seen their real exchange rate appreciate because of the capital inflows resulting from the reform. This has led to pressure by the agricultural lobbies for protection (e.g., in Chile, Colombia, and New Zealand). Consequently, in order to ensure that the reforms are not reversed, governments should carefully manage the short-term component of these large capital flows.

14

The Political Framework for Agricultural Policy Decisions

ROBERT H. BATES

 T. W. Schultz once stated, "Once there are investment opportunities and efficient incentives, farmers will turn sand into gold" (Schultz 1976, 5). Schultz and others are quick to point out that governments in the developing areas often provide distorted economic incentives and that their agricultural policies constitute a major reason for low levels of food production. I shall draw on my earlier work (Bates 1981) to discuss why governments act as they do.

Agricultural policy can be defined as the set of decisions taken by governments that influence the prices farmers confront in the markets which determine their incomes. The level of farm revenues is determined in part by the prices at which sales are made in markets for agricultural commodities. The prices which farmers must pay for farm inputs help to determine their costs and thus, in combination with revenues, the money value of their incomes from farming. And the real value of farm incomes, in turn, is determined by the prices which farmers must pay for consumer items.

THREE APPROACHES TO POLICY ANALYSIS

Research throughout the developing world suggests that governmental policy tends to be antithetical to the interests of most farmers. Governments tend to lower the prices farmers receive for produce. They tend to shelter domestic manufacturers from meaningful levels of economic competition originating both at home and abroad, thereby raising the prices farmers must pay for consumer items. And, while governments often subsidize the price of farm inputs, these subsidies tend to be captured by the larger farmers. The incomes of most farmers are thus adversely affected by the agricultural policies of Third World governments.

Governmental policies thus tend to weaken production incentives for farmers.

ROBERT H. BATES is Eaton Professor of the Science of Government, Harvard University.

Originally titled "The Political Framework for Price Policy Decisions." Reprinted from *Food Policy: Frameworks for Analysis and Action*, edited by Charles Mann and Barbara Huddleston, by permission of Indiana University Press and the author.

When governments do emphasize production, moreover, they attempt to secure higher output by building projects rather than by raising prices. And when governments do offer positive incentives for increased production, they tend to do so by lowering costs rather than by increasing gross revenues, that is, by subsidizing the prices of farm inputs rather than by raising the prices of commodities.

Why do Third World governments tend to adopt these kinds of policies? There are several approaches to explaining the behavior of governments, and I will review three of them.

Maximizing Social Welfare

The first explanatory approach is the one most often adopted by economists. It treats governments as agencies whose job is to maximize the social welfare; public policy is viewed as a set of choices made by governments to secure society's best interests. In poor societies, this approach holds, the social interest is best served by development, and the behavior of governments is analyzed in terms of its impact on this overriding objective.

There are many problems with this approach. One is its lack of explanatory power. Its basic method is to account for the behavior of governments in terms of social objectives. But a given objective can often be secured through a variety of policy instruments, and noting the underlying objective of a policy program often does not account for the particular choice of instrument. To secure increased food production, for example, governments could pay higher prices to farmers expending the same amount of resources as on food production projects. Under most circumstances, the former would be the more efficient way of securing this social objective, but the latter is more often chosen. Noting the social objectives of government does not account for this systematic bias in governmental policy.

Not only does the approach possess low explanatory power, but when it does make strong predictions, it is often wrong. For example, governments want low-priced food. In the name of this objective, they often strive to impose low food prices. But this choice of policy instrument weakens economic incentives, resulting in lower production and higher food prices. The instrument chosen thus produces an effect precisely opposite to that desired. The objective thus cannot be cited as its cause.

In response to problems such as these, policy analysts often invoke other considerations. They treat the failure of particular governmental policies as "mistakes" and call for "more information" or "better training" for decision makers; or they note that governments often have multiple, often conflicting objectives and so treat the failure to maximize one set of objectives as evidence of efforts to optimize a larger, more complex set. Both responses represent efforts to preserve the welfare-maximizing model of policy formation.

The deeper problem is that unless one is prepared to treat a government as a single, unitary actor—that is to treat it as a single decision maker, be it a planner or a dictator—it is impossible to secure from a government a coherent statement of its objectives that possesses even the most limited set of desirable properties. In this area of policy analysis, the Nobel Prize–winning work of Theodore Schultz (1976) should be coupled with that of Kenneth Arrow (1951). Any approach that treats govenments as agencies for maximizing the best interests of society should be regarded as a normative enterprise rather than as an effort at explanation.

POLICY AS A BARGAINING OUTCOME FOR PRIVATE PRESSURE GROUPS

The pluralist view of policy formation provides an alternative to the assumption of welfare maximization. According to this approach, governments do not pursue transcendent social interests; rather, they respond to private demands. Public policy is regarded as an outcome of political competition among organized groups.

In applying this approach to agricultural policy, we can note forces that shape both the demand and supply of pricing policies. On the demand side, what is striking is the intensity of the pressures for low-priced food. One reason is clear: because urban consumers in the less developed countries are poor, they spend much of their incomes on food. In Africa, for example, urban consumers often spend between 50 and 60 percent of their disposable incomes on food. Changes in the price of food therefore make a major impact on the economic well-being of urban dwellers, and they pay close attention to the issue of food prices.

Another reason is that urban consumers possess the capacity forcefully to register their preferences on the body politic. Urban consumers are geographically concentrated and strategically located. Because of their geographic concentration, they can be organized quickly; and because they control such basic facilities as transport, communications, and public services, they can impose deprivations on others. They are, therefore, an influential force in politics.

The demand for low-priced food is powerful, moreover, because it can form the basis for the formation of coalitions. It is not only the worker who cares about the price of food; it is also the employer. Employers care about food prices because food is a wage good; with higher food prices, wages must rise and, all else being equal, profits fall. Governments care about food prices not only because they are employers in their own right but also because as owners of industries and promoters of industrial development programs they seek to protect industrial profits. Indicative of the significance of these interests is that in Africa, at least, the unit that sets agricultural prices often resides not in the ministry of agriculture but in the ministry of finance or commerce.

When urban unrest begins among food consumers, political discontent often rapidly spreads to upper echelons of the polity; it comes to include those whose incomes come from profits, not wages, and those in charge of major bureaucracies. Political regimes that are unable to supply low-cost food are seen as dangerously incompetent and as failing to protect the interests of key elements of the social order. In alliance with the urban masses, influential elites are likely to shift their political loyalties and to replace those in power. Thus it was that protests over food shortages and rising prices formed a critical prelude to the coup that unseated Busia in Ghana and led to the period of political maneuvers and flux that threatened to overthrow the government of Arap Moi in Kenya.

Many of the factors which account for the potency of the demand for low-priced food suggest why it is not countered by equally strong demands by producers. A prime factor is the cost of organization: while low for urban dwellers, it is high for farmers, who are more numerous and widely scattered. Another is the lack of natural allies, particularly at the upper reaches of the polity. While the ties between governments and rural producers are close in some developing areas, they tend not to be in Africa, and this situation may account for the relatively more adverse set of pricing policies which have been adopted by governments in that continent.

Also important are the factors affecting the supply of public policy. One such factor is the quantity of public resources. A lower bound is placed on low-priced policies by the government's capacity to make up for domestic food shortages; foreign exchange constraints, for example, place limits on food imports. Another factor is the character of the nation's political institutions. Where Third World governments are subject to competitive elections, for example, the evidence suggests they are more sensitive to rural interests, for farmers constitute a political majority in many developing countries. Where there are representative assemblies whose members are accountable to constituencies, then, once again, political pressures will arise for the provision of favorable policies for farmers, for farm districts tend to outnumber urban constituencies in most developing areas. These representative institutions—elections and assemblies—help to offset the anti-farmer bias inherent in pure pressure group politics, as discussed above. At least as important as representative institutions, however, are bureaucracies, particularly those that regulate agricultural markets. Once formed, such bureaucracies secure the resources to reward politicians and thereby come to perpetuate the programs they administer. The agencies in charge of markets accumulate political power, and their vested interests in the government's agricultural programs help to perpetuate these policy commitments even in the face of clear evidence that the policies have failed. Clearly, in understanding agricultural policies, we need to know more about these agencies.

The primary strategy of the pluralist approach, then, is to look at the factors that influence the way in which public demands are processed into public policy. From the pluralist viewpoint, the problem of government is the problem of representation. Viewed in this light, the limitations of the approach become obvious, for in agricultural policy a very small subset of relevant interests receives representation. A third perspective is required—one that explains how governments get away with institutionalizing the interests of political minorities. In nations where commonly over 50 percent of the gross domestic product and over 70 percent of the labor force are in agriculture, how can governments remain in power while maintaining agricultural programs which violate the interests of most farmers?

USING PUBLIC POLICY TO RETAIN POLITICAL POWER

The third approach views governments as agencies that seek to stay in power. It underscores the features of agricultural programs that let governments organize political followings and disorganize political opposition, particularly in the rural areas. This approach—which for want of a better term we can label a hegemonic approach to policy analysis—also stresses two general points: that economic inefficiency can be politically useful and that government-controlled markets can be employed as instruments for political power. Economically suboptimal programs, in short, can be politically attractive.

An approach that stresses the role of public policy as a means of retaining political power is useful in explaining several otherwise puzzling aspects of agricultural policy. In seeking increased food production, for example, governments often favor project-based policies over price-based policies. We have already seen that price-based policies can be politically costly—they are resisted by urban interests—but what is also important is that price-based policies offer few political benefits to governments attempting to organize support in the rural areas. For the benefits of higher prices can be reaped by both the supporters and the opponents of governments in power. Projects, however, can be targeted; their benefits can be conferred on those who support the government and withheld from political opponents. Project-based programs thus often provide superior resources to those who seek to organize the rural areas.

Another example illustrates the same point. In seeking increased food production, governments appear far more willing to manipulate incentives by manipulating prices in a way that lowers farm costs than in one that increases farm revenues. We have already discussed one reason for this: the high political costs and low political benefits of offering higher prices for agricultural commodities. Another reason is that subsidy programs create resources for organizing. When governments lower input prices, private sources of supply withdraw from the market, levels of demand increase, and there is excess demand at the government prices. Under such circumstances, markets do not clear, and those in charge of the farm input program achieve the capacity to ration. Those in charge can then employ the program to build an organization. They can target the program's benefits to the politically faithful and withhold them from political opponents. They can also use the program to disorganize. In Ghana, for example, a chief means of breaking the resistance by cocoa farmers to the government's low cocoa prices following self-government was the politicization of farm input programs and the distribution of subsidized farm inputs through the politically loyal faction of farm organizations. Combined with outright coercion, the political manipulation of the supply of farm inputs made it in the private interest of farmers to support a government whose agricultural programs, taken as a whole, violated the interests of agriculture.

Market intervention creates the capacity for political organization in other ways. When governments maintain bureaucracies to lower farm prices, for example, they can use regulated markets to build political machines. Those in charge of the market can selectively grant rights of entry into it, and those who reap the economic rewards from access to the artificially cheapened commodities become their clients and supporters.

SUMMARY

I have moved away from a form of analysis which views policy as the result of efforts to maximize the social welfare. I have moved instead to a set of approaches that looks at public policy as a solution to political problems. The general theme of this chapter, then, is that politicians are rational actors, but they are solving problems that do not take a purely economic form. What appear as economic costs may often offer political benefits: noncompetitive rents or inefficient projects, for example, may be politically attractive in that they offer tools for building loyal organizations.

What economists may evaluate as bad policy, then, is not necessarily the result of poor training, obduracy, or other deficiencies on the part of policy makers. Rather, policy makers may simply be solving a different problem than are economists. As policy analysts, it behooves us to represent explicitly the political problem as perceived by the policy maker and to use our analytic techniques to solve it, both in order to offer better explanations of government behavior and to advocate better policy more effectively.

REFERENCES

Arrow, Kenneth. 1951. *Social Choice and Individual Values*. New York: John Wiley.

Bates, Robert H. 1981. *Markets and States in Tropical Africa: The Political Basis of Agricultural Policies*. Berkeley and Los Angeles; University of California Press.

Schultz, T. W. 1976. *Transforming Traditional Agriculture*. New York: Avon Books.

15

Food, Economics, and Entitlements

AMARTYA SEN

ECONOMICS AND THE ACQUIREMENT PROBLEM

What may be called "instant economics" has always appealed to the quick-witted layman impatient with the slow-moving economist. This is particularly so in the field of hunger and food policy. Of course, the need for speed is genuinely important in matters of food, and the impatience is, thus, easy to understand. But instant economics is also highly deceptive, and especially dangerous in this field. Millions of lives depend on the adequacy of the policy response to the terrible problems of hunger and starvation in the modern world. Past mistakes of policy have been responsible for the death of many millions of people and the suffering of hundreds of millions, and this is not a subject in which short-cuts in economic reasoning can be taken to be fairly costless.

One common feature of a good deal of instant economics related to food and hunger is impatience with investigating the precise mechanisms for acquiring food that people have to use. People establish command over food in many different ways. For example, while a peasant owning his land and the product of his labor simply owns the food produced, a wage laborer paid in cash has to convert that wage into a bundle of goods, including food, through exchange. The peasant does, as it were, an exchange with "nature," putting in labor, etc., and getting back the product, viz., food. The wage laborer does repeated exchanges with others in the society—first, his labor power for a wage and then the wage for a collection of commodities, including food. We cannot begin to understand the precise influences that make it possible or not possible to acquire enough food, without examining the conditions of these exchanges and the forces that govern them. The same

AMARTYA SEN is master of Trinity College, Cambridge University.

This chapter represents a shortened version of the fourth Elmhirst Lecture given at the triennial meeting of the International Association of Agricultural Economists, Malaga, Spain, 26 August 1985. Reprinted from *Lloyd's Bank Review*, no. 160 (1986):1–20. Copyright © The International Association of Agricultural Economists, 1986, and reprinted by permission of Gower Publishing Company Ltd., and Gower Publishing Company. Published with minor omissions by permission of the author.

applies to other methods of acquiring food, for example, through sharecropping and getting a part of the produce, through running a business and making a profit, through selling services and earning an income, and so on. I shall call the problem of establishing command over commodities, in this case food, the "acquirement problem." It is easy to establish that the acquirement problem is really central to questions of hunger and starvation in the modern world.

The acquirement problem is often neglected not only by non-economists, but also by many economists, including some great ones. For example, Malthus in his famous *Essay on the Principle of Population as It Affects the Further Improvement of Society* (1798) leaves the acquirement problem largely unaddressed, though in his less known pamphlet *An Investigation of the Cause of the Present High Price of Provisions* (1800), which deals with more short-run questions, Malthus is in fact deeply concerned precisely with the nitty-gritty of this problem.[1] The result of this neglect in the former work is not without practical consequence, since the popularity of the Malthusian approach to population and food, and of the particular metric of food output per head extensively used in the *Essay on Population,* has tended to give that metric undue prominence in policy discussions across the world.

Malthusian pessimism, based on the expectation of falling food output per head, has not been vindicated by history. Oddly enough, what can be called "Malthusian optimism," that is, *not* being worried about the food problem so long as food output grows as fast as — or faster than — population, has often contributed substantially to delaying policy response to growing hunger (against a background of stationary or rising food output per head). This is a serious enough problem in the case of intensification of regular but non-extreme hunger (without starvation deaths but causing greater proneness to morbidity and mortality), and it can be quite disastrous in the context of a famine that develops without a decline in food output per head, with the misguided focus leading to a hopelessly delayed response of public policy. While Malthus's own writings are by no means unique in focusing attention on the extremely misleading variable of food output per head, "Malthusian optimism," in general, has been indirectly involved in millions of deaths which have resulted from inaction and misdirection of public policy.[2] While fully acknowledging the great contribution that Malthus has made in highlighting the importance of population policy, this negative feature of his work, related to his own bit of instant economics, must also be recognized.

The neglect of the acquirement issue has far-reaching consequences. For many years rational discussion of the food problems of the modern world was distracted by undue concentration on the comparative trends of population growth and the expansion of food output, with shrill warnings of danger coming from very respectable quarters.[3] The fear of population outrunning food output on a global scale has certainly not been realized, and world food output per head has steadily risen.[4] This has, however, gone hand in hand with intensification of hunger in some parts of the world. In many — though not all — of the affected countries, food output per head has in fact fallen, and the anxiety about these countries has often been anchored to the statistics of food output per head, with Malthusian worries translated from the global to the regional or country level. But a causal analysis of the persistence and intensification of hunger and of the development of famines does, in fact, call for something more than attention being paid simply to the statistics of food output per head.

I shall have more to say on the policy questions presently, but before that I would like to discuss a bit further the nature and implications of the acquirement problem. I shall also discuss some arguments that relate to studying food and hunger in terms of what in my book *Poverty and Famines*[5] was called the "entitlement approach."[6] That approach has been extensively discussed, examined, criticized, applied as well as extended, and I have learned a lot from these contributions.[7] But the approach has also been occasionally misinterpreted, and, given the importance of the subject of food policy and hunger, I shall permit myself the self-indulgence of commenting—*inter alia*—on a few of the points that have been made in response to my earlier analysis.

FAMINES AND ENTITLEMENTS

The entitlement approach provides a particular focus for the analysis of famines. It does not specify one particular causation of famine—only the general one that a famine reflects widespread failure of entitlements on the part of substantial sections of the population. Such failure can arise from many different causes.

The entitlement of a person stands for the set of different alternative commodity bundles that the person can acquire through the use of the various legal channels of acquirement open to someone in his position. In a private ownership market economy, the entitlement set of a person is determined by his original bundle of ownership (what is called his "endowment") and the various alternative bundles he can acquire starting respectively from each initial endowment, through the use of trade and production (what is called his "exchange entitlement mapping"). This is not the occasion to go into the formal characterizations of endowments, exchange entitlement mappings, entitlement sets, etc., which were discussed in *Poverty and Famines*.

A person has to starve if his entitlement set does not include any commodity bundle with enough food. A person is reduced to starvation if some change, either in his endowment (e.g., alienation of land, or loss of labor power due to ill health) or in his exchange entitlement mapping (e.g., fall in wages, rise in food prices, loss of employment, drop in the price of the goods he produces and sells), makes it no longer possible for him to acquire any commodity bundle with enough food. I have argued that famines can be usefully analyzed in terms of failures of entitlement relations.

The advantages of the entitlement approach over more traditional analysis in terms of food availability per head were illustrated with case studies of a number of famines, for example, the Bengal famine of 1943, the Ethiopian famines of 1973 and 1974, the Bangladesh famine of 1974, and the Sahel famines in the early seventies.[8] In some of these famines food availability per head had gone down (e.g., in the Sahel famines); in others there was no significant decline—even a little increase (e.g., in the Bengal famine of 1943, the Ethiopian famine of 1973, the Bangladesh famine of 1974). That famines can occur even without any decline in food output or availability per head makes that metric particularly deceptive. Since food availability is indeed the most commonly studied variable, this is a source of some policy confusion. It also makes "Malthusian optimism" a serious route to disastrous inaction. But the point of entitlement analysis is not only to dispute the focus on food availability, but more positively also to provide a general approach for understanding and investigating famines through focusing on variations in endowments and exchange entitlement mappings.

Famine can be caused by various different types of influences, and the common predicament of mass starvation does not imply any one common fundamental cause. Droughts, floods, general inflationary pressure, sharp recessionary loss of employment, and so on, can all in their own way deprive large sections of the population of entitlement to adequate food. A decline in food output or availability can, of course, be one of the major influences on the development of a famine, but even when that is the case (indeed even when food availability decline is the primary proximate antecedent), a serious study of the causal mechanism leading to the famine and the precise form it takes will require us to go into the behavior of the determinants of the entitlements of the different sections of the population.

In *Poverty and Famines,* two broad types of famines were distinguished from each other, viz. boom famines and slump famines. A famine can, of course, occur in a situation of general decline in economic activity (as happened, for example, in the Wollo province of Ethiopia in 1973, due to a severe drought). But it can also occur in overall boom conditions (as happened, for example, in the Bengal famine of 1943, with a massive expansion of economic activity related to war efforts). If economic expansion is particularly favorable to a large section of the population (in the case of the Bengal famine, primarily the urban population, including that of Calcutta), but does not draw into the process another large section (in the Bengal famine, much of the rural laboring classes), then that uneven expansion can actually make the latter group lose out in the battle for commanding food. In the food battle the devil takes the hindmost, and even a boom condition can lead to some groups losing their command over food because of the worsening of their *relative* position vis-à-vis the groups favored by the boom.

THE ENTITLEMENT APPROACH AND ECONOMIC TRADITIONS

It is important to emphasize that the entitlement approach is consistent with many different *detailed theories* of the actual causation of a famine. While the approach identifies certain crucial variables, different theories of the determination of the values of these variables may all be consistent with the general entitlement approach. For example, the entitlement approach does not specify any particular theory of price determination, but relative prices are quite crucial to the entitlements of various occupation groups. The entitlement approach by itself does not provide—nor is it intended to provide—a detailed explanation of any famine, and such an explanation would require supplementation by more specific theories of movements of prices, wages, employment, etc., causing particular shifts in the entitlements of different occupation groups.[9]

What the entitlement approach does is to take up the acquirement problem seriously. Rather than arbitrarily making some implicit assumption about distribution (such as equal division of the available food, or some fixed pattern of inequality in that division), it analyzes acquirement in terms of entitlements, which in a private ownership economy is largely a matter of ownership and exchange (including, of course, production, i.e., exchange with nature). I would claim that this is not in any way a departure from the old traditions of economics. It is, rather, a reassertion of the continuing concern of economics with the mechanism of acquiring commodities. If I had the courage and confidence that Gary Becker shows in his distinguished work in calling his own approach "*the* economic approach,"[10] I would have called the entitlement approach by the same bold name. While the price of timidity is to shy away from assertive naming, I would nevertheless claim that economic traditions stretching back centuries do, in fact, direct our attention to entitlements in analyzing problems of wealth, proverty, deprivation, and hunger.

This is clear enough in Marx's case,[11] but the point is often made that Adam Smith was a great believer in the simple theory of food availability decline in explaining all famines and that he would have thus had little patience for discussion of entitlements and their determinants. Indeed, it is true that in his often-quoted "Digression Concerning the Corn Trade and Corn Laws" in Book IV of the *Wealth of Nations,* Adam Smith did remark that "a dearth never has arisen from any combination among the inland dealers in corn, nor from any other cause but a real scarcity, occasioned sometimes, perhaps, and in some particular places, by the waste of war, but in by far the greatest number of cases, by the fault of the season."[12] However, in understanding the point that Adam Smith is making here, it is important to recognize that he is primarily denying that traders could cause famine through collusion, and he is disputing the view that famines often follow from artificial shortages created by traders, and asserting the importance of what he calls "a real scarcity." I shall have the occasion to take up this aspect of Smith's observation presently when I discuss the issue of anti-famine policy.

We have to look elsewhere in the *Wealth of Nations* to see how acutely concerned Adam Smith was with the acquirement problem in analyzing what he called "want, famine and mortality." I quote Smith from the chapter called "Of the Wages of Labour" from Book I of the *Wealth of Nations:*

> But it would be otherwise in a country where the funds destined for the maintenance of labour were sensibly decaying. Every year the demand for servants and labourers would, in all the different classes of employments, be less than it had been the year before. Many who had been bred in the superior classes, not being able to find employment in their own business, would be glad to seek it in the lowest. The lower class being not only over-

stocked with its own workmen, but with the over-flowings of all the other classes, the competition for employment would be so great in it, as to reduce the wages of labour to the most miserable and scanty subsistence of the labourer. Many would not be able to find employment even upon these hard terms, but would either starve, or be driven to seek a subsistence either by begging, or by the perpetration perhaps of the greatest enormities. Want, famine, and mortality would immediately prevail in that class, and from thence extend themselves to all the superior classes. [13]

Here Adam Smith is focusing on the market-based entitlement of laborers, and its dependence on employment and real wages, and explaining famine from that perspective. This should, of course, come as no surprise. In denying that artificial scarcity engineered by collusive traders can cause famine, Adam Smith was in no way closing the door to the economic analysis of various different real influences on the ability of different groups to command food in the market, in particular the values of wages and employment.

Perhaps it is useful to consider another argument presented by another great classical economist, viz. David Ricardo, attacking the view that a famine cannot occur in a situation of what he calls "superabundance." This was in a speech that Ricardo wrote for delivery in Parliament in 1822, using the third person for himself as if the speech is reported in the *Hansard,* though in the event Ricardo did not actually get to deliver the speech. The reference is to the famine conditions then prevailing in Ireland, and Ricardo examines the point made by another member of Parliament that this could not be the case, since there was superabundance of food in Ireland at that time.

But says the honble. gentn. the people are dying for want of food in Ireland, and the farmers are said to be suffering from superabundance. In these two propositions the honble. gentn. thinks there is a manifest contradiction, but he Mr. R. could not agree with him in thinking so. Where was the contradiction in supposing that in a country where wages were regulated mainly by the price of potatoes the people should be suffering the greatest distress if the potato crop failed and their wages were inadequate to purchase the dearer commodity corn? From whence was the money to come to enable them to purchase the grain however abundant it might (be) if its price far exceeds that of potatoes. He Mr. Ricardo should not think it absurd or contradictory to maintain that in such a country as England where the food of the people was corn, there might be an abundance of that grain and such low prices as not to afford a renumeration to the grower, and yet that the people might be in distress and not able for want of employment to buy it, but in Ireland the case was much stronger and in that country there should be no doubt there might be a glut of corn, and a starving people. [14]

There is indeed nothing surprising in the fact that economists should be concerned with the acquirement problem and dispute the instant economics that overlooks that aspect of the food problem based on confusing supply with command, as the "honourable gentleman" quoted by David Ricardo clearly did. It is a confusion that has recurred again and again in actual discussions of the food problem, and the need to move away from instant economics to serious analysis of the acquirement problem and the entitlement to food is no less today than it was in Ricardo's time. [15]

It is not my purpose to assert that the entitlement approach is flawless as an economic approach to the problem of hunger and starvation. Several "limitations" of the entitlement approach were, in fact, noted in *Poverty and Famines,* including ambiguities in the specification of entitlement, the neglect of nonlegal transfers (e.g., looting) in the disposition of food, the importance of tastes and values in causing hunger despite adequate entitlement, and the relevance of disease and epidemic in famine mortality which extends far beyond the groups whose entitlement failures may have initiated the famine.

To this, one should also add that in order to capture an important part of the acquirement problem, to wit, distribution of food within a family, the entitlement approach would have to be extended. In particular, notions of perceived "legitimacy" of intrafamily distributional patterns have to be brought into the analysis, and its causal determinants analyzed.[16]

Further, if the focus of attention is shifted from famines as such to less acute but possibly persistent hunger, then the role of choice from the entitlement set becomes particularly important, especially in determining future entitlement. For example, a peasant may choose to go somewhat hungry now to make a productive investment for the future, enhancing the entitlement of the following years and reducing the danger of starvation then. For entitlement analysis in a multiperiod setting, the initial formulation of the problem would require serious modification and extension.[17]

These changes and amendments can be systematically made without losing the basic rationale of introducing entitlement analysis to understand the problem of hunger and starvation in the modern world. The crucial motivation is to see the centrality of the acquirement problem and to resist the short-cuts of instant economics, no matter how respectable its source.

POLICY ISSUES

Famine Anticipation and Action

Focusing on entitlements and acquirement rather than simply on food output and availability has some rather far-reaching implications for food policy. I have tried to discuss some of these implications elsewhere, but I would like to pick a few issues here for brief comment. In particular, the problems of famine anticipation and relief are among the most serious ones facing the turbulent and traumatic world in which we live, and I shall comment on them briefly from the perspective that I have been outlining.

So far as famine anticipation is concerned, the metric of food output and availability is obviously defective as a basis, for reasons that follow from the preceding discussion. In fact, the anticipation of famines and their detection at an early stage have often in the past been hampered by undue concentration on this index, and specifically by what we have been calling "Malthusian optimism." Early warnings, as they are sometimes called, may not come at all from the output statistics, and it is necessary to monitor other variables as well, which also influence the entitlements of different vulnerable groups. Employment, wages, prices, etc., all have very direct bearing on the entitlements of various groups.

It is also important to recognize that famines can follow from many *different* types of causal processes. For example, while in a boom famine food prices will sharply rise, in a slump famine they may not. If the economic change that leads to mass starvation operates through depressing incomes and purchasing powers of large groups of people, food prices may stay low—or rise only relatively little, during the process of pauperization of these groups. Even when the slump famine is directly related to a crop failure due to, say, a drought, there may possibly be only a relatively modest rise in food prices, if the supply failure is matched by a corresponding decline in purchasing power due to the same drought. Indeed, it is easy to see that in a fully peasant economy in which food is eaten precisely by those who grow it, a crop failure will subtract from demand what it deducts from supply. The impoverished peasants would of course later be thrown into the rest of the economy—begging, looking for jobs, etc.—but they will arrive there without purchasing ability, and thus need not cause any rise in food prices even later. Actual economies are not, of course, that pure, but the impact on prices is very contingent on the relative weights of the different types of system and organization that make up the affected economy.[18]

Neither food output, nor prices, nor any other variable like that can be taken to be an invariable clue to famine anticipation, and once again there is no substitute to doing a serious economic analysis of the entitlements of all the vulnerable groups. All these variables have possible significance, and it is a question of seeing them as contingently important in terms of what they could do to the ability of different groups to acquire food. The search for some invariable indicator on the basis of which even the economically blind could see an oncoming famine sufficiently early is quite hopeless.

One of the major influences on the actual prevention of famine is the speed and force with which early hunger is reported and taken up in political debates. The nature and freedom of the news media, and the power and standing of opposition parties, are of considerable importance in effective prevention of famines.[19] But if the aim is to anticipate a famine even before early reports of hunger, that object cannot be satisfied by some mechanical formula on an "early warning system." The various information on prices, wages, outputs, etc., have to be examined with an economic understanding of the determinants of the entitlements of the different occupation groups and of the rich variety of ways in which the entitlements of one group or another can be undermined.

The different processes involved not only vary a good deal from each other, they may also be far from straightforward. For example, in various famines some occupation groups have been driven to the wall by a fall in the relative price of the food items they sell, for example, meat sold by pastoral nomads in Harerghe in the Ethiopian famine of 1974, fish sold by fishermen in the Bengal famine of 1943. These groups may survive by selling these food items and buying cheaper calories through the purchase of grains and other less expensive food. A decline in the relative price of meat or fish will, of course, make it easier for the richer parts of the community to eat better, but it can spell disaster for the pastoralist and the fisherman. To make sense of them as signals of turmoil, the observed variables have to be examined in terms of their specific roles in the determination of entitlements of vulnerable groups.

RELIEF, FOOD, AND CASH

Turning now from the anticipation to the relief of famines, the traditional form of relief has, of course, been that of providing free food in relief camps and distribution centers. There can be no doubt that relief in this form has saved lives in large scale in various famines around the world. But to understand precisely what free food distribution does, it may be useful to distinguish between two different aspects of the act of providing, which are both involved in the food relief operation. One is to give the destitute the *ability* to command food, and the other is to give him this ability in the actual form of *food itself*. Though they are integrated together in this form of relief, they need not in general be thus combined. For example, cash relief may provide the ability to command food without directly giving the food.

A person's ability to command food has two distinct elements, viz., his "pull" and the supplier's "response." In the price mechanism the two elements are integrally related to each other. But in terms of the logistics of providing the person with food, the two elements may, in some contexts, be usefully distinguishable. If a person has to starve because he has lost his employment and has no means of buying food, then that is a failure originating on the pull side. If, on the other hand, his ability to command food collapses because of absence of supply, or as a result of the cornering of the market by some manipulative traders, then this is a failure arising on the response side.

One way of understanding what Adam Smith was really asserting (an issue that was briefly touched on earlier) is to see his primary claim as being one about the nature of "response failure" in particular, saying nothing at all about "pull failure." His claim was that a response failure will arise only from what he called "a real scarcity," most likely due to natural causes, and not from manipulative actions of traders. He may or may not have been right in this claim, but it is important to note that in this there is no denial of the possibility of "pull failure." Indeed, as is shown by his own analysis of "want, famine and mortality" arising from unemployment and falling wages (I quoted a passage from this earlier), Smith did also outline the possibility of famine originating on the pull side. There is nothing particularly puzzling or internally inconsistent in Smith's various pronouncements on famine, if we distinguish between his treatment of pull and that of response. It is not the case, as is often asserted, that Adam Smith believed that hunger could not arise without a crop failure. Also he was not opposed to public support for the deprived, and in particular he was not opposed to providing relief through the Poor Laws (though he did criticize the harshness of some of the requirements that were imposed on the beneficiaries under these laws).

Smith's point that response failure would not arise from collusive action of traders has a direct bearing on the appropriate form of famine relief. If his point is correct, then relief could just as easily be provided by giving the deprived additional income and leaving it to the traders to respond to the new pull through moving food to the cash recipients. It is arguable that Smith did underestimate the extent to which traders can and do, in fact, manipulate markets, but at the same time the merits of cash relief do need serious examination in the context of assessing policy options.

Cash relief may not, of course, be quick enough in getting food to the starving in a situation of severe famine. Directly moving food to the starving may be the only immediate option in some situations of acute famine. There is also the merit of direct food distribution that it tends to have, it appears, a very immediate impact on nutrition, even in nonfamine, normal situations, and it seems to do better in this respect than relief through income supplementation. These are points in favor of direct relief through food distribution. There is the further point that cash relief is arguably more prone to corruption, and that the visibility of direct food distribution does provide a better check. And the point about the possibility of manipulative actions of traders cannot, also, by any means be simply dismissed. These are serious points in favor of direct food distribution. But cash relief does have many merits as well.

First, the government's inefficiency in transporting food could be a considerable barrier to famine relief, as indeed some recent experiences have shown. In addition to problems of bureaucracy and red tape, there is the further problem that the transport resources (i.e., vehicles, etc.) in the possession of the private sector may sometimes be hard to mobilize, whereas they would be drawn into use if the actual trading and moving is left to the profit-seeking private sector itself. There is here a genuine pragmatic issue of the speed of response, and it cannot be brushed aside by a simple political judgment one way or the other.

Second, as was observed in the Wollo famine in 1973 and the Bangladesh famine of 1984, and most spectacularly in the Irish famines of the 1840s, food often does move *out* of the famine-stricken regions to elsewhere. This tends to happen especially in some cases of slump famine, in which the famine area is short of effective demand. Since such "food countermovement" tends to reflect the balance of pulls of different regions, it may be preventable by distributing cash quickly enough in the famine-affected region.

Third, by providing demand for trade and transport, cash relief may help to regenerate the infrastructure of the famine-stricken economy. This has some merit in contrast with ad hoc use of transitory public intervention, which is not meant to continue, and the lasting benefits from expansion of normal trade and transport may be considerable for the local economy.

Fourth, it is arguable that cash relief is more usable for development investment needed for productive improvement, and this cannot be sensibly organized in relief centers. Even "food for work" programs, which can help in this direction, may sometimes be too unwieldy, given the need for flexibility for such investment activities.

Fifth, living in relief camps is deeply disruptive for normal family life as well as for pursuing normal economic activities. Providing cash relief precisely where the people involved normally reside and work, without having to move them to relief camps, may have very considerable economic and social advantages. Judging from the experience of an innovative "cash for food" project sponsored by UNICEF in Ethiopia, these advantages are indeed quite real.[20]

This is not the occasion to try to form an overall judgment of the "net" advantage of one scheme over another. Such judgments would have to be, in any case, extremely contingent on the exact circumstances of the case. But the general distinction between the "pull" aspect and the "response" aspect of entitlement failures is of immediate relevance to the question of the strategy of famine relief. Adam Smith's long shadow fell over many famines in the British Empire over the last two hundred years, with Smith being cited in favor of inaction and letting things be. If the analysis presented here is accepted, then inaction reflected quite the wrong reading of the implications of Smith's economic analysis. If his analysis is correct—and the honors here are probably rather divided—the real Smithian issue in a situation of famine is not "intervention versus nonintervention," but "cash relief versus direct food relief." The force of the arguments on Smith's side cannot be readily dismissed, and the experience of mismanagement of famine relief in many countries has done nothing to reduce the aptness of Smith's question.

FOOD SUPPLY AND FOOD PRICES

In comparing the merits of cash relief with food distribution, it was not assumed that there would be more import of food with the latter than with the former. That question—of food imports from aboard—is a quite distinct one from the form that relief might take. It is, however, arguable that in a famine situation direct food distribution is more thoroughly dependent on food import from abroad than a cash relief scheme need be. This is to some extent correct, though direct food distribution may also be based on domestically acquired food. But if we compare food distribution combined *with* food imports, on the one hand, and simple cash relief *without* such imports, on the other, then an arbitrary difference is brought into the contrast which does not belong there. In fact, the issue of food import is a separate one, which should be considered on its own.

This relates to an issue that has often been misunderstood in trying to work out the implications of the entitlement approach to hunger and famines, and in particular the implications of recognizing the possibility that famines can occur without any decline in food availability per head. It has sometimes been argued that if a famine is not caused by a decline in food availability, then there cannot be a case for food imports in dealing with the famine.[21] This is, of course, a non sequitur, and a particularly dangerous piece of nonsense. Consider a case in which some people have been reduced to starvation not because of a decline in total supply of food, but because they have fallen behind in the competitive demand for food in a boom famine (as happened, for example, to rural laborers in the Bengal famine of 1943). The fact is that the prices are too high for these victim groups to acquire enough food. Adding to the food supply will typically reduce prices and help these deprived groups to acquire food. The fact that the original rise in prices did not result from a fall in availability but from an increase in total demand does not make any difference to the argument.

Similarly, in a slump famine in which some group of people has suffered a decline in their incomes due to, say, unemployment, it may be possible to help that group by reducing the price of food through more imports. Furthermore, in each case import of food can be used to break a famine through public relief measures. This can be done either directly, in the form of food distribution, or indirectly through giving cash relief to the famine victims combined with releasing more food in the market to balance the additional demand that would be created. There are, of course, other arguments to be considered in judging pros and cons of food imports, including the important problem of incentives for domestic food producers. But to try to reject the case for food imports in a famine situation on the simple ground that the famine has occurred without a decline in food availability (if that is the case) is to make a straightforward mistake in reasoning.

A more interesting question arises if in a famine situation we are, for some reason, simply not in a position to get more food from abroad. Would a system of cash relief then be inflationary, and thus counterproductive? The answer is it would typically be inflationary, but not necessarily counterproductive. Giving the famine victims more purchasing power would add to the total demand for food. But if we want a more equal distribution of food, with some food moving from others to the famine victims, then the only way the market can achieve this (when the total supply is fixed and the money incomes of others cannot be cut) is through this inflationary process. The additional food to be consumed by the famine victims has to come from others, and this may require that prices go up to induce others to consume less, so that the famine victims—with their new cash incomes—can buy more. Thus, while having a system of cash reliefs is not an argument against food imports in a famine situation, that system can have some desirable consequences *even when* food imports are, for some reason, not possible. If our focus is on enhancing the entitlements of famine victims, the creation of some inflationary pressure—within limits—to redistribute food to the famine victims from the rest of the society may well be a sensible policy to pursue.

ENTITLEMENTS AND PUBLIC DISTRIBUTION

So far in this lecture my concentration on policy matters has been largely on what may be called short-run issues, including the anticipation and relief of famines. But it should be clear from the preceding analysis, with its focus on acquirement and entitlements, that long-run policies have to be geared to enhancing, securing, and guaranteeing entitlements, rather than to some simple formula like expanding food output.

I have discussed elsewhere the positive achievements of public food distribution policies in Sri Lanka and China, and also in Kerala in India, along with policies of public health and elementary education. [22] The role of Sri Lanka's extensive "social welfare programmes" in achieving high living standards has been the subject of some controversy recently. It is, of course, impossible to deny that, judged in terms of such indicators of living standard as life expectancy, Sri Lanka's overall achievement is high (its life expectancy of 69 years is higher than that of any other developing country—even with many times the GNP per head of Sri Lanka). But by looking not at the *levels* of living but at their rate of *expansion* over a selected period, to wit 1960–78, it has been argued by Surjit Bhalla and others that Sri Lanka has performed only "in an average manner." Armed with these findings (based on international comparisons of expansion of longevity, etc., over 1960–78), the positive role of Sri Lanka's wide-based welfare programs has been firmly disputed (asking, on the contrary, the general question: when does a commitment to equity become excessive?). [23]

The basis of this disputation, however, is extremely weak. The period 1960–78 is one in which Sri Lanka's social welfare programs themselves did not grow much, and indeed the percentage of GNP expended on such programs *came down sharply,* from 11.8 in 1960–61 to 8.7 by 1977. [24] If the expansion of sowing is moderate, and so is the expansion of reaping, that can scarcely be seen as a sign of the ineffectiveness of sowing!

The really fast expansion of Sri Lanka's social welfare programs came much earlier, going back at least to the forties. Food distribution policies (e.g., free or subsidized rice for all, free school meals) were introduced in the early 1940s, and health intervention was also radically expanded (including taking on the dreaded malaria). Correspondingly, the death rate too fell from 21.6 per thousand in 1945 to 12.6 in 1950, and to 8.6 by 1960 (all this happened *before* the oddly chosen period 1960–78 used in Bhalla's much-publicized "international comparisons" of expansions). There is nothing in the picture of "expansion" that would contradict the fact of Sri Lanka's exceptional performance, if one does look at the right period, that is, one in which its social welfare programs were, in fact, radically expanded, which happened well before 1960.

The diverse policy instruments of public intervention used in Sri Lanka relate closely to "food policy" in the wider sense, affecting nutrition, longevity, etc., going well beyond the production of food. Similar relations can be found in the experience of effective public distribution programs also in other regions, for example, China and Kerala. It is right that the "food problem" should be seen in these wider terms, involving not only the production of food, but also the entitlements to food and to other nutrition-related variables such as health services.

PRODUCTION AND DIVERSIFICATION

The problem of production composition in achieving economic expansion is also, *inter alia,* an important one in long-run food policy. This complex problem is often confounded with that of simply expanding food output as such, treating it as largely a matter of increasing food supply. This is particularly so in the discussions of the so-called African food problem. It is, of course, true that food output per head in sub-Saharan Africa has been falling in recent years, and this is certainly one of the major factors in the intensification of hunger in Africa. But food production is not merely a source of food supply in Africa, but also the main source of means of livelihood for large sections of the African population. It is for this reason that food output decline tends to go hand in hand with a collapse of entitlements of the masses in Africa.

The point can easily be seen by comparing and contrasting the experience of sub-Saharan Africa in terms of food output per head vis-à-vis those of some countries elsewhere. Take Ethiopia and the Sahel countries, which have all suffered so much from famines. Between 1969–71 and 1980–82, food output per head has fallen by five percent in Chad and Burkina Faso, seven percent in Senegal, 12 percent in Niger, 17 percent in Mali, 18 percent in Ethiopia, and 27 percent in Mauritania.[25] These are indeed substantial declines. But in the same period, and according to the same source of statistics, food output per head has fallen by five percent in Venezuela, 15 percent in Egypt, 24 percent in Algeria, 27 percent in Portugal, 29 percent in Hong Kong, 30 percent in Jordan, and 38 percent in Trinidad and Tobago. The contrast between starvation in sub-Saharan Africa and nothing of the sort in these other countries is not, of course, in the least difficult to explain. Unlike the situation in these other countries, in sub-Saharan Africa a decline in food output is associated with a disastrous decline in entitlements, because the incomes of so many there come from growing food, because they are generally poor, and because the decline of food output there has not been outweighed or even balanced by increases in nonfood (e.g., industrial) output. It is essential to distinguish between (1) food production as a source of income and entitlement, and (2) food production as a source of supply of the vital commodity food. If the expansion of food production should receive full priority in Africa, the case for it lies primarily in the role of food production in generating entitlements rather than only supply.

There are, of course, other reasons as well for giving priority to food production, in particular the greater security that the growers of food might then have, since they would not be dependent on market exchange for acquiring food. This argument has been emphasized by many in recent years, and it is indeed an important consideration, the relevance of which is brought out by the role of market shifts in contributing to some of the famines that have been studied. But this type of uncertainty has to be balanced against uncertainties arising from other sources, in particular those related to climatic reasons. In the very long run the uncertainty of depending on unreliable weather conditions in parts of sub-Saharan Africa may well be eliminated by irrigation and afforestation. However, for many years to come this is a serious uncertainty, which must be taken into account along with other factors in the choice of investment policy in sub-Saharan Africa. An argument that is often encountered in public discussion in various forms can be crudely put like this: "Food output in parts of sub-Saharan Africa has suffered a lot because the climate there is so unreliable for food production; therefore let's put all our resources into food production in these countries." This is, of course, a caricature, but even in somewhat more sophisticated forms, this line of argument as a piece of economic reasoning is deeply defective. One does not put all one's eggs in the same highly unreliable basket. The need is surely for diversification of the production pattern in a situation of such uncertainty.

CONCLUDING REMARKS

I have tried to comment on a number of difficult policy problems. The entitlement approach on its own does not resolve any of these issues. But by focusing on the acquirement problem, and on the major variables influencing acquirement, the entitlement approach provides a general perspective that can be fruitfully used to analyze the phenomenon of hunger as well as the requirements of food policy. I have tried to illustrate some of the uses of the entitlement approach and have also discussed what policy insights follow or do not follow from it. The policy issues discussed have included problems of anticipation and relief of famines, forms of relief to be provided (including food distribution versus cash relief), the role of food supply and food prices in famine relief, and long-run strategies for eliminating vulnerability to famines and starvation (with particular reference to Africa).

I have also claimed that the entitlement approach is, with a few exceptions, in line with very old traditions in economics, which have been, in their own way, much preoccupied with the acquirement issue. The challenges of the terrible economic problems of the contemporary world relate closely to those traditional concerns and call for sustained economic analysis of the determination and use of entitlements of diverse occupation groups.

NOTES

1. On the importance of the latter document, which has received much less attention than the former, see my *Poverty and Famines* (Oxford: Clarendon Press, 1981, Appendix B).

2. This issue is discussed in my article "The Food Problem: Theory and Policy," *Third World Quarterly* 4 (1982).

3. The Club of Rome, despite its extremely distinguished leadership, has been responsible for some of the more lurid research reports of doom and decline. However, a later study sponsored by the club undertaken by H. Linnemann, *MOIRA: A Model of International Relations in Agriculture* (Amsterdam: North-Holland, 1981) shows the picture to be both less gloomy and more easily influenced by policy. See also K. Parikh and F. Rabar, eds., *Food for All in a Sustainable World* (Laxenburg, Austria, IIASA, 1981), especially on the role of policy.

4. See, for example, FAO, *The State of Food and Agriculture 1984* (Rome, 1985).

5. See also my "Starvation and Exchange Entitlements: A General Approach and Its Application to the Great Bengal Famine," *Cambridge Journal of Economics* 1 (1977); and "Ingredients of Famine Analysis: Availability and Entitlements," *Quarterly Journal of Economics* 95 (1981).

6. Note that the use of the expression "entitlement" here is descriptive rather than prescriptive. A person's entitlements as given by the legal system, personal circumstances, etc., need not command any

moral endorsement. This applies both to the opulent entitlements of the rich and to the meager entitlements of the poor.

7. Particularly from Kenneth J. Arrow, "Why People Go Hungry," *New York Review of Books* 29 (15 July 1982); Christopher Bliss, "The Facts About Famine," *South* (March 1982); Keith Griffin, "Poverty Trap," *Guardian* (7 October 1981); Teresa Hayter, "Famine for Free," *New Society* (15 October 1981); Vijay Joshi, "Enough to Eat," *London Review of Books* (19 November 1981); Robert M. Solow, "Relative Deprivation?", *Partisan Review* 51 (1984).

8. See *Poverty and Famines,* chapters 6–10.

9. See *Poverty and Famines,* chapters 6–10. See also Peter Svedberg, "Food Insecurity in Developing Countries: Causes, Trends and Policy Options," UNCTAD, 1984; Martin Ravallion, "The Performance of Rice Markets in Bangladesh during the 1974 Famine," *Economic Journal* 92 (1985); Qaisar M. Khan, "A Model of Endowment Constrained Demand for Food in an Agricultural Economy with Empirical Applications to Bangladesh," *World Development* 13 (1985).

10. See Gary S. Becker, *The Economic Approach to Human Behavior* (Chicago: University of Chicago Press, 1976); and Becker, *A Treatise on the Family* (Cambridge: Harvard University Press, 1981).

11. See, for example, the discussion on wages and capital in *Capital,* vol. I (London: Sonnenschein, 1887, parts 6 and 7).

12. Adam Smith, *An Inquiry into the Nature and Causes of the Wealth of Nations,* Book IV, chapter 5, b.5, in the edition edited by R. H. Campbell and A. S. Skinner (Oxford: Clarendon Press, 1976, vol. 1, p. 526).

13. Smith, *Wealth of Nations,* Book I, chapter 8, pp. 90–91.

14. *The Works and Correspondence of David Ricardo,* edited by P. Sraffa, with the collaboration of M. H. Dobb (Cambridge: Cambridge University Press, 1971, vol. 5, pp. 234–35).

15. See Lance Taylor's illuminating critique, "The Misconstrued Crisis: Lester Brown and World Food," *World Development* 3 (1975).

16. The consequences of particular perceptions of "legitimacy" of intrafamily distributions do have something in common with those of legal relationships. Using that perspective "*extended* exchange entitlement" relations, covering both interfamily and intrafamily distributions, have been explored in an integrated structure in my paper, "Women, Technology and Sexual Division," *Trade and Development Review* no. 6, 1985, UNCTAD, Geneva. The interrelations may be of real importance in understanding sex bias, e.g., the effect that outside earnings of women have on the divisions with the family. On this see also Ester Boserup's pioneering study, *Women's Role in Economic Development* (London, Allen and Unwin, 1970); and my *Resources, Values and Development* (Oxford: Blackwell, 1984, essays 15, 16, 19 and 20).

17. See *Poverty and Famines,* p. 50, footnote 11. For some important and original ideas in this direction, see Peter Svedberg, "The Economics of Food Insecurity in Developing Countries" (Stockholm: Institute for International Economic Studies, 1985, mimeographed).

18. In the Ethiopian famine in Wollo in 1973, food price rises seem to have been relatively moderate. Indeed, in Dessie, the capital of Wollo, the mid-famine food prices seem to have been comparable with prices outside the famine-affected province. There was more of a price rise in the rural areas, but again apparently not a catastrophic rise, and prices seemed to come down relatively quickly. On the importance of prices as a monitoring device for famine anticipation, see J. A. Seaman and J. F. J. Holt, "Markets and Famines in the Third World," *Disasters* 4 (1989); and P. Cutler, "Famine Forecasting: Prices and Peasant Behaviour in Northern Ethiopia," *Disasters* 8 (1984): 48–56. See also B. Snowdon, "The Political Economy of the Ethiopian Famine," *National Westminster Bank Quarterly Review* (November 1985).

19. On this see my "Development: Which Way Now?" *Economic Journal* 93 (1983), reprinted in *Resources, Values and Development,* 1984.

20. See B. G. Kumar, "The Ethiopian Famine and Relief Measures: An Analysis and Evaluation," UNICEF, 1985. See also Wendy A. Bjoerck, "An Overview of Local Purchase of Food Commodities (LPFC)," UNICEF, 1984; and R. Padmini, "The Local Purchase of Food Commodities: 'Cash for Food' Project, Ethiopia," UNICEF, 1985.

21. For a forceful presentation of this odd belief, see Peter Bowbrick's paper (with a truly flattering title), "How Professor Sen's Theory Can Cause Famines," presented at the Agricultural Economics Society Conference, 1985, at the Annual Conference of the Development Studies Association. For a revised version of Bowbrick's paper see P. Bowbrick, "The Causes of Famine: A Refutation of Professor Sen's Theory," *Food Policy* 11 (1986) and my reply, "The Causes of Famine: A Reply," *Food Policy* 11 (1986).

22. See my "Public Action and the Quality of Life in Developing Countries," *Oxford Bulletin of Economics and Statistics* 43 (1981); and "Development: Which Way Now?" *Economic Journal* 93 (1983).

23. See Surjit Bhalla, "Is Sri Lanka an Exception? A Comparative Study of Living Standards," World Bank, 1985, to be published in T. N. Srinivasan and P. Bardhan, eds., *Rural Poverty in South Asia* (Columbia University Press, vol. 2). Bhalla's findings have been used for drawing negative policy conclusions regarding social welfare programs, by several economists (e.g., Hla Myint, "Growth Policies and Income Distribution," discussion paper, World Bank, March 1985; and Jagdish Bhagwati, "Growth and Poverty," text of the Center for Advanced Study of International Development Lecture, Michigan State University, spring 1985).

24. These figures are given by Bhalla himself in a different context. He does not give the figure for 1978, but in his table the percentage had further dropped to 7.7 by 1980. Other sources confirm these overall declining trends during the 1960s and 1970s taken together.

25. *World Development Review 1984* (Oxford: Oxford University Press, 1984, table 6).

IV

Agricultural Transformation and Rural Economic Development

Introduction

 The 1990s have been a period of turbulent and unprecedented change in the global economy and the political landscape. The rapid movement towards more open markets has achieved impressive economic gains in many countries, such as Chile, Indonesia, Thailand, and China. But despite the contribution of higher economic growth rates to improving the welfare of many people, there are still one billion poor in the world in the late nineties, and about half to two-thirds of them live in rural areas. Higher rates of economic growth in Latin America have been accompanied by an increase in the number of the rural poor (Huddle 1997). Africa remains the poorest part of the world economy, and many African countries have yet to generate a reliable food surplus (from own production or via export earnings), which is one of the foundations of political and economic stability. Even in Southeast Asia, the economic crisis of the late 1990s has drawn into question whether the rapid pace of economic growth this region experienced up to 1997 was sustainable.

Part IV addresses the fundamental challenges of increasing food and agricultural production and promoting rural economic development in low- and middle-income countries. It draws on the vast literature about getting agriculture moving, rural institutions, food security, and sustainable production. Eleven chapters are new and four are key contributions from the second edition. The fifteen essays are grouped into three interrelated sections: learning from experience, institutional and human capital, and technology development and sustainability.

In chapter 16, James Bonnen introduces part IV by analyzing the need to coordinate and carefully sequence investments in human capital, technology, and institutional reforms in the design of an agricultural development strategy. Drawing heavily on the experience of the United States, he points out that the payoffs to investments in any single activity, such as basic research, extension, or farming systems research, will be low unless there is a high degree of coordination with investments in complementary activities. Yet, given the scarcity of resources in most developing countries, not all investments can be made simultaneously. Hence, the question of the sequence in which investments are made becomes critical. Bonnen emphasizes the long-term institution building and human-capital improvement required for a highly productive agricultural sector. But he points out that institution building must go beyond research and training institutes to include complementary organizations that address problems of soil and water conservation, credit, rural infrastructure, and market regulation. Some of these organizations will be public, some private, with the mix depending on a nation's history and political philosophy.

In chapter 17, Hans Binswanger reviews the painful lessons gleaned from the failure of community development projects in the fifties and of area development and integrated rural development projects in the seventies and eighties. These lessons are invaluable for designing rural economic development programs (Holdcroft 1984). Because the absolute number of poor increased in many developing countries in the eighties and nineties, the World Bank and Inter-American Bank recently reiterated that poverty reduction is their central goal. But rural poverty is a major problem that is not being addressed in many liberalization programs (de Janvry 1996).

The contribution of a rural-oriented strategy to poverty alleviation is highlighted by a World Bank study that distilled the results of thirty-three household expenditure surveys conducted in India over the forty years between 1951 and 1991 (Ravillion and Datt 1996). The authors show that (1) urban growth had no discernible impact on rural poverty, (2) rural-to-urban migration did not significantly reduce poverty, and (3) both the urban and rural poor gained from rural-sector growth. The policy implication for countries in the early stages of development is that agricultural and rural development can contribute to reducing both urban and rural poverty. But many countries such as South Africa are giving priority to the expansion of urban industrialization and housing rather than emphasizing investments to help the rural poor (Eicher and Rukuni 1996).

Agribusiness and contract farming are now being widely debated in development and donor circles. In chapter 18, Yujiro Hayami discusses the evolution of peasant (smallholder) and plantation production systems and the recent spread of contract farming as a means of helping the landless and sub-family farms gain access to resources (land, credit) and improved technology by entering into contracts with plantations and large-scale farms. Contract farming is spreading rapidly in Asia, Latin America, and parts of Africa. Its growth reflects the increasing globalization of agribusiness and the need to meet the tighter specifications that have been established for food and fiber products sold in industrialized countries. Meeting these tight product specifications requires increased vertical coordination between farmers and exporters, which contract farming provides. There is, however, insufficient research on the economic, political, and environmental aspects of contract farming and agribusinesses (Barham, Carter, and Sigelko 1995; Jaffee and Morton 1995).

The second section of part IV includes five essays on institutional and human capital. We start with agrarian structure, the size of farm and land reform. During the 1950s and 1960s, most economists investigating land tenure concluded that tenure reforms were often necessary to give smallholders incentives to invest in land improvements and to adopt new technologies that required more purchased inputs.[1] Although the 1960s and early 1970s witnessed a number of land reforms in Latin America and Asia, by the late 1970s land reform in most parts of the world was stalled (Dorner 1992; Thiesenhusen 1995). But the topic of land reform is a burning issue in countries that have dualistic agricultural sectors, such as Zimbabwe (Rukuni 1994) and South Africa (Van Zyl, Kirsten and Binswanger 1996; Deininger and Binswanger 1995). In chapter 19, Binswanger and Miranda Elgin address two questions—land reform and farm size. Land reform, although still important in political rhetoric, is seldom implemented today. After reviewing the experience of reforms during the past four decades, the authors conclude that land reform is unlikely to be a major tool for improving the welfare of the poor, because of political resistance by large farmers and plantation owners. Hence, other measures have to be developed to improve the access of the rural poor to land, including land registration (Feder and Feeny 1993), land settlement, tenancy reform (Hayami and Otsuka 1993), contract farming (Porter and Phillips-Howard 1997; Eicher and Rusike 1995), and helping the poor increase rural nonfarm incomes.

Turning to the economics of farm size, Binswanger and Elgin draw on the definitive study by Berry and Cline (1979) showing that, in many countries, productivity is higher on small farms than large farms: family members have a higher incentive to work on their own farms because they receive a share of profits, there are no hiring and search costs for family labor, monitoring costs are lower, and each family member takes a share of the risk. Many other factors, such as land quality, also contribute to the inverse relation between farm size and productivity (Carter 1984). But in some countries, large estates and plantations coexist with small farms. The usual justification for plantations is that these large firms can more efficiently perform the tight coordination between harvesting, processing, and international marketing.

In chapter 20, Nobel laureate T. W. Schultz reiterates Alfred Marshall's dictum that "knowledge is the most powerful engine of production; it enables us to subdue nature and satisfy our wants." Considered the father of human capital theory, Schultz has a straightforward message: "Investment in improving population *quality* can significantly enhance the economic prospects and welfare of poor people."[2] Traditionally, investments have been focused on improving the income-earning skills of men. In 1970 Boserup wrote an influential book, *Women's Role in Economic Development,* that identified the contributions of women to the rural economy, the differential impact of development projects on men and women, and hence the need to invest in improving women's income-earning skills and access to resources.

In chapter 21, Mayra Buvinić demonstrates the substantial economic contributions of women to the rural economy, analyzes the failure of many traditional development projects to reach women, and examines the record of women-in-development projects. She shows that many projects aimed at increasing women's incomes have often "misbehaved" and become sidetracked into providing welfare services and training in "traditional female skills (sewing, cooking, and crafts)." Learning from these failures, many donors shifted to microenterprise and microfinance projects for women (Deere and Leon 1987). Buvinić examines the issues in designing such projects and concludes that, above all, women in developing countries need to increase their productivity and income in agriculture and related rural enterprises in order to improve their own and their families' welfare.

In the 1990s the debate on women was broadened to include gender.[3] Strategic issues in gender analysis include improving the productivity of smallholder farming, income generation via microenterprise projects, and the human capital formation that results from removing the racial, class, and institutional barriers that keep various family members from gaining access to land titles, microfinance, and education (Birdsall and Londoño 1997).

The role of agricultural extension in developing countries has generated a great deal of passion and controversy in development circles over the past fifty years. The debate intensified during the 1990s because of the pressure to downsize public extension services and the apparent success of the privatization of extension in a number of industrial countries, including the United Kingdom, the Netherlands, and New Zealand. The training and visit (T&V) extension model has been aggressively promoted by its founder, Daniel Benor (1987) and the World Bank (1994). But numerous critics have raised questions about the sustainability of the model (Goodell 1983; Chambers, Pacey, and Thrupp 1989; Chambers, Scoones, and Thompson 1994; and Antholt 1994). In India, Feder, Lau and Slade (1987) found that T&V had no significant influence on rice production. Rukuni (1996) raises questions about the fiscal sustainability of T&V extension in southern Africa. Picciotto and Anderson (1997) raise questions about Bindlish and Evenson's evaluation (1993) of the T&V system in Kenya.[4] Because of the intensity of the debate surrounding extension in an era of policy reform and privatization, we include a new paper by Charles Antholt, "Agricultural Extension in the Twenty-first Century," as chapter 22. Antholt reports that many Asian countries, such as Bangladesh, have moved beyond T&V to more pluralistic and cost-effective systems.[5] Research is urgently needed on the economics of alternative public, private, and voluntary extension models.[6]

The book next turns to credit and microfinance. Development theorists during the 1950s viewed the lack of physical capital as a crucial constraint on both agricultural and industrial growth. Concern about capital shortages in agriculture grew during the 1960s as the Green Revolution technology, with its heavy reliance on purchased inputs, was introduced into many countries. This concern led to greatly expanded efforts to channel subsidized credit to poor farmers, and donors poured an estimated $5 billion into rural credit projects in the 1960s and 1970s. The major debate of the 1960s and 1970s centered on whether specialized lending agencies should subsidize interest rates to small farmers in order to offset the administrative costs and risks of lending to small farmers, the alleged monopoly profits in private capital markets and the price distortions in other parts of the economy, such as low farmgate prices due to heavy agricultural taxation. Many researchers argued that subsidized interest rates were an extremely inefficient means of counteracting price distortions, because they undermined incentives for rural savings mobilization and worsened income distribution. The pioneering research of scholars such as Adams, Graham, and Von Pischke (1984) helped convince many donors and governments to deemphasize subsidized agricultural credit and to charge positive real rates of interest.

Timothy Besley, in chapter 23, discusses the economic causes and consequences of market failure in credit markets that arise from high transaction costs and imperfect information (e.g., adverse selection, moral hazard) and the arguments for government action to intervene in rural credit markets.[7] In chapter 24, Marguerite Robinson draws on her research on microfinance in Indonesia and describes the rise and decline of the old credit paradigm—subsidized credit— and the rise of the new paradigm of sustainable finance. Robinson describes the evolution of three banking organizations in Indonesia that are providing sustainable microfinance to small-scale firms: the BDB, a private bank; BRI, a state-owned commercial bank; and village banks. She compares the BRI's local banking system in Indonesia with the Grameen Bank in Bangladesh.

Despite substantial publicity about the "success" of the Grameen model and its applicability in other parts of the world, there is still a lack of definitive data on the long-term sustainability of the Grameen Bank. Many skeptics feel that the Grameen Bank in Bangladesh is still dependent on donor support and that it might not be fiscally sustainable.[8] There is also a gap between the promotion of microfinance and empirical research to back up some of the claims. For example, Otero and Rhyne (1994) contend that the new world of microenterprise finance "has the potential to do in finance what the Green Revolution has done in agriculture—provide access on a massive scale to the poor" (1). In Africa, Buckley (1997) challenges the "uncritical enthusiasm that lies behind much of the proselytizing of microfinance for informal sector enterprises" (1081). On the basis of field research in Kenya, Malawi, and Ghana, Buckley argues that the question of sustainability of microfinance has not been answered in Africa.

Small-scale industries and microfinance are currently in the limelight because of their employment potential and their ability to help the poor, especially women. Carl Liedholm, in chapter 25, reviews empirical studies from the 1970s to the 1990s and confirms that micro and small enterprises (MSEs) are major sources of output, employment, income, and intermediate demand for agricultural products in many poor countries. Although MSEs are defined as firms employing up to fifty workers (usually unpaid family workers, apprentices, and part-time workers), most MSEs are micro firms employing no more than ten workers. Because of the interdependencies between agriculture and rural nonfarm enterprises, the profitability of nonfarm enterprises is crucially linked to the growth of farm income. Since farmers generate the largest share of rural incomes, policies that increase agricultural growth have an important indirect effect on the demand for the products and services of MSEs (Reardon, Crawford, and Kelly 1994).

Despite the importance of rural small-scale industries in terms of their efficiency and rural income and employment generation, there are few widely applicable policy measures to assist small-scale firms other than "leveling the playing field" between small- and large-scale firms by removing discriminatory tariffs, taxes, and licensing requirements for small-scale firms and supplying credit and technical assistance to the MSEs. Most of these interventions are supply driven. Tendler and Amorim (1996) argue that demand-assisted small enterprise growth (helping MSEs to identify and respond to existing and emerging markets) is more effective than the supply-assisted (e.g., credit, technical assistance) model that is promoted by many governments and nongovernmental organizations. Liedholm stresses the need to link rural small-scale industries, financing, and marketing initiatives, but more research is urgently needed on microfinance and the dynamics of the growth of rural industries (Kirsten 1995; Machethe, Reardon, and Mead 1997).

The third section in part IV includes five essays on technology development and sustainability. Sustainability is an important issue because crop yields have been declining on experiment stations across Asia and it will require a long-term research program to discover how to reverse the decline. In southern Africa, declining soil fertility is a major constraint on increasing maize yields (Kumwenda et al. 1997). The International Institute of Tropical Agriculture (IITA), in Nigeria, launched research on alternatives to shifting cultivation soon after it was established in 1967. But after thirty years of research it still has not developed an alternative to shifting cultivation that is profitable to smallholders on a recurring basis and is sustainable in biological terms.

Vernon Ruttan, in chapter 26, points out that sustainability is difficult to define, the research agenda is fraught with conceptual difficulties, the demand for policy guidance is far ahead of the knowledge base and it will take time for research on sustainability to achieve results. Ruttan outlines three critical research issues that must be answered before designing institutions and technologies to achieve sustainable growth of agricultural production. Thomas Reardon (chapter 27) discusses Africa's struggle to deal with the competing advice from agriculturalists and environmentalists on the three-way competition for land and natural resources: food and agricultural production, livestock grazing, and public and private parks for tourists. Reardon argues that increasing agricultural productivity and sustainability are interwoven, and he discusses policies and institutions that might be employed to achieve an intensified and sustainable agriculture. He questions the euphoria surrounding the LISA (low-input sustainable agriculture) model and suggests that successful technology development should incorporate relevant components of LISA-type models as well as selected use of purchased inputs.[9]

In chapter 28, Michael Morris and Derek Byerlee voice concern that the Asian food production struggles of the 1960s may reappear because of "signs that the recent period of rapid growth in Asian agriculture may be ending," the decline of the cereals area in India and China, and the decline in the rate of growth in cereal yields. They point out the importance of the spread of modern varieties in nonirrigated areas over the past ten to fifteen years (Byerlee 1996; David and Otsuka 1994). The authors argue that the three prime movers of future technical change in agriculture are agricultural research, technology transfer systems, and economic policies that support agriculture. They stress the increasing role of private sector research and seed industry development in Asia (Pray and Echeverria 1991; Pray and Umali-Deininger 1997).

In chapter 29, Prabhu Pingali addresses the ecological consequences of the rice Green Revolution in Asia. Pingali is addressing a critical problem, as attested by two respected agronomists who recently concluded that "soil quality is deteriorating in the most productive agricultural systems in Asia" (Cassman and Harwood 1995). Others have argued that the pesticides used in rice paddies are also endangering the health of farmers (Antle and Pingali 1994; Pingali and Gerpacio 1997).

The Green Revolution strategy worked exceptionally well until the mid-eighties, when rice productivity slowed down in the intensively cultivated areas across Asia. This slow down was caused by falling real world rice prices in the 1980s and intensification-induced factors. The declining world rice price encouraged farmers to shift land out of rice into more profitable crops and to use less fertilizer and other inputs on rice. Pingali argues that rice intensification (movement from one rice crop per year to two or three on the same land) has contributed to the degradation of the paddy ecology and the consequent declining productivity. To address this problem, Pingali calls for a shift in research attention from a fixation on increasing rice yields to a more holistic approach to managing the agricultural resource base in the long run, that is, how to develop a sustainable farming system for the twenty-first century.

The literature on "appropriate technology" is replete with policy advice but short on empirically based economic, social, and environmental analysis. Although Peter Timmer's essay (chapter 30) was written in the early seventies about an Indonesian policy debate, it is still useful for teaching purposes, because it illustrates the type of economic analysis that is useful in selecting technologies appropriate in low-wage economies. When Timmer undertook his analysis, the government of Indonesia was considering importing several large, capital-intensive milling facilities in order to "modernize" the Javanese rice-processing industry. Timmer shows that if Indonesia had imported technology appropriate to high-wage countries like the United States (large rice-processing mills), it would have resulted in much higher milling costs and increased unemployment, as expensive imported capital displaced inexpensive domestic labor. Using neoclassical economic analysis, Timmer demonstrates the superiority, from an efficiency standpoint, of the small-scale rice mills adopted spontaneously in Java during the late 1960s. These mills were more efficient than both large, capital-intensive facilities and hand-pounding of rice.

In their comment on Timmer's paper, William Collier et al. point out that, although the small mills may have been economically efficient, the costs and benefits of shifting from hand-pounding to small mechanized mills were borne very unevenly. The major cost to Indonesian society was in the form of increased unemployment among the low-income village women who previously had hand-pounded the paddy, while the benefits were in the form of lower consumer rice prices and increased incomes for rice millers. The Timmer–Collier et al. interchange raises the issue of how to develop mechanisms in low-wage economies to compensate those hurt by technical change. The exchange also demonstrates the large array of detailed engineering, economic, and social data needed to quantify production and income-distribution consequences of technical change and to arrive at a policy recommendation based on facts, rather than slogans such as "small is beautiful," "appropriate technology," and "intermediate technology."

NOTES

1 Most authors argued that land ownership per se was not necessary for small farmers to be technologically dynamic; many improvements could be achieved by reforming rental agreements.

2. See Schultz 1995; Idachaba 1995; Strauss 1990; and Strauss and Thomas (1995).

3. See Razavi 1997; Udry et al. 1995; Gladwin 1996; Buvinic, Gwin, and Bates 1996; Quisumbing 1996; Adesina and Djato 1997; and Palmer-Jones and Jackson 1997.

4. See Picciotto and Anderson 1997 and Bindlish and Evenson 1993 and 1997.

5. See Chowdhury and Gilbert 1996 for a discussion of the rise and fall of T&V extension in Bangladesh and the movement toward a more pluralistic and cost-effective system.

6. Recent literature on agricultural technology adoption and extension includes Feder and Feeny 1993; Anderson 1994; Evenson 1994; Farrington 1995; Ban and Hawkins 1996; Eponou 1996; Due, Magayanae, and Temu 1997; Byerlee and Heisey 1996; and Pray and Umali-Deininger 1998.

7. For pioneering studies of transactions costs and credit see Stiglitz 1989; Udry 1990; Aleem 1990; and Barham, Boucher, and Carter 1996.

8. For a history of the origins of the Grameen Bank see Yunus 1997. A World Bank study has pulled together the best practices from microfinance programs in Thailand, Indonesia and Bangladesh (Yaron, Benjamin, and Piprek 1997).

9. In Africa, the debate over fertilizer use ranges from Norman Borlaug's promotion of the use of inorganic fertilizer and "higher yield" agriculture to LISA advocates who recommend the sole use of manure and organic matter. Heisey and Mwangi (1997) offer an intermediate strategy, recommending moderate doses of inorganic fertilizer. See Marglin 1996 for a discussion of the economic impetus behind the search for "alternative agriculture." Also see Pretty, Thompson, and Hinchcliffe 1996.

REFERENCES

Adams, Dale W., Douglas Graham, and J. D. Von Pischke. 1984. *Undermining Rural Development with Cheap Credit.* Boulder, Colo.: Westview Press.

Adesina, Akinwumi A., and Kouakou K. Djato. 1997. "Relative Efficiency of Women as Farm Managers: Profit Function Analysis in Côte d'Ivoire." *Agricultural Economics* 16:47–53.

Aleem, Irfan. 1990. "Imperfect Information, Screening, and the Costs of Informal Lending: A Study of a Rural Credit Market in Pakistan." *The World Bank Economic Review* 4:329–49.

Anderson, Jock, ed. 1994. *Agricultural Technology: Policy Issues for the International Community.* Wallingford, U.K.: CAB International.

Antholt, Charles H. 1994. "Getting Ready for the Twenty-First Century: Technical Change and Institutional Modernization in Agriculture." Technical Paper no. 217. Washington, D.C.: World Bank.

Antle, John M. and Prabhu L. Pingali. 1994. "Pesticides, Productivity, and Farmer Health: A Philippine Case Study." *American Journal of Agricultural Economics* 76:418–30.

Ban, van den, A. W., and H. S. Hawkins. 1996. *Agricultural Extension.* Second edition. Oxford: Blackwell Science.

Barham, Bradford L., Stephen Boucher, and Michael R. Carter. 1996. "Credit Constraints, Credit Unions, and Small-Scale Producers in Guatemala." *World Development* 24 (5): 793–806.

Barham, Bradford L., Michael R. Carter, and Wayne Sigelko. 1995. "Agro-export Production and Peasant Land Access: Examining the Dynamic between Adoption and Accumulation." *Journal of Development Economics* 46:85–107.

Benor, Daniel. 1987. "Training and Visit: Back to Basics." In *Agricultural Extension Worldwide: Issues, Practices, and Emerging Priorities,* edited by William Rivera and Susan Schram, 137–48. London: Croom Helm.

Berry, R. A., and William R. Cline. 1979. *Agrarian Structure and Productivity in Developing Countries.* Baltimore: Johns Hopkins University Press.

Bindlish, Vishva, and Robert Evenson. 1993. *Evaluation of the Performance of T&V Extension in Kenya.* Agriculture and Rural Development Series no. 7. Washington, D.C.: World Bank.

———. 1997. "The Impact of T&V Extension in Africa: The Experience of Kenya and Burkina Faso." *World Bank Research Observer* 12 (2): 182–201.

Birdsall, Nancy, and Juan Luis Londoño. 1997. "Asset Inequality Matters: An Assessment of the World Bank's Approach to Poverty Reduction." *American Economic Review* 87 (2): 32–37.

Boserup, Ester. 1970. *Women's Role in Economic Development.* New York: St. Martin's Press.

Buckley, G. 1997. "Microfinance in Africa: Is It Either the Problem or the Solution." *World Development* 25 (7): 1081–93.

Buvinić, Mayra, Catherine Gwin, and Lisa M. Bates. 1996. *Investing in Women: Progress and Prospects for the World Bank.* Baltimore: Johns Hopkins University Press.

Byerlee, Derek. 1996. "Modern Varieties, Productivity, and Sustainability: Recent Experience and Emerging Challenges." *World Development* 24 (4): 697–718.

Byerlee, Derek, and Paul W. Heisey. 1996. "Past and Potential Impacts of Maize Research in Sub-Saharan Africa: A Critical Assessment." *Food Policy* 21 (3): 255–77.

Carter, Michael. 1984. "Identification of the Invisible Relationship between Farm Size and Productivity." *Oxford Economic Papers* 36:131–45.

Cassman, K. G., and R. R. Harwood. 1995. "The Nature of Agricultural Systems: Food Security and Environmental Balance." *Food Policy* 20 (5): 439–54.

Chambers, Robert, Arnold Pacey, and Lori Ann Thrupp. 1989. *Farmer First: Farmer Innovation and Agricultural Research.* London: Technology Publications.

Chambers, Robert, Ian Scoones, and John Thompson. 1994. *Beyond Farmer First: Rural People's Knowledge, Agricultural Research and Extension Practice.* London: Intermediate Technology.

Chowdhury, Mrinal K., and Elon H. Gilbert. 1996. *Reforming Agricultural Extension in Bangladesh: Blending Greater Participation and Sustainability with Institutional Strengthening.* Agricultural Research and Extension Network Paper no. 61. London: ODI.

David, Cristina C., and Keijiro Otsuka, eds. 1994. *Modern Rice Technology and Income Distribution in Asia.* Boulder, Colo.: Lynne Rienner Publishers.

Deere, Carmen Diana, and Magdalena Leon. 1987. *Rural Women and State Policy: Feminist Perspectives on Latin American Agricultural Development.* Boulder, Colo.: Westview Press.

Deininger, Klaus, and Hans P. Binswanger. 1995. "Rent Seeking and the Development of Large-Scale Agriculture in Kenya, South Africa, and Zimbabwe." *Economic Development and Cultural Change* 43 (3): 493–522.

de Janvry, Alain. 1996. "Seven Theses in Support of Successful Rural Development." Paper presented at Workshop on Approaches to Rural Poverty Alleviation in SADC Countries, 12–22 February, Cape Town, South Africa.

Dorner, Peter. 1992. *Latin American Land Reforms in Theory and Practice: A Retrospective Analysis.* Madison: University of Wisconsin Press.

Due, J. M., F. Magayanae, and A. A. Temu. 1997. "Gender Again—Views of Female Agricultural Extension Officers by Smallholder Farmers in Tanzania." *World Development* 25 (5): 713–25.

Eicher, Carl K., and Mandivamba Rukuni. 1996. "Reflections on Agrarian Reform and Capacity Building in South Africa." Staff Paper no. 96-3, Department of Agricultural Economics, Michigan State University, East Lansing.

Eicher, Carl K., and Joseph Rusike. 1995. "Introduction—Agribusiness in Eastern and Southern Africa." *African Rural and Urban Studies* 2 (2/3): 7–28.

Eponou, Thomas. 1996. *Partners in Technology Generation and Transfer: Linkages between Research and Farmers' Organizations in Three Selected African Countries.* Research Report no. 9. The Hague: ISNAR.

Evenson, Robert E. 1994. "Analyzing the Transfer of Agricultural Technology." In *Agricultural Technology: Policy Issues for the International Community,* edited by Jock R. Anderson, 165–78. Wallingford, U.K.: CAB International.

Farrington, John. 1995. "The Changing Public Role in Agricultural Extension." *Food Policy* 20 (6): 537–44.

Feder, Gershon, and David Feeny. 1993. "The Theory of Land Tenure and Property Rights." In *The Economics of Rural Organization: Theory, Practice, and Policy,* edited by Karla Hoff, Avishay Braverman, and Joseph E. Stiglitz, 240–58. New York: Oxford University Press.

Feder, G., L. J. Lau, and R. H. Slade. 1987. "Does Agricultural Extension Pay? The Training and Visit System in Northwest India." *American Journal of Agricultural Economics* 69 (3): 677–86.

Gladwin, Christina H. 1996. "Gender in Research Design: Old Debates and New Issues." In *Achieving Greater Impact from Research Investments in Africa,* edited by Steven A. Breth. Mexico City: Sasakawa Africa Association.

Goodell, Grace E. 1983. "Improving Administrators' Feedback Concerning Extension, Training, and Research Relevance at the Local Level: New Approaches and Findings from Southeast Asia." *Agricultural Administration* 13:39–55.

Hayami, Y., and K. Otsuka. 1993. *The Economics of Contract Choice: An Agrarian Perspective.* Oxford: Clarendon Press.

Heisey, Paul W., and Wilfred Mwangi. 1997. "Fertilizer Use and Maize Production." In *Africa's Emerging Maize Revolution,* edited by Derek Byerlee and Carl K. Eicher, 193–211. Boulder, Colo.: Lynne Rienner Publishers.

Holdcroft, Lane. 1984. "The Rise and Fall of Community Development, 1950–65: A Critical Assessment." In *Agricultural Development in the Third World,* edited by Carl K. Eicher and John M. Staatz, 46–58. Baltimore: Johns Hopkins University Press.

Huddle, Donald L. 1997. "Review Article: Post-1982 Effects of Neoliberalism on Latin American Development and Poverty: Two Conflicting Views." *Economic Development and Cultural Change* 45, no. 4 (July): 881–97.

Idachaba, Francis S. 1995. "Human Capital and African Agricultural Development." In *Agricultural Competitiveness: Market Forces and Policy Choice. Proceedings of the Twenty-Second International Conference of Agricultural Economists, Harare, Zimbabwe, 22–29 August 1994.* edited by G. H. Peters and Douglas D. Hedley, 540–53. Aldershot, U.K.: Dartmouth Publishing.

Jaffee, Steven, and John Morton. 1995. *Marketing Africa's High-Value Foods.* Dubuque, Iowa: Kendall-Hunt.

Kirsten, J. F. 1995. "Rural Non-farm Enterprises: A Vehicle for Rural Development in South Africa." *Agrekon* 34 (4): 198–204.

Kumwenda, John D. T., Stephen R. Waddington, Sieglinde S. Snapp, Richard B. Jones, and Malcolm J. Blackie. 1997. "Soil Fertility Management in Southern Africa." In *Africa's Emerging Maize Revolution,* edited by Derek Byerlee and Carl K. Eicher, 157–72. Boulder, Colo.: Lynne Rienner Publishers.

Machethe, Charles L., Thomas Reardon, and Donald Mead. 1997. "Promoting Farm-Nonfarm Linkages for Employment of the Poor in South Africa: A Research Agenda Focused on Small-Scale Farms and Agroindustry." *Development Southern Africa* 14 (3): 377–94.

Marglin, Stephen A. 1996. "Farmers, Seedsmen, and Scientists: Systems of Agriculture and Systems of Knowledge." In *Decolonizing Knowledge: From Development to Dialogue,* edited by Frédérique Apffel-Marglin and Stephen A. Marglin, 185–248. Oxford: Clarendon Press.

Otero, María, and Elisabeth Rhyne, eds. 1994. *The New World of Microenterprise Finance: Building Healthy Financial Institutions for the Poor.* West Hartford, Conn.: Kumarian Press.

Palmer-Jones, Richard, and Cecile Jackson. 1997. "Work Intensity, Gender, and Sustainable Development." *Food Policy* 22 (1): 39–62.

Picciotto, Robert, and Jock Anderson. 1997. "Reconsidering Agricultural Extension." *World Bank Research Observer* 12 (2): 249–59.

Pingali, Prabhu, and Roberta V. Gerpacio. 1997. "Living with Reduced Insecticide Use for Tropical Rice in Asia." *Food Policy* 22 (2): 107–18.

Porter, Gina, and Kevin Phillips-Howard. 1997. "Comparing Contracts: An Evaluation of Contract Farming Schemes in Africa." *World Development* 25 (2): 227–38.

Pray, Carl E., and Ruben G. Echeverria. 1991. "Private-Sector Agricultural Research in Less-Developed Countries." In *Agricultural Research Policy: International Quantitative Perspectives,* edited by P. Pardey et al., 343–96. Cambridge: Cambridge University Press for ISNAR.

Pray, Carl E., and Dina Umali-Deininger. 1998. "Private Agricultural Research: Will It Fill the Gap?" *World Development* 26 (3).

Pretty, Jules N., John Thompson, and Fiona Hinchcliffe. 1996. *Sustainable Agriculture: Impacts on Food Production and Challenges for Food Security.* London: International Institute for Environment and Development.

Quisumbing, Agnes R. 1996. "Male-Female Differences in Agricultural Productivity: Methodological Issues and Empirical Evidence." *World Development* 24 (10): 1579–95.

Ravallion, Martin, and Gaurav Datt. 1996. "How Important to India's Poor is the Sectoral Composition of Economic Growth?" *World Bank Economic Review* 10 (1): 1–25.

Razavi, S. 1997. "Fitting Gender into Development Institutions." *World Development* 25 (7): 1111–25.

Reardon, Thomas, Eric W. Crawford, and Valerie Kelly. 1994. "Links between Nonfarm Income and Farm Investment in African Households: Adding the Capital Market Perspective." *American Journal of Agricultural Economics* 76 (5): 1172–76.

Rukuni, Mandivamba (Chairman). 1994. *Report of the Commission of Inquiry into Appropriate Agricultural Land Tenure Systems.* Vol. 1, *Main Report;* Vol. 2, *Technical Reports;* Vol. 3, *Methods, Procedures, Itinerary, and Appendices.* Harare, Zimbabwe: Commission of Inquiry.

———. 1996. "A Framework for Crafting Demand-Driven National Agricultural Research Institutions in Southern Africa." Staff Paper no. 96-76, Department of Agricultural Economics, Michigan State University, East Lansing.

Schultz, T. Paul. 1995. "Human Capital and Economic Development." In *Agricultural Competitiveness: Market Forces and Policy Choice. Proceedings of the Twenty-Second International Conference of Agricultural Economists, Harare, Zimbabwe, 22–29 August 1994,* edited by G. H. Peters and Douglas D. Hedley, 523–39. Aldershot, U.K.: Dartmouth Publishing.

Stiglitz, Joseph E. 1989. "Financial Markets and Development." *Oxford Review of Economic Policy* 5 (4): 55–68.

Strauss, John. 1990. "Households, Communities, and Preschool Children's Nutrition Outcomes: Evidence from Rural Cote d'Ivoire." *Economic Development and Cultural Change* 38:231–61.

Strauss, John, and Duncan Thomas. 1995. "Health and Labour Productivity: Sorting Out the Relationships." In *Agricultural Competitiveness: Market Forces and Policy Choice. Proceedings of the Twenty-Second International Conference of Agricultural Economists, Harare, Zimbabwe, 22–29 August 1994,* edited by G. H. Peters and Douglas D. Hedley, 570–90. Aldershot, U.K.: Dartmouth Publishing.

Tendler, Judith, and Mônica Alves Amorim. 1996. "Small Firms and Their Helpers: Lessons on Demand." *World Development* 24 (3): 407–26.

Thiesenhusen, William C. 1995. *Broken Promises: Agrarian Reform and the Latin American Campesino.* Boulder, Colo.: Westview Press.

Udry, Christopher. 1990. "Credit Markets in Northern Nigeria: Credit as Insurance in a Rural Economy." *World Bank Economic Review* 4:251–69.

Udry, Christopher, John Hoddinott, Harold Alderman, and Lawrence Haddad. 1995. "Gender Differentials in Farm Productivity: Implications for Household Efficiency and Agricultural Policy." *Food Policy* 20 (5): 407–23.

Van Zyl, Johan, J. Kirsten, and H. P. Binswanger. 1996. *Agricultural Land Reform in South Africa: Policies, Markets, and Mechanisms.* New York: Oxford.

Yaron, Jacob, McDonald Benjamin, and Gerda Piprek. 1997 (February draft). "Rural Finance: Issues, Design, and Best Practices," Agriculture and Natural Resources Department, World Bank, Washington, D.C.

Yunus, Muhammad. 1997. "The Grameen Bank Story: Rural Credit in Bangladesh." In *Reasons for Hope: Instructive Experiences in Rural Development,* edited by A. Krishna, N. Uphoff, and M. J. Esman, 9–24. West Hartford, Conn.: Kumarian Press.

World Bank. 1994. *Agricultural Extension: Lessons from Completed Projects.* Washington, D.C.: World Bank.

16

Agricultural Development: Transforming Human Capital, Technology, and Institutions

JAMES T. BONNEN

INTRODUCTION

Increased agricultural productivity is commonly explained solely in terms of technological change. Technology, in turn, is often seen as the exclusive product of research and development. Both notions are erroneous. Implicit in the attitudes of many scientists is the even more erroneous belief that "basic research" is the true and ultimate source not only of all technology but of all increased productivity. This frequently produces the view that everything else is of some lower order of scientific interest and importance to society, and thus to be relegated to second-rate minds, that is, to bureaucrats, politicians, applied researchers, and other inferior orders.

Conscious technological innovation predates science by centuries, and even today we often produce new technologies without recourse to science, especially basic science. In any case, the origins of specific changes in productivity are more complex and multiple than is commonly appreciated. Many criticisms of agricultural research arise out of confusion over the sources of agricultural productivity, as well as from a profound ignorance of the characteristics imposed on the search for agricultural productivity by its biological nature.

This chapter argues that increases in productivity arise not from technological change alone but from institutional innovation, improvements in human capital, as well as changes in the availability of biological and physical capital. Any careful reading of the history of the development of agriculture and its institutions and people will demonstrate this. Moreover, the data on returns to agricultural research have independently begun to substantiate this view (Evenson, Waggoner, and Rut-

JAMES T. BONNEN is professor emeritus of agricultural economics, Michigan State University.

Reprinted from *U.S.-Mexico Relations: Agriculture and Rural Development,* edited by Bruce F. Johnston, Cassio Luiselli, Celso Cartas Contreras, and Roger D. Norton, 1987, pp. 267–300. Copyright © 1987 by the Board of Trustees of the Leland Stanford Junior University. Published with revisions and deletions by permission of Stanford University Press and the author.

tan 1979; Ruttan 1982, 237–61). The chapter also illustrates these points by describing the evolution of the system of developmental institutions in U.S. agriculture, and it examines the significance of the organizational characteristics of this system for other nations.

RELATIONSHIPS BETWEEN SCIENCE, TECHNOLOGY, HUMAN CAPITAL, AND INSTITUTIONS

Change in productivity, as measured by economists, is the unexplained residual in output after accounting for conventional inputs (land, labor, capital, etc.). This residual is attributable both to new technology and to the new human capital and institutional innovations that are almost invariably preconditions for or adaptive complements to any technological innovation. Because technology, human capital, and institutional innovations tend to be complementary inputs in production, it is impossible to separate their relative influences with much accuracy. In some recent studies of the returns to agricultural research, variables for human capital and technological change have been introduced into regression models to explain changes in agricultural productivity and to measure the internal rates of return to these investments. To my knowledge, no one has yet found a way even crudely to conceptualize and represent separately in such models the aggregate effect of institutional innovations.[1]

Institutional innovation seems to depend on prior human capital accumulation, just as technological innovation does (Schultz 1968; Shaffer 1969). Both are embodied human capital. Like technological changes, institutional innovations represent a change not just in the opportunity sets of individuals or groups but in the aggregate or social opportunity set. Thus, institutional changes are transformations of social production functions in much the same sense that technological changes are transformations of the production functions of conventional economic theory. The problem is how to conceptualize and measure production functions in society's marketplace for social and political transactions.

I will not dwell long on human capital. Anyone who does not now appreciate what the quality of the human agent means to productivity growth and development has missed one of the most important dimensions of the economic literature over the last 20 years. In the United States, the land-grant colleges' historical contribution in educating farmers, providing broad access to higher education, forcing high schools into existence nationwide, and helping to create science as a profession by introducing it into college curricula cannot be overemphasized. Before there can be science, scientists must be trained. Indeed, the leadership that created the land-grant system and the U.S. Department of Agriculture (USDA) came not from farmers, but primarily from an educated middle class of professionals— lawyers, clergy, doctors, and journalists—who shared a faith in the idea of progress and saw access to education as the road to individual opportunity, as well as the primary assurance of a vital democratic social order. Educated professionals created and then staffed the USDA, the land-grant colleges, and other public universities. These institutional innovations eventually made a significant difference in the economic productivity of the United States. In short, the slow accumulation of human capital in an educated middle class preceded and led to an institutional innovation, the land-grant-USDA system, which in turn led to a greater accumulation in human capital through the growing access to higher education and through agricultural research and extension. New science-based agricultural technologies have flowed from and were preceded by many decades of investment in human capital and related institutional innovation. This has been an iterative and interactive development process without a clearly conceived blueprint.

The concept of human capital in its modern form is the intellectual contribution of Nobel laureate Theodore W. Schultz. Improvements in human capital increase the ability of the human agent to identify, define, and deal with problems, or as Schultz puts it, "the ability to deal with disequilibria" (Schultz 1975). In the development of agriculture, this ability to deal with disequilibria shows up dramatically in the early contribution of improved farm management to agricultural productivity. As new agricultural technologies are introduced, factor combinations inevitably are left in less-than-optimal proportions. Many scientists and traditional farmers commonly attribute to the new technology the productivity that farmers in the aggregate could never have realized if they had not taught themselves and been taught how to make rational economic decisions. The traditional practices of farmers are invariably made inefficient in some degree by technical change. Continuous technical change makes traditional practices obsolete, and to achieve efficiency requires a conscious system of management decision based on economic as well as biological and physical science knowledge—that is, farm management.

Thus, new technologies not only arise out of prior investments in human capital and institutions but have a potential for increasing productivity that generally cannot be realized until the new technologies are combined with some appropriate, complementary improvement in agricultural institutions and in the human agents managing agriculture. Whereas new institutions generally depend on prior human capital accumulation, improved human capital frequently depends on prior institutional innovation. The creation of farm management research and extension in the United States as a function of the college of agriculture was a prerequisite to improving the farmers' ability to capitalize on the stream of new physical and biological technologies that began to flow from science in this century.[2] Thus, the factors of technology, individual human capability, institutions, and biophysical capital, interact in a continuing process of innovative disturbance in one factor, followed by the managed adaptation of the other factors to find a new, more efficient equilibrium of resource use.

Under such conditions, it is a major intellectual misunderstanding to attribute the entire increment of any increase in productivity to one factor, as is commonly done in agriculture in discussing the role of technology in transforming productivity. An even greater misunderstanding allows the media and some scientists to talk about basic science as if it were the only factor necessary to create new technologies. As important as basic science is, this is a naive understanding of the development process. Basic science must be interactively linked with various types of applied research and that linked in turn with technology development and ultimately with technology- and knowledge-transfer mechanisms. If these other activities or linkages are missing, some basic science knowledge will remain undeveloped or be developed so slowly that significant part of its value will be lost, and the social return to that investment in basic science reduced or lost. As a consequence, some of the potential growth in productivity is lost to society (Knutsen and Tweeten 1979).

To extract the full potential in productivity, the creation of knowledge and its development must be coordinated and interlinked in some systemic manner all the way to its use. This cannot be achieved accidentally or solely by market forces. To achieve the highest potential levels of productivity requires a sustained national policy with clear goals to guide the development of the necessary public and private institutions and to assure the investments in human capital and institutions that are prerequisite to, as well as complements in, creating new technologies.

In their organization and evolution, the developmental institutions of U.S. agriculture directly reflect this understanding of the relationship between scientific knowledge, effective technology development and use, investments in human capital, and institutional development. It is the creative process of innovative disruption and selective adaptation that the system of developmental institutions in U.S. agriculture historically managed so well. To understand the lessons for the potential of science and the sources of productivity in agriculture, we must understand the system of developmental institutions.

THE U.S. SYSTEM OF DEVELOPMENTAL INSTITUTIONS

Man, not science, transformed U.S. agriculture. Men and women, acting through the institutions they had created, developed scientific knowledge, changed human values and aspirations, modified old institutions and built new ones as they saw the need, and step by step transformed the productivity and welfare of U.S. farmers. A set of diverse institutions supporting public policy slowly evolved around a common goal of agricultural development. By the 1930s it constituted a coherent, science-based system that subsequently transformed U.S. agriculture.

Five sets of institutions compose the core of this developmental system. These are (1) a web of diverse farmer organizations, (2) the land-grant colleges of agriculture, (3) the U.S. Department of Agriculture, (4) the private-sector markets and firms that provide purchased inputs to farmers and market farm products as well, and (5) the political bodies, federal and state, responsible for agricultural policy. These last two sets of institutions, one private and the other public, help coordinate the other three and provide closure to the social system. If separate institutions are to constitute a system with a common purpose, their behavior must be coordinated. Private markets provide the information necessary to coordinate the marketing decisions of farmers and agribusiness firms as well as the purchasing decisions of public institutions. However, it is national, state, and local governments that set many of the rules for markets. Governments, of course, provide the financial support and the policy direction to coordinate the public institutions of agriculture. Since the nineteenth century, as the fundamentally different institutions of agriculture coalesced into a single system for agricultural development, these two quite different coordination processes have behaved as one interactive, tension-ridden communications and coordination system. Over time these public and private institutions and policies have become more and more interactive, until now their embrace is so intimate and longstanding that the line between public and private is often difficult to draw. In short, the public and private institutions of U.S. agriculture are part of and respond to signals out of both of these coordination processes.

THE BIRTH OF NEW INSTITUTIONS, 1850–1880

The institutions that evolved into a developmental system in U.S. agriculture were created during the middle decades of the nineteenth century and grew quite separately until the 1880s. The first farm organization to have an impact on national economic and farm policy matters was the Patrons of Husbandry, commonly called the Grange. Founded in 1867, the Grange grew rapidly during the 1870s as the forces of agrarian discontent fed on depressed economic conditions. The first land-grant college, Michigan State University, was established in 1855. The Morrill Act, creating a national system of land-grant colleges, was enacted by Congress in 1862. Most of the colleges were in place by 1880, except in the West. The U.S. Department of Agriculture was founded the same year the land-grant system was established; but in the early years it followed its own evolutionary course, focusing almost exclusively on developing a research program while the colleges were struggling to develop a curriculum. These early decades were a period of great conflict, in which agrarian leaders fought over the need for and the nature of the institutions that had been created. Battles raged inside and around each institution over its appropriate activities, organizational form, and social purpose. Survival was a daily battle, especially in the colleges. Great struggles over what an appropriate agricultural curriculum should be took place through the 1870s and 1880s between practical men, who saw agriculture as a vocation, and a small but growing body of scientists and professionals, who believed in the potential of science for transforming agriculture. This stuggle lasted well into the twentieth century (Bonnen 1962). The curriculum and organization that finally evolved was a compromise between science and a vocational commitment to farming and its improvement.

GROWING LINKS BETWEEN INSTITUTIONS, 1880–WORLD WAR I

Attempts to apply science to agriculture forced a search for appropriate organizational forms. The first U.S. agricultural experiment station (an innovation borrowed from Germany) was established as an independent institution in Connecticut in 1875. Further efforts by agricultural leaders with an understanding of the potential for science in agriculture led to congressional passage of the Hatch Act of 1887, providing federal funds for the establishment of stations in all the states and for an office in the USDA to coordinate the flow of scientific knowledge between the two systems (True 1929).

Legislation of this kind requires consensus, coordinated effort, and political activity. The consensus and the movement that led to the Hatch Act grew out of annual informal meetings between representatives of the colleges and the USDA during the early 1880s. In 1887, the colleges formalized their collaboration by establishing the Association of American Agricultural Colleges and Experiment Stations, subsequently renamed the American Association of Land-Grant Colleges. Legislation raising the Department of Agriculture to cabinet status (1889) was this coalition's next legislative achievement. The Adams Act (1906) strengthened the support for experiment stations, especially in basic science, and clarified the USDA and land-grant college roles in agricultural research.

From 1897 to 1913, scientific agricultural research came to full maturity within the USDA. A systematic structure of applied and problem-oriented bureaus was created. The organizational structures of the USDA and the land-grant colleges were now strikingly similar, and they were staffed by a similar cadre of scientists. By the beginning of World War I, the USDA was the world's finest agricultural research organization. Although it had been assigned regulatory activities as early as 1884, its primary functions were agricultural research and education (Baker et al. 1963).

In 1914 Congress passed the Smith-Lever Act, which established a national extension system organized on roughly the same pattern as the research system, with the USDA and the colleges linked in a loose structure for coordination. The American Association of Land-Grant Colleges was the early political arm of this coalition of federal and state research and educational organizations. The USDA worked toward the same goals in the formal budget processes of the executive and legislative branches. The Congress and its agricultural committees grew accustomed to dealing with the USDA, the land-grant colleges, and the farm organizations as clientele of federally funded agricultural research and education programs. In sum, the period from the 1880's through World War I was one of growing interdependence and institutional linkage between these research and education institutions.

A fundamental change in the system had begun to take place in the early 1900s, when the colleges experimented with full-time representatives at the county level to extend to farmers the growing body of new scientific knowledge. The Smith-Lever Act of 1914 transformed this idea into a national system of county extension agents, financed from federal, state, and local (county) government sources but responsible to a director of agricultural extension in the state colleges of agriculture. An agency was created within the USDA to assist in coordination of the system. The existence of this linkage to the local level created for the land-grant colleges and for the USDA a grass-roots organization that communicated new agricultural technologies and knowledge directly to farmers in a systematic and continuing way, while sending back to the colleges and the USDA information about farming problems that needed research and policy attention.

THE SYSTEM MATURES, 1920–1950

The early county extension agents were frustrated in their efforts to get farmers interested in learning how to improve farm practices. After a brief national debate, extension began organizing farm bureaus in the local chambers of commerce for this purpose. They recruited the more progressive, often better-educated farmers and gave them special attention. Once organized, these farmers wanted to influence national policy. This quickly led to the organization of state farm bureaus and, in 1920, to the American Farm Bureau Federation (AFBF), which pursued the economic and business interests of members at state and national levels. The AFBF opened an office in Washington, D.C., and quickly became the dominant farm organization in the United States.

Although the land-grant college extension agents created the county farm bureaus as their political action arm, the AFBF soon controlled the local and state farm bureaus as well as the county extension offices. When the Farm Bureau spoke, the colleges, the USDA, and the U.S. Congress all listened intently. County agents did not travel to Washington to represent extension; the AFBF's state president took care of that chore. The AFBF generally supported the interests of the land-grant colleges and the USDA, as well as those of the more successful farmers. This awkward marriage ultimately led to a separation of the public extension and private farm organization structures.

The rise of politically effective modern farm organizations, especially the AFBF, strengthened political support for the colleges but complicated life for their presidents and deans of agriculture. Conflicts arose between educational objectives and farmers' political goals and eventually led to a physical, financial, and organizational separation of the county farm bureaus from the land-grant college county extension offices. A strong political coalition remains to this day in many states in which the American Farm Bureau is the only or the dominant general farm organization. And the history of close ties with the politically strong Farm Bureau have made relations between the colleges and other general farm organizations difficult at best.

The experience gained from nineteenth-century failures in farm organization became the basis for their success in the twentieth century. Unlike the nineteenth-century farm organization, the contemporary farm organization is an interest group that is careful not to compete with political parties. Its business activities are managed quite separately from its lobbying and other political activities. Business services at advantageous prices are made available only to members, which stabilizes membership and ensures a continuing organizational base for political and policy activities (Olson 1971; Salisbury 1970).

Since the 1930s the National Farmer's Union, the American Farm Bureau Federation, and, on occasion, the National Grange have had a substantial impact on national agricultural policy decisions. Other, more recently formed general farm organizations are the National Farmers Organization and the American Agriculture Movement.

Modern farm organizations have considerable economic and political strength at the national, state, and county levels. By the late 1920s, farmers had become one of the best-organized economic groups in the United States. The extremely low farm prices that prevailed during the 1920s led to what was known as the "farm bloc" in the U.S. Congress, a coalition of senators and congressmen from farm states who were backed by and responsive to the farm organizations. Although the farm bloc was a loose coalition, it represented an absolute majority of both the House and the Senate.

CHARACTERISTICS OF THE SYSTEM OF DEVELOPMENTAL INSTITUTIONS

The system of developmental institutions that evolved in U.S. agriculture up through the 1940s had several key characteristics that contributed to the great increase in the productivity and adaptive capability of U.S. agriculture. First and perhaps *most* significantly, it was a *system* of institutions linked one to another in various ways. It is interesting how much this aspect is discussed and how little it is understood. Its significance, however, has not escaped the notice of astute observers.

> Perhaps agriculture's strongest claim to consideration as a scientific undertaking has come with the rise of cybernetics, or systems theory—the theory of how the diverse elements of systems interact through time to produce change. Even in oral traditions, agriculture has always been perceived as a system; hundreds of generations of farmers have understood the interaction of stock, soil, water supply, climate, supply and demand. Today these elements are understood better than ever; they can be quantified; they can even be controlled. More than ever, the science of agriculture stands at the center of a broader system integrating human society and its physical environment. The further study of this system demands the coordination of all the sciences from physics to sociology (Mayer and Mayer 1974).

ARTICULATED LINKAGE OF INSTITUTIONAL COMPONENTS

The performance of a successful institutional system comes to more than the sum of its parts. To say that a set of institutions is a system is to say that its individual components are interlinked or articulated, that the separate institutions are connected, that they communicate and cooperate in action to achieve some common goal. This does not mean that U.S. agricultural institutions have pursued or now pursue totally compatible or common goals. They are not mechanical but human social systems, after all. In the United States there has in fact been a continuing tension and contest between the USDA, the land-grant colleges, and farm organizations over their appropriate roles and activities. In research, the USDA and the state colleges, as well as the various experiment stations, have competed for federal funds ever since the states first began to expand their experiment stations. Farmer organizations periodically tell colleges of agriculture what they should be teaching and researching and on occasion even try to tell them what they should not be teaching and researching. In turn, the colleges attempt to instruct farmers and their organizations on the appropriate policies and roles for farmer action. Much of this tension is constructive. Indeed, it is through such continuing tension and the associated communication between institutions that the commonality of goals is repeatedly rediscovered, adapted to change, and revalidated.

A constructive tension holds the system in place and allows it to adapt to changes in the economic and political environment. But periodically the tension becomes excessive and destructive, threatening the very fabric of the system. So far the system has proved quite durable, although it is rarely without some serious problems, usually the result of prior policy or decision failures or a failure to recognize problems early enough.

The system of institutions exists by virtue of various types of articulated linkage that join differing functions and levels of the system. The U.S. college of agriculture is an institution that internally manages three very different functions: research, teaching, and extension. Here the linkage is internal to a single organization and is administered by one officer, the dean, although there are great variations across the states in degree of decentralization and delegation of authority. This direct linkage produces far more complementarity, coordination, and thus productivity than can be extracted from systems where each of these functions— teaching, research, and extension— is embedded in a separate institution that is a creature of national government and controlled by a different ministerial bureaucracy. Farmers tend to distrust and ignore information delivered by a bureaucracy that is also responsible for national agricultural policies. Extension has enough difficulty maintaining credibility with farmers when it restricts itself to an educational role.

The problems and conditions of production agriculture are location specific, embedded in local ecosystems. Research agendas that are set unilaterally in national capitals by organizations without interactive linkage to state and local levels rarely reflect regional or local research priorities and problems. To have a locally governed institution for teaching, extension, and research working from a common knowledge base appears to have a high payoff in agricultural productivity. These functions are usually well integrated in the U.S. system, since researchers and on-campus extension specialists do almost all the teaching and the extension specialist often does much of the applied research and is usually housed with researchers in the same academic department. Again, there has been quite a bit of variation historically, but the system is converging at present on a model in which all three functions are integrated and administered at the departmental level in colleges of agriculture.[3]

There are fifty states in the U.S. and about sixty land-grant colleges. Coordinating a group of this diversity has never been easy, but it has repeatedly achieved major goals. When the Hatch Act of 1887 established a national system of state experiment stations and when the Smith-Lever Act of 1914 established a national system of state extension services, two small offices, the Cooperative State Research Service and the Federal Extension Service, were created within the USDA to facilitate communication and to manage the transfer of congressional appropriations to the states. The National Association of State Universities and Land-Grant Colleges meets annually and is a forum for debate and policy formation between the various states and regions, as well as between the states and the USDA's research and extension managers. The USDA's top political leaders once participated effectively in this forum, but no longer do so.

The agricultural colleges and the USDA, thus are held together in a loosely coordinated structure. At the national level this system integrates and coordinates basic science for agriculture, applied research, technology development, extension, and the formal education of scientists and other agricultural professionals. Finally, and just as importantly, it must be recognized that this system is also coordinated and linked through markets and the political process at both the state and the national level. Indeed, these last two sources supply, validate, and sustain some of the most important values that drive this system of developmental institutions.

Historically, a strong, if uneven, political commitment has been made at the state level to education and research in agriculture. At the national level, a strong continuing commitment has been made to education (1862), research (1887), and extension (1914), and to the institution building involved in creating these means to achieve improved agricultural productivity and welfare. In addition, very important and highly complementary national public investments have been made in developing institutions and programs for farm credit, soil conservation, reclamation and water development, rural electrification, rural free delivery of mail, rural roads and highways, market regulation, and market stabilization. This investment in infrastructure facilitated the industrialization of agriculture, the growth of agricultural markets, and the increase in agricultural productivity. The returns to agricultural research would have been lower without these physical, human, and institutional investments—and vice versa.

In short, basic research, although necessary, is not sufficient to achieve high levels of agricultural productivity. The same is true of all other elements: applied research and technology development, extension of knowledge and technologies to the private sector including farmers, education for farmers and scientists, credit, electricity, and so forth. The most important issue is the systematic integration of decisions about institutional development and the combination, timing, and coordination of the various factors. Failure to link together in the same goal-driven system public and private decisions about investments in basic science, applied research, technology development, extension, and education will reduce the level of productivity that can be extracted from a given social investment in agriculture or in any other industrial sector.

DECENTRALIZATION OF DECISION MAKING

Another obvious characteristic of the U.S. agricultural support system is decentralization. Although it is a national system, authority is not concentrated solely at the national level. This is an important strength of the system, not because decentralization is inherently superior organizationally to centralization, but because decentralization is responsive to the nature of the problems the system addresses. First, to manage agricultural research or almost anything else over an area as large as the United States requires some decentralization of decision making for the sake of both efficiency and effectiveness. However, decentralization is particularly suitable for research that must deal with countless combinations of climatic conditions, soils, topography, flora, and fauna. The creation of basic scientific knowledge is only the first step toward greater national agricultural productivity. Basic scientific research creates potential that cannot be fully realized until it is successfully adapted to many specific ecosystems. This requires extensive adaptive research and technology development—that is, applied research. In addition, to get new technologies and knowledge adopted by farmers often requires further adaptive work in the sense of devising extension strategies to deal with historical differences in farming practice as well as ethnic and other cultural differences. The private sector faces the same problem in technology development and transfer.

While articulation of the system of developmental institutions is necessary, to keep many diverse functions coordinated, decentralization is necessary for the successful adaptation of science and technology to the highly varied local ecospheres that characterize agricultural production. There are, in addition, all sorts of political, cultural, and social variations that make it necessary to accommodate the institutional structure to local polities and resources to ensure a politically inclusive, legitimized, and coordinated system. To do otherwise in the United States would leave fifty subnational polities free to develop potentially conflicting, duplicate, and, in the aggregate, inefficient agricultural policies.

Many of the states, finding that a single experiment station was inadequate to deal with the multiple ecosystems within their borders, established multiple field stations or substations to work on different soil types, specific crops or animal products, and other problems peculiar to a local area. There were well over 350 such substations in the United States in 1981 (USDA 1981). Thus, the U.S. system is far more decentralized than the existence of fifty to sixty "state experiment stations" would imply.

CONSENSUAL DECISION MAKING

A less obvious characteristic of the U.S. system is that decisions that affect all or large parts of the system must be developed by consensus, if they are to be accepted as legitimate and implemented effectively. Unilateral power plays to achieve something that substantially affects the whole system generally create excessive conflict and end in failure. Attempts at unilateral or external command do not work in systems of separate institutions held together by a few common goals and the tensions of interdependence. Given the steady relative decline of federal support for agricultural research in the U.S., further attempts to command the system from the federal level are likely to cause the states to consider opting out of the system rather than cooperating.

BALANCED PURSUIT OF BASIC AND APPLIED RESEARCH

Another characteristic of U.S. agriculture institutions is the combination and management of societal problem solving and the pursuit of science for its own sake in a single system. The pragmatism and political expediency necessary to sustain effective societal problem solving involve organization, values and expectations that are inconsistent with the organization, values and expectations associated with the scientific pursuit of knowledge for its own sake. When managed in the same system, they exist in a perpetual tension. Nevertheless, the productivity achieved in agriculture has arisen from the sustained linkage of these functions and the management of the resulting tensions to maintain a workable balance.

The four characteristics discussed above—a well-articulated linkage of institutional components, a decentralization of decision making, consensual decision making, and a balanced pursuit of basic and applied science, technology development, and transfer—are not unique to the U.S. system; they are fundamental to the success of science-based developmental systems throughout the world.

But there are two serendipitous elements in the evolution of the U.S. system that should be noted. The first is that the legislation that established the nationwide system of land-grant colleges in 1862 came well before that which established the nationwide system of experiment stations in 1887. Had the timing been reversed, the research function might have been assigned to institutions independent of the colleges, as has been done in most countries. The same is true of extension. With the land-grant colleges in command of the state's agricultural science resources and "political turf," it was logical for the Congress to establish the extension service in 1914 as part of the existing agricultural system; but it might have been otherwise.[4]

Equally important is the fact that the Morrill Act did not establish colleges just to teach agriculture. It set forth the broad goal of improving the welfare of the working classes and ensuring their social equity and political freedom in the face of the growing concentration of economic and political power in an industrializing nation. This egalitarian vision, combined with the pragmatism of the strong vocational commitment to the welfare of the farm family, constrained and balanced the inherent intellectual narcissism that can turn a university into a gaggle of isolated disciplines and an engine of social elitism. The "land-grant idea" has been a great force for both democracy and national development in U.S. history. These values have given cohesion and purpose to the developmental institutions of U.S. agriculture.

The other major serendipitous element in the development of the U.S. system is the relatively small size of most of the states. This created a very decentralized system from the beginning, ensuring systematic research on many different ecosystems and an adaptive capability that the agricultural research programs of many industrialized nations do not have even today.

CONCLUSIONS

One of the clear lessons from successful agricultural development the world over is necessity of a centralized national investment in agricultural research complemented by and coordinated with a decentralized capacity in adapting agricultural research to the highly varied local ecospheres within which agriculture is practiced. Together this is what the land-grant colleges and the USDA originally accomplished. Their performance was magnificent. The focus of the USDA today, however, is on the immediate economic benefits created by special programs that are controlled or fought over by a growing swarm of special interest groups. As a consequence, the attention of USDA political leadership is no longer on research and education. The USDA neglects its own research functions, which today constitute a declining force within the agricultural science research community. Congress also appears neither to understand nor care much about agricultural research policy today. National research has faltered, and research budgets have all but ceased to grow in real terms since 1967. The federal commitment to agricultural research has faded and now appears to lie in the balance. Without an effective national agricultural research policy and without an influential national research focus, coordination of the agricultural research system has been deteriorating slowly for decades. This is primarily a failure of political institutions and political leadership, but the institutions of agricultural science also seem increasingly to lack a coherent vision of a politically viable future. However, one must now face the fact that agricultural research has become the most critical investment in achieving and maintaining national competitiveness in agriculture. This is the consequence of the growing dominance of highly competitive global markets and a reduction of agricultural protectionism in industrial nations.

Clearly, a developing nation that cannot sustain long-term institution building and human capital improvement will never have a highly productive, industrialized agriculture. Just as clearly, long-term institution building and human capital accumulation must involve more than the research and educational institutions. Physical capital and conventional input development are necessary for soil and water conservation, reclamation, and development; for long-term, intermediate, and short-term credit; for rural roads, mail service, and eventually electronic communications; and for the development of modern market institutions, common market standards, regulation, and, if necessary, market stabilization. These investments improve the capacity and productivity of agriculture and thereby the productivity of agricultural research as well.

Some institutional development will be public, some private. The mix will differ depending on a nation's history, institutions, and political philosophy. One lesson to be learned from past failures is to avoid extreme, exclusive ideological commitment either to free market capitalism or to socialism, with their demands that institution building take place entirely in the private sector or entirely in the public sector. The search for complementarities between public and private roles and a pragmatic focus on problem solving appear to form a more effective and more efficient approach. The U.S. experience also involved a partnership between public universities and state and national research institutions. If the universities do not do some of the basic research in agriculture, where does the next generation of well-trained scientists come from? Some applied research, the benefits of which spill over to the entire nation, must be done at the national level, if it is to get done at all. These are some of the lessons from the U.S. experience. Despite all its free enterprise values and rhetoric, the United States has imposed significant government regulation on and has socialized important activities of its agricultural sector. Despite a major investment in a national, centralized R&D institution (the USDA), the United States also developed a decentralized, location-specific R&D capacity to contend with the diverse ecosystems inherent in nature.

The evolution of the developmental system of institutions in U.S. agriculture was a pragmatic process of piecing together solutions to problems identified at state, local, and national levels. It used existing institutions and created new ones, public and private, to achieve results that reflected interests and needs at all levels of organization. It was a decision-making process in which all the major institutions shared the common nineteenth- and early twentieth-century goal of increasing human welfare through greater agricultural productivity. They made major national decisions by mobilizing a consensus, not by command. This takes a strong commitment by individuals and institutions to a reasonably common set of specific social values. It also requires strong and sustained leadership. One cannot, after setting off on an institution-building path, reverse directions or reorganize every few years to let some politician "put his stamp on things" or to test some new ideology or theory of public accountability. Unilateral changing of the rules in the middle of the game of long-term institutional development breeds suspicion and conflict instead of cooperation and leads to a breakdown in the linkage between separately governed institutions. If this occurs, some of the benefits of decentralization are eventually lost as cooperation across institutions and levels of government decays, and the system's ability to extract the full potential of increased productivity from any social investment declines.

There are large differences between the situation faced by the United States and those of other nations in developing a modern agricultural sector. The United States is a large continental land mass. It is exceptionally well endowed with natural resources and is blessed with a good climate for agriculture. Until about World War I, labor was short but land very plentiful. U.S. political institutions were democratic in a Western European, mostly Anglo-Saxon, tradition, while its economic institutions were free-market oriented and capitalistic.

Agricultural development across the world has many common requirements, even though the opportunity sets nations face can be quite different. A small nation with few ecosystems and climatic variations to deal with has much less need for decentralization of its agricultural institutions. If it is very small, it may face problems of a resource base too small to sustain all of the scientific specializations needed for a fully effective agricultural research effort. Thus, many small Third World countries need to develop an efficient capacity to borrow, screen, and adapt technologies from neighboring countries, regions, and the international research system.

Nations less well endowed than the U.S. face many more constraints. A poor country cannot invest in everything at once. So the question of the most effective sequencing of complementary investments becomes critical to successful development.

By the middle of the nineteenth century the United States was highly literate and by the twentieth century was a well-educated society, so collecting market information to allow agricultural markets to function more efficiently was possible very early in U.S. development. The U.S. legal system, building on British common law traditions, protected property rights in transactions, reducing many of the risks and costs of commerce.

The fundamental lesson is clear. It takes more than research to increase productivity. It takes more than basic research. It takes an articulated-systems approach that coordinates a broad research investment with the creation of biological and physical capital, new human capital, new technologies, and an adaptive response to their use. It takes sustained national policy and institution building focused on clear common goals over long periods of time.

NOTES

1. Some models do, however, provide limited insights into the impact of certain institutional characteristics of a research system, such as its degree of decentralization and/or articulation, on returns to investments in agricultural research. See, for example, Evenson, Waggoner, and Ruttan 1979.

2. The same reasoning applies to all major educational investments made in U.S. agriculture in both the public and the private sector.

3. In a few states—California, Maine, and the southern states—extension was originally organized separately from research at the academic department level. Extension followed a different evolutionary path in the South than in the rest of the United States.

4. Seaman Knapp, the "father" of modern extension, was adamantly opposed to putting county agents under the control of the deans of agriculture, whose objectives he saw as parochial and generally limited to their own states. Knapp wanted to make the extension system part of the U.S. Department of Agriculture, an organizational model similar to that followed in most countries today. He died before Congress passed the Smith-Lever Act of 1914, establishing a national extension system controlled at the state level by individual colleges of agriculture.

REFERENCES

Baker, Gladys L., Wayne Rasmussen, Vivian Wiser, and Jane M. Porter. 1963. *Century of Service: The First 100 Years of the U.S. Department of Agriculture*. Washington, D.C.: U.S. Department of Agriculture.

Bonnen, James T. 1962. "Some Observations on the Organizational Nature of a Great Technological Payoff." *Journal of Farm Economics* 44, no. 5: 1279–94.

———. 1980. "Observations on the Changing Nature of National Agricultural Policy Decision Processes, 1946–76." In *Farmers, Bureaucrats and Middlemen: Perspectives on American Agriculture*, edited by Trudy H. Peterson, 309–27. Washington, D.C.: Howard University Press.

Evenson, Robert E., Paul E. Waggoner, and Vernon W. Ruttan. 1979. "Economic Benefits from Research: An Example from Agriculture." *Science* 205, no. 14: 1101–7.

Heinz, John P. 1962. "The Political Impasse in Farm Support Legislation." *Yale Law Journal* 71:945–70.

Knutson, Marlys, and Luther G. Tweeten. 1979. "Toward an Optimum Rate of Growth in Agricultural Production Research and Extension." *American Journal of Agricultural Economics* 61, no. 1:70–76.

Lowi, Theodore J. 1965. "How Farmers Get What They Want." In *Legislative Politics U.S.A.*, edited by Theodore J. Lowi, 132–39. Boston: Little, Brown.

Mayer, Andre, and Jean Mayer. 1974. "Agriculture and the Island Empire." *Daedalus* 103, no. 3:83–95.

Office of Technology Assessment (OTA). 1981. "An Assessment of the United States Food and Agricultural Research System." Washington, D.C.: Office of Technology Assessment, pp. 201–6.

Olson, Mancur. 1971. *The Logic of Collective Action.* Cambridge: Harvard University Press.

Rasmussen, Wayne D. 1977. "Technology and American Agriculture: An Historical View." In *Technology Assessment: Proceedings of an ERS Workshop, April 20–22, 1976*, pp. 20–25. Washington, D.C.: USDA Economic Research Service, AGERS-31.

Ruttan, Vernon W. 1982. *Agricultural Research Policy.* Minneapolis: University of Minnesota Press.

Salisbury, Robert H. 1970. "An Exchange Theory of Interest Groups." In *Interest Group Politics in America*, edited by Robert H. Salisbury, 32–67. New York: Harper and Row.

Schultz, Theodore W. 1968. "Institutions and the Rising Economic Value of Man." *American Journal of Agricultural Economics* 50, no. 5: 1113–22.

———. 1975. "The Value of the Ability to Deal with Disequilibria." *Journal of Economic Literature* 13, no 3: 827–46.

Shaffer, James D. 1969. "On Institutional Obsolescence and Innovation—Background for Professional Dialogue on Policy." *American Journal of Agricultural Economics* 51, no. 2: 245–67.

True, Alfred Charles. 1929. *A History of Agricultural Education in the United States, 1785–1925.* USDA Miscellaneous Publication, no. 36. Washington, D.C.: U.S. Department of Agriculture.

U.S. Department of Agriculture (USDA). 1981. *1980–81 Directory of Professional Workers in State Agricultural Experiment Stations and Other Cooperating State Institutions.* Agricultural Handbook 305. Washington, D.C.: USDA.

17

Agricultural and Rural Development: Painful Lessons

HANS P. BINSWANGER

INTRODUCTION

Some countries have adopted successful agricultural and rural development strategies as if by accident, and have stayed with them. Other countries experienced dramatic failures and some painful learning experiences before they abandoned poor policies. Some continue to cling to misguided prescriptions of the past, supported by political equilibria that do not provide adequate voice to large segments of their rural populations. Severe external shocks and adverse policies of developed countries have often contributed to their poor performance. Poor agricultural and rural development performance has retarded economic growth and increased poverty, both rural and urban.

During the early days of "development economics"—in the 1950s—rural poverty was often explained by the backwardness of traditional smallholder agriculture. The sector was considered to have almost no potential for development. It is therefore not surprising that the solution to the reduction in rural poverty was almost universally seen as being associated with urban growth and rural-to-urban migration. It was assumed that rural population and employment would decline, if not in absolute terms, at least as a proportion of the labor force.

The promised elimination of rural poverty via migration to the cities has not materialized. Today many developing countries have two to three times as many poor rural people as in 1950. Much of the massive population transfer to the cities has been into the informal sector and into slum areas. Most of these coun-

HANS P. BINSWANGER is the senior policy adviser for agriculture and natural resources in the World Bank in Washington, D.C.

This paper is a revised and condensed version of the Simon Brandt Address delivered by the author on September 21, 1994, at the thirty-second annual meeting of the Agricultural Economics Association of South Africa, in Pretoria. It was previously published in *Agrekon* 33, no. 4 (1994): 165–74, and is published, with omissions and revisions, by permission of the Agricultural Economics Association of Southern Africa and the author. These remarks are not an official position of the World Bank but represent the author's own views.

tries are characterized by high rates of rural violence and urban crime, and many of these countries have undergone decades of land-related uprisings and land invasions. Finally, many smallholders who cannot gain access to land via purchase, rental, or land reform eventually turn to environmentally destructive cultivation of marginal land, petty trading activities, or to crime (Heath and Binswanger 1996).

This paper discusses rural poverty and the rural development programs designed to alleviate it. The failures of integrated rural development and its explanations are analyzed in historical perspective. The next section examines ways in which countries can foster rural development via administrative, fiscal, and political decentralization and the empowerment of their rural poor. The paper then summarizes the key policies for promoting agricultural growth, rural development, and poverty reduction.

THE POVERTY REDUCTION IMPACT OF AGRICULTURAL GROWTH

Agricultural growth can have a major impact on poverty reduction. This has been amply demonstrated. Agricultural growth reduces consumer prices of nontradable and semitradable foods (unless their markets are heavily protected or monopolized, of course). It can generate rapid growth of rural employment and self-employment in rural areas. The corresponding tightening of the labor market raises rural wages and has spillover effects on urban informal sector wages. These points were forcefully made by Johnston and Mellor (1961). The modest government support that smallholders require in research, extension, infrastructure and marketing can usually produce many jobs at a very low budget cost per job.

The mechanisms by which agricultural growth reduces urban poverty include the reduction of urban food prices and the positive impact of rural growth on the real wage of unskilled and semiskilled urban workers. Rural wages rise because rapid agricultural growth fuels the demand for labor, both in agricultural production and in the rural nonfarm sector. These rural wage rate increases are transmitted to the urban wage because rising rural wages reduce the labor supply to urban areas. These wage effects exceed those from manufacturing growth, especially in economies where the rural sector is still large, because of the higher labor intensity of agricultural relative to manufacturing growth (Ravallion and Datt 1994).

A few countries, such as Taiwan, Indonesia, Malaysia, and Thailand, have had spectacular successes in generating agricultural growth and reducing rural poverty. China joined this group in 1978 when it abandoned farm collectives. This group of countries either had or later reformed their large-scale ownership holdings into owner-operated family farms, with the exception of those growing plantation crops. Countries with plantation crops pursued smallholder strategies based on contract farming and steadily increased the share of these crops grown by smallholders. They either invested heavily in agricultural infrastructure or, in the case of China, inherited the investment from the period of collectivization. They also have invested heavily in agricultural technology for smallholders and have largely refrained from heavily subsidizing credit. They have either not taxed or only lightly taxed their agricultural sectors via indirect or direct discrimination. These countries have experienced rapid agricultural growth, modernization of technology, and sharp reductions in rural poverty. For example, China's agricultural growth has been in excess of 5 percent per annum for the last seventeen years, which must be one of the greatest agricultural growth episodes in world history. Yet the average farm size is half a hectare, fragmented into an average of nine plots.

However, most developing countries have been unable to develop and implement an agricultural development strategy that generated growth and attacked rural poverty. For example, many countries have heavily subsidized their modernizing commercial farm sectors and achieved rapid agricultural "modernization." But during this process they have prematurely evicted workers from their agricultural sectors, only to find them unemployed or underemployed in rural and urban slums. In most of Eastern Europe and Central Asia, a disastrous pursuit of large-scale and collective farming has led to an inefficient and fiscally unsustainable farm sector, which contributed to the downfall of the communist regimes. They are a long way from realizing the growth and employment potential of an efficient private farm sector based on family farms, competitive private marketing, and other agricultural services. In all the countries where discredited policy recommendations have not been abandoned, the attempt to achieve rapid agricultural growth has failed spectacularly, as in many African countries or Argentina, with catastrophic results for the rural poor (Eicher and Rukuni 1996).

Another group of countries inherited unequal land ownership distribution at the end of World War II and did very little to change the situation via land reform. They include Brazil, Colombia, Guatemala, and South Africa. These countries imposed relatively modest taxation on their agricultural sectors and concentrated the bulk or almost all of their public sector support on their large-scale farming sectors. This support took the form of subsidized farm credit, infrastructure investment without cost recovery, and assistance in marketing via parastatals or statutory monopoly rights (Deininger and Binswanger 1995). Most Central American countries pursued similar policies until the early 1980s, when the policies led to civil war. These countries successfully abolished "feudal" land-labor relations in their large-scale farming sectors and modernized them into large-scale commercial farms, although at a heavy fiscal cost (de Janvry 1981). Without question, these countries have fostered a dynamic, technologically sophisticated, and politically articulate class of commercial farm owners. But at the same time, most of their smallholders have sunk deeper into poverty, except where special rural development efforts were made. Since rural labor has been largely excluded from participation in the modernization process, the landless and near landless have migrated and become slum dwellers in rural towns and the cities. The fiscal burden of supporting the technologically sophisticated but economically inefficient large-scale farming sectors has proved to be unsustainable in all of these countries. Credit and other subsidies have been substantially reduced, tax privileges are threatened, and protection at the border or via monopolies is being eliminated. Farm land prices have declined. This process has recently been studied in detail in South Africa (van Zyl, Kirsten, and Binswanger 1996).

To summarize, agricultural growth can have a major impact on poverty reduction; but only a few countries, such as Taiwan, Indonesia, Malaysia, Thailand and China, have been able to develop and implement an agricultural strategy that achieves both agricultural growth and poverty reduction.

RURAL DEVELOPMENT AND POVERTY REDUCTION: WHAT HAVE WE LEARNED?

PERSISTENT RURAL POVERTY

Poverty continues to be concentrated in rural areas in Asia, Africa, and Latin America. Poverty data across country and over time are often not comparable. The World Bank has recently completed poverty assessments for fifty-nine countries. In forty-seven of the fifty-nine countries, rural areas have a higher proportion of poor people than urban areas. The absolute number of rural poor also exceeds the absolute number of urban poor in forty-seven of the fifty-nine countries. Of the 700 million poor people in these fifty-nine countries, 72 percent reside in rural areas. A recent study of Kenya reveals that 80 percent of the population and 90 percent of the poor live in rural areas (World Bank 1995). Nutrition and anthropometric data consistently show that the rural populations are less well fed than the urban ones, so the findings of the head counts are not simply statistical artifacts. It is indeed ironic that the poorly nourished are concentrated in rural areas where food is produced (Ravallion and Bidani 1994). To summarize, the overwhelming concentration of poverty in rural areas comes across despite reservations about data quality. A substantial decline in rural poverty has occurred only in countries which have consistently pursued a smallholder-friendly agricultural development strategy. In all other countries today there are many more rural poor than there were forty-five years ago. In many countries the number of rural poor has doubled or tripled.

THE BANKRUPTCY OF THE URBAN STRATEGY

The time is long overdue for declaring bankrupt the notion that urban development can solve rural poverty. In most of the developing world, the rural areas today contain many more poor people than they did in 1950, when the urban strategy first became fashionable, in many countries two to three times as many. In many countries where rural poor populations have shifted to urban slums, urban poverty is seen today as a more severe problem than rural poverty, ignoring the fact that it is the premature shedding of labor from the commercial farm sector that has been a root cause of the urban poverty problem.

Some advocates of a development strategy suggest that it is highly unlikely that the urban poor will find rural livelihoods attractive. This ignores several factors. First, many of the urban poor have grown up in rural areas and maintain links to them, which they activate in times of hardship in urban areas. Second, in many countries, urban people who become unemployed during periods of recession return temporarily or permanently to rural areas, especially if they have land rights or can work on the farms of relatives or acquaintances. Third, rural populations continue to grow, despite migration, in all but the most advanced developing countries, providing a new supply of farm workers and operators. Finally, just because a country has proceeded so long on an erroneous path does not imply that a drastic course correction would not be beneficial.

THE EVOLUTION OF WORLD BANK POLICY

Ever since the World Bank made rural poverty reduction a priority, in the early 1970s, it has advocated a smallholder development strategy as the primary way to attack rural poverty. By and large the Bank has followed its own prescription in lending via integrated rural development programs and in subsector programs for irrigation, research, and extension.

However, the smallholder strategy did not generate unqualified support, even among Bank staff. It was not applied in Bank support for agricultural credit, which primarily subsidized credit for medium- to large-scale farmers (World Bank 1993; Binswanger and Khandker 1995). While these credit projects tried to limit subsidies and direct more credit to smallholders, good intentions were rarely realized in practice. This led to a sharp reduction of agricultural credit projects by the Bank and partly explains the decline in agricultural lending by the Bank.

Since the early to mid-1970s, Bank policy has also been supportive of land reform. Several attempts were made to translate this commitment into lending programs—for example, in the Philippines, Zimbabwe, and Brazil—but the political climate did not permit this. The Bank's commitment to land reform has been reaffirmed in the *World Development Report 1995*. The demise of the Cold War, the fiscal unsustainability of large-scale commercial farm sectors, and new approaches to land reform may reopen opportunities in this area.

THE FAILURE OF INTEGRATED RURAL DEVELOPMENT PROJECTS

The opposition to land reform in many countries in the 1960s and 1970s has made integrated rural development directed at smallholders a second-best smallholder strategy (de Janvry 1981). The Bank has financed many rural development programs and projects, including an integrated package of support to smallholder agricultural development for a specific area or region. Some of these projects were called area development projects. The projects typically consisted of synergistic interventions in agricultural extension, research (if technology was not available), marketing, input supply, credit, rural roads, water supply and electricity infrastructure, and small-scale irrigation. Sometimes the projects included social infrastructure such as primary schools and health centers. These project interventions were planned by technicians from the countries, with assistance of Bank teams. Methods for beneficiary consultations were developed and applied. Execution of the components was generally delegated to government organizations, often highly centralized ministries or parastatals. Since coordination proved difficult, project management units were established. These units were staffed by Bank-selected professionals and maintained authority over the disbursement of funds and supervision of procurement and implementation efforts in the project area.

Many integrated rural development (IRD) projects in the seventies and eighties were unsuccessful, because they encountered the following problems (World Bank 1987):

Adverse policy environment. It quickly became apparent that many IRD projects, when pursued in an adverse policy environment for agriculture as a whole or for smallholders, amounted to pushing on a string, and could not succeed. Reform of the policy environment was seen as a prior condition for success. The greater success rate of integrated rural development projects in Asia compared to Latin America and Africa is attributed to a more favorable policy environment in Asia.

Lack of government commitment. Many governments did not provide the counterpart funding required for implementation of the programs, despite assurances agreed upon during negotiations.

Lack of appropriate technology. This proved to be an important problem in rainfed areas, especially in Africa, where there was little history of past commitment to agricultural research, or where colonial research efforts had decayed. Some integrated rural development projects included research components, but most failed to develop improved technologies. Also, many of these research components undermined the national agricultural research systems by depriving them of talented researchers.

Neglect of institutional development. Many IRD projects set up project coordination units, sometimes staffed by expatriates. However, this approach postponed the development of a local and district-level institutional capacity to plan, execute, and monitor rural development programs.

Lack of beneficiary participation. The programs were often designed in a top down approach within which beneficiaries were not given authority for decision making or program execution. Even if they were consulted in advance, they could not be sure that their preferences were being given adequate weight. Most often, therefore, they chose the only decision making option they had, voting with their feet and not participating in the project.

The complexity or coordination problem. It is ironic that complexity should have become the Achilles heel of rural development. After all, building rural roads, small-scale infrastructure, and providing agricultural extension are dramatically simpler tasks than the construction of large-scale irrigation infrastructure or ports, where the Bank did not encounter a coordination problem. The coordination problem emerged as a consequence of delegating subprogram execution to government bureaucracies or parastatals, which were typically highly centralized and had their own objectives. Many of them were out of touch with beneficiaries, who could much more easily have coordinated the relatively simple tasks at the local level, where the issues are often quite simple and information is readily available. Indeed, one might classify integrated rural development as the last bastion of central planning, swept away by reality like all other central planning schemes.

The frequent poor performance of integrated rural development projects has left in disarray experts within and outside the Bank who are interested in rural poverty reduction. The Bank has retreated from the ambitious IRD agenda of the 1970s into the support of subsector-specific programs or projects, each dealing with a specific component of rural development, such as agricultural extension, small-scale irrigation, rural roads, primary education, and health care. This means that support for rural poverty reduction has become highly selective, even spotty, within the Bank's program. Nowhere has it been possible to support the full array of interventions that are required for successful rural poverty reduction.

The worst consequence of the failure, however, has been the Bank's inability to advise countries on policies and programs that would enable them to successfully implement rural development programs and reduce rural poverty. Policy advice rightfully concentrates on eliminating direct and indirect distortions, supporting infrastructure and social investment in rural areas and for the poor, implementing land reform, reducing interventions via parastatals, strengthening agricultural research and extension, etc. How to implement the investment and support strategies that are recommended in the rural areas of entire countries is left unanswered. By withdrawing from rural development the Bank has left the complexity and other problems of implementation in the hands of the country governments. The rural development programs have not disappeared just because the Bank has withdrawn from them.

ALTERNATIVES TO INTEGRATED RURAL DEVELOPMENT

ADMINISTRATIVE AND FISCAL DECENTRALIZATION

Many countries have tried to find alternatives to integrated rural development. Most of these initiatives deal with decentralization, administrative and/or fiscal aspects, and greater involvement of beneficiaries (discussed below; see Parker 1995 for a full discussion of decentralization issues). The first approach has been privatization of infrastructure and service delivery to the private sector, especially of marketing functions. This relieves the government of a fiscal burden and often improves the delivery of services once the private sector has taken over the functions. The private sector can provide most production and infrastructure services to large-scale entrepreneurial sectors, often at a lower cost than government could. However, partial or full government finance is required for poverty-reducing rural development efforts based on a small farmer strategy.

Another approach is channeling resources for specific small-scale productive or social projects to beneficiary groups, either directly or through nongovernmental organizations (NGOs). This approach has flourished in countries where bureaucratic or political institutions have been severely discredited, for example, in Zambia and South Africa. Governments, bilateral donors, and multilateral lenders have increasingly resorted to this method. Social funds delegate planning and execution to beneficiary groups or their NGO agents, but they leave ultimate approval and disbursement authority with central project units, the social fund administrators.

A more radical evolution of rural development programs has taken place in Mexico and Colombia and recently, on a pilot basis, in Brazil, where the programs have evolved into matching-grant mechanisms that can serve rural municipalities or districts or poor beneficiary groups without necessarily losing their multisectoral approach. Matching grants will be further discussed below. Within these programs, genuine decision making power over project funds is delegated to municipalities or beneficiary groups, through such mechanisms as municipal funds. Within certain budget limits the municipalities are empowered to choose from a menu of poverty-reducing community projects. Project selection takes place according to rules that increase transparency of decision making to the ultimate beneficiaries and assist in proper targeting to the poorer groups.

Many countries have recently gone much further with administrative and fiscal decentralization of rural development. Administrative decentralization can take place via deconcentration of administrative powers in government bureaucracies and/or by delegation or devolution of rural development functions to lower-levels of government or to communities. Fiscal decentralization involves the assignment of revenue sources to lower-levels of government and/or the transfer of resources to such governments.

An extremely successful fiscal and administrative decentralization effort occurred in China in the late 1970s, along with the elimination of collective farms and the reduction of farm taxation. In China all revenues are collected by local entities and shared with higher-level governments. The extraordinary rural development performance that followed has already been commented on. However, the central government has found itself in great fiscal difficulties and is currently reforming the tax and revenue-sharing system to resolve the fiscal imbalances that have emerged.

However, decentralization has also had its failures (Crook and Manor 1994; Meenakshisundaram 1994). In Ghana and the Ivory Coast, elected local governments were created, but the resulting enthusiasm dissipated rapidly, because the new local governments were starved for resources. In Brazil, the 1988 constitution raised the percentage of the government's fiscal resources available to states and municipalities, through changes in tax assignment and revenue sharing from about 57 to 83 percent of total fiscal revenues. It did so without assigning many additional responsibilities to these levels, and this assignment of revenue without responsibility only deepened the fiscal crisis of the central government. The constitutional changes also did not reform the matching or conditional grant systems of the central ministries, missing a major opportunity to influence spending of lower-level jurisdictions in socially productive ways (Bomfim and Shah 1991).

The following lessons emerge from these experiences with decentralization:

- Decentralization is not a simple panacea or a recipe. It matters how it is put together. The many different elements—fiscal, administrative, and political—must be consistent with each other to avoid fiscal imbalances, failure, or backlash.
- Decentralization is politically difficult, since most bureaucrats and central politicians tend to oppose the implied loss of power.
- Decentralization appears to work better if it has preceded or accompanies delegation of responsibility, by placing professional staff into local offices.
- Decentralization cannot work if elected governments are not given adequate fiscal powers or transfers from higher-level governments.

These lessons do not imply that centralization works better. There is plenty of evidence that it does not, viz. the failed integrated rural development strategy. However, they do imply that decentralization must be done deliberately, consistently, and carefully.

EMPOWERING THE POOR

Another lesson emerging from these experiences is that consulting the poor is not enough to empower them for their own development, even if it is done with the most genuine intentions. Nor is administrative and fiscal decentralization sufficient. In Karnataka, India, for example, the decentralization effort improved the match of development expenditures with local preferences, accelerated implementation without increasing costs, and made local government employees such as teachers more assiduous in their attendance. It also reduced the amount, if not the frequency, of corruption, by shifting it from the state level to lower levels. However, it neither improved nor reduced the effectiveness with which development programs were targeted to the poor (Crook and Manor 1994).

Additional steps will be required:

1. The first is the earmarking of conditional or matching-grant resources for poverty-alleviating projects or programs and the delegation of their execution to poor communities, where technically feasible.

2. The second is to strengthen the political representation of poor and disadvantaged groups in local political bodies, as has been done by reserving seats for women and scheduled and backward casts in the constitutional reform of the Panchayat Raj system in India (Meenakshisundaram 1994).

3. Where such constitutional change is not feasible, as in Mexico and Brazil, the rules of earmarked matching-fund systems can be designed to ensure greater representation. In Mexico all decisions of fund allocations must be taken in open assemblies at the municipal level, and a proportion of the funds is allocated to outlying settlements, which usually are poorer than the municipal headquarters (Fox 1996). In Brazil a special municipal council has been created for the allocation and administration of the funds; this ensures adequate statutory representation of poor rural communities in these nonelected bodies.

4. Accountability to the poor can also be improved by adding rules that encourage openness and transparency, such as representation of small farmers, women, and rural workers on boards of research stations, supervisory committees of extension systems, or on land or labor committees that deal with rural land and labor issues.

MARKET-ASSISTED LAND REFORM

Even when countries attempted land reform, they often entrusted it to a centralized land ministry or to a parastatal, a land reform institute. The government acquired land via expropriation, with or without compensation, depending on the historical development of legal provisions. Much of the land was legally acquired after it had already been invaded by the program, and the arrangement amounted to regularization of a *fait accompli*. These arrangements were costly and slow.

Where land was acquired or regularized by purchase, a bilateral bargaining game ensued between each of the sellers and the government, in which each could threaten to use provisions of the law to improve its bargaining position. Economic theory does not suggest any reason to expect such a process to lead to low acquisition prices if the sellers are wealthy and the government is under political pressure from the peasants. Where land was expropriated with no or minimal compensation, each case led to protracted legal battles, frittering away the energies of the peasants and the land reform agency alike into thousands of legal battles.

Disillusion with the slow pace of reform projects often led to loss of political momentum and erosion of the budget for land acquisition. Using these processes it took Mexico sixty some years after the end of the revolution of 1910 to complete the task of redistribution. And Mexico has been the most successful of all Latin American countries in transferring land in a peaceful manner.

Market-assisted land reform avoids the bilateral bargaining game and leads to competition on both sides, the buyer groups and the sellers. It avoids years of delays associated with disputes about compensation levels. It privatizes and thereby decentralizes the essential processes. The process should not be left unsupervised. District land committees, reporting to regional and national committees, are a promising device. Parties will ultimately have to be provided with recourse to the courts. This can be ensured by a decentralized land or agrarian court system, to which parties can appeal disputes that cannot be resolved through arbitration or by the land committees.

The conditions for market-assisted land reform to work are well known (e.g., van Zyl, Kirsten, and Binswanger 1996): partial grants to enable beneficiaries to buy land without starting out with impossible debt-equity ratios, (2) a decentralized structure capable of assisting with the provision of infrastructure and social and agricultural services,and (3) policies and programs that do not reward large-scale farming via privileges.

EMPLOYMENT GENERATION

Rural employment can be generated by insisting that rural infrastructure be constructed with labor-intensive techniques. Many countries have gradually improved their ability to ensure this via their contracting procedures and other means. Employment generation programs are also a useful tool, especially during periods of macroeconomic recession, sharp agricultural price declines, or drought. Zambia and other countries have shown how such programs can be implemented in a decentralized way, with much involvement of NGOs and community groups.

Employment generation may also be needed where there are few agricultural or nonagricultural development opportunities and where, nevertheless, an immobile labor force is unemployed and poor. They may be immobile because of legal or economic limitations on migration; in the case of poor women, it is because they also have child-rearing responsibilities.

SUMMARY

The potential of agriculture and rural development to increase economic growth and reduce poverty has been fully realized in only a small number of countries. Why most countries have failed in this regard is a topic of a growing political economy literature, recently reviewed by Binswanger and Deininger (1997). The debate about the causes is likely to continue.

There has long been a consensus in the agricultural economics and development economics profession on what elements of an agricultural and rural development strategy and the associated policies would generate agricultural growth and reduce rural poverty. These professionals have examined the development theories, measured the impacts of various development policies, and painstakingly sifted through the experiences of many countries in an effort to fathom what makes the difference between success and failure.

There is broad professional consensus supporting the following key policy elements of a strategy to achieve agricultural and rural development and reduce rural poverty (Binswanger and Landell-Mills 1995):

- The foreign exchange, trade, and taxation regime should not discriminate against agriculture but should tax it lightly, preferably using the same progressivity and instruments as it applies to the urban economy.
- An strategy that promotes an open economy, employment intensiveness, and a small farmer orientation is both economically efficient and most likely to reduce poverty, both rural and urban.
- Providing privileges or reducing competition in output, input, and credit markets is costly to consumers and taxpayers and ends up hurting small farmers and the rural poor, even if such an effect is unintended.
- In countries where land is unequally distributed, a rural development strategy requires a substantial prior or concurrent effort at land reform. Constraining land rental and insisting on expropriation without compensation has a perverse impact on the rural poor. Centralized ministries or parastatal bureaucracies are not good at implementing land reforms.
- Rapid technological progress is essential for agricultural growth. Achieving it requires both private sector involvement and government financing of agricultural research (strategic research, smallholder crops, sustainable systems and techniques, etc.) and smallholder extension where private firms have little incentive to enter.
- Rural areas require substantial investments in economic and social infrastructure, and in health, education, and nutrition. Concentrating these investments in urban areas is not less costly and misses an important opportunity.
- Successful and cost-effective implementation of agricultural and rural development programs requires the mobilization of the skills, talents, and labor of the rural population, through decentralized administrative, fiscal, and political systems conducive to their genuine participation and through private sector involvement.
- The needs of women farmers and workers must be incorporated in strategy and program design.
- A special effort is required in the design of decentralized mechanisms so that the poor can effectively participate in project decision making, execution and supervision, and accountability. Otherwise, rural elites will appropriate most of the benefits of the rural development programs.

These lessons have been acquired with much pain for people of the developing world. These lessons can be ignored only at a high social cost—for economic growth, for the fiscal balance, for the environment, for the rural and urban poor, and for social peace.

REFERENCES

Binswanger, Hans P., and Klaus Deininger. 1997. "Explaining Agricultural and Agrarian Policies in Developing Countries." *Journal of Economic Literature* 35 (4): 1958–2005.

Binswanger, Hans P., and Shahidur Khandker. 1995. "The Impact of Formal Finance on the Rural Economy of India." *Journal of Development Studies* 32 (2): 234–62.

Binswanger, Hans P., and Pierre Landell-Mills. 1995. "The World Bank's Strategy for Reducing Poverty and Hunger: A Report to the Development Community." Environmentally Sustainable Development Studies and Monographs Series no. 4, World Bank, Washington, D.C.

Bomfim, Antulio, and Anwar Shah. 1991. *Macroeconomic Management and the Division of Powers in Brazil: Perspectives for the Nineties.* Washington, D.C.: Country Economics Department, World Bank.

Crook, Richard, and James Manor. 1994. "Enhancing Participation and Institutional Performance: Democratic Decentralization in South Asia and West Africa." London: Overseas Development Administration.

de Janvry, Alain. 1981. *The Agrarian Question and Reformism in Latin America.* Baltimore: Johns Hopkins University Press.

Deininger, Klaus, and Hans P. Binswanger, 1995. "Rent Seeking and the Development of Large-Scale Agriculture in Kenya, South Africa, and Zimbabwe." *Economic Development and Cultural Change* 43 (3): 493–522.

Eicher, Carl K., and Mandivamba Rukuni. 1996. "Reflections on Agrarian Reform and Capacity Building in South Africa." Staff Paper no. 96-3, Department of Agricultural Economics, Michigan State University, East Lansing.

Fox, Jonathan, and Josefina Aranda. 1996. *Decentralization and Rural Development in Mexico: Community Participation in Oaxaca's Municipal Funds Program.* Monograph Series no. 42, Center for U.S.–Mexico Studies, University of California, San Diego.

Heath, John, and Hans P. Binswanger. 1996. "Natural Resource Degradation Effects of Poverty and Population Growth Are Largely Policy-Induced: The Case of Colombia." *Environment and Development Economics.* Vol. 1, part 1 (February).

Johnston, Bruce F., and John Mellor. 1961. "The Role of Agriculture in Economic Development." *American Economic Review* 51 (4): 566–93.

Meenakshisundaram, S. S. 1994. *Decentralisation in Developing Countries.* New Delhi: Concept Publishing.

Parker, Andrew. 1995. "Decentralization: The Way Forward for Rural Development?" Policy Research Working Paper no. 1475, World Bank, Washington, D.C.

Ravallion, Martin, and Benu Bidani. 1994. "How Robust Is a Poverty Profile?" *World Bank Economic Review* 8 (1): 75–102.

Ravallion, Martin, and Gaurav Datt. 1994. "How Important to India's Poor Is the Urban-Rural Composition of Growth?" Policy Research Department, World Bank, Washington, D.C.

van Zyl, Johan, Johann Kirsten, and Hans P. Binswanger, eds. 1996. *Agricultural Land Reform in South Africa: Policies, Markets, and Mechanisms.* Capetown: Oxford University Press.

World Bank. 1987. *World Bank Experience with Rural Development: 1965–1987.* (Operations Evaluation Study 6883.) Washington, D.C.: World Bank.

———. 1993. *Poverty Reduction Handbook.* Washington, D.C.: World Bank.

———. 1995. *Kenya: Poverty Assessment.* (Report 13152-KE.) Washington, D.C.: World Bank.

———. 1995. *World Development Report 1995.* Washington, D.C.: World Bank.

18

The Peasant in Economic Modernization

YUJIRO HAYAMI

Peasants—self-employed tillers of soil, whose farm production is based mainly on family labor as an integral part of household activities—have been for thousands of years and still are today the majority of mankind. Their production mode represents a sharp contrast with the large internal organization of modern corporate firms characterized by a hierarchy of employees.

The style of peasant farming, apparently archaic relative to modern corporate activities, has often led to a presumption that the peasantry is a remnant of feudal society and bound to disappear as modernization proceeds. As a corollary, it has been argued that consolidation of peasants into large farm enterprises is desirable or necessary for promoting agricultural productivity growth consistent with modern economic development.

This perspective has been waning recently, partly because of the disastrous experience of collective farming in former socialist economies, as well as repeated failures in the attempt to develop large farms as both state and private enterprises in developing economies (Eicher and Baker 1992; Johnson and Ruttan 1994). Concurrently, the high potential of peasants to achieve productivity growth has been recognized with the successful diffusion of modern high-yielding varieties and related inputs—the so-called Green Revolution in Asia. Yet, pessimism about peasant agriculture persists and tends to distort the development strategy toward favoring large farm estates (Binswanger and Rosenzweig 1986; Deininger and Feder 1995; Eicher and Rukuni 1996).

More ambiguous is the role of peasants in industrial and commercial development. The traditional view from Karl Marx to W. Arthur Lewis has assumed peasants to be the source of an industrial reserve army for assuring the horizontal supply of labor to the emerging modern industrial sector. The possibility of peasants' displaying entrepreneurship in industrial and commercial activities has been to-

YUJIRO HAYAMI is professor of international economics at the Aoyama-Gakuin University, Tokyo. Previously published in the *American Journal of Agricultural Economics* 78, no. 5 (1996): 1157–67. Copyright © 1996 American Agricultural Economics Association.

tally neglected. However, rural industrialization in the early modernization phase in Japan as well as recent developments in the village-township enterprises in postreform China strongly suggest the possibility of rural-based economic development with proper exploitation of peasants' entrepreneurial abilities.

In this paper the major controversy concerning the nature and fate of the peasantry in the course of modern economic development is reviewed. Second, strengths and weaknesses of the peasant system are reviewed in comparison with the plantation system. Third, the impact of commercialization on peasants is investigated, with a focus on the relationship between peasants and middlemen. Finally, the possibility of rural-based economic development by mobilizing peasants' entrepreneurship in commerce and industry is examined and policies to enhance this process are explored.

THE AGRARIAN QUESTION

Since the outset of "modern economic growth" á la Kuznets, the nature and fate of peasantry have been the subjects of a major controversy. Pessimism about peasant agriculture as being incompatible with modern development needs first found expression in the work of Arthur Young and other exponents of "new husbandry" in England from the time of the Agricultural Revolution in the eighteenth century to the era of "high farming" in the nineteenth century (Ernle 1961).

In their view, small peasant farmers were constrained by village-community regulations on crop rotation and, therefore, were unable to shift from the open three-field system to the Norfolk crop-rotation system. With the enclosure of peasants' plots into large, private farms leased to innovative tenant operators, the advantage of the new crop rotation could be properly exploited. By this arrangement, fallowed lands were planted with fodder crops, such as clover and turnips, which increased the livestock-carrying and, hence, the stable-manure-supplying capacity, which in turn augmented soil fertility and crop yields.

This popular view on the productivity-increasing effect of the Second Enclosure Movement in eighteenth-century England, together with the serious labor-displacement experienced in the First Enclosure Movement of the fifteenth to sixteenth centuries, by which peasants' holdings were consolidated into sheep farms for commercial wool production, provided the basis for Karl Marx's theory on the demise of peasantry. Marx predicted that peasants would be displaced by large capitalistic farm firms using labor-saving machinery and, therefore, would be forced to seek employment in the labor market. This was nothing but an extension of the general process of capitalist development in which the majority of self-employed, small producers owning small productive assets ("means of production") are proletarianized.

The subsequent German censuses of 1882 and 1895 were a shock for Marxists, because there was no indication in the census data that small farms had been displaced by large ones. This anomaly, which was called the "Agrarian Question," ignited a major controversy. Some tried to defend the Marxian orthodoxy. Karl Kautsky (1899), among others, reasserted the superiority of large farms in Germany and other European economies, and argued that the eventual demise of peasantry was delayed because of peasants' desperate efforts to continue farming by working harder and reducing consumption against competition from capitalist farms.[1] In another effort, Vladimir Lenin (1899) tried to show that polarization of peasantry into large commercial farmers employing landless laborers was, in fact, in progress in Russia.

In the other camp, so-called revisionists, such as Eduardo Bernstein (1899) and Eduardo David (1903), argued that the Marxian theory of proletarianization does not apply to agriculture because of the inherent difficulty of labor enforcement in agricultural production. In urban industries, work is standardized and easy to monitor. The biological process of agricultural production, however, is subject to infinite ecological variations. Different ways of handling crops or animals are often necessary because of slight differences in temperature and soil moisture. The dispersal of agricultural operations over wide spaces adds to the difficulty of monitoring. Therefore, small family farms will continue to be more productive than large farms dependent on hired labor, despite development of the capitalist system in other sectors of the economy.[2]

The Agrarian Question continued to fuel a major debate from the late nineteenth to the early twentieth century on the choice of socialist political programs (Mitrany 1951). Looking back from a century later there is little doubt about which side withstood the historical test. In all the advanced market economies in western Europe, North America, and Japan, family farms have continued to be the dominant form of agricultural production organization. Their size of operation has increased in terms of farming area and capital input applied. However, corporate farms based on hired labor organized according to a management hierarchy have, until recently, been the exception.

Several production function studies have found significant scale economies in agriculture in advanced economies (Griliches 1964; Hayami and Ruttan 1985; Hayami and Kawagoe 1989). However, the continued dominance of family farms implies that the range of increasing returns has been limited within the size that could be managed mainly by family labor. The increase in farm size has been motivated by a drive to equate the average income of family members engaged in farm production with that of nonfarm employees (Kislev and Peterson 1981). Expansion has been supported by technological innovation geared toward increasing the optimum farm size. The nuclear family farm has continued to be optimum because scale economies arising from the use of indivisible inputs such as large-scale machinery are countervailed by scale diseconomies from the use of hired labor, according to the logic of the revisionists.

In fact, the history of the Agricultural Revolution in England, on the basis of which the Marxian orthodoxy was formulated, has now been drastically redrawn. The iconoclastic study by Robert Allen (1992) convincingly shows that the enclosure in the eighteenth century resulted in no significant gain in agricultural productivity and that the major increase in land productivity had been brought about by yeomen (small independent farmers constituting an upper stratum of the British peasantry) during the seventeenth century, before their lands were enclosed. Agricultural stagnation in former socialist economies under farm collectivization promoted by the Marxist doctrine might have been a bad replica of the true enclosure history.[3]

PEASANTS AND PLANTATIONS

While the Agrarian Question has already been resolved for advanced market economies, it still resounds in developing economies. The issue has often been discussed around the relative efficiency of peasants versus plantations.[4]

The term "plantation" refers here to large farms based on hired wage labor, which were initially established in developed economies by Western colonizers for the purpose of extracting tropical agricultural products for export to home countries.[5] A traditional paradigm, developed under colonialism, had been to identify the plantation sector as a modern enclave geared for the international market, and the peasant sector as dominated by subsistence orientation and irresponsive to profit incentives created by changes in market demands and technological opportunities (Boeke 1953). This stereotyped view has been debunked simultaneously by three great development economists, Theodore W. Schultz (1964), Hla Myint (1965), and W. Arthur Lewis (1969, 1970).

Schultz convincingly argued that peasants in traditional agriculture are rational and efficient in resource allocation and that they remain poor not because they are irresponsive to economic incentives but because only limited technical and market opportunities are available to which they can respond. Myint, drawing mainly on the experience of Southeast Asia, demonstrated how peasants responded vigorously to market incentives in opening new lands for cultivation of export cash crops while maintaining subsistence food crop production. This observation for the Southeast Asian case was found by Lewis to be no exception in tropical development from the late nineteenth to the early twentieth century.

A conventional explanation for the establishment of a plantation system is the scale economies inherent in the production of tropical export crops (Baldwin 1956). However, there are only a few crops capable of generating sufficiently strong scale economies to justify plantation production (Pim 1946; Wickizer 1951, 1960; Lim 1968; Hayami, Quisumbing, and Adriano 1990, chaps. 5 and 6). In fact, one can find an example of every so-called plantation crop being grown successfully by peasants somewhere in the world.

Significant increasing returns emerge only at the levels of processing and marketing activities. The vertical integration of a large farm unit with a large-scale central processing and/or marketing system is called for because of the need to supply farm-produced raw materials in a timely schedule. A typical example is fermented "black tea." The manufacturing of black tea at a standardized quality for export requires a modern machine plant into which fresh leaves must be fed within a few hours after plucking (Wickizer 1951, 1960). The need for close co-ordination between farm production and processing underlies the pervasive use of the plantation system for black tea manufacture. Unfermented "green tea," in contrast, remains predominantly the product of peasants in China and Japan.

In the case of bananas grown for export, harvested fruits must be packed, sent to the wharf, and loaded to a refrigerated boat within a day. A boatful of bananas that can meet the quality standards of foreign buyers must be collected within a few days (Hayami, Quisumbing, and Adriano 1990). Therefore, the whole pro-duction process from planting to harvesting must be precisely controlled so as to meet the shipment schedule. Although the plantation system has a decisive ad-vantage for this export production, bananas for domestic consumption are usu-ally produced by peasants.

On the other hand, for the crops for which centralized processing and mar-keting are not necessary, plantations have no significant advantage over peasants. Typical examples are cocoa and coconuts. The fermentation of cocoa and the drying and smoking of coconuts to make copra can be handled in small lots with no large capital requirement beyond small indigenous tools and facilities. These crops are grown predominantly by peasants.

Sugar is frequently cited as a classic case of scale economies stemming from the need of coordination between farm production and large-scale central pro-cessing (Binswanger and Rosenzweig 1986). Efficient operation of a centrifugal sugar mill requires the steady supply of a large amount of cane over time. Co-ordination of production, from planting to harvesting, with processing is re-quired. This coordination, however, need not be as stringent as for tea and ba-nanas. The rate of sugar extraction decreases as the processing of cane is delayed, but this loss is in no way comparable to the devastating damage that delayed pro-cessing has on the quality of tea and bananas. Sugar cane can be hauled from relatively long distances and stored for several days. Therefore, the need for ver-tical integration is not so large, and the necessary coordination can be achieved through contracts of a sugar mill with cane growers on the time and quota of cane delivery. In fact, an efficient sugar industry with smallholders has devel-oped in Australia and Taiwan. In tropical Asia, too, sugar production has been carried out in the peasant system, in India and Thailand.

Another explanation for the use of the plantation system is the advantage of large estate farms in accessing capital. Because of this, it has been argued that plantations have an advantage in regard to tree crops characterized by long ges-tation periods from planting to maturity (Binswanger and Rosenzweig 1986). However, the opportunity costs of labor and capital applied to formation of the tree capital are not necessarily high for peasants. Typically, they plant the trees in hitherto unused lands. If such lands are located near their residence, they open new lands for planting by means of family labor at low opportunity cost during the idle season for the production of food crops on farm lands already in use. When they migrate to frontier areas, a typical process is to slash and burn jun-gles and plant subsistence crops such as maize, potatoes, and upland rice, together with tree seedlings. Such complex intercropping is difficult to manage with hired labor in the plantation system.

Therefore, even in the export boom of tropical cash crops under colonialism from the nineteenth century to the early twentieth century, the plantation system failed to make inroads in regions where indigenous populations had established family farms (Lewis 1970). Western traders found it more profitable to purchase tropical agricultural commodities from peasant producers in exchange for imported manufactured commodities than to produce these commodities themselves in the plantation system. This was particularly convenient during the nineteenth century, when the industrial revolutions in the Western nations made it possible for these countries to produce and supply manufactured products at much lower cost than if these products had been produced by the manufacturing sector in the tropical economies (Resnick 1970).

The establishment of plantations in less developed economies became a necessity when the demand for tropical products by the industrialized nations continued to rise, although the regions in the less developed economies physically suited for the production of these products had no significant peasant population that could produce and trade these commodities. Opening frontier lands for the production of new crops entailed high capital outlays. Virgin lands had to be cleared and developed, and physical infrastructure, such as roads, irrigation systems, bridges, and docking facilities, had to be constructed. Capital, in the form of machinery and other equipment, had to be imported and redesigned to suit local situations. Laborers were not only imported from the more populous regions but also had to be trained in the production of these crops.

The establishment of plantations thus requires huge initial capital investment. For the investors to internalize gains from investment in infrastructure, the farm size inevitably must be large. Viewed from this perspective, it follows that the plantation system evolved not because it was generally a more efficient mode of productive organization than the peasant mode but because it was the most effective type of agricultural organization for extracting the economic benefit accruing from the exploitation of sparsely populated virgin areas. From this perspective, it is easy to understand why the same crop is grown mainly by peasants in one place and mainly by plantations in another. For example, for sugar cane production in the Philippines, the peasant mode is more common in old settled areas of Luzon, and the plantation system predominates in the newly opened Negros (Hayami, Quisumbing, and Adriano 1990, chap. 5).

Thus, the efficiency of the plantation relative to the peasant system is high in the initial opening-up process of land-abundant and labor-scarce economies. However, several negative aspects of plantations become significant as tropical economies shift from the land-abundant to the land-scarce stage after the completion of the opening-up process.

First, the plantation system tends to substitute capital for labor. This is because of the inherent difficulty in supervising wage laborers in spatially dispersed and ecologically diverse farm operations.

Second, agricultural lands tend to be cultivated less intensively in a plantation system that employs mainly wage labor and produces essentially a monoculture crop. Complicated crop rotation and crop-livestock combinations are more difficult to manage in the command system. This implies that both labor input and income per hectare are lower in the plantations. In contrast, small-sized family farms tend to cultivate land more intensively.

Third, plantations usually specialize in a single crop. This bias for the production of a monocrop reduces the flexibility of these productive organizations, their ability to respond to changing demand by shifting to the production of other crops. Moreover, continual cultivation of a single crop tends to result in soil degradation and an increase in pest incidence; counterapplication of fertilizer and chemicals causes serious stress on the environment and human health.

Fourth, the specialization of plantation workers in specific tasks inhibits the development of their managerial and entrepreneurial capacity (Baldwin 1956; Myint 1965; Beckford 1972).

Fifth, the plantation system is the source of class conflict between the laborers and the managers and capitalists. The presence of a plantation enclave in rural economies where the peasant mode of production predominates has often strained relationships in rural communities. In terms of the criterion of social stability, therefore, the plantation system is no match for the system of relatively homogeneous small producers owning small assets, however small they might be.

These disadvantages can be mitigated if the plantation system is reorganized into the "contract farming" system. In contract farming, an agribusiness firm (or cooperative) manages processing and marketing but contracts with peasant farmers for the supply of farm products. The firm provides technical guidance, credit, and other services to peasants in return for production pledged to the firm. In this way the system can take advantage of peasants in farm-level production without sacrificing scale economies in processing and marketing. A major advantage of this system is to tap not only the muscle labor but also the management ability of rural people in developing economies. The high efficiency of this system has been illustrated by the fact that Thailand, which relatively recently began producing canned pineapple by this system, has surpassed the Philippines, formerly the world's leading exporter of canned pineapple, whose production is based on the plantation system.

While negative aspects of plantations have loomed larger over time, direct government controls on their operations will likely prove damaging to both national development and the well-being of rural people. The entrepreneurship and management capability of agribusiness enterprises, including multinational corporations, in the area of agricultural marketing and processing are very valuable inputs, which can be dispensed with only at a very high cost. The rational approach, therefore, should be to design an inducement mechanism toward establishing an agrarian organization that adequately combines the entrepreneurial and managerial abilities of both peasants and agribusiness firms.

A policy designed in this direction might include the gradual phasing out of special treatments to agribusiness plantations such as public land leases at favorable terms and special allocation of import licenses and foreign exchange, and the stricter application of labor and environment codes to the corporate farms. At the same time, government must invest in education, research, and extension for developing the capability of small growers to operate the contract farming scheme effectively.[6]

PEASANTS AND MIDDLEMEN

The same policy prescription can be envisaged for the relation between peasants and middlemen. It is a deeply rooted popular belief that middlemen exploit peasants by means of monopoly or monopsony pricing and usury. This suspicion against middlemen is common in East Africa and Southeast Asia, where export-import business in major port cities was mainly handled by European firms, while collection of tropical export products from inland villages and distribution of imported consumption goods there were largely carried out by non-European ethnic minorities (Indians and Chinese). Such an ethnic division of labor originally could have been based on the comparative advantage of the native population in primary production in the natural-resource-rich economies suddenly opened to international trade. However, it was inevitable for the natives to develop strong anti-middleman sentiment and ideology as they continued to be excluded from the main current of commercial activities. Thus, as Leon Mears (1981, 133) described for Indonesia, even after independence, "it is not unusual to hear judgment . . . that farmers or consumers are exploited by the market control exercised by ethnic Chinese middlemen. At times one even hears that all private traders are exploitative and discouraging to producers."

This stereotype, however, has not stood up under empirical tests. Almost all substantive empirical studies, including the classic work for export cash crops in West Africa by Bauer (1954) and two major studies for food crops in India by Lele (1971) and in Africa by Jones (1968a), have produced results inconsistent with the hypothesis of marketing inefficiency and middleman exploitation.[7] These studies unanimously show that entry to agricultural marketing activities is open and competition among middlemen is intense in developing economies in the absence of government control, so that marketing margins are largely consonant with the costs associated with marketing activities; wide price gaps across areas and fluctuation over seasons are not caused by monopolistic behavior by traders and speculators but arise mainly from the high costs of transport and storage as well as insufficient market information services.

The fundamental contribution of trading activities to the development of the peasant economy has been neglected, relative to the importance to such factors as capital formation, rural education, agricultural research, and land reform. It must be recognized that profitable opportunities created by new technology and improved infrastructure, such as roads, cannot be exploited without the activities of middlemen. While solely motivated for their own profit, middlemen, in effect, provide essential support for peasants: Traders both large and small create new opportunities. With their knowledge of the requirements of local, regional, and export markets, traders provide outlets for farm products. They buy the traditional products and at the same time acquaint farmers with new products and the methods of growing them. Further, they make available to them the necessary inputs such as seeds, fertilizers, and implements. Thus the traders encourage new wants, convey new opportunities, and help farmers to take advantage of them. The activities of traders set in motion and maintain the process by which participation in the exchange economy replaces subsistence production (Bauer and Meier 1994, 139).

When governments attempted to constrain or even to replace private trading with state trading based on the folklore of exploitative middlemen, disastrous consequences were inevitable, as evident from the experience of marketing boards and parastatals in several African economies (Bauer 1954; Hopkins 1973; Bates 1983; Jones 1987; Lele and Christiansen 1989).[8]

This does not mean that government necessarily should leave the existing system of marketing as it is. A wide scope exists for reducing transportation costs through government investment in roads and railways. Moreover, improvements in transportation and communication by public investments are critically important for reducing trade risk and transaction costs and thereby promoting new entry and competition in marketing. Development of institutions for the service of market information, such as grading, standardization of measures and weights, commodity exchange, crop forecasting, and regular quotations of market prices through mass media, as well as more fundamental institutions for the protection and enforcement of property rights and contracts, can contribute much to reductions in trade risks and transaction costs.

If the activities of middlemen in the countryside of developing economies were supported by these government services, the healthy development of peasant economy would be greatly promoted. The problem is that "most governments under-invest in this infrastructure and over-invest in their own enterprises and efforts to carry out agricultural marketing directly. If policymakers trusted their peasants more and feared middlemen less, this government bias could be reversed. Most policymakers have never met a peasant, much less one with entrepreneurial skills engaged in risky trading activities (Timmer 1993, xi)."

PEASANT ENTREPRENEURSHIP IN COMMERCE AND INDUSTRY

Indeed, the popular belief that peasants are exploited through the marketing process assumes implicitly that middlemen belong to a social group alienated from the peasantry. Peasants have been considered always to be passive to market forces and to have neither the desire nor the ability to participate in commercial and industrial activities.

This view found a typical expression in Clifford Geertz's anthropological study in Indonesia (1963). Based on observations in East Java and Bali, he concluded that the entrepreneurship for nonfarm business activities that may induce social modernization cannot emerge fro..n "the immediate purview of village social structure" but is limited to the population with "extra-village status," such as ethnic Arab traders in the East Javanese town and traditional rulers in the Balinese town (Geertz, 148–49).

If the Geertz thesis is valid, the case of Indonesia represents a sharp contrast to the historical experience of Japan. In the initial stage of modern economic growth in Japan, wealthy peasants, who typically cultivated a part of their land by themselves and rented out the other part, actively participated in trading and manufacturing; this process had begun already in the feudal Tokugawa period, in response to the gradual development of the market economy, and it accelerated with Japan's opening to foreign trade and national unification by the Meiji Restoration in 1868 (Smith 1956, 1959, 1988). Contributions of these small-scale, rural-based enterprises to the national economy were no less significant than those of large, modern corporations developed by urban entrepreneurs who emerged from the preindustrial merchant class (such as Mitsui and Sumitomo) and the ex-warrior class (such as Yataro Iwasaki, the founder of Mitsubishi). In fact, until the turn of the century—or even later until about World War I—rural and national economic development is considered to have been supported, to a large extent, by the commercial and industrial activities of those rural entrepreneurs (Rosovsky and Ohkawa 1961; Tussing 1966). This development of rural-based enterprises had made conditions for industrialization in modern Japan less capital intensive than in other latecomers to modern economic growth (Smith 1959, chap. 1).

What I myself observed in a field study of agricultural marketing in Indonesia during 1986–90, as reported in Hayami and Kawagoe 1993, was contrary to the image developed by Geertz. Both in long-settled Java and newly opened Sumatra, indigenous entrepreneurs belonging to the upper peasantry actively engaged in the marketing and processing businesses. These village-based traders in upland Java have been overtaking town-based ethnic Chinese traders in the interregional transshipment of such commodities as corn and soybeans by effectively mobilizing a large number of small collectors who belong to the lower ranks of the peasantry. In the highly complicated and risky operation of commercial vegetable marketing for the metropolis, they have become dominant. Owner-operators of local tobacco factories have applied to their businesses modern marketing techniques, such as grading and the use of brand names, for reducing product quality uncertainty and transaction costs, without ever attending business school. In the transmigration area in Sumatra, too, peasant entrepreneurs have been following the developments in Java, in response to improvements in transportation and communication infrastructure. All these activities by the agents of peasant marketing in Indonesia resemble those of "rural capitalists" (Smith 1956) in Japan, who emerged from the *gono* (wealthy peasant) class and supported Japan's emergence as a modern industrial state.

The strength of these village-based traders is their ability to enforce contracts with farmers and lower-rank collectors by means of the village community tie. This advantage is especially large in connection with perishable commodities like vegetables, for which close coordination between farm-level collection and bulk shipment to urban markets is required (Hayami and Kawagoe 1993, chap. 4). This coordination is enforced by such means as long-term contracts involving credit tying, which are difficult for urban-based traders, lacking the community mechanism of enforcement, to organize.[9] Thus, if they are appropriately linked with international agribusiness or trading firms, while supported by public agricultural research and extension, they could well become an effective instrument for bringing Indonesian agriculture up to the status of a major supplier to the rapidly expanding world market for horticultural products.

There is little doubt that Geertz's pessimism about Indonesian peasants' entrepreneurship does not stand up under empirical tests today.

TOWARD RURAL-BASED DEVELOPMENT

What will be the role of peasant entrepreneurs as economies continue to advance to higher stages? The question arises as to what their fate will be in the event of successful economic modernization. Their marketing organization, as documented in Japan's history and as observed in Indonesia today, is a decentralized hierarchy of many self-employed informal agents tied by customary trade practices and informal contracts, where vertical integration is typically absent. In the low-income stage of economic development, the system is highly efficient in economizing the use of scarce capital and management input while making intensive use of labor having a low opportunity cost. This system's efficiency depends, to a large extent, on the dualistic structure characterized by differentials in wage and interest rates across firm sizes. Will this system become inefficient and be replaced by vertically integrated large corporations when the economy advances to a stage at which the factor market dualism is eliminated?

The experience of the Japanese economy in the past three decades may shed some light on this question. Within a decade of high economic growth from the mid-1950s, the dualistic structure was largely eliminated (Minami 1973). Yet, small-scale family enterprises have survived and have even been strengthened (Kiyonari 1980; Patrick and Rohlen 1987). Advantages of small- and medium-scale enterprises, such as high incentives for entrepreneurs and flexibility in employment and staffing, have increased in correspondence to the increased need for small-lot production of differentiated products, as the Japanese economy has advanced to a stage characterized by high per capita income and diversified consumer demands. Large corporations in Japan continue to prefer subcontracting to vertical integration. Coordination between parent company and small or medium firms has been developed with such precision that the subcontracting system is integrated inseparably in Toyota's famous *kanban* (just-in-time) system. In this system the subcontractors deliver the supply of their parts and materials to the assemblers precisely at the time when the parts are used, so that no inventory accumulates in the assembling plant even for small-lot production of many differentiated products. The improved subcontracting system is now considered a major organizational innovation that underlies the strength of Japanese industries, especially the automobile industry (Abegglen and Stalk 1985; Asanuma 1985, 1988; Wada 1991).

Is there any strong reason to doubt whether entrepreneurial and managerial skills now being learned in the countryside of Indonesia through the marketing of peasants' products will provide the basis of a modern subcontracting system and thereby support the advancement of the Indonesian economy to a higher regime of development? Indeed, the relationship between the transshippers of vegetables to metropolitan markets and their agents engaged in collection from farmers, which I observed in rural Indonesia, is very similar to Toyota's *kanban* system (Hayami and Kawagoe 1993, chap. 4). Are there insurmountable cultural and social barriers for peasant entrepreneurs in Indonesia to follow the development of their Japanese counterparts?

If the emergence of peasant entrepreneurs in Indonesia has followed the same pattern as in Japan, is there any reason to suspect that they will be incapable of becoming a major carrier of modern commerce and industry when Indonesia advances to a regime of higher economic development? Does not the same question apply to other developing economies?

The iconoclasm by T. W. Schultz has established a consensus in our profession that peasants in developing economies are not tradition-bound, irrational creatures but are highly responsive to economic opportunities and perfectly capable of carrying out modern agriculture. We must now recognize that they also can be a basis of modern commerce and industry if appropriate policies will be taken to support, rather than constrain, their entrepreneurship.

NOTES

Useful comments from Keijiro Otsuka and Vernon Ruttan are gratefully acknowledged.

1. Kautsky's argument is similar to the theory of Alexander Chayanov (1925) on the point of the strong resilience and viability of peasants because of the application of family labor to farm production beyond the equilibrium between market wage rates and labor's marginal productivities. However, unlike Kautsky, who reasserted the demise of peasantry along the Marxian orthodoxy, Chayanov argued its persistence, a position similar to the revisionists'.

2. This perspective has been elaborated by a number of modern economists, from John Brewster to Hans Binswanger and Mark Rosenzweig, so it has been established as a current orthodoxy.

3. Stalin collectivized family farms into *kolkhoz* partly based on the Marxian doctrine (Mitrany 1951) but more importantly with the intention of utilizing the collective farms for compulsory procurement of foodstuff at low prices for urban industrial workers (Tang 1967). The consequence was a shift of status for Russia from a major exporter of foodgrains to a major importer after World War II.

4. This section draws heavily on Hayami 1994.

5. In a broader definition, for example, by Jones (1968b), farm estates based on forced labor, such as slavery, corvée, and serfdom, instead of free wage labor may also be called plantations. Estates based on forced labor were established typically before the onset of the industrial revolution in Eu-

rope and North America. They had a major impact on the southern United States and Latin America (hacienda), as well as Eastern Europe (such as the Junker estates in Prussia) but had little effect in Asia. The plantations dealt with in this paper are those established in tropical Asia in the late nineteenth to the early twentieth century. From the beginning their operations were based on wage laborers, even though many laborers were imported from densely populated economies such as China and India under long-term contracts, often tied by credit, akin to debt peonage.

6. In this connection the debate on the role of food crop versus cash crop, which has been heated especially in Africa, should be reconsidered. The traditional emphasis on export cash crops under the colonial regime was initially inherited by newly independent governments. However, since Africa shifted from being a net food exporter to being an importer in the early 1970s, the reallocation of resources to the food sector has been strongly (often emotionally) advocated (Rodney 1994, Lappé and Collins 1977, Twose 1984). Correspondingly, both international and national supports on cash crop research, which was relatively well developed in the colonial regime, have been drastically reduced (Eicher and Baker 1992; Eicher and Rukuni 1996). While the importance of public research on food crops cannot be overemphasized, the total neglect of export crop research on the popular presumption that it serves for the profit of agribusiness alone is counterproductive to the benefit of small peasant producers. It is important to recognize that cash crops are an important source of income for peasants in Africa as well as other developing regions and that peasants' participation in cash crop production increases their entitlement to foods, thereby enhancing their food security (Drèze and Sen 1989). Research on cash crops, especially nontraditional export crops such as flowers, fruits, and vegetables for which world demands have been expanding very rapidly, would be highly effective in the promotion of food security in low-income economies (Islam 1990).

7. The same conclusion has been drawn from numerous individual commodity studies, including Hirsch on sugar in India, Ruttan (1969) on rice and corn in the Philippines, Mears (1974) on rice in the Philippines, Scott (1985) on potatoes in Peru, Hayami and Kawagoe on upland crops, and Akiyama and Nishio (1996) on cocoa in Indonesia.

8. For example, farm producers' shares of export FOB prices for cocoa for 1980–88 were less than 60 percent in the countries in which marketing was handled by state marketing boards, such as Ghana, Cameroon, and Côte d'Ivoire, whereas those of countries with no marketing board, such as Brazil and Indonesia, were higher than 80 percent. Within Indonesia, producers' shares were much higher for commodities with little government intervention, such as cocoa and coffee, than for sugar, which was controlled by the state procurement agency (BULOG) (Akiyama and Nishio 1996, 10–11).

9. I must caution, however, that the community mechanism can produce multiple equilibria depending on different social and cultural conditions, as predicted by Akerlof (1984). Unlike many parts of Asia, close kinship relationships in African villages serve as a mechanism of tolerating credit defaults rather than enforcing repayment (Kennedy 1988; Platteau 1996). This tradition might be one of the major factors underlying poorer performances in capital accumulation and economic growth in Africa than in East Asia for the past several decades.

REFERENCES

Abegglen, J. C. and G. Stalk, Jr. 1985. *Kaisha: The Japanese Corporation.* New York: Basic Books.

Akerlof, G. A. 1984. *An Economic Theorist's Book of Tales.* Cambridge: Cambridge University Press.

Akiyama, T., and N. Nishio. 1996. *Indonesia's Cocoa Boom: Hands-Off Policy Encourages Smallholder Dynamism.* Policy Research Working Paper 1580, World Bank, Washington, D.C.

Allen, R. C. 1992. *Enclosure and the Yeoman: The Agricultural Development of the South Midlands 1450–1850.* Oxford: Oxford University Press.

Asanuma, B. 1985. "Organization of Parts Purchases in the Japanese Automobile Industry." *Japanese Economic Studies* 13:32–35.

———. 1988. "Manufacturer-Supplier Relationships in Japan in the Concept of Relation-Specific Skill." *Journal of Japanese and International Economics* 3:1–30.

Baldwin, R. E. 1956. "Patterns of Development in Newly Settled Regions." *Manchester School of Economic and Social Studies* 24:161–79.

Bates, R. H. 1983. *Markets and States in Tropical Africa.* Berkeley: University of California Press.

Bauer, P. T. 1948. *The Rubber Industry.* London: Longman and Green.

———. 1954. *West African Trade: A Study of Competition, Oligopoly and Monopoly in a Changing Economy.* Cambridge: Cambridge University Press.

Bauer, P. T., and G. M. Meier. 1994. "Traders and Development." In *From Classical Economics to Development Economics,* edited by G. M. Meier, 135–43. New York: St. Martin's Press.

Beckford, G. L. 1972. *Persistent Poverty: Underdevelopment in Plantation Economies of the Third World.* New York: Oxford University Press.

Bernstein, E. 1899. *Die Voraussetzungen des Socialisums und die Aufgaben der Socialdemokratie.* Stuttgart: Dietz.

Binswanger, H. P., and M. R. Rosenzweig. 1986. "Behavioral and Material Determinants of Production Relations in Agriculture." *Journal of Development Studies* 22–23:503–39.

Boeke, J. S. 1953. *Economics and Economic Policy of Dual Societies as Exemplified by Indonesia.* New York: Institute of Pacific Relations.

Brewster, J. M. 1950. "The Machine Process in Agriculture and Industry." *Journal of Farm Economics* 32:69–81.

Chayanov, A. Y. 1966. *Theory of Peasant Economy,* edited by D. Thorner, B. Kerblay, and R. E. F. Smith. Homewood, Ill.: Richard D. Irwin. (Original pub. 1925.)

David, E. 1903. *Socialismus und Landwirtschaft.* Berlin: Socialistschen Monastshefte.

Deininger, K., and G. Feder. 1995. "Revolt and Reform in Agricultural Land Relations." *Handbook of Development Economics.* Vol. 3B, edited by J. Behrman and T. N. Srinivasan, 2659–2772. Amsterdam: Elsevier.

Drèze, J. and A. K. Sen. 1989. *Hunger and Public Action.* Oxford: Clarendon Press.

Eicher, C. K., and D. C. Baker. 1992. "Agricultural Development in Sub-Saharan Africa: A Critical Survey." In *Survey of Agricultural Development Literature.* Vol. 4, *Agriculture in Economic Development,* edited by L. Martin, 3–328. Minneapolis: University of Minnesota Press.

Eicher, C. K. and M. Rukuni. 1996. "Reflections on Agrarian Reform and Capacity Building in South Africa." Staff Paper no. 96-3, Department of Agricultural Economics, Michigan State University, East Lansing.

Ernle, Baron R. E. 1961. *English Farming: Past and Present.* London: Heinemann Educational Books and Cass and Co. (Original pub. 1912.)

Geertz, C. 1963. *Peddlers and Princes.* Chicago: University of Chicago Press.

Griliches, Z. 1964. "Research Expenditures, Education, and the Aggregate Agricultural Production Function." *American Economic Review* 54:961–74.

Hayami, Y. 1994. "Peasant and Plantation in Asia." In *From Classical Economics to Development Economics,* edited by G. M. Meier. New York: St. Martin's Press.

Hayami, Y., and T. Kawagoe. 1989. "Farm Mechanization, Scale Economies and Polarization." *Journal of Development Economics* 31:221–39.

———. 1993. *The Agrarian Origins of Commerce and Industry: A Study of Peasant Marketing in Indonesia.* London: Macmillan; New York: St. Martin's Press.

Hayami, Y., M. A. Quisumbing, and L. S. Adriano. 1990. *Toward an Alternative Land Reform Paradigm: A Philippine Perspective.* Quezon City, Philippines: Ateneo de Manila University Press.

Hayami, Y., and V. W. Ruttan. 1985. *Agricultural Development: An International Perspective,* rev. ed. Baltimore: Johns Hopkins University Press.

Hopkins, A. G. 1973. *An Economic History of West Africa.* New York: Columbia University Press.

Islam, N. 1990. *Horticultural Exports of Developing Countries: Past Performances, Future Prospects, and Policy Issues.* Washington, D.C.: International Food Policy Research Institute.

Johnson, N. L. and V. W. Ruttan. 1994. "Why Are Farms So Small?" *World Development* 22: 691–706.

Jones, W. O. 1968a. *Marketing Staple Food Crops in Tropical Africa.* Ithaca: Cornell University Press.

————. 1968b. "Plantations." *International Encyclopedia of the Social Sciences.* New York: Macmillan and Free Press.

————. 1987. "Food-Crop Marketing Boards in Tropical Africa." *Journal of Modern African Studies* 25:375–402.

Kautsky, K. 1899. *Die Agrarfrage.* Stuttgart: Dietz.

Kennedy, P. 1988. *African Capitalism: Struggle for Ascendancy.* Cambridge: Cambridge University Press.

Kislev, Y., and W. Peterson. 1981. "Prices, Technology, and Farm Size." *Journal of Political Economy* 90:578–95.

Kiyonari, T. 1980. *Chusho Kigyo Dokuhon* [Textbook of small and medium-scale industries]. Tokyo: Toyokeizaishimposha.

Kuznets, S. 1966. *Modern Economic Growth.* New Haven: Yale University Press.

Lappé, F. M., and J. Collins. 1977. *Food First: Beyond the Myth of Scarcity.* Boston: Houghton Mifflin.

Lele, U. 1971. *Food Grain Marketing in India.* Ithaca: Cornell University Press.

Lele, U., and R. E. Christiansen. 1989. *Markets, Marketing Boards, and Cooperatives in Africa: Issues in Adjustment Policy.* MADIA Discussion Paper 11, World Bank, Washington, D.C.

Lenin, V. I. 1960. *The Development of Capitalism in Russia: The Process of Formation of a Home Market for Large-Scale Industry.* Vol. 3 of *Lenin, Collected Works,* 4th ed. Moscow: Foreign Languages House. (Original Pub. 1899.)

Lewis, W. A. 1969. *Aspects of Tropical Trade, 1883–1965.* Stockholm: Almquist and Wiksel.

————. 1970. "The Export Stimulus." In *Tropical Development, 1880–1913,* edited by W. A. Lewis, 13–45. London: Allen and Unwin.

Lim, Y. 1968. "Impact of the Tea Industry on the Growth of the Ceylonese Economy." *Social and Economic Studies* 17:453–67.

Marx, K. 1970. *Capital: A Critique of Political Economy.* Vol. 1 of *The Process of Capital Production.* Chicago: Kerr. (Original pub. 1867.)

Mears, L. A. 1974. *Rice Economy of the Philippines.* Quezon City: University of the Philippines Press.

————. 1981. *The New Rice Economy of Indonesia.* Yogyakarta, Indonesia: Gadjah Mada University Press.

Minami, R. 1973. *The Turning Point in Economic Development: The Japanese Experience.* Tokyo: Kinokuniya.

Mitrany, D. 1951. *Marx against the Peasant.* Durham: University of North Carolina Press.

Myint, H. 1965. *The Economics of Developing Countries.* New York: Praeger.

Patrick, H. R. and T. P. Rohlen. 1987. "Small-Scale Family Enterprises." In *The Political Economy of Japan.* Vol. 1 of *The Domestic Transformation,* edited by K. Yamamura and Y. Yasuba, 331–84. Stanford, Calif.: Stanford University Press.

Pim, A. 1946. *Colonial Agricultural Production.* London: Royal Institute of International Affairs; New York: Oxford University Press.

Platteau, J. P. 1996. "Traditional Norms as an Obstacle to Economic Growth in Tribal Societies." Mimeograph, CRED Faculty of Economics, University of Namur, Belgium.

Resnick, S. A. 1970. "The Decline in Rural Industry under Export Expansion: A Comparison among Burma, the Philippines, and Thailand, 1870–1938." *Journal of Economic History* 30:51–73.

Rodney, W. 1974. *How Europe Underdeveloped Africa.* Washington, D.C.: Howard University Press.

Rosovsky, H., and K. Ohkawa. 1961. "The Indigenous Components in the Modern Japanese Economy." *Economic Development and Cultural Change* 9:476–501.

Ruttan, V. W. 1969. "Agricultural Product and Factor Markets in Southeast Asia." *Economic Development and Cultural Change* 17:501–19.

Schultz, T. W. 1964. *Transforming Traditional Agriculture.* New Haven: Yale University Press.

Scott, G. J. 1985. *Markets, Myths, and Middlemen: A Study of Potato Marketing in Central Peru.* Lima, Peru: International Potato Center.

Smith, T. C. 1956. "Landlords and Rural Capitalists in the Modernization of Japan." *Journal of Economic History* 16:165–68.

————. 1959. *The Agrarian Origins of Modern Japan.* Stanford, Calif.: Stanford University Press.

————. 1988. *Native Sources of Japanese Industrialization, 1750–1920.* Berkeley: University of California Press.

Tang, A. M. 1967. "Agriculture in the Industrialization of Communist China and the Soviet Union." *Journal of Farm Economics* 49:1118–34.

Timmer, C. P. 1993. "Foreword." In *Agrarian Origins of Commerce and Industry,* edited by Y. Hayami and T. Kawagoe. New York: St. Martin's Press.

Tussing, A. 1966. "The Labor Force in Meiji Economic Growth: A Quantitative Study of Yamanashi Prefecture." *Journal of Economic History* 26:59–92.

Twose, N. 1984. *Cultivating Hunger: An Oxfam Study of Food, Power, and Poverty,* Oxford: Oxfam.

Wada, K. 1991. "The Development of Tiered Inter-firm Relationships in the Automobile Industry: A Case Study of Toyota Motor Corporation." *Japanese Yearbook on Business History* (August): 23–47.

Wickizer, V. D. 1951. *Coffee, Tea, and Cocoa: An Economic and Political Analysis.* Stanford, Calif.: Stanford University Press.

————. 1960. "The Smallholder in Tropical Export Crop Production." *Food Research Institute Studies* 1:49–99.

Young, A. 1774. *Political Arithmetic.* London: Nicoll.

19

Reflections on Land Reform and Farm Size

HANS P. BINSWANGER AND MIRANDA ELGIN

INTRODUCTION

Land reform gives poor people ownership rights or permanent cultivation rights to specific parcels of land. It makes sense when it increases their income, consumption, or wealth. And it fails if their consumption does not increase—or is reduced.

The Zamindari Abolition Act for Eastern India and the postwar land reforms in Iran, Japan, and China are outstanding examples of successful land reforms. China's creation of family farms from collectives—under the household responsibility system—in 1978 and the Philippines' tenancy reform in 1972 are other examples of successful land reforms. Neither provided ownership rights to the farmers or tenants, but they did provide permanent cultivation rights; and by fixing ceilings on rents, they gave farmers a portion of the land rent. Under both of these reforms, agricultural productivity started to grow faster. Between 1978 and 1984 output in Chinese agriculture increased by 61 percent. Otsuka's study (1988) of the impact of the 1962 Philippines Land Reform Code and its implementation in 1973 concludes that the reform has successfully broken up large ownership holdings. The result has been greater social equity and higher agricultural productivity, as tenants adopt the modern seed technology.

Another success is Kenya's Land Settlement program in the 1960s. Soon after independence, with funding from the British, the government bought large estates from white farmers, subdivided the land into small farms, and redistributed them to the African farmers. Incomes and productivity shot up almost immediately.

By contrast, Algeria's nationalization of French estates in 1964 created large cooperative farms that gave few direct incentives to workers. The state retained ownership of the land and appointed managers to run the farms. It paid cooperative members what amounted to a wage, giving them neither ownership nor cultivation

HANS P. BINSWANGER is an agricultural economist with the World Bank, Washington, D.C. MIRANDA ELGIN is a consultant to the World Bank.

Originally titled "What Are the Prospects for Land Reform," this paper was presented at the Twentieth International Conference of Agricultural Economists, Buenos Aires, 24–31 August 1988. It is reprinted by permission of the International Association of Agricultural Economists and the authors.

rights. Consequently, the real rate of growth in agriculture fell from 1 percent a year in the 1960s to 0.2 percent in the period 1969/71 to 1978/80 (Cleaver 1982).

Today, in recognition of this failure, the Algerian government is reforming the state farm sector. Under its 1987 land reforms, the government dismantled the state farms—which had about 60 percent of the country's agricultural potential—and replaced them with about 25,000 newly formed collectives. These new collectives give permanent and inheritable cultivation rights to groups and individual households. But the sudden switch in policy has yet to convince farmers of the permanency of their new land rights. And the lack of government guarantees in the law may mean that investments and the maintenance of land improvements will remain suboptimal.

WHY DOES LAND REFORM MAKE ECONOMIC SENSE?

If efficient small farms replace inefficient large farms, there is a benefit. But if smaller farms are not as efficient, there is a loss. Berry and Cline (1979) have shown that, in many countries, productivity is higher on small farms than larger farms (table 1). However, many question whether these findings really mean that transfers of land from large to small farms increase output. Some critics have tried to show that the observed differences in efficiency disappear when differences in land quality are accounted for, arguing that larger farms often are on poorer quality land. Bhalla (1983) used the Indian Fertilizer Demand Survey to try to eliminate the land quality differences statistically. He found that when soil quality variables are introduced, the inverse relationship declines for almost all the states. This de-

TABLE 1
PRODUCTIVITY DIFFERENCES BY FARM SIZE FOR SELECTED COUNTRIES

Farm Size[a] *(Hectares)*	*Northeast Brazil[b]*	*Punjab, Pakistan[c]*	*Muda, Malaysia[d]*
Small farm	563 (10.0–49.9)	274 (5.1–10.1)	148 (0.7–1.0)
Largest farm	100 (500+)	100 (20+)	100 (5.7–11.3)

SOURCE: Berry and Cline 1979.

[a] 100 = largest farm size compared with second smallest farm size. Second smallest farm size used in calculations to avoid abnormal productivity results often recorded for the smallest plots.

[b] Table 4-1, Berry and Cline 1979. Northeastern Brazil, 1973: Production per Unit of Available Land Resource, by Farm Size Group (p. 46). Index taken using average gross receipts/area for size group 2 (small) and 6 (large), averaged for all zones excluding zone F, where sugarcane and cocoa plantations skew productivity average for large farms.

[c] Table 4-29. Relative Land Productivity by Farm Size: Agricultural Census and FABS Survey-based Estimates Compared, 1968–69 (p. 84). Index taken using value added per cultivated acre for second smallest size group and largest.

[d] Table 4-48. Factor Productivity of Muda River Farms by Size, Double Croppers, 1972–73 (p. 117). Index taken from value added in agriculture/relong (0.283 ha = 1 relong).

cline is observed for both the magnitude and the significance of the coefficient for land. Kutcher and Scandizzo's (1981) similar work in Northeast Brazil shows that productivity differences between large and small farms do decline, but that they do not disappear. Even after adjusting for the proportion of farmland used for crops and for land value, they still came up with declines in productivity with respect to farm size, with an average elasticity of -0.69 (excluding the humid Southeast, where sugarcane and cocoa plantations skew productivity in most large farms).

WHY SMALL FARMS ARE MORE EFFICIENT THAN LARGE FARMS

Binswanger and Rosenzweig's theoretical study (1986) shows that the main reason for the lower productivity of large farms is that they use more hired labor than do smaller family farms, and family workers are cheaper and more efficient than hired workers. First, family members receive a share of profits and therefore have more incentive than hired wage workers to work for given supervision. Second, there are no hiring and search costs for family labor. And third, unlike hired labor, each family member takes a share of the risk.

The diseconomies of scale associated with hired labor can be partly circumvented by rental markets for land. Over the course of history, most large land owners have realized that family labor is cheaper than hired labor. So, rather than manage hired labor, they rent their land to tenants, taking advantage of the lower cost of family labor. Even if the optimum farm operation is small, the size of land holdings can be large since it is fairly simple to subdivide and rent out smaller holdings.

The subdivision of plantations into small tenant farms in the southern United States after the Civil War illustrates this point. When cheap slave labor became unavailable, the Southern farmers soon found that output and incomes rose if they subdivided and rented out their holdings. Similarly, the Zamindars in Eastern India, and the landlords in China, Japan, Taiwan, and Iran all developed closely supervised, subdivided holdings that they rented out. The systems allowed the landowners to circumvent the higher labor cost of large farming operations and to take advantage of cheap family labor.

Tenancy has its own incentive problems, because sharecroppers do not receive their marginal product. But here, too, landlords have ways to structure their contracts with tenants to circumvent or minimize these problems. The landlords might share in the cost of fertilizers and seeds, tightly supervise the operations of farms, and provide the tenant with credit.

Although these ways of restructuring contracts can reduce the incentive problems, they cannot overcome them. Shaban (1987) shows that in six South Indian villages, inputs and outputs per acre are higher on the owned plots of a mixed sharecropper than on fully sharecropped plots. The difference ranges between 19 and 55 percent for inputs and is 33 percent for output. These differences may be upper bounds, because mixed sharecroppers have the opportunity to divert inputs from the sharecropped plots to their own plots. Otsuka and Hayami's (1988) review shows that the difference between plots of pure sharecroppers and pure owner-operators are smaller. The upshot of the long debate is that tenants are less efficient than owners, but not as much as expected.

Where large landlords have used whole farm tenants on a large scale and constituted a hated class of absentee owners, land reform has succeeded. Land reforms in Iran, Japan, and Taiwan, and under the Zamindari Abolition Act in India were a simple transfer of the land to the former tenant. The reforms owe their success to the fact that the farmers knew the land, had draft animals, family labor, implements, and farm management skills. Today, there are almost no such large-scale opportunities left.

Collective farms suffer from the same labor disincentives as hired labor. These effects are often aggravated by an ideological reluctance to use piece rates and other output-based payment systems. In addition, households in collectives have to take savings and investment decisions jointly—an extremely difficult task if there are wide differences in preferences for consumption over time.

The size of these disincentives can be enormous. A large proportion of Soviet agricultural output is produced not by the state and collective farms but by plots allocated to individuals. Comparing productivity on collectively and privately farmed plots is complicated because the product mix differs and land quality may not be the same. Moreover, inputs may be diverted from collectively managed plots to private plots. Nevertheless the productivity differences are so large as to be noteworthy. Private household plots in the USSR, held by 23 million families (Shamelev 1982), account for only 3 percent of the total sown area, but they produce more than 25 percent of gross agricultural output. These private plots produce more than 30 percent of the country's total meat and milk and around 60 percent of the fruit and vegetables (Johnson and Brooks 1983). In China, agricultural output rose by 61 percent between 1978 and 1984, following the introduction of the household responsibility system. Data on post-1978 Chinese agricultural performance suggest that just over three-quarters of the measured productivity increase is due to change in individual incentives and the remainder to price increases to farmers.

Decollectivization could, as it did in China, substantially increase productivity in, for example, the Ethiopian State farms, the Soviet Union, some Eastern European systems, and Vietnam. The problems of resettlement or of financing a reform do not arise in centrally planned states, since the governments own the land, the farmers are present, and it is a simple matter to redistribute the land to members of the collectives.

MECHANIZATION AND PRODUCTIVITY

Karl Marx and his followers believed that, as in manufacturing, the economies of scale associated with agricultural mechanization were so large as to make the family farm obsolete. Without question, lumpy inputs such as draft animals or tractors give rise to initial economies of scale of farm holdings—that is, the average costs decrease as the size of the holdings increase. And technical change implies that larger tractors and machines operate at lower unit costs, so optimum operational farm sizes will increase.

So, does mechanization make very small *ownership* holdings obsolete? No. Small owners can rent out their land rather than sell it—and still keep the advantage of owning the land to raise credit (Binswanger and Rosenzweig 1984, 1986). Again, tenancy makes the ownership distribution partly independent of the operational distribution. So, the initial economy of scale associated with machines does not imply that reverse land reform is needed in areas with many small ownership holdings.

Moreover, rental markets for machines can circumvent the economies of scale inherent in machines—but only partly. In the late nineteenth century, mechanical threshers in European agriculture were too large for individual farms. Since threshing can be done at any time of the year, the machines would rotate between farms during the winter months, threshing the individual farm's output. Similarly, today's expanded use of threshers in developing countries reflects a well-developed, efficient rental market for threshers. Tractors are widely rented out to small farms for ploughing in Asia, Africa, and Latin America, but the markets are not as problem-free as for threshers (World Bank 1984). Rental markets are often infeasible for time-bound operations, such as seeding in dry climates, or harvesting where climatic risks are high. Farmers compete for first service and prefer to own their own machines.

Rental markets for machines figure prominently in recent decollectivization efforts. In China, the responsibility system has generated very small farms. Some households specialize in renting machines to these small farms. The system assumes that rental markets for equipment can completely overcome the economies of scale inherent in large equipment. That may be over-optimistic, and some farms seem to be growing in size. Conversely, in Algeria, the 1987 land reforms reduced farm sizes from 1,000 to 80 hectares per farm. The government hoped that these 80 hectare farms would be large enough to use a complete set of machinery. However, Krafft, Rogers, and Rooney (1988) suggest that without rental markets, the small farms cannot use the machines to full capacity. They predict that the increased pressure for a rental market will lead to some households or collectives switching out of farming and specializing in machine rentals.

As Hanumantha Rao (1977) showed, the negative relationship between farm size and productivity initially disappeared with the introduction of tractors in northwest India. But once the size of operational holdings rose, small farms re-emerged with higher productivity rates than large farms. Economies of scale for machines increase the minimum efficient farm size, but by less than expected, because of rental markets.

MODERN TECHNOLOGY, MANAGEMENT, AND FARM SIZE

Management, like a machine, is an indivisible and lumpy input. So the need for management initially gives rise to economies of scale: the better the manager, the larger the optimal farm size. The argument goes like this: modern fertilizer, pesticides, credit, and marketing require modern managerial skills. Therefore optimal farm sizes will tend to increase with technical change.

But too much can be made of this. Some management skills can be rented. If technology becomes too complex, farmers can hire private extension officers by the hour or the day to advise them. The training and visit (T and V) agricultural extension system has been a successful way of reaching and advising small farmers on new technology (Feder and Slade 1984). Another solution to the management problem is contract farming, where large firms provide technical advice, finance, and marketing services to small farmers.

Once again, however, rental markets for management and alternative contractual arrangements can circumvent the lumpiness of management skills only partly: actual farming decisions and the supervision of labor cannot be bought in a market. Managers have to do these tasks themselves. Nor is there any substitution for the important plot-specific experience of the farmer or manager. So the minimal *operational* size for farms may rise over time with the introduction of machines and other technology.

CAN PLANTATIONS BE REDISTRIBUTED?

We have just discussed why small farms are more efficient than large farms. Then why are there plantations—large operational farms—using permanent or semipermanent hired workers rather than family labor? The explanation is that for certain crops, economies of scale in processing and marketing are transmitted to the farm via the necessity of tight coordination between harvesting and processing.

Consider the coordination between harvesting and processing. For products that are easily stored in raw form, such as wheat and rice, a large mill can simply buy the grain at harvest time in the open market and store it for milling throughout the year. This shows that economies of scale in processing alone are not a sufficient condition for plantations—explaining why plantations or contract farming for wheat and other foodgrains have never survived.

In contrast with wheat, the harvesting and processing of sugarcane must be well coordinated. If cut cane is left unprocessed for more than 12 hours, the sugar is lost to fermentation. So the manager must carefully stagger the planting and harvesting to keep the sugar factory operating throughout a large part of the year. Some of the cane must be planted at sub-optimal times of the year, when farmers would be unwilling to do so without compensation. To get around this problem, sugar factories run their own plantations, using a single manager who decides on the tradeoffs between the costs of growing cane and the costs of processing it.

The coordination problems of growing and processing bananas for export are an extreme example. Mature bananas must be put into a cold boat within 24 hours of their harvest to arrest further ripening. This represents an immense challenge for the plantation and the shipping company. The coordination is possible if the planter operates a large enough number of plantations in a given area to ensure that a boat will get filled and if he can be sure that a boat will arrive when the bananas mature. So, some of the world's largest owner-operations are banana companies whose holdings include dozens of plantations operated by hired managers. Local banana markets, by contrast, can be served by trucks or rail. These markets are usually served by small owner-operators.

Contract farming can, depending on the crop, substitute for the plantation. For sugarcane, contracting with small farmers is widespread throughout India, Thailand, for example. For bananas, however, the quality controls are so rigorous that contract farming is less feasible. Hayami, Adriano, and Quisumbing (1987) have proposed redistributing the Philippine banana plantations to smallholders, who would then produce under contract. The proposal is to create farms of perhaps 20 to 30 hectares, but this farm size would preclude distribution of land to the poor. Holdings of 5 to 6 hectares are too small to meet the demands of tightly scheduled contracts. In Central America, when legislation prevented the multinationals from owning large plantations, the major banana companies increased their supplies from contract farms. But these farms typically have hundreds of hectares, and their contracts are so tight that they are virtually managed by the multinationals. For this reason, the proposal to split the banana plantations into small operational holdings would be unlikely to lead to an internationally competitive banana industry.

REMAINING OPPORTUNITIES FOR LAND REFORM

Most of the large ownership holdings operated by tenants have disappeared or been reformed—those in India, Iran, and China, to name a few. Left are the agricultural systems that are difficult to reform for political and economic reasons. Where large farms—30–40 hectares—are interspersed with medium and smaller farms, as in parts of South Asia, large farms are owner-operated and are difficult to reform. The same is true of collective farms in the Soviet Union, Eastern Europe, Vietnam, and Ethiopia. As we just described, plantations cannot easily be distributed without efficiency losses.

The only remaining opportunities for reform are the large-scale farms in Brazil, Nicaragua, Guatemala, and other Latin American countries, and in Zimbabwe and South Africa. During colonial times, landowners in these countries ousted the native populations from much of the most fertile areas and forced them into generally infertile mountain or dryland areas. As late as 1964 in Zimbabwe, less than six thousand white farmers consolidated their occupation of nearly half the land—and it was the best land—leaving 800,000 African farms on the other half, which was poor quality land. Despite attempts since 1979 to reform and resettle the African farmers, the situation remains largely unchanged. The sizes of the large estates in these countries exceed what could be justified by the economies of scale of machines or management skills. Farm size productivity differences between these estates and smallholdings are often huge, providing strong economic justification for land reform.

However, land reform in these countries would require resettlement which is a complex process. First, the resettled people have to acquire capital and farming skills appropriate to the new area. This is an important difference between resettlement and simply giving the land to preexisting tenants. Second, the settlers may not be compatible ethnically. Third, new settlements of this kind require costly infrastructure and support services.

Some of these problems can be avoided. Large Latin American farms used to be operated with tenants, hired labor, or as Haciendas. Under the hacienda system, wage-earning laborers are given small plots of land for their own cultivation. In the last 30 years, however, tenants and workers have been driven off these holdings (de Janvry and Sadoulet 1986). Ironically, they have been driven off by well-meaning but perverse reforms—tenancy and labor law reforms. In Brazil, for example, the 1964 Estatuta da Terra imposed ceilings on fixed rents, limits on the share of output that an owner could obtain from the tenant, and provisions giving security to long-term tenants, leading to a practical loss of ownership. In addition, labor laws made it illegal for workers to receive payments in kind. Under such circumstances, any rational owner would try to evict tenants and long-term workers. Alternatively, owners might try to sell their land, but subsidies for mechanization and for credit have provided impressive "gifts" to large farmers. The government's policy mix has encouraged large farmers to mechanize or convert to ranching and to shed laborers and tenants, systematically destroying the poor's opportunities for employment or self-employment.

HOW TO PAY FOR LAND TRANSFERS

SPECIAL PROBLEMS OF POOR FARMERS

Despite the difficulties of reforming these remaining systems of large farms, the economic benefits would probably be large. The question then remains, If small farms are so much more efficient, why do small, poor farmers not buy land from large farmers? The main reason is that even under ideal circumstances, they cannot buy that land without curtailing their consumption, because they have no equity.

Given a perfect market situation, the value of land reflects the present value of agricultural profits, capitalized at the opportunity cost of capital. If the poor have to use credit to buy land at its present value, the only income stream they have available for consumption is the imputed value of family labor. They must use the remaining profits to pay for the loan. If the poor can get the same wage in the labor market, they are not any better off as landowners than they would be as workers. This example is, moreover, an ideal situation, in which the interest rate paid by the poor is equal to the interest rate that the most creditworthy borrowers can get. The poor generally have to pay higher interest rates and therefore have to reduce consumption below what they could have earned in the labor market.

If, in a less than ideal situation, the value of the land exceeds the capitalized agricultural profits, the poor must cut consumption below the imputed value of family labor to pay for the land. Anything that drives the land price above the capitalized value of the agricultural income stream thus makes it impossible for the poor to buy land without reducing consumption.

In most real world situations, several other income streams are capitalized into the land price. First, with populations growing and the demand for land increasing, some of the expected future real appreciation of the land price is capitalized into the current land price. The only way a poor person could have access to that income stream is by selling off a small parcel of land every year to pay for his interest cost. This is clearly infeasible for smallholders.

Second, where land ownership becomes attractive as a hedge against inflation, an inflation premium is built into the real land price, as is clearly shown by Brandao and Rezende (1988) for Brazil.

Third, tax breaks are often capitalized in the land price. Most countries exempt agricultural income from income tax; and even where there is no general exemption, depreciation allowances are so generous that nobody with agricultural income pays any income tax on it. But, since the poor have a zero tax rate anyway, they receive no such benefit from the income tax break.

Fourth, owners of large holdings have a cost advantage in securing credit, even in the absence of credit subsidies, and these credit cost advantages are capitalized into land values as well (Binswanger and Rosenzweig 1986). Official credit systems often allocate the bulk of credit to large farmers, further increasing this credit cost advantage. Brandao and Rezende (1988) demonstrate econometrically how these credit subsidies are capitalized into land prices.

In sum, real future appreciation, inflation premium, income tax exemptions, and credit cost advantages of large ownership holdings raise the land price far beyond the capitalized value of agricultural profits. Agricultural economists know this problem well. When they try to compute the overall rate of return of capital invested in agriculture, they usually find that the opportunity cost of capital exceeds the rate of return in agriculture. In Switzerland the ratio is 5:1. And according to every farm management study in India, agriculture is unprofitable when measured at the opportunity cost of capital. Given this situation, the productivity advantage of the small farmers would have to be immense to enable the assetless poor to finance land purchases out of agricultural profits. So, a land market generally cannot substitute for a land reform.

Making a Land Reform Stick

If governments introduce a land reform into a distorted environment that favors large farms, one would expect the recipients—small farmers—to sell out to the large farmers, defeating the purposes of land reform. Because such distortions as income tax exemptions or credit distortions favor the rich, a precondition for a land reform is the prior elimination of all distortions favoring large farms. For example, to institute a land reform under the current policy regime in Brazil would be foolhardy. Tough policy choices eliminating explicit and implicit subsidies to large farmers must be made in order for a land reform to stick.

Progressive Land Taxes and the Land Market

With a progressive land tax, the price of land in large ownership holdings would drop. Could governments impose a large enough land tax to reduce land prices to a level that the poor could afford? The World Bank has considered this idea in Zimbabwe, and a land tax has been proposed as the main component of a Philippine land reform. Brazil actually has a progressive land tax in place.

In principle, governments can impose a large enough land tax to offset any non-agricultural premium on land prices in large farms. But this is unlikely to benefit the truly poor, because they still need some equity capital to buy the land. Even under the best of circumstances, a progressive land tax redistributes land from the rich to the middle class. And circumstances are seldom the best, because governments have used land taxes to try to raise agricultural productivity, cutting the tax rate for large farms that use land intensively or are very productive. In Brazil, farmers can cut their land tax rate in half by converting idle land or land under forestry into pasture; with modest crop production, they can cut their land tax almost to zero. So, all the Brazilian system does is provide an additional incentive to ranching or extensive crop production.[1] It does not increase the number of land sales from large farmers to small farmers.

HAVING BENEFICIARIES PAY FOR A LAND REFORM

If governments cannot use the voluntary land market to reform the size of land holding, can the beneficiaries of compulsory reform be made to pay? Here again the typical proposal is for the Philippines and Brazil. The state buys the land and compensates the owners at market prices with land reform bonds, instead of cash. It services the interest and principal payments, which it then recovers from the beneficiaries. Sometimes, private agencies, like the Guatemala Rural Development Foundation, execute such programs of land redistribution. The private agency buys large estates, subdivides them, and sells the plots to settlers. Of course, if the land price contains any premium reflecting nonagricultural income streams, the beneficiaries of these schemes will not be able to pay.

If such schemes are implemented in the face of these problems, there are three likely outcomes. First, the beneficiaries default and the program stops. Many ambitious land reform plans simply peter out; this has been a common outcome in Latin American countries (de Janvry and Sadoulet, 1989). Second, bonds may have built-in features that erode their real value over time. So, although landowners receive their nominal value, time erodes the real market value and the government makes no compensation for this loss. Most landowners naturally oppose such thinly disguised expropriation. Third, governments may fail to repay loans from foreign lenders, making the programs effectively funded by a grant.

Since the beneficiaries of a land reform cannot pay for their land, the land purchases must be financed by foreign grants, internal tax revenues, or inflationary monetary expansion, or by a combination of the three. The grants provide the equity that the poor lack. Credit to beneficiaries can play a supplementary but only minor role.

Because the poor cannot pay for land reform, we believe that the outlook for land reform is very bleak. Landowners will oppose any form of open or disguised expropriation, foreign grants will not materialize, and governments will not allocate domestic resources for the purpose.

INCREASING THE OPPORTUNITIES FOR THE POOR
IN AGRICULTURE

Many governments have tried to improve the tenancy terms of poor sharecroppers by legislation, but these attempts have largely had perverse results. First, owners have many ways of getting around the legislation—say, by reducing the size of plots allocated to tenants or by reducing credit, fertilizer, or other inputs they might provide the tenant. Second, if owners cannot circumvent the laws, they expel tenants and revert to self-cultivation. As discussed earlier, the impact of many of these tenancy reforms has reduced the welfare of tenants.

If land reform cannot be financed and tenancy reform leads to perverse results, other policies and programs must be pursued to assist the landless poor and small farmers. Such approaches, far from being new, are the standard fare of small farmer development programs, and they have enjoyed much success. They continue to be valid, and they should be pursued:

First, governments should reform the policies that favor large farmers and that lead to large land premiums over the capitalized value of agricultural profits. Also, they should eliminate income tax exemptions for agriculture and subsidized credit for large farmers.

Second, governments should eliminate explicit and implicit subsidies to machines. As an example, the 1986 U.S. Tax Reform Act lengthened the recovery rates on such depreciable assets as agricultural machinery from five to seven years and repealed the investment tax credit for farmers.

Third, governments should undo perverse tenancy reforms and perverse labor laws, allowing people to rent out their land again or make more intensive use of labor. Hayami's proposal for the newly planned reforms in the Philippines calls explicitly for the abolition of all constraints on tenancy. In Latin America, the abolition of such constraints would greatly benefit self-employment in agriculture.

Fourth, governments should redistribute the land they already own, but with some reasonable ceilings on the size of holdings. In the Brazilian Amazon, squatters can obtain up to 3,000 hectares of land if they clear trees from half of it. This accelerates deforestation and drastically reduces the land available to smallholders. A more sensible policy would be a land ceiling of 50 to 100 hectares. A good example of a successful redistribution scheme, using a smaller land allocation, is the U.S. Homestead Act, which opened the Midwest to settlers in the nineteenth century.

Fifth, efforts should be made to give smallholders adequate titles. Even if their claims to the land are secure, they cannot compete for official credit without titles. Gershon Feder's 1988 study of land titling in Thailand shows how large the disadvantages can be for small farmers lacking deeds of ownership. As mentioned earlier, the recent land reforms in Algeria have not given firm guarantees of land tenure to the new farmers, so the farmers there will continue to have difficulty in raising loans from banks.

Sixth, special efforts should be devoted to programs that assist small farmers.

Very popular in the 1970s, these projects are still an integral part of the World Bank's poverty alleviation strategy. Such schemes as area development programs, the T and V extension programs, and the large dairy projects along the lines of the Anand Dairy Cooperative have done much to help small farmers. Despite these successes, discussion in recent years has often focused on failed small farm projects. These occurred where general economic policies were stacked against the farm sector or where the project design was excessively complex for the implementation capacity of the agricultural services. In sub-Saharan Africa, many projects have also focused on zones with very little agroclimatic potential and where no new high pay-off technology exists. So the failures do not put in question the small farmer development programs, but rather provide lessons of how better to design them.

CONCLUSION

Land reform is unlikely to be a major tool for improving the welfare of the poor in developing countries. Even where it would make a lot of economic sense, it will not happen, because the beneficiaries cannot pay for the land reform, implying the need for confiscating appropriations or imposing large tax costs, neither of which is politically palatable. Consequently, other measures have to be devised to improve poor people's access to land or to increase their income from agriculture. But these measures can help small farmers only if governments abandon policies that favor large farms and that put premiums on land prices. A much stronger commitment from governments and agencies is thus needed to tackle these policy issues and thereby reduce incentives to accumulate large ownership holdings, increase agricultural production, and assure greater equity and self-employment in agriculture.

NOTES

1. This is one measure which de Janvry and Sadoulet (1989) describe as part of the state's strategy to force large farmers to modernize as an alternative to land reform. Other elements of the strategy are the credit subsidies discussed earlier in this paper.—ED.

REFERENCES

Berry, R. A., and W. R. Cline. 1979. *Agrarian Structure and Productivity in Developing Countries.* Baltimore: Johns Hopkins University Press.

Bhalla, G. S. 1983. *The Green Revolution and the Small Peasant: A Study of Income Distribution among Punjab Cultivators.* New Delhi: Concept Publishers.

Binswanger, H. P., and M. R. Rosenzweig, eds. 1984. *Contractual Arrangements, Employment, and Wages in Rural Labor Markets in Asia.* New Haven: Yale University Press.

———. 1986. "Behavioural and Material Determinants of Production Relations in Agriculture." *Journal of Development Studies* 22, no. 3 (April).

Brandao, A., and G. Rezende. 1988. "The Behavior of Land Prices and Land Rents in Brazil." Paper presented at the Twentieth International Conference of Agricultural Economists, Buenos Aires, August 24–31.

Cleaver, Kevin M. 1982. *Agricultural Development Experience of Algeria, Morocco, and Tunisia: A Comparison of Strategies for Growth.* Washington, D.C.: World Bank.

de Janvry, Alain, and Elisabeth Sadoulet. 1989. "A Study in Resistance to Institutional Change: The Lost Game of Latin American Land Reform." *World Development* 17, no. 9 (September): 1397–1408.

Feder, G. 1988. "The Implications of Land Registration and Titling in Thailand." Paper presented at the Twentieth International Conference of Agricultural Economists, Buenos Aires, August 24–31.

Feder, G., and R. Slade. 1984. *Aspects of the Training and Visit System of Agricultural Extension in India: A Comparative Analysis.* Staff Working Paper 656. Washington, D.C.: World Bank.

Hayami, Y., L. S. Adriano, and A. R. Quisumbing. 1987. *Agribusiness and Agrarian Reform: A View from the Banana and Pineapple Plantations.* Los Baños, University of the Philippines, November.

Johnson, D. G., and K. M. Brooks. 1983. *Prospects for Soviet Agriculture in the 1980s.* Bloomington: Indiana University Press.

Krafft, N., R. Rogers, and C. Rooney. 1988. "Algeria After Land Reform: Implementing the Break-up of the State Farms." Washington, D.C.: World Bank.

Kutcher, G. P., and P. L. Scandizzo. 1981. *The Agricultural Economy of Northeast Brazil.* Washington, D.C.: World Bank.

Otsuka, Keijiro. 1988. *The Determinants and Consequences of Land Reform Implementation in the Philippines.* Los Baños: International Rice Research Institute.

Otsuka, Keijiro, and Yujiro Hayami. 1988. "Theories of Share Tenancy: A Critical Survey." *Economic Development and Cultural Change* 37, no. 1 (October): 31–68.

Rao, Hanumantha. 1977. *Technological Change and Distribution of Gains in Indian Agriculture.* New Delhi: Macmillan.

Shaban, R. A. 1987. "Testing between Competing Models of Sharecropping." *Journal of Political Economy* 95 (5): 893–920.

Shamelev, G. 1982. "Social Production and Personal Household Plots." *Problems of Economics* 25 (June): 39–54.

World Bank. 1984. *Agricultural Mechanization—A Comparative Historical Perspective.* Washington, D.C.: World Bank.

20

Investing in People

THE ECONOMICS OF BEING POOR

Most people in the world are poor. If we knew the economics of being poor, we would know much of the economics that really matters. Most of the world's poor people earn their living from agriculture. If we knew the economics of agriculture, we would know much of the economics of being poor.

Economists find it difficult to comprehend the preferences and scarcity constraints that determine the choices poor people make. We all know that most of the world's people are poor, that they earn a pittance for their labor, that half and more of their meager income is spent on food, that they reside predominantly in low-income countries, and that most of them earn their livelihood in agriculture. What many economists fail to understand is that poor people are no less concerned about improving their lot and that of their children than rich people are.

What we have learned in recent decades about the economics of agriculture will appear to most reasonably well informed people to be paradoxical. Agriculture in many low-income countries has the potential economic capacity to produce enough food for the still-growing population and also improve the income and welfare of poor people significantly. The decisive factors of production in improving the welfare of poor people are not space, energy, and cropland; the decisive factors are *the improvement in population quality and advances in knowledge*.

In recent decades the work of academic economists has greatly enlarged our understanding of the economics of human capital, especially the economics of research, the responses of farmers to new and profitable production techniques, the connection between production and welfare, and the economics of the family. Development economics has, however, suffered from several intellectual mistakes. The major error has been the presumption that standard economic theory is inadequate for understanding low-income countries and that a separate economic theory is needed. Models developed for this purpose were widely acclaimed, until it be-

THEODORE W. SCHULTZ is professor emeritus, Department of Economics, University of Chicago, and a Nobel laureate.

This chapter is based on his Nobel lecture, given 8 December 1979, Stockholm, Sweden, copyright © the Nobel Foundation, 1979. Reprinted from *Investing in People: The Economics of Population Quality*, 1981; with minor omissions, by permission of the University of California Press and the author.

came evident that they were at best intellectual curiosities. Some economists reacted by turning to cultural and social explanations for the alleged poor economic performance of low-income countries, although cultural and behavioral scholars are understandably uneasy about this use of their studies. Increasing numbers of economists have now come to realize that standard economic theory is as applicable to the scarcity problems that confront low-income countries as to the corresponding problems of high-income countries.

A second mistake is the neglect of economic history. Classical economics was developed when most people in Western Europe were barely scratching out subsistence from the poor soils they tilled and were condemned to a short life span. As a result, early economists dealt with conditions similar to those prevailing in low-income countries today. In Ricardo's day, about half of the family income of laborers in England went for food. So it is today in many low-income countries. Marshall tells us that "English labourers' weekly wages were often less than the price of a half bushel of good wheat" (Marshall 1920) when Ricardo published his *Principles of Political Economy and Taxation* (1817). The weekly wage of a ploughman in India is currently somewhat less than the price of two bushels of wheat (Schultz 1980). Knowledge of the experience and achievements of poor people over the ages can contribute much to an understanding of the problems and possibilities of low-income countries today. Such understanding is far more important than the most detailed and exact knowledge about the surface of the earth, or of ecology, or of tomorrow's technology.

Historical perception of population is also lacking. We extrapolate global statistics and are horrified by our interpretation of them—mainly that poor people breed like lemmings headed toward their own destruction. Yet when people were poor in our own social and economic history, that is not what happened. Expectations of destructive population growth in today's poor countries are also false.

LAND IS OVERRATED

A widely held view—the natural earth view—is that the land area suitable for growing food is virtually fixed and the supply of energy for tilling the land is being depleted. According to this view, it is impossible to continue producing enough food for the growing world population. An alternative view—the social-economic view—is that man has the ability and intelligence to lessen his dependence on cropland, traditional agriculture, and depleting sources of energy and to reduce the real costs of producing food for the growing world population. By means of research, we discover substitutes for cropland which Ricardo could not have anticipated, and, as incomes rise, parents reveal a preference for fewer children, substituting quality for quantity of children, which Malthus could not have foreseen. Ironically, economics, long labeled the dismal science, shows that the bleak natural earth view with respect to food is not compatible with history, which demonstrates that we can augment resources by advances in knowledge. I agree with Margaret Mead: "The future of mankind is open-ended." Mankind's future is not foreordained by space, energy, and cropland. It will be determined by the intelligent evolution of humanity.

Differences in the productivity of soils do not explain why people are poor in long-settled parts of the world. People in India have been poor for ages, both on the Deccan Plateau, where the productivity of the rainfed soils is low, and on the highly productive soils of South India. In Africa, people on the unproductive soils of the southern fringes of the Sahara, on the somewhat more productive soils on the steep slopes of the Rift landform, and on the highly productive alluvial lands along and at the mouth of the Nile all have one thing in common: they are very poor. Similarly, the much-publicized differences in land-population ratio throughout the low-income countries do not produce comparable differences in poverty. What matter most in the case of farmland are the incentives and associated opportunities farm people have to augment the effective supply of land by investments that include the contributions of agricultural research and the improvement of human skills. An integral part of the modernization of the economies of high- and low-income countries is *the decline in the economic importance of farmland and a rise in that of human capital—skills and knowledge.*

Despite economic history, economists' ideas about land are still, as a rule, those of Ricardo. But Ricardo's concept of land, "the original and indestructible powers of the soil," is no longer adequate, if ever it was. The share of national income that accrues as land rent and the associated social and political importance of landlords have declined markedly over time in high-income countries, and they are also declining in low-income countries.

Why is the Ricardian law of rent (which treats it as a result rather than a cause of prices) losing its economic sting? There are two primary reasons: first, the modernization of agriculture has over time transformed raw land into a vastly more productive resource than it was in its natural state; second, agricultural research has provided substitutes for cropland. With some local exceptions, the original soils of Europe were poor in quality. They are today highly productive. The original soils of Finland were less productive than the nearby western parts of the Soviet Union, yet today the croplands of Finland are superior. Japanese croplands were originally much inferior to those in Northern India; they are greatly superior today. In both high- and low-income countries these changes are partly the consequence of agricultural research, including the research embodied in purchased fertilizers, pesticides, insecticides, equipment, and other inputs. There are new substitutes for cropland, or land augmentation. The substitution process is well illustrated by corn: the corn acreage harvested in the United States in 1979, 33 million acres less than in 1932, produced 7.76 billion bushels, three times the amount produced in 1932.

THE QUALITY OF HUMAN AGENTS IS UNDERRATED

While land per se is not the critical factor in being poor, the human agent is: investment in improving population quality can significantly enhance the economic prospects and welfare of poor people. Child care, home and work experience, the acquisition of information and skills through schooling, and other investments in health and schooling can improve population quality. Such investments in low-income countries have been successful in improving economic prospects wherever they have not been dissipated by political instability. Poor people in low-income countries are not prisoners of an ironclad poverty equilibrium that economics is unable to break. No overwhelming forces nullify all economic improvements and cause poor people to abandon the economic struggle. It is now well documented that in agriculture poor people do respond to better opportunities.

The expectations of human agents in agriculture—farm laborers and farm entrepreneurs who both work and allocate resources—are shaped by new opportunities and by the incentives to which they respond. These incentives, explicit in the prices farmers receive for their products and in the prices they pay for producer and consumer goods and services, are greatly distorted in many low-income countries. The effect of these government-induced distortions is to reduce the economic contribution that agriculture is capable of making.

Governments tend to introduce distortions that discriminate against agriculture because internal politics generally favor urban at the expense of rural people, despite the much greater size of the rural population (Schultz 1978). The political influence of urban consumers and industry enables them to exact cheap food at the expense of the vast number of rural poor. This discrimination is rationalized on the grounds that agriculture is inherently backward and that its economic contribution is of little importance despite the "Green Revolution." The lowly cultivator is presumed to be indifferent to economic incentives and strongly committed to traditional ways of cultivation. Rapid industrialization is viewed as the key to economic progress. Policy gives top priority to industry and keeps foodgrains cheap. It is regrettable but true that this doctine is still supported by some donor agencies and rationalized by some economists in high-income countries.

Farmers the world over, in dealing with costs, returns, and risks, are calculating economic agents. Within their small, individual, allocative domain they are entrepreneurs tuning so subtly to economic conditions that many experts fail to recognize how efficient they are (Schultz 1964). Although farmers differ in their ability to perceive, interpret, and take appropriate action in responding to new information for reasons of schooling, health, and experience, they provide the essential human resource of entrepreneurship (Welch 1970; Evenson and Kislev 1975). On most farms women are also entrepreneurs in allocating their time and using farm products and purchased goods in household production (Schultz 1974). Allocative ability is supplied by millions of men and women on small-scale producing units, for agriculture is in general a highly decentralized sector of the economy. Where governments have taken over this entrepreneurial function in farming, they have been unsuccessful in providing an effective allocative substitute capable of modernizing agriculture. The allocative roles of farmers and farm women are important and their economic opportunities matter.

Entrepreneurship is also essential in research, always a venturesome business, which entails organization and allocation of scarce resources. The very essence of research is that it is a dynamic venture into the unknown or partially known. Funds, organizations, and competent scientists are necessary, but not in themselves sufficient. Research entrepreneurship is required, be it by scientists or by others engaged in the research sector of the economy. Someone must decide how to distribute the limited resources available, given the existing state of knowledge.

THE INEVITABILITY OF DISEQUILIBRIA

The transformation of agriculture into an increasingly productive state, a process commonly referred to as modernization, entails adjustments in farming as better opportunities become available. The value of the ability to deal with disequilibria is high in a dynamic economy (Schultz 1975). *Such disequilibria are inevitable.* They cannot be eliminated by law, by public policy, and surely not by rhetoric. Governments cannot efficiently perform the function of farm entrepreneurs.

Future historians will no doubt be puzzled by the extent to which economic incentives have been impaired during recent decades. The dominant intellectual view is antagonistic to agricultural incentives, and prevailing economic policies depreciate the function of producer incentives. D. Gale Johnson (1978) has shown that the large economic potential of agriculture in many low-income countries is not being realized. Technical possibilities have become increasingly favorable, but the economic incentives that are required for farmers in these countries to realize this potential are in disarray, either because the relevant information is lacking or because the prices and costs farmers face have been distorted. For want of profitable incentives, farmers have not made the necessary investments, including the purchase of superior inputs. Intervention by government is currently the major cause of the lack of optimum economic incentives.

ACHIEVEMENTS IN POPULATION QUALITY

I now turn to measurable gains in the quality of both farm and nonfarm people. Quality in this context consists of various forms of human capital. I have argued elsewhere that while a strong case can be made for using a rigorous definition of human capital, it will be subject to the same ambiguities that continue to plague capital theory in general, and the concept of capital in economic growth models in particular (Schultz 1972). Capital is two-faced, and what these two faces tell us about economic growth, which is a dynamic process, are, as a rule, inconsistent stories. It must be so because the cost story is a tale of sunk investments; for example, once a farmer invests in horse-drawn machinery, such machinery has little value for use with tractors. The other story pertains to the discounted value of the stream of services such capital renders, which changes with the shifting sands of growth. But worse still is the assumption, underlying capital theory and the aggregation of capital in growth models, that capital is homogeneous. Each form of capital has specific properties: a building, a tractor, a specific type of fertilizer, a

tube well, and many other forms not only in agriculture but also in all other production activities. As Hicks has taught us, this capital homogeneity assumption is the
disaster of capital theory (Hicks 1965). It is demonstrably inappropriate in analyzing the dynamics of economic growth afloat on capital inequalities because of the
differences in the rates of return, whether capital aggregation is in terms of factor
costs or in terms of the discounted value of the lifetime services of its many parts.
Nor would a catalogue of all existing growth models prove that these inequalities
are equals.

But why try to square the circle? If we were unable to observe these inequalities,
we would have to invent them, because *they are the mainspring of economic
growth*. They are the mainspring because they are the compelling economic signals
of growth. One of the essential parts of economic growth is thus concealed by such
capital aggregation.

The value of additional human capital depends on the additional well-being that
human beings derive from it. Human capital contributes to labor productivity and
to entrepreneurial ability valuable in farm and nonfarm production, in household
production, in the time and other resources that students allocate to their education,
and in migration to better job opportunities and better locations in which to live.
Such ability also contributes importantly to satisfactions that are an integral part of
current and future consumption.

My approach to population quality is to treat quality as a scarce resource, which
implies that it has an economic value and that its acquisition entails a cost. The key
to analyzing the human behavior that determines the type and amount of quality
acquired over time is the relation between the returns from additional quality and
the cost of acquiring it. When the returns exceed cost, population quality will be
enhanced. This means that an increase in the supply of any quality component is a
response to a demand for it. In this supply-demand approach to investment in population quality, all quality components are treated as durable, scarce resources useful over some period of time.

My hypothesis is that the returns on various quality components are increasing
over time in many low-income countries; the returns that entrepreneurs derive
from their allocative ability rise; so do the returns on child care, schooling, and
improvements in health. Furthermore, the rates of return are enhanced by reductions in the cost of acquiring most of these quality components. Over time, the
increased demand for quality in children, and on the part of adults in enhancing
their own quality, favors having and rearing fewer children (Becker and Tomes
1976). The movement toward quality thus contributes to the solution of the population problem.

INVESTMENT IN HEALTH

Human-capital theory treats everyone's state of health as a stock, that is, as
health capital, and its contribution as health services. Part of the quality of the
initial stock is inherited and part is acquired. The stock depreciates over time and at

an increasing rate in later life. Gross investment in human capital entails acquisition and maintenance costs, including child care, nutrition, clothing, housing, medical services, and care of oneself. The service that health capital renders consists of "healthy time" or "sickness-free time" which contributes to work, consumption, and leisure activities (Williams 1977; Grossman 1972).

The improvements in health revealed by the longer life span of people in many low-income countries have undoubtedly been the most important advance in population quality. Since about 1950, life expectancy at birth has increased 40 percent or more in many of these countries. The decline in mortality among infants and very young children is only part of this achievement. The mortality of older children, youths, and adults is also down.

Ram and Schultz deal with the economics of these demographic developments in India (Ram and Schultz 1979). The results correspond to those in other low-income countries. From 1951 to 1971, life expectancy at birth of males increased by 43 percent in India, and that of females by 41 percent. For both males and females, life spans over the life cycle after age ten, twenty, and on to age sixty, were also decidedly longer in 1971 than in 1951.

The favorable economic implications of these increases in life span are pervasive. While the satisfactions that people derive from longer life are hard to measure, Usher (1978) has devised an ingenious extension of economic theory to determine the utility that people derive from increases in life expectancy. His empirical analysis indicates that the additional utility increases substantially the value of personal income (Usher 1978).

Longer lifespans provide additional incentives to acquire more education, as investments in future earnings. Parents invest more in their children. More on-the-job training becomes worthwhile. The additional health capital and the other forms of human capital tend to increase the productivity of workers. Longer life results in more years of participation in the labor force, and brings about a reduction in "sick time." Better health and vitality in turn lead to more productivity per man-hour at work.

The Ram-Schultz study provides evidence of the gains in the productivity of agricultural labor in India realized as a consequence of improvements in health. Most telling is the productivity effect of the "cycle" that has characterized the malaria program.

INVESTMENT IN EDUCATION

Education accounts for much of the improvement in population quality. But in reckoning the cost of schooling, the value of the work that young children do for their parents must be included. Even for very young children during their first years of school, most parents sacrifice the value of the work that children traditionally perform (Rosenzweig and Evenson 1977). Another distinctive attribute of schooling is what might be called the vintage effect, as more education per child is achieved. Starting from widespread illiteracy, older people continue through life with little or no schooling, whereas the children on entering adulthood are the beneficiaries of schooling.

The population of India grew about 50 percent between 1950–51 and 1970–71. School enrollment of children aged six to fourteen rose over 200 percent, and the rate of increase in secondary schools and universities was much higher. Since schooling is primarily an investment, it is a serious error to treat all educational outlays as current consumption. This error arises from the assumption that schooling is solely a consumer good. It is misleading to treat public expenditures on schooling as "welfare" expenditures, and a use of resources that has the effect of reducing "savings." The same error occurs in the case of expenditures on health, both on public and private account.

Expenditures on schooling, including higher education, are a substantial fraction of national income in many low-income countries. These expenditures are large relative to the conventional national accounting measures (concepts) of savings and investment. In India, the proportional cost of schooling in relation to national income, savings, and investment is not only large, but has tended to increase substantially over time.

THE HIGHLY SKILLED

In assessing population quality, it is important not to overlook the increases in the stock of physicians, other medical personnel, engineers, administrators, accountants, and various classes of research scientists and technicians.

The research capacity of a considerable number of low-income countries is impressive. There are specialized research institutes, research units within governmental departments, industrial sector research, and ongoing university research. Scientists and technicians are university trained, some of them in universities abroad. Research areas include, among others, medicine, public health (control of communicable diseases and the delivery of health services), nutrition, industry, agriculture, and even some atomic-energy research. I shall touch briefly on agricultural research, because I know it best and because it is well documented.

The founding and financing of the international agricultural research centers, originally initiated by the Rockefeller Foundation in cooperation with the government of Mexico, is an institutional innovation of a high order. But these centers, good as they are, are not a substitute for national agricultural research enterprises, as demonstrated by the increases in the number of agricultural scientists in twenty-two selected low-income countries between 1959 and 1974. All told, the number of man-years devoted to agricultural research in these countries increased more than three times during this period. By 1974, there were over 13,000 such scientists, ranging from 110 in the Ivory Coast to over 2,000 in India (Boyce and Evenson 1975). Indian agricultural research expenditures between 1950 and 1968 also more than tripled in real terms. An analysis by states within India shows that the rate of return has been approximately 40 percent, which is high indeed compared to the returns from most other investments to increase agricultural production (Evenson and Kislev 1975).

While there remains much that we do not know about the economics of being poor, our knowledge of the economic dynamics of low-income countries has advanced substantially in recent decades. We have learned that poor people are no less concerned about improving their lot and that of their children than those of us who have incomparably greater advantages. Nor are they any less competent in obtaining the maximum benefit from their limited resources. Population quality and knowledge matter. A good number of low-income countries have a positive record in improving population quality and in acquiring useful knowledge. These achievements imply favorable economic prospects, provided they are not dissipated by politics and governmental policies that discriminate against agriculture. As Alfred Marshall wrote, "knowledge is the most powerful engine of production; it enables us to subdue Nature and satisfy our wants."

Even so, most people throughout the world continue to earn a pittance from their labor. Half, or even more, of their meager income is spent on food. Their life is harsh. Farmers in low-income countries do all they can to augment their production. What happens to these farmers is of no concern to the sun, or to the earth, or the behavior of the monsoons and the winds that sweep the face of the earth; farmers' crops are in constant danger of being devoured by insects and pests: Nature is host to thousands of species that are hostile to the endeavors of farmers. Nature, however, can be subdued by knowledge and human abilities.

NOTE

I am indebted to Gary S. Becker, Milton Friedman, A. C. Harberger, D. Gale Johnson, and T. Paul Schultz for their helpful suggestions, as well as to my wife, Esther Schultz, for her insistence that what I thought was stated clearly was not clear enough.

REFERENCES

Becker, Gary S., and Nigel Tomes. 1976. "Child Endowments and the Quality of Children." *Journal of Political Economy* 84, part 2 (August): S143–S162.

Boyce, James K., and Robert E. Evenson. 1975. *National and International Agricultural Research and Extension Programs.* New York: Agricultural Development Council.

Evenson, Robert E., and Y. Kislev. 1975. *Agricultural Research and Productivity.* New Haven: Yale University Press.

Grossman, M. 1972. *The Demand for Health.* National Bureau of Economic Research, Occasional Paper, no. 119. New York: Columbia University Press.

Hicks, John. 1965. *Capital and Growth.* Oxford: Oxford University Press.

Johnson, D. Gale. 1978. "International Prices and Trade in Reducing the Distortions of Incentives. In Schultz, *Economics of the Family,* 195–215.

Marshall, Alfred. 1920. *Principles of Economics,* 8th ed. New York: Macmillan.

Ram, Rati, and Theodore W. Schultz. 1979. "Life Span, Health, Savings and Productivity." *Economic Development and Cultural Change* 27 (April): 399–421.

Rosenzweig, Mark R., and Robert E. Evenson. 1977. "Fertility, Schooling and the Economic Contribution of Children in Rural India." *Econometrica* 45 (July): 1065–79.

Schultz, Theodore W. 1964. *Transforming Traditional Agriculture*. New Haven: Yale University Press. Reprinted New York: Arno Press, 1976; Chicago: University of Chicago Press, 1983.

———. 1972. "Human Capital: Policy Issues and Research Opportunities." In *Human Resources*. New York: National Bureau of Economic Research.

———, ed. 1974. *Economics of the Family: Marriage, Children and Human Capital*. Chicago: University of Chicago Press.

———. 1975. "The Value of the Ability to Deal with Disequilibria." *Journal of Economic Literature* 13 (September): 827–46.

———. 1978. "On Economics and Politics of Agriculture." In *Distortions of Agricultural Incentives*, edited by T. W. Schultz, 3–23. Bloomington, Ind.: Indiana University Press.

———. 1980. "On the Economics of the Increases in the Value of Human Time over Time." In *Economic Growth and Resources*. Vol. 2, *Trends and Factors*, edited by R. C. O. Matthews. London: Macmillan.

Usher, Dan. 1978. "An Imputation to the Measure of Economic Growth for Changes in Life Expectancy." In *The Measurement of Economic and Social Performance*, edited by Milton Moss, 193–236. New York: National Bureau of Economic Research.

Welch, Finis. 1970. "Education in Production," *Journal of Political Economy* 78 (January-February): 35–59.

Williams, Alan. 1977. "Health Service Planning." In *Studies in Modern Economic Analysis*, edited by M. J. Artis and A. R. Nobay, 301–5. Edinburgh: Blackwell.

21

Projects for Women: Explaining Their Misbehavior

MAYRA BUVINIĆ

THE PROBLEM

The practice of assisting women in developing countries gained impetus with the designation of the United Nations' Decade for Women (1975–85) and with the allocation of special budgets within the UN system for this purpose. However, it is difficult to assess the impact of the Development Decade for Women on the original mandate, because there is a dearth of sound project evaluation and implementation studies. But it is evident that project implementation has lagged far behind achievements in research and policy (Staudt 1982; Buvinić, Lycette, and McGreevey 1983). While policies that incorporate the results of research and stress the importance of economic programs for women are often firmly in place, a welfare orientation has prevailed in the execution of projects for low-income women throughout the decade (Rogers 1979; Weeks-Vagliani 1984). It has been observed that male planners are frequently reluctant to implement, or even downright hostile to, projects for women that have an economic base, and this has been used to explain the prevalence of welfare action for women (Abdullah and Zeidenstein 1982; Zeidenstein 1977). Negative male attitudes can account for the absence of economic projects for women, but they fail to adequately explain the preference for welfare projects and the discrepancy that exists between economic-oriented policy and welfare-oriented action.

Purely welfare projects are those designed to deliver information, education, and sometimes free handouts (money, food, technology) to poor women in their roles as homemakers, reproducers, and child rearers. Examples are projects in maternal and child health, hygiene, nutrition, home economics, and home-based

Mayra Buvinić is chief of the Women and Development Program Unit and Special Advisor on Violence, for the Inter-American Bank, Washington, D.C.

Originally titled "Projects for Women in the Third World: Explaining Their Misbehavior." Previously published in *World Development* 14, no. 5 (1986): 653–64; published, with omissions and minor editorial revisions, by permission of Elsevier Science Ltd., Oxford, England, and the author.

appropriate technologies. Income-generation designs, in contrast, involve teaching a new skill or upgrading income-generating skills women already have and providing some of the resources needed to use the skills in the production of marketable goods and services.

To understand the persistence of welfare action for women without resorting to attitudinal explanations, this essay analyzes the characteristics and the environment of projects for women in developing countries. The project observations used to derive and illustrate the analysis are based on the work of the International Center for Research on Women (ICRW). The observations, therefore, were not drawn from a representative sample of projects, and the analysis does not presume to represent or do justice to the universe of projects for women but attempts to explain a particular type of project behavior. It is worth noting that successful (economic-oriented) exceptions to the category of projects examined here do exist and that they have become more frequent in recent years.[1]

PROJECT ILLUSTRATIONS

In 1979 a private voluntary agency set up an income-generation project for rural women in Western Province in Kenya. A group of fifty women was organized into a cooperative to produce potholders from banana fiber rings, for sale in Nairobi. Two years later the women were losing 0.50 Kenya shillings (US$0.05) for every potholder they produced and sold, not even including the implicit cost of their labor. (The unit cost of the fiber was 3.00 shillings and the retail price of the potholders was 2.50 shillings.) Moreover, capital that had been donated to finance and replicate the project through a revolving fund had been depleted. The project, nonetheless, continued operating.

A year earlier a similar situation had evolved in San José, Costa Rica. In this case thirty-eight poor urban women had received a donation of five industrial sewing machines, had taken an industrial sewing course, and had produced a stockpile of children's school uniforms. Unfortunately, not a single uniform had been sold. Aside from their labor, the women had invested cash for rental of a work space and purchase of materials and were deeply in debt.

A new project in a squatter settlement on the outskirts of Lima, Peru, promises to share with the Kenya and Costa Rica efforts the same bleak economic future. Under the project, seven to eight women are receiving group training to produce skirts for sale in the local market. The cost of the denim fabric used to make one skirt, however, is 1,000 soles (US$0.45) more than the highest retail price at which the skirts can be sold (7,000 soles). The women, some of whom have worked at the sewing training center for as long as two years without pay, are unlikely ever to make a profit on the sale of these clothes.

PROJECT BEHAVIOR AND MISBEHAVIOR[2]

The above observations do not illustrate instances of aberrant project behavior; on the contrary, they exemplify the typical unfolding of an income-generation project design for poor women in the developing world. These projects survive their financial misfortunes only because social or community development goals (i.e., the ideal of forming a community-based working group) take precedence over or replace production concerns when women are involved as project beneficiaries.

But if these examples illustrate the typical intervention aimed at women, they also reveal a pattern of project behavior that contradicts stated policies on women, the objectives of most projects, and the economic needs voiced by poor women. This contradiction between stated government policy and action is evident in the case of Honduras. In 1979 the great majority of projects for women sponsored by the government and private agencies shared the objective of integrating women into the country's productive programs; however, they also shared the inability to realize this aim. The Honduran 1979–83 Five-Year Development Plan included a section on women that identified the expansion and improvement of women's participation in the economy as an important goal (CONSUPLANE 1978). However, a follow-up review in 1981 showed that most government programs continued to concentrate on the promotion of traditionally feminine, sex-segregated, low-productivity activities for women (Youssef and LeBel 1981).

An integrated rural development effort in the Bolivian highlands illustrates the discrepancy between blueprints and action at the project level. One of the project's primary goals was to modernize the herd management and shearing practices of Bolivian peasants, in order to increase alpaca and llama wool production. Information collected during project appraisal revealed that herding and shearing were women's work, and as a result, the design of the project was revised to include a production-oriented women's component. In implementation, however, the component was redirected towards developing women's skills in nutrition, cooking, and embroidery. In the course of the project many supervision teams stressed, with little success, the need to direct women's activities away from those that supported their role as wives and mothers and to concentrate, instead, on the productive roles and expressed economic needs of women. Project documents reveal repeated recommendations that women be included in farmer-training courses and receive information on modern veterinary practices, but these were never implemented (Buvinić and Nieves 1982).

The average intervention does not respond to the importance women beneficiaries assign to income generation when voicing the needs they hope projects will address, nor does it respond to the more objective assessment of needs that emerges when analyzing economic participation statistics (Dixon 1980; Jain 1980; Chen 1984). Women's economic motivation is reflected in these statistics by their increased participation in the work force and underscored by their predominance in low-level, low-paying occupations and their substantial responsibility for the economic welfare of their families (Youssef, Sebstad, and Nieves 1980).

But there is a gap between the policy goals of increasing women's productivity and incomes and the implementation of projects for poor women throughout the world.[3] During the 1975–85 period many projects for women were modified, in the course of their implementation, to assume social and welfare tasks. Explaining the misbehavior of projects that assume welfare features in their execution, despite their stated economic objectives, can shed light on the apparent contradiction between the willingness of policy makers to acknowledge the importance of women's economic roles in development policy and the inability to follow this policy through to implementation.

THREE RELATED EXPLANATIONS

A hierarchy of three factors helps explain project misbehavior and defines both the specific and more general dimensions of this implementation problem. The welfare slant in the execution of women's projects is accounted for, first, by project design characteristics that are shared by a majority of interventions and that interfere with the execution of production objectives but may facilitate the implementation of social aims. Second, these characteristics are, in turn, the result of the expertise in the welfare sector of the agencies that implement women's projects and are affected by historical asymmetries in the growth of women and development agencies. Third, the institutional choices and the more general preference for welfare action are influenced by the lower financial and social costs that are involved in the execution of welfare policies in comparison with economic-oriented policies for women in developing countries.

PROJECT CHARACTERISTICS

A review of the recent literature shows that the standard project for women has design features that interfere with the execution of production objectives but may facilitate the implementation of social ones.

The Standard Design

The typical women's project that gained popularity in the past decade is small-scale, situation-specific, and uses limited financial and technical resources. It is implemented by women, many of whom are volunteers with little technical expertise, and it benefits only women. The intended target group is poor women in urban and rural communities, but project tasks usually require beneficiaries to volunteer their time and labor, which tends to exclude those with heavy demands on their time and the poorest women, who cannot afford to make these investments (e.g., women who head households). The typical project works with groups of five to forty women; groups that wish to undertake economic activities are often legalized as cooperatives. This involves substantial group participation and includes awareness-raising through group discussions, human development training, and/or training in stereotypical female skills such as sewing, knitting, cooking, and gardening. Lastly, the typical project involves group activities through which women attempt to apply the skills they have learned for income generation. Because of the type of training offered, income generation is in areas that are time consuming and have no income potential. Groups survive the financial failure that often occurs by replacing economic goals with social ones, and projects fall back onto a variety of social group actions.

The standard design can respond either to welfare or production concerns. These two different orientations could lead to two very different kinds of projects for women, but in reality welfare and income-generation distinctions blur in the execution phase. Because many income-generating projects fail to achieve their intended economic goals, they end up with community development objectives. Likewise, many welfare projects will make some attempt to increase incomes, particularly when poor women voice their need to earn money. The choices that are made in the standard design regarding the nature of the task, staff composition, group participation, and the use of volunteer labor interfere with production objectives and contribute, in project execution, to their translation into welfare realities.

Misjudging Simple and Familiar Tasks

It is well established that the likelihood of successful project implementation increases when interventions are clearly defined, short-term, have a single objective, and provide a single service. Successful execution is more likely when tasks required from project participants are not too numerous, too complex, or too unfamiliar (Cleaves 1980; Tendler 1982; Esman and Uphoff 1984). In fact, it has been observed that women's projects are often more successful when women participants are required to perform familiar tasks (Dixon 1980).

Common wisdom judges that stereotypical Western female tasks are both simple and familiar to poor women elsewhere and are, therefore, easily transferable. It is no surprise that they should predominate in the execution of projects for low-income women. In reality, however, female-appropriate tasks are not simple nor are they as familiar to low-income women as they are assumed to be. This is one of the most immediate and salient features that emerges from field observation of women's projects, and it was evident in 1980 in a sewing session for a group of low-income women in San José, Costa Rica. Women in the project were being taught how to measure and translate these measures into dress patterns that would be used to cut the fabric. Pattern drawing (as taught) was extremely complex and required drawing skills, spatial ability, and more than basic mathematics knowledge (percentages and fractions). It was clear that most of the women in the group could not follow the lesson, because it was too difficult and unfamiliar to them.

The training course for women in the rural development project in Bolivia cited earlier provides a good illustration of the complexity of traditionally female tasks. As noted in a supervision report, "All went well with the course but *too many* themes were included—for example, nutrition and cooking, embroidery, sewing, knitting and crochet, paper and paper maché, and flower making" (Buvinić and Nieves 1982, 25). These tasks were not only diverse but also highly unfamiliar to highland rural women whose main functions are to herd and shear animals, manage household finances, and supervise the day-to-day activities of the household.

Underestimating the difficulty of stereotypical female tasks and overestimating their transferability induces project misbehavior—that is, it prompts project implementers who want to see successful projects for women to choose welfare rather than productive activities. It is true that productive tasks are not inherently easy, but the difficulty of welfare tasks is underrated, because they are identified as traditionally female activities, while productivity tasks are often misjudged as being more difficult than they are for poor women.

Volunteer Staff and the Need for Technical Expertise

Women volunteers still staff a significant proportion of the productive projects for women being carried out in low-income countries today. Their generalist background is inadequate for the execution of economic programs and steers projects into the social rather than the income-earning sectors (Tendler 1982; Esman and Uphoff 1984). Volunteerism also perpetuates women's lower status among project implementers, since the overwhelming majority of male development project staff are paid.

It is commonly believed that, because of cultural proscriptions, the staff of these projects must be women. This belief has been put into practice in low-income countries, though its validity has gone largely untested. At the same time, it is clear that the lack of technical expertise of volunteer women staff is a major hindrance to the success of projects directed to increase women's productivity and income. It has been repeatedly observed that economic need breaks down the cultural restrictions imposed on women's mobility and the work they do and are allowed to do (Sundar 1983; Chen 1984). It is, therefore, highly likely that the cultural need to have female staff interacting with clients will vary with the degree of poverty of the beneficiary group, the nature of the project, and the task required of the staffperson. While it may be necessary to have women staff implement programs for women in sensitive family relations areas, such as family planning, it does not seem necessary and it may be counterproductive to have women staff address low-income women in areas such as agricultural extension where a communicator with a perceived higher status (i.e., a male extensionist) may be more credible, and therefore more effective, than one with a perceived lower status (i.e., a female extensionist).[4] In this latter case, however, work incentives need to be built in to guard against sex biases that may affect the behavior of the male communicator.

Participation, Volunteer Labor, and a Biased Clientele

The standard design of a women's project relies on a participatory style to identify felt needs and arrive at group decisions, while economic programs instead require centralized decision making for successful implementation. The participatory working style of women's projects is associated in the implementation literature with the successful execution of social rather than economic objectives (Tendler 1982; Esman and Uphoff 1984; Samuel 1982). The preference for this working style can, therefore, help explain the survival of projects that succeed with reference to social criteria despite financial failure.

The time required for group participation and the demands to donate voluntary labor in the standard women's design tend to replicate the regressive effect observed in many community development projects and to exclude women who have greater than average demands on their time or are the poorest (Tendler 1982). Field observations repeatedly show that, in the typical women's project, women who are relatively better off and do not need to work for a living are self-selected for project participation. It is highly likely that women who head households, who often are the poorest and have the most time constraints (because they have to undertake both home- and market-production roles and generally have fewer family members who can help them with income-generating tasks), will exclude themselves from projects that require time for group discussion, participation, or voluntary labor. These requirements in women's projects promote the selection of beneficiaries who can afford to undertake social tasks and, therefore, will go along with the transformation of productive goals into welfare activities.

INSTITUTIONS AND THEIR LEGACY

The standard design used in women's projects throughout the Third World is a direct product of the institutions that have been most frequently called upon to implement these projects. The nature of implementing institutions has determined the choice of project styles.

Project Illustrations

A small private organization of mostly women volunteers in Costa Rica that had effectively lobbied for women's legal rights was approached by an international development agency to design and implement a large, innovative project that would raise poor women's productivity and income in rural Costa Rica. It was determined that credit needed to be a key component of the project but that the organization did not have the institutional capacity to manage a sizeable loan and implement a credit program for poor women. Women volunteers were proficient at teaching traditional female skills (i.e., cooking, sewing, knitting) but had little experience in dealing with fund disbursements and balance sheets. Understandably, the organization was hesitant to undertake the project as it was conceived, and changed its productive orientation during implementation.

These circumstances are typical of women's projects and help to explain the redirection of projects to welfare actions in the execution stage: the women-based institutions that are chosen to implement women's projects are organizationally capable of executing welfare-oriented but not production-oriented projects; since these institutions want to execute successful projects, their most rational option is to translate production objectives into welfare actions.

The History of Women and Development Agencies

This limitation of women's agencies came about in part because women's organizations developed in the parallel worlds of development and relief agencies in the post–World War II period. Maendeleo ya Wanawake, the largest women's voluntary association in Kenya, was set up by a small group of European women in the early 1950s to promote the advancement of African women and to raise African living standards. Maendeleo was organized following a Western philanthropic model in which white, middle-class female volunteers provided assistance to rural women's clubs in welfare-oriented matters. Maendeleo began early on to Africanize its staff, but the particular volunteer and relief legacies remained. Maendeleo, which coordinates women's clubs around the country and has an approximate membership of 40,000 women, is still primarily staffed by local volunteers who perform charitable and welfare activities (Wipper 1975). In recent years, however, Maendeleo has expanded its scope of work to include the implementation of income-generating projects, but it still uses volunteers and only a small paid staff to undertake the productive projects (Lycette and Buvinić 1981).

The roots of Maendeleo are not unique; like women's organizations elsewhere in low-income countries, it was influenced by the post–World War II relief movement. In Chile and Brazil, for example, national women's organizations were first constituted in the 1920s to fight for women's suffrage and other legal rights; they disappeared within the decade and were revitalized only after World War II, for charity purposes (Kirkwood 1982; Schmink 1981). In East Bengal upper-class Muslim women started forming organizations in 1916. While only a handful of women participated during the early decades, after 1950 women joined in greater numbers, to provide relief to destitute women and carry out welfare-oriented policies (Jahan 1979). The All India Women's Conference (AIWC) was founded in 1926 and, like similar organizations elsewhere, was established to contribute to the general progress and welfare of women and children. With more than 100,000 members, AIWC now fulfills its mandate by, among other things, organizing conferences and undertaking educational and social welfare programs and services (Self and Girling 1983).

The end of World War II and the ensuing reconstruction of Europe brought about the creation of two parallel approaches in development assistance: on the one hand, the approach of economic growth, represented institutionally by the World Bank and its affiliates; on the other hand, an emphasis on emergency relief, with the proliferation of international and national private voluntary agencies (Ayres 1983; Bolling 1982). Poor women and their children became a main target of welfare programs operated by the international private voluntary agencies. Relief agencies often relied on, and therefore promoted, national volunteer organizations of upper- and middle-class women to implement their programs— that is, to distribute relief to poor women and children.

Because their objective was relief, women's institutions were organized as effective mechanisms for distributing services and free goods. Thus, they needed a large constituency and a large staff to reach this constituency, and they found that volunteers could do the job well and cheaply. Mothers' clubs, which were created during this period in developing countries, were instrumental in the relief efforts of women's organizations. Aside from those undertaking relief work, however, most women's organizations stagnated between 1950 and 1970. It was only in the late 1970s that new organizations were created and existing women's organizations revised their charters to include economic and feminist objectives.

The 1970s witnessed two major events that would have profound repercussions on programs for poor women. These were changes in the theory and practice of economic development, and the United Nations' designation of a Women's Decade, starting in 1975 with International Women's Year (IWY). Realizing that capital and technology transferred from the industrialized countries had not filtered down to the poor in developing societies and had not spread from modern enclaves to traditional sectors in these societies, development agencies established new strategies, designed to directly improve standards of living among the poor. In his address to the World Bank Board of Governors in 1973, Robert McNamara, then president of the Bank, made explicit the need to redirect the investments made by development agencies from projects that focused purely on economic growth to those that would also attempt to reduce poverty. International and national relief agencies soon followed suit, initiating their transformations into private development foundations.

The worlds of relief and economic growth started to merge as the World Bank invested heavily in social sectors and took the lead in research on basic human needs, and private voluntary organizations professionalized their staffs and implemented small-scale programs in economic development. These agencies were slow, however, in shifting the orientation of their work with women from relief to development (Tendler 1982). While women were a focus of economic development research, because of their importance in meeting basic family needs, in development action, projects for women remained the last bastions of relief interventions. In part, this can be attributed to the institutional legacy from the world of relief.

International Women's Year brought to world attention the concerns of women in industrialized and developing countries, assigned legitimacy to work on women's issues in economic development, and enticed small but critical budget allocations from international development agencies with which to undertake work on the subject. It became appropriate for development agencies to include in their antipoverty portfolios projects intended to improve the situation of poor women in developing countries. Some women's organizations in existence since the 1950s started to revise their aims and were in a position to implement these new projects. However, these organizations had been developed and were organizationally better suited to implementing relief rather than production. The asymmetry in the growth of women and development agencies and the motivation that women-only institutions have to expand and do what they know how to do best helps to explain the welfare orientation of projects for women in these countries.

THE POLITICAL ECONOMY OF WOMEN'S PROJECTS

The factors that condition the choice of implementing institutions complete the explanation of why projects for women misbehave. Women-based institutions that carry out development projects for women do not operate in a vacuum but in the context of international and national development agencies; these technical agencies are run by men who decide development priorities and the allocation of development resources. The choice of women-only institutions to implement women's programs is, in part, due to the belief that women staff should work with women beneficiaries; more importantly, however, it is the result of the reluctance of technical development agencies to both allocate significant financial resources to projects for women and to implement production-oriented women's projects. Women-based institutions are willing to do the job, and do it cheaply. Behind the development agencies' resistance are the actual and perceived costs and benefits to men-based development agencies (and related social institutions) of welfare versus productive action for poor women.

Approaches to Women's Place in Society

Until the international women's movement emerged in the early 1970s, a family model had guided the treatment of women in economic development work for more than two decades. The movement adopted an alternative definition of women's place in society, an action that further polarized deep-seated views and created controversy in many quarters, but also offered a new women-oriented model on which to base the study of women and the design of projects for them. The different social costs associated with each approach have affected the execution of projects for poor women in developing countries in important and largely unrecognized ways.

The family approach defines motherhood as the most important role for women in society and the most effective role for them in economic development. The unit of concern is the mother-child dyad, both in research and in action. In research, this approach led to the first serious efforts to study women in the context of economic development by exploring the effects of variables related to women's status (e.g., education and labor force participation) on fertility differentials and on health and nutrition patterns. The earliest social science literature on women's status variables is found in the fields of population, health, and nutrition studies. In action, the model calls for interventions directed toward women's reproductive and home production roles, since it is assumed that the prevailing sexual division of labor makes it most efficient to allocate development investments to women in their functions as childbearers, child rearers, and homemakers. Maternal and child welfare, nutrition education, and food distribution programs are examples of such interventions.

This family model, with an emphasis on the mother-child dyad, is used across the ideological spectrum. Capitalist and Marxist orientations, at opposite ends of this spectrum, share a family-centered view of women's place but differ on the factors that are believed to cause the poverty of mothers and children (i.e., whether poverty is attributable to individual or structural factors) and the action that will be effective in alleviating this poverty (i.e., relief interventions or revolutions) (Kirkwood 1982).

International Women's Year in 1975 promoted the recognition of women's productive roles in society as well as their contribution to economic growth and development. IWY also offered a model that centered on women as the unit of analysis and emphasized antipoverty and equity considerations in research and action.

The equity perspective in the woman-oriented model is concerned with inequality between women and men, in both the private and public spheres of life and across socioeconomic groups. It seeks the origin of women's subordination in the context of the family as well as in relationships between women and men in the marketplace. Economic development questions and objectives derive from the basic hypothesis of the negative impact of economic growth on women; these issues are important but so are equality issues that transcend the development field. In research, the equity perspective uses qualitative techniques and participatory methods as well as more standard analytical tools, and relies on theoretical frameworks from sociology, anthropology, and economics. In action, this approach guides the design of a wide range of programs for women that includes awareness groups organized for the purpose of understanding women's subordination, sex education and information classes for women of different socioeconomic groups, and credit programs for low-income women.

The poverty perspective deals with a more restrictive set of concerns. It centers on women's socioeconomic roles within low-income groups, relates women's situation to poverty, and emphasizes the goal of poverty reduction. It attributes the origins of women's poverty and inequality with men to their lack of access to private ownership of land and capital and to sexual discrimination in labor and capital markets. In research, the woman-centered poverty approach tries to quantify women's poverty and demonstrate that sexual inequality promotes economic inefficiencies and perpetuates poverty in developing countries. In action programs, this approach concentrates on increasing poor women's employment and income-generation options (e.g., skills training programs) and providing women with access to productive resources (e.g., credit). The poverty focus restricts action programs to women in low-income groups.

Anticipated Costs and Competition for Scarce Resources

In a world with finite development resources that are largely controlled by men, welfare and relief programs for women that emerge from the family model represent little or no threat to existing budget and power allocations as compared to the threat posed by production-oriented strategies that are guided by either poverty or equity concerns. Within this latter category, equity-oriented strategies imply greater costs than poverty-oriented ones.

Welfare action is supported by monies traditionally set aside for the purpose and, since this action is directed exclusively toward women in their roles as mothers and childbearers, it operates in a sex-segregated environment where, by definition, there is no possibility of competition with men for the goods or services offered. Productive interventions, by contrast, have the potential to pit women against men in the project environment. These interventions are bound to be perceived as more costly than welfare ones since they have the potential to create a situation in which women will compete with men for scarce development resources. Operations within a poverty-oriented framework restrict this competition between the sexes to development resources that have been earmarked for poverty programs, while equity-oriented action expands the range of resources that is subject to competition and includes, among other things, the budgets allocated for staffing development agencies.

Productive strategies are, therefore, less attractive than welfare strategies because they have the potential to redistribute resources from men to women—in other words, they carry the risk of a "zero-sum" situation, either because reducing inequalities will add costs to programs or because of the potential appropriation of economic resources by women. The fear that programs for poor women will reduce the already insufficient amount of aid allocated to poor men is reflected in the argument frequently made by project implementers that interventions designed to insure poor women's access to productive resources, such as credit, should be subordinated to similar actions directed towards men. A further corollary is that action for women may imply changes in the balance of power between men and women within the family, since productive interventions have the potential to modify the sexual division of labor within households, a division that preserves traditional cooperative arrangements that benefit male over female family members. (The concern with changes within the family was evident in an interview with a high-level official in a planning ministry who was favorably disposed to economic action for poor women. He supported the strategy of giving women access to resources so they could earn more money and contribute to family income but added the qualifier that women should never earn more than men, since this would have negative repercussions within the home.)

Because welfare action is aimed mainly at women and children and operates in effectively sex-segregated environments, it is believed that these actions will be appropriate to women, will not impinge on men, and—most important—will not take resources away from men. Welfare programs are perceived as "positive-sum" situations in which nobody loses.

It follows from the above discussion that the design of interventions to increase earnings of female heads of household among the poor and of women in female-only occupations somewhat reduces the fear of redistribution in poverty-oriented programs, since in both situations there is a measure of sex segregation and therefore lack of competition with men. There is little, however, that can reduce the risk of zero-sum outcomes and unwelcome social changes within families in programs with an equity focus, since these programs imply the possibility that women will take over some assets or resources in the home and in the market.

Action for poor women, therefore, is conditional on the assessment that investments in women will not affect or cut back on development investments in poor men. The result is that welfare designs are preferred by development experts and practitioners.

SOLUTIONS AND REMAINING HURDLES

The misbehavior of development projects for low-income women has historical roots in the creation of separate economic development and relief agencies after World War II. The translation of production objectives into welfare action is in part the rational response of implementing agencies with a capacity for, and often a history of, success in the welfare sector and limited experience in economic development.

The central policy question is how to maintain a specific emphasis on women that tackles both poverty and equity issues without setting up separate women's programs that command only a fraction of development resources and deny women access to development expertise. The dilemma emerges from the fact that while women-only agencies and women-specific programs tend to further isolate poor women from the economic benefits of projects, full integration of women's objectives into the development programs of male-based technical development agencies risks the submersion of women's priorities during implementation or the possibility that project resources directed to women will be monopolized by male beneficiaries. In addition, the concern for equity calls for the growth and professionalization, rather than the disappearance, of women-only institutions with expertise in economic development. A solution to this dilemma is to unlock the institutional potential of women-based and integrated agencies in specialized and complementary areas. It is clear that an element necessary for increasing the rate of success of productive strategies for women is institutional development that considers the strengths and weaknesses of existing agencies and the risks of misbehavior and submersion.[5]

NOTES

I wish to thank the Rockefeller Foundation for inviting me to finalize this essay under the Foundation's Resident Program for Scholars, at the Villa Serbelloni, Bellagio, Italy.

1. Examples include the Self-Employed Women's Association (SEWA) in Ahmedabad, India, the Grameen Bank in Bangladesh, and the PRODEM credit program of the Fundacion Ecuatoriana de Desarrollo in Quito, Ecuador. All three are intermediary agencies set up to respond to existing demand for credit by poor female and male micro entrepreneurs. Aside from having a single-purpose orientation, they have sufficient financial resources to serve a large clientele, and they rely on paid staff rather than volunteers.

2. The term "misbehavior" was used by Hirschman (1967) to address departures of project execution from project design.

3. See Dhamija 1981 for a review of projects in Africa, Dixon 1980 for projects supported by US-AID, and Cohn, Wood, and Haag 1981 for projects supported by the Peace Corps.

4. The psychology of social influence shows consistently that high status communicators are more credible than low status one. See Bem 1970.

5. For further analysis of the incorporation of women's issues into development projects, see Buvinić, Gwin, and Bates 1996.

REFERENCES

Abdullah, T. A., and S. A. Zeidenstein. 1982. *Village Women of Bangladesh: Prospects for Change.* New York: Pergamon Press.

Ayres, L. 1983. *Banking on the Poor: The World Bank and World Poverty.* Cambridge: MIT Press.

Bem, D. J. 1970. *Beliefs, Attitudes, and Human Affairs,* Belmont, Calif.: Brooks/Cole.

Bolling, R., with C. Smith. 1982. *Private Foreign Aid: U.S. Philanthropy for Relief and Development.* Boulder, Colo.: Westview Press.

Boserup, E. 1970. *Women's Role in Economic Development.* New York: St. Martins's Press.

Buvinić, M., C. Gwin, and L. M. Bates. 1996. *Investing in Women: Progress and Prospects for the World Bank.* Baltimore: Johns Hopkins University Press.

Buvinić, M., M. Lycette, and W. P. McGreevey, eds. 1983. *Women and Poverty in the Third World.* Baltimore: Johns Hopkins University Press.

Buvinić, M., and I. Nieves. 1982. "Elements of Women's Economic Integration: Project Indicators for the World Bank." Report prepared for the World Bank, Office of the Adviser on Women in Development, International Center for Research on Women, Washington, D.C.

Chen, M. A. 1984. *A Quiet Revolution: Women in Transition in Rural Bangladesh.* Cambridge, Mass.: Schenkman.

Cleaves, P. S. 1980. "Implementation amidst Scarcity and Apathy: Political Power and Policy Design." In *Politics and Policy Implementation in the Third World,* edited by M. Grindle. Princeton: Princeton University Press.

Cohn, S., R. Wood, and R. Haag. 1981. "U.S. Aid and Third World Women: The Impact of Peace Corps Programs." *Economic Development and Cultural Change* 29 (4): 795–811.

CONSUPLANE. 1978. "Plan Nacional para la Incorporacion de la Mejer al Desarrollo." Propuesta preliminar elaborada por el Departamento de Promocion Social de CONSUPLANE. Tegucigalph, Honduras, CONSUPLANE.

Dhamija, J. 1981. "Women and Handicrafts: Myth and Reality." *SEEDS Pamphlet Series.* New York: SEEDS.

Dixon, R. 1980. "Assessing the Impact of Development Projects on Women." *AID Evaluation Discussion Paper no. 8.* Washington, D.C.: U.S. Agency for International Development.

Esman, M. J., and N. T. Uphoff. 1984. *Local Organizations.* Ithaca, N.Y.: Cornell University.

Hirschman, A. 1967. *Development Projects Observed.* Washington, D.C.: Brookings Institution.

Jahan, R. 1979. "Public Policies, Women, and Development: Reflections on a Few Structural Problems," In *Women and Development: Perspectives from South and Southeast Asia,* edited by R. Jahan and H. Papanek, 54–70. Dhaka: Bangladesh Institute of Law and International Affairs.

Jain, D., assisted by N. Singh and M. Chand. 1980. *Women's Quest for Power: Five Indian Case Studies.* Ghaziabad, India: Vikas.

Kirkwood, J. 1982. "Feminismo y participación política en Chile." Documento de Trabajo, Programa FLACSO, no. 159. Santiago, Chile, FLASCO.

Lycette, M., and M. Buvinic. 1981. "Maendeleo ya Wanawake's Role in Promoting Income Generation Activities for Women in Kenya." Memo to Ned Greeley—USAID Kenya, December 23.

Rogers, B. 1979. *The Domestication of Women: Discrimination in Developing Societies.* New York: St. Martin's Press.

Samuel, P. 1982. *Managing Development Programs: The Lessons of Success.* Boulder, Colo.: Westview Press.

Schmink, M. 1981. "Women in Brazilian Abertura Politics." *Signs* 7:115–34.

Self, J., and R. Girling. 1983. "Reaching Poor Women: A Training Plan for Organizational Development in India." Report prepared for USAID/India, International Center for Research on Women, Washington, D.C.

Staudt, K. A. 1982. "Bureaucratic Resistance to Women's Programs: The Case of Women in Development," In *Women, Power, and Politics,* edited by E. Boneparth, 263–79. New York: Pergamon Press.

Sundar, P. 1983. "Women's Employment and Organization Modes." *Economic and Political Weekly* 18 (48): 171–75.

Tendler, J. 1982. "Turning Private Voluntary Organizations into Development Agencies: Questions for Evaluation." *AID Program Evaluation Paper no. 12.* Washington, D.C.: U.S. Agency for International Development.

Weeks-Vagliani, W. 1984. "The Integration of Women in Development Projects." Paris, Organization for Economic Co-operation and Development.

Wipper, A. 1975. "The Maendaleo ya Wanawake Organization: The Co-optation of Leadership." *African Studies Review* 18:99–120.

Youssef, N., and A. LeBel. 1981. "Exploring Alternative Employment and Income Generation Opportunities for Honduran Women: Analysis and Recommendations." Report prepared for USAID/Honduras, International Center for Research on Women, Washington, D.C.

Youssef, N., J. Sebstad, and I. Nieves. 1980. "Keeping Women Out: A Structural Analysis of Women's Employment in Developing Countries." Mimeograph. International Center for Research on Women, Washington, D.C.

Zeidenstein, G. 1977. "Including Women in Development Efforts." In *The Population Council Annual Report 1977.* New York: Population Council.

22

Agricultural Extension in the Twenty-first Century

CHARLES H. ANTHOLT

In a world undergoing structural adjustment and market liberalization, the dominant public organizations serving agriculture (research, extension, credit) are being challenged to look for less costly and more pluralistic systems that can be privatized or served by nongovernmental organizations (NGOs). The United Kingdom, the Netherlands, and New Zealand, for example, are privatizing their agricultural extension systems, and the ripple effect of privatization is spilling over into foreign aid programs in Asia, Africa, and Latin America. In light of this rapidly changing global economic environment, there is a need to carefully examine the changing public and private roles of extension in developing countries. This chapter focuses on a number of complex issues facing public extension services, including the relevancy, responsiveness, and cost effectiveness of alternative extension models for developing countries in the twenty-first century.

The three objectives of this chapter are to trace the historical evolution of agricultural extension from 1945 to 1995, to examine the special problems facing extension in developing countries in the late 1990s, and to discuss alternative extension models for the twenty-first century. Special attention will be directed to Asia, because many Asian countries have had twenty to twenty-five years of experience with T&V (training and visit) extension programs.

HISTORICAL OVERVIEW

In the 1950s most agricultural extension services in newly developing countries were focused on export commodities, because that had been their focus during colonialism. But with the advent of foreign aid programs during the 1950s, agricultural extension advisers "swarmed over the developing world bringing U.S. and European 'know-how' to farmers of the tropics" (Evenson 1984, 350). These advisers and information specialists assumed that the simple act of strengthening national public extension services would lead to more rapid trans-

CHARLES H. ANTHOLT is a consultant living in the state of Washington.

fer and adoption of imported and existing technologies (i.e., technologies on the shelf) and to increased food production. The decade of the fifties has been described as the "golden age of extension," because there was a high degree of confidence in the ability of Western agricultural technology to solve the needs of the "hungry, poor, and ignorant" in the developing world (Britan 1985). The problem of developing agriculture was seen as one of accelerating the rate of growth of agricultural output and productivity via what came to be known as the "diffusion model" of agricultural development (Rogers 1962). In that model the process was conceived as a hierarchical, unidirectional process; it provided to traditional agricultures new technology, usually from the West, which was delivered to farmers by extension workers in departments of agriculture (Kearl 1991).

However, the results of village-level studies in the 1950s and early 1960s documented that peasant farmers were "poor but efficient," and that the lack of profitable technology was a major cause of agricultural stagnation. Schultz's pioneering book *Transforming Traditional Agriculture* (1964) drew on these studies to challenge the extension/diffusion model and urged developing countries and donors to shift their resources from extension to building agricultural research capacity. The rapid adoption of Green Revolution wheat and rice varieties in the late 1960s reinforced Schultz's basic argument by demonstrating the willingness and ability of small-scale farms to adopt new technology. These experiences, plus a number of studies that documented high returns to investments in agricultural research, gave rise to a better understanding of the critical role of research in developing countries. This shift in emphasis to research and technology development was reinforced by studies of the failure of agricultural extension to get agriculture moving in Latin America in the 1950s (Mosher 1957; Rice 1971). Likewise, the rise and fall of community development programs in Asia in the fifties and early sixties severely wounded the extension/diffusion model of agricultural development (Holdcroft 1984). The diffusion model obscures the fact that farmers are innovators, not just passive receptacles of information. This perception of farmers as receptacles of information limits the ability of extension institutions to be farm and farmer orientated (Roling 1991). Perhaps equally important has been this model's failure to promote farmers' involvement in determining the agendas, evaluating the performance, and financially supporting extension institutions.

Unfortunately, both of these legacies (diffusion and technology generation) generally reinforced the limited, linear, and sequential view of how information and knowledge need to be developed and made accessible to farmers—that is, from basic science to applied science to technological innovations to farmer recommendations. Nevertheless, in the early 1970s, after the first flush of the Green Revolution, there was a sense among many agriculturalists that there was a backlog of technology yet to be moved to farmers. It therefore followed that it was necessary to increase the intervention capacity of extension through more staff, more training, more buildings, more motorcycles, etc. At the same time, it was generally agreed that increased discipline in managing extension personnel would be needed to move this backlog of technology to farmers.

The T&V approach to extension management was introduced by Daniel Benor in 1967 in Turkey (Benor 1987). The aim of the T&V approach was to reform the *management* of extension systems and turn a cadre of poorly supervised, poorly motivated, and poorly trained field agents into effective technology transfer agents, through fortnightly training of agents, who then made regular visits to farmers, conveying clear extension messages (Hulme 1991). While the World Bank had supported agricultural extension from 1964, Bank support for extension increased rapidly in the seventies in Asia, and in Africa in the eighties. By 1989 the Bank, through freestanding extension projects and extension components in other projects, had disbursed about $3 billion, primarily using the T&V model (or a somewhat modified T&V model) for reforming and strengthening of agricultural extension services (World Bank 1994).

ASSESSMENT OF EXTENSION PERFORMANCE

We shall summarize two major strands of literature in drawing lessons from extension experience. The first is a World Bank global assessment of Bank-funded extension projects that were completed and evaluated covering a fifteen-year period, 1977–92. The second draws on Asia's experience with the training and visit model of agricultural extension.[1] We turn now to the World Bank's global evaluation.

Lessons from World Bank Extension Projects, 1977–1992

The most comprehensive global review of agricultural extension in developing countries was completed by the Operations Evaluation Department (OED) of the World Bank in 1994 (World Bank 1994). Between 1977 and 1992 the Bank committed US$3 billion to extension projects. The OED review covered 107 Bank-funded extension projects that had been completed and evaluated. Some of the issues that are currently of great concern to agriculturalists and environmentalists (e.g., the role of women, environmental concerns, and the role of NGOs) were not extensively treated in the evaluation. Since the quantification of the impact of extension in economic terms is normally not undertaken in either ex ante or ex post evaluation of extension projects,[2] the Bank evaluators used subjective methods to assess the relevance, efficiency, and efficacy of different extension approaches in meeting project objectives.

The highlights of the World Bank review of the 107 completed extension projects were as follows:

- The extension projects supported by the Bank performed as well as the Bank's agricultural sector portfolio as a whole. However, funding shortfalls were "common phenomena"; in over 70 percent of freestanding projects sustainability was considered either uncertain or unlikely.

- Insufficiency of relevant technology was frequently a problem, linkages with research were generally weak, and "with few exceptions" little attention was given in project design or implementation to enlisting the participation of farmers in problem definition, problem solving, and extension programming.

The evaluation identified the following limitations of the T&V approach:

- The model was rigid and was often not appropriate, given the variation in cultural, historical, and institutional factors among and within countries.
- Problems of recurrent cost funding, lack of appropriate technology, and deficiencies in staff quality threatened the long-term sustainability of extension programs.
- The T&V concept of using a contact farmer as the primary recipient of extension visits (for subsequent transfer of technology to other farmers) was not very effective and was often replaced with farmer groups.
- A top down approach to delivering extension messages was often based on standard packages of recommendations that ignored the heterogeneity among farmers.

The findings of the OED study did not "support a single extension model [with] sufficient superior qualities to justify its uniform adoption in an extension service in all smallholder farmer circumstances" (World Bank 1994). The major implication of this important conclusion is that more attention should be given to the client, what Robert Chambers has coined the "farmer first" approach of developing appropriate technology (Chambers 1983). More emphasis should also be given to pre-project analysis. This experimental and participatory approach to designing country-specific extension models is consistent with the proposal for a new project cycle, which relies on cycles of experimentation, evaluation, learning, and redesign prior to mainstreaming (de Capitani and North 1994).

ASIA'S EXPERIENCE WITH T&V EXTENSION

The second body of literature and experience that can be used to evaluate the performance of various extension systems is Asia's experience with the training and visit approach. There can be no question that the T&V approach has had considerable influence on extension services in Asia, despite the controversy and the debate about it (Roberts 1980; Howell 1988). Perhaps the most useful result of the debate concerning T&V has been the focusing of attention on the more systemic problems of extension, not just the organization and management arrangements used (Hulme 1991).

Nevertheless, there is widespread dissatisfaction with T&V and extension in general in Asia. The literature makes it clear that a number of observers, researchers, and evaluators have reached conclusions that need to be debated in order to help design more appropriate extension models for the twenty-first century. Some of the more important findings are:

- In Pakistan T&V had no impact in the Punjab province (Khan, Sharif, and Sarwar 1984). T&V focused too much on process and not enough on "increasing the relevance of technology messages and different methods of transferring them to farmers" (Bartlett 1987).
- In Indonesia T&V was unable to make an impact in non-rice, dryland, multisystem crops (Pusat Pengembangan Agribisnis 1989).
- In rainfed and less well-endowed areas of Andhra Pradesh, India, T&V was found to have no effect on agricultural productivity (Sanghi 1989). In comparing the relative growth in wheat yields and agricultural gross domestic product for Haryana, which used T&V, with Punjab, a non-T&V state, it cannot be concluded that T&V made a difference, in spite of the attention, additional investment, and new life that T&V brought to extension in the Haryana (Antholt 1990). A recent review of West Bengal, Bihar, Kerala, Maharashtra, and Tamil Nadu in India could not identify a clear causal connection between incremental productivity and incremental investment in establishing the T&V system. This is true in spite of ten years of effort and the provision of relatively intensive extension services to farmers in three of the states—Maharashtra, Kerala, and Tamil Nadu (World Bank 1991a).
- After ten years, T&V in the Terai of Nepal was found to have had no impact on changing wheat yields, the principal winter season thrust area for extension (World Bank 1992).
- Thailand moved to a "participatory farmer planning" approach after trying T&V for five years in the early 1980s (Chumsri 1992). While rice yields increased by 1.0–1.7 percent per year in the ten years after the introduction of T&V in 1980, and crop diversification and cropping intensity also increased, these changes could not be linked reliably to the investments in extension (World Bank 1991b).
- In 1984, Malaysia decided T&V was not a workable model and changed to a market-driven commercial approach linked to groups (Abas 1992).

There are two additional, general observations about T&V that also need to be made:

- First, T&V projects almost universally have been associated with large increases in government staff. In the Indian state of Tamil Nadu, for example, the number of village extension officers increased from 1,730 to 4,000; in Madhya Pradesh the number increased from 6,932 to 14,525. These extension departments historically have had problems providing sufficient operational funds for travel, demonstrations, etc., and expanding staff makes this problem even more acute. Lack of operational funds tends to perpetuate itself, because it severely limits extension's ability to be responsive to client needs. Under those circumstances, extension is unable to establish the political base necessary to ensure long-term financial support above what is necessary to meet salary needs.
- Secondly, T&V projects have tended to further institutionalize hierarchical

tendencies already existing for top down, centralized management, despite clear aims to the contrary. Bureaucrats appreciated the T&V approach because it was a new means by which to hold staff accountable (Sims and Leonard 1990). Similarly, research in Pakistan found that "the pattern of internal communication in the Department of Agriculture is asymmetric (geared to control rather than to create an understanding) and top to bottom" (Nayman 1988). Observers in Indonesia noted that the top down flow of information, which stemmed from national planning objectives, did not necessarily reflect the objectives of farmers (Drysdale and Shute 1989), and, because of the limitations inherent in a centrally controlled and centrally managed extension service, extension was unable to deal effectively with the site-specific needs of farmers' problems and opportunities (Fisher 1988; Manwan et al. 1988). Given the seasonality of work loads, the heterogeneity of agroecological systems, changing market conditions, and the difficulties of travel, extension services must be decentralized and made more flexible—and more timely (Moris 1988; Antholt 1991).

Kearl (1991) found that, despite its high visibility and controversial reviews, the T&V approach is no longer at the center of discussion. He suggested that T&V is too narrow a model for most situations and therefore of limited utility, particularly under circumstances of considerable farm-level heterogeneity. But Kearl did not go far enough. Not only is the model too narrow, but T&V's management response to the problems of extension has failed to address adequately the underlying systemic problems confounding extension, for example, lack of relevant technology, poorly trained and poorly motivated staff, and insufficient operational resources (Antholt 1991). In most Asian extension systems, the criticism of T&V needs to be redirected to the underlying systemic problems facing extension. Unfortunately, there has been a delay in the recognition and confrontation of the more fundamental issues facing extension.

Further debate concerning T&V is not likely to be very fruitful. T&V needs to be put behind and attention turned to developing public and private services that are relevant, responsive, and cost-effective with respect to enhancing the knowledge base of farmers.

POLICY ISSUES AND CHOICES

GENERAL CONSIDERATIONS

Governments and donors have been reasonably generous in supporting research and extension since the 1960s. Given the strategic importance of technical change in agriculture, it is important to be concerned about the continuation of support for these activities. Nevertheless, with increasing frequency there is a level of frustration and fatigue expressed at the seemingly never-ending discussions about, and projects for, extension. The frustration and fatigue are acknowledged, but given the lack of alternatives to science-based, knowledge-intensive paths for further agriculture development, it is argued, these anxieties must not detract from future support by donors and host countries.

We start by pointing out once again the importance of getting the technology right in the first instance, whether it is evolved over time by farmers themselves, borrowed directly from other parts of the world, or borrowed and then locally adapted. Indeed, this need and the need to have a competent, first-rate capacity to seek out and adapt or to develop technology, are strategic needs for most countries that are dependent significantly on their agricultural sectors. That is not to say that other factors—such as macroeconomic policies, commodity price policies, infrastructure development, input availabilities—can be ignored. But given the current and future demands on agriculture in Asia, there is no alternative but to rely heavily on developing institutions, public and private, that are creative, foster excellence, and are entrepreneurial and agile in the use of scientific resources to solve old problems or meet new opportunities. And that does not imply business as usual.

Secondly, we need also to be reminded that "extension is only one of a number of factors that contribute to increased farm productivity" (Cernea, Coulter, and Russell 1984). This is not to say that extension can be ignored, or that new investments in extension are not needed; but it does put a premium on ensuring that extension services are as relevant, responsive, and cost-effective as possible. In hindsight, it is clear that too much emphasis was given to expanding extension services, particularly in the number of staff, and not enough emphasis was placed on the qualitative dimensions of extension. Consequently there remains much to do, and in some cases to undo, to ensure that farmers rapidly become better acquainted with better technology, learn important principles and practices, and learn how to organize to help themselves—and all in an affordable, sustainable manner.

ACCOUNTABILITY TO FARMERS

The most important policy initiative that is needed in extension is to shift the primary focus of power and responsibility for extension to the clients. To borrow Robert Chambers' phrase, we need to "put the farmer first" (Chambers 1983). There is abundant evidence that the "normal" incentive system facing government employees, even under the most enlightened circumstances, puts a premium on not making a mistake and on length of service but not necessarily on service to clients, particularly small farmers. This is not acceptable and does not have to be taken as inevitable. Sims and Leonard (1990) found that the most important determinant of extension success is the strength of farmer organization.

The opposite side of the accountability coin is expecting the beneficiaries of extension to be responsible for some of the support, even if it is only a proportion of total costs. This is important for three reasons. First, it gives the beneficiaries ownership and drawing rights on the services. Second, it takes some of the financial pressure off the central government and therefore gets at the issue of financial sustainability. Lastly, if ownership and responsibility rest with clients, the basis for more demand-driven, responsive service is established. An example of this is the National Farmers' Association of Zimbabwe (Amanor and Farrington 1991).

Another scenario using this approach might be for extension departments to develop cooperative or contractual agreements with local bodies, as in China. Under such arrangements local organizations might take responsibility for provision of their own extension services, but the center would reimburse the local entities for some percentage of their costs. Alternatively, as in some areas of China or in Ecuador (Van Crowder 1991), an arrangement to share in the output of the farming enterprise can be devised.

Another alternative is seen in Chile: contracting with private firms or NGOs for the provision of extension services. The government's role is to lay out the ground rules for service, select consultant firms through competitive bidding, evaluate performance, and subsidize the cost of the services. Consultants carry out the technical extension services, and farmers contract with the firm of their choice (Venenzian 1992). The exact form is not so important, but the bottom line must result in putting farmers in the driver's seat.

The exact nature of the accountability and responsibility relationships will vary from country to country. This does not matter. Of central importance is the need to ensure that the relevance and responsiveness of extension, as viewed by farmers, clearly and meaningfully affects the welfare of extension personnel involved. Furthermore, it needs to be ensured that farmers have some responsibility for support as well. This does not mean that a farmer is charged every time extension workers stop by, but it does mean going beyond talking about putting farmers first to developing practical, tangible means to do so. Perhaps more applicable for Asia, however, is the Chilean model, which basically relies on the private advisory services for frontline extension work, although there is cost-sharing between the government and farmers, the proportion of which is dependent on the amount of land owned by the farmer.

Contemporary extension organizations, particularly their leadership, should take the lead in developing the environment necessary for encouraging private companies, local communities, NGOs, and groups to assume greater responsibility for some of the extension functions. However, it is important for extension leadership to take the lead, in order to control the pace and shape of this kind of change. Not to do so is to invite others to take the lead. Surely the forces of change stemming from budgetary constraints or the movements toward greater decentralization that are going on, as in Indonesia, Philippines, Karnatake state in India, and Sri Lanka, will dictate these changes. However, given the conservative tendencies and internal interests of ministries of agriculture, this is unlikely to happen without outside encouragement.

MANAGEMENT

There is a management crisis in public extension systems. Improving management of agricultural public services is an often-stated objective for most governments, but at any given point in time the particular issues and tactics change. For example, in extension, T&V was a management response to problems perceived to be important in the late 1960s and the 1970s. However, as Nogueira (1990) notes, a management response such as T&V, which in effect seeks to reinforce centralized management, never really could be a viable response given the multiplicity of participants, the location-specificity of agriculture, the formidable information constraints and the need for high levels of discretionary capability and authority. For these reasons, and the other systemic problems with extension pointed out by Antholt (1991), particularly the availability of technology and the incentive structures facing extension agents in the field, a management response to extension has proved insufficient. Indeed, such a response is a misdiagnosis of the nature of the problems facing extension and not the right solution.

However, we do not mean to suggest that management issues do not need to be tackled. Rather, efforts directed at better management only pay off significantly if the more problematic, systemic issues of extension can be dealt with first. The problem is that, too often, a management response such as T&V or adoption of the form (but not the substance) of the U.S. land grant system is thought to be sufficient. Clearly that is not the case.

The size and complexity of almost all Asian public sector extension services have grown by orders of magnitude since the early 1960s. India, for example, has 88,000 extension workers. Unfortunately, most of the basic management systems used there have been more or less brought forward from even older management systems, and those primarily were concerned with control. Consequently, over time the management practices of public sector extension organizations have reduced flexibility and added to institutional rigidities.

RESEARCH-EXTENSION LINKAGES

The synergism between extension and research is well known and well recognized, but in practice there is often a lack of cooperation between research and extension. The systemic reasons for this lack of cooperation are well understood. Kaimowitz (1991) identifies five mechanisms to enhance linkages between research and extension: (1) integrate the organization, (2) establish liaison units, (3) organize committees for coordination purposes, (4) have members of the respective institutions carry out joint activities, and (5) communicate better. The implications of these tactical options are discussed extensively and sufficiently elsewhere (Sims and Leonard 1990; Roling 1991; Kaimowitz 1991; Eponou 1993). What is required now is something more than monthly meetings and technical committees.

In countries where there is institutional separation between research and extension, none of the mechanisms Kaimowitz mentions, including integration, seem to have been particularly successful. Nevertheless, one step toward breaking down these boundaries would be to make it professionally advantageous for individual scientists and extension personnel to have assignments in each other's organizations. But this is only one step and it may not prove any more success-ful than some of the other mechanisms that have been tried. In any case, the bot-tom line is that the incentive environment facing research and extension profes-sionals, and their respective institutions, has to provide value to those individuals and institutions who enhance research and extension linkages. Institutional rigidities and the lack of a universal prescriptive solution to this problem will make such enhancement difficult. The seriousness of the disjunction between re-search and extension clearly needs to be recognized. That is seldom the case. There also must be widespread political support and pressure, particularly from the clients, for satisfactory resolution of the issue.

RECRUITMENT

In the long run, extension systems most certainly will be called on to do more with less. It is not unreasonable to expect the overall numbers of extension per-sonnel in government service to decline by more than 50 percent from today's levels. Since the core staff who will be in place ten to fifteen years from now will be recruited in the next few years, it is imperative that the standards of re-cruitment be reviewed and revised. Given the likely demands of agriculture in the early part of the twenty-first century, new professionals must have a capaci-ty to (1) work under complex and fluid circumstances with little supervision, (2) listen to and learn from farmers, (3) diagnose farmers' problems effectively, (4) communicate effectively and work with farmers and farm groups, and (5) pre-sent options, based on principles of good agricultural practices, that widen the range of choices available to farm families.

A bachelor of science degree is not always essential for an extension adviser. For example, Lionberger and Chang (1970) found that 95 percent of the exten-sion agents in Taiwan had a vocational agriculture background. This would not be possible in South Asia, where vocational schools are generally substandard. On the other hand, B.Sc. degrees in South Asia do not have much practical con-tent. Under these circumstances it is particularly important that practical farm-ing experience be given a fair amount of weight in the recruitment process. Li-onberger and Chang also found that nine out of ten Taiwanese extension agents were brought up on farms.

A significant percentage of the future extension staff should be female.[3] While this chapter does not address the gender issue specifically, relevant, responsive, and effective extension services in the twenty-first century need to have the ca-pacity to serve male and female farmers and the needs of rural households. Therefore, from both the qualitative dimension and the gender perspective, re-cruitment of women extension workers is a policy issue of considerable impor-tance. Given that most extension systems are stuck with the current staffing pro-file, that is, a low level of competency as well as a male-dominated cadre that is likely to weigh the systems down for some time, it is essential to change the re-cruitment system in the near future.

Beyond T&V Extension: Insights from Bangladesh

Bangladesh's experience with extension is of general interest to agricultural scientists, donors, and students because the government has moved beyond T&V and developed a new national extension strategy that is less costly, more demand-driven, more decentralized, and relies heavily on NGOs. A recent paper by Chowdhury and Gilbert (1996) pulls together the main lessons from Bangladesh's extension experience over the past twenty years, traces the rise and fall of T&V, and summarizes the components of the new national extension strategy that is now being implemented. The authors raise a number of concerns about the future willingness of the government extension agents and the NGOs to work together and the skills required for effective participation of NGOs; and they point out that "nurturing, patience and persistence" will be required by both the government and NGOs to operationalize the new strategy.[4]

Bangladesh is a nation of about 118 million people in a land area about the size of the state of Wisconsin in the United States. In the mid-1970s, Bangladesh had six different agencies under the Ministry of Agriculture providing extension advice to farmers about crop production. Because of the confusion and the duplication inherent in this system, the government reorganized its extension service in 1977 and introduced the T&V system with World Bank support, charging the system with helping to increase agricultural production. The basic features of the T&V system were first introduced in the northwest region of the country and then expanded to forty-six of the sixty-four districts by 1982. With World Bank assistance, the government increased the number of extension workers and provided improved mobility and supervision. By 1991 the system covered the entire country, and the overall ratio of extension worker to farm families was approximately 1:1,000.

In practice the T&V system fit in well with the bureaucratic norms of the public sector, where programs were planned at the center. The T&V approach was also consistent with the development thinking of the 1970s, in which the state played a central role in development and little attention was given to the possible contribution of NGOs in extension activities or to private firms in input delivery and marketing.[5] The T&V emphasized regular extension agent and farmer training, regular contact with extension and research staff, and it provided improved transport and housing to extension workers. However, the T&V system had several major weaknesses, including its emphasis on delivering routine messages to farmers and failing to take farmers' constraints and priorities into account. Also, the use of contact farmers proved to be ineffective, and the program proved to be costly and was not financially sustainable. Finally, the impact of T&V on agricultural production in Bangladesh was mixed. Several scholars have argued that the improvements in agricultural production and productivity that occurred were largely traceable to the expansion of farmer networks and the spread of shallow tube wells, coupled with the dramatic increase in the use of fertilizer and the spread of new rice varieties, particularly *pajam*—not an "approved" or extension promoted variety.

In 1991 the shortcomings of the T&V system of extension were acknowledged in the design of an Agricultural Support Services Project (World Bank 1991c). The project design report "called for a fundamental change in the approach from that of a supply-driven, top-down approach to one that was bottom-up and demand-driven (i.e., reflecting the needs articulated by farmers)" (Chowdhury and Gilbert 1996).

Chowdhury and Gilbert concluded that the demise of T&V in Bangladesh was traceable as much to the changing view of the state in development as to the shortcomings of the model itself. They report that "the government together with donors is no longer willing or able to continue to support the extension service at current levels."

Bangladesh's new extension strategy includes the following reforms and institutional innovations: greater decentralization of authority and accountability from the center to the districts; use of groups of farmers rather than contact farmers; demand-driven extension methods and recommendations; broader participation of the private sector, including NGOs; a sharper focus on the disadvantaged, including women; and greater emphasis on financial sustainability. Although these reforms and innovations appear to be headed in the right direction, Chowdhury and Gilbert note that "there is still no clear vision of the roles of NGOs and private commercial firms in providing extension services for farmers" and that the "sustainability of new extension approaches is especially problematic at this stage of the process." They also point out that greater decentralization may adversely offset accountability and that "the extent to which field extension workers are accountable to clients at the local level appears to be mainly a matter of their own choosing."

CONCLUSION

The challenges of growth, sustainability, and poverty facing Asian agricultural systems remain. Hence the strategic importance of agricultural extension is greater than ever. These challenges will need to be met in a faster-moving, more interdependent world, in which public sector support is likely to be less generous. It seems clear that thinking about agricultural extension services needs to have conceptual horizons broader than the conventional public sector. It also follows that more attention needs to be given to financing.

The time for change is now, given the long gestation periods for institutional modernization. Below are some general parameters for the future that will provide useful guidance for contemporary policy changes and investment initiatives.

- Farmers need to come first. This means placing real ownership of, and accountability for, public extension organizations into the hands of the client community, particularly farmers (but agribusiness as well).
- Competition in provision of extension services needs to be fostered through pluralism in the provision of extension services.

- Pluralism means redefining the role of the public and private sectors in extension and, in particular, enhancing the role of the private sector through privatization, particularly of frontline extension.
- Mechanisms for public support—for example, vouchers, cost sharing, local taxes—need to be developed whereby farmers, farm organizations, and farming communities can draw on public resources to be used by them for extension services of their choice (public or private).
- Current public extension systems need to be downsized.

Leadership and initiative from the public sector, agribusiness, and farmers will be required in order to achieve these changes. Donors can help as well. Difficult decisions are called for. It will not be easy for the public sector to downsize, develop an institutional and personal stake in how farmers view their performance, and accept the increasing role of the private sector. Farmers and agribusiness, on the other hand, will have to recognize that to own, control, and obtain the benefits they want from these services, the previous "free lunch" is not good enough, and that for the future they must take some responsibility for support of extension. That is not to say the public sector will be unimportant, but that in the future the public sector needs to confine itself to those activities it must do, such as informational activities that have significant economies of scale, and to being a catalyst in seeing that extension services are adequate, available, relevant, and responsive to the needs of farmers and agribusiness.

NOTES

This chapter draws on Antholt 1990, 1991, 1992, and 1994. The views expressed are those of the author and do not necessarily reflect the official views of the World Bank.

1. The major public agricultural institutions supporting agriculture in Africa (e.g., research, extension, credit, fertilizer delivery) are currently being subjected to careful scrutiny in light of policy reforms and a reduction in the size of the state bureaucracy. For a discussion of agricultural research and extension issues in sub-Saharan Africa see Eicher 1989, Cleaver 1993, and Rukuni 1996.

2. For a survey of studies of the economics of extension see Birkhaeuser, Evenson, and Feder 1991. A team studying two similar districts in India found a high probability of at least a 15 percent return on the incremental investment in T&V (Feder, Lau, and Slade 1987).

3. In Bangladesh 560 of the 12,000 extension workers were female in the early nineties (Chowdhury and Gilbert 1996).

4. These operational issues are remarkably similar to those identified by Farrington (1995) and by Rukuni (1996) in southern Africa.

5. There are an estimated 30,000 NGOs in Bangladesh of which more than 6,000 are registered with the government's NGO Bureau.

REFERENCES

Abas, M. 1992. "Strengthening Extension Capacity in Developing Countries." Paper, University of the Philippines, Los Baños.

Amanor, K., and J. Farrington. 1991. "NGOs and Agricultural Technology Development." In *Agricultural Extension: Worldwide Institutional Evolution and Forces for Change,* edited by William Rivera and Dan Gustafson. New York: Elsevier.

Antholt, Charles H. 1990. "Strategic Issues for Agricultural Extension in Pakistan: Looking Back to Look Ahead." In proceedings from a seminar entitled "Productivity through Agricultural Extension in Pakistan," Islamabad, March.

———. 1991. "Agricultural Extension in the Twenty-first Century: Lessons from South Asia." In *Agricultural Extension: Worldwide Institutional Evolution and Forces for Change,* edited by William Rivera and Dan Gustafson. New York: Elsevier.

———. 1992. "Relevancy, Responsiveness, and Cost-Effectiveness: Lessons for Agricultural Extension in the Twenty-first Century." Revised version of a paper presented at the seminar "Strengthening Extension Capacity in Developing Countries," University of the Philippines, Los Baños, February 17–22.

———. 1994. "Getting Ready for the Twenty-first Century: Technical Change and Institutional Modernization in Agriculture." Technical Paper no. 217, World Bank, Washington, D.C.

Bartlett, A. 1987. *Baluchistan Agricultural Extension and Adaptive Research Project: Modifying the Training and Visit System.* Islamabad, Pakistan: National Agricultural Research Center Training Institute.

Benor, Daniel, 1987. "Training and Visit: Back to Basics." In *Agricultural Extension Worldwide: Issues, Practices and Emerging Priorities,* edited by William Rivera and Susan Schram, 137–48. London: Croom Helm.

Birkhaeuser, Dean, Robert E. Evenson, and Gershon Feder. 1991. "The Economic Impact of Agricultural Extension: A Review." *Economic Development and Cultural Change* 39 (3): 607–50.

Britan, Gerald M. 1985. "AID's Experience in Agricultural Extension." Paper presented to the Joint Committee for Agricultural Research and Development, Washington, D.C.

Cernea, M. M., J. Coulter, and J. Russell. 1984. *Agricultural Extension by Training and Visit: The Asian Experience.* Washington, D.C.: World Bank.

Chambers, Robert, 1983. *Rural Development: Putting the Last First.* London: Longman.

Chowdhury, Mrinal K., and Elon H. Gilbert. 1996. "Reforming Agricultural Extension in Bangladesh: Blending Greater Participation and Sustainability with Institutional Strengthening." Agricultural Research and Extension Network. Paper no. 61. London: Overseas Development Institute.

Chumsri, S. 1992. Comments made at the seminar "Strengthening Extension Capacity in Developing Countries," University of the Philippines, Los Baños, February 17–21.

Cleaver, Kevin, 1993. "Making Agricultural Extension Work in Africa." In *Policy Options for Agricultural Development in Sub-Saharan Africa,* edited by Nathan C. Russell and Christopher R. Dowswell, 75–82. Mexico, D.F.: CASIN/SAA/Global 2000.

de Capitani, Alberto, and Douglass C. North. 1994. "Institutional Development in Third World Countries: The Role of the World Bank." Human Resources Working Paper, World Bank, Washington, D.C.

Drysdale, A. M., and J. C. M. Shute. 1989. "Efficiency and Effectiveness of Agricultural Extension in Indonesia: A Case Study." *Journal of Extension Systems* 5 (2) December.

Eicher, Carl K. 1989. *Sustainable Institutions for African Agricultural Development.* Working Paper no. 19. The Hague: ISNAR.

Eponou, Thomas. 1993. *Partners in Agricultural Technology: Linking Research and Technology Transfer to Serve Farmers.* ISNAR Research Report no. 1, ISNAR, The Hague.

Evenson, Robert E. 1984. "Benefits and Obstacles in Developing Appropriate Agricultural Technology." In *Agricultural Development in the Third World,* edited by Carl K. Eicher and John M. Staatz, 348–61. Baltimore: Johns Hopkins University Press.

Farrington, John, 1995. "The Changing Public Role in Agricultural Extension." *Food Policy* 20 (6): 537–44.

Feder, G., L. J. Lau, and R. H. Slade. 1987. "Does Agricultural Extension Pay? The Training and Visit System in Northwest India." *American Journal of Agricultural Economics* 69:677–86.

Fisher, Larry A. 1988. Priorities for Marginal Farmers and Marginal Lands: Reflections on Challenges and Opportunities for the Ford Foundation. Memo to David Winder, Resident Representative, Ford Foundation, June 2, Jakarta.

Holdcroft, Lane. 1984. "The Rise and Fall of Community Development, 1950–65: A Critical Assessment." In *Agricultural Development in the Third World,* edited by Carl K. Eicher and John M. Staatz, 46–58. Baltimore: Johns Hopkins University Press.

Howell, J. 1988. "Training and Visit Extension in Practice." Occasional Paper 8, Overseas Development Institute, London.

Hulme, David. 1991. "Agricultural Extension Services as Machines: The Impact of the Training and Visit Approach, Agricultural Extension Worldwide: A Critical Turning Point." In *Agricultural Extension: Worldwide Institutional Evolution and Forces for Change,* edited by William Rivera and Dan Gustafson. New York: Elsevier.

Kaimowitz, David. 1991. "The Evolution of Links between Research and Extension in Developing Countries." In *Agricultural Extension: Worldwide Institutional Evolution and Forces for Change,* edited by William Rivera and Dan Gustafson. New York: Elsevier.

Kearl, Bryant, 1991. "Evolution in Thinking about the Extension Function." Unpublished paper based on the March 28–30, 1991 meeting of the Association for International Agricultural and Extension Education, St. Louis, Missouri.

Khan, M., M. Sharif, and M. Sarwar. 1984. "Monitoring and Evaluation of Training and Visit System of Agricultural Extension in Punjab, Pakistan." Lahore, Pakistan: Economics Research Institute.

Lionberger, Herbert, and H. C. Chang. 1970. *Farm Information for Modernizing Agriculture: The Taiwan System.* New York: Praeger.

Manwan, Ibrahim, Krisnawati Suryanata, David S. McCauley, and M. Husein Sawit. 1988. "Kepas Study on an Agro-ecosystems Approach to Dealing with Diversity in the Uplands of East Java: Summary and Conclusions." In *An Agrosystems Approach to Dealing with Diversity in the Uplands of Java: Results of an Agrosystems Analysis in the Uplands of East Java,* edited by Ibrahim Manwan et al.. Jakarta, Indonesia: Agency of Agricultural Research and Development, and the Ford Foundation.

Moris, Jon R. 1988. "The Demand System in Agricultural Extension." London: Overseas Development Institute.

Mosher, Arthur T. 1957. *Technical Co-operation in Latin American Agriculture.* Chicago: University of Chicago Press.

Nayman, Oguz B. 1988. "Seekers of Light." An Evaluation of Official and Non-official Sources of Agricultural Information, Lahore, Punjab, Pakistan." Colorado State University Project.

Nogueira, Martinez, 1990. "The Effect of Changes in State Policy and Organization on Agricultural Research and Extension Links: A Latin American Perspective." In *Making the Link: Agricultural Research and Technology Transfer in Developing Countries,* edited by David Kaimowitz. Boulder, Colo.: Westview Press.

Pusat Pengembangan Agribisnis. 1989. *The Study and Evaluation of the Training and Visit System and Selected Extension Methods, Republic of Indonesia.* Jakarta: Ministry of Agriculture.

Rice, E. B. 1971. "Extension in the Andes: An Evaluation of Official U.S. Assistance to Agricultural Extension Services in Central and South America." AID Evaluation Paper no. 3A, Agency for International Development, Washington, D.C.

Roberts, Nigel, ed. 1989. *Agricultural Extension in India.* Washington, D.C.: World Bank.

Rogers, Everett M. 1962. *Diffusion of Innovations.* New York: Free Press.

Roling, Niels. 1991. "The Emergence of Knowledge Systems Thinking: The Changing Perception of the Relationships between Innovation, Knowledge Process, and Institutions in the Search for an Effective Diagnostic Framework," Department of Extension Science, Agricultural University Wageningen, Wageningen, The Netherlands.

Rukuni, Mandivamba. 1996. "A Framework for Crafting Demand-Driven National Agricultural Research Institutions in Southern Africa." Staff Paper no. 96–76, Department of Agricultural Economics, Michigan State University, East Lansing.

Sanghi, N. K. 1989. "Changes in the Organization of Research on Dryland Agriculture." In *Farmer First: Farmer Innovation and Agriculture Research,* edited by R. Chambers et al. London: Intermediate Technology Publications.

Schultz, Theodore W. 1964. *Transforming Traditional Agriculture.* New Haven: Yale University Press.

Sims, Holly, and David Leonard, 1990. "The Political Economy of the Development and Transfer of Agricultural Technologies." In *Making the Link: Agricultural Research and Technology Transfer in Developing Countries,* edited by David Kaimowitz. Boulder, Colo.: Westview Press.

Van Crowder, L. 1991. "Extension for Profit: Agents and Sharecropping in the Highlands of Ecuador." *Human Organization* 50 (1).

Venenzian, Eduardo L. 1992. *Agricultural Research in a Growing Economy: The Case of Chile, 1970–1990.* Washington, D.C.: Agriculture Division, Technical Department, Latin American and Caribbean Regional Office, World Bank.

World Bank. 1991a. "Agricultural Research and Extension in India." *OED Precis.* Washington, D.C.: Operations Evaluation Department, World Bank.

———. 1991b "Project Performance Audit Report, Thailand: National Agricultural Extension II Project (Loan 1752-IND)." Washington, D.C.: Operations Evaluation Department, World Bank.

———. 1991c. "Staff Appraisal Report, Bangladesh." Washington, D.C.: World Bank.

———. 1992. "Projected Performance Report, Nepal -Agricultural Extension and Research Project (Cr. 1100-NEP), Hill Food Production Project (Cr. 1101-NEP) and Cash Crop Development Project (Cr. 1339-NEP)." (Draft.) Washington, D.C.: Operations Evaluation Department, World Bank.

———. 1994. *Agricultural Extension: Lessons from Completed Projects.* Washington, D.C.: World Bank.

23

How Do Market Failures
Justify Interventions
in Rural Credit Markets?

TIMOTHY J. BESLEY

Understanding of the economic causes and consequences of market failure in credit markets has progressed a great deal in recent years. This article draws on these developments to appraise the case for government intervention in rural financial markets in developing countries and to discover whether the theoretical findings can be used to identify directives for policy.

Before debating the when and how of intervention, the article defines market failure, emphasizing the need to consider the full array of constraints that combine to make a market work imperfectly. The various reasons for market failure are discussed and set in the context in which credit markets function in developing countries. The article then looks at recurrent problems that may be cited as failures of the market justifying intervention. Among these problems are enforcement; imperfect information, especially adverse selection and moral hazard; the risk of bank runs; and the need for safeguards against the monopoly power of some lenders. The review concludes with a discussion of interventions, focusing on the learning process that must take place for financial markets to operate effectively.

Interventions in rural credit markets in developing countries are common and take many forms. Chief among them is government ownership of banks; India and Mexico, for example, nationalized their major banks in 1969 and 1982, respectively. In these cases the government can compel its banks to set up branches in rural areas and to lend to farmers. Governments in other countries, such as Nigeria, have imposed a similar obligation on commercial banks (see Okorie 1990). So the presence of a bank in a particular area is not sufficient reason to assume that the bank has chosen to operate there or that it is operating profitably.

TIMOTHY J. BESLEY is professor of economics at the London School of Economics.

Previously published in The World Bank Research Observer 9, no. 1 (1994): 27–47. Published with minor editorial revisions by permission of the World Bank and the author.

Regulations have also affected the day-to-day operation of banking. Straight-forward subsidization of credit is a standard policy in many countries; one example is the system established by the government of the Philippines in which low-interest loans are financed by a low interest rate paid on deposits (World Bank 1987). Charging below-market interest rates generates excess demand for credit, and as a result bank operations have often been governed by rules for the selective allocation of credit; the Masagna-99 program that targeted rice farmers in the Philippines is a case in point. More generally, Filipino banks were required to allocate 25 percent of all loans to the agricultural sector, and the government has also limited their flexibility to set interest rates and lend according to private profitability. Foreign and private banks in India have also faced restrictions on the extent of their lending activity (India 1991).

Various governments have also required that lenders insure their loan portfolios. The apex agricultural bank in India has insured loans in agriculture for amounts up to 75 percent of outstanding overdues. Similar policies were pursued in Mexico, where the principal agricultural lender has had its loan portfolio compulsorily insured by a government-owned insurer. Because default rates on rural loans are typically quite high, such schemes also provide an explicit subsidy to rural financial institutions.

Thus, it seems fair to say that rural credit markets in developing countries have rarely operated on a commercial basis. Substantial subsidies are often implicit in the regulation schemes. A traditional view would see these interventions as part and parcel of development policy throughout much of the postwar era: an actively interventionist government controlling the commanding heights of the economy and taking the lead in opening up new sectors.

It is widely recognized that such policies, particularly below-market interest rates and selective allocation of credit, are not without cost. One view, associated with McKinnon (1973), is that these policies lead to financial repression: without a market allocation mechanism, savings and credit will be misallocated. Thus, it became popular to argue for financial liberalization and relaxation of government regulations, especially those that held interest rates on loans below market-clearing levels.

This type of intervention was also criticized by the Ohio State University group on the grounds that many of the policies were not consistent with such objectives as helping the poor (see, for example, Adams, Graham, and Von Pischke 1984). The group pointed to two central facets of many government-backed loan programs: first, default rates were typically very high, and, second, much of the benefit of these programs appeared to go to the wealthier farmers.

Criticism of existing policies has led to considerable rethinking about intervention in rural credit markets in developing countries. In particular, the view has gained ground that interventions should be restricted to cases where a market failure has been identified; this view is investigated here. The objective is to consider whether and how interventions can be—or are being—used to make up for shortcomings of existing (formal and informal) markets to allocate credit.

WHAT ARE MARKET FAILURES?

A market failure occurs when a competitive market fails to bring about an efficient allocation of credit. Credit, like other goods, has supply and demand. Some individuals must be willing to postpone some consumption so that others can either consume (with a consumption loan) or invest (with an investment loan). The price of credit—the interest rate at which a loan is granted—must therefore be high enough for some individuals to postpone their consumption and low enough for individuals who take out loans to be willing to repay, given their current consumption needs or investment opportunities.

In an idealized credit market, loans are traded competitively and the interest rate is determined through supply and demand. Because individuals with the best investment opportunities are willing to pay the highest interest rates, the best investment opportunities should theoretically be selected. Such a loan market would be efficient, in the standard economic sense of *Pareto efficiency;* that is, the market is efficient when it is not possible to make someone better off without making someone else worse off (no Pareto *improvement* is possible). Allowing two individuals to trade typically generates such an improvement. If one has an investment opportunity and no capital, for example, and the other has some capital, both may gain by having the second individual lend to the first. They need only find some way to share the gains from their trade for both to benefit. Both must be at least equally well off with the trade for them to participate in it voluntarily.

An outcome is thus Pareto efficient when all Pareto improvements are exhausted—which happens for credit when the loans cannot be reallocated to make one individual better off without making another worse off. In particular, Pareto efficiency is achieved when an individual who gets a loan has no incentive to resell it to another and become a lender himself.

The first fundamental welfare theorem says that competitive markets with no externalities yield a Pareto-efficient outcome. But the standard model of perfect competition, where large numbers of buyers and sellers engage in trade without transactions costs, has some deficiencies as a model for credit markets, both in theory and in practice. The waters are muddied in credit markets by the issue of repayment, because a debtor may be unable to repay (for instance, if he is hit by a shock such as bad weather or a fire) or unwilling to repay (if the lender has insufficient sanctions against delinquent borrowers). For the latter contingency, credit markets require a framework of legal enforcement. But if the costs of enforcement are too high, a lender may simply cease to lend—a situation that may well arise for poor farmers in developing countries.

Credit markets also diverge from an idealized market because information is imperfect. A lender's willingness to lend money to a particular borrower may hinge on having enough information about the borrower's reliability and on being sure that the borrower will use the borrowed funds wisely. The absence of good information may explain why lenders choose not to serve some individuals.

Efficiency in the allocation of credit has to be examined in light of these practical realities. Suppose, for example, that a bank is considering providing credit for a project to someone who, after receiving the loan, will choose how hard to work to make his project successful. If the project is successful, then the loan is repaid, but if it fails, the individual is assumed to default. As the size of the loan increases, the borrower's effort is likely to slacken, because a larger share of the proceeds of the project go to the bank. If the bank cannot monitor the borrower's actions (perhaps because doing so is prohibitively costly), a bigger loan tends to be associated with a lower probability of repayment. A bank that wants to maximize profits is therefore likely to offer a smaller loan than it would if monitoring were costless. This may result in less investment in the economy and, in comparison with a situation in which information is costless, would appear to entail a reduction in efficiency. With full information, the bank should be willing to lend more, to the advantage of both the borrower and the lender. Thus, tested against the benchmark of costless monitoring, there appears to be a market failure—that is, the market has not realized a potential Pareto improvement.

In the real world, monitoring is not costless and information and enforcement are not perfect. A standard of efficiency impossible to achieve in the real world is not a useful test against which to define market failure. The test of efficiency should still be that a Pareto improvement is impossible to find, but such an improvement must be sought taking into account the imperfections of information and enforcement that the market in question has to deal with—that is using the concept of *constrained Pareto efficiency.* By this standard, the outcome described above, where the lender reduced the amount lent to a borrower because of monitoring difficulties, could in fact be efficient in a constrained sense. The information problem may still have an efficiency cost to society, but from an operational point of view that cost has no relevance.

The argument that problems in credit markets result in a lower level of output, and perhaps too much risk-taking relative to some ideal situation in which information is freely available, is frequently used to justify subsidized credit or the establishment of government-owned banks in areas that appear to be poorly served by the public sector. This argument is a non sequitur and should be resisted whenever encountered. In thinking about market failure and constrained Pareto efficiency, the full set of feasibility constraints for allocating resources needs to be considered. In this article, market failure is taken to mean the inability of a free market to bring about a constrained Pareto-efficient allocation of credit, in the sense defined above (see Dixit 1987 for a sample formal analysis). The rest of the article examines the implications of this concept.

Applying the criterion of constrained Pareto efficiency narrows the field for market failure, but it still leaves room for a fairly broad array of cases in which resources could end up being inefficiently allocated. In the illustration of Pareto improvement used above, only the well-being of the two individuals involved in a trade was considered. But if externalities enter the picture—in other words, if a third party is affected, possibly negatively, by the decision of the other two—a

Pareto improvement is clearly not guaranteed, even if the two principals are made better off. It is well known that markets operate inefficiently if there are externalities (see Greenwald and Stiglitz 1986 for a general discussion), and specific types of externalities may particularly afflict credit markets. One important role for government policy to improve the working of credit markets is to deal impartially with externality problems.

SIGNIFICANT FEATURES OF RURAL CREDIT MARKETS

What makes rural credit markets in developing countries different from other credit markets? The three principal features distinguished here—collateral security, underdevelopment in complementary institutions, and covariant risks—characterize all credit markets to some extent. The distinction is in degree rather than in kind; these problems are felt much more acutely in rural credit markets, and in developing countries, than in other contexts in which credit markets operate. That is why those governments have regarded policy initiatives in this area as important.

Scarce Collateral

One solution to the repayment problem in credit markets is to have the borrower put up a physical asset that the lender can seize if the borrower defaults. Such assets are usually hard to come by in rural credit markets, partly because the borrowers are too poor to have assets that could be collateralized and partly because poorly developed property rights make appropriating collateral in the event of default difficult in rural areas of many developing countries. Improving the codification of land rights is often suggested, therefore, as a way to extend the domain of collateral and improve the working of financial markets. This idea is discussed in greater detail below.

Underdeveloped Complementary Institutions

Credit markets in rural areas of developing countries also lack many features that are taken for granted in most industrial countries. One obvious example is a literate and numerate population. Poorly developed communications in some rural areas may also make the use of formal bank arrangements costly for many individuals. In addition, complementary markets may be missing. The virtual absence of insurance markets to mitigate the problems of income uncertainty is a typical example. If individuals could insure their incomes, default might be less of a problem. Another way to mitigate default problems is to assemble individual credit histories and to sanction delinquent borrowers. Such means of enforcing repayment are commonplace in more developed economies, but they require reliable systems of communication among lenders that seldom exist in rural areas of developing countries.

Deficiencies in complementary institutions are mostly ancillary to the credit market and suggest policy interventions of their own. Programs that raise literacy levels may improve the operation of credit markets yet could be justified without reference to the credit market. The benefits to credit markets should, theoretically, figure in cost-benefit analyses of such interventions, but in practice it might be too difficult to quantify the value of those benefits with any precision.

Covariant Risk and Segmented Markets

A special feature of agriculture, which provides the income of most rural residents, is the risk of income shocks. These include weather fluctuations that affect whole regions as well as changes in commodity prices that affect all the producers of a particular commodity. Such shocks affect the operation of credit markets if they create the potential for a group of farmers to default at the same time. The problem is exacerbated if all depositors simultaneously try to withdraw their savings from the bank. This risk could be averted if lenders held loan portfolios that were well diversified. But credit markets in rural areas tend to be segmented, meaning that a lender's portfolio of loans is concentrated on a group of individuals facing common shocks to their incomes—in one particular geographic area, for example, or on farmers producing one particular crop, or on one particular kinship group.

Segmented credit markets in the rural areas of developing countries often depend on informal credit, such as local moneylenders, friends and relatives, rotating savings, and credit associations. Informal credit institutions tend to operate locally, using local information and enforcement mechanisms.

The cost of segmentation is that funds fail to flow across regions or groups of individuals even though there are potential gains from doing so, as when needs for credit differ across locations. For example, a flood may create a significant demand for loans to rebuild, but because credit institutions are localized, such flows may be limited. Deposit retention schemes, which require that some percentage of deposits raised be reinvested in the same region, or the practice of unit banking may exacerbate the segmentation. Finding the optimal scope of financial intermediaries may require a trade-off. Local lenders may have better information and may be more accountable to their depositors than large, national lenders. However, the latter may have better access to well-diversified loan portfolios.

ENFORCEMENT PROBLEMS

Arguably, the issue of enforcing loan repayment constitutes the central difference between rural credit markets in developing countries and credit markets elsewhere. In this article, a pure enforcement problem is defined as a situation in which the borrower is able but unwilling to repay. Most models of credit markets discussed below do not concern themselves with enforcement and assume that, where projects are sufficiently profitable, loan repayment is guaranteed.

Enforcement problems are broadly of two kinds. First, the lender must attempt to enforce repayment after a default has occurred. But for this to be worthwhile, the lender must reap a benefit from enforcement that exceeds the cost. And the costs of sanctions, such as seizing collateral, may not be the only cost involved. It is sometimes argued that rich farmers who fail to repay are not penalized because the political costs are too high (see, for example, Khan 1979). Furthermore debt forgiveness programs—where a government announces that farmers are forgiven their past debts—are quite frequent. They have been common in Haryana State in India (see *India Today* 1990), for example, and *The Economist* (1992) has documented them in Bangladesh. So borrowers, aware that they can default on a loan with impunity, come to regard loans as grants, with little incentive to use the funds wisely.

Second, enforcement problems are exacerbated by the poor development of property rights mentioned earlier. In both industrial and developing countries, many credit contracts are backed by collateral requirements, but in developing countries the ability to foreclose on many assets is far from straightforward. Land—which, as a fixed asset, might be thought of as an ideal candidate to serve as collateral—is a case in point. In many countries property rights to land are poorly codified, which severely limits its usefulness as collateral. Rights to land are often usufructual, that is, based on using the land, and have limited possibilities for transfer to others, such as a lender who wishes to realize the value of the land as collateral. Reclaiming assets through the courts is similarly not a well-established and routine procedure. (For a general discussion of land rights issues and collateralization in three African countries, see Migot-Adholla and others 1991).

The difficulties of enforcement also help explain the widespread use of informal financial arrangements in developing countries. Such arrangements can replace conventional solutions, such as physical collateral, with other mechanisms, such as social ties (social collateral) (Besley and Coate 1991). Informal sanctions may persuade individuals to repay loans when formal banks are unable to do so. Udry (1990), for instance, cites cases of delinquent borrowers' being debarred from village ceremonies as a sanction.

Governments can help solve the collateral problem by improving the codification of property rights. In many countries, particularly in Africa, governments have taken steps to improve land registration. Whether these actions have the desired effect is debatable, especially in the short run, where attempts to codify rights may lead to disputes and increased land insecurity (Attwood 1990). Such programs also raise tricky ethical questions about the extent to which countries should be encouraged to adopt Western legal notions of property. In addition, the link between improved property rights and improvements in the workings of credit markets, while intuitively clear, is not yet firmly established from empirical work. Interesting studies in this direction on Thailand (Feder, Onchan, and Raparla 1988) and on Ghana, Kenya, and Rwanda (Migot-Adholla and others 1991) explore the connections among property rights, investment, and credit.

In some important respects the government is itself part of the enforcement problem; indeed, government-backed credit programs have often experienced the worst default rates. In their pursuit of other (particularly distributional) objectives, governments have often failed to enforce loan repayment. Governments are often reluctant to foreclose on loans in the agricultural sector, in part because the loans are concentrated among larger, politically influential farmers (see, for example, Neri and Llanto 1985, on the Philippines). As a result, borrowers take out loans in the well-founded expectation that they will not be obliged to repay them and consequently come to regard credit programs solely as a pot of funds to be distributed among those lucky enough to get "loans." This lack of sanctions weakens incentives for borrowers to invest in good projects and strengthens those for rent seeking.

Appropriation of benefits by the richer, more powerful farmers has been a particular problem of selective credit schemes. The greater the credit subsidy, the higher the chances that the small farmer will be rationed out of the scheme (Gonzalez-Vega [1984] describes this as the "iron law of interest rate restrictions"). The evidence on this exclusion of small farmers is quite strong (see, for example, Adams and Vogel 1986). Given the political constituencies that governments have to serve, they are unlikely to be able to enforce repayments under certain conditions in programs that they back. Witness the reaction of the U.S. government, which, in the face of crises in the U.S. farm credit program, tends to protect the influential farming constituency by not foreclosing on delinquent borrowers or by helping them refinance their loans. A strong case may be made for privatizing credit programs to separate them from the government budget constraint. As noted above, state-owned banks are a common institution in developing countries.

The problem of weak government resolve is not confined to cases where the government actually sets up and runs the programs. Governments in various Indian states have made debt-forgiveness declarations binding on private creditors. Such practices, along with bailouts of bankrupt credit programs, give the wrong signals to borrowers if they engender expectations that bad behavior will ultimately be rewarded by debt's being forgiven. Ultimately, the government's ability to commit itself credibly to a policy of imposing sanctions on delinquent borrowers is a significant aspect of the political economy of credit programs.

IMPERFECT INFORMATION

As discussed earlier, credit markets can face significant problems that rise from imperfect information. This section examines information problems that cause market failure from the perspective of constrained Pareto efficiency. The two main categories of information problem discussed are adverse selection and moral hazard.

Adverse Selection

Adverse selection occurs when lenders do not know particular characteristics of borrowers; for example, a lender may be uncertain about a borrower's preferences for undertaking risky projects. (For analyses of credit markets under such conditions, see Jaffee and Russell 1976 and Stiglitz and Weiss 1981.) One much-discussed implication is that lenders may consequently reduce the amount that they decide to lend, resulting in too little investment in the economy. Ultimately, credit could be rationed.

The typical framework for analyzing such problems is as follows. Suppose that the projects to which lenders' funds are allocated are risky and that borrowers sometimes do not earn enough to repay their loans. Suppose also that funds are lent at the opportunity cost of funds to the lenders (say, the supply price paid to depositors). Lenders will thus lose money because sometimes individuals do not repay. Therefore, lenders must charge a risk premium, above their opportunity costs, if they wish to break even. However, raising the interest rate to combat losses is not without potentially adverse consequences for the lender.

Suppose (as do Stiglitz and Weiss 1981) that all projects have the same mean return, differing only in their variance. To make the exposition easier, suppose also that all borrowers are risk neutral. The adverse selection problem is then characterized as individuals having privately observed differences in the riskiness of their projects. If the interest rate is increased to offset losses from defaults, it is precisely those individuals with the least risky projects who will cease to borrow first. This is because these individuals are most likely to repay their loans and hence are most discouraged from borrowing by facing higher interest rates. By contrast, those who are least likely to repay are least discouraged from borrowing by higher interest rates. Profits may therefore decrease as interest rates increase beyond some point. A lender may thus be better off rationing access to credit at a lower interest rate rather than raising the interest rate further.

The key observation here is that the interest rate has two effects. It serves the usual allocative role of equating supply and demand for loanable funds, but it also affects the average quality of the lender's loan portfolio. For this reason lenders may not use interest rates to clear the market and may instead fix the interest rate, meanwhile rationing access to funds.

A credit market with adverse selection is not typically efficient, even according to the constrained efficiency criterion discussed above. To see this, consider what the equilibrium interest rate would be in a competitive market with adverse selection. Because all borrowers are charged the same interest rate, the average probability of repayment over the whole group of borrowers, multiplied by the interest rate that they have to pay, must equal the opportunity cost of funds to the lender. Each borrower thus cares about the average repayment rate among the *other* borrowers, because that rate affects the interest rate that he or she is charged. But an individual who is deciding whether or not to apply for a loan may ignore the fact that doing so affects the well-being of the other borrowers—which generates an externality as described above.

Situations of adverse selection give a lender an incentive to find ways to separate borrowers into different groups according to their likelihood of repayment. One device for screening out poor-quality borrowers is to use a collateral requirement (Stiglitz and Weiss 1986). If the lender demands that each borrower put up some collateral, the high-risk borrowers will be least inclined to comply because they are most likely to lose the collateral if their project fails. Given the scarcity of collateral and the difficulty of foreclosure discussed earlier, sorting out high-risk borrowers is certainly difficult and may be impossible. The discussion that follows therefore assumes that the lender is unable to distinguish between those borrowers who are likely to repay and those who are not.

The Stiglitz-Weiss model (1981) of the credit markets seems relevant for thinking about formal lending in a rural context, where it is reasonable to suppose that banks will not have as much information as their borrowers. The model also appears to yield an unambiguous policy conclusion that lending will be too low from a social point of view. In fact, it can be shown that a government policy that expands lending—through subsidies, for example—raises welfare in this model by offsetting the negative externality that bad borrowers create for good ones and by encouraging some of the better borrowers to borrow. In other words, adverse selection examined in the context of Stiglitz and Weiss's model argues for government intervention on the grounds of an explicit account of market failure.

How robust is their conclusion? DeMeza and Webb (1987) enter a caveat: instead of supposing that projects have the same mean, they suppose that projects differ in their expected profitability, with good projects more likely to yield a good return. They also suppose, as do Stiglitz and Weiss, that the lender does not have access to the private information that individuals have about the projects they are able to undertake. At any given interest rate, set to break even at the average quality of project funded, DeMeza and Webb show that some projects with a negative social return will be financed. Thus, the competitive equilibrium has socially excessive investment levels. A corollary developed by DeMeza and Webb is that government interventions—such as a tax on investment—to restrict the level of lending to a competitive equilibrium are worthwhile.

Both the Stiglitz-Weiss and DeMeza-Webb analyses conclude that the level of investment will be inefficient, but they recommend opposite policy interventions as a solution. The conflicting recommendations would not be especially disquieting except that the differences between the models are not based upon things that can be measured with precision but on assumptions about the project technology, for example, whether the mean return of the project is held fixed. So it is hard to know which of the results would apply in practice.

Moral Hazard

The Stiglitz-Weiss model of credit markets can also be extended to allow for moral hazard, a problem that can arise when lenders are unable to discern borrowers' actions. The central risk for the lender is that individuals who are in debt might slacken their efforts to make the project successful or they might change the type of project that they undertake. Borrowing money to invest in a project shares the risk between lender and borrowers: if the project fails and the loan is not repaid, the lender bears the cost of the loan. There is a tendency, therefore, for the borrower to increase risk-taking, reducing the probability that a loan will be repaid.

Moral hazard is elaborated by Stiglitz and Weiss in their model where all projects have identical mean returns but different degrees of risk. As with their adverse selection model, they find that an increase in interest rates affects the behavior of borrowers negatively, reducing their incentive to take the actions conducive to repaying their loans. Riskier projects are more attractive at higher interest rates because, at the higher rate, the borrower will prefer a project that has a lower probability of being repaid. Once again, a higher interest rate may have a counterproductive effect on lenders' profits because of its adverse effects on borrowers' incentives. Stiglitz and Weiss again suggest the possibility of credit rationing—restricting the amount of money lent to an individual to correct incentives.

In cases of moral hazard, it is not clear-cut that the outcome is inefficient. Individuals who increase the riskiness of their projects when they are more indebted affect only their own payoff.[1] Thus, restrictions on the amount that an individual can borrow need not constitute a market failure, even though in a framework that allows for heterogeneous borrowers, such restrictions might compound the problems of adverse selection discussed above. There is no inefficiency from incentive effects if the lender is able to impose the cost of increased risk-taking on the borrower and no one else. This conclusion assumes, however, that the borrower borrows from a single lender.

In reality, that assumption may not hold (see, for example, Bell, Srinivasan, and Udry 1988). Some borrowers obtain funding for a project from more than one lender, very often mixing formal and informal lenders. Each lender typically prefers that the others undertake any monitoring that has to be done, and the monitoring may then be less vigorous and effective than otherwise. And if borrowers undertake several projects funded from different sources, effort on each project may not be separable, so that the terms of each loan contract may affect the payoff to the other lenders.

It is unclear whether either of these difficulties leads to too much or too little lending relative to the efficient level. Depending on the exact specification of the model, one can obtain a result in either direction, which from a policy viewpoint compounds the ambiguities found in the analysis of adverse selection. These arguments suggest the possibility of efficiency gains if a borrower deals with a single lender. Such an arrangement could internalize the externalities that arise when more than one lender is involved in a project.

Moral hazard may also lead to externalities in related markets, an obvious example being insurance. Individuals who have income insurance may make no effort to repay their loans, so that default ends up as a transfer from the insurer to the lender—a scenario reminiscent of the experience of some countries (for example, Mexico, as documented by Bassoco, Cartas, and Norton 1986).

The incentive effects of moral hazard need not in themselves argue for government intervention in credit markets, but if they are combined with multiple indebtedness, outcomes are likely to be inefficient, and government intervention designed to deal with such externalities may increase efficiency.

Investing in Information

The discussion has so far assumed that the amount of information available to lenders is unalterable, but lenders have many opportunities to augment information. They can, for instance, investigate the quality of projects and monitor their implementation. That information is costly does not necessarily imply that outcomes are inefficient (see Townsend 1978); one has to ask first whether lenders are likely to collect and process information efficiently. The answer may be negative if the "public good" nature of information is taken seriously. There seems to be no evidence that this theoretical possibility is practically important in rural areas of developing countries. Furthermore, the experience of industrial countries suggests that markets have effectively created mechanisms for generating information about borrowers that help to circumvent the public good problems. Private and independent credit-rating agencies have existed in the United States since the middle of the nineteenth century (Pagano and Jappelli 1992).

For rural financial markets of developing countries, lack of expertise in project appraisal and the high costs of monitoring and assessment relative to the size of a loan may mean that people are excluded from the credit market, even though they have projects that would survive a profitability test based on complete information. Braverman and Guasch (1989) suggest that the cost of processing small loans can range from 15 to 40 percent of the loan size (see also Adams, Graham, and Von Pischke 1984). But these kinds of transactions costs do not necessarily lead to inefficient exclusion from the credit market. It is at least possible that they reflect the real economic cost of serving a clientele where information is scarce. Whether there is an inefficiency depends on whether the human capital and other factors that go into appraising loans are priced at their true economic costs. If not, the high figures for transactions costs discussed by Braverman and Guasch might indicate inefficiency.

The point is a reminder that parallel market failures may be important. If markets that provide inputs for the credit market are also imperfect, credit will be allocated inefficiently. From a policy viewpoint, therefore, the question is whether policy ought not be focused on the real problem, rather than on the proximate problem of misallocated credit.

The Effect of Redistribution

The arguments discussed above explain why allocation of credit can be suboptimal. This section develops the idea that the distribution of capital in the economy becomes tied together with efficiency in such situations. Suppose that there are two individuals, one with a worthwhile project to invest in and the other with some capital. If the one with the capital is uncertain about the quality of the other's project, he may be unwilling to lend enough for the project to reach its full potential. But if capital is redistributed—that is, if the person with the project now has the capital as well—the project is more likely to be undertaken because the investor does not have to allow for the risk posed by inadequate information. (For a formal analysis of such redistribution, see Bernanke and Gertler 1990.) Clearly, there is no Pareto improvement, because one individual now has less capital; however, the information problems in the economy are now reduced. The outcome would be quite different in the absence of information problems, when it should not much matter which of the individuals owns the capital because each has full information about the quality of the investment project.[2]

When lenders face information problems, therefore, the distribution of assets matters for other than purely distributional reasons, which may help explain why such things as land redistribution can enhance growth. If severe information problems beset credit markets, land redistribution is tantamount to a redistribution of assets that can enhance investment by reducing the costs of information imperfections—assuming, of course, that the individuals to whom assets are redistributed really have access to superior investment technologies. Binswanger and Rosenzweig (1990) argue for that assumption on the basis of evidence that small farmers have good investment opportunities that go unexploited because of high risk and limited access to credit. Their argument is not, however, based on efficiency. It is either a straightforward redistribution argument, or it might be justified by adopting a social welfare function that attached special importance to investment.

In practice, there is little doubt that many arguments in favor of intervention in credit markets are motivated by a belief that those who have few assets nonetheless have good investment opportunities. Unwillingness of lenders with little information about the poor to lend is thought to be costly in terms of investment efficiency. Sometimes intervention in credit markets emerges as an alternative to redistributing assets. Intervention may make sense for both political and incentive reasons, but it may have little to do with market failure as defined here.

Relevance of Imperfect Information Arguments for Rural Financial Markets

It seems obvious that the analysis of information problems has general relevance for rural financial markets in developing countries, because it is hard to imagine that unobservable actions and characteristics do not play some part in the way in which the formal credit sector deals with farmers. The concern here is to examine more precisely what institutional features of rural financial markets can be explained by information imperfections and how these features can be related to arguments for government intervention.

For example, information imperfections are potentially important in explaining the segmentation of credit markets. Information flows are typically well established only over relatively close distances and within social groups, making it likely that financial institutions, at least indigenous ones, will tend to work with relatively small groups. Among such groups, characteristics of individuals tend to be well known, and monitoring borrowers' behavior may be relatively inexpensive. Such considerations also suggest why informal finance is used so extensively in rural areas.[3]

This claim is consistent with the many studies of informal rural financial markets available, several of which are collected in a special issue of the *World Bank Economic Review* (vol. 4, no. 3, September 1990). For example, Udry's study of Nigeria (1990) finds that individuals tend to lend to people they know in order to economize on information flows. Similar evidence has been found for Thailand (see Siamwalla et al. 1990) and Pakistan (see Aleem 1990). The fact that individuals form into groups is not inconsistent with efficiency in investment decisions once enforcement costs and information difficulties are recognized, although there may be a case for facilitating flows of funds across segmented groups.

In contrast to small local lenders, formal institutions can usually intermediate funds over larger groups. Formal institutions suffer from greater problems of imperfect information, however, and are most susceptible to the kinds of inefficiencies discussed above. In this context, the formal sector naturally suffers a greater default problem.

One view says that the informal sector serves as lender of last resort to those who are unable to obtain finance in the formal sector—the people to whom the formal bank is reluctant to lend because of their characteristics and the cost of collecting information about them. A related argument is that the transactions costs of lending to this group are prohibitive, very often because the loans they demand are so small. This, by itself, does not argue for any kind of intervention, but shifting more people to the formal sector—through government subsidization of loans in the formal sector, for example—could bring a beneficial externality by making market segmentation easier to overcome. The argument for reducing the size of the informal sector does, however, rest crucially on the belief that a formal bank has a comparative advantage in certain activities, such as managing loan portfolios across areas.

OTHER ARGUMENTS FOR INTERVENTION

Other functions that are often advanced as properly within the purview of government are protecting depositors, establishing safeguards against monopoly, and disseminating know-how and innovation in credit markets.

Protecting Depositors

Much regulation in credit markets is directed toward the relationship between a lender and the ultimate owners of the funds that are lent, depositors in many cases. Indeed, creating an environment in which savings can be mobilized in the form of deposits is an essential part of operating an efficient credit market. Depositors typically are concerned about the safety of their deposits as well as the return that those deposits yield.

Providing reliable receptors of savings in rural areas of developing countries may seem especially problematical because of the covariant risk discussed earlier. Particular problems arise if all depositors wish to retrieve their savings at the same time, which may lead to bank runs. This problem is compounded if the withdrawals occur when borrowers are having difficulty repaying their loans. In such situations market segmentation becomes particularly costly if it prevents funds from flowing toward regions where demands for retrieving deposits are greatest. The farm credit program in the United States, established with such issues in mind, provides a clearinghouse for funds to flow between regions. The program was necessitated, however, by restrictive legislation that disallowed branch banking in favor of unit banking, a kind of legislated segmentation of the credit market.

The economics literature studies cases in which depositors withdraw funds en masse, causing the bank to collapse. Two different views emerge on the efficiency of such situations. In Diamond and Dybvig's analysis (1983), bank runs are inefficient. They are modeled as resulting from a loss of confidence. Once depositors lose confidence, a run becomes a self-fulfilling prophecy, because if depositors expect others to withdraw funds in a hurry, it is rational to follow suit, for fear that the bank will be bankrupt if they wait. The result is a cascading collapse of the bank. Such losses of confidence need not have anything to do with a fundamental change in the economy. The whims of depositors are enough to lead to collapse.

Calomiris and Kahn (1991), among others, take an alternative view. They argue that bank runs are triggered by depositors who monitor the bank and have good information about its financial health. Because deposits are returned on a first-come-first-served basis, the more diligent depositors are able to withdraw their funds if they suspect that the bank's loan portfolio is bad. A run can develop if the uninformed depositors see the informed ones deserting the bank. Thus, in this view, bank runs are the natural product of a process in which banks are disciplined by their depositors and need not be associated with any efficiency cost.

Governments in many countries have used the threat of bank runs to justify regulation. Reserve requirements (for example, where a given amount of assets must be held in the central bank) and liquidity ratios are sometimes imposed on commercial lenders—nominally to protect depositors, but quite often in practice to exert monetary control by the central bank or to finance the government's budget cheaply. Another mechanism for protecting depositors is loan portfolio insurance, often used with agricultural loans.

In the United States federal deposit insurance is designed to protect depositors against bank failures. Opinion is divided about the efficacy of this policy response. According to one view, deposit insurance reduces monitoring of banks by depositors, and the quality of lenders' loan portfolios may deteriorate as a result. Even if bank runs occur entirely at the whim of depositors, deposit insurance could still bring adverse consequences if insured lenders change their behavior—for example, by increasing their lending toward riskier projects. Trying to relax credit market segmentation is arguably preferable to expanding deposit insurance (Calomiris 1989). The aim is to provide some direct way to shift funds toward regions that have experienced negative income shocks affecting a banks' clientele. Guinnane (1992) gives an interesting account of how the "Centrals" intermediated funds between credit cooperatives in nineteenth-century Germany, directing funds to those cooperatives in need. In contemporary developing countries, systemic shocks, such as those resulting from fluctuations in commodity prices, may threaten the integrity of a regional financial system if flows of funds are poor.

Providing some assurances to depositors is a prerequisite to building financial institutions that mobilize local savings. Local institutions, such as credit cooperatives, make it relatively easy for depositors to monitor the behavior of lenders and even borrowers (Banerjee, Besley, and Guinnane 1994). Credit programs that are entirely externally financed cannot use this method of accountability. The trade-off is between avoiding covariant risk and encouraging local monitoring of lender and borrower behavior. The appropriate policy response to the problem of bank runs is far from clear. The U.S. experience suggests that building clearing-houses for interregional flows of funds may have merits, but this approach has the drawback, particularly for developing countries, of requiring a complex network of institutions that may be costly to build and maintain.

In sum, protecting depositors is an important dimension of government regulation in rural credit markets. The trade-off is between protecting depositors and blunting their incentives to monitor lenders. Two main types of intervention appear justified on this count. The first is deposit insurance, and the second is building structures to intermediate funds across groups and regions, thereby reducing credit market segmentation.

Market Power and Intervention in Rural Credit Markets

Market power may lead to inefficiencies in credit markets if trade is restricted to maximize profits and if goods are not priced at marginal cost. Thus, monopolies are often subject to regulation. There are good reasons to expect market power to develop in credit markets. In a world of imperfect information, those with privileged access to information may obtain some market power as a result. Village moneylenders are a case in point, and they are often held up as archetypal monopolists because of their ability to exploit local knowledge.

Market power may also be important because, as lenders grow larger, their ability to diversify risk improves and their lending activities take on monopolistic tendencies. In effect, this gives a decreasing average cost curve to the industry. One might, therefore, expect a market structure with a few large lenders, each of whom is able to intermediate funds for a large group of borrowers. This scenario may not characterize rural areas of developing countries very well because of the high costs of getting the information needed to operate across many different localities. Experience does suggest, however, that these large lenders in rural areas may attempt to use their market power (see, for example, Lamberte and Lim 1987 on the Philippines).

Monopoly does not always lead to an inefficiency. If the monopolist-lender is able to discriminate in the price charged to each borrower, the lender will be able to extract all of the consumer surplus from each borrowers. Monopoly power has no efficiency cost in this case; it pays the monopolist to lend to the point where the marginal value of credit to each borrower is the same (a "discriminating monopoly" outcome). In that case loans will be made efficiently, even though they will be designed to extract all of the surplus from borrowers and the lender may be labeled as exploitative (for a discussion of these issues, see Basu 1989).

The usual monopoly inefficiency, where lenders restrict funds to increase their profits, arises only when loan arrangements cannot be tailored to each individual. In this case an argument for intervention can be made. Direct regulation of interest rates is one obvious option, but village moneylenders who operate informally may be difficult to regulate. Nonetheless, usury laws are common. A second option is to reduce the monopoly power of established sources by providing alternative sources of credit. The system of credit cooperatives established in rural India was motivated this way. To consider the rationale for such policies, one needs to understand why, if moneylenders were making a profit, no one else attempted to enter these markets. One possibility is that moneylenders were effectively able to deter entry in ways that could not be regulated directly; another is that the costs of setting up and running credit institutions in rural areas were prohibitive. One could argue for subsidizing rural credit institutions as an indirect way of reducing market power, but experience has shown that it is very hard to make such schemes function effectively. The moneylenders' ability to collect information and enforce repayment is real and must be replaced by an institutional structure that can fulfill these functions equally effectively.

Learning to Use Financial Markets

The operation of financial markets in more developed countries has evolved over a long period and has entailed a learning process whose importance cannot be underestimated. That process can be thought of as a period of acquiring the human and organizational capital that is basic to the functioning of financial markets.

This learning process can be related to the case for intervention in two ways. One is based simply on asymmetric information between citizen and government. A government may have a better sense than its citizens of the pitfalls and problems associated with different financial structures and is arguably in a better position to observe past experience at home and abroad. The intervention called for here, then, is provision of information to potential operators of financial institutions. In practice, providing information can be difficult and costly in comparison with either setting up institutions as demonstration projects or subsidizing successful projects. The scope of arguments based upon the government knowing best is potentially wide, and acknowledging that range may be the thin end of a large wedge. Such arguments may, however, be used to justify intervention on efficiency grounds. The market failure arises because agents are uninformed about what has worked elsewhere, and the aim is to avoid a costly search and learning process.

Another learning-based argument for intervention might hold that individuals learn from the experience of others within a country. An inefficiency might develop if individuals hang back waiting for others to try things out. The slow diffusion of certain agricultural technologies has often been attributed to a reluctance to be the first user. An obvious role for government intervention is to subsidize early innovators. Thus, experiments in institutional design, such as the Grameen Bank in Bangladesh, might serve as prime candidates for subsidization. Such arguments appear only to justify subsidizing new ventures, however, and subsidies should be phased out along the way. The creation of vested interests raises tricky political economy issues.

CONCLUDING REMARKS

Enforcement difficulties, imperfect information, protection of depositors, market power, and learning arguments all have implications for government intervention in rural credit markets.

Where enforcement is an issue, governments may intervene by strengthening property rights to increase the scope and effectiveness of collateral, although this is not a direct intervention in the credit market. But government might be as much a part of the problem as the solution in this context, because many government-backed credit schemes fail to sanction delinquent borrowers.

Deposit insurance is an obvious option for protecting depositors, but it may blunt the incentives depositors have to monitor the performance of lenders. Measures intended to facilitate the flow of funds across groups and regions may be preferable to deposit insurance schemes.

Monopoly power may create tension because information is concentrated in lenders' hands, but market power (for example, of village moneylenders) is not necessarily socially inefficient, even though its redistributive consequences may be considered repugnant. Providing credit alternatives may be a reasonable response from the perspective of distributional concerns but, again, might have relatively little to do with market failure.

In summary, there may be good arguments for intervention, and some may be based on market failure. But as one unpacks each argument, the realization grows that, given the current state of empirical evidence on many relevant questions, it is impossible to categorically assert that an intervention in the credit markets is justified. Empirical work that can speak to these issues is the next challenge if the theoretical progress on the operation of rural credit markets is to be matched by progress in the policy sphere.

NOTES

This article was originally prepared for the Agricultural Policies division of the World Bank. The author is grateful to Dale Adams, Harold Alderman, Charles Calomiris, Gershon Feder, Franque Grimard, Karla Hoff, Christina Paxson, J. D. Von Pischke, Christopher Udry, and seminar participants at the World Bank and Ohio State University for comments and to Sanjay Jain for assistance in preparing the first draft.

1. A caveat to this is the case in which returns to borrowers are correlated and the lender is not risk neutral. In that case, the break-even interest rate for all borrowers depends on the decision of all borrowers as to effort, and an externality similar to that discussed for the adverse selection case obtains.

2. The argument is really a bit more subtle. Redistribution would still have potential income effects that might affect willingness to bear risk; a rich individual might be more willing than a poor one to undertake a risky project. Such influences could mean that, even without an information problem, individual circumstances could affect the decision of how much to invest in the project. The argument in the text is exactly correct only with risk-neutral individuals.

3. Stiglitz (1990) argues that this characteristic could be harnessed in group lending programs that encourage peer monitoring.

REFERENCES

Adams, Dale W., Douglas H. Graham, and J. D. Von Pischke, eds. 1984. *Undermining Rural Development with Cheap Credit.* Boulder, Colo.: Westview Press.

Adams, Dale W., and Robert C. Vogel. 1986. "Rural Financial Markets in Developing Countries: Recent Controversies and Lessons." *World Development* 14:477–87.

Aleem, Irfan. 1990. "Imperfect Information, Screening, and the Costs of Informal Lending: A Study of a Rural Credit Market in Pakistan." *World Bank Economic Review* 4, no. 3 (September): 329–50.

Attwood, David A. 1990. "Land Registration in Africa: The Impact on Agricultural Production." *World Development* 18 (May): 659–71.

Banerjee, Abhijit V., Timothy Besley, and Timothy W. Guinnane. 1994. "Thy Neighbor's Keeper: The Design of a Credit Cooperative, with Theory and a Test." *Quarterly Journal of Economics* 109 (2): 491–515.

Bassoco, Luz Maria, Celso Cartas, and Roger D. Norton. 1986. "Sectoral Analysis of the Benefits of Subsidized Insurance in Mexico." In *Crop Insurance for Agricultural Development,* edited by Peter Hazell, Carlos Pomerada, and Alberto Valdes. Baltimore: Johns Hopkins University Press.

Basu, Kaushik. 1989. "Rural Credit Markets: The Structure of Interest Rates, Exploitation, and Efficiency." In *The Economic Theory of Agrarian Institutions,* edited by Pranab Bardhan. Oxford: Oxford University Press.

Bell, Clive, T. N. Srinivasan, and Christopher Udry. 1988. "Agricultural Credit Markets in the Punjab: Segmentation, Rationing, and Spillovers." Yale University.

Bernanke, Ben, and Mark Gertler, 1990. "Financial Fragility and Economic Performance." *Quarterly Journal of Economics* 105 (February): 87–114.

Besley, Timothy J., and Stephen Coate. 1991. "Group Lending Repayment Incentives and Social Collateral." RPDS Discussion Paper 152, Woodrow Wilson School, Princeton University.

Binswanger, Hans T., and M. R. Rosenzsweig. 1990. "Are Small Farmers Too Poor to Be Efficient?" World Bank, LAC Technical Department, Washington, D.C.

Braverman, Avishay, and J. Luis Guasch. 1989. "Institutional Analysis of Credit Co-operatives." In *The Economic Theory of Agrarian Institutions,* edited by Pranab Bardhan. Oxford: Oxford University Press.

Calomiris, Charles W. 1989. "Deposit Insurance: Lessons from the Record." *Federal Reserve Bank of Chicago Economic Perspectives* (May–June): 10–30.

Calomiris, Charles W., and Charles M. Kahn. 1991. "The Role of Demandable Debt in Structuring Optimal Bank Arrangements." *American Economic Review* 81 (3, June): 497–513.

DeMeza, David, and David C. Webb. 1987. "Too Much Investment: A Problem of Asymmetric Information." *Quarterly Journal of Economics* 102 (May): 281–92.

Diamond, Douglas W., and Philip W. Dybvig. 1983. "Bank Runs, Deposit Insurance, and Liquidity." *Journal of Political Economy* 91 (June): 401–19.

Dixit, A. K. 1987. "Trade and Insurance with Moral Hazard." *Journal of International Economics* 23 (November): 201–20.

Economist. 1992. "Begum Zia's Burden." April 4.

Feder, Gershon, Tongroj Onchan, and Tejaswi Raparla. 1988. "Collateral Guarantees and Rural Credit in Developing Countries: Evidence from Asia." *Agricultural Economics* 2:231–45.

Gonzalez-Vega, Claudio. 1984. "Credit-Rationing Behavior of Agricultural Lenders: The Iron Law of Interest-Rate Restrictions." In *Undermining Rural Development with Cheap Credit,* edited by Dale W. Adams, Douglas H. Graham, and J. D. Von Pischke. Boulder, Colo.: Westview Press.

Greenwald, Bruce, and Joseph E. Stiglitz. 1986. "Externalities in Economies with Imperfect Information and Incomplete Markets." *Quarterly Journal of Economics* 101 (May): 229–64.

Guinnane, Timothy W. 1992. "Financial Intermediation for Poor Borrowers: The Case of German Credit Cooperatives, 1850–1914." Yale University.

India, Government of. 1991. *Report of the Committee on the Financial System.*

India Today. 1990. "Bluff and Bluster." March, 31:45.

Jaffee, Dwight, and Thomas Russell. 1976. "Imperfect Information, Uncertainty, and Credit Rationing." *Quarterly Journal of Economics* 90:651–66.

Khan, A. 1979. "The Comilla Model and the Integrated Rural Development Programme in Bangladesh: An Experiment in 'Cooperative Capitalism.'" *World Development* 7:397–422.

Lamberte, Mario B., and Joseph Lim. 1987. "Rural Financial Markets: A Review of the Literature." Working Paper 87-02, Philippine Institute for Development Studies, Manila.

McKinnon, Ronald. 1973. *Money and Capital in Economic Development.* Washington, D.C.: Brookings Institution.

Migot-Adholla, Shem, Peter Hazell, Benoit Blarel, and Frank Place. 1991. "Indigenous Land Rights Systems in Sub-Saharan Africa: A Constraint on Productivity?" *World Bank Economic Review* 5, no. 1 (January): 155–75.

Neri, Purita F., and Gilbert M. Llanto. 1985. "Agricultural Credit Subsidy." *CB Review* (Central Bank of the Philippines) 37 (October): 8–16.

Okorie, Aja. 1990. "Rural Banking in Nigeria: Determining Appropriate Policy Variables." ARSSS Research Report 9. Winrock International Institute for Agricultural Development, Morrilton, Ark.

Pagano, Marco, and Tullio Jappelli. 1992. "Information Sharing in the Market for Consumer Credit." Università di Napoli.

Siamwalla, Ammar, et al. 1990. "The Thai Rural Credit System: Public Subsidies, Private Information, and Segmented Markets." *World Bank Economic Review* 4 (3, September): 271–96.

Stiglitz, Joseph E. 1990. "Peer Monitoring and Credit Markets." *World Bank Economic Review* 4 (3, September): 351–66.

Stiglitz, Joseph E., and Andrew Weiss. 1981. "Credit Rationing in Markets with Imperfect Information." *American Economic Review* 71:393–419.

———. 1986. "Credit Rationing and Collateral." In *Recent Developments in Corporate Finance,* edited by Jeremy S. S. Edwards and Colin P. Mayer. London: Cambridge University Press.

Townsend, Robert. 1978. "Optimal Contracts and Competitive Markets with Costly State Verification." *Journal of Economic Theory* 21:265–93.

Udry, Christopher. 1990. "Credit Markets in Northern Nigeria: Credit as Insurance in a Rural Economy." *World Bank Economic Review* 4, no. 3 (September): 251–71.

World Bank. 1987. *The Philippines: A Framework for Economic Recovery.* Washington, D.C.

24

Microfinance: The Paradigm Shift from Credit Delivery to Sustainable Financial Intermediation

MARGUERITE S. ROBINSON

INTRODUCTION

More than 80 percent of the world's population does not have access to financial services from institutions, either for credit or for savings.[1] Among them, of course, are nearly all the poor of the developing world. Although there is a large demand for microfinance worldwide, banks typically believe that providing small loans and deposit services would be an unprofitable activity for them. The problem is exacerbated by the low level of influence of the poor who require microfinance. Accordingly, institutional commercial microfinance has remained at a low level (Rosenberg 1994, 2). From the borrower's point of view, the crucial words in microcredit are "access" and "cost." Subsidized loan programs provide cheap credit, but they do not provide lower-income households with widespread *access* to credit. Informal moneylenders, in aggregate, provide wide access, but generally at very high *cost* to the borrower. On the savings side, the poor need secure, convenient, voluntary savings services, with instruments that provide liquidity and returns. These are frequently unavailable at the local level—from either the formal or the informal sector. Since government and donor funds can supply only a tiny fraction of global microfinance demand, financial intermediation by self-sufficient institutions is the *only* way that financial services can be supplied to lower-income people worldwide.

Microfinance refers to small-scale financial services for both credit and deposits that are provided to people who farm or fish or herd; operate small or microenterprises where goods are produced, recycled, repaired, or traded; perform

MARGUERITE S. ROBINSON is an Institute Fellow at the Harvard Institute for International Development.

services; work for wages or commissions; gain income from renting out small amounts of land, vehicles, draft animals, or machinery and tools; and to other individuals and local groups in developing countries, in both rural and urban areas.

Where available, sustainable institutions that provide microfinance increase the options of the working poor by helping them to reduce risk, improve management and productivity, obtain higher returns on investment, and improve the quality of their lives. Savings services permit people to store excess liquidity for future use and to obtain returns on their assets. Credit services enable the use of anticipated income for present investment or consumption. However, sustainable institutions providing commercial financial intermediation at the local level are very rare.[2]

The services of financial institutions, of course, cannot meet the needs of all of the poor. Destitute, hungry people at the lowest levels of the poor are often not yet bankable, even by the standards of institutions that provide microfinance. Such people need food, and they need employment and/or government or donor assistance in starting or improving microenterprises. Over time they can then become clients of institutions providing commercial microfinance.

This chapter concerns the working poor who already have microenterprises or other income sources that would enable them to participate in, and benefit from, commercial institutions providing microfinance.[3] However, it is important also to draw attention to the relations between sustainable microfinance and poverty alleviation—both direct and indirect. When microfinance is provided at commercial rates through profitable, sustainable institutions, it can contribute to: (1) a direct improvement in the economic activities, political empowerment, and the quality of life of the working poor; (2) increased employment of the poor; and (3) a shift of government and donor support from credit subsidies to poverty alleviation. The productivity, incomes, and quality of life of hundreds of millions of people could be substantially increased if they had access to institutional savings and credit facilities delivered locally.

This chapter (1) documents that self-sufficient institutions can provide microfinance profitably, with large-scale outreach to lower-income clients; (2) demonstrates a recent shift in the microfinance paradigm from credit delivery to commercial financial intermediation; (3) analyzes the reasons why financial institutions can provide credit to the working poor at lower interest rates and total costs than many informal commercial lenders; (4) discusses the development of sustainable microfinance systems in Indonesia; (5) contrasts the approach used in Indonesia with that of the Grameen Bank in Bangladesh; and (6) considers the policy implications of the new paradigm.

THE PARADIGM SHIFT

A shift from subsidized credit delivery programs to commercial financial intermediation is under way internationally. We examine here the rise and decline of the old approach and the emergence of a new paradigm.

THE RISE AND DECLINE OF THE OLD PARADIGM: SUBSIDIZED CREDIT

During the 1960s and 1970s, governments and donors promoted large-scale subsidized rural credit programs in developing countries. Since it was assumed that subsidized credit was required to stimulate agricultural growth, agricultural finance came to be treated essentially as a subsidized crop input. This approach was based on the (unexamined) assumptions that poor farmers needed credit for productive inputs, that they could not save enough for the inputs they required, and that they could not afford to pay the full cost of credit. Therefore, subsidized credit programs would be required for the adoption of new agricultural technologies; the technologies would then enable farmers to produce more crops, increase their incomes, and repay their loans. It was further assumed that, in general, lower-income people did not save, or preferred to save in nonfinancial forms. Therefore, savings mobilization would require that people be taught financial discipline. As a result, compulsory saving is often required as a condition of obtaining a subsidized loan.

The assumptions, however, were at variance with reality. By the late 1960s and early 1970s, serious difficulties with subsidized credit programs had begun to become apparent; by the late 1970s, criticisms of the rationale behind these policies filled the development literature.[4] The distortions and failures of subsidized rural credit programs included the following:

1. Credit subsidies tend to encourage corruption and to be captured by wealthier and more influential households.
2. The diffusion of many agricultural innovations in developing countries does not depend on formal credit.
3. Subsidized credit programs frequently have high default rates and large losses.
4. Credit subsidies, channeled to local elites, buy political support for governments and once offered, are difficult to dislodge.
5. In many cases subsidized credit depresses savings mobilization and the development of sustainable financial institutions.

The original subsidized credit approach focused on rural credit, especially for farmers. However, it later became evident that subsidized credit had similar effects on small and microenterprises and led to the perpetuation of a policy environment in which most lower-income borrowers, both rural and urban, were typically unable to gain access to institutional credit (Castello, Stearns, and Christen 1991; Robinson 1992, 1994a; Rhyne and Rotblatt 1994).

Perhaps the most deleterious aspect of subsidized credit is that, by definition, it restricts the range of financial services available and the number of clients served. In developing countries, successful mobilization of voluntary savings and effective microcredit programs have tended not to occur together. This is largely because of the long-prevailing mode of credit subsidies. For example, the Grameen Bank of Bangladesh has been successful in lending to the poor and recovering its loans; however, since Grameen does not mobilize voluntary savings effectively and is not sufficiently viable to attract commercial investment, the bank remains subsidy dependent. The subsidy-dependent microcredit model can work for particular institutions at particular times, but it is not sustainable in the long term and not affordable on the global scale. Since subsidy-dependent institutions are capital constrained, they cannot meet demand.

The opposite model is also prevalent: mobilizing rural savings that are reinvested elsewhere. For example, many rural bank branches in India and China have mobilized large amounts of voluntary savings. Yet in China, and until 1996 in India, the spread between the interest rates on loans and deposits was too small for profitable lending to small borrowers. Therefore, most of these savings have been invested or deposited in urban banks, while microcredit demand remains largely unmet.

Under both models, financial institutions have not—and cannot—meet the demand for *microfinance*—credit *and* savings services. Even the best of the institutions that operate with subsidized loan portfolios are effective *either* in capturing savings *or* in providing loans. *They cannot afford to be effective in both because they do not have a large enough spread to cover the operating and financial costs that would be required. Sustainable microfinance has occurred only in systems that provide commercial financial intermediation.*

THE EMERGENCE OF THE NEW PARADIGM: SUSTAINABLE FINANCIAL INTERMEDIATION

In the past two decades, Indonesia has turned on its head the conventional wisdom about local finance. Bank Dagang Bali (BDB), a private bank in Indonesia, first demonstrated that banks serving the microfinance market can be profitable without subsidy. The Bank Rakyat Indonesia (BRI), a large state-owned commercial bank, demonstrated that the demand for microfinance can be met on a large scale by sustainable institutions; and Indonesia's village-owned banks demonstrated that commercial microfinance can be provided profitably on a small scale by community-owned financial institutions. Together, they have demonstrated that widespread, locally available financial services can have important effects on social and economic development. The combination of the wide outreach of these institutions and their financial viability has made Indonesia the center of sustainable microfinance. These institutions provide the working poor with access to microcredit at costs well below those available from informal lenders.

Microcredit: Access and Cost

Substantial evidence exists to show that sustainable financial institutions can profitably deliver microcredit to large numbers of borrowers at about 5 to 30 percent of the interest rates charged by informal commercial lenders to lower-income borrowers. Informal lenders in many developing countries currently charge a "flat" monthly interest rate of from 5 percent to more than 40 percent on the original loan balance.[5] They typically offer the lower rates to better-off and more influential borrowers, while, in general, the higher rates are charged to the poorer borrowers, who have the fewest alternatives. In contrast, the BRI in Indonesia provides loans through its local banking system at a flat monthly interest rate that is at or below 1.5 percent on the original balance of the loan.[6] No additional fees are charged to borrowers who repay on time.

The crucial point is that lower-income borrowers who borrow from moneylenders generally pay much higher interest rates for credit than would be necessary if commercial microfinance were widely available through institutions. This is of particular significance because the high rates of informal lenders tend to constrain microenterprise growth and because the volume of informal commercial credit is very large in developing countries worldwide.[7]

Why Do Informal Commercial Lenders Charge High Interest Rates?

Informal lending is of two main types: commercial (loans from moneylenders, traders, employers, commodity wholesalers, landlords) and noncommercial (loans from friends, relatives, neighbors, and some forms of rotating savings and credit associations). While noncommercial loans from friends, kin, neighbors, and so forth are common and usually carry no (or low) financial interest, they often entail other kinds of social, political, and economic obligations. Noncommercial informal credit tends to be available for small amounts for short terms, for emergencies, or for special occasions and specific purposes, such as land purchase, weddings, or house construction for a young couple. However, the capital for such loans is usually limited, and the amounts are often inadequate or the terms inappropriate for production credit for agriculture, local industries, trade, or services.

Informal commercial lenders, however, typically provide credit that can be used for both production and consumption—but at high cost to the lower-income borrower. The prevalence of high-interest rates in informal credit markets is so well documented that the literature is filled with debates as to why these rates are so high. There are two main arguments.[8]

The first, and older, view is that informal credit markets are noncompetitive and that monopolistic moneylenders charge high interest rates, extracting substantial profits. A variant of the monopolistic moneylender is the lender whose primary aim is not to extract interest payments but to force the borrower to default. The so-called "malicious moneylender" is widely viewed as a myth (Von Pischke 1991, 174), yet there is considerable evidence, dating from at least the 1920s until the present, in support of the argument that some informal commercial lenders gain monopoly profits, collected in money, land, or labor.[9]

There is also substantial evidence to support the opposing position, that most rural lenders are neither exploitive nor malicious.[10] It is argued that they are providers of important financial services in rural areas. Operations of moneylenders "are frequently more cost-effective and useful to the poor than those of the specialized farm-credit institutions, cooperatives and commercial banks that governments use to supplant moneylenders. . . . The emerging perspective is that informal financial arrangements are generally robust and socially useful. . . . Widespread use of informal finance suggests that it is well suited to most rural conditions" (Von Pischke, Adams, and Donald 1983, 8).

As discussed in the volume edited by Von Pischke, Adams, and Donald, this conclusion assumes that the high interest rates for informal commercial loans reflect the lenders' transaction costs and risk.[11] One view is that "the high cost of administering small loans and persistent repayment problems lead to high interest rates in informal rural money markets in the developing world" (Bottomley 1983, 243). However, another view, also widespread, is that risk premiums and transaction costs do not explain the high interest rates charged—because, in fact, these costs are low! Thus, "informal intermediaries . . . survive on the basis of competitiveness, financial viability and low cost operations" (Bouman 1989, 9). Germidis, Kessler, and Meghir (1991) also find that transaction costs and risks in the informal sector are low. Reasons cited include low overhead, low default risk, good and cheap information on the creditworthiness of potential borrowers, and interlinked credit contracts.

Are the transaction costs and risks of informal commercial lenders high or low? The answer, of course, is that they are both—depending upon the circumstances. Lenders' transaction costs can be expensive, and lenders may charge high prices when they cannot diversify risk. Transaction costs and risks, especially for repeat borrowers, can also be low. There is considerable variation in informal financial markets, as was pointed out by Millard Long three decades ago (1968): "In most Asian countries, the agricultural credit markets . . . are not classifiable either as fully competitive or fully monopolized. Competition may prevail in one village market while the next is under the control of a single lender. Even within a village one borrower may have several sources of loans, while another lacking alternatives may be forced to pay monopolized rates" (276).[12]

The presence or absence of "malicious moneylenders" is not an issue of myth or reality; such lenders represent one end of a continuum within informal financial markets. It has been extensively documented that some informal moneylenders are malicious and exploitive, and that many are not. The latter provide useful financial services; the relevant question is, Does the borrower need to pay such high interest rates?

Malicious moneylenders, transaction costs, and risk premiums can all be causes of high interest rates. However, none of these, nor even all of them together, explains satisfactorily the widespread persistence of high interest rates in informal rural credit markets. The reason that informal commercial lenders charge high interest rates, especially to lower-income borrowers, is that *informal credit markets are not competitive, as is widely assumed, but are in fact explained by a variant of monopolistic competition.*

Informal credit markets tend to consist of many small monopolies or quasi monopolies generated by the dynamics of local-level socioeconomic processes and associated information flows. The dynamics of these markets are best explained by monopolistic competition, except that in this case monopoly profits can be maintained over the long term. Lenders, even over time, do not usually compete for the same borrowers. Therefore, the constraint on lenders tends not to be the availability of funds; the constraint is on the number of borrowers over whom the lender can maintain sufficient control to minimize the default rate.

Informal commercial lenders of all types understand well that lending beyond their sphere of influence and control of information can lead to high default, and thereby to a lowering of the quality of the loan portfolio. Such lenders typically provide credit to their commodity suppliers, employees, tenants, and others with whom they have interlinked transactions. These linkages, combined with local political alliances, create information flows that are both channeled and constrained by local-level social processes. It is the networks through which these interlinked transactions are conducted, and the associated political, business, social, and kin-based relationships of the locality, that typically provide the information flows and controls that enable lenders to recover their loans with relatively low risk.

While local business networks and political alliances provide control mechanisms, they also provide constraints that effectively limit the number of borrowers per lender. The prevalence of loans linked to transactions in other markets is related to a widely reported characteristic of local credit: informal commercial lenders typically provide credit to relatively small numbers of borrowers (usually well under 50, often under 20, and very rarely over 100, each).[13] Credit rationing is practiced by moneylenders all over the world—not necessarily because of capital constraints, but because of limits on the number of potential borrowers from whom the lender can collect. As Aleem observed from a study of the Chambar rural credit market in Pakistan: "Each lender in this environment is perceived by borrowers to be offering a different product; thus, each faces a downward-sloping demand curve, which gives him some flexibility to price according to his own circumstances. Equilibrium in this model involves a distortion in the market; there are too many lenders in relation to the size of the informal credit market. . . . This observation of 'too many lenders' is not unique to the Chambar market. Similar observations have been made in studies of credit markets in other countries" (1993, 148–49).

Thus, local politics, market linkages, and the structure of information transfers often serve to limit the number of borrowers per lender, and to maintain high interest rates in the informal commercial credit market. Aleem makes the important point that, "because of these [information] imperfections [in the market] the lender does not have an incentive to cut interest rates to increase his market share, even when rates are well above his marginal cost of lending" (150).

For lenders, market entry is limited primarily by their access to borrowers operating within the area in which the lender holds political influence and controls good information and by the number of individuals with whom the lender can maintain transactions in other markets. Under these general conditions, lenders and borrowers tend to maintain long-term relationships. Borrowers face risks in changing informal lenders and are reported to do so only rarely.[14] Thus, informal commercial lenders tend not to compete for clients, or to compete imperfectly. The pattern of numerous small quasi monopolies reflects primarily local information flows and lenders' perceptions of their abilities to collect loans with low risk.

Yet, despite massive documentation to the contrary, the widespread assumption of a competitive informal credit market persists. For example, Bouman states, "One should not expect monopoly profits to be terribly important [in informal rural finance] since there are few barriers to entry into informal financial intermediation and competitive forces generally prevail" (1984, 243). There is considerable evidence to demonstrate that the latter is not true. A similar view: "Monopoly profits of the sort implied by these examples would surely attract vigorous competition that would severely erode returns" (Von Pischke 1991, 185). But what Von Pischke describes generally does not happen. Since lenders typically do not want to expand their market shares, they often have no incentive to lower interest rates. Therefore, loan terms that translate into high annual interest rates are widespread, well-entrenched, and accepted by the many poor borrowers who have no better options.

Lower-income borrowers generally have no other credit options for financing their productive activities because: (1) if such a borrower turns to another informal lender, he or she is likely to face significant risk for similar credit terms (the new lender may choose not to lend to the borrower, while the old lender may hear about the defection and cut off the borrower's credit [Robinson 1988]); (2) subsidized credit programs tend to bypass most lower-income borrowers; and (3) institutional commercial credit is typically unavailable at the local level. While noncommercial loans from friends, kin, and neighbors may be available, such loans are normally unsuited to ongoing finance of the borrowing household's productive activities. In the absence of an institutional alternative that provides access to commercial credit, such borrowers tend to stay with their informal commercial lenders, despite the high cost the borrowers pay for credit. The extensive evidence of monopolistic competition seems to have been largely ignored in the enthusiasm of the 1970s and 1980s for the elimination of intervention in rural credit markets, since the assumption of a competitive informal credit market was made an important part of that argument. In their seminal statements opposing credit subsidies, Adams, Von Pischke, and others sometimes lost sight of the difference between intervention and subsidy and tended to assume that removal of formal-sector interventions would leave behind local, informal competitive credit markets. As Siamwalla commented: "This critical literature [in Von Pischke, Adams, and Donald (1983)] stressed the distortions introduced by government policies [for credit subsidies] and, in doing so, tended to idealize the informal credit markets that did exist or that might have existed in absence of the massive government intervention in the credit market. There was a presumption that an intervention-free rural financial market would approximate the perfect competition model" (Siamwalla et al. 1993, 170).

Interventions and credit subsidies should not be confused. Removal of credit subsidies is essential for the development of competitive credit markets. However, removal of the subsidies will not, in itself, generally result in competitive microfinance. Interventions in local financial markets are important, primarily because the information that institutional microfinance can be profitable has not yet reached most parts of the developing world. Thus, Indonesia began to have competitive credit markets at the local level only *after* the government intervened in order to enable Bank Rakyat Indonesia's local banking system to become profitable; BRI's success then motivated other financial institutions to compete in the same market.

The widespread pattern of monopolistic competition in the informal commercial market—independent of whether or not the lenders are "malicious"—provides an important reason for institutional participation in local financial markets. In most developing countries, however, the reason for such intervention has rarely been understood. The result is that the poor pay far higher total costs for credit than would be required if conveniently located financial institutions were to provide them microcredit at commercial rates. *The difference to a poor borrower between paying a moneylender a flat monthly interest rate on the original loan balance of 20 or 30 percent or paying a financial institution a monthly flat rate of 1.5 percent, can be the growth of the borrower's enterprise.*

However, governments, and donor agencies have had little incentive to build sustainable institutions to provide microfinance at the local level because of the many widespread, but mistaken, assumptions. A policy maker is unlikely to give priority to the development of sustainable microfinance institutions if he or she believes that institutions cannot provide financial services at the local level because informal lenders have better information, meet demand, and benefit the poor; that the institution will adversely select its borrowers and have a high level of default; and that the working poor cannot or will not save in a financial institution, and that therefore the institution cannot be capitalized with savings. In Indonesia, and increasingly in other countries, all of these assumptions have been shown to be wrong. Nevertheless, these views persist.

The success of BRI in operating a profitable system of financial intermediation at the local level throughout Indonesia has, for the first time, engendered extensive competition from other financial institutions of many types. It is thus the *formal* sector, not the informal sector, that has the potential to make local financial markets competitive.

How Can Formal Financial Institutions Charge Lower Interest Rates?

There are three main reasons that formal financial institutions can provide commercial microfinance at interest rates much lower than those of informal commercial lenders. First, in contrast to informal commercial lenders, institutions providing commercial microfinance have an incentive to attain wide client outreach. Such institutions, for which the lending of money is a business (and not a way of retaining commodity suppliers, employees, or political supporters), price their loan products on commercial principles. They also provide incentives and training to staff in order to expand the institution's microfinance business and its profitability. In informal commercial markets, on the other hand, lenders typically lend only to a small number of borrowers over whom they already have some control through long-term interlinked transactions (in their roles as commodity buyer, employer, landlord, etc.) and from whom they can easily collect. The lending role is usually subordinate to the other relationship. If A, a long-term rice supplier to and borrower from rice merchant and lender B, goes to lender C for a loan, C is unlikely to lend to A so long as A remains linked with lender B. Lender C also wants to lend only to those whom he or she controls, and C will usually decide that loan collection in lender B's turf is too risky. Thus, informal commercial lenders generally have no incentive to lower their interest rates, because they know the borrowers linked with them cannot easily find another informal lender. However, informal lenders know that banks will not take away their suppliers or employees, and they are often (but not always) willing that their borrowers receive bank credit.

Second, banks and other formal-sector institutions providing commercial microfinance can benefit from their financial intermediation, from economies of scale, and from better protection against co-variant shocks.

Third, financial institutions with well-trained and motivated staff can obtain better information about larger numbers of lower-income borrowers than can an individual moneylender. This is so for the following reasons:

1. Voluntary savings services can provide the institution with good information about the economic activities and the character of large numbers of savers—who are also potential borrowers. This helps to keep loan repayment rates high and to lower the bank's costs for loan transactions.
2. Moneylenders are often clients of the financial institutions and may be willing to trade information for prime customer status.
3. Staff of bank branches are generally local people who maintain social and political relationships and who, in aggregate, have access to multiple local information flows.
4. In group lending programs, the peer group helps to screen borrowers and to recover payments.

For these reasons, institutions providing commercial microfinance can offer loans to creditworthy lower-income borrowers at much lower interest rates than the borrowers would normally pay to moneylenders. Because such institutions maintain many small branches located in areas convenient for the customers, and because they offer loans with simple procedures, borrowers' transaction costs tend to be relatively low. While these costs may still be higher than the transaction costs of borrowing from moneylenders, the total cost of borrowing from banks, especially for poorer borrowers, is generally far lower than the cost of borrowing from informal commercial lenders.

From the perspective of the financial institution, three aspects of sustainable microfinance—all apparently counter-intuitive to many bankers, politicians, and policy makers—are crucial to the new paradigm.

First, in order to combine wide coverage with institutional sustainability, interest rates for small loans must be significantly *higher* than the rates charged by large urban bank branches. This reflects the inescapable fact that the delivery of microfinance services at scattered locations is more expensive than providing larger loans and deposits in centrally located urban banks. Thus, the spread between loan and deposit interest rates must be sufficient to cover all the (nonsubsidized) financial costs, nonfinancial costs, and risk.

Second, the interest rates of self-sufficient microfinance institutions are highly attractive to lower-income borrowers at the local level because they represent a small fraction of the rates typically charged by informal lenders.

Third, there is vast unmet demand in developing countries for savings services that are delivered at the local level and that offer a combination of security, convenience, liquidity, confidentiality, access to loans, returns, and good service. In Indonesia, both BDB and BRI finance *all* their loans from locally mobilized savings.

THE DEVELOPMENT OF SUSTAINABLE MICROFINANCE IN INDONESIA

Indonesia, with a population of 190 million, is the world's fourth most populous country. It has a diverse economy, and the average annual economic growth since 1980 has been about 8 percent. In 1996 GDP per capita was about US$1,000. There has been a sharp reduction in the number of people below the poverty line, from over 60 percent in the 1960s to about 12 percent in 1996.

Viable microfinance comes in different forms. The three Indonesian financial institutions discussed below—a small private bank (BDB), a large state-owned commercial bank (BRI), and Badan Kredit Desa (BKD), a century-old network of village-owned banks, now supervised by BRI—all provide microfinance profitability without subsidy.

BANK DAGANG BALI, A SMALL PRIVATE BANK

The Bank Dagang Bali was opened in 1970 by I Gusti Made Oka and Sri Adnyani Oka, a husband and wife who had long previous experience as micro entrepreneurs and informal commercial lenders (Robinson 1995d). In 1968, the Okas used this knowledge to create a secondary market bank, Bank Pasar Umum (BPU), to provide financial services to lower-income people.

The BPU provided loans for a one-month term, with interest of 8 percent a month and a 3 percent fee for each loan. Loan repayments were collected in daily installments, and the capital was immediately re-lent. BPU became profitable very quickly because the Okas, with their extensive knowledge of the local financial market, knew that there was large demand for both savings and credit services and that they could undercut moneylenders by a wide margin.

By 1970, after two years of operation, the BPU had made Rp 15 million in profits (about $41,345), and the Okas decided to open a private bank in addition to the BPU. They borrowed an additional Rp 5 million (about $13,782) from the local provincial bank. With their initial capital of Rp 20 million (about $55,127) from the BPU profits and the bank loan, the Okas opened the Bank Dagang Bali—the second private bank in Bali—in September 1970. As of December 31, 1996, BDB—still a solely owned private bank—operated eight branches, eighteen subbranches, and four smaller offices that served as deposit collection points. All but two of the branches are located in Bali; the other two are in Jakarta and Surabaya, Indonesia's largest cities. The bank, which serves over 350,000 clients, had about $115 million in deposits and about $95 million in loans outstanding as of December 31, 1996. The annual effective interest rates on most small loans is about 30 percent, and repayment rates are typically above 98 percent. BDB has been profitable every year since it opened, and it is fully self-sufficient. During the 1990s, annual before-tax profits have ranged from about $1 million to about $1.7 million.

BDB is extremely active on the savings side of its microfinance activities and provides many services, including the maintenance of daily routes to visit customers at home or place of work. All savings are voluntary; savings are not required to obtain loans.

BANK RAKYAT INDONESIA, A LARGE STATE-OWNED COMMERCIAL BANK

Each of Indonesia's five state-owned commercial banks has traditionally held special responsibilities in addition to its general banking activities. The special assignment of Bank Rakyat Indonesia has been the provision of agricultural credit in rural areas. The bank also provides commercial, corporate, and international banking services. Since this paper concerns BRI's local banking division, the term "BRI" refers here only to the bank's local banking system.[15] In the early 1970s, BRI established over 3,600 small bank units at the subdistrict level throughout the country. Savings accounts were offered in BRI's unit banks beginning in the mid-1970s. However, the annual interest rates, set by the government for state-owned banks (12 percent for loans and 15 percent for most deposits) discouraged the units from undertaking effective savings mobilization.

BRI's bank units were originally set up as a channeling agent for subsidized loans to farmers under BIMAS, the credit component of Indonesia's massive program to achieve rice self-sufficiency.[16] Originally, all units were located in rural areas. However, in 1989 unit banks were added in lower-income urban areas. Thus, the term "local banking" refers here to microfinance services delivered at the local level in both rural and urban areas.

The initial approach to financial intermediation at the local level through BRI's unit banking system was similar to that found in many developing countries whose rural banking programs were designed under the old paradigm: institutional credit was subsidized, the credit program was poorly planned, the low-interest BIMAS loans typically bypassed the poor, arrears and losses were high, and deposits were low. During 1983, BRI's unit banking system sustained a loss of $28 million, and the bank gave serious consideration to closing down the system. However, the Indonesian government began a series of major financial reforms in 1983. The first of these, in June 1983, permitted government banks to set their own interest rates on most loans and deposits. Subsequent financial deregulation provided an enabling environment in which BRI could transform its subsidized local banks into a sustainable system of financial intermediation, operating at the subdistrict level in both rural and urban areas.

Since January 1984, BRI's local bank units have offered the KUPEDES program of general rural credit.[17] Most Indonesian households have multiple income sources, and KUPEDES loans are provided for any viable productive activity, including services and trade. The loans are often used, in fact, for financing several activities within one household. KUPEDES loans from about US$11 to about $11,000 are available to any borrower deemed creditworthy. Loan terms up to two years for working capital and three years for investment capital are available.

In 1995, a new set of deposit and savings accounts was introduced at BRI's unit banks. These accounts offer the depositor security at convenient bank locations, and customers can choose among instruments offering different ratios of liquidity and returns. BRI's local banking system broke even at the end of 1985 after only two years of commercial operation, and the system has been profitable every year since 1986. At the end of 1996, in BRI's 3,595 local bank units, there was about US$1.7 billion in KUPEDES credit outstanding to about 2.5 million borrowers (table 1). The KUPEDES long-term loss ratio as of the same date was 2.2 percent. The low rate of arrears is attributable primarily to the fact that borrowers repay promptly because they want to retain the option to reborrow; there is also a monetary incentive for prompt repayment. For many KUPEDES borrowers, the only alternative is to borrow from the informal commercial market at much higher interest rates.

TABLE 1
BANK RAKYAT INDONESIA'S UNIT BANKING SYSTEM:
PERFORMANCE INDICATORS 1993–1996

	1993	1994	1995	1996
Total real value of loans outstanding (billions US $)[a]	$1.20	$1.34	$1.53	$1.74
Total number of loans outstanding (millions)	1.9	2.1	2.3	2.5
Long-term loss ratio[b]	3.1%	2.6%	2.3%	2.2%
Total real value of savings (billions US $)[a]	$2.66	$2.86	$2.89	$3.03
Total number of deposit accounts (millions)	11.4	13.1	14.5	16.1
Return on assets	3.4%	5.2%	6.5%	5.7%
Total number of units	3267	3388	3512	3595
Percentage of profitable units	89.3%	93.7%	95.7%	94.9%

[a]In 1996 prices
[b]The ratio of the cumulative amount due but unpaid since the opening of the unit, to the total amount due.

From the early 1970s until the financial deregulation of June 1983, BRI's unit banking system had mobilized only about $17 million in savings nationwide in more than 3,600 unit banks. This was widely attributed within the government and the formal financial sector to the lack of local demand for financial services, the absence of "bank-mindedness," and the mistrust of banks that were assumed to characterize Indonesia's rural population. These assumptions were wrong. As of December 1996, the unit banking system held deposits of about $3 billion in about 16.1 million deposit accounts.

BRI's success in local banking since 1984 is based on:

1. an extensive organizational reform within the bank that created a unit banking division;
2. use of scarce high-level management resources for microfinance development;
3. a spread between loan and deposit interest rates that enables institutional profitability;
4. convenient, secure unit bank locations at the local level;
5. a simple, uniform, and appropriately designed and priced set of instruments and services;
6. simple, transparent reporting procedures;
7. a system under which each unit operates as a "profit center," with the staff receiving performance incentives based on the unit's outreach and profitability;
8. a well-designed and well-implemented supervision process;
9. the creation of a specialized staff training program that emphasizes knowledge of local markets and responsibility at the local unit bank level; and
10. respect for, and close relations with, the units' predominantly rural, lower-income clients.

THE BADAN KREDIT DESA, A BRI-SUPERVISED NETWORK OF VILLAGE BANKS

In addition to the activities of its local banking system, BRI supervises and in some cases provides commercial loans to capitalize a network of traditional village banks in Java and Madura known collectively as the Badan Kredit Desa system and individually as BKDs. Begun in 1896 under the Dutch colonial government, these banks are owned by their respective village governments. At the end of 1995, the BKD system served over 750,000 clients. There are 4,806 BKDs in active operation; each provides financial services on a commercial basis within its own village, usually on a weekly basis. BRI's units are located at the subdistrict level, serving the villages of the subdistrict, while the BKDs reach deeper into their own villages. Most BKD loans are for short terms, usually for 10 to 12 weeks and for amounts below $75. Interest rates set by the respective local governments are typically at least double the BRI bank unit rates. Establishing a savings account is a condition of receiving a loan.

While most BKDs finance their loans from retained earnings, they can borrow at a commercial rate from BRI in order to finance their loan portfolios. BKDs with excess liquidity (derived mostly from profits) can deposit these at BRI and obtain interest on the deposits. Profits in 1995 for the total BKD network were about $7 million.

SUSTAINABLE MICROFINANCE IN INDONESIA: SUMMARY

Financial services are widely available to lower-income clients throughout Indonesia. BDB finances the greatest range of clients, while BRI's local banking system serves by far the largest number of microfinance clients. In addition, the village banks, the BKDs, provide loans and offer deposit facilities to even poorer clients than those typically served by BDB and BRI. Although the Indonesian financial institutions discussed here represent widely varying institutional structures, they have important underlying commonalities:

- The institutions provide financial services profitably to large numbers of the working poor.
- Interest rates for loans are higher than those normally charged by large urban Indonesian banks, reflecting the higher costs involved in financial intermediation when services are delivered at the local level.
- Loan arrears are low. There are a number of factors involved, but the most important is that the terms of the loan are attractive to borrowers—who want to repay so that they can retain the option to reborrow.
- In BRI and BDB, where voluntary savings are permitted and compulsory savings are not required, deposits finance all loans. In the BKDs, retained earnings and commercial loans finance the loan portfolio.
- Activities are restricted entirely to financial services; no community development, social services, client training, or other nonfinancial activities are carried out by these institutions.
- All the institutions are self-sufficient and operate without subsidy.

BRI'S LOCAL BANKING SYSTEM AND THE GRAMEEN BANK OF BANGLADESH: A COMPARISON

BRI's local banking system and the Grameen Bank of Bangladesh are the two largest indigenous banks in the world providing microfinance in their respective countries. A comparison will be useful in helping to explore policy issues. Grameen is a well-known, subsidized model of successful microfinance delivery, and it represents a different approach from that of the Indonesian banks.

Since Grameen is a special bank that provides only microfinance, while BRI's local banking activities are carried out by a division of a larger commercial bank, the comparison made here is between Grameen Bank and BRI's local banking division. In order to provide comparability between the two, most of the data used here are from Yaron, Benjamin, and Piprek 1997, where uniform adjustments to the financial reports from both institutions have already been made. Information has also been included from Christen, Rhyne, and Vogel 1995 and from more recent data provided by BRI's local banking division.

The Grameen figures, however, are difficult to obtain and to interpret. There are discrepancies among the various recent sources,[18] and the terms used in those sources are not always clearly defined. Despite the difficulties with data, the overall comparison between the two institutions is clear-cut and important. There are both substantial similarities and fundamental differences in the philosophies and the operations of these two banks.

The 1995 population in Bangladesh was 120 million and in Indonesia 193 million, while the per capita GNP was $240 for Bangladesh and $980 for Indonesia (World Bank 1997b). Both the BRI unit banks and Grameen began their present banking activities in the mid-1980s and by the end of 1995 held a roughly comparable number of outstanding loans—2.06 million for Grameen and 2.3 million for BRI (table 2). Grameen provides group loans, while BRI's unit banking system offers individual loans. However, both deliver small loans locally, and both have high repayment rates.

Both banks serve poor borrowers, although Grameen reaches the poorest borrowers directly, while BRI reaches them primarily through the BKDs. The BKDs and Grameen both require savings from all borrowers. However, Grameen deposits much of its savings in fixed and short-term accounts in other banks and uses subsidized funds to finance its loan portfolio. In contrast, BRI uses its deposits to finance its entire KUPEDES loan portfolio.

Since Bangladesh is a poorer country than Indonesia, the average loan balance at Grameen ($140) was considerably smaller than at BRI ($617). However, the average loan balance as a percentage of GNP per capita was similar: 63.6 percent for Grameen and 70.1 percent for BRI. BRI's local banking system and the Grameen Bank both serve large numbers of low-income borrowers, although in different ways, and both recover their loans. There are, however, some major differences between the microfinance activities of the two banks.

INSTITUTIONAL PURPOSE AND PERFORMANCE

The Grameen Bank maintains an integrated approach in which both social services and credit are provided to members (Khandker 1993, 1; Khandker, Khalily, and Khan 1995, 12). Thus, in addition to its financial operations, Grameen Bank provides services such as training of members in health, nutrition, family planning, and livestock and poultry care; promotion of seedling distribution, tree planting, and kitchen gardens; and operation of schools and day care centers. BRI's services are limited to financial intermediation.

Grameen's 1995 annual effective interest rate for loans was about 20 percent, while at BRI's local banking system the rate was about 32 percent. According to a 1994 study, salary costs for lending operations as a percentage of average annual loan portfolio at BRI (5.0 percent) were less than half those of Grameen (11.2 percent). Other administrative costs as a percentage of portfolio at BRI (2.1

TABLE 2
INDICATORS OF OUTREACH AND SUSTAINABILITY OF THE GRAMEEN BANK
AND BRI UNIT BANKS (1995)

	Grameen Bank	*BRI Unit Banks*
Country population (1994) (millions)	117.9	190.4
Country GNP/capita (1994) (US$)	$220	$880
Average inflation (1994)	4.6%	8.9%
Number of branches	1,056	3,512 (plus 423 village posts
Number of staff	12,268	17,174
Annual effective interest rate	20%	32%
Real effective interest rate	14.7%	21.2%
Average loan balance (US$)	$140	$617
Average loan balance as percenatge of GNP/capita	63.6%	70.1%
Number of loans outstanding (millions)	2.06	2.3
Value of loans outstanding (millions US$)	$289	$1,419
Number of savings accounts (millions)	2.06	14.5
Value of deposits (millions US$)	$133.3[a]	$2,675
Value of average savings accounts (US$)	$65	$185
Total savings as a percentage of outstanding loans	46.1%	188.5%
Return on assets	0.14%[b]	6.5%

SOURCES: Country data are from World Bank 1996. Data for the Grameen Bank are from Yaron, Benjamin, Piprek 1997. Data for BRI are from Bank Rakyat Indonesia. All data represent 1995 end-of-year figures except where otherwise noted.

[a]Data on the value of Grameen's savings are difficult to interpret. This figure is an estimate based on a comparison of multiple sources (see Yaron, Benjamin, Piprek 1997; Khandker, Khalily, and Khan 1995; World Bank 1997b; and Christen, Rhyne, and Vogel 1995).

[b]Grameen's 1995 reported ROA of 0.14 was positive only because of the substantial subsidies the bank received.

percent) were well below the Grameen figure of 5.7 percent (Rhyne and Rotblatt 1994, table 7). The operating costs of the two banks reflect the different services provided to customers.

Grameen serves its members; BRI serves the public. Grameen calls its customers "beneficiaries"; BRI calls its customers "clients." In 1995 Grameen had 2.06 million members who were both borrowers and savers; BRI's unit banks had 2.3 million borrowers and 14.5 million savings and deposit accounts.[19] The BRI local banking system maintains over three times the number of branch offices as Grameen. BRI and the BKDs together have about eight times as many local offices as Grameen.

The philosophies of the two banks concerning savings mobilization are very different. The Grameen Bank uses the slogan: "Savings is an integral part of lending" (Khandker 1993, 4). Believing that its members must be taught to save, Grameen requires savings from its members. This is thought to "promote the financial discipline of the poor" (5). Grameen reportedly accepts savings from nonmembers, but the number of such savers and the value of their deposits are not known (Rhyne and Rotblatt 1994, 13).

In contrast, BRI does not assume that savings is part of lending but believes rather that lending and savings are both integral parts of financial intermediation. BRI assumes that the working poor save and that if a bank offers savings instruments and services appropriate for their demand, many poor clients will save in the bank voluntarily. BRI understands also that the microfinance market is large, and that at a given time, savings services will be demanded by more people than credit services. Accordingly, BRI's local banks provide savings services to the public.

The approaches of the two institutions are reflected in their respective performances and degrees of sustainability. At Grameen, the value of outstanding loans at the end of 1995 was $289 million; at BRI it was $1.4 billion. As of December 31, 1995, Grameen had about $133 million in savings compared with $2.7 billion for BRI's local banking division. BRI's 6:1 ratio of the number of savings accounts to number of loans, in comparison with Grameen's 1:1 ratio, highlights the difference between requiring savings from members and mobilizing voluntary savings from the public.

SUSTAINABILITY

BRI's local banking system is not subsidized and has been profitable and self-sufficient every year since 1986. All the loans in the system are financed by its deposits. While the system received subsidies for aspects of institution building (initial capital, unit bank infrastructure, training, buildings, and technical assistance), its KUPEDES loan portfolio was never subsidized. In contrast, while Grameen requires savings, the savings do not finance most of the loans, and the bank is unable to leverage commercial funds. The institution remains dependent on low-cost funds and is not fully self-sufficient.

The primary subsidies Grameen receives are in the form of interest-free loans or concessional interest rates on loan capital obtained from donors. The government also provides subsidized loans. Of Grameen's nearly $74 million in foreign capital in 1994, most was received interest free, with the remainder provided at an interest rate of 2 percent per year (Morduch 1997). Moreover, a study of the Grameen Bank conducted by the World Bank and the Bangladesh Institute of Development Studies estimated that in 1993, foreign funds represented nearly 75 percent of total resources available for Grameen (Khandker, Khalily, and Khan 1995). However, more recently "the Grameen Bank has seen steady increases in the amount of subsidized capital obtained, but with a recent shift toward borrowing from the Central Bank" (Morduch 1997, 29).

Thus, in contrast to BRI's unit banking system, where there are no subsidies and where the 1995 return on assets of 6.5 percent is calculated on a commercial banking basis, Grameen's 1995 return of 0.14 percent was positive only because of the substantial subsidies that the bank received (see table 2).

A USAID study of eleven successful microfinance programs (Christen, Rhyne, Vogel 1995) analyzed the levels of sustainability of each institution (see note 2). The Grameen Bank was classified as operationally self-sufficient but not covering the commercial costs of loanable funds. BRI's unit banking system was classified as fully self-sufficient, with revenues covering all costs and risks.

While both banks help to finance rural development, BRI's unit banking system is economically sustainable. Grameen has played an important role in the development of institutional microfinance by demonstrating on a large scale that the poor are good credit risks. However, its approach to microfinance requires continuing subsidies. Grameen could become self-sufficient if it raised its interest rate on loans. A move towards sustainability would also be helped by separating its financial from its social services, mobilizing voluntary savings from the public, and using the savings to finance its loans.

DEVELOPING SUSTAINABLE MICROFINANCE: POLICY IMPLICATIONS

The new commercial microfinance model challenges the widespread assumption that subsidies are required for microfinance in developing countries. Since government and donor funds can supply only a small fraction of global microfinance demand, financial intermediation by self-sufficient institutions is the *only* way that financial services can be provided to lower-income people worldwide.

While the Grameen Bank has helped large numbers of poor people, this bank currently depends on continuing donor and government injections of low-cost funds. The microfinance model developed in Indonesia, however, is sustainable and does not require infusions of government subsidy or foreign aid. Also, unlike Grameen, BRI does not promote replications of itself. BRI's approach is rather to explain the underlying principles of sustainable microfinance to its many international visitors, demonstrate its methods, and show its results. It is left to the visitors to adapt what is suitable in the context of their own countries. Many institutions in the developing world are in various stages of adapting the principles of the Indonesian approach to the special circumstances found in their countries.

The World Bank's Operations Evaluation Department identifies the reasons for the success of BRI's local banking system:

> The program succeeded because the banks loaned at market rates, used income to finance their operations, kept operating costs low, and devised appropriate savings instruments to attract depositors. By mobilizing rural savings . . . [the local banking system] was not only provided . . . with a stable source of funds, it also kept financial savings in rural areas, thus helping development growth in the countryside. Other reasons for success included: the simplicity of loan designs, which enabled the banks to keep costs down; effective management at the unit level, backed by close supervision and monitoring by the center; and appropriate staff training and performance incentives. (*World Bank News* 1996, 6)

IMPLICATIONS FOR GOVERNMENTS

Microfinance made widely available is an effective and crucial tool for poverty alleviation; it is appropriately provided by commercial institutions. Credit subsidies, which are capital-constrained, serve in fact to prevent access to credit on a global scale by the working poor who could make good use of commercial loans. However, other tools are required for the poorest of the poor, who have prior needs. The provision of food, employment, health services, and other basic requirements needed for overcoming desperate poverty are appropriately financed by government and donor subsidies and grants; these tools are properly the responsibility of ministries of social welfare, health, labor, and others, as well as of private charities.

Can the commercial approach to microfinance be successful in poorer countries like Bangladesh, as well as in higher-income, faster-growing economies like Indonesia's? The answer appears to be yes. There are several reasons. First, the Grameen Bank and other financial institutions providing microcredit in Bangladesh have proven that there are many poor borrowers who can use credit productively and who repay loans promptly. Second, commercial microcredit is already working in Bangladesh. The Association for Social Advancement (ASA), a highly successful nongovernmental organization, provides microcredit in Bangladesh at commercial interest rates. Until August 1995, ASA's annual effective interest rate was 31.8 percent; as of June 1995 ASA reported 267,500 active borrowers with loans from $50 to $175. In August 1995, the rate was reduced to 24.4 percent (Rutherford 1995, 95–99). ASA's approach to setting interest rates is similar to that of BRI, which reduced its KUPEDES interest rates in 1995 (see note 6). Start-up costs and early mistakes can be expensive for institutions starting commercial microfinance. Therefore, pricing loans higher at the beginning, improving efficiency, and then decreasing interest rates later is a sensible strategy.

Third, other very poor countries, such as Tanzania (1994 per capita GNP: $140) and India (1994 per capita GNP: $320), have been able to mobilize large amounts of savings in their rural banks and are presently involved in large rural banking reforms designed to move them towards the commercial microfinance model. It appears that there is similar potential in Bangladesh (Rutherford 1995).

Can borrowers in poor countries pay the interest rates needed for the lending institution to become sustainable? There is substantial evidence that poor borrowers around the world already pay far higher interest rates to moneylenders than the rates needed for institutional viability. In addition, financial institutions using the group-lending approach in poor countries tend to allow the group to lend its money to its members at a rate fixed by the particular group. Frequently these loans are provided at a substantially higher interest rate than that received by the group; thus, the end borrower is already paying a nonsubsidized interest rate.

The demand for commercial credit and savings services among the working poor is massive in developing countries, and meeting this demand through commercial microfinance is one of the most powerful tools in the poverty alleviation toolbox.

For commercial microfinance to be successful, however, government must undertake an enabling and supportive role. This includes regulation, supervision, and education of the public, as well as recognizing and rectifying earlier mistakes. In Indonesia, the minister of finance played a crucial role in developing the first large-scale system of commercial microfinance through BRI's unit banking system. He describes what led to the project:

> By the early 1980s we began to realize that, year after year, the subsidies and the arrears of our subsidized rural credit programs were large, the programs were inefficient, and the loans generally did not reach the intended borrowers. In brief, our approach to local finance was ineffective and unsustainable. Not only were our subsidized credit programs not a driving force for rural development, they were actually slowing it down! Having recognized the severe deficiencies of these programs, we decided, in 1983, to begin a new program for rural finance that would be based on principles of commercial finance. (Wardhana, forthcoming)

Many governments and institutions are becoming increasingly aware that, while there are important lessons to be learned from Grameen's successes in credit delivery to the poor, the model is not affordable on a global scale. It is particularly important that the governments of larger countries be well-informed about the crucial differences between institutional commercial microfinance and donor-driven credit delivery systems. For example, in India the central bank has taken the lead in identifying the problems in the country's subsidized credit programs and the losses that have occurred over decades in rural banks. In 1996, India deregulated interest rates and allowed commercial banks and regional banks to set their own interest rates. Plans are now under way for restructuring the regional rural banks into sustainable financial intermediaries.

IMPLICATIONS FOR DONORS

Donors can help the emergence of commercial microfinance in a variety of ways. First, donors should not provide funds for on-lending at subsidized interest rates. Microcredit programs that offer subsidized loans to borrowers undercut the institutions that provide commercial microfinance, thus harming the effort to meet microfinance demand on a large scale. Second, donors should insist that financial and social services be funded separately and differently. The former should be financed commercially. The latter, where appropriate, can be funded by donors. Third, donors can help to identify institutions that are potentially qualified for commercial microfinance and are committed to attaining self-sufficiency. These institutions can be provided with grants and concessional loans, not for their continuing loan portfolios, but rather for their institutional development. Fourth, when necessary and feasible, donors should use their influence with governments to assist the latter in introducing appropriate regulations, or deregulation, and in developing supervisory bodies that can provide suitable oversight for institutions offering commercial microfinance. Fifth, donors can disseminate "best practices" in microfinance through workshops, training courses, and study tours. In recent years there has been a shift in these directions on the part of many donors.

IMPLICATIONS FOR SOCIAL AND ECONOMIC DEVELOPMENT

Only institutional commercial microfinance can combine relatively low-cost credit with sustainability and wide outreach in the provision of financial services to the working poor. Therefore, the shift from donor-assisted credit delivery programs to sustainable financial intermediation is essential if microfinance demand is to be met on the global scale. Meeting this demand matters for several reasons.

Clients of institutions that offer microcredit at commercial interest rates and provide returns on deposits can improve the management of their financial affairs, raise productivity, and achieve enterprise growth and diversification. Financial institutions providing commercial microfinance can become fully self-sufficient without subsidy, enabling wide outreach to lower-income clients. Governments benefit from reduced subsidies and reduced losses and from the increased social and economic development that results from sustainable microfinance. The economy benefits from increased production and from the new resources made available for investment. Overall, the widespread availability of financial services to the working poor could stimulate economic growth, increase equity, and improve the quality of life for hundreds of millions of people.

NOTES

The research discussed here has been supported by the Indonesian Ministry of Finance, the United States Agency for International Development, the Consultative Group to Aid the Poorest, the World Bank, the United Nations Development Program, the Ford Foundation, the Calmeadow Foundation (Toronto), and others. The author is grateful to Peter Fidler for his assistance in the research and preparation of this chapter. An early version of this paper was presented at the meeting "Financial Services and the Poor: U.S. and Developing Country Experiences" sponsored by USAID and held at the Brookings Institution, on September 28–30, 1994. Parts of the "Introduction" section are adapted from Robinson 1997b, and parts of the section on policy implications are adapted from Robinson 1996.

1. See Christen, Rhyne, and Vogel 1995 and Rosenberg 1994 for discussion.

2. What are the characteristics of a sustainable microfinance program? A USAID study of sustainability in eleven microfinance programs in developing countries (Christen, Rhyne, and Vogel 1995) found the institutions to be located along a sustainability continuum that ranged from a new institution in which revenues did not yet cover operating costs to institutions that were fully self-sufficient without subsidy. The study divided the continuum into three levels of sustainability: (1) institutions in which revenues from interest and fees do not cover operating costs, (2) institutions in which revenues cover operating costs but do not cover the commercial costs of loanable funds, and (3) fully self-sufficient institutions that cover all costs and risks. "Sustainable," therefore refers to level 3 institutions; their revenues cover both nonfinancial and financial costs calculated on a commercial basis. Such institutions are profitable without subsidy, and a return on equity can be expected that is equivalent to returns that can be obtained in the private sector.

3. The term "working poor" as used here denotes those poor people who have sufficient income and opportunity to make use of, and to repay, micro-loans. It is recognized, however, that some people who are not yet bankable by microfinance institutions do work, often very hard.

4. For overviews and bibliographies concerning the problems of subsidized rural credit programs, see, among others, Donald 1976; Von Pischke, Adams, and Donald 1983; Adams, Graham, and Von Pischke 1984; Von Pischke 1991; and Gonzalez-Vega 1993.

5. See Germidis, Kessler, and Meghir 1991 and Robinson 1994a for extensive references on informal commercial lenders charging interest rates in this range in developing countries throughout the world.

6. A flat interest rate on the original balance of 1.5 percent per month (approximately equivalent to 32 percent annual effective rate on the declining balance for a twelve-month loan) was charged from the beginning of BRI's general purpose credit program (KUPEDES) in 1984, until 1995. In 1995, a range of flat interest rates from 1 to 1.5 percent per month was instituted (equivalent to annual effective rates from 26 to 32 percent). Inflation remained at or below 10 percent throughout this period.

7. See Germidis, Kessler, and Meghir 1991 for a review of studies concerning the share of formal and informal credit in rural areas of developing countries. See also Von Pischke 1991; Hoff, Braverman, and Stiglitz 1993; and Ghate et al. 1993.

8. For a review of the debates, see Von Pischke 1991; and Germidis, Kessler, and Meghir 1991.

9. For discussion of monopolistic and exploitative money lending, see, among others, Darling 1978; Indian School of Social Sciences 1976; Rao 1977; Sharma 1978; Vyas 1980; Marla Sarma 1981; Kamble 1982; Roth 1983; and Robinson 1988. See Robinson 1994a for further references.

10. See Von Pischke, Adams, and Donald 1983; and Von Pischke 1991.

11. For discussion of transaction costs and risk, explaining the interest rates of rural lenders in relation to these, see Bottomley 1983; Tun Wai 1980; Adams and Graham 1981; Wilmington 1983; Singh 1983; Von Pischke, Adams, and Donald 1983; Vogel 1984; Adams and Vogel 1986; Bouman 1989; Von Pischke 1991. See Siamwalla et al. 1993 for an opposing view. For discussion of lender transaction costs in linked and unlinked loans, see Floro and Yotopoulos 1991.

12. See also Floro and Yotopoulos (1991); they demonstrate that lender transaction costs vary, depending on a number of interlinked variables.

13. See Robinson 1994a for early references concerning the widespread practice whereby many lenders operate in rural credit markets, each lending to relatively small numbers of borrowers. For more recent examples, see Ladman and Torico 1981 for Bolivia; Harriss 1983 for India; Bouman 1984 for Sri Lanka; Varian 1989 for Bangladesh; Siamwalla et al. 1993 for Thailand; Aleem 1993 for Pakistan; and Carstens 1995 for Mexico. See also Bell and Srinivasan 1985; Von Pischke 1991; and Floro and Yotopoulos 1991.

14. See Robinson 1988; Aleem 1993; Siamwalla et al. 1993.

15. For the development of BRI's local banking system, see Sugianto 1989; Patten and Rosengard 1991; Robinson 1992, 1994a, 1994b, 1995a, 1995b, 1997b, and 1997c; and Sugianto and Robinson forthcoming. For comparative studies that include BRI, see Yaron 1992; Otero and Rhyne 1994; Rhyne and Rotblatt 1994; and Christen, Rhyne, and Vogel 1994.

16. Improved national BIMAS (an acronym for Bimbingan Massal, or Mass Guidance) was begun during the 1970–71 wet season.

17. KUPEDES is an acronym for Kredit Unum Pedesaan (General Rural Credit).

18. Sources used for Grameen Bank data are drawn from: Hossain 1988; Fuglesang and Chandler 1993; Yaron 1992; Hubbard 1994; Rhyne and Rotblatt 1994; Christen, Rhyne, and Vogel 1994; Khandker, Khalily, and Khan 1995; Yaron, Benjamin, and Piprek 1997; and Robinson 1995c, 1996, 1997a, and 1997b.

19. Fixed deposit accounts constitute 10.1 percent of total unit bank deposits and 6.5 percent of the total number of accounts as of December 31, 1995. The rest of the funds are held in various types of savings instruments. The terms "deposit" and "savings" are used synonymously in this chapter.

REFERENCES

Adams, Dale, and Douglas H. Graham. 1981. "A Critique of Traditional Agricultural Credit Projects and Policies." *Journal of Development Economics* 8 (3): 347–66.

Adams, Dale, Douglas H. Graham, and John D. Von Pischke. 1984. *Undermining Rural Development with Cheap Credit*. Boulder, Colo.: Westview Press.

Adams, Dale, and Robert C. Vogel. 1986. "Rural Financial Markets in Low Income Countries: Recent Controversies and Lessons." *World Development* 14(4): 477–87.

Aleem, Irfan. 1993. "Imperfect Information, Screening and the Costs of Informal Lending: A Study of a Rural Credit Market in Pakistan." In *The Economics of Rural Organization: Theory, Practice, and Policy,* edited by Karla Hoff, Avishay Braverman, and Joseph E. Stiglitz, 131–53. New York: Oxford University Press.

Bell, C., and T. N. Srinivasan. 1985. "An Anatomy of Transactions in Rural Credit Markets in Andhra Pradesh, Bihar, and Punjab." Mimeograph. World Bank, Washington, D.C.

Bottomley, Anthony. 1983. "Interest Rate Determination in Underdeveloped Rural Areas." In *Rural Financial Markets in Developing Countries: Their Use and Abuse,* edited by John D. Von Pischke, Dale Adams, and Gordon Donald, 243–50. Baltimore: Johns Hopkins University Press.

Bouman, F. J. A. 1984. "Informal Saving and Credit Arrangements in Developing Countries: Observations from Sri Lanka." In *Undermining Rural Development with Cheap Credit,* edited by Dale Adams, Douglas H. Graham, and John D. Von Pischke, 232–47. Boulder, Colo.: Westview Press.

———. 1989. *Small, Short and Unsecured: Informal Rural Finance in India.* Delhi: Oxford University Press.

Carstens, Catherine Mansell. 1995. *Las Finanzas Populares en Mexico: El Redescubrimiento de un Sistema Financiero Olvidado.* Mexico City: Institute Technologico Autonome de Mexico.

Castello, Carlos, Katherine Stearns, and Robert Christen. 1991. "Exploring Interest Rates: Their True Significance for Microentrepreneurs and Credit Programs." Discussion Paper no. 6, ACCION International, Cambridge, Mass.

Christen, Robert, Elisabeth Rhyne, and Robert Vogel. 1995. "Maximizing the Outreach of Microenterprise Finance: An Analysis of Successful Microfinance Programs." USAID Program and Operations Assessment Report no. 10, USAID, Washington, D.C.

Darling, Malcolm L. 1978. *The Punjab Peasant in Prosperity and Debt.* (Fourth edition, originally published 1925). Columbia, Mo.: South Asia Books.

Donald, Gordon. 1976. *Credit for Small Farmers in Developing Countries.* Boulder, Colo.: Westview Press.

Floro, Sagrario L., and Pan A. Yotopoulos. 1991. *Informal Credit Markets and the New Institutional Economics: The Case of Philippine Agriculture.* Boulder, Colo.: Westview Press.

Fuglesang, Andreas, and Dale Chandler. 1993. *Participation as Process—What We Learned from Grameen Bank, Bangladesh.* Dhaka: Grameen Bank.

Germidis, Dimitri, Dennis Kessler, and Rachel Meghir. 1991. *Financial Systems and Development: What Role for the Formal and Informal Financial Sectors?* Paris: Development Centre of the Organization for Economic Co-operation and Development.

Ghate, Prabu, Arindam Das-Gupta, Mario Lamberte, Mipon Poapongaskorn, Dibyo Prabowo, and Atiq Rahman. 1993. *Informal Finance: Some Findings from Asia.* New York: Oxford University Press.

Gonzalez-Vega, Claudio. 1993. "From Policies to Technologies, to Organizations: The Evolution of the Ohio State University Vision of Rural Financial Markets." Economics and Sociology Occasional Paper no. 2062, Rural Finance Program, Ohio State University, Columbus.

Harriss, Barbara. 1983. "Money and Commodities: Their Interaction in a Rural Indian Setting." In *Rural Financial Markets in Developing Countries: Their Use and Abuse,* edited by John D. Von Pischke, Dale Adams, and Gordon Donald, 233–41. Baltimore: Johns Hopkins University Press.

Hoff, Karla, Avishay Braverman, and Joseph E. Stiglitz, eds. 1993. *The Economics of Rural Organization: Theory, Practice, and Policy.* New York: Oxford University Press.

Hossain, Mahabub. 1988. "Credit for Alleviation of Rural Poverty: The Grameen Bank in Bangladesh." Research Report no. 65, International Food Policy Research Institute, Washington, D.C.

Hubbard, Joan Meyer. 1994. "Grameen Bank: A Profile." Paper presented at the Conference on Financial Services and the Poor: U.S. and Developing Country Experiences, Brookings Institution, Washington, D.C., September 28–30.

Indian School of Social Sciences, Calcutta. 1976. *Bonded Labour in India.* Calcutta: India Book Exchange.

Kamble, N. D. 1982. *Bonded Labour in India.* New Delhi: Uppal Publishing House.

Khandker, Shahidur. 1993. "Grameen Bank and Its Impact on the Poor." World Bank and Bangladesh Institute of Development Studies. Mimeograph.

Khandker, Shahidur, Baqui Khalily, and Zahed Khan. 1995. "Grameen Bank: Performance and Sustainability." World Bank Discussion Paper no. 206, World Bank, Washington, D.C.

Ladman, Jerry, and José Torrico. 1981. "Informal Credit Markets in the Valle Alto of Cochabamba, Bolivia." In *1981 Proceedings of the Rocky Mountain Council on Latin American Studies Conference,* edited by J. Brasch and S. Rouch, 83–89. Lincoln: University of Nebraska.

Long, Millard. 1968. "Interest Rates and the Structure of Agricultural Credit Markets." *Oxford Economics Papers* 20 (1): 276–87.

Morduch, Jonathan. 1997. "The Microfinance Revolution." (Draft.) Cambridge: Harvard Institute for International Development.

Otero, Maria, and Elizabeth Rhyne, eds. 1994. *The New World of Microenterprise Finance: Building Healthy Financial Institutions for the Poor.* West Hartford, Conn.: Kumarian Press.

Patten, Richard H., and Jay K. Rosengard. 1991. *Progress with Profits: The Development of Rural Banking in Indonesia.* San Francisco: International Center for Economic Growth and the Harvard Institute for International Development.

Rao, G. Hanumantha. 1977. *Caste and Poverty: A Case Study of Scheduled Castes in a Delta Village.* Malikpuram: Savithri Publications.

Rhyne, Elisabeth, and Linda S. Rotblatt. 1994. *What Makes Them Tick? Exploring the Anatomy of Major Microenterprise Finance Organizations.* Monograph Series no. 9, ACCION International, Cambridge, Mass.

Robinson, Marguerite S. 1988. *Local Politics: The Law of the Fishes.* Delhi: Oxford University Press.

———. 1992. "Rural Financial Intermediation: Lessons from Indonesia." Discussion Paper no. 434, Harvard Institute for International Development, Cambridge, Mass.

———. 1994a. "Financial Intermediation at the Local Level: Lessons from Indonesia, Part Two." Discussion Paper no. 482, Harvard Institute for International Development, Cambridge, Mass.

———. 1994b. "Savings Mobilization and Microenterprise Finance: The Indonesian Experience." In *The New World of Microenterprise Finance: Building Healthy Financial Institutions for the Poor,* edited by Maria Otero and Elizabeth Rhyne, 27–54. West Hartford, Conn.: Kumarian Press.

———. 1995a. "Indonesia: The Role of Savings in Developing Sustainable Commercial Financing of Small and Micro-Enterprises" In *New Perspectives on Financing Small Businesses in Developing Countries,* edited by Ernst Brugger and Sarath Rajapatirana, 147–74. San Francisco: ICS Press.

———. 1995b. "Leading the World in Sustainable Microfinance: The 25th Anniversary of BRI's Unit Desa System." Jakarta: Bank Rakyat Indonesia.

———. 1995c. "The Paradigm Shift in Microfinance: A Perspective from HIID." Discussion Paper no. 510, Harvard Institute for International Development, Cambridge, Mass.

———. 1995d. "Where the Microfinance Revolution Began: The First 25 Years of the Bank Dagang Bali." GEMINI Working Paper no. 53, Development Alternatives and USAID, Bethesda, Md.

———. 1996. "Addressing Some Key Questions on Finance and Poverty." *Journal of International Development* 8 (2): 153–61.

———. 1997a. "Introducing Savings in Microcredit Institutions: When and How?" CGAP Focus Note no. 8, CGAP Secretariat, World Bank, Washington, D.C.

———. 1997b. "Microfinance in Indonesia" *The UNESCO Courier,* Paris, UNESCO, 24–27.

———. 1997c. "The Microfinance Revolution: Sustainable Finance for the Poor." Unpublished manuscript.

Rosenberg, Richard. 1994. "Beyond Self-Sufficiency: Licensed Leverage and Microfinance Strategy." (Draft.) Washington, D.C.: USAID.

Roth, Hans-Dieter. 1983. *Indian Moneylenders at Work: Case Studies of the Traditional Rural Credit Markets in Dhanbad District, Bihar.* New Delhi: Manohar.

Rutherford, Stuart. 1995. *ASA: The Biography of an NGO.* Dhaka: Association for Social Advancement.

Sarma, Marla. 1981. *Bonded Labour in India: National Survey on the Incidence of Bonded Labour.* New Delhi: Biblia Impex Private.

Sharma, Miriam. 1978. *The Politics of Inequality: Competition and Control in an Indian Village.* Honolulu: University Press of Hawaii.

Siamwalla, Ammar, et al. 1993. "The Thai Rural Credit System and Elements of a Theory: Public Subsidies, Private Information, and Segmented Markets." In *The Economics of Rural Organization: Theory, Practice, and Policy,* edited by Karla Hoff, Avishay Braverman, and Joseph E. Stiglitz. New York: Oxford University Press.

Singh, Karam. 1983. "Structure of Interest Rates on Consumption Loans in an Indian Village." In *Rural Financial Markets in Developing Countries: Their Use and Abuse,* edited by John D. Von Pischke, Dale Adams, and Gordon Donald, 251–54. Baltimore: Johns Hopkins University Press.

Sugianto. 1989. "Kupedes and Simpedes." *Asia Pacific Rural Finance* July–September: 12–14.

Sugianto, and Marguerite S. Robinson. Forthcoming. "Commercial Banks as Microfinance Providers." Bangkok: APRACA.

Tun Wai, U. 1980. "The Role of Unorganized Financial Markets in Economic Development and in the Formulation of Monetary Policy." *Savings and Development* 4, no. 4.

Varian, Hal R. 1989. "Monitoring Agents with Other Agents." Center for Research on Economic and Social Theory, Working Paper no. 89-18, Department of Economics, University of Michigan, Ann Arbor.

Vogel, Robert C. 1984. "The Effect of Subsidized Agricultural Credit on Income Distribution in Costa Rica." In *Undermining Rural Development with Cheap Credit,* edited by Dale Adams, Douglas H. Graham, and John D. Von Pischke, 133–45. Boulder, Colo.: Westview Press.

Von Pischke, John D. 1991. *Finance at the Frontier: Debt Capacity and the Role of Credit in the Private Economy.* Washington, D.C.: World Bank.

Von Pischke, John D., Dale Adams, and Gordon Donald, eds. 1983. *Rural Financial Markets in Developing Countries: Their Use and Abuse.* Baltimore: Johns Hopkins University Press.

Vyas, N. N. 1980. *Bondage and Exploitation in Tribal India.* Jaipur: Rawat Publications.

Wardhana, Ali. Forthcoming. "Introduction." In "The Microfinance Revolution: Sustainable Finance for the Poor," by Marguerite S. Robinson.

Wilmington, Martin W. 1983. "Aspects of Money Lending in Northern Sudan." In *Rural Financial Markets in Developing Countries: Their Use and Abuse,* edited by John D. Von Pischke, Dale Adams, and Gordon Donald, 255–61. Baltimore: Johns Hopkins University Press.

World Bank. 1996. *World Development Report.* New York: Oxford University Press.

———. 1997a. *World Development Report.* Washington, D.C.: World Bank.

———. 1997b. "An Inventory of Selected Microfinance Institutions in South Asia." Sustainable Banking with the Poor (series). Washington, D.C.: World Bank.

World Bank News. 1996. "KUPEDES: Indonesia's Model Small Credit Program." Precis no. 104, Operations Evaluation Department, World Bank, Washington, D.C.

Yaron, Jacob. 1992. *Assessing Development Finance Institutions: A Public Interest Analysis.* Discussion Paper no. 174, World Bank, Washington, D.C.

Yaron, Jacob, McDonald Benjamin, and Gerda Piprek. 1997. *Rural Finance: Issues, Design, Best Practices.* (Draft.) Agricultural and Natural Resources Department, World Bank, Washington, D.C.

25

Micro and Small Enterprises and the Rural Poor

CARL LIEDHOLM

The role of micro and small enterprises (MSEs) in providing productive employment and earning opportunities in rural areas has become a hotly debated topic among development economists, policy makers, and members of international donor agencies.[1] This heightened interest has paralleled the increased realization that MSEs could be an important vehicle for achieving equity and employment objectives. The widespread attention focused on innovative microenterprise credit schemes, such as the Grameen Bank in Bangladesh, reflects this realization.

MSEs, however, have been overlooked for many years by policy makers in developing countries. This is understandable, because such enterprises typically are hidden from view and are easily missed in official surveys. Consequently, they have tended to be undercounted and their contribution to the economy has often been unappreciated. Fortunately, a number of recent studies, using innovative survey techniques, have now begun to illuminate the important dynamic of rural MSEs in development.[2]

The purpose of this chapter is to fill in the gap in the literature on rural micro and small enterprises in low-income countries. A descriptive profile of these enterprises will be presented first, followed by an examination of the determinants of the role of rural MSEs in development. The important growth contributions of these enterprises, incorporating the latest empirical findings, will then be considered. The major policy and project assistance issues will be discussed in the final section.

DESCRIPTIVE PROFILE

Micro and small enterprises include all enterprises engaged in nonprimary activities,[3] where at least 50 percent of the output is sold. Although there is no universally accepted size classification for MSEs, the typical definition, and the one utilized here, includes firms with up to fifty workers (including unpaid family

CARL LIEDHOLM is professor of economics at Michigan State University.

workers, working proprietors, apprentices, and part-time workers). Microenterprises cover the smaller end of the MSE range and typically include enterprises with ten or fewer workers.

MAGNITUDE

Just how significant are rural MSEs in developing countries? The evidence available from national population censuses, as well as a recent series of innovative establishment surveys indicates that MSEs provide an important source of primary rural employment in developing countries. On the basis of population censuses for forty-three countries, Haggblade and Hazell (1989) found that rural MSEs accounted for 14 percent of full-time employment in Africa, 26 percent in Asia, and 28 percent in Latin America. Recent surveys in six African countries (Botswana, Kenya, Lesotho, Malawi, Swaziland, Zimbabwe) indicate that somewhat over 20 percent of the labor force is primarily employed in MSEs in these countries (Liedholm and Mead 1995).

Such figures provide a minimal estimate of the magnitude of primary employment in MSEs in rural areas. First, they generally reflect the employment characteristics of the rural villages with populations below five thousand; if the larger rural towns were included, the rural nonfarm percentage would be higher.[4] Second, measurement errors contribute to a systematic undercounting of nonfarm activities. In some African countries rural respondents will report farming to be their main occupation even if they engage in this activity only part time. In addition, women's participation in MSEs is often substantial, but frequently it is not measured or included in labor-force figures. Female entrepreneurs, in fact, frequently outnumber men as owners or operators of MSEs in Africa and Latin America (Liedholm and Mead 1995). Since they typically operate out of the home, however, females are much more likely to be "invisible entrepreneurs."

These primary employment statistics also understate the magnitude of rural MSEs, because they fail to reflect farmers engaged in MSE activities on a part-time or seasonal basis. Data on secondary employment are not generally available for most countries. The limited evidence indicates that 10–20 percent of the rural male labor force undertakes MSE work as a secondary occupation. In western Nigeria, for example, 20 percent of the rural males engaged in nonfarm work on a part-time basis, while in Sierra Leone, Afghanistan, and Korea the figures were 11 percent, 16 percent, and 20 percent, respectively (Chuta and Liedholm 1979).

There are significant monthly variations in the amounts of rural farm and MSE employment over the agricultural cycle. Farm and nonfarm employment move in opposite directions. There is no period when MSE employment disappears; thus, MSE employment does compete somewhat with farm employment during periods of the peak agricultural demand for labor. Data from Nigeria reveal that the peak in nonfarm labor use is nine times the use in the slack periods (Norman 1973). The fluidity of labor between a number of activities on a seasonal basis is a striking feature of rural households.

To summarize, MSEs provide a source of primary or secondary employment for 30 to 50 percent of the rural labor force in developing nations.[5] Consequently, in terms of employment, MSE activities are quantitatively an important component of the rural economy that should not be overlooked in the design of rural development policies or programs.

In view of the magnitude of MSE employment, it is not surprising that MSEs also provide an important source of income for rural households. Evidence from countries where information on rural incomes is available indicates that MSE earnings account for 30 to 50 percent of total rural household income (Haggblade and Hazell 1989). In Sierra Leone, for example, MSE income was found to provide 36 percent of rural household income, while in Taiwan the comparable figure was 43 percent (Chuta and Liedholm 1979).

INCOME DISTRIBUTION

Does the income generated by rural MSEs provide an important source of income for the poorest rural households and, if so, does it serve to reduce income inequality in rural areas? Recent studies have begun to provide some clues.

Empirical studies of rural households typically find a U-shaped relationship between income from MSEs and total income. Earnings from MSEs play an important role in the incomes of the rural poor, particularly those with little or no land. Rural households with less than half a hectare of land, for example, typically generate over 50 percent of their income from MSEs, and this income provides them with a vital margin of support (Liedholm and Kilby 1989). But many of the MSE activities of the rural poor, such as weaving, knitting, and trading, yield a low return in contrast to the typically higher returns generated by the MSE activities of the wealthy, and thus their effect on overall income distribution is not certain.

The empirical findings on the effect of MSE income on overall income inequality in rural areas, in fact, are somewhat mixed. The evidence from Asia and from some parts of Africa indicates that MSE income reduces inequality (Adams and Alderman 1992, and Liedholm and Kilby 1989). Yet the opposite result is reported in recent findings from the Sahel region of Africa, where poor households have limited access to MSE opportunities (Reardon and Taylor 1996).

COMPOSITION

What are the most important types of MSE activities? Amid wide variation, the composition of rural MSE employment typically includes one-third manufacturing and one-third commerce, with services, mining, and construction making up the remainder (Haggblade and Liedholm 1992). More recent figures for six African countries indicate that over 90 percent of rural MSE employment is concentrated in these two sectors, with manufacturing accounting for 50 percent and commerce accounting for 43 percent (Liedholm and Mead 1995).[6]

The relative importance of rural manufacturing activity as a component of the rural economy may appear surprising. Even more surprising, perhaps, is the strength of rural manufacturing relative to its urban counterpart. Indeed, there is evidence that employment in micro and small manufacturing enterprises in rural areas typically exceeds that in urban manufacturing enterprises, both small and large (Liedholm and Mead 1987). In Sierra Leone 86 percent of the total manufacturing employment and 95 percent of the manufacturing establishments were located in rural areas (Chuta and Liedholm 1985). The percentages of rural industrial employment in other countries range from 70 percent in Bangladesh (Bangladesh Institute of Development Studies 1979) to 67 percent in Jamaica (Davies et al. 1979) and 63 percent in Malaysia (World Bank 1978b). These figures may actually understate the magnitude of rural industrial activity, because country censuses often fail to pick up the very small rural enterprises.

Within rural manufacturing, three activities have consistently been identified as the most important: (1) textiles and wearing apparel, (2) food and beverages, and (3) wood and forest products. These "big three" categories typically generate over 75 percent of MSE manufacturing employment in developing countries (Liedholm and Mead 1987).

SIZE

What is the average size of these rural MSEs? In most countries, the majority of rural MSEs are found to be micro firms, which employ up to ten workers (Chuta and Liedholm 1979). In many countries, in fact, it is the one-person rural MSE that predominates. A recent review of the findings from MSE surveys in six African countries found that 65 percent of MSEs were one-person firms (Liedholm and Mead 1995). Self-employment is a central element in many of these rural economies, reinforcing the notion that MSEs are potentially an important target group for policy makers concerned with helping the rural poor.

DETERMINANTS OF THE ROLE OF RURAL MSEs

What are the main determinants of the existing patterns and the growth prospects of rural MSE employment and income? Answers to these questions can be found by focusing on the factors influencing the demand for and supply of these activities.

DEMAND PROSPECTS

Several important issues relate to the nature of the demand for the goods and services produced by rural MSEs. One crucial issue, on which there has been a divergence of opinion, is whether the demand for these activities increases as rural incomes increase. Hymer and Resnick (1969) have argued that rural MSEs produce inferior goods, in the sense that the demand for them would be expected to decline as rural incomes rise. Mellor (1976), Chuta and Liedholm (1979), and various International Labour Office missions (1972, 1974), on the other hand, have contended that there is a strong, positive relationship between income and the demand for these activities. Recent research, based on analyses of household expenditure surveys in Asia and Africa, however, provides support for the latter position (King and Byerlee 1978; Liedholm and Kilby 1989; Haggblade and Hazell 1989).

Another demand-related issue is whether there are strong backward and forward linkages between rural MSEs and other sectors of the economy, particularly agriculture. Hirschman (1958) has contended that linkages between agriculture and other sectors are quite weak,[7] while others, such as Mellor (1976) and Tomich, Kilby, and Johnston (1995), have argued that the linkages between rural MSEs and agriculture are or could be potentially very strong under conditions of rapid agricultural growth. The available empirical evidence indicates that these linkages are important and that their magnitude is related to the size distribution of farms and the type of agricultural strategy adopted. The capacity among small producers to meet the specific tool and equipment needs of small farmers is particularly noteworthy (Liedholm and Kilby 1989). Rural MSEs are influenced by the pattern of agricultural growth and can themselves influence the course and rate of agricultural development. Finally, there is some empirical and analytical evidence that the international market is an important component of demand for certain types of rural MSE products (see Chuta and Liedholm, 1979).

Supply Factors

With respect to supply, the key issue is whether rural MSEs in developing countries are efficient users of economic resources, particularly when compared with their larger-scale, urban counterparts. Both partial and comprehensive measures of economic efficiency have been used in attempting to answer this question.

The labor-capital (labor intensity) and the output-capital (capital productivity) ratios are the economic efficiency measures most frequently used in empirical studies. These partial efficiency measures are based on the assumption that labor is abundant and capital is the only scarce resource. Virtually all the aggregate and most industry studies reveal that MSEs generate more employment per unit of scarce capital than do their larger-scale counterparts. The available evidence on relative capital productivities is somewhat limited and more mixed.

Only a few studies have used one of the analytically more correct comprehensive economic efficiency measures, in which all scarce resources are included in the analysis and are evaluated at "shadow" or social prices that reflect their scarcity values in the economy. The findings of such studies, which have been limited to manufacturing activity only, are mixed. Moreover, rural manufacturing activities are rarely examined explicitly in these analyses.

To assist in filling this void, Liedholm and Kilby (1989) used a social benefit-cost analysis to compare the relative efficiency of small rural manufacturing enterprises with their larger-scale urban counterparts in Sierra Leone, Honduras, and Jamaica. The ratio of the enterprise's value added to the cost of its capital and labor, both valued at their shadow or "social" prices, was used to measure economic efficiency.[8] The key finding from this three-country analysis was that the small rural manufacturing enterprises were found to use fewer resources per unit of output than their larger-scale counterparts in a majority of the industry groups considered. In over two-thirds of the industrial groups examined, the social benefit-cost ratios of the small rural firms not only exceeded one but also were greater than the comparable ratios for the large-scale firms in those particular industries and countries. These findings, while not conclusive, do indicate that small rural industries are economically viable in several lines of activity.

The efficiency of individual rural firms, however, varies by their production characteristics, particularly their size, input composition, and location. A review of various rural industry surveys (Liedholm and Mead 1987) reveals some important patterns. The rural firms most likely to be economically efficient tend to possess a number of characteristics, many of which can be discerned on the basis of visible evidence. A key finding is that economic efficiency is lowest for one-person firms but increases substantially for firms with between two and five workers. A small increase in size, particularly an increase from one to two workers, is thus associated with a sizeable increase in productivity. Higher efficiency firms also tend to use hired workers, operate in workshops away from the home, operate in localities with more than 2,000 inhabitants, and are involved in selected product lines with better economic prospects, such as tiles, furniture, baking, and repair activities. Judiciously and cautiously applied, such indicators can provide the analyst with useful insights into those types of rural industries most likely to be economically viable.

GROWTH POTENTIAL

What are the growth prospects for rural MSEs? Employment data, the only indicator routinely available, suggest that rural MSE activity has generally increased across continents over time (Anderson 1982; Chuta and Liedholm 1979; Haggblade and Hazell 1989). Recent surveys in Africa indicate that during the 1980s, the expansion of employment in MSEs absorbed around 30 percent of the increase in the working age population (Mead 1994).

MSEs are in a constant state of flux. Two general components of enterprise growth must be analyzed if the complex changes taking place are to be captured. The first is net firm creation, which itself reflects two offsetting elements: firm starts (births) and firm closures (deaths). The second is net firm expansion, which incorporates the expansion and contraction of existing firms. Empirical evidence on new business starts from recent surveys in five African countries and the Dominican Republic, however, reveal that the annual birth rate of rural MSEs averages over 20 percent (Liedholm and Mead 1995). This rate is substantially higher than the 10 percent annual rate typically reported for such enterprises in the industrialized countries and would suggest that there is no shortage of entrepreneurs in developing countries willing to incur the risk of establishing businesses.

Almost 80 percent, of the new firms being created are one-person establishments, the least efficient and remunerative size of microenterprise. There is also evidence that new starts are inversely related to the level of economic activity (Daniels 1995), indicating that most of these new starts are created by people with few options.

MSE death rates also appear to be high. The annual rate of closure of rural microenterprises in the Dominican Republic, the only country for which accurate annual figures exist, exceeded 20 percent in the early 1990s (Cabal 1995). A profile of these closed microenterprises in rural areas, however, has begun to emerge from Liedholm and Mead's study of such enterprises in five African countries and the Dominican Republic (1995). First, only about one-half of the closures were caused by business failures. The remainder of the firms closed for personal reasons, such as bad health or retirement; because better options became available; or because the government forced them to close. Second, most of the closures that were caused by business failure occurred in the initial years of operation. Indeed, over 50 percent of rural enterprise closures in Zimbabwe, Swaziland, Botswana, and Kenya had taken place before the end of the business's third year.

Third, a systematic analysis of closure patterns of rural microenterprises in Zimbabwe, Swaziland, and the Dominican Republic provides a picture of the characteristics of enterprises that are most likely to close (Liedholm and Mead 1995). The results indicate that a rural MSE was more likely to close during any given year, holding all other variables constant, if it: (1) did not grow; (2) started large, not small; (3) operated in the trading sector; or (4) operated out of the home. It is noteworthy that the gender of the entrepreneur was not a factor in closures due to business failures.

What about MSE growth due to net firm expansion? One of the striking findings to emerge from recent surveys is the high overall rate of growth exhibited by the existing MSEs located in rural areas. In comparable baseline surveys conducted in seven African countries, the annual compound employment growth rate of rural MSEs since start-up was found to be 6.9 percent in localities with fewer than 2,500 inhabitants and 8.8 percent in rural towns with from 2,500 to 20,000 inhabitants (Liedholm, McPherson, and Chuta 1994). Similarly high growth rates have been reported in the Dominican Republic (Cabal 1995).

These rapid growth rates are even more impressive, however, when it is realized that the vast majority of rural MSEs did not grow at all. In the surveyed countries mentioned previously, only slightly more than one-quarter of all new MSEs expanded, while about two-thirds remained the same size. For rural MSEs as a whole, growth is the exception rather than the rule, and expansion growth is being propelled by a minority of the enterprises.

Among the rural MSEs that did grow, over 85 percent started very small (one to four workers) and added fewer than four workers. Only one percent of these very small enterprises ultimately graduated from this microenterprise seedbed and ended up with ten or more workers. Thus, most of the expansion was due to the addition of just a few workers by large numbers of the growing MSEs.

When an existing rural MSE expands by adding only one or two workers, however, this is likely to be associated with a sharp increase in its economic efficiency as well as its net income. Most new microenterprise start-ups are one-person enterprises, which empirical studies have indicated are the least efficient size category (see above). If some of these microenterprises subsequently expand, adding even one more worker, they will be moving into a size category where their economic efficiency as well as their net income are likely to be significantly higher. Recent empirical evidence from Africa indicates that about one-quarter of the new rural jobs have come from a net expansion of existing firms and three-quarters from new starts (Mead 1994).

Given the economic significance of expansion, what are the characteristics of those rural microenterprises that expand and how, if at all, do they differ from the characteristics of those that do not grow? The results of a systematic analysis of determinants of employment growth of existing rural microenterprises in five African countries (Botswana, Kenya, Lesotho, Swaziland, and Zimbabwe) make it possible to provide a profile of the type of microenterprise most likely to expand (Liedholm, McPherson, and Chuta 1994). One important finding is that the rural microenterprises that are youngest and smallest at start-up are the ones most likely to generate more expansion jobs per firm, a powerful finding for those concerned with employment creation. Another significant result is the evidence that, after controlling for other variables, male-headed enterprises are more likely to grow more rapidly than are those run by females. In addition, rural enterprises operating in the service and manufacturing sectors are more likely to experience higher growth than those in trading. Rural enterprises operating in commercial districts or at the roadside were more likely to grow more rapidly than those operating out of the home. Related studies in such countries as Kenya (Parker 1995), Zimbabwe (McPherson 1996), and the Dominican Republic (Cabal 1995) have also provided evidence that human capital factors significantly affect microenterprise expansion. Specifically, vocational training, experience (typically a minimum of seven years), and at least a secondary school level of formal education are found to contribute to MSE expansion.

Finally, at the more macro level, there is evidence of a positive relationship between the level of economic activity and the level of rural MSE expansion (Liedholm, McPherson, and Chuta 1994; Liedholm and Mead 1995). These expansion jobs are not only more likely to endure but are also more likely to provide higher incomes than those that arise from new business starts.

MAJOR POLICY AND DIRECT PROJECT ASSISTANCE ISSUES

Given the favorable characteristics of rural MSEs with respect to employment, income generation, and income distribution issues, governments as well as non-government organizations are showing increasing interest in incorporating these activities into their development strategies. MSEs are assisted by general policy measures that affect the environment in which they operate and by direct project assistance. Some of these measures attack the MSEs' demand constraints while others attack their supply constraints (Tendler and Amorim 1996).[9]

GENERAL POLICY MEASURES

A panoply of general governmental policies affect the efficiency, employment, and size distribution of MSEs in the rural economy. These policies typically influence MSEs through their product markets, the demand side, or their resource markets, primarily capital and labor.

Agricultural growth policies loom large among the demand side policies that importantly influence MSEs. Since the rural households' income elasticity of demand for rural MSE goods is positive and agriculture generates the largest share of rural incomes, policies designed to increase agricultural growth have an important indirect effect on the demand for these activities. Consequently, government actions ranging from improvements in the terms of trade between agriculture and the larger-scale urban sector to specific investment programs and policies designed to increase, directly or indirectly, agricultural production and income can lead to an expansion of employment in existing rural MSEs.

The nature and composition of these agricultural policies and programs should also be considered, however, since they can have important, differential effects on the demand for products from rural MSEs. There is some evidence that higher-income rural residents have a somewhat lower income elasticity of demand for rural industrial products than do lower-income individuals, the majority of whom are small-scale farmers (see King and Byerlee 1978; Haggblade and Hazell 1989). Moreover, the agricultural inputs, such as tractors and fertilizers, used by large-scale, high-income farmers are less likely to be produced in rural localities than are the inputs used by the small-scale farmers (see Tomich, Kilby and Johnston 1995).[10] Consequently, policies and programs designed to benefit a large number of small-scale farmers are likely to generate a larger demand for rural MSE activities and services than those designed to benefit a few large-scale farmers.

With respect to resource markets, policies often generate input price distortions that have significant, though often unintended, negative effects on rural MSEs. This is because the overall policy environment in most countries is not neutral with respect to firm size and location and is typically biased against small rural MSEs (Haggblade, Liedholm and Mead 1986). Consequently, great care must be exercised in policy choices, as many government actions seemingly unrelated to rural MSEs can inadvertently have adverse effects on them. Two of the major sources of input price distortions, interest and tariff rates, will be discussed here.

With respect to interest rates, two distinct capital markets—the formal and the informal—exist in most developing countries. Banks and similar institutions constitute the formal market, while moneylenders, raw-material suppliers, and purchasers constitute the bulk of the informal market. Interest rates vary widely between the two. Official interest rates, where government-imposed ceilings frequently exist, generally run from 10 percent to 20 percent, while the informal rates are frequently 100 percent or more per year (see Chuta and Liedholm 1979). Particularly under inflationary conditions, the formal real rates become very low, sometimes negative. Thus, not surprisingly, banks have tended to lend only to the established, large-scale firms, which may appear to the banks to pose lower risks and incur lower lending costs. Most of the recipients are urban-based, and their operations have tended to become more capital-intensive than they would have been had they been forced to borrow at the opportunity cost of capital. The removal of interest rate ceilings can constitute a step towards ensuring that interest rates for borrowers of all sizes more closely approximate the opportunity cost of capital.

The import duty structure can also be an important cause of a difference in treatment for urban large-scale industries compared with rural MSEs. For most developing countries, import duties are lowest for heavy capital goods and become progressively higher through intermediate and consumer durable goods categories. Yet, many items classified as intermediate or consumer goods in tariff schedules are capital goods for rural small-scale firms. In Sierra Leone the sewing machine, an important capital item for tailoring firms, was classified as a luxury consumer good and taxed accordingly (Chuta and Liedholm 1985).

Further escalating the distortion in capital cost is the frequent practice of granting concessions or even total waivers of import duties on capital goods or raw materials for specified periods as an inducement for industrial development. In some cases, small firms may technically qualify for similar concessions but may be unaware of this opportunity or, even when they are aware of it may find the process of obtaining the concessions so complicated and time consuming that it is not economical for them to exercise the option. In many other cases small firms do not even qualify.

DIRECT PROJECT ASSISTANCE

Projects rather than policy reforms have been the primary vehicle used to date by governments and nongovernmental organizations for fostering rural enterprise growth. Rural MSEs are difficult targets to reach through direct project assistance, however. The firms are numerous, widely dispersed, and not easy to assist in a cost-effective manner. Given the already large number of new starts and the high attrition rate in the early years of the life of MSEs, new firms would seem to be a particularly problematic target group. Moreover, virtually all rural enterprise surveys reveal that only a tiny fraction of the entrepreneurs have heard of the projects intended for them and even fewer have been aided by them. These same studies indicate that the constraints facing such firms, and thus the types of direct assistance needed, vary from industry to industry and from country to country. Most of the direct project assistance used to promote rural MSEs has taken the form of supply-side interventions: the provision of credit, technical and management assistance, and common facilities, usually industrial estates. Relatively few have focused on the demand or market constraints facing MSEs (Tendler and Amorim 1996).

Financial Assistance

Credit assistance is one of the most frequently used mechanisms to aid rural small-scale industries. An important task in the designing of such assistance is determining the extent of effective demand for this credit by MSEs. Some evidence appears to indicate that this demand is quite sizeable. Rural entrepreneurs, for example, when asked directly to identify their greatest assistance needs and greatest perceived bottleneck, will usually list credit and capital first (see Kilby, Liedholm, and Meyer 1984). There is also evidence that for many types of rural industrial enterprises the rates of return on existing capital are substantial. These high rates of return indicate that the potential demand for credit could be quite large.

Yet, other evidence indicates that the rural MSEs' demand for credit may be less extensive than indicated above. Detailed analyses undertaken in Sierra Leone (Chuta and Liedholm 1985) and Kenya (Harper 1978) revealed that although entrepreneurs perceived the lack of credit to be the crucial bottleneck, other problems, such as poor management or difficulties procuring raw materials, proved to be the crucial constraints facing many enterprises. Unless these other difficulties are recognized and dealt with, the simple provision of credit could, at a minimum, be wasteful and could actually harm rural MSEs by inducing overcapitalization.

Another demand issue relates to the composition of the credit demand from rural MSEs. In particular, is the credit demand primarily for fixed or working capital? The composition of credit demand does appear to vary somewhat depending on the size, life-cycle position, and type of rural MSE. For the smallest enterprises, which account for the bulk of this sector, the primary demand is for working capital.[11] It is important to ascertain how much of the apparent working capital demand is simply a manifestation of some other problem, such as a raw-material shortage, inadequate management, or a lack of demand for final products.

An important credit delivery issue centers on determining the appropriate channel for providing financial services to rural MSEs. In most developing countries, formal credit institutions such as commercial banks, specialized small enterprise banks, specialized divisions of development banks, credit unions, and cooperative and worker banks have typically been used to channel funds to these enterprises. Although such devices as rediscounting facilities, guarantees, and ear-marking of funds are frequently introduced to entice these formal institutions to expand their lending to rural industrial enterprises, it is unclear whether these inducements have been successful in significantly expanding the amount of formal credit available to these enterprises, particularly the smaller ones. There continues to be a huge gap between the formal supply of finance and the demand for this finance on the part of MSEs. The vast majority of these rural MSEs have never even applied for funds from formal credit institutions. Most of their capital is obtained from family or internal sources.[12]

Several innovative credit schemes, however, have been quite successful in providing financial resources to even the smallest rural MSEs. Among them are the Grameen Bank in Bangladesh (Houssain 1988) and the Bank Rakyat Indonesia in Indonesia. They reflect the important paradigm shift from donor and government-funded subsidized credit to sustainable financial intermediation. There are several characteristics common to these schemes. First, loans are provided primarily for working capital rather than for fixed capital. Second, loans are screened in locally based institutions, primarily on the basis of the borrower's character. Third, loans are initially made for small amounts and for short periods to encourage and facilitate high repayment rates (Otero and Rhyne 1994).

NONFINANCIAL ASSISTANCE

Nonfinancial direct assistance to rural MSEs involves the delivery of such things as technical, managerial, and infrastructure services as well as the frequently overlooked marketing services. It is frequently argued that the rural firm's demand for such service is generally quite small and that a large volume of resources ends up being concentrated on a relatively limited clientele.

Most nonfinancial assistance projects have not been particularly successful in terms of benefit-cost analysis (see Liedholm and Mead 1987). Nevertheless, successful projects possessed several common characteristics. First, the projects addressed situations in which a single missing ingredient needed to be supplied to the firm (see Kilby 1979). An implication of this finding is that projects assisting existing firms are more likely to be successful than those attempting to establish new firms. Second, the successful projects were industry specific and task specific. Third, before these projects or schemes were launched, surveys were undertaken to uncover the demand for the activity and the number and type of missing ingredients. Fourth, successful projects tended to be built on proven existing institutions, even informal ones. Finally, recent experience has shown that the use of a subsector approach, to study a particular sector such as furniture, can be an effective approach for identifying cost-effective intervention points (Liedholm and Mead 1995).

SUMMARY

International donor agencies and the governments of many developing nations are devoting increased attention to a previously neglected component of the rural economy, rural micro and small enterprises. MSEs provide a source of primary or secondary employment for 30–50 percent of the rural labor force in many developing nations. Consequently, in terms of employment, MSE activities are quantitatively an important component of the rural economy and should not be overlooked in the design of rural development policies or programs. The empirical evidence also indicates that these activities not only generate a significant amount of rural employment and output but also provide an important source of income for poor rural households. Moreover, there is mounting evidence that several kinds of rural MSEs may be more economically efficient than their larger-scale urban counterparts and that many of these productive efficiencies can be obtained when existing MSEs expand by adding one or two workers. A key finding is that economic efficiency is lowest for one-person firms but increases substantially for firms with two to five workers. A small increase in size, particularly an increase from one to two workers, is thus associated with a sizeable increase in productivity. With judicious governmental policies and carefully formulated direct assistance measures, the dynamic contribution of rural MSEs in providing employment and income to rural households can be significantly enhanced.

NOTES

1. India and China began in the 1950s to introduce policies and programs to foster village and cottage industries. In India, cottage or household-type industries, which generally employed traditional technologies, frequently stressed the goal of absorbing surplus labor; these enterprises were frequently protected and subsidized and were not always closely linked with local demands or the agricultural sector. In China, communally organized industries using improved techniques were designed to meet local demands and were generally closely linked to the agricultural sector (see Gupta 1980).

2. Data collection innovations have made it possible to be more precise about the patterns of MSE birth, survival, growth, and closure. These include "closed" MSE surveys, as well as continuous panel and modified baseline MSE surveys that provide information about the growth of enterprises since start-up. These new survey techniques, which were undertaken as part of the GEMINI project supported by USAID and under the overall supervision of researchers from Michigan State University, have been conducted in twelve countries: Botswana, Kenya, Malawi, Swaziland, Zimbabwe, Lesotho, Niger, Nigeria, South Africa, Guinea, Jamaica, and the Dominican Republic.

3. Nonprimary activities exclude agriculture, forestry, hunting and fishing, mining and quarrying, but include the transformation, transport, and marketing of agricultural products.

4. See, for example, the evidence cited in World Bank 1978a. The dividing line between "rural" and "urban" is arbitrary, particularly in census data collected in most countries. The boundary lines are often framed in terms of urbanization characteristics rather than minimum size or occupational structure; consequently, settlements of a few thousand are often classified as "urban." The United Nations definition of "rural areas" includes localities with fewer than twenty thousand inhabitants.

5. The figure may be as high as 50 percent in some countries. Luning (1967), in a survey of villages in northern Nigeria, reports that 48 percent of the employed males engaged either full time or part time in rural nonfarm activities, while Norman (1973) reports that in the same area 47 percent of male labor time was devoted to these activities.

6. Agricultural processing and marketing activities are reflected in these figures; fishing and livestock activities are not. See Chuta and Liedholm 1979 for more details.

7. Hirschman perceived few linkages, because he implicitly used a two-sector model in which all rural activities were labeled "agriculture," and he was writing in the 1950s in the context of a technologically stagnant agriculture.

8. The primary data were generated from detailed small-scale industry surveys, in which hundreds of rural firms in each country were interviewed twice weekly over a twelve-month period to obtain daily information on revenues and costs. For data on the profits and productivity of small-scale industries in other countries see Liedholm and Mead 1987. The information on the large-scale enterprises was obtained from the worksheets used to construct the industrial censuses. Among the industry groups examined were baking, clothing, shoes, furniture, and metal products.

9. Tendler and Amorim 1996 characterizes those interventions that focus on MSE supply side con-

straints as "supply driven" and those that focus on demand side constraints as "demand driven." They argue that demand-driven support provided by large customers—firms, traders, government agencies, and state enterprises—is more likely to stimulate sustained MSE growth than the typical supply-driven intervention.

10. Small-scale farms are also more likely to use primarily smaller, rural-based agricultural processing establishments, while large-scale farms might be expected to make more use of larger-scale, urban-based processing plants.

11. See Kilby, Liedholm, and Meyer, 1984.

12. For a review of alternative institutional arrangements see Kilby, Liedholm and Meyer 1984. In Haiti, 94 percent had never applied (Haggblade, Defay, and Pitman 1979), while in Sierra Leone the figure was 96 percent (Chuta and Liedholm 1985).

REFERENCES

Adams, R. H., and H. Alderman. 1992. "Sources of Income Inequality in Rural Pakistan," *Oxford Bulletin of Economics and Statistics* 54 (4): 591–608.

Anderson, D. 1982. "Small Industry in Developing Countries: A Discussion of Issues." *World Development* 10 (11): 913–48.

Bangladesh Institute of Development Studies. 1979. "Rural Industries Study Project-Phase I Report." Mimeograph, BIDS, Dacca.

Cabal, Miguel. 1995. "Growth, Appearances and Disappearances of Micro and Small Enterprises in the Dominican Republic." Ph.D. dissertation, Michigan State University.

Chuta, Enyinna, and Carl Liedholm. 1979. "Rural Non-Farm Employment: A Review of the State of the Art." Michigan State University Rural Development Paper no. 4, Department of Agricultural Economics, Michigan State University, East Lansing.

———. 1985. *Employment and Growth in Small-Scale Industry: Empirical Evidence and Policy Assessment from Sierra Leone.* New York: St. Martin's Press.

Daniels, Lisa. 1995. "Entry and Exit Behavior and Growth Patterns among Small-Scale Enterprises in Zimbabwe." Ph.D. dissertation, Michigan State University.

Davies, Omar, Yacob Fisseha, Annette Francis, and Claremont Kirton. 1979. "A Preliminary Analysis of the Small-Scale, Non-Farm Sector in Jamaica." Mimeograph. Small-Scale Enterprise Survey Unit, Institute of Social and Economic Research, University of the West Indies, Kingston, Jamaica.

Gupta, Devendra. 1980. "Government Policies and Programmes of Rural Industrialization with Special Reference to the Punjab Region of Northern India." World Employment Research Paper WEP 2–37/WP5, International Labour Organization, Geneva.

Haggblade, Stephen, Jacques Defay, and Bob Pitman. 1979. "Small Manufacturing and Repair Enterprises in Haiti: Survey Results." Rural Development Series Working Paper no. 4, Department of Agricultural Economics, Michigan State University, East Lansing.

Haggblade, Stephen, and Peter Hazell. 1989. "Agricultural Technology and Farm-Nonfarm Growth Linkages." *Agricultural Economics* 3 (4): 345–64.

Haggblade, Stephen, and Carl Liedholm. 1992. "Agriculture, Rural Labor Markets and the Evolution of the Rural Non-farm Economy." In *Sustainable Agricultural Development: The Role of International Cooperation,* edited by G. Peters and B. Stanton, assisted by G. J. Tyler, 542–57. Aldershot, U.K.: Dartmouth Publishing.

Haggblade, Stephen, Carl Liedholm, and Don Mead. 1986. "The Effect of Policy and Policy Reform on Non-Agricultural Enterprises and Employment in Developing Countries: A Review of Past Experiences." EEPA Discussion Paper no. 1, Harvard Institute for International Development, Cambridge, Mass.

Harper, Malcolm. 1978. "Consultancy for Small Business." London: Intermediate Technology Publications.

Hirschman, A. O. 1958. *The Strategy of Economic Development.* New Haven: Yale University Press.

Houssain, Makabub. 1988. "Credit for Alleviation of Rural Poverty: The Grameen Bank in Bangladesh." Research Report no 5, International Food Policy Research Institute, Washington, D.C..

Hymer, Stephen, and Stephen Resnick. 1969. "A Model of an Agrarian Economy with Nonagricultural Activities." *American Economic Review* 59 (4): 493–506.

International Labour Office. 1972. "Employment, Incomes, and Equality: A Strategy for Discovering Productive Employment in Kenya." Geneva: ILO.

———. 1974. "Sharing in Development: A Programme of Employment, Equity, and Growth for the Philippines." Geneva: ILO.

Kilby, Peter. 1979. "Evaluating Technical Assistance." *World Development* 7 (3): 309–23.

Kilby, Peter, Carl Liedholm, and Richard Meyer. 1984. "Working Capital and Nonfarm Rural Enterprises." In *Undermining Rural Development with Cheap Credit,* edited by Dale Adams and John D. Von Pischke, 266–83. Boulder, Colo.: Westview Press.

King, Robert P., and Derek Byerlee. 1978. "Factor Intensities and Locational Linkages of Rural Consumption Patterns in Sierra Leone." *American Journal of Agricultural Economics* 60:197–206.

Liedholm, Carl, and Peter Kilby. 1989. "Nonfarm Activities in the Rural Economy." In *The Balance between Industry and Agriculture in Economic Development,* vol . 2, edited by J. Williamson and V. Panchamukhi. New York: St. Martin's Press.

Liedholm, C., M. McPherson, and E. Chuta. 1994. "Small Enterprise Growth in Rural Africa." *American Journal of Agricultural Economics* 76 (5): 1177–82.

Liedholm, Carl, and Don Mead. 1987. "Small-Scale Industries in Developing Countries: Empirical Evidence and Policy Implications." MSU International Development Papers no. 9, Michigan State University, East Lansing.

———. 1995. "The Dynamic Role of Micro and Small Enterprises in the Development Process" GEMINI Final Report #1, Private Agencies Collaborating Together, Washington, D.C.

Luning, H. A. 1967. "Economic Aspects of Low Labor-Income Farming." Agricultural Research Report no. 699, Centre for Agricultural Publications and Documentations, Wageningen, The Netherlands.

McPherson, M. 1996. "Growth of Micro and Small Enterprises in Southern Africa." *Journal of Development Economics* 48 (21): 253–77.

Mead, Donald. 1994. "The Contribution of Small Enterprises to Employment Growth in Southern and Eastern Africa." *World Development* 22 (12): 1881–94.

Mellor, John W. 1976. *The New Economics of Growth.* Ithaca: Cornell University Press.

Norman, David W. 1973. "Methodology and Problems of Farm Management Investigations: Experiences from Northern Nigeria." African Rural Employment Paper no. 8, Department of Agricultural Economics, Michigan State University, East Lansing.

Otero, M. and B. Rhyne. 1994. *The New World of Microenterprise Finance.* West Hartford, Conn.: Kumarian Press.

Parker, Joan. 1995. "Patterns of Business Growth: Micro and Small Enterprises in Kenya." Ph.D. dissertation, Michigan State University.

Reardon, T. and J. Taylor. 1996. "Agroclimatic Shock, Income Inequality, and Poverty." *World Development* 24 (5): 901–14.

Tendler, Judith, and M. Amorim. 1996. "Small Firms and Their Helpers: Lessons on Demand." *World Development* 24 (3): 407–26.

Tomich, Thomas, P. Kilby, and B. Johnston. 1995. *Transforming Agrarian Economies.* Ithaca, New York: Cornell University Press.

World Bank. 1978a. "Rural Enterprise and Nonfarm Employment." Washington, D.C.: World Bank.

———. 1978b. "Employment and Development in Small Enterprises." Washington, D.C.: World Bank.

26

Constraints on the Design of Sustainable Systems of Agricultural Production

VERNON W. RUTTAN

Contemplation of the world's disappearing supplies of minerals, forests and other exhaustible assets has led to demands for regulation of their exploitation. The feeling that these products are now too cheap for the good of future generations, that they are being selfishly exploited at too rapid a rate, and that in consequence of their excessive cheapness they are being produced and consumed wastefully, has given rise to the conservation movement. (Hotelling 1931)

When confronted with the task of defining sustainable agriculture, one's natural inclination is to finesse (Hopper 1987, 5). This inclination to avoid definition reflects the fact that sustainability has emerged as an umbrella under which a large number of movements with widely disparate reform agendas have been able to march while avoiding confrontation over their often mutually inconsistent agendas.

DEFINITIONS OF SUSTAINABILITY

In spite of the advantages of avoiding defining a term which has apparently been adopted precisely because of its ambiguity, it is useful to trace the evolution of the concept. The term was probably first advanced in 1980 by the International Union for the Conservation of Nature and National Resources (Pearce, Markandya, and Barbier 1989, xii; Lélé 1991). Prior to the mid-1980s it had achieved its widest currency among critics of "industrial" approaches to the process of agricultural development (Harwood 1990, 3–19). Proponents had traveled in a number of rhetorical vehicles, such as biodynamic agriculture, organic

Vernon W. Ruttan is Regents Professor in the Department of Applied Economics and the Department of Economics, University of Minnesota, St. Paul.

Previously published in *Ecological Economics* 10 (1994): 209–19, by Elsevier Science, Amsterdam, The Netherlands. Copyright © 1994 Elsevier and the author. Published with minor editorial revisions by permission of the author.

431

agriculture, farming systems, appropriate technology and, more recently, regenerative and low-input agriculture (Dahlberg 1991).

Writing in the early 1980s, Gordon K. Douglass identified three alternative conceptual approaches to the definition of agricultural sustainability (Douglass 1984, 3–29). One group defined sustainability primarily in technical and economic terms—the capacity to supply the expanding demand for agricultural commodities on increasingly favorable terms. For this group, primarily mainstream agricultural and resource economists, the long-term decline in the real prices of agricultural commodities represented evidence that the growth of agricultural production had been following a sustainable path.

Douglass identified a second group, which regards agricultural sustainability primarily as an ecological question: "an agricultural system which needlessly depletes, pollutes, or disrupts the ecological balance of natural systems is unsustainable and should be replaced by one which honors the longer-term biophysical constraints of nature" (2). Among those advancing the ecological sustainability agenda there is a pervasive view that present population levels are already too large to be sustained at present levels of per capita consumption (Goodland 1991).[1]

A third group, traveling under the banner of "alternative agriculture," places its primary emphasis on sustaining not just the physical resource base but a broad set of community values (National Research Council 1989). It often views conventional science-based agriculture as an assault, not only on the environment, but on rural people and rural communities. Its adherents take as a major objective the strengthening or revitalization of rural culture and rural communities guided by the values of stewardship and self-reliance and an integrated or holistic approach to the physical and cultural dimensions of production and consumption.

By the mid-1980s the sustainability concept was diffusing rapidly from the confines of its agroecological origins to include the entire development process. The definition that has achieved the widest currency was that adapted by the Bruntland Commission (World Commission on Environment and Development 1987, 43): "Sustainable development is development that meets the needs of the present without compromising the ability of future generations to meet their own needs."

The Bruntland Commission's definition represented a deliberate attempt to expand the concept of sustainability to take into account the need to respond to the growth in demand for agricultural and other natural resource–based products arising out of population and income growth. But the Bruntland Commission's definition also raises the possibility that it may be necessary for those of us who are alive today, particularly those of us living in the more affluent societies, to curb our level of material consumption in order to accommodate growth in consumption in less affluent societies to avoid an even more drastic decline in the consumption levels of future generations. This is not a welcome message to societies that find it difficult to discover principled reasons for the contemporary transfer of resources across political boundaries in support of efforts to narrow the distance between the levels of living of rich and poor nations or rich and poor people (Ruttan 1989a).

Our historical experience, at least in the West, often causes us to be skeptical about our obligations to future generations. It was only a generation ago that Robert Solow, one of our leading growth theorists, noted in his Richard T. Ely Address to the American Economic Association: "We have actually done quite well at the hands of our ancestors. Given how poor they were and how rich we are, they might properly have saved less and consumed more" (Solow 1974, 9). In most of the world the ancestors have not been so kind!

In spite of the challenge to current levels of consumption in the developed countries, it is hard to avoid a conclusion that the popularity of the Bruntland Commission's definition is due, at least in part, to its being so broad that it is almost devoid of operational significance. The sustainability concept has undergone what has been referred to as "establishment appropriation." It is now experiencing the same natural history as earlier reform efforts. Initially a "progressive" rhetoric is advanced by critics as a challenge to the legitimacy of dominant institutions and practices. If the groups and symbols involved are sufficiently threatening to the dominant institutions, these institutions will attempt to respond to these challenges by appropriating or embracing the rhetoric themselves. "In so doing these dominant institutions—such as the World Bank and the agricultural universities—are typically able to demobilize the movement" (Buttel 1991, 7).

Buttel argues that sustainability has been embraced both by radical reformers and neoconservatives because it removes the focus from achieving greater participation of the poor in the dividends from economic growth to protecting an impersonal nature from the destructive forces of growth (9). Runge (1992) presents a more positive perspective on the move by the traditional agricultural and development communities to embrace the sustainability concept. He visualizes sustainability as an integrative concept that can facilitate the synthesis of the research and policy agendas of the environmental, agricultural, and development communities.

SUSTAINABLE AGRICULTURAL SYSTEMS IN HISTORY

It is not uncommon for a social movement to achieve the status of an ideology while still in search of a methodology or a technology. If the reform movement is successful in directing scientific and technical effort in a productive direction, it becomes incorporated into normal scientific or technical practice. If it leads to a dead end, it slips into the underworld of science, often to be resurrected when the conditions that generated the concern again emerge on the social agenda.

Research on new uses for agricultural commodities is one example. It was promoted in the 1930s under the rubric of chemurgy and in the 1950s under the title of utilization research as a solution to the problem of agricultural surpluses. It lost both scientific and political credibility because it promised more than it could deliver. "Integrated pest management" represents a more fortunate example. This term emerged in the 1960s as an alternative to chemical-intensive pest control strategies and was appropriated in the 1970s as a rhetorical device to paper over the differences between ecologically oriented and economically oriented entomologists. After two decades of scientific research and technology development there are now packages of practice consistent with the definition of integrated pest management (Palladino 1989).

In the case of sustainable agricultural systems, we are able to draw on several historical examples of systems that proved capable of meeting the challenge of achieving sustainable increases in agricultural production. One example is the forest and bush fallow (or shifting cultivation) systems practiced in most areas of the world in premodern times and today in many tropical areas (Pingali, Bigot, and Binswanger 1987). At low levels of population density, these systems were sustainable over long periods of time. As population density increased, short fallow systems emerged. Where the shift to short fallow systems occurred slowly, as in Western Europe and East Asia, systems of farming that permitted sustained growth in agricultural production emerged. Where the transition to short fallow has been forced by rapid population growth the consequence has often been soil degradation and declining productivity.

A second example can be drawn from the agricultural history of East Asian wet rice cultivation (Hayami and Ruttan 1985, 280–98). Traditional wet rice cultivation resembled farming in an aquarium. The rice grew tall and rank. It had a low grain-to-straw ratio. Most of what was produced, straw and grain, was recycled in the form of animal and human manures. Mineral nutrients and organic matter were carried into and deposited in the fields with the irrigation water. Rice yields rose continuously, though slowly, even under a monoculture system.

A third example of sustainable agriculture was the system of integrated crop-animal husbandry that emerged in Western Europe in the late Middle Ages to replace the medieval two- and three-field systems (van Bath 1963; Boserup 1965). The "new husbandry" system emerged with the introduction and intensive use of new forage and green manure crops. These in turn permitted an increase in the availability and use of animal manures. This permitted the emergence of intensive crop-livestock systems of production through the recycling of plant nutrients in the form of animal manures to maintain and improve soil fertility.[2]

These three systems, along with similar systems based on indigenous technology, have provided an inspiration for the emerging field of agroecology. But none of the traditional systems, while sustainable under conditions of slow growth in demand, has the capacity to respond to modern rates of growth in demand—in the 3 to 5 percent per year range—generated by some combination of rapid increase in population and in growth of income (Hayami and Ruttan 1985, 41–42). In the presently developed countries the capacity to sustain the necessary increases in agricultural production will depend largely on capacity for institutional innovation. If capacity to sustain growth in agricultural production is lost, it will be a result of political and economic failure. It is quite clear, however, that the scientific and technical knowledge is not yet available that will enable farmers in most tropical countries to meet the current demand their societies are placing upon them nor to sustain the increases that are currently being achieved. In these countries, achievement of sustainable agricultural surpluses is dependent on advances in scientific knowledge and on technical and institutional innovation (TAC/CGIAR 1989).

THE TECHNOLOGICAL CHALLENGE TO SUSTAINABILITY

One might ask why concern about the sustainability of modern agricultural systems has emerged with such force toward the end of the twenty-first century. The first reason is the unprecedented demands that growth of population and income are imposing on agricultural systems. Prior to the beginning of this century almost all increases in food production were obtained by bringing new land into production. By the first decades of the next century almost all increases in food production must come from higher yields—from increased output per hectare.

Historical trends in the production and consumption of the major food grains could easily be taken as evidence that one should not be excessively concerned about the capacity of the world's farmers to meet future food demands. World wheat prices have declined since the middle of the last century. Rice prices have declined since the middle of this century. These trends suggest that productivity growth has been able to more than compensate for the rapid growth in demand arising out of growth in population and income, particularly during the decades since World War II. But the past may not be an effective guide to the future. The demands that the developing countries will place on their agricultural producers arising out of population growth and the growth in per capita consumption will, until well into the middle of the next century, be exceedingly high.

A second reason for concern about sustainability is that the sources of future productivity growth are not as apparent as we move toward the early years of the twenty-first century as they were a quarter-century ago. It seems apparent that the gains in agricultural production that will be required over the next quarter-century will be achieved with much greater difficulty than those in the immediate past (Ruttan 1989b, 1994). The incremental responses to the increases in fertilizer use have declined. Expansion of irrigated areas has become more costly. Maintenance research, the research required to prevent yields from declining, is rising as a share of research effort (Plucknett and Smith 1986). The institutional capacity to respond to these concerns is limited, even in the countries with the most effective national agricultural research and extension systems. In many developing countries there has been considerable difficulty in maintaining the agricultural research capacity that had been established in the 1960s and 1970s (Eicher 1994).

Within another decade, advances in basic knowledge may create new opportunities for advancing agricultural technology that will reverse the urgency of some of the above concerns. Institutionalization of private sector agricultural research capacity in some developing countries is beginning to complement public sector capacity (Pray 1987). It is possible that advances in molecular biology and genetic engineering will soon begin to release the constraints on productivity growth in the major food- and feedgrains.[3] But advances in agricultural technology will not be able to eliminate what some critics tend to view as a subsidy from outside the agricultural sector. Transfers of energy in the form of mineral fuels, pathogen and pest control chemicals, and mineral nutrients will continue to be needed to sustain growth in agricultural production—and in much larger quantities—until well into the middle of the next century. Over the very long run scarcity, reflected in rising real prices, of phosphate fertilizer and fossil fuels is likely to become the primary resource constraint on sustainable growth in agricultural production (Desai and Gandhi 1990; Chapman and Barker 1991).

The third concern is about the environmental spillover from agricultural and industrial intensification. The spillover effects from agricultural intensification include the loss of soil resources due to erosion; water-logging and salinization; surface and groundwater contamination from plant nutrients and pesticides; resistance of insects, weeds, and pathogens to present methods of control; and the loss of land races and natural habitats (Conway and Pretty 1991). If agriculture is forced to continue to expand into more fragile environments, problems such as soil erosion and desertification can be expected to become more severe. Additional deforestation will intensify problems of soil erosion, species loss, degradation of water quality and will contribute to the forcing of climate change. There can no longer be much doubt that the accumulation of carbon dioxide (CO_2) and other greenhouse gases—principally methane (CH_4), nitrous oxide (N_2O), and chlorofluorocarbons (CFCs)—has set in motion a process that will result in a rise in global average surface temperature and changes in rainfall patterns over the next 30 to 60 years. These changes can be expected to impose substantial adaptation demands on agricultural systems. The systems that will have the least capacity to adapt will be in countries with the weakest agricultural research and natural resource management capacity—principally in the humid and semi-arid tropics (Ruttan 1992).

It should be apparent that a major issue over the next half-century for most developing countries, including the formerly centrally planned economies, will be how to generate and sustain the advances in agricultural technology that will be needed to meet the demands that these societies will place on these agricultural sectors. This objective appears to be in direct conflict with the world view of many of the leading advocates of sustainable development. Sustainable development is a concept that implies limits, both to the assimilative capacity of the environment and to the capability of technology to enhance human welfare. To the sustainable development community, the capacity of the environment to assimilate pollution from human production and consumption activity is the ultimate limit to economic growth (Batie 1989, 1085). But this is not a problem that has emerged only during the second half of the twentieth century. Throughout history humankind has been continuously challenged by the twin problems of how to obtain adequate sustenance and how to manage the disposal of what in recent literature has been referred to as "residuals." Failure to make balanced progress along both fronts has at times imposed serious constraints on society's growth and development (Ruttan 1971, 707).

I differ in one fundamental respect from those who are advancing the sustainability agenda. It seems clear to me that the capacity of a society to solve either the problem of sustenance or the problems posed by the production of residuals is inversely related to population density and the rate of population growth, and it is positively related to the society's capacity for innovation in science and technology and in social institutions (Ruttan 1971, 788). I am exceedingly concerned that the bilateral and multilateral assistance agencies, in their rush to allocate resources in support of a sustainability agenda, will fail to sustain the effort needed to build viable agricultural research capacity in the tropics.

THREE UNRESOLVED ANALYTICAL ISSUES

In this section I identify three unresolved analytical issues that must be confronted before a commitment to sustainability can be translated into an internally consistent reform agenda.

THE ISSUE OF SUBSTITUTABILITY

Our knowledge about the role of technology in widening the substitutability among natural resources and between natural resources and reproducible capital is clearly inadequate. Economists and technologists have traditionally viewed technical change as widening the possibility of substitution among resources—of fertilizer for land, for example (Solow 1974; Goeller and Weinberg 1976). The sustainability community rejects the "age of substitutability" argument. The loss of botanical genetic resources is viewed as a permanent loss of capacity. The elasticity of substitution among natural factors and between natural and man-made factors is viewed as exceedingly low (James, Nijkamp, and Opschoor 1989; Daly 1991). When considering the production of a particular commodity—for example, the substitution of fertilizer for land in the production of wheat—this is an argument over the form of the production function. But substitution also occurs in the production of a different product that performs the same function or fills the same need as another—of fiber optic cable for conventional copper telephone wire, or fuels with higher hydrogen to carbon ratios for coal, for example.

The argument about substitutability, while inherently an empirical issue, is typically argued on theoretical or philosophical grounds. It is possible that historical experience or advances in future modeling may lead toward some convergence of perspectives, but the scientific and technical knowledge needed to fully resolve disagreements about substitutability will always lie in the future (Costanza 1989). Yet, the issue is exceedingly important. If a combination of capital investment and technical change can continuously widen opportunities for substitution, imposing constraints on present resource use could leave future generations less well off. On the other hand, when real output per unit of natural resource input is narrowly bounded—cannot exceed some upper limit that is not too far from where we are now—then catastrophe is unavoidable.

Obligations toward the Future

The second issue that has divided traditional resource economists and the sustainability community is how to deal analytically with the obligations of the present generation toward future generations. The issue of intergenerational equity is at the center of the sustainability debate (Pearce, Markandya, and Barbier 1989, 23–56; Solow 1991). Environmentalists have been particularly critical of the approach used by resource and other economists in valuing future benefit and cost streams. The conventional approach involves the calculation of the "present value" of a resource development or protection project by discounting the cost and benefit stream by some "real" rate of interest—an interest rate adjusted to reflect the costs of inflation. It is World Bank policy (but not always practice) to require a 10–15 percent rate of return on projects. These higher rates are set well above long-term real rates of interest (historically less than 4 percent) in order to reflect the effect of unanticipated inflation and other risks associated with project development and implementation. An attempt is made in this way to avoid unproductive projects.

The critics insist that this approach results in a "dictatorship of the present" over the future. At conventional rates of interest the present value of a dollar of benefits fifty years into the future approaches zero. "Discounting can make molehills out of even the biggest mountain" (Batie 1989, 1092). Solow has made the same point in more formal terms. He notes that if the marginal profit—marginal revenue less marginal cost—to resource owners rises more slowly than the rate of interest, resource production and consumption is pushed nearer in time and the resource will be quickly exhausted (Solow 1974, 3).

A question that has not been adequately answered is whether, as a result of the adoption of a widely held sustainability "ethic," the market-determined discount rates would decline toward the rate preferred by those advancing the sustainability agenda.[4] Or will it be necessary to impose sumptuary regulations—constraints on current consumption—in an effort to induce society to shift the income distribution more strongly toward future generations? It seems clear to me that in most countries efforts to achieve sustainable growth must involve some combination of higher contemporary rates of saving—that is, deferral of present consumption in favor of future consumption—and more rapid technical change, particularly the technical changes that will enhance resource productivity and widen the range of substitutability among resources.[5] But will this be enough? I suspect not! What should be done given the inability of economic theory to provide satisfactory tools to deal analytically with obligations toward the future? My own answer is that we should take a strategic approach to the really large issues—how much should we invest to reduce the probability of excessive climate change, for example. We should continue to employ conventional cost-benefit analysis to answer the smaller questions, such as when to develop the drainage systems needed to avoid excessive build-up of water and salinity in an irrigation project.

INCENTIVE-COMPATIBLE INSTITUTIONAL DESIGN

A third area where knowledge needs to be advanced is the design of institutions that are capable of internalizing—within individual households, private firms and public organizations—the costs of actions that generate the negative spillover effects—the residuals—that are the source of environmental stress. Under present institutional arrangements important elements of the physical and social environment continue to be undervalued for purposes of both market and nonmarket transactions. Traditional production theory implies that if the price to a user of an important resource is undervalued it will be overused. If the price of a factor—the capacity of groundwater to absorb pollutants, for example—is zero, it will be used until the value of its marginal product to the user approaches zero. This will be true even though its use may be imposing large social costs on society.

The dynamic consequences of failure to internalize spillover costs are even more severe. In an environment characterized by rapid economic growth and changing relative factor prices, failure to internalize resource costs will bias the direction of technical change. The demand will grow more rapidly when a resource is priced below its social cost than in a situation where substitution possibilities are constrained by existing technology. As a result, "open access" resources will undergo stress or depletion more rapidly than in a world characterized by a static technology or even by neutral (unbiased) technical change.

The process is clearly apparent in U.S. agriculture. Federal farm programs encourage farmers to grow a small group of selected program crops, to grow these crops on a continuous basis, and to use more chemical intensive methods in production (General Accounting Office 1990). The capacity of the environment to absorb the residuals from crop and livestock production has been treated as a free good. As a result, scientific and technical innovation has been overly biased toward the development of land substitutes—plant nutrients and plant protection chemicals and management systems that reflected the overvaluation of land and the undervaluation of the social costs of the disposal of residuals from agricultural production processes (Runge et al. 1990).

The design of incentive compatible institutions—institutions capable of achieving compatibility among individual, organizational, and social objectives—remains at this stage an art rather than a science. The incentive compatibility problem has not been solved even at the most abstract theoretical level.[6] This deficiency in institutional design capacity is evident in our failure to design institutions capable of achieving contemporary distributional equity, either within countries or among rich and poor countries. It impinges with even greater force on our capacity to design institutions capable of achieving intergenerational equity.

AN UNCERTAIN FUTURE

We are far from being able to design either an adequate technological or institutional response to the issue of how to achieve sustainable growth in agricultural production. In spite of the large literature in agronomy, agricultural economics, and related fields there is no package of technology that is available to transfer to producers that can assure the sustainability of growth in agricultural production at a rate that will enable agriculture, particularly in the developing countries, to meet the demands that are being placed on them (National Research Council, 1991, 1993; Rosenberg and Eisgruber 1992; Vosti and Reardon 1997). Sustainability is appropriately viewed as a guide to future agricultural research agendas rather than as a guide to practice (Ruttan 1988). As a guide to research it seems useful to adhere to a definition that would include (1) the development of technology and practices that maintain or advance the quality of land and water resources, and (2) the improvement in the performance of plants and animals and advances in production practices that will facilitate the substitution of biological for chemical technology. The research agenda on sustainable agriculture needs to explore what is biologically feasible without being excessively limited by present economic constraints.

At present the sustainability community has not been able to advance a program of institutional innovation or reform that can provide a credible guide to the organization of sustainable societies. We have yet to design the institutions that can assure intergenerational equity. Few would challenge the assertion that future generations have rights to levels of sustenance and amenities that are at least equal to those of the present generation. They also should expect to inherit the improvements in institutional capital—including scientific and cultural knowledge—needed to design more productive and healthy environments.

My conclusion with respect to institutional design is similar to that which I have advanced in the case of technology. Economists and other social scientists have made a good deal of progress in the analysis needed for course correction, but their capacity to contribute to institutional design remains limited. The problem of designing incentive-compatible institutions—institutions capable of achieving compatibility among individual, organizational, and social objectives—has not been solved at even the most abstract theoretical level, which means that institutional design is proceeding in an ad hoc trial and error fashion—and that the errors continue to be expensive. Institutional innovation and reform should represent a high priority research agenda.

NOTES

1. This view stems in part from a naïve carrying capacity interpretation of the potential productivity of natural systems (Raup 1964).

2. In his study of sustainable agriculture in the Middle Ages, Jules N. Pretty (1990, 1) notes that "manorial estates survived many centuries of change and appear to have been highly sustainable agricultural systems. Yet this sustainability was not achieved because of high agricultural productivity—indeed it appears that farmers were trading off low productivity against the more highly valued goals of stability, sustainability and equitability."

3. For an argument that the results of genetic engineering can be expected to undermine sustainable methods of farming, see Hindmarsh 1991.

4. The question of the impact of the use of a positive discount (or interest) rate on resource exploitation decisions is somewhat more complex than often implied in the sustainability literature. High rates of resource exploitation can be consistent with either high or low interest rates (Norgaard 1991; Price 1991). As an alternative to lower discount rates, Mikesell (1991) suggests taking resource depletion into account in project cost-benefit analysis.

5. In Norgaard 1991 and Norgaard and Howarth 1991, the authors argue that decisions regarding the assignment of resource rights among generations should be based on equity rather than efficiency. When resource rights are reassigned between generations, interest rates will change to reflect the intergenerational distributions of resource rights and income. I interpret these arguments as saying that if present generations adopt an ethic that causes them to save more and consume less, the income distribution will be tilted in favor of future generations. This is, however, not the end of the story. A decline in marginal time preference has the effect of lowering the rate of interest. Improvement in investment opportunities resulting, for example, from technical change will have the effect of increasing the demand for investment and thus raising interest rates (Hirshleifer 1970, 31–45, 113–16).

6. The concept of incentive compatibility was introduced in a paper by Hurwicz (1972). In that paper he showed that it was not possible to specify an informationally decentralized mechanism for resource allocation that simultaneously generated efficient resource allocation and incentives for consumers to honestly reveal their true preferences. For a review of the literature in this area, see Groves, Radner, and Reiter 1987. For a discussion of the difficulties of achieving incentive compatibility in natural resources and environmental policy and management, see Young 1992. For a set of case studies illustrating successful efforts to reduce the transaction costs involved in institutional design and maintenance, see Ostrom 1990.

REFERENCES

Batie, Sandra S. 1989. "Sustainable Development: Challenges to the Profession of Agricultural Economics." *American Journal of Agricultural Economics* 71 (5): 1083–1101.

Boserup, Ester. 1965. *Conditions of Agricultural Growth.* Chicago: Aldine.

Buttel, F. 1991. "Knowledge Production, Ideology, and Sustainability in the Social and Natural Sciences." Paper presented at the Conference on Varieties of Sustainability, Asilomar, California, May 10–12.

Chapman, D., and R. Barker. 1991. "Environmental Protection, Resource Depletion, and the Sustainability of Developing Country Agriculture." *Economic Development and Cultural Change* 39 (4): 723–37.

Conway, G. R., and J. N. Pretty. 1991. *Unwelcome Harvest: Agriculture and Pollution.* London: Earthscan Publications.

Costanza, R. 1989. "What Is Ecological Economics?" *Ecological Economics* 1:1–7.

Dahlberg, K. A. 1991. "Sustainable Agriculture: Fad or Harbinger." *BioScience* 41:337–40.

Daly, H. E. 1991. "From Empty World Economics to Full World Economics: Recognizing an Historical Turning Point in Economic Development." In *Environmentally Sustainable Economic*

Development: Building on Bruntland," edited by R. Goodland, H. Daly, and S. El-Serafy, 18–26. Environment Working Paper no. 4, World Bank, Washington, D.C.

Desai, G. M., and V. Gandhi. 1990. "Phosphorous for Sustainable Agricultural Growth in Asia: An Assessment of Alternative Sources and Management." In *Phosphorous Requirements for Sustainable Agriculture in Asia and Oceana.* Los Baños, Philippines: International Rice Research Institute.

Douglass, G. K., ed. 1984. *Agricultural Sustainability in a Changing World Order.* Boulder, Colo.: Westview Press.

Eicher, Carl K. 1994. "Building Productive National and International Agricultural Research Systems." In *Agriculture, Environment and Health: Toward Sustainable Development into the 21st Century,* edited by Vernon W. Ruttan, 77–103. Minneapolis: University of Minnesota Press.

General Accounting Office. 1990. *Alternative Agriculture: Federal Incentives and Farmers Options.* Washington, D.C.: GAO.

Goeller, H. E., and A. M. Weinberg. 1976. "The Age of Substitutability." *Science* 191:683–89.

Goodland, R. 1991. "The Case That the World Has Reached Limits." In *Environmentally Sustainable Economic Development: Building on Bruntland.* Environment Working Paper no. 46, edited by R. Goodland, H. Daly, and S. El-Serafy, 5–17, World Bank, Washington, D.C.

Groves, T., R. Radner, and S. Reiter, eds. 1987. *Information, Incentives, and Economic Mechanisms.* Minneapolis: University of Minnesota Press.

Harwood, R. R. 1990. "A History of Sustainable Agriculture." In *Sustainable Agricultural Systems,* edited by C. A. Edwards, R. Lal, P. Madden. R. H. Miller, and G. House. Ankeny, Iowa: Soil and Water Conservation Authority.

Hayami, Yujiro, and Vernon W. Ruttan. 1985. *Agricultural Development: An International Perspective,* 2nd ed. Baltimore: Johns Hopkins University Press.

Hindmarsh, R. 1991. "The Flawed 'Sustainable' Promise of Genetic Engineering." *Ecologist* 21:196–205.

Hirshleifer, J. 1970. *Investment, Interest, and Capital.* Englewood Cliffs, N.J.: Prentice Hall.

Hopper, W. D. 1987. "Sustainability, Policies, Natural Resources, and Institutions." In *Sustainability Issues in Agricultural Development: Proceedings of the Seventh Agricultural Sector Symposium,* edited by T. J. Davis and I. A. Schirmer. Washington, D.C.: World Bank.

Hotelling, H. 1931. "The Economics of Exhaustible Resources." *Journal of Political Economy* 39:137–75.

Hurwicz, L. 1972. "On Informationally Decentralized Systems." In *Decision and Organization,* edited by C. G. McGuire and R. Radner, 297–336. Amsterdam: North Holland.

James, D. E., P. Nijkamp, and J. B. Opschoor. 1989. "Ecological Sustainability in Economic Development." In *Economy and Ecology: Toward Sustainable Development,* edited by F. Archibugi and P. Nijkamp, 27–48. Dordrecht, The Netherlands: Kluwer.

Lélé, S. M. 1991. "Sustainable Development: A Critical Review." *World Development* 19 (6): 607–21.

Mikesell, R. F. 1991. "Project Evaluation and Sustainable Development." In *Environmentally Sustainable Economic Development: Building on Bruntland,* Environment Working Paper no. 46, edited by R. Goodland, H. Daly, and S. El-Serafy, 54–60. Washington, D.C.: World Bank.

National Research Council. 1989. *Alternative Agriculture.* Washington, D.C.: National Academy Press.

———. 1991. *Sustainable Agriculture Research and Education in the Field.* Washington, D.C.: National Academy Press.

———. 1993. *Sustainable Agriculture and the Environment in the Humid Tropics.* Washington, D.C.: National Academy Press.

Norgaard, R. B. 1991. "Sustainability as Intergenerational Equity: The Challenge to Economic Thought and Practice." World Bank Report no. DP 7, World Bank, Washington, D.C.

Norgaard, R. B., and R. B. Howarth. 1991. "Sustainability and Discounting the Future." In *Ecological Economics: The Science and Management of Sustainability,* edited by R. Costanza, 88–101. New York: Columbia University Press.

Ostrom, Elinor. 1990. *Governing the Commons: The Evolution of Institutions for Collective Action.* Cambridge: Cambridge University Press.

Palladino, P. S. A. 1989. "Entomology and Ecology: The Ecology of Entomology." Ph.D. dissertation, University of Minnesota, Minneapolis.

Pearce, D., A. Markandya, and E. B. Barbier. 1989. *Blueprint for a Green Economy.* London: Earthscan.

Pingali, Prabhu, Y. Bigot, and Hans P. Binswanger. 1987. *Agricultural Mechanization and the Evolution of Farming Systems in Sub-Saharan Africa.* Baltimore: Johns Hopkins University Press.

Plucknett, D. H., and N. J. H. Smith. 1986. "Sustaining Agricultural Yields." *BioScience* 36 (1): 40–45.

Pray, Carl E. 1987. "Private Agricultural Sector Research in Asia." In *Policy for Agricultural Research,* edited by Vernon W. Ruttan and Carl E. Pray, 411–31. Boulder, Colo.: Westview Press.

Pretty, J. N. 1990. "Sustainable Agriculture in the Middle Ages: The English Manor." *Agricultural History Review* 3 (1): 1–19.

Price, C. 1991. "Do High Discount Rates Destroy Tropical Forests?" *Journal of Agricultural Economics* 42 (1): 77–83.

Raup, H. M. 1964. "Some Problems in Ecological Theory and Their Relation to Conservation." *Journal of Ecology* 52:19–28.

Rosenberg, E., and L. M. Eisgruber. 1992. "Sustainable Development and Sustainable Agriculture: A Partially Annotated Bibliography with Emphasis on Economics." Working Paper 92-101, Graduate Faculty of Economics, Oregon State University, Corvallis.

Runge, C. Ford. 1992. "A Policy Perspective on the Sustainability of Production Environments: Toward a Land Theory of Value." In *Future Challenges for National Agricultural Research: A Policy Dialogue.* The Hague: International Service for National Agricultural Research.

Runge, C. Ford., R. D. Munson, E. Lotterman, and J. Creason. 1990. *Agricultural Competitiveness, Farm Fertilizer, Chemical Use and Environmental Quality.* St. Paul, Minn.: Center for International Food and Agricultural Policy, University of Minnesota.

Ruttan, Vernon W. 1971. "Technology and the Environment." *American Journal of Agricultural Economics* 53 (5): 707–17.

———. 1988. "Sustainability Is Not Enough." *American Journal of Alternative Agriculture* 3:128–30.

———. 1989a. "Why Foreign Economic Assistance?" *Economic Development and Cultural Change* 37 (2): 411–24.

———, ed. 1989b. "Biological and Technical Constraints on Crops and Animal Productivity: Report on a Dialogue." Staff Paper P89-45, Department of Agricultural and Applied Economics, University of Minnesota, St. Paul.

———, ed. 1992. *Sustainable Development and the Environment: Perspectives on Growth and Constraints.* Boulder, Colo.: Westview Press.

———, ed. 1994. *Agriculture, Environment and Health: Sustainable Development into the Twenty-First Century.* Minneapolis: University of Minnesota Press.

Solow, R. M. 1974. "The Economics of Resources or the Resources of Economics." *American Economic Review* 64 (2): 1–14.

———. 1991. "Economists Perspective." J. Seeward Johnson Lecture, Woods Hole Oceanographic Institution, Marine Policy Center, Woods Hole, Massachusetts, June 14.

Technical Advisory Committee/Consultative Group on International Agricultural Research (TAC/CGIAR). 1989. *Sustainable Agricultural Production: Implications for International Research.* Rome: Food and Agriculture Organization.

van Bath, S. H. S. 1963. *The Agrarian History of Western Europe, A.D. 500–1850.* London: Edward Arnold.

Vosti, S., and T. Reardon, eds. 1997. *Sustainability, Growth, and Poverty Alleviation: A Policy and Agroecological Perspective.* Baltimore: Johns Hopkins University Press.

World Commission on Environment and Development. 1987. *Our Common Future.* Bruntland Commission. New York: Oxford University Press.

Young, M. D. 1992. *Sustainable Investment and Resource Use: Equity, Environmental Integrity, and Economic Efficiency.* Park Ridge, N.J.: Parthenon.

27

African Agriculture: Productivity and Sustainability Issues

THOMAS REARDON

Rural Africa is struggling to develop sustainable agricultural production systems to cope with increasing population pressure on land and water resources. The struggle is intense because crop yields are stagnating, the resource base is degrading, and public support to agriculture has declined, with cuts in fertilizer subsidies, rural credit, and equipment programs. Nevertheless, agricultural productivity must be raised substantially and sustained, by enhancing and protecting the farm resource base. Yet, there is a common misperception that the productivity and sustainability (i.e., the growth and environment) agendas can and should be pursued separately.

The thesis of this paper is that productivity and sustainability are interwoven and that they should be pursued together. The chapter proceeds as follows. First, I define productivity and sustainability and discuss both issues in historical perspective in Africa. Second, I analyze the choice of technology for pursuing productivity and sustainability in African agriculture. Third, I go beyond technological considerations to discuss the policies and institutions that are required to sustainably intensify African agriculture. I conclude by assessing policy and research implications.

DEFINING AND MEASURING PRODUCTIVITY AND SUSTAINABILITY

Agricultural productivity is measured in terms of average (or marginal) "factor productivity." The latter is the output derived from the use of a unit of the factor (land, labor, or capital), conditioned by the technology and the quantity and quality of other factors used. When the sum (weighted by prices) of output of all crops and livestock of the farm (or sector) is in the numerator, and the amount used of all factors (weighted by prices) is in the denominator, one has an index of "total factor productivity." When a single factor is in the denominator (with one or more outputs) one has "partial factor productivity."[1]

THOMAS REARDON is associate professor of agricultural economics, Michigan State University.

"Sustainability," by itself, is a vague term. It does not make explicit what is to be sustained, for how long, at what level, or by whom. In the early 1980s, sustainability advocates focused on sustaining local ecosystems and recommended farming at low intensity, with minimum tillage and no external inputs. Hence, low-input sustainable agriculture (LISA) was equated with agricultural sustainability (Ruttan 1990). The concept of ecological sustainability was broadened in the late 1980s to include meeting the needs of rural households (Consultative Group for International Agricultural Research 1988). Social scientists, such as Chambers (1988), emphasized the rural household's priority of sustaining its "livelihood," rather than a particular activity or resource. Later, Reardon and Islam (1989) observed that ecological sustainability and livelihood sustainability are not necessarily compatible. They argued that both sustainability and productivity advocacy groups

> might be missing what the rural household really wants. In a degrading and unstable environment, the priority of the household may well be to diversify away from farming. It may want to maximize present earnings in cropping and invest the surplus in livestock and off-farm enterprises. Off-farm earnings might not be reinvested in cropping, but instead be used to diversify further. The above possibility is often neglected by both agricultural researchers and environmentalists who assume that a rural household in regions at environmental risk is first and foremost a *farming* household. The implication of their assumption is that innovations that can improve the farm resource base are automatically attractive to households. It is precisely in the areas at greatest risk where this assumption is least tenable (53).

The concepts of productivity and sustainability can be usefully linked, however, for any activity, including agriculture, and at any level, including the field, the whole farm, or the set of the household's livelihood activities. Lynam and Herdt (1989) define sustainability as "stable and growing total factor productivity."

HISTORICAL PERSPECTIVE ON PRODUCTIVITY AND SUSTAINABILITY ISSUES IN AFRICA

Agricultural productivity and sustainability (under the name of soil conservation) have been major themes of research in Africa since the 1920s (Food and Agriculture Organization 1973). Colonial researchers experimented with and extended soil conservation practices, planting of legumes, and crop-livestock farming.[2] After many countries achieved independence in the early 1960s, there was a "boom" in studies of smallholder agriculture, including farm management and farming systems.

We forget how farsighted and deep the literature on productivity and environment in Africa was in the 1960s and 1970s. The emphasis was on improved techniques and inputs to raise labor productivity in land-abundant areas with shifting cultivation. There was strong interest in settlement schemes that would introduce farmers to "modern agriculture" and provide fertilizer and seed. World

Bank teams urged governments to subsidize fertilizer use, to spur adoption of its use by farmers. These debates in the 1960s were a precursor to the current debate on whether improved input use can be intensified without subsidies and whether subsidies can be fiscally sustainable (Johnston 1964). Other scholars emphasized the importance of the development of input and output markets to raise farm productivity. Yet others raised questions about the proper mix of state and private involvement in input and output marketing and about the environmental effects of various interventions (Jones 1965). Finally, agricultural economists pointed to the need to study the farm household and the farming system (Norman 1973).

Nevertheless, conditions have substantially changed over the past three decades in rural Africa. Land constraints have increased in many areas formerly thought to be land abundant. With an overall population growth rate of 2.7 percent a year, rural population density has risen and fallow periods have decreased (Binswanger and Pingali 1988). Degradation of farmlands, pastures, and forests has exacerbated land constraints. Moreover, the rural economy has, to a great extent, become monetized and commercialized, with farm households buying and selling crops and allocating family labor to nonfarm activities.

Moreover, in many areas, crop yields are stagnant, food imports are increasing, and export market share has declined over the past two decades (Agcaoili and Rosegrant 1994). For most food crops and in most areas, Africa has not yet generated a sustained Green Revolution.[3] More than a decade of structural adjustment policies have produced mixed results in agriculture, including a general reduction in public services for farmer support and access to improved inputs such as fertilizer.

In the late 1980s, sustainability emerged as a critical issue in African policy circles, because of famine, growing evidence of land degradation, deforestation, and desertification, and because of a rebirth of concern in developed countries for the environment. These forces translated into pressure on foreign assistance agencies to undertake environment programs, and, in their interactions with African policy makers, to insist on the urgency of addressing environmental problems. However, the international environmentalist community has tended to cast the sustainability agenda as one of conserving endangered species and virgin forests and wetlands, and reducing the intensity of farmland use through the pursuit of LISA (Pretty 1995).

Yet African governments, agricultural researchers, and farmers have often viewed raising farm productivity as the immediate, pressing challenge. Although sustainability issues are of increasing concern to African policy makers (witness the recent creation of environment ministries in some countries, although often at the behest of donors), environment issues are still viewed as "second generation problems." That is, they tend to see solutions to environmental problems as helping long-term economic growth but not solving the first-generation problem—i.e., the need to increase food production (Idachaba 1987). Moreover, because of fiscal constraints, national agricultural research systems (NARS) are finding it difficult to maintain on-going research in plant breeding and agronomy. These factors explain why many NARS are reluctant to channel their shrinking resources to the relatively uncharted realm of sustainability research (Rukuni 1996).

The concern over food production and short-term survival is also of central concern to the farm household, the main actor in reconciling productivity and sustainability. Since small-scale farmers have immediate food security objectives, they may be forced to relegate to second priority investments in resource conservation with a medium- to long-run payoff. Nevertheless, productivity and sustainability can be compatible on the African farm and can reenforce each other.

PRODUCTIVE AND SUSTAINABLE TECHNOLOGY PATHS UNDER INCREASING POPULATION PRESSURE

African farmers have traditionally pursued shifting cultivation in response to population growth and declining soil fertility. As population pressure increased, they simply opened new land, by extending farming into forests, wetlands, hillsides, and pastures. This path is still common in land-abundant countries such as Zaire, where the extensification path is going to be "sustainable" for a long time (until all the forest is cut). Yet environmentalists often try to stop farmers in land-abundant areas from pushing into forests and wetlands, because it destroys valuable biodiversity. Farmers in these land-abundant areas choose technologies that use land and save labor, while environmentalists want farmers to see the land as a constraining factor and choose land-saving and labor-using technologies (such as LISA). The cat-and-mouse game that often results is an attempt by African governments and nongovernmental organizations (NGOs) to bar farmers from using forests.

Nevertheless, the land-extensive path is quickly becoming unsustainable or is no longer practical in much of Africa, where land scarcity is increasing as the forest or wetland is exhausted or the farmer is barred from using it, or when soil degradation in the "extensive margin" undermines crop yields over time.

Rising land scarcity under population pressure will become the norm for most of Africa in the twenty-first century. Under rapid population growth, farmers "intensify" by changing their farm technologies toward greater intensity of labor and/or capital use, relative to land. This change of technology as factor scarcities change is predictable from the induced innovation theory (Boserup 1965; Hayami and Ruttan 1985). Unfortunately, in response to declining farm size in places such as Malawi, Rwanda, and parts of the Sahel, many farmers are reducing fallow periods and increasing planting density through intercropping, without a concurrent increase in the use of farm capital. Farm capital is broadly defined as chemical inputs, organic matter, equipment, and land-conservation infrastructure.

Many farmers have been forced onto this capital-deficient path for the following reasons. First, structural adjustment programs have reduced input subsidies and public agricultural services (input provision, output distribution, credit, extension); private sector response to the change has been slow or partial, leaving a serious gap in access to inputs and credit (Rukuni 1996; Dembélé 1996). Second, the disappearance of pasture has reduced herds and thus access to manure. Third, many farmers are too poor to purchase inputs except in cash-crop areas and among households that earn off-farm income. Fourth, price instability caused by rainfall variation and underdeveloped product markets makes input use risky.[4]

The consequences of pursuing the capital-deficient path can be devastating. Intensification with inadequate use of farm capital causes rapid soil degradation in fragile tropical soils and undermines both productivity and sustainability. In Senegal, for example, fertilizer use became less profitable to farmers in the 1980s as the subsidy was removed. Although Senegal's currency was devalued in 1994 and peanut prices were raised, fertilizer use is still unprofitable. To compensate for degrading soils, farmers have been steadily increasing peanut seed density. This has led to a further decline in yields and more degradation, hence a vicious circle (Kelly et al. 1996). In Rwanda, farms that have intensified with inadequate use of farm capital have more eroded soils and lower land productivity than farms that have used chemical fertilizer, organic matter, and land improvements (Byiringiro and Reardon 1996).

The key technological issue is what *type* of intensification technology farmers choose, and whether it is financially profitable, sufficiently productive to meet crop output (including food) needs, and can be sustained on the resource base of the agroclimatic zone.

There are two broad technological options for intensification: LISA, which uses little inorganic fertilizer and equipment, and intensification technologies that combine elements of LISA with the use of fertilizer and equipment. I will show that the relative emphasis given to each path will differ by agroclimatic zone. In the more fragile agroclimates, LISA is more appropriate, while in the more favorable agroclimates, crop output growth and soil fertility needs will best be served by supplementing the organic matter application and soil conservation techniques of LISA with capital-using intensification, in order to meet the goals of productivity, sustainability, and agricultural growth.

LISA: LOW-INPUT SUSTAINABLE AGRICULTURE

LISA is a revival of the organic farming movement of the mid-1800s in Germany (Ruttan 1990). Many environmentalists and some agriculturalists are currently urging African farmers to pursue traditional LISA systems that use minimum tillage, labor-intensive recycling of nutrients by alley cropping, green manuring, and composting, and little or no chemical fertilizer, pesticides, or herbicides.

LISA has been promoted in Africa because of the hypothesis that farmers cannot afford risky chemical inputs and that using chemical inputs as well as tillage is harmful to the environment. Elwell, cited in Low (1993), argues that in Zimbabwe annual plowing and inorganic fertilizers have undermined soil fertility and soil integrity. Nicou and Charreau (1985) maintain that deep tillage (using animal traction) can break down fragile soils and lead to erosion and accelerated burning of organic matter. They recommend zero or minimum tillage. Spencer and Polson (1997) argue that chemical fertilizer has become unprofitable in the humid tropics since the withdrawal of fertilizer subsidies during structural adjustment, and that farmers should pursue LISA.

Nevertheless, there is growing evidence that in many parts of Africa LISA practices *by themselves* do not enable farmers to achieve both productivity and sustainability goals (Low 1993). Although the LISA model is well suited for fragile areas that support livestock grazing, LISA has the potential to increase food output by only about 1 percent a year, which falls far short of meeting Africa's 3.0 to 3.5 percent annual growth in food demand (Ruttan 1990). If LISA systems are unable to meet family food security needs, many farmers will cultivate hillsides and fragile lands. The environmental damage caused by this type of extensification may exceed the beneficial effects of low doses of inorganic fertilizer and minimum tillage. Tribe (1994) notes that if a LISA food-production strategy rather than the Green Revolution food-production model had been pursued in South Asia since the 1960s, 44 million hectares that are now under forest would instead have been plowed and cropped. This suggests that biodiversity has been enhanced in Asia by the yield-increasing and land-saving Green Revolution model.

Third, LISA advocates in Africa are, like Don Quixote, "jousting with windmills" when they worry about the effects of chemical fertilizers on the environment in most countries. In 1993, African farmers used an average of only 10 kilograms of inorganic fertilizers per hectare, as compared to 83 kilograms per hectare in all developing areas (Heisey and Mwangi 1997). Besides, fertilizer use has fallen over the past decade as subsidies have been reduced or eliminated. Rather, the low use of chemical fertilizer is a major reason for *worry,* from the environmental perspective and from the food-production perspective. Even manure, a key component in most LISA systems, is in short supply in many countries (e.g., Rwanda, Malawi, and Zimbabwe), because increasing population pressure has prompted clearing of pasture lands for farming.

Fourth, many LISA techniques, such as hand weeding, recycling organic matter, and alley cropping, are labor intensive. The evidence is mixed on the farm profitability of these practices. On the one hand, there is evidence of farmer adoption of LISA-type land improvements that are profitable, where there are farmers with land constraints due to rapid population growth. On the other hand, there is evidence that the returns to family labor in some LISA techniques are lower than in alternative on-farm and off-farm uses of labor.[5]

The latter point raises the critical issue of the profitability of some labor-using techniques, among them LISA, as well as of risky inputs such as chemical fertilizer. There has been a tendency for LISA advocates to equate subsistence agriculture with "sustainability," yet there is increasing evidence from field surveys that African farmers tend to use *very little* organic matter or chemical fertilizers, or labor-intensive soil conservation measures on low-return, subsistence-food crops—even if agronomists or environmentalists recommend that they do so. Evidence (from such diverse settings as Burkina Faso, Ghana, Kenya, Rwanda, Tanzania, and Zimbabwe[6]) shows that the most common use of manure, chemical fertilizer, and land-improvement measures is on commercialized crops (food or nonfood) with relatively high and stable returns.

Recent studies have shown that subsistence food crops and commercialized crops can be complementary rather than competitive. For example, animal traction equipment that was purchased mainly for use on the cash crops is sometimes also used to prepare land for the subsistence food crops. In many countries fertilizer acquired through cash crop schemes is sometimes available to subsistence crops either through "turning away" a portion of the fertilizer from the cash crops to the subsistence crops or as plot residues from the commercial crop grown in the field the year before (in a rotation system). Also, marketing and farm management skills acquired in commercial crop production can benefit subsistence crop production. (For illustrations from Mali, see Dione 1989, and from Ghana, see al Hassan, Kydd, and Warner 1996.)

Nontraditional variants of LISA that are already in use in parts of Asia are being studied and recommended for Africa (Pretty 1995). These include biological methods, for instance, integrated pest management, rhizobium inoculants, and biotechnology, which promise much higher productivity than traditional LISA techniques. There are, however, obstacles to their adoption in Africa. First, many of these new biological technologies are not really low-input. Some of the technologies require increased labor use, as well as public expenditures on research, extension, and other support systems. This can make them more expensive overall than conventional yield-increasing technologies (Oram 1997). Second, use of these biological technologies is in its infancy for the crops and conditions in Africa; it will take several decades before the practices will have been tested, adapted, and proven to be cost-effective. The research expenditures for the transfer and adaptation of these methods will be extremely costly for small countries in Africa with strained research budgets (Herdt 1991).

To summarize, it is important for policy makers, farmers, and donors to pursue a middle path between regarding LISA as a panacea and seeing it as irrelevant to Africa's needs. In countries dominated by pasture (e.g., Botswana), mixed farming, or fragile areas, LISA practices like mulching and alley cropping can maintain grazing ecosystems and add organic matter through nutrient recycling. The challenge is to help farmers combine *profitable* LISA practices with the selective use of farm capital, such as inorganic fertilizer, equipment (animal traction equipment, tied ridgers), and soil conservation infrastructure. This is discussed below.

Farm Capital Intensification

A substantial increase in the use of farm capital is the most promising path to achieving both productivity and sustainability in all but the most fragile agroclimates in Africa. Farm capital includes nonlabor variable inputs that enhance soil fertility (both organic matter, like manure, mulch, and compost, and chemical fertilizer) and soil-conservation and water-retention infrastructure (e.g., bunding, terracing, tied ridging, anti-erosion ditches). Examples of combinations of these enhancements include contour bunding combined with use of manure and fertilizer in the semi-arid tropics (see Matlon and Adesina 1997), and terracing, fertilizer, and mulching in the hillside tropics (see Clay, Reardon, and Kangasniemi 1998).

Farm-capital intensification is productive and sustainable because the elements of the set of farm capital are complementary. For example, soil conservation measures can prevent runoff of organic matter and chemical fertilizers during periods of heavy rainfall, increasing the profitability of fertilizer and other purchased inputs. Also, organic matter needs to accompany chemical fertilizer use for cation exchange to occur (Matlon and Spencer 1984).

Sanders, Shapiro, and Ramaswamy (1996) report that farm-capital intensification often takes place in two stages. The first stage involves the labor-intensive application of manure and construction of traditional land improvements (planting grass strips, digging anti-erosion ditches, constructing earthen bunds). The second stage involves increased use of chemical fertilizer, improved—and more capital-intensive—land conservation techniques (such as tied ridging using modified animal traction equipment). Yet, whether farmers move to this second stage will depend on policy and institutional support, profitability, and access to cash and labor to purchase or produce the farm capital. This is discussed in the next section.

POLICY AND INSTITUTIONAL SUPPORT FOR INTENSIFICATION WITH FARM CAPITAL

Intensification with substantial use of farm capital is expensive for a poor African farmer and requires a critical combination of incentives and capacity at the farm level. Such investments will take place where: (1) agriculture is commercializing, input and output markets are accessible, and investments in intensification are profitable because returns are high and stable; (2) population pressure is high; (3) labor (family or hired) is available to undertake the labor-intensive tasks of constructing soil conservation capital (collecting rocks for bunds, building terraces, etc.), collecting and distributing manure; and (4) where farmers have cash to buy fertilizer, animal traction equipment and carts to haul manure and rocks for bunds, and to hire labor and install tubewells. These four conditions are now being fulfilled in the coffee-and-banana zones in Rwanda (Clay, Reardon, and Kangasniemi 1998), in the coffee-and-horticulture zones of Kenya (Tiffen, Mortimore, and Gichuki 1994), and in the maize-and-cotton zones of the semi-arid West Africa (Savadogo, Reardon, and Pietola 1995). These examples all include combining a cash crop (traditional or nontraditional) with a food crop, and with access to a growing market. It is important to note, however, that government policies, investments, and institutions have been a prerequisite for farmers to invest in these successful intensification areas. Four points are particularly noteworthy in that regard.

First, increasing farm capital and rural infrastructure is critical to sustainable intensification. Rural infrastructure needs are particularly important in feeder roads, trucks to haul rocks for bunds, dams and culverts, wells, and small-scale irrigation infrastructure. These public goods increase the profitability and feasibility of farm- and merchant-level private investments. An important lesson from the Green Revolution in Asia was the importance of a political commitment by governments to make massive road and irrigation investments; this has so far been lacking in Africa.

Moreover, increasing the access of the landless and near-landless to land is crucial, especially in dual agricultural systems such as South Africa, Kenya, Namibia, and Zimbabwe. Large farms tend to have higher yields than small farms in places where policy distortions give the former disproportionate access to land, inputs, and credit (e.g., Côte d'Ivoire [see Adesina and Djato 1996] and South Africa [see van Zyl, Binswanger, and Thirtle 1995]). Correcting these distortions and leveling the playing field will help small-scale farmers pursue farm-capital intensification.

Second, access of farmers to inputs through well-functioning input markets is crucial. It is today often argued that fertilizer and seed prices have adjusted to "nondistorted values" after devaluation and removal of subsidies and that a reduced use of these inputs is more efficient because financial profitability to farmers has dropped. However, fertilizer use needs to increase to maintain soil fertility and to meet food output needs, and if it does, financial returns may then be out of sync with economic returns and the longer-term interest of Africa. A choice needs to be made between two difficult paths. African governments could simply take current financial returns as "given" and let farmers reduce input use, with consequent harm to productivity, sustainability, and national food security. This pathway will not be politically acceptable if food production lags and food prices increase. The preferred option is for African governments to improve input markets infrastructure so as to lower transaction costs, and to improve the efficiency and profitability of fertilizer and seed use. Moreover, an economic case can be made for selected subsidies in certain circumstances (Sanders, Shaprio, and Ramaswamy 1996).

Third, it is important to reform macroeconomic policies so that they create an incentive environment for farmers. Nevertheless "getting prices right" is necessary but not sufficient where there are obstacles to farm investment posed by the lack of physical infrastructure and weak farmer support organizations.

Fourth, it is necessary to build farmers' capacity to invest in intensification by helping them obtain access to credit and nonfarm income. There are two means to this end. On the one hand, rebuilding more sustainable rural credit institutions is a priority (Rukuni 1996). On the other hand, cash incomes have become *critical* since the dismantlement of many public credit programs in the 1980s. Promotion of small rural nonfarm employment and businesses will not only provide rural employment and cash for on-farm investments[7] but also provide farm inputs, increase the demand for crops through downstream production linkages and expenditure linkages, and reduce pressure on the land by offering alternative income sources to farmers. Nonfarm income is, however, very unequally distributed in rural Africa; that inequality can translate in the longer run into increasing inequality in farm productivity and land and asset holdings as land markets and land titling proceed (Reardon 1998).

CONCLUSIONS

The present debate in the international community juxtaposes the promotion of agricultural productivity and, more broadly, economic growth, against environmental protection and sustainability. This conflict, which has invaded Africa, is a waste of time, and even destructive. African farmers, who constitute the majority of the population, are caught in the middle of this clash, and their pressing needs are often being forgotten.

On the one hand, the conditions of structural adjustment grants and loans have made fertilizer and, in some cases, seed more expensive and harder to obtain. The upshot is that it is harder for farmers to intensify production on the land they have. On the other hand, the new environmental conditionality programs (limiting access to protected forests and wetlands) bar farmers from pursuing production on new land. As a result, farmers are caught in a bind, but with growing food needs bearing down on them.

Nevertheless, the biodiverse forests and wetlands are in danger *unless* agriculture is intensified—that is, that the needed growth in food output is produced on current farmland rather than by cutting into virgin forests. Regulation and edict will not keep desperate families out of virgin land and game parks if they cannot survive on their current farmland.

The exclusive reliance on low-input sustainable agriculture will be unable to meet the 3 to 5 percent projected growth in food demand in Africa. Therefore, if food production with low-input methods is inadequate to keep up with food demand, African governments will be forced to increase food imports or farmers will simply push into forests and hillsides.

Without question, LISA is the most appropriate intensification path for many fragile areas in Africa; but in most agroecologies of Africa, a combination of LISA and farm-capital intensification approaches will be required to meet both food production and sustainabilty goals. This will require increasing the use of chemical fertilizer, organic matter, and improved seed, in combination with increasing investments in soil conservation and small-scale irrigation.

Identifying which technology path to pursue is complicated, because farm investments are determined by incentives and capacity. Incentives to invest in agricultural intensification are influenced by macroeconomic policies. The capacity of farmers to pursue alternative technological pathways is critically conditioned by public investments in rural infrastructure, improvements in input and output markets, credit policy, and promotion of nonfarm enterprises (especially those linked to agriculture, such as agroindustry). The challenge is to develop innovative, cost-effective public, private, and NGO agricultural support services and a favorable macroeconomic environment.

NOTES

I am grateful to USAID's Africa Bureau (Sustainable Development Division, Food Security and Productivity Unit) for support for this work.

1. Calculation of total factor productivity for many areas of Africa is hampered by lack of data for factor prices (e.g., because of missing or incomplete data on land, manure, or labor markets) and land quality, which should be reflected in the denominator but which are usually not available (Kelly et al. 1995).

2. See Eicher and Baker 1982 and Stocking 1985 for literature reviews.

3. Exceptions include hybrid maize for large-scale farms in Zimbabwe in the 1960s and in the first half of the 1980s for smallholders, in Kenya in the 1960s, and in Malawi, Zambia, Zimbabwe, Nigeria, and Ghana in the 1980s and 1990s; cocoa in Côte d'Ivoire and Ghana; cotton in French-speaking West Africa; and improvements in cassava (Lele, van de Walle, and Gbetibouo 1989; Enete, Nweke, and Okorji 1995; Byerlee and Eicher 1997).

4. Kumwenda et al. 1997, Clay, Reardon, and Kangasniemi 1997; Kelly et al. 1996; Sanders, Shapiro, and Ramaswamy 1996; Dembélé 1996; and Heisey and Mwangi 1997; Reardon et al. 1994.

5. Examples of LISA-type improvements include terraces in Kenya's Machakos district (Tiffen, Mortimore, and Gichuki 1994), alley farming in land-constrained humid areas of Nigeria, the *zai* (traditional water-retention technique) in Burkina Faso (Sanders, Shapiro, and Ramaswamy 1996), and alley cropping in densely populated areas of southeastern Nigeria (Jabbar, Larbi, and Reynolds 1996). Low (1986) notes that in Swaziland in the late 1970s, there was rapid adoption of hybrid maize and fertilizer, because they were labor saving and land augmenting, and farmers were then able to use freed labor to work off-farm where the returns were greater.

6. In Burkina Faso, farmers use thirteen times more manure on cotton and maize (the cash crops) than on sorghum and millet (subsistence foodgrains) (Savadogo, Reardon, and Pietola 1995). In Zimbabwe, farmers mainly use improved tillage practices and fertilizers where there are profitable cash crops (Mudimu 1996). In northern Ghana, fertilizer use is low on average and quite variable, but fertilizer tends to be applied only to crops that are for sale (hybrid maize, cotton, rice) and not to the subsistence food crops (sorghum, millet, cowpea) (al Hassan, Kydd, and Warner 1996). In the highland tropics of Tanzania, farmers confine fertilizer use and soil conservation practices to cash crops (Semgalawe 1997), as they do in Rwanda (Clay, Reardon, and Kangasniemi 1997) and in Kenya (Tiffen, Mortimore, and Gichuki 1994).

7. For a review of survey evidence of reinvestment of nonfarm income in farm capital in Africa see Reardon, Crawford, and Kelly 1994.

REFERENCES

Adesina, A. A., and K. K. Djato. 1996. "Farm Size, Relative Efficiency, and Agrarian Policy in Côte d'Ivoire: Profit Function Analysis of Rice Farms." *Agricultural Economics* 14 (2): 93–102.

Agcaoili, M. C., and M. W. Rosegrant. 1994. *World Production of Cereals, 1966–90.* 2020 Vision Brief 3. Washington, D.C.: International Food Policy Research Institute.

Binswanger, H., and P. Pingali. 1988. "Technological Priorities for Farming in Sub-Saharan Africa." *Research Observer* 3 (1): 81–98.

Boserup, Esther. 1965. *The Conditions of Agricultural Growth: The Economics of Agrarian Change under Population Pressure.* Chicago: Aldine.

Byerlee, Derek, and Carl K. Eicher, eds. 1997. *Africa's Emerging Maize Revolution.* Boulder, Colo.: Lynne Rienner Publishers.

Byiringiro, F., and T. Reardon. 1996. "Farm Productivity in Rwanda: Effects of Farm Size, Erosion, and Soil Conservation Investments." *Agricultural Economics* 15:127–36.

Chambers, R. 1988. "Sustainable Rural Livelihoods: A Key Strategy for People, Environment and Development." In *The Greening of Aid,* edited by C. Conroy and M. Litvinoff. London: Earthscan Publications.

Clay, D., T. Reardon, and J. Kangasniemi. 1998. "Sustainable Intensification in the Highland Tropics: Rwandan Farmers' Investments in Soil Conservation and Soil Fertility." *Economic Development and Cultural Change* 46:(2): 351–77.

Consultative Group for International Agricultural Research (CGIAR), Technical Advisory Committee (TAC). 1988. *Sustainable Agricultural Production: Implications for International Agricultural Research.* Washington, D.C.: CGIAR, World Bank.

Dembélé N. N. 1996. "Implications of Market Reform for Fertility Technology Development and Implementation in Sub-Saharan Africa with Special Reference to the Soil Fertility Management Initiative in Burkina Faso." Mimeograph. International Fertilizer Development Center—Africa, Ouagadougou, Burkina Faso.

Dione, J. 1989. *Informing Food Security Policy in Mali: Interactions between Technology, Institutions, and Market Reforms.* Ph.D. dissertation, Department of Agricultural Economics, Michigan State University, East Lansing.

Eicher, C. K., and D. Baker. 1982. *Research on Agricultural Development in Sub-Saharan Africa: A Critical Survey.* MSU International Development Paper no. 1, Department of Agricultural Economics, Michigan State University, East Lansing.

Enete, A. A., F. I. Nweke, and E. C. Okorji. 1995. "Trends in Food Crop Yields under Demographic Pressure in Sub-Saharan Africa: The Case of Cassava in Southeast Nigeria." *Outlook on Agriculture* 24 (4): 249–54.

Food and Agriculture Organization. 1973. *Shifting Cultivation and Soil Conservation in Africa.* Rome: FAO.

al Hassan, R., J. Kydd, and M. Warner. 1996. *Review of Critical Issues for Natural Resources Policy in Ghana's Northern Region,* Briefing Paper 4, Project on the Dynamics of Smallholder Agriculture in the Guinea Savannah Zone of West Africa, with particular reference to Northern Region Ghana, Wye College, Ashford, U.K.

Hayami, Y., and V. Ruttan. 1985. *Agricultural Development: An International Perspective,* 2nd ed. Baltimore: Johns Hopkins University Press.

Heisey, P. W., and W. Mwangi. 1997. "Fertilizer Use and Maize Production." In *Africa's Emerging Maize Revolution,* edited by D. Byerlee and C. K. Eicher. Boulder, Colo.: Lynne Rienner Publishers.

Herdt, R. W. 1991. "Perspectives on Agricultural Biotechnology Research for Small Countries." *Journal of Agricultural Economics* 42 (3): 298–308.

Idachaba, F. S. 1987. "Sustainability Issues in Agriculture Development." In *Sustainability Issues in Agricultural Development: Proceedings of the Seventh Agricultural Sector Symposium,* edited by Ted J. Davis and Isabelle A. Schirmer. Washington, D.C.: World Bank.

Jabbar, M. A., A. Larbi, and L. Reynolds. 1996. *Alley Farming for Improving Small Ruminant Productivity in West Africa: ILRI's Experiences.* Socioeconomics and Policy Research Working Paper no. 20, International Livestock Research Institute, Addis Ababa, Ethiopia.

Johnston, B. F. 1964. "The Choice of Measures for Increasing Agricultural Productivity: A Survey of Possibilities in East Africa." *Tropical Agriculture* 41 (2): 91–113.

Jones, W. O. 1965. "Environment, Technical Knowledge, and Economic Development in Tropical Africa." *Food Research Institute Studies* 5 (2): 101–16.

Kelly, V., B. Diagana, T. Reardon, M. Gaye, E. Crawford. 1996. *Cash Crop and Foodgrain Productivity in Senegal: Historical View, New Survey Evidence, and Policy Implications,* MSU International Development Paper, no. 20, Department of Agricultural Economics, Michigan State University, East Lansing.

Kelly, V., J. Hopkins, T. Reardon, E. Crawford. 1995. *Improving the Measurement and Analysis of African Agricultural Productivity: Promoting Complementarities between Micro and Macro Data.* MSU International Development Paper no. 16, Department of Agricultural Economics, Michigan State University, East Lansing.

Kumwenda, J. D. T., S. R. Waddington, S. S. Snapp, R. B. Jones, and M. J. Blackie. 1997. "Soil Fertility Management in Southern Africa." In *Africa's Emerging Maize Revolution,* edited by D. Byerlee and C. K. Eicher. Boulder, Colo.: Lynn Rienner Publishers.

Lele, U., N. van de Walle, and M. Gbetibouo. 1989. *Cotton in Africa: An Analysis of Differences in Performance.* MADIA Working Paper, World Bank, Washington, D.C.

Low, A. 1986. *Agricultural Development in Southern Africa: Farm-household Economics and the Food Crisis.* London: James Curry.

———. 1993. "The Low Input, Sustainable Agriculture (LISA) Prescription: A Bitter Pill for Farm Households in Southern Africa." *Project Appraisal* 8 (2): 97–101.

Lynam, J. K., and R. W. Herdt. 1989. "Sense and Sustainability: Sustainability as an Objective in International Agricultural Research." *Agricultural Economics* 3:381–98.

Matlon, P., and A. Adesina. 1997. "Agricultural Growth and Sustainability—Prospects for Semi-arid West Africa." In *Sustainability, Growth, and Poverty Alleviation: A Policy and Agroecological Perspective,* edited by S. Vosti and T. Reardon. Baltimore: Johns Hopkins University Press.

Matlon, P., and Spencer, D. S. C. 1984. "Increasing Food Production in Sub-Saharan Africa: Environmental Problems and Inadequate Technological Solutions." *American Journal of Agricultural Economics* 66 (5): 671–76.

Mudimu, G. 1996. "An Analysis of Incentives for Adopting Soil and Moisture Conservation Tillage Practices by Smallholder Farmers in Zimbabwe: A Case Study of Kandeya Communal Land." Mimeograph. Department of Agricultural Economics and Extension, University of Zimbabwe, Harare.

Nicou, R., and Charreau, C. 1985. "Soil Tillage and Water Conservation in Semi-Arid West Africa." In *Appropriate Technologies for Farmers in Semi-Arid West Africa,* edited by H. Ohm and J. Nagy. West Lafayette, Ind.: Purdue University.

Norman, D. W. 1973. *Economic Analysis of Agricultural Production and Labor Utilization among the Hausa in the North of Nigeria.* African Rural Employment Paper no. 4, Michigan State University, East Lansing.

Oram, P. 1997. "Institutions and Technical Change." In *Sustainability, Growth, and Poverty Alleviation: A Policy and Agroecological Perspective,* edited by S. Vosti and T. Reardon. Baltimore: Johns Hopkins University Press.

Pretty, J. N. 1995. *Regenerating Agriculture: Policies and Practice for Sustainability and Self-Reliance.* London: Earthscan Publications.

Reardon, T. 1997. "Using Evidence of Household Income Diversification to Inform Study of the Rural Nonfarm Labor Market in Africa." *World Development* 25 (5): 735–48.

Reardon, T., E. Crawford, and V. Kelly. 1994. "Links between Nonfarm Income and Farm Investment in African Households: Adding the Capital Market Perspective." *American Journal of Agricultural Economics* 76 (5): 1172–76.

Reardon, T., and N. Islam. 1989. "Issues of Sustainability in Agricultural Research in Africa." In *Proceedings of the Symposium on the Sustainability of Production Systems in Sub-Saharan Africa,* Agricultural University of Norway, Ås, Norway, 4–7 September 1989.

Reardon, T., V. Kelly, E. Crawford, K. Savadogo, T. Jayne. 1994. *Raising Farm Productivity in Africa to Sustain Long-Term Food Security.* Staff Paper no. 94-77, Department of Agricultural Economics, Michigan State University, East Lansing.

Rukuni, M. 1996. "A Framework for Crafting Demand-driven National Agricultural Research Institutions in Southern Africa." Staff Paper no. 96-76, Department of Agricultural Economics, Michigan State University, East Lansing.

Ruttan, V. 1990. "Models of Agricultural Development." In *Agricultural Development in the Third World,* 2nd edition, edited by C. K. Eicher and J. Staatz. Baltimore: Johns Hopkins University Press.

Sanders, J., B. Shapiro, and S. Ramaswamy. 1996. *The Economics of Agricultural Technology in Semiarid Sub-Saharan Africa.* Baltimore: Johns Hopkins University Press.

Savadogo, K., T. Reardon, and K. Pietola. 1995. "Mechanization and Agricultural Supply Response in the Sahel: A Farm-Level Profit Function Analysis." *Journal of African Economies* 4 (3): 336–77.

Semgalawe, Z. M. 1997. *Soil Conservation and Agricultural Sustainabilty: The Case of North-Eastern Mountain Slopes, Tanzania.* Doctoral dissertation, Department of General Economics, Wageningen University, The Netherlands.

Spencer D. S. C., and R. Polson. 1997. "Agricultural Growth and Sustainability: Conditions for Their Compatibility in the Humid and Sub-Humid Tropics of Africa." In *Sustainability, Growth, and Poverty Alleviation: A Policy and Agroecological Perspective,* edited by S. Vosti and T. Reardon. Baltimore: Johns Hopkins University Press.

Stocking, M. 1985. "Soil Conservation Policy in Colonial Africa." *Agricultural History* 59:148–61.

Tiffen, Mary, M. Mortimore, and F. Gichuki. 1994. *More People, Less Erosion: Environmental Recovery in Kenya.* Chichester: Wiley.

Tribe, D. 1994. *Feeding and Greening the World: The Role of International Agricultural Research.* Wallingford, U.K.: CAB International.

van Zyl, J., H. Binswanger, and C. Thirtle. 1995. *The Relationship between Farm Size and Efficiency in South African Agriculture.* Policy Research Working Paper 1548, Agriculture and Natural Resources Department, World Bank, Washington, D.C.

28

Maintaining Productivity Gains in Post–Green Revolution Asian Agriculture

MICHAEL MORRIS AND DEREK BYERLEE

INTRODUCTION

World food security depends to a large extent on the productivity of Asian farmers. With approximately three billion inhabitants, Asia is home to 55 percent of the world's population and produces about 40 percent of the total global cereal supply. Agriculture in Asia has a long and rich history, one that has been marked by a series of technological achievements that today allow the region's vast population to be fed from a comparatively small share of the world's cultivated area. The most impressive food production gains have come during the past three decades, when many Asian countries achieved food self-sufficiency even as population and income growth increased sharply.

Asia's ability to feed itself in years to come will depend crucially on continued growth in the production of cereals, especially rice and wheat, which contribute the bulk of the region's food supply (table 1). Asia's irrigated lowland cropping systems, in which most cereals production is concentrated, were transformed beginning in the 1960s by the so-called Green Revolution, which was based on input-responsive semidwarf varieties of rice and wheat (referred to here as modern varieties, or MVs). When grown with increased levels of fertilizer and an assured water supply, MVs led to a sharp jump in yields and provided significantly higher incomes for millions of farmers who adopted the technology.

Today, there are signs that the recent period of rapid growth in Asian agriculture may be ending. Expansion in the area planted to cereals, once a major source of production gains, has slowed dramatically across the region as a whole, and cereals area has actually begun to decline in China and India, the two most popu-

MICHAEL MORRIS is an agricultural economist at CIMMYT, Mexico.

DEREK BYERLEE is principal economist, Rural Development Department, World Bank, Washington, D.C.

TABLE 1
PROJECTED GROWTH IN PRODUCTION AND COMSUMPTION OF CEREALS, SOUTH ASIA, EAST ASIA, AND SOUTHEAST ASIA, 1990–2020

	Population		Projected Production Growth (%)				Projected Consumption Growth (%)				Total Cereal Deficit, 2020 (M t)
	1990 (millions)	1990–2020 (annual growth)	Rice	Wheat	Maize	Total Cereals	Rice	Wheat	Maize	Total Cereals	
South Asia	1115	1.7	2.3	2.2	2.0	2.2	2.3	2.6	2.2	2.3	−13
East Asia[a]	1227	0.9	0.8	1.9	2.0	1.5	0.9	1.9	2.2	1.8	65
Southeast Asia	441	1.5	2.0	1.0	1.8	1.9	1.8	2.6	2.5	2.0	26
Total Asia[a]	2783	1.7	1.7	2.0	2.0	1.8	1.7	2.2	2.2	1.9	79

SOURCES: Population: United Nations 1993. Cereals consumption: International Food Policy Research Institute 2020 Vision data base (baseline scenario projections).
[a]Excluding Japan.

TABLE 2
AVERAGE ANNUAL GROWTH IN AREA, YIELD,
PRODUCTION OF CEREALS, ASIA, 1966–95

	1966–75	*1976–85*	*1986–95*
All cereals			
Area	0.7	0.0	−0.1
Yield	2.8	3.9	2.3
Production	3.5	3.9	2.2
Rice (paddy)			
Area	1.1	0.2	0.2
Yield	2.1	3.5	1.5
Production	3.2	3.7	1.8
Wheat			
Area	2.4	1.2	0.6
Yield	4.6	5.4	2.1
Production	7.0	6.6	2.6
Maize			
Area	1.2	0.0	0.6
Yield	3.2	3.9	3.4
Production	4.4	3.9	4.0

SOURCE: U.N. Food and Agriculture Organization Agrostat database, 1995.
NOTE: South Asia, Southeast Asia, and East Asia, excluding Japan.

lous countries. Cereals yields continue to rise, but the rate of yield growth has slowed (table 2). In addition, the more intensive use of purchased inputs needed to maintain and extend productivity gains is undermining the profitability of food grain production and inflicting damage to the natural resource base upon which agriculture depends.

Policy makers concerned with food production in Asia face a daunting task, because extremely high rates of agricultural productivity growth will be needed to feed a population that is not only increasing rapidly in many countries but in many cases also experiencing income growth. To complicate matters, the technologies used to achieve future productivity gains will have to accommodate a much broader range of technical, economic, and social concerns than in the past. Future technologies must be evaluated not only in terms of their ability to raise productivity but also in terms of their long-term sustainability.

This chapter reviews the recent history of technical change in rice and wheat in the intensively irrigated cropping systems of Asia and examines the prospects for maintaining productivity growth in the post–Green Revolution era. The chapter is divided into three sections. First, selected evidence is briefly reviewed on current trends in production, input use, and productivity. Second, potential sources of future productivity growth are discussed. Third, implications are drawn regarding the three likely prime movers of future technical change in Asian agriculture: agricultural research, technology transfer systems, and economic policies that support agriculture.

RECENT TRENDS IN INPUT USE AND PRODUCTIVITY

During the next century, Asia's food supply will have to be produced on a shrinking land base. The land frontier in Asia has already been exhausted in many densely populated regions, and urbanization is eating away at the remaining supply of agricultural land. This means that farmers will have to further intensify cereal production on land which in many cases is already being double- and triple-cropped. Meanwhile, yield growth has slowed noticeably in the intensively cultivated irrigated zones where the Green Revolution technologies made their initial dramatic impacts.[1]

In the past, farmers in Asia have alleviated growing pressure on land by intensifying the use of inputs, as happened during the 1960s and 1970s following the release of rice and wheat MVs. The rapid diffusion of MVs throughout densely populated irrigated areas of Asia is well known. Less well known is the fact that use of MVs subsequently spread into rainfed areas, as is evidenced by the steady growth in the area planted to MVs which has continued up to the present. Currently, the total area planted to rice and wheat MVs far exceeds the irrigated area planted to these two crops, especially in India, confirming that MVs have moved well beyond the irrigated zones into rainfed areas.

The varietal diffusion process has generally proceeded in two stages. *Type A varietal changes* occurred when the original MVs, developed at the international rice and wheat research centers (IRRI and CIMMYT), first replaced traditional varieties (TVs), leading to a sharp jump in productivity.[2] *Type B varietal changes* continue to occur as newer MVs periodically replace older MVs (usually at least once per decade), allowing productivity gains to be sustained over an extended period. Many of these newer MVs were developed by national research institutes to fit specific local environments. While they generally have been much less visible than the first Green Revolution MVs, the newer MVs (now involving at least three generations) have made substantial cumulative contributions to productivity growth. Often they have also provided greatly improved pest and disease resistance, as well as better grain quality.

Most MVs perform relatively well under unfavorable production conditions, but they express their full yield potential only with favorable management. Because of their responsiveness to inputs, MVs became an important catalyst for the adoption of complementary inputs, especially fertilizer, which over the past three decades has been the largest source of growth in food production in Asia. Use of fertilizer was additionally encouraged by a decline in global fertilizer prices and by subsidies introduced in many countries to encourage increased application. From a very small base in the 1960s, fertilizer use in Asia expanded to the point that it now accounts for nearly half of total world fertilizer consumption. Fertilizer application levels in many irrigated lowland areas are now at or above recommended levels. Emphasis is being placed on the efficient management of existing doses, rather than on increasing application rates.

Because intensive monocropping of rice had led to a rapid buildup in insect populations, and because many of the early rice MVs lacked resistance to important pests, the introduction and spread of rice MVs precipitated a sharp increase in the use of pesticides. But after rising steadily for several decades, pesticide application rates on rice have recently started to decline in some Asian countries, as health and safety effects have become more apparent, leading to more widespread use of integrated pest management practices (Raheja 1995). Pest management was and continues to be less of a problem in wheat than in rice, partly because wheat is less prone to insect pest attack, and partly because the early wheat MVs incorporated resistance to major diseases.

The diffusion of MVs also stimulated investment in irrigation, leading to a surge in irrigated area during the 1960s and 1970s. However, growth in irrigated area has slowed in recent years, for two main reasons. First, many Asian irrigation systems have become degraded through lack of maintenance, so a considerable portion of irrigation investment now must be devoted to rehabilitating existing systems rather than to constructing new ones. Second, most of the zones that can be irrigated at comparatively low cost have already been identified, so further expansion of irrigation capacity tends to be technically challenging and correspondingly more expensive. The increasing costliness of irrigation means that net returns to foodgrain production are often too low to justify installing irrigation facilities exclusively to grow cereals. Opportunities for profitable investment still exist, but it is clear that most of the "easy" opportunities have already been exploited.

STAGES OF TECHNICAL CHANGE: A STYLIZED VIEW

The process of agricultural intensification in Asia can be depicted as occurring in several stages, distinguished by the development and diffusion of technologies to substitute for emerging factor scarcities. According to this view, technical change in Asia's land-intensive cereals production systems proceeds through the following four stages (Byerlee 1992):

1. *Pre–Green Revolution Phase.* Traditional varieties (TVs) are cultivated using negligible amounts of external inputs; productivity growth is modest, and the main source of production increases is more extensive use of land and water resources (e.g., expansion in area planted, a shift to more fertile land, investment in irrigation infrastructure).
2. *Green Revolution Phase.* A technological breakthrough in the form of input-responsive MVs provides the potential for a dramatic increase in land productivity, expressed in the form of higher crop yields.
3. *First Post–Green Revolution Phase (Input Intensification Phase).* Farmers increase their use of purchased inputs (e.g., fertilizer) and capital (e.g., tube wells, machinery) to substitute for increasingly scarce land and labor.
4. *Second Post–Green Revolution Phase (Input Efficiency Phase).* Farmers use improved information and management skills to substitute for higher

input use, leading to more efficient utilization of inputs while contributing to the sustainability of the resource base.

These stylized stages of technical change can be depicted in the framework of a conventional production function (figure 1). During the Green Revolution Phase, the introduction of MVs shifts the production function upwards (TV to MV_1), increasing crop response to complementary inputs such as fertilizer and irrigation water and leading to a one-time surge in productivity (A to B). Initially, farmers operate well below the production frontier MV_2. During the First Post–Green Revolution Phase, input use intensifies as farmers become more familiar with the technology, as input markets improve, and/or as input subsidies are introduced. This allows them to move along the (suboptimal) production function (B to C), using higher levels of complementary inputs to improve the allocative efficiency of production. Finally, during the Second Post–Green Revolution Phase, farmers approach the new production frontier (MV_2) by increasing the technical efficiency with which they use inputs. Depending on the strategy followed by farmers, use of complementary inputs may increase (D) or decrease (E) during this phase. An additional dynamic element to be considered in interpreting technical change in Asia is that the production frontier MV_2 can shift over time (not shown in figure 1) (upward, due to development of new land-saving technologies [e.g., newer MVs], or downward, due to natural resource degradation).

In Asia, observed changes in rates of growth of output, input use, and total factor productivity (TFP) have been consistent with this stylized view of techni-

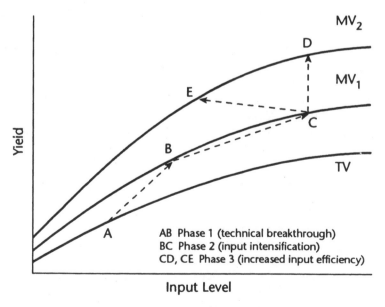

Fig. 1. Phases of Technical Change in Asian Agriculture (Source: Byerlee 1992.)

TABLE 3
SOURCES OF PRODUCTIVITY GROWTH BY STAGE OF TECHNICAL CHANGE

Phase	Output Growth Rate	Input Growth Rate	TFP Growth Rate	Main Source of TFP Growth
1 Pre–Green Revolution	low	low	low	
2 Green Revolution	high	high	high-medium	First generation MVs
3 First Post–Green Revolution (intensification)	high-medium	medium	medium	Second generation MVs Labor-saving technologies
4 Second Post–Green Revolution (increased efficiency)	medium-low	low	medium	Third-generation MVs Labor-saving technologies Efficient imput management

cal change (table 3). Many parts of Asia are still in the First Post–Green Revolution Phase, as is evidenced by the persistence of a large technical efficiency gap for wheat and rice, which has been estimated at about 30 percent (Ali and Byerlee 1991). This technical efficiency gap can be attributed to several factors, the most important of which appear to be weak adaptive research and extension capacity, as well as deficiencies in farmers' technical knowledge and level of education (Hussain and Byerlee 1995). Some evidence suggests that the technical efficiency gap gradually narrows through time as farmers gain additional experience with improved technologies and fine-tune their management practices; this narrowing of the technical efficiency gap corresponds to the Second Post–Green Revolution Phase, which is now under way in some areas with the adoption of input-efficient practices, such as integrated pest management and reduced tillage.

But the fit between the theory and the evidence is not perfect. One major inconsistency involves observed changes in rates of total factor productivity growth. During the transition from the First Post–Green Revolution Phase (input intensification) to the Second Post–Green Revolution Phase (input efficiency), TFP growth should account for a large and increasing share of output growth and may even exceed output growth if input use declines due to greater efficiency of input use. However, the record in Asia has been mixed on this score, and in recent years some regions that by now should be well into the Second Post–Green Revolution Phase have experienced low TFP growth coupled with rapid expansion in input use (Pingali and Heisey 1996).[3] Evidence of negligible productivity growth in intensively cultivated rice-wheat systems has been reported by Cassman and Pingali (1995) and Murghai (1996) for the Indian state of Punjab; these authors attribute stagnating productivity to changes in the physical and chemical properties of soils repeatedly flooded for rice cultivation then dried for growing wheat. Recurring outward shifts of the production frontier attributable to continual adoption of newer MVs thus can be partially or perhaps even completely offset by downward shifts caused by long-term resource degradation (e.g., loss of soil fertility due to nutrient mining). This emerging evidence of a slowdown in TFP growth serves as a warning that future efforts to increase food production in Asia will need to give greater attention to maintaining the quality of the resource base.

INSTITUTIONAL CHALLENGES

Since most of the easy gains from the original Green Revolution technologies have already been realized in Asia, particularly in areas where MVs have been widely adopted, there will be diminishing payoffs to further intensification using current input-based strategies. In many irrigated lowland areas, adoption of MVs is now virtually complete, fertilizer application rates are approaching optimal levels, with low marginal returns to additional application, and the potential for affordable irrigation is largely exhausted. By implication, if food production is to keep pace with projected increases in demand, new sources of productivity growth will have to be tapped. Future productivity growth is likely to come from three main sources: agricultural research, technology transfer systems (extension and education), and agricultural support policies. However, as the following section makes clear, major institutional challenges will have to be overcome if the potential of each of these three sources of future productivity growth is to be fully realized.

AGRICULTURAL RESEARCH

The four phases of technical change described earlier are useful in thinking about how the products and information needed from agricultural research systems have changed over the years and how they will continue to change in the future. During the initial phases of the Green Revolution (phases 2 and 3), production technologies were largely input-based, and researchers focused on providing MVs and standardized technical packages that could be extended to farmers in blanket fashion. Strong local crop breeding efforts were needed to adapt modern varieties to niches determined by agro-climatic conditions and cropping patterns; national program plant breeders also helped to preserve host plant resistance to mutating insect pests and diseases. During the Second Post–Green Revolution Phase (phase 4), new approaches to research are required in order to develop the sophisticated, site-specific management information needed to improve input use efficiency and manage the natural resource base in the context of increasingly complex cropping systems.

Over the long term, the challenge for researchers will be to continue to shift the production frontier upward (outwards) through development of new technologies. The major source of upward movement has been and will continue to be varietal improvement. Since the Green Revolution, plant breeders have been able to raise the yield potential of wheat MVs at a rate of about 1 percent per year. In rice, yield gains have been less dramatic, but recent technological breakthroughs may enable more substantive shifts. Hybrid rice, which was developed in China in the 1970s and has recently been introduced into other irrigated areas of Asia, has resulted in one-time yield gains averaging 15 percent. The International Rice Research Institute's much publicized effort to develop so-called "super rice" by drastically modifying plant architecture is expected to produce a similar breakthrough in the next few years.

Much has been made of the potential of biotechnology to deliver technological breakthroughs in plant breeding. While certainly important, biotechnology is unlikely to generate another Green Revolution in the major cereal crops. In the short-to-medium term, the main value of biotechnology will be to lower the cost of conventional plant breeding by providing molecular markers which will allow rapid identification of plants that carry (or lack) genes for specific traits. Also, biotechnology is likely to enhance yield stability by allowing genes to be transferred from unrelated species into commercial cultivars. But for the next decade or so, the only traits that are likely to be inserted successfully into cereal crops are those conferred by a single gene or by very few genes, such as improved pest resistance and improved herbicide resistance. To date, insect resistance has received the greatest amount of attention in the developing world's biotechnology laboratories. Genetically engineered rice MVs with new sources of resistance to several major pests are expected within the next few years. Biotechnology has also proved useful in developing maize hybrids with genes for insect resistance; these hybrids will soon be available in Asia.

Yet, even if the remaining technological challenges can be overcome and genetic transformation techniques live up to their considerable promise as tools for applied plant breeding, there are many legal barriers to be overcome. Concerned that transgenic plants could have negative effects on human health or the environment, many countries have been reluctant to sanction their use, and throughout most of the developing world it is still not possible even to test transgenic plants (except sometimes in strictly controlled isolation facilities). In addition, many of the tools and products of biotechnology have been developed in the private sector and are considered proprietary. Considering the enormous sums that private firms have invested in biotechnology research, most of them are unwilling to grant access to their proprietary tools and products unless they receive compensation (e.g., through licensing fees, royalty payments, or material transfer agreements). For a number of reasons, then, commercial use of transgenics remains a distant prospect.[4]

These technological challenges underline the critical importance of increasing investment in agricultural research. After growing rapidly during the post–Green Revolution period, public investment in agricultural research in the developing countries of Asia during the past decade has stagnated, at about 0.5 percent of agricultural value added, much lower than in countries that have generated rapid technical change on a sustained basis. The increasing commercialization of agriculture in many Asian countries has encouraged greater private investment in agricultural research, but private-sector research tends to be narrowly targeted on certain types of technology, such as hybrid seed. Other critically important areas, especially basic research activities with limited commercial applications, remain underfunded.

With funding for agricultural research likely to remain scarce, research managers will have to identify research strategies that optimize the use of scarce human and capital resources. In seeking to identify efficient strategies, research managers will be forced to make difficult tradeoffs between short- and long-term objectives. One key issue involves the relative emphasis to be placed on the development of embodied technologies (such as new seeds with enhanced input efficiency) versus the development of disembodied technologies (such as integrated pest management practices). On the one hand, committing additional resources to efforts to embody more traits in seed necessarily means committing fewer resources to efforts to develop new technologies capable of increasing the rate at which the production frontier is pushed upward (Traxler et al. 1994). But on the other hand, the cost involved in transferring embodied technologies to small-scale farmers is usually quite small, and the technical knowledge and skills needed to use them may be modest compared to that required for using disembodied technologies.

These strategic issues have important implications for the organization of agricultural research. In the years following the Green Revolution, research managers in national research systems in Asia moved quickly to adopt the commodity-based research strategy, which had been popularized by the international agricultural research centers (IARCs).[5] In most cases, highest priority was assigned to plant breeding research designed to develop second- and third-generation MVs, along with variety-specific management practices to enable these MVs to express their superior genetic potential. The number of scientists engaged in crop-breeding activities rose rapidly. By 1990, the level of investment in varietal improvement research in Asia (expressed in terms of numbers of scientists per million tons of crop output) was as high as in many industrialized countries. Judging by the number of MVs developed and adopted, many of the specialized rice and wheat research programs launched during and immediately after the Green Revolution period have been very successful. Despite their record of past achievement, however, most of these programs are unlikely to be as effective in the future, because farmers' technology needs are changing. Future productivity growth in Asia's intensively cultivated cereal cropping systems will come mainly from the adoption of improved crop and resource management practices that are designed to close the remaining yield gap, to increase the efficiency of input use, and to arrest or reverse the degradation of soil and water resources (Byerlee and Pingali 1995). Currently, most national research institutions in Asia are not well organized to address these complex problems, which are threatening to undermine the sustainability of intensive cropping systems. Organizational changes will thus be needed to build multidisciplinary, systems-oriented teams of researchers capable of working more closely with farmers to explore innovative crop and resource management technologies (Hobbs and Morris 1996).

TECHNOLOGY TRANSFER SYSTEMS: EXTENSION AND EDUCATION

As Asian agriculture moves forward into the post–Green Revolution era, knowledge and management skills will grow in importance relative to increased use of inputs as means of improving productivity. Numerous studies have shown that many of the variables associated with the technical efficiency gap relate to farmers' knowledge and management abilities (e.g., farmers' contacts with extension, technical knowledge, and education). The increasing information intensity of improved management practices requires new and more effective strategies for their transfer.

Given the complexity of many new information-intensive technologies, the technology transfer process will in future pose a much greater challenge than in the past, when the emphasis often was on strengthening input distribution systems. The increasing reliance of farmers in industrialized countries on computerized planning systems and on farm- and crop-management software provides a glimpse of where modern agriculture in Asia is heading. In the many regions throughout Asia where farm size is too small to justify using such technologies at the farm level, ways will have to be found to employ them at the village level. Such technologies could include soil- and tissue-testing equipment, pest-identification kits, and, in the future, computers for accessing expert management systems.

Farmers will increasingly turn to a range of sources for obtaining improved technical information, including the traditional extension system, input dealers, NGOs, farmer organizations, and even paid consultancies. Public sector extension services will have to be considerably upgraded if they are to provide field staff with the advanced training and equipment needed to bring better decision aids to farmers. Beginning in the 1970s, the training and visit (T&V) system promoted by the World Bank was institutionalized in many countries, particularly in South Asia. Although the T&V system met with some successes, like many other extension approaches it remained heavily oriented toward the promotion of input intensification, rather than toward the promotion of practices designed to increase input efficiency.

In many countries, the effectiveness of extension efforts has also been constrained by poor linkages between extension agents and researchers, by the inability of researchers to provide appropriate information, and by heavy reliance on a "recipe" approach to delivering extension messages, emphasizing adoption of technological packages. In the future, extension services will have to give greater emphasis to their educational role; only by understanding the scientific basis of new technologies will farmers be able to adjust them to their own circumstances. The recent success achieved in several Asian countries in training farmers to employ integrated pest management practices for rice demonstrates the value of this approach for improving input-use efficiency (in this case by sharply reducing input use). For example, in Indonesia, use of pesticides on rice increased rapidly after the Green Revolution with intensification of cultivation and the associated buildup of insect populations. Encouraged by extension and pesticide dealers, farmers developed the practice of routine spraying, as an insurance measure. Eventually, growing recognition of the health and environmental costs of excessive pesticide use caused the Indonesian government to launch a campaign to increases farmers' knowledge about pesticide use and pest dynamics. By carrying out regular insect scouting exercises and resorting to pesticides only on an as-needed basis, Indonesian farmers were able to reduce their use of pesticides dramatically. The campaign was extremely cost effective; a one-time investment of about US$40 per farmer resulted in annual savings in pesticide costs of about US$18 per farmer (Wiebers 1996).

Some management practices will require community collaboration to be effective (e.g., water management, certain types of pest management). Since individual farmers will have little incentive to adopt these practices unless their neighbors do as well, in order to avert market failure in the demand for information it will be necessary to develop community organizations capable of making collective decisions and acting upon them. This underlines the importance of diversifying the sources of technology dissemination to include private input suppliers, specialized consultants, farmer organizations, and NGOs.

Complicating the issue of transferring a wider array of increasingly complex information is the fact that Asian farmers are poorly educated relative to the stage of technological development of agriculture in which they are working. Studies have shown that returns to investment in education, especially primary education, are high in post–Green Revolution agriculture (Hussain and Byerlee 1995). Because farmers are frequently functionally illiterate (particularly in South Asia), they can derive little from written information. Investment in rural schooling, as well as in the institutional changes needed to make schooling more effective, have failed to keep pace with the demands imposed by increasingly complex agricultural technologies. Although improved extension services can partially substitute for low levels of education, the effectiveness of extension services is greatly increased in the presence of higher levels of education, which allow the use of a wider array of educational media. Higher levels of education also increase farmers' demand for information and improve the efficiency with which farmers are able to adapt information to local situations.

AGRICULTURAL SUPPORT POLICIES

At each stage in Asia's Green Revolution, the process of technical change was encouraged by programs and policies designed to induce farmers to change their practices. During the Green Revolution and after, these programs and policies encouraged adoption of MVs and complementary inputs, especially fertilizer and irrigation (Foster and Rosenzweig 1996). In most countries, adoption incentives were provided through input subsidies or through supervised credit programs (often also subsidized). Food production was also promoted through public investment in rural infrastructure (irrigation systems, roads, marketing facilities) and through supports to producer prices (Hayami and Ruttan 1985).

Although supporting policies continue to play an important role in Asian agriculture, an accumulating body of evidence suggests that the kinds of policy measures favored in the past have outlived their usefulness. High profile food production campaigns such as the Masagna 99 program in the Philippines and the many rice and wheat campaigns in selected districts of India have succeeded in increasing production, but they have also generated fiscal costs that are proving difficult to sustain. In India, for example, fertilizer subsidies originally introduced to boost cereal production now account for over 80 percent of public sector investment in agriculture and have crowded out investment in high-priority areas such as irrigation and agricultural research.

In areas where the use of MVs and associated inputs is already intensive, input subsidies can actually be counterproductive. Removal of these subsidies gives farmers a major incentive to move toward more efficient use of inputs. This has been demonstrated in Indonesia, where removal of pesticide subsidies combined with a massive program of farmer education in integrated pest management has led to a substantial reduction in pesticide use on rice (Wiebers 1996).

At the same time, new types of supporting policies are needed to foster changes in the way technologies are created and delivered to farmers. A good example involves policies relating to the protection of intellectual property rights (IPR) for agricultural technologies. Governments in many Asian countries appreciate the importance of IPR laws in stimulating private sector research, but they also realize that IPR laws are a mixed blessing. Predictably, with more attention being paid to protecting intellectual property, most private breeding programs have become less willing to exchange germplasm, and even some public breeding institutes have adopted more restrictive policies. This trend has been accelerated by the decline in government support for research, which has forced many public breeding programs to look for alternative sources of funding; the sale of proprietary germ plasm is an obvious attraction. Thus, in seeking to design and implement effective IPR policies, governments are struggling to strike a balance between providing enough protection to stimulate desirable levels of private sector investment while safeguarding the interests of economically disadvantaged groups of the population.

New types of supporting policies will also be important in promoting the development and dissemination of information-based technologies, many of which have attributes associated with so-called public goods. Private companies consequently have difficulty earning profits from the production and sale of information-based technologies, which means they have little incentive to invest in them. As a result, public research institutes generally must take the lead in their development, and the public sector has an important role in creating public awareness efforts and in training.

CONCLUSIONS

During the past three decades, extraordinarily rapid technical change in Asia's agricultural sector has allowed cereal production growth to keep pace with a steadily expanding population, while at the same time boosting rural incomes and reducing real prices paid by consumers for major food staples (David and Otsuka 1994). The process of technological change experienced in Asia during and after the Green Revolution can be disaggregated into four distinct phases. Prior to the release of modern varieties of rice and wheat, traditional varieties were cultivated using negligible amounts of external inputs; productivity growth was modest, and production increases came mainly from greater use of land and water resources (phase 1). The initial adoption of MVs, which began in the 1960s, pushed the yield frontier upward and stimulated rapid increases in the use of external inputs, leading to a sharp jump in productivity (phase 2). Following the widespread diffusion of MVs, input use continued to increase steadily, reaching high levels in many areas and reducing potential payoffs to further input intensification (phase 3). Most irrigated lowland areas are now undergoing a process of technical change driven by the need to improve input efficiency, with farmers using improved information to substitute for inputs (phase 4). Although information-based technologies in many cases are proving successful, a critical question is whether upward shifts of the production frontier are being offset by degradation of the resource base.

With the potential of the Green Revolution technologies now largely exhausted, new technologies will be needed to ensure continuing productivity growth in Asia's intensively cultivated cropping systems. The distinct features of these new technologies will require significant changes in the organization of agricultural research, in the design of technology transfer strategies, and in the implementation of policies to encourage technical change.

Agricultural research will need to be more decentralized, more strongly farmer-oriented, and more closely linked to the technology dissemination process. Greater farmer participation will be needed to adapt technologies to local circumstances, to improve the efficiency of technology transfer activities, and to ensure the accountability of public research and extension organizations. Research will have to be conducted within a systems framework that integrates information on several crops and management practices within a farming system. Farmer organizations will increase in importance relative to individual farmers, because many new informational technologies will have to be managed at the district and village levels.

In the area of technology dissemination, the emphasis will have to shift from communication to education. Instead of merely seeking to deliver specific messages to farmers, extension agents will have to concentrate on providing farmers the knowledge and skills needed to better manage information-intensive technologies such as integrated pest management. The goal must be to increase farmers' demand for information by strengthening their ability to seek and process information from diverse sources and to adapt it to their own specific circumstances. The use of sophisticated computer-based technologies and decision aids will increase, particularly in specialized technical areas such as soil testing, tissue analysis, and pest scouting. The fact that information-based technologies will place a premium on literacy and education levels could increase inequalities among farmers much more than occurred during the Green Revolution. Because education is unequally distributed in the farming population, wealthier farmers are likely to benefit disproportionally from information-based technologies, because of their greater ability to access information.

Finally, agricultural support policies also will have to change to accommodate the emerging information-based technologies. In particular, it will be necessary to shift the bulk of public expenditures from input subsidies to increased investment in public good aspects of technology development and dissemination.

NOTES

1. There is still much scope for increasing cereal yields in rainfed areas, especially through investment in irrigation, which would diffuse existing technologies more widely.

2. Traditional varieties include locally developed varieties selected by farmers, and improved tall varieties developed by plant-breeding programs during the pre–Green Revolution period.

3. Most studies suggest a TFP growth of around 1–2 percent annually, with at least half of the gains being attributed to adoption of MVs (Evenson and McKinsey 1991; Sidhu and Byerlee 1991; Kumar and Mruthyunjaya 1992; Murghai 1996; Jha and Kumar 1996).

4. The Rockefeller Foundation invested roughly $100 million in rice biotechnology research from 1985 to 1995 (R. Herdt, personal communication). Eight new genes for pest resistance have been inserted into rice to date.

5. In India, where commodity-oriented research programs predated the creation of the IARC system in the 1960s, the success of the IARC model served to validate the strategy that had already been implemented.

REFERENCES

Ali, M., and D. Byerlee. 1991. Economic Efficiency of Small Farmers in a Changing World: A Survey of Recent Evidence. *Journal of International Development* 3 (1): 1–27.

Byerlee, D. 1992. Technical Change, Productivity, and Sustainability in Irrigated Cropping Systems of South Asia: Emerging Issues in the Post–Green Revolution Era. *Journal of International Development* 4 (5): 477–96.

Byerlee, D., and P. Pingali. 1995. "Asian NARSs: Frustrations and Fulfillments." In *Agricultural Competitiveness: Market Forces and Policy Choice. Proceedings of the Twenty-Second International Conference of Agricultural Economists. Harare, Zimbabwe, 22–29 August, 1994,* edited by G. H. Peters and D. Hedley. Aldershot, U.K.: Dartmouth Publishing.

Cassman, K. G., and P. L. Pingali. 1995. Extrapolating Trends from Long-Term Experiments to Farmers' Fields: The Case of Irrigated Rice Systems in Asia. In *Agricultural Sustainability in Economic, Environmental, and Statistical Terms,* edited by V. Barnett., R. Payne and R. Steiner. London: John Wiley and Sons.

David, C., and K. Otsuka, eds. 1994. *Modern Rice Technology and Income Distribution in Asia.* Los Baños, Laguna, Philippines: International Rice Research Institute.

Evenson, R. E., and J. W. McKinsey. 1991. "Research, Extension, Infrastructure, and Productivity Change in Indian Agriculture." In *Research and Productivity in Asian Agriculture,* edited by R. E. Evenson and C. E. Pray, 158–84. Ithaca: Cornell University Press.

Foster, A., and M. R. Rosenzweig. 1996. "Technical Change and Human-Capital Returns and Investments: Evidence from the Green Revolution." *American Economic Review* 86 (4): 931–53.

Hayami, Y., and V. W. Ruttan. 1985. *Agricultural Development: An International Perspective.* Revised and expanded edition. Baltimore: Johns Hopkins University Press.

Hobbs, P., and M. L. Morris. 1996. "Meeting South Asia's Future Food Requirements from Rice-Wheat Cropping Systems: Priority Issues Facing Researchers in the Post–Green Revolution

Era." Natural Resources Group Paper 96-01, International Maize and Wheat Improvement Center (CIMMYT), Mexico, D.F.

Hussain, S. S., and D. Byerlee. 1995. "Education and Farm Productivity in Post–Green Revolution Asia." In *Agricultural Competitiveness: Market Forces and Policy Choice. Proceedings of the Twenty-Second International Conference of Agricultural Economists. Harare, Zimbabwe, 22–29 August, 1994,* edited by G. H. Peters and D. Hedley. Aldershot, U.K.: Dartmouth Publishing.

Jha, D., and P. Kumar. 1996. "Rice Production and Impact of Rice Research in India." Paper presented to the International Conference on the Impact of Rice Research, Bangkok, Thailand, sponsored by the International Rice Research Institute and the Thailand Development Research Institute.

Kumar, P., and Mruthyunjaya. 1992. Measurement Analysis of Total Factor Productivity Growth in Wheat. *Indian Journal of Agricultural Economics* 47 (3): 451–58.

Murghai, R. 1996. "Diversity in Agricultural Growth and Technical Change: A District-wide Analysis of the Punjab and Haryana Growth Experience." Draft. Agricultural and Natural Resources Department, World Bank, Washington, D.C.

Pingali, P. L., and P. W. Heisey. 1996. "Cereal Crop Productivity in Developing Countries: Past Trends and Future Prospects." Paper presented at the conference *Global Agricultural Science Policy to the Twenty-first Century,* Melbourne, Australia, 26–28 August.

Pray, C. E. 1991. "Determinants of Output and Productivity Growth in Eastern India: Implications for Future Governments." Mimeograph. Department of Agricultural Economics, Cook College, Rutgers University.

Raheja, A. K. 1995. "Practice of Integrated Pest Management in South and South-east Asia." In *Integrated Pest Management in the Tropics: Current Status and Future Prospects,* edited by A. Mengech, K. N. Saxena, and H. N. B. Gopala. Chichester: John Wiley.

Sidhu, D. S., and D. Byerlee. 1991. Technical Change and Wheat Productivity in Post–Green Revolution Punjab. *Economic and Political Weekly* 26 (52): A159–A166.

Traxler, G., J. Falck-Zepeda, J. I. Ortiz-Monasterio, and K. Sayre. 1994. "Production Risk and the Evolution of Varietal Technology." *American Journal of Agricultural Economics* 76 (1): 1–7.

United Nations. 1993. *World Population Prospects: The 1992 Revision.* New York: United Nations.

Wiebers, U. 1996. *Integrated Pest Management and Pesticide Management in Developing Asia.* World Bank Technical Paper no. 211, World Bank, Washington, D.C.

29

Confronting the Ecological Consequences of the Rice Green Revolution in Tropical Asia

PRABHU L. PINGALI

 The Green Revolution strategy for increasing food production in Asia was based on the intensification of the lowlands through massive investments in irrigation infrastructure and in crop research. It was presumed that the lowlands were resilient to intensification pressures and would sustain rice output growth over the long term. This strategy was meant to relieve pressures on the fragile uplands by creating employment opportunities in the lowlands. The strategy worked exceptionally well for rice, up to the mid-1980s (Dalrymple 1986; Herdt and Capule 1983). Since then rice productivity growth has slowed down in the intensively cultivated areas across Asia (Rosegrant and Pingali 1994).

The aggregate rice output growth rate for Asia increased from 2.1 percent per annum during 1955–65 to 2.9 percent per annum during 1965–80, surpassing the annual population growth rate of 2.3 percent. Area expansion contributed to nearly one-third of Asian rice output growth in the 1960s and one-fifth in the 1970s. Rapid yield growth from 1965 to 1980, due to the adoption of modern rice varieties, was the primary contributor to rice output growth. In the past decade, however, the growth in aggregate rice output has declined to 1.5 percent per annum. Rice yield growth in Asia also declined sharply in the 1980s, from an annual growth rate of 2.6 percent in the 1970s to 1.5 percent during the period beginning in 1981.

The slowdown in rice productivity growth in Asia since the 1980s has been caused by world price–induced factors and intensification-induced factors. The world rice price has been on a declining trend in real terms since 1900, a decline that has sharpened in the 1980s (Mitchell 1987). The declining price of rice has caused a direct shift of land out of rice and into more profitable cropping alternatives, and has slowed the growth in input use and yields. Probably more im-

PRABHU L. PINGALI is the director of the economics program, CIMMYT (International Maize and Wheat Improvement Center), Mexico, D.F.

portant in the long run, the declining world price has caused a slowdown in investment in rice research and irrigation infrastructure (Rosegrant and Pingali 1994).

Does intensification of irrigated land use, independent of world rice price effects, lead to a long-term decline in rice productivity? Intensification is defined here as the permanent movement from one rice crop per year followed by a dry season fallow, to two or three consecutive rice crops per year on the same land. This chapter argues that the practice of intensive rice monoculture itself contributes to the degradation of the paddy ecology and hence to declining productivity. The consequences of intensification on the paddy resource base can be observed only over the long term and vary by agroclimatic and management factors.

This chapter attempts to (1) provide evidence on productivity decline in the high potential irrigated rice lands of Asia, (2) highlight potential ecological and environmental causes of productivity decline, and (3) relate food self-sufficiency policies, pursued by most Asian countries, to the degradation of the paddy resource base.

INTENSIFICATION AND RICE PRODUCTIVITY DECLINE

Evidence from experiment stations across Asia indicates that even with the best scientific management available, crop yields have been declining over time. Experiment station yield trends provide a clear case of intensification-induced degradation of the paddy resource base, since they are not influenced by prices and other policy factors. Understanding the factors that contribute to the degradation of the paddy resource base from experiment station experiences could provide useful information for sustaining rice productivity on farmers' fields. Reversing the current trends in productivity decline on farmers' fields would, however, require innovations in technology, land management practices, as well as policies.

PRODUCTIVITY DECLINE ON EXPERIMENT STATIONS

The best illustration of the consequences of intensification, independent of world rice price effects, can be found in the examination of yield trends from long-term trials conducted on experiment stations. The objective of long-term trials is to monitor maximum yields obtained over time, holding input levels and crop management practices constant. The long-term continuous cropping experiment conducted by the International Rice Research Institute (IRRI) in the Philippines is an excellent example of such trials. This experiment, set up in 1963, has been monitoring the yield impact of rice monoculture (with three crops per year) and as of 1993 had completed eighty-nine consecutive crops on the same plot (Cassman et al. 1994). Table 1 presents yield trends from this as well as other long-term trials in the Philippines, India, Thailand, and Bangladesh. The trends indicate that, holding input levels constant, even with the best available cultivars

TABLE 1
ANNUAL GROWTH IN RICE YIELD POTENTIAL FOR SELECTED ASIAN COUNTRIES

Country and Survey Site	Wet Season (%)	Dry Season (%)
Philippines (1966–68)		
IRRI	−1.29	−1.28
Maligaya Rice Research and Training Center	−1.01	+0.15
Visayas Rice Experiment Station	+0.18	+0.18[a]
Bicol Rice and Corn Experiment Station	−0.62	−0.38
India (1969–89)		
Coimbatore	−0.27[a]	0.44[a]
Raipur	−1.41	—
Pantnagar	−0.89	—
Rajendranagar	0.12[a]	—
Mandya	−1.11	—
Bangladesh (1977–88)		
Comilla	−1.80	—
Joydebpur	−0.13[a]	—
Thailand (1977–90)		
Chiang Mai	2.30	—
Suphan Buri	−2.50	—
Chiang Rai	−1.80	—
Vietnam (1977–89)		
Hanoi	−3.35	—
Maylaysia (1980–87)		
Tuaran, Sabah	−3.37	—
Indonesia (1978–90)		
Sukamandi	—	0.99
Nepal		
Bhairahawa (1977–88)	−1.77	—
Paruwanipur (1977–82)	−2.99	—
Pakistan		
Muingara, Swat (1985–90)	5.09	—
D. I. Khan (1979–85)	−4.57	—

SOURCE: Growth rates for the Philippines were estimated using the data from the long-term fertility trials conducted at the listed experiment stations. Growth rates estimates for the other countries used basic data from the International Network for Germplasm Exchange in Rice.

[a]Not significantly different from 0.0%.

and scientific management, yields decline over the long term. The declining yield trend in long-term experiments has been documented by Flinn and De Datta (1984), Pingali (1994), Cassman and Pingali (1995) and Cassman et al. (1994).

IRRI started releasing modern rice varieties in the mid-1960s. IR-8 was the first of the modern varieties widely grown in Asia. At the time of its release in 1966, IR-8 yielded as much as 10 tons per hectare in the dry season and 6 t/ha in the wet season at IRRI's experimental farm in Laguna, Philippines. At that time, farmers in the neighborhood of IRRI growing traditional rice varieties were getting yields of 2.0–2.5 t/ha (International Rice Research Institute 1967). Since its initial release, the yields of IR-8 have been declining even when grown under scientific management on the IRRI farm. Flinn, De Datta, and Labadan (1982) estimate that since 1966 the wet-season yields of IR-8 have declined by 0.2 t/ha per year and the dry season yields have declined by 0.26–0.47 t/ha/yr. The most commonly attributed cause of this decline is the greatly increased insect and disease pressure to which IR-8 is not resistant. (Insect and disease infestations have risen with the growth in intensive rice production across Asia. See below.)

Following the introduction of IR-8, 40 more modern rice varieties have been released in the Philippines. These varieties have better insect and disease resistance, shorter crop duration, and to some extent better eating quality than IR-8. However, none of the later varieties has been able to match the initial yield potential of IR-8.[1] Indeed, De Datta et al. (1979) report that in recent years rice yields of over 9 t/ha are rarely recorded at IRRI. Perhaps more disturbing is the observation by Flinn and De Datta (1984) that the highest yields obtained from the nitrogen response trials have been exhibiting a long-term decline. They estimate the decline at an annual rate of 0.10–0.16 t/ha in both the wet and dry seasons. Figure 1 charts the highest wet and dry season yields obtained in the nitrogen response experiment for the years 1966–91. Flinn and De Datta (1984) also provide evidence of yield stagnation or decline in both the wet and dry seasons in three other experiment stations in the Philippines in addition to IRRI.

Pingali, Moya, and Velasco (1990) updated the Flinn and De Datta analysis for all four stations by expanding the long-term yield response data set to include

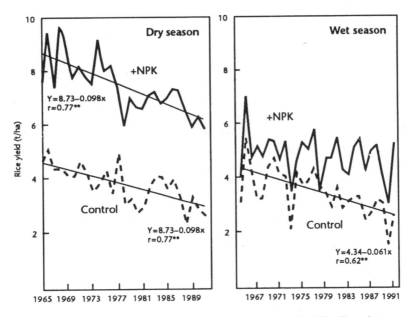

Fig. 1. Yield Trends of Highest-Yielding Variety in Long-Term Fertility Experiment at IRRI Research Farm, Laguna Province, Philippines. (Source: Cassman and Pingali 1995. Notes: Treated plots received nitrogen (N), phosphorus (P), and potassium (K) inputs in each crop cycle (+NPK). Control plots received no fertilizer-nutrient inputs. There was no significant trend in wet season. Notation ** indicates significance at 0.05.)

all years up to 1988. A significant negative yield trend was found for the wet season for three of the four locations and for two of the four locations for the dry season. The exceptions, VRES for both seasons and PhilRice for the dry season, exhibited stagnant yield trends.

Similar long-term yield declines have been observed in experiment stations in India, Bangladesh, Thailand, and Indonesia. Long-term fertilizer experiments conducted in four locations in India, from 1972 to 1982, found declining long-term yields in two locations and stagnant yields in two locations (Nambiar and Ghosh 1984). Table 1 provides data on five additional experiment station yield trends from India over a twenty-year period. Negative trends are observed in three of the five stations and the two remaining stations have stagnant yields.

Long-term yield declines have been witnessed in eleven years of continuous rice cropping at Maros, Indonesia (International Network 1987) and ten years of continuous rice cropping in Thailand (Gypmantasiri et al. 1980). Table 1 also presents data from three research stations in Thailand and two in Bangladesh. Negative trends are evident in all but one case.

Declining experiment station yields, holding constant input levels and crop management practices, could indicate one or both of the following: (1) the genetic potential of later-generation varieties is lower than earlier varieties; (2) the productive potential of the paddy resource base itself has been declining over time. Substantial evidence exists now to indicate that the genetic potential of latter-day varieties is not different from early-generation varieties (see Khush 1990; Cassman et al. 1994). In fact yields of over 10 tons have been recorded for IR-72, a variety released in the early 1990s. Current evidence seems to indicate clearly a long-term degradation of the paddy resource base (Cassman et al. 1994; Cassman and Pingali 1995). Estimates of nitrogen response functions using data from the long-term trials at IRRI show a significant downward shift of these functions over time while the slope remains the same.

Several hypotheses have been generated and are being tested for explaining the long-term yield decline under continuous cropping on experiment stations. These hypotheses are: (1) long-term decline in soil nitrogen supply due to intensive cropping on water-saturated soils, (2) increased incidence of diseases, with high nitrogen use, and (3) buildup of soil pests, especially nematodes that hamper root growth. Do these hypotheses also explain productivity trends on farmer fields? Yes and no. No, because there could be several other factors operating on farmer fields—inefficient irrigation water use, poor quality irrigation water, lower human capital and limited ability to diagnose post–Green Revolution problems, etc. On farmer fields, issues such as salinity buildup and micronutrient deficiencies could be just as important as soil nitrogen supplying capacity.

FARM-LEVEL YIELD STAGNATION AND PRODUCTIVITY DECLINE

Experiment station yield trends can be used as a means of forecasting future farm-level productivity trends. The essential message from the experiment station results is that, under intensive rice monoculture systems, productivity over the long-term is difficult to sustain, even with the best scientific management. For the intensively cultivated irrigated lowlands of Asia, which have been under rice monoculture systems over the past two decades, one should expect signs of declining productivity.

At the farm level, declining yield trends are usually not observed, since input levels are not held constant over time. However, in areas where intensive rice monoculture has been practiced over the past two to three decades, one does observe stagnant yields and/or declining trends in partial factor productivities, especially for fertilizers, and declining trends in total factor productivities (Pingali, Moya, and Velasco 1990; Pingali 1992; Cassman and Pingali 1995).

Yield Trends

It is difficult to assess trends in farm performance and the technical efficiency of farmers over time using time-series data on national average yields, because these data are based on the pooling of heterogeneous rice-growing environments (Herdt 1988; Barker and Herdt 1985). However, if countries are stratified by cropping intensities, it turns out that the rate of deceleration in yields is higher for countries with higher cropping intensities (table 2). These are invariably countries with an exhausted land frontier which sought output growth through land-augmenting technical change; China, Korea, and the Philippines are examples. Rapid growth in yields during the decade of the 1980s came from an increase in intensification in the low-intensity countries such as Laos, Nepal, and

TABLE 2
COMPARISON OF ANNUAL GROWTH RATE
IN RICE YIELD BY CROPPING INTENSITY
FOR SELECTED COUNTRIES IN ASIA

	1970–80 (%)	*1980–92 (%)*
High-Intensity Areas		
Pakistan	0.58	−0.65
Japan	0.20	1.04
China (incl. Taiwan)	2.41	2.31
Indonesia	2.93	2.17
Republic of Korea	2.72	1.32
Malaysia	1.48	0.19
Philippines	3.72	1.84
Vietnam	−1.18	3.35
Sri Lanka	1.73	0.96
India	1.44	2.92
Low-Intensity Areas		
Thailand	−0.68	0.40
Laos	0.25	4.45
Nepal	−0.74	2.43
Myanmar	4.32	−0.23
Cambodia	−3.44	2.97
Bangladesh	2.13	2.66

SOURCE: Basic data from International Rice Research Institute 1990.

Cambodia (table 2). India and Vietnam were exceptions to the above trends, due to an increase in irrigation infrastructure during the 1980s in India's case (Rosegrant and Pingali 1994) and policy reforms of the mid-1980s in Vietnam's (Pingali and Xuan 1992).

Within each country, a comparison of yield and productivity trends by provinces, stratified by cropping intensities, gives a better assessment of the state of intensive rice monoculture systems. Table 3 provides a province-level comparison of yield trends for Bangladesh, India, and the Philippines. The essential point that comes out of this comparison is that in the irrigated, high-intensity rice provinces of these countries, growth rate in yields is decelerating. In several instances, yields in the late 1990s are not significantly different from those in the early 1980s. Yields have actually fallen in some instances. For provinces with lower levels of irrigation investments, yield growth has been stagnant through the entire Green Revolution period.

The long-term impact of intensive monoculture systems on productivity can be best assessed using farm-level panel data sets. Long-term farm-level data that can be used to discern trends in productivity are rare throughout Asia. The exception are the long-term farm monitoring data from Laguna and Central Luzon provinces in the Philippines, which were collected by IRRI's Social Sciences Division from 1966 to 1990. The "cost of cultivation" surveys conducted in India

TABLE 3
COMPARISON OF YIELD TRENDS IN THE HIGH- AND LOW-INTENSITY
PROVINCES OF SELECTED ASIAN COUNTRIES

	High-Intensity Areas (%)			Low-Intensity Areas (%)	
Bangladesh					
	1970–80	*1980–87*		*1970–80*	*1980–87*
Dhaka	2.09	0.18	Faridpur	1.15	3.43
Comilla	1.12	1.87	Dinajpur	0.85	2.29
India					
	1970–80	*1980–88*		*1970–80*	*1980–88*
Andhra Pradesh	2.61	1.94	Madhya Pradesh	0.06	2.86
Haryana	4.46	−0.85	Orissa	3.63	2.34
Punjab	4.60	0.70	West Bengal	1.28	4.53
			Bihar	0.51	4.02
Philippines					
	1970–80	*1980–91*		*1970–80*	*1980–91*
Central Luzon	4.96	1.02	Northern Mindanao	2.24	2.84
Bicol	3.68	1.60	Western Mindanao	8.36	2.17
Southern Tagalog	2.94	2.79			

Sources: For Bangladesh: *Yearbook of Agricultural Statistics of Bangladesh* (various years), Bangladesh Bureau of Statistics, Ministry of Planning, Government of the People's Republic of Bangladesh, Dhaka. For India: (1960) India Central Statistical Organization, Statistical Abstract; (1961–1984) India Directorate of Economics and Statistics, *All India Estimate of Rice* (various issues); (1985–88) India Directorate of Economics and Statistics, *Agricultural Situation in India* (various issues). For the Philippines: Bureau of Agricultural Statistics, Department of Agriculture, Manila.

are a close approximation to long-term farm data sets. Two intensively cultivated locations were selected from these data sets for comparison with the Philippines. The Indian locations are the Ludhiana District in the State of Punjab and the Krishna District in Andhra Pradesh.

Yield trends within these selected domains indicate patterns that are similar to the aggregate national and regional trends in rice output: (1) there was a dramatic increase in yields following the rapid adoption of modern rice varieties and management practices in the 1960s; (2) yields continued to increase in the second decade after adoption; and (3) stagnant or declining yield trends are indicated in the most recent decade.

Growth in Input Use and Factor Productivity

By themselves, long-term farm-level yield trends do not tell the complete story, because farmers tend to maintain yields with increasing levels of inputs per hectare. Therefore, while an increase in yields may be observed at the farm level, it may be coming at the cost of a proportionately greater increase in input use. National data across Asia indicate that the rate of growth in yields has been substantially smaller than the rate of growth in fertilizer use over the past three decades (table 4).

Consider the following intensively cultivated rice bowls of Southeast Asia: Central Luzon, Philippines; Central Plains, Thailand; and West Java, Indonesia, for the period 1980–89. Farm panel data sets for each of these locations indicate that in the 1980s the rate of growth in yields was lower than the rate of growth in input use (Pingali 1992). Table 4 provides several additional examples of increased nitrogen input requirements for sustaining yields under intensive-cultivation systems. The increase in inputs required for maintaining yield levels indicates declining partial factor productivities. Evidence from provincial data sets and from farm-level panel data sets from the Green Revolution provinces across Asia indicate a consistent pattern of declining partial factor productivity of

TABLE 4
COMPARISON OF ANNUAL GROWTH IN RICE YIELD
AND GROWTH IN NITROGEN INPUT USE
FOR SELECTED ASIAN COUNTRIES

	Rice Yield (%)	Nitrogen Use (%)
Bangladesh (1968–89)	1.59	10.03
India (1961–91)	2.04	9.76
Myanmar (1962–92)	2.80	12.16
Nepal (1961–91)	0.38	15.38
Vietnam (1976–92)	3.52	10.62

SOURCES: International Rice Research Institute 1990; AGROSTAT, IRRI, Los Baños, Laguna, Philippines; Planning Management and Evaluation Division, Agriculture Corporation, Myanmar; *Statistical Yearbook* (various years), Socialist Republic of Vietnam.

chemical fertilizers and also a decline in total factor productivity over time (Pingali, Hossain, and Gerpacio 1997).

Where intensification is not associated with a change in the inherent productivity of the paddy resource base, declining factor productivity indicates a movement along a production function. Where intensification leads to reduced productivity of the resource base, declining factor productivities signify both a shift downward of the production function and a movement along the new production function. Cassman and Pingali (1995) provide empirical evidence on the downward shift of production functions over time in the intensive rice monoculture areas of Laguna and Central Luzon in the Philippines. The next section discusses the changes in the paddy ecology that occur as a consequence of long-term intensive rice monoculture and have a negative effect on the inherent productivity of the paddy resource base.

ECOLOGICAL CONSEQUENCES OF INTENSIFICATION

Intensive rice monoculture on the lowlands results in the following changes in production systems: (1) rice paddies are flooded for most of the year without adequate drying time; (2) there is an increased reliance on inorganic fertilizers; (3) planting schedules become asymmetrical; and (4) there is a greater uniformity in the varieties cultivated. Over the long term, these changes impose significant ecological costs because of their negative biophysical impacts (table 5). The economic impacts of these biophysical changes include declining trends in total factor productivity, reduced profitability of rice cultivation, and greater externalities imposed on the environment and on human health as a result of increased pesticide use.

Ecological consequences of rice monoculture systems vary by agroclimatic condition, soil type, and the source and quality of irrigation water. The following, however, are the most common ecological consequences: (1) changes in soil nutrient status, nutrient deficiencies, and increased incidence of soil toxicities; (2) formation of a hardpan (subsoil compaction); (3) increased pest buildup and pest-related yield losses; and (4) buildup of salinity and waterlogging. A brief description of each of these problems is given and the possibilities for reversing them are discussed below. At the farm level, long-term changes in the biophysical environment are manifested in terms of declining total factor productivity, profitability, and input efficiencies.

Changes in Soil Nutrient Status

The most commonly observed effect of intensive rice monoculture systems is a decline in the partial factor productivity of nitrogen fertilizer. Recent work at IRRI (Cassman et al. 1994) indicates that this effect is due to a decline in the nitrogen-supplying capacity of intensively cultivated wetland soils. In addition, there is an increased incidence of phosphorus, potassium, and micronutrient de-

TABLE 5
INTENSIFICATION-INDUCED DEGRADATION OF THE IRRIGATED LOWLANDS

Resource Base Degradation	Possible or Probable Causes	Farm level Indicators of Resource Degradation
Build-up of salinity or waterlogging	Poor design of irrigation systems (poor drainage) Intensive use of irrigation water	Reduced yields and/or reduced factor productivities Reduced cropping intensities Abandoned paddy lands in the extreme
Increased incidence of soil toxicities and micronutrient deficiencies	Long-term flooding or water saturation of paddy soils Increased reliance on low-quality irrigation water Depletion due to continuous rice monoculture Long-term flooding or water saturation on paddy soils	Reduced yields and/or reduced factor productivities Reduced yields and/or reduced factor productivities
Hardpan (subsoil compaction)	Increased frequency of puddling (wet tillage)	Reduced flexibility non-rice crop production in the dry season
Changes in soil nitrogen supplying capacity	Changes in organic matter quantity and quality due to slower rate of decomposition in continuously flooded soil	Declining efficiency of nitrogen fertilizer use
Increased pest buildup and pest-related yield losses	Continuous rice monoculture Increased asymmetry of planting schedules Greater uniformity in varieties cultivated	Increased pesticide use

ficiency, due to a lack of nutrient balance in the fertilizers applied (De Datta, Gomez, and Descalsota 1988).

Dynamics of Soil Nitrogen Supply

Fertilized rice obtains 50–80 percent of its nitrogen requirement from the soil; unfertilized rice obtains an even larger portion from the soil, mainly through the mineralization of organic matter (De Datta 1981). The nitrogen-supplying capacity of the soil depends on the previous cropping history and residue management, the quantity and quality of organic matter in the soil, and the moisture regime, which affects the composition and activity of the microflora and -fauna that govern the decomposition of soil's organic matter and of crop residues. In continuous cropping of flooded soils with two and sometimes three crops each year, organic matter is conserved or increased even when all straw is removed at harvest, because of the large carbon inputs from the aquatic biomass, such as the green and blue green algae, and because the rate of organic matter decomposition is slower than in dry soils. Despite this conservation, the soil's nitrogen-supplying capacity decreases over time, because of chemical changes in the organic matter and effects of flooding on microbial activity in the soil (Cassman et al. 1994). The soil's capacity to provide nitrogen to the plant declines with continuous (two to three crops per year) flooded rice cultivation systems.

Declining soil nitrogen supply results in declining factor productivity of chemical nitrogen, since soil nitrogen is a natural substitute for chemical nitrogen. Holding fertilizer levels constant, intensive rice culture can, over time, reduce the soil's ability to meet the plant's nitrogen requirement, especially in the later period of crop growth, thereby affecting crop yields. Farmers have been applying more chemical fertilizers to maintain their yield levels. Declining soil nitrogen supply is not caused by the prolonged use of chemical fertilizers, but rather because of the intensive rice monoculture system itself. This is evident when one looks at the yield trends on long-term continuous cropping experiments without chemical nitrogen use; the yields on these plots are also declining over time (Cassman et al. 1994).

The magnitude of yields forgone due to declining soil nitrogen supply is estimated by Cassman and Pingali (1995) to be around 30 percent, over a twenty-year period, at all nitrogen levels. How can these trends in nitrogen productivity be reversed? The primary leverage point is in the cropping system, a break in the continuous flooded rice cycle with a dry season non-rice crop (a crop that does not require standing water). In the southern coastal plains of China, a cropping system consisting of two crops of rice followed by a crop of barley or soybeans, practiced over eighteen years, has maintained a high and stable crop yield (Kundu and Ladha 1995). The choice of the crop grown in the dry season determines the level of contribution of the crop rotation to enhanced soil nitrogen supplying capacity. In the double rice cropped areas of India, growing a short duration legume such as cowpeas or mungbeans as part of the rotation (after the second crop of rice) increased yields by 1 t/ha and saved 30 kg N/ha.

Macronutrient Deficiencies

In addition to nitrogen, phosphorus and potassium are the two other macronutrients demanded by the rice plant. Phosphorus and potassium deficiencies are becoming widespread across Asia in areas not previously considered to be deficient. These deficiencies are directly related to the increase in cropping intensity and the predominance of year-round irrigated rice production systems. For example, in China it is estimated that about two-thirds of agricultural land is now deficient of phosphorus, while in India nearly one-half of the districts have been classified as low in available phosphorus (Stone 1986; Tandon 1987; Desai and Gandhi 1989). Desai and Gandhi note that this is due to the emphasis on nitrogen alone rather than a balanced application of all macronutrients required for sustaining soil fertility. The result of unbalanced application of fertilizers has been a decline in the efficiency of fertilizer use over time (Desai and Gandhi 1989; Stone 1986; Ahmed 1985).

Micronutrient Deficiencies and Soil Toxicities

Perennial flooding of ricelands and continuous rice monoculture leads to increased incidence of micronutrient deficiencies and soil toxicities. Zinc deficiency and iron toxicity are the ones most commonly observed in the tropics. Waterlogging and salinity buildup aggravate these problems. In Asia, zinc deficiency is regarded as a major limiting factor for wetland rice cultivation on about 2 million hectares (Ponnamperuma 1974). Soils not initially of low zinc content also show signs of induced zinc deficiency as a consequence of rice monoculture. Drainage, even if temporary, helps alleviate this deficiency by increasing zinc availability (Lopes 1980; Moormann and van Breemen 1978).

Most ricelands do not start off with any soil toxicities; however, toxicities may build up in some soils due to continuous flooding, increased reliance on poor quality irrigation water, and impeded drainage. Some toxicities are related directly to chemical content and pollutants in the incoming irrigation water. Pollutant concentrations in irrigation water have been increasing due to the degradation of the watersheds that replenish the irrigation systems (De Vera 1992), industrial pollutants discharged into the river system (Castañeda and Bhuiyan 1988), and increased pumping of brackish groundwater.

Rice researchers in Asia and U.S.-based rice researchers familiar with Asia ranked phosphorus, zinc, and sulphur deficiencies as the top three soil-related problems of rice production in South and Southeast Asia. These problems accounted for forgone production of 5 million, 3.6 million, and 2.5 million tons of rice per year respectively (Barker and Duff 1986; Herdt and Riely 1987). Salinity was ranked the fourth and accounted for forgone production of 2 million tons, while iron toxicity accounted for forgone production of 1.6 million tons of rice annually. Jointly these soil-related problems account for approximately 14 million tons of rice production forgone annually, around 10 percent of the total rice produced in Asia.

Once diagnosed at the farm level, micronutrient deficiencies are relatively straightforward to correct. Zinc deficiencies can be corrected by adding zinc, for instance. Diagnosis is not easy though; quite often micronutrient deficiencies are misdiagnosed as pest-related damage. In the case of soil toxicities, farm-level diagnosis is equally complicated, and corrective actions are not as straightforward. In both cases, however, the problem ought to be attacked at the cause rather than the cure stage. Periodic breaks in rice monoculture systems and improved water use efficiency contribute to reducing the incidence and magnitude of the above problems.

Long-Term Changes in Soil Physical Characteristics

Seasonal cycles of puddling (wet tillage) and drying, over the long term, lead to the formation of hardpans in paddy soils. "Hardpan" refers to compacted subsoil that is 5–10 cm thick at depths of 10–40 cm from the soil surface. Compared to the surface soil, a hardpan has higher bulk density and less medium to large-sized pores. Permeability is generally lower than that of the overlying and deeper horizons. The formation of hardpans makes it difficult to grow non-rice crops after rice in a cropping system; for the rice crop, it contributes to impeded root growth and ability to extract nutrients from the subsoil and leads to the buildup of soil toxicities, due to the perennially waterlogged condition of the soil layer above it.

A striking example of the problem of hardpans is seen in the rice-wheat cropping system in South Asia. With the advent of short-duration rice and wheat varieties, over 12 million hectares of paddy lands are grown to wet season rice followed by a dry season wheat crop (Hobbs and Morris 1996). The productivity of the wheat crop is affected by the poor establishment of wheat after puddled rice. Breaking the hardpan by deep tillage and improving soil structures through the incorporation of organic matter affects the productivity of the subsequent rice crop by reducing the water-holding capacity of the soil. Intensification has thus reduced the flexibility of dry season crop choice by changing the physical structure of the soil.

LOSSES FROM PESTS

The use of purchased inputs to protect plants from pests was unimportant for rice prior to the mass introduction of modern varieties. Farmers had traditionally relied on host plant resistance, natural enemies, cultural methods, and mechanical methods such as handweeding. Relatively minor pests—leaffolder, caseworm, armyworm, and cutworm—started to cause noticeable losses in farmers' fields as the area planted to modern varieties increased. The green leafhopper and brown planthopper became major problems, the former as a vector of the rice tungro virus and the latter as a direct result of insecticides' killing its natural enemies (Teng 1990). Soil pests, especially root nematodes, have also increased with intensification (Prot et al. 1992). Pest buildup in irrigated rice systems is related to continuous rice cultivation, increased asymmetry of planting, uniformity of varieties cultivated, and injudicious pesticide use. Heong, Aquino, and Barrion (1992) argue that prophylactic pesticide application has led to the disruption of the pest-predator balance and a resurgence of pest populations later in the crop season. The health and environmental consequences of injudicious insecticide use are documented in Pingali and Roger (1995); Antle and Pingali (1994); Pingali, Marquez, and Palis (1994); and Rola and Pingali (1993).

Injudicious and indiscriminate pesticide application is related to policies that have made these chemicals easily and cheaply accessible. Rola and Pingali (1993) have argued that pesticide use has been promoted by policy makers' misperceptions of pests and pest damage. Policy makers commonly perceive that intensification of rice cultivation and modern variety use necessarily lead to increases in pest-related crop losses and that modern rice production is therefore not possible without high levels of chemical pest control.

Perceptions of high crop losses are based on experiences from early modern varieties that were susceptible to pest damage. Most varieties released since the mid-1970s are highly resistant to a broad spectrum of pest infestations, yet the perception of a close link between modern varieties and pesticides persists. This perception has led to the promotion of pesticide use through subsidies and credit programs. Pesticide mismanagement, disruption of the pest-predator balance, increased pest-induced losses, as well as health and environmental externalities are the result. When health externalities were explicitly accounted for, Rola and Pingali found that the positive production benefits of applying insecticides were overwhelmed by the increased health costs.

Even with appropriate policies, there are two areas of growing concern with respect to intensification and pesticide use. The first is the increasing incidence of plant diseases, especially in association with high fertilizer use. The second is the growing incidence of pest resistance to chemicals, especially by plant pests— weeds. Farmers striving for high yields usually apply high levels of chemical fertilizers. The resulting luxuriant and dense rice canopy is more susceptible to disease infestations, such as blast, sheath blight, and bacterial blight (Teng 1990). High disease incidences have been observed in Japan, Korea, Vietnam, and China. Fungicide use has been increasing in these areas, and other parts of Asia are expected to follow suit as higher yields are sought there.

The increasing importance of herbicides in Asian rice production, with the shift from transplanting to direct seeding, brings with it a concern for changes in weed ecology and possible emergence of herbicide resistance. Moody (1994) has reported the increased incidence of "red rices" in direct seeded areas in the Philippines. These weedy forms of rice are taller than cultivated rice, they lodge, and they have different grain characteristics. Rice seeds carried on the farm from season to season become the main reservoir of weed seeds and the main cause of farm-level weed buildup over time. In countries with high rice herbicide use, such as the United States, there are signs that some of the weed species are becoming resistant to herbicides. As herbicide use increases in Asia, such trends may also emerge.

SALINITY AND WATERLOGGING

"The long-term viability of irrigated agriculture (especially in the semi-arid and arid zones) becomes one of salt management—devising strategies to prevent salts from accumulating either in the irrigated area or downstream" (National Academy of Science 1989, 96). Intensive use of irrigation water in areas with uneven toposequence and poor drainage can lead to continual recharge of groundwater and a consequent rise in the water table. In the semi-arid and arid zones, this leads to salinity buildup, and in the humid zone, to waterlogging. Salinity is induced by an excess of evapotranspiration over rainfall, causing a net upward movement of water through capillary action and the concentration of salts on the soil surface. High water tables prevent the flushing of salts from the surface soil. Postel (1989) estimates that 24 percent of the irrigated land worldwide suffers from salinity problems, with India, China, the United States, Pakistan, and the republics of the former Soviet Union being the most affected. In the short term, salinity buildup leads to reduced yields, while in the long term it can lead to abandoning of paddy lands (Samad et al. 1992; Postel 1989; Mustafa 1991)[2]. Poor irrigation system design is a primary cause of salinity problems.

In the humid zone, induced salinity buildup is not as serious a problem, because the greater rainfall flushes out the accumulated salts. However, excessive water use and poor drainage cause problems of waterlogging in this zone. Waterlogged fields have lower productivity because of lower decomposition rates of organic matter, lower nitrogen availability, and accumulation of soil toxins. These issues are discussed further below.

Can Salinity Problems Be Reversed?

Once salinity has set in, reversing it becomes very difficult and expensive. Salts have to be flushed out of the soil and drained out of the area. This process requires large quantities of fresh water and a drainage system. Often, retiring saline lands from irrigated agriculture may be more cost-effective than trying to fix them. The opportunity costs of fresh water are very high, both for agricultural and nonagricultural purposes; hence desalinization may not be the socially optimal use of this water. Similarly, the returns on investing scarce national resources in drainage systems are higher for systems that are part of on-going production efforts than those aimed at rehabilitating land that has gone out of production due to salinization.

The problem of induced salinity ought to be managed by addressing the causes of the problem; these are poor system design and inefficient use of irrigation water. For systems that are already in place, improving water use efficiency would lead to a significant slowdown in salinity buildup. An essential component in improving water use efficiency is pricing irrigation water at its "true" cost (Pingali, Hossain, and Gerpacio 1997). For new irrigation projects, drainage systems have to be planned and budgeted right from the start, even if this means facing the reality that many new systems may not be cost-effective.

INTENSIFICATION POLICIES: WHERE DID THEY GO WRONG?

Ironically, the very policies that encouraged increased food supply through intensive monoculture systems also contributed to the declining sustainability of these systems. Rice policies operated under two presumptions: (1) that the lowlands were resilient to intensification pressures and that they could sustain productivity growth indefinitely, and (2) that modern technology provided a "silver bullet" solution to food supply problems of Asia. Traditional farming systems were sustainable because of their lower intensities of cultivation and because they benefited from a stock of farmers' technical knowledge about the crop and paddy resource base that had been built over millennia. Neither science nor farmer knowledge was able to predict the changes imposed on the biophysical resource base by intensification and the use of modern technology.

Massive investments in irrigation infrastructure were essential for the success of the Green Revolution. Without these investments, rapid growth in productivity would not have been possible. However, in retrospect it is clear that many of the irrigation systems were poorly designed. Drainage investments were deliberately left out of irrigation projects to keep the cost down (National Academy of Sciences 1989). The long-term environmental costs of irrigation investments were rarely accounted for, and hence the social returns from these investments were overestimated. Timmer (1991, 9) states that "the track record of incorporating environmental and public health costs into the design and evaluation of irrigation projects is dismal, whether the projects were funded by external donors such as the World Bank or came directly from the country's own budget."

It was not just the design of irrigation systems that was problematic; errors in system management, water allocation, and water pricing also contributed to environmental costs of irrigated agriculture. Water was, and still is, essentially "free," and therefore is used beyond the social optimum. Increasing water use efficiency offers substantial environmental benefits and does not adversely affect yields, yet this leverage for improving the sustainability of the resource base was not used anywhere in Asia.

The dual goals of food self-sufficiency and sustainable resource management are often mutually incompatible. Policies designed for achieving food self-sufficiency tend to undervalue goods not traded internationally, especially land and labor resources. As a result, food self-sufficiency in countries with an exhausted land frontier can come at a high environmental cost.

Government intervention in the rice market, especially through output price support and input subsidies, provided farmers with incentives for increasing rice productivity. In addition to highly subsidized irrigation water, Asian farmers benefited from "cheap" fertilizers, pesticides, and credit (see Monke and Pearson 1991 for an example of Indonesian price policy). The net result was that rice monoculture systems were extremely profitable through the decades of the 1970s and the 1980s, despite a long-term decline in the real world rice price throughout this period.

Input subsidies directly affect crop management practices at the farm level; they reduce farmer incentives for improving input use efficiency. Improving farm-level technical efficiencies requires farmer investment in learning about the technology and how best to use it. Where input prices are kept low through government intervention, farmers do not have the incentive to spend the time to learn about methods of increasing technical efficiency. The injudicious use of fertilizers, of pesticides, and of water are cases in point. The persistence of inefficient input use has led to several of the ecological problems discussed earlier in this chapter.

Rice production policies of the Green Revolution era were enormously successful in moving the food deficit countries of Asia to food self-sufficiency, and in some cases to food surplus. These policies were often unidimensional and formulated in a crisis mind set. The need today is for a more holistic approach to food production policies that explicitly accounts for externalities and long-term system sustainability.

CONCLUSIONS

The current problems of sustaining productivity growth in the Asian lowlands indicate that these areas are as susceptible to environmental degradation as the more fragile uplands. Intensification's environmental impacts on the lowlands, although not easily observed, tend to have a significant long-term effect on food production and food supply. For instance, if current rice yields on the irrigated lowlands of Asia dropped by 5 percent, the impact on total rice production would be 36 million tons per year.

The problem of sustainability of agriculture in the lowlands does not emerge because of the technology being used but rather because of the intensity of land use itself and the choice of crops. Intensive rice monoculture systems over the long term are not sustainable without adequate changes in current technologies and management practices. Just because rice has been sustainably cultivated in China, Japan, and elsewhere in Asia for centuries does not mean that the problems discussed above are not serious. In these countries, until recently, one crop of rice was grown per year, and the fallow period during the dry season allowed the land to be rejuvenated.

The problems with sustaining productivity growth have come about because people have inadequately understood and responded to the physical, biological, and ecological consequences of agricultural intensification. The focus of research resources ought to shift from a fixation on yield improvements to a holistic approach to the long-term management of the agricultural resource base. When yield per hectare is used as the only measure of productivity growth and the "true" costs of production are not considered, then research resource allocation will be biased away from understanding the systemic problems causing productivity stagnation or decline. It is unlikely that there will be quick answers for reversing the current negative trends in productivity growth. Sustained research investments are essential.

Sustaining productivity gains in the post–Green Revolution era will have to come from more efficient use of inputs, including land and labor. Technologies for enhancing input efficiencies (such as better fertilizer management, integrated pest management) are more knowledge-intensive and location-specific than the modern seed-fertilizer technology that was characteristic of the Green Revolution. Productivity gains accrue to farmers who have the ability to learn about the new technologies, discriminate among technologies offered to them by the research system, adapt the technologies to their particular environmental conditions, and provide supervision to ensure the appropriate application of the technology. Profitable adoption of knowledge-intensive input management technologies will depend on the value of input savings relative to the cost of additional time required for learning and decision making.

The Green Revolution strategy of increasing lowland productivity has to a large extent relieved the pressure on the uplands by providing employment opportunities for migrant labor. However, if the current trend towards stagnation and decline in lowland productivity persists, then one could expect a decline in employment opportunities in the lowlands, and hence an increased pressure on the uplands.

NOTES

1. There is no evidence to indicate that for irrigated rice adding more plant traits has resulted in any yield sacrifice.
2. Parallel incidences of salinity buildup in U.S. irrigated lands can be found in National Academy of Sciences 1989.

REFERENCES

Ahmed, N. 1985. Fertilizer Efficiency and Crop Yields in Pakistan. *Phosphorus in Agriculture* 89:17–32.

Antle, J. M., and P. L. Pingali. 1994. "Pesticides, Productivity, and Farmer Health: A Philippine Case Study." *American Journal of Agricultural Economics* 76 (3): 418–30.

Barker, R., and J. B. Duff. 1986. *Constraints to Higher Rice Yield in Seven Rice Growing Environments in South and Southeast Asia.* Mimeograph. International Rice Research Institute, Los Baños, Laguna, Philippines.

Barker, R., and R. W. Herdt, with B. Rose. 1985. *The Rice Economy of Asia.* Washington, D.C.: Resources for the Future; and Los Baños, Laguna, Philippines: International Rice Research Institute.

Cassman, K. G., S. K. De Datta, D. C. Olk, J. Alcantara, M. Samson, J. Descalsota, and M. Dizon. 1994. "Yield Decline and Nitrogen Balance in Long-term Experiments on Continuous Irrigated Rice Systems in the Tropics." *Advances in Soil Science,* Special Issue.

Cassman, K. G., and P. L. Pingali. 1995. "Extrapolating Trends from Long-term Experiments to Farmers' Fields: The Case of Irrigated Rice Systems in Asia." In *Agricultural Sustainability: Economic, Environmental, and Statistical Considerations,* edited by V. Barnett, R. Payne, and R. Steiner, 63–84. Chichester, New York: John Wiley and Sons.

Castañeda, A. R., and S. I. Bhuiyan. 1988. "Industrial Pollution of Irrigation Water and Its Effects on Riceland Productivity." *Philippine Journal of Crop Science* 13 (1): 27–35.

Dalrymple, D. G. 1986. *Development and Spread of High Yielding Rice Varieties in Developing Countries.* Washington, D.C.: Agency for International Development.

De Datta, S. K. 1981. *Principles and Practices of Rice Production.* New York: Wiley-Interscience Publication, John Wiley & Sons.

De Datta, S. K., F. V. Garcia, W. P. Abilay Jr., J. M. Alcantara, A. Mandac, and V. P. Marciano. 1979. "Constraints to High Yields, Nueva Ecija, Philippines." In *Constraints to the Adoption of Modern Rice Technology in Asia,* 191–234. Los Baños, Laguna, Philippines: International Rice Research Institute.

De Datta, S. K., K. A. Gomez, and J. P. Descalsota. 1988. "Changes in Yield Response to Major Nutrients and in Soil Fertility under Intensive Rice Cropping. *Soil Science* 146:350–58.

Desai, G. M., and V. Gandhi. 1989. "Phosphorus for Sustainable Agriculture Growth in Asia: An Assessment of Alternative Sources and Management." In *Proceedings of the Symposium on Phosphorus Requirements for Sustainable Agriculture in Asia and Pacific Region,* International Rice Research Institute, Los Baños, Laguna, Philippines, March 6–10.

De Vera, M. V. M. 1992. "Impact of Upper Watershed Destruction on the Performance of National Irrigation Systems in the Philippines." Master's thesis, College of Economics and Management, University of the Philippines, Los Baños.

Flinn, J. C., and S. K. De Datta. 1984. "Trends in Irrigated Rice Yields under Intensive Cropping at Philippine Research Stations." *Field Crops Research* 9.

Flinn, J. C., S. K. De Datta, and E. Labadan. 1982. "An Analysis of Long-term Rice Yields in a Wetland Soil." *Field Crops Research* 5 (3): 201–16.

Gypmantasiri, P., A. Wiboonpongse, B. Rerkasem, I. Craig, K. Rerkasem, L. Ganjarapan, M. Titayawaan, M. Seetisarn, P. Thani, R. Jaisaard, S. Ongprasert, and T. Radanachaless. 1980. *An Interdisciplinary Perspective of Cropping Systems in the Chiang Mai Valley: Key Questions for Research.* Faculty of Agriculture, University of Chiang Mai, Chiang Mai, Thailand.

Heong, K. L., G. B. Aquino, and A. T. Barrion. 1992. "Population Dynamics of Plant and Leafhoppers and Their Natural Enemies in Rice Ecosystem in the Philippines." *Crop Protection* 11: 371–79.

Herdt, R. W. 1988. Increasing Crop Yields in Developing Countries. *Proceedings of the 1988 Meeting of the American Agricultural Economics Association,* 30 July–3 August, Knoxville, Tennessee.

Herdt, R. W., and C. Capule. 1983. *Adoption, Spread, and Production Impact of Modern Rice Varieties in Asia.* Los Baños, Laguna, Philippines: International Rice Research Institute.

Herdt, R. W., and F. Riely. 1987. "International Rice Research Priorities: Implications for Biotechnology Initiatives." Paper presented at the Rockfeller Foundation Workshop on Allocating Resources for Developing Country Research, Bellagio, Italy, 6–10 July.

Hobbs, P., and M. Morris. 1996. *Meeting South Asia's Future Food Requirements from Rice-Wheat Cropping Systems: Priority Issues Facing Researchers in the Post–Green Revolution Era.* Natural Resource Group Working Paper 96-01, CIMMYT, Mexico, D.F.

International Network for Sustainable Rice Fertility. 1987. *Annual Report.* Los Baños, Laguna, Philippines: International Rice Research Institute.

International Rice Research Institute. 1967. *Annual Report.* Los Baños, Laguna, Philippines: IRRI.

———. 1990. *World Rice Statistics.* Los Baños, Laguna, Philippines: IRRI.

Khush, G. S. 1990. *Varietal Needs for Different Environments and Breeding Strategies.* Los Baños, Laguna, Philippines: International Rice Research Institute.

Kundu, D. K., and J. K. Ladha. 1995. "Efficient Management of Soil and Biologically Fixed N^2 in Intensively Cultivated Rice Fields." *Soil Biology and Biochemistry* 27 (4/5): 431–39.

Lopes, A. S. 1980. "Micronutrients in Soils of the Tropics as Constraints to Food Production." In *Priorities for Alleviating Soil-Related Constraints to Food Production in the Tropics.* Jointly sponsored and published by the International Rice Research Institute, Los Baños, Laguna, Philippines, and the New York State College of Agriculture and Life Sciences, Cornell University, Ithaca.

Mitchell, D. O. 1987. *Factors Affecting Grain Prices.* Washington, D.C.: World Bank.

Monke, E., and S. Pearson. 1991. "Introduction." In *Rice in Indonesia,* edited by S. Pearson, W. Falcon, P. Heytens, E. Monke, and R. Naylor. Ithaca, N.Y.: Cornell University Press.

Moody, K. 1994. "Postplanting Weed Control in Direct-seeded Rice." In *Proceedings of the National Workshop on Direct Seeding Practices and Productivity,* edited by A. H. Ali, 249–65. Penang, Malaysia: Malaysian Agricultural Research and Development Institute.

Moormann, F. R., and N. van Breemen. 1978. *Rice: Soil, Water, Land.* Los Baños, Laguna, Philippines: International Rice Research Institute.

Mustafa, U. 1991. "Economic Impact of Land Degradation (Salt Affected and Waterlogged Soils) on Rice Production in Pakistan's Punjab." Ph.D. dissertation, College of Economics and Management, University of the Philippines, Los Baños.

Nambiar, K. K. M., and A. B. Ghosh. 1984. *Highlights of Research of a Long Term Fertilizer Experiment in India (1971–82).* LTFE Research Bulletin no. 1, Indian Agricultural Research Institute, New Delhi.

National Academy of Sciences. 1989. *Irrigation-Induced Water Quality Problems: What Can Be Learned from the San Joaquin Valley Experience?* Washington, D.C.: National Academy Press.

Pingali, P. L. 1992. "Diversifying Asian Rice Farming Systems: A Deterministic Paradigm." In *Trends in Agricultural Diversification: Regional Perspectives,* edited by J. Anderson, 107–26. Paper no. 180, World Bank, Washington, D.C.

————. 1994. "Technological Prospects for Reversing the Declining Trend in Asia's Rice Productivity." In *Agriculture Technology Policy Issues for the International Community,* edited by J. Anderson, Chap. 21. Washington, D.C.: Agricultural Policies Division, Agricultural and Rural Development Department, World Bank.

Pingali, P. L., M. Hossain, and R. V. Gerpacio. 1997. *Asian Rice Bowls: The Returning Crisis.* Wallingford, U.K.: CAB International.

Pingali, P. L., C. B. Marquez, and F. G. Palis. 1994. "Pesticides and Philippine Rice Farmer Health: A Medical and Economic Analysis." *American Journal of Agricultural Economics* 76 (August): 587–92.

Pingali, P. L., P. F. Moya, and L. E. Velasco. 1990. *The Post–Green Revolution Blues in Asian Rice Production: The Diminished Gap between Experiment Station and Farmer Yields.* Social Science Division Paper no. 90-01, International Rice Research Institute, Los Baños, Laguna, Philippines.

Pingali, P. L., and P. A. Roger, eds. 1995. "Impact of Pesticides on Farmer Health and Rice Environment." Los Baños, Laguna, Philippines: International Rice Research Institute; and Kluwer Academic Publishers, Norwell, Massachusetts.

Pingali, P. L. and V. T. Xuan. 1992. "Vietnam: De-collectivization and Rice Productivity Growth." *Economic Development and Cultural Change* 40 (4): 697–718.

Ponnamperuma, F. N. 1974. "Micronutrient Limitations in Acid Tropical Rice Soils." In *Soil Management in Tropical America,* edited by E. Bornemisza and A. Alvarado, 330–47. Raleigh: Soil Science Department, North Carolina State University.

Postel, S. 1989. "Water for Agriculture: Facing the Limits." *Worldwatch Paper 93,* December.

Prot, J. C., I. R. S. Soriano, D. M. Matias, and S. Savary. 1992. "Use of Green Manure Crops in Control of *Hirschmanniella mucronata* and *H. oryzae* in Irrigated Rice." *Journal of Nematology* 24:127–32.

Rola, A. C., and P. L. Pingali. 1993. *Pesticides, Rice Productivity, and Farmers' Health: An Economic Assessment.* Los Baños, Laguna, Philippines: World Resources Institute and International Rice Research Institute.

Rosegrant, M. W., and H. P. Binswanger. 1994. "Markets in Tradeable Water Rights: Potential for Efficiency Gains in Developing Country Water Resource Allocation." *World Development* 22 (11): 1613–25.

Rosegrant, M. W., and P. L. Pingali. 1994. "Policy and Technology for Rice Productivity Growth in Asia." *Journal of International Development* 6 (6): 665–88.

Samad, M., D. Merrey, D. Vermillion, M. Fuchs-Carsch, K. Mohtadullah, and R. Lenton. 1992. "Irrigation Management Strategies for Improving the Performance of Irrigated Agriculture." *Outlook on Agriculture* 21 (4): 279–86.

Stone, B. 1986. "Chinese Fertilizer Application in the 1980s and 1990s: Issues of Growth, Balances, Allocation, Efficiency, and Response." In *China's Economy Looks Toward the Year 2000,* Volume 1, 453–93. Washington, D.C.: Congress of the United States.

Tandon, H. L. S. 1987. *Phosphorus Research and Agricultural Production in India.* New Delhi: Fertilizer Development and Consumption Organization.

Teng, P. S. 1990. *IPM in Rice: An Analysis of the Status Quo with Recommendations for Action.* Report to the International IPM Task Force, Los Baños, Laguna, Philippines: International Rice Research Institute.

Timmer, C. P. 1991. *Agriculture and the State: Growth, Employment, and Poverty in Developing Countries.* Ithaca, N.Y.: Cornell University Press.

United States Department of Agriculture. 1954. *Diagnosis and Improvement of Saline and Alkali Soils.* Agricultural Handbook no. 66. Washington, D.C.: USDA.

30

Choice of Technique in Rice Milling on Java

C. PETER TIMMER

INTRODUCTION

A technological revolution has swept across Java virtually unnoticed. As recently as 1971 informed estimates assumed that as much as 80 percent of Java's rice crop was hand-pounded, both for subsistence consumption and for local marketings. The figure now (1973) is certainly less than 50 percent and may well be as little as 10 percent— there are no direct statistics from which to judge. The number of small mechanical rice processing facilities has increased dramatically. The economic and social impacts are only beginning to be felt, and any assessments of these changes in the countryside and villages are necessarily for the future.

This article will try to answer three questions about the recent changes in rice processing: (1) What has happened, in rough quantitative terms? (2) What explains the shift from hand-pounding to small rice mills and why not to larger mills? and (3) What has happened to rural employment with the decline of hand-pounding? The secondary data are taken from an anonymous report from the Asian Development Bank (ADB),[1] a Rice Marketing Study (cited in this paper as RMS) prepared by a U.S. consulting firm,[2] and two publications by the author.[3]

TECHNOLOGY CHOICES

Three rice processing techniques are in use in Indonesia: hand-pounding, small rice mills, and large rice mills. The overall patterns of what has happened technologically to rice milling in the past few years are very clear: hand-pounding has declined drastically. But the large-scale mills have not been the beneficiaries of the decline in hand-pounding. Rather, a whole new rice-milling industry has sprung up, composed of an assortment of machinery but with one overriding

C. PETER TIMMER is Dean of the Graduate School of International Relations and Pacific Studies at the University of California, San Diego.

This paper and the following comment and reply are reprinted from *Bulletin of Indonesian Economic Studies* 9, no. 2 (1973), with omissions and minor editorial revisions, by permission of the publisher— the Research School of Pacific Studies of the Australian National University—and the authors.

characteristic: all of the facilities are small in scale and labor-intensive. A quote from ADB, *Rice Processing Report,* makes the point explicitly:

> Why pay more than 40,000 Dollars for a large rice mill when the same output can be attained by a small mill with an investment of 7,400 Dollars? Naturally the cheap unit requires far more labour, but that does not count much in a country where a mill labourer is paid Rp 100–150 (U.S. Dollars 0.24 to 0.36) per working day. The differences in rendement (extraction) rate (less than 1 percent) and broken percentage (around 3 percent) are also insignificant compared to the high debt service for the large-scale mill.

The type of machinery used to mill rice—from wooden pounding pole and pestle to large-scale multistage mills with bulk storage and drying—is, then, a function of labor and capital costs. The results of a formal economic analysis of the question of choice of technique in rice milling strongly confirm the "common sense" of the quote above.[4] Both the methodology and the results of the analysis are presented below.

The analytical technique is purposefully textbookish: the aim is not to confuse the choice of technique issue with fancy methodology but to be as simple-minded as the problem will allow. Consequently, an isoquant has been constructed that represents several different techniques, in terms of relative capital/labor ratios, of producing a unit amount of value added in rice processing. After going step by step through the data, the assumptions and the manipulations, we end up with a standardized isoquant in the two dimensions of investment cost and labor cost.

Five different processing techniques form the basis of the analysis: hand-pounding (HP); small rice mills (SRM); large rice mills (LRM); small bulk facilities (SBF); and large bulk facilities (LBF). The first three techniques are at present in operation in Indonesia—hand-pounding is millennia old. The small rice mills can be thought of as ranging from the now obsolete double Engelberg-type huller/polisher combinations to the smaller self-contained Japanese rice milling units and rubber roll huskers connected to Engelberg-type or pneumatic polishers. All these together are taken as the class "small rice mills." They do not have mechanical drying equipment but rely solely on sun drying. Consequently, the small rice mills (SRM) are assumed to suffer high physical (and monetary) losses during processing, not so much in the milling per se but from a lack of control in drying.

Fewer "large rice mills" are seen in Indonesia, although all the older multistage milling equipment fits this category if mechanical drying facilities are also available. The major feature of this category is the combined use of mechanical and sun drying with modern milling equipment, either Japanese-type or conventional multi-stage.

The fourth and fifth techniques—bulk facilities—represent proposed improvements to the Indonesian rice processing sector. "Bulk facilities" is a shorthand way of describing a rice mill/storage system. The rice mill produces high-quality milled rice which is stored in vertical silos of varying capacity. No example of either the small bulk facility or the large bulk facility exists at present in Indonesia, although even the larger facility is not large by international grain-handling standards. The small bulk facilities have a milling and drying capacity of three tons per hour and forty-five hundred tons of vertical steel storage. The large bulk facilities can process nine tons of rough rice per hour and contain fifteen thousand tons of bulk storage in vertical steel silos for rough rice and conventional multi-stage gradual-reduction milling machinery. A continuous-flow dryer attached has a capacity of twenty tons per hour.

CONSTRUCTING UNIT ISOQUANTS

The data and calculations necessary to construct a unit isoquant in value added by rice processing are presented in table 1. The isoquant is drawn in the two dimensions of total investment cost and number of unskilled workers needed to run each facility. A "budget" or "iso-cost" line can then be drawn tangent to the isoquant in order to determine the optimum capital/labor ratio for rice processing. Since the capital axis is in total investment cost and not in annualized capital charges, it is necessary to convert annual laborers' wages into a lifetime "wage fund." This is done by discounting a laborer's annual earnings for his lifetime (fifty years) by an appropriate discount rate (12 percent, 18 percent, or 24 percent) to calculate the present value of the cost of a laborer.

Three basic steps are necessary to construct the isoquant, and all three are carried out in table 1. The "Data Per Unit" section simply reports capacity, investment cost, and number of manual laborers required per operating shift for each facility. These data are then standardized in terms of one thousand tons of rough rice input per year. The data for the small rice mill do not change, since its initial capacity was one thousand tons per year, but each of the larger facilities is scaled down to a comparable one-thousand-ton capacity. Obviously, it is not possible to install one-twentieth of a large bulk facility, but this technique merely keeps the numbers manageable without losing any of the scale economies of the larger facilities. Conceptually it is equally possible to use the large bulk facility capacity of 21,600 tons as the standard and multiply the number of smaller units to be on a comparable basis. Nothing is lost by keeping the numbers smaller and more manageable.

PHYSICAL AND MONETARY CONVERSIONS

The next step is to convert the one thousand tons of rough rice input per facility into a value of output. There are two parts to the process: a physical conversion and a monetary conversion. Table 1 shows the conversion rates for both processes. The first is merely the rendement or extraction rate. How much milled rice does each facility produce per ton of rough rice? No fixed rates are really applicable, since this extraction rate depends so critically on quality of

TABLE 1

DERIVATION OF A UNIT ISOQUANT IN VALUE ADDED FROM RICE PROCESSING

	Hand-Pounding HP (s)[a]	Small Rice Mill SRM (s)[a]	Large Rice Mill LRM (s/m)[a]	Small Bulk Facility SBF (m)[a]	Large Bulk Facility LBF (m)[a]
			Data per Unit		
Milling capacity (tons per year)[b]	—	1,000[c]	2,500[d]	7,200	21,600
Investment cost (U.S. dollars)[e]	0	$8,049[c]	$90,511[d]	$453,283	$2,605,926
Operative laborers (number per shift)	—	12[c]	16[d]	27	39
		Data per 1,000 Tons of Rough Rice Input per Year			
Investment cost (U.S. dollars)	0	$8,049	$36,204	$62,956	$120,645
Operative laborers (number)	22.00[f]	12.00	6.40	3.75	1.81
Milled rice output (tons)	570	590	630	650	670
Market price (Rp/kg)	40.0	45.0	48.0	49.5	50.0
Value of output (million Rp)	22.8	26.6	30.2	32.2	33.5
Value added[g] (million Rp)	4.8	8.6	12.2	14.2	15.5
		Data per Rp 10 Million in Value Added per Year			
Investment cost (U.S. dollars)	0	$9,359	$29,675	$44,335	$77,835
Operative laborers (number)	45.83	13.95	5.25	2.64	1.17

[a]The *s* in parentheses indicates that the facility uses sun drying; *m* indicates mechanical drying.

[b]Milling capacity is measured in tons of rough rice input per year, assuming the facility can operate 2,400 hours per year.

[c]The technical and cost data for the small rice mill relate specifically to a locally manufactured flash-type husker with an input capacity of three-quarters of a ton per hour linked to an Engelberg-type polisher with an input capacity of half a ton per hour. A thresher shed and sun-drying pad are provided, but no additional storage capacity. This facility is taken as "representative" of the entire range of small rice milling facilities.

[d]The technical and cost data for the large rice mill relate specifically to a Japanese self-contained milling unit integrated with 756 tons of rough rice storage capacity: 300 tons in bagged storage and 456 tons in upright bulk steel bins. A mechanical dryer with three-quarters ton per hour capacity is provided along with a sun-drying pad. The milling capacity is 1.0 to 1.1 tons per hour of rough rice.

[e]Costs of building and machinery (including a diesel-powered thresher) are included, but not land.

[f]This assumes that one worker hand-pounds about 150 kg of *gabah* (unhusked rice) per day, with a yield of approximately 95 kg of rice.

[g]Value added is calculated assuming a *gabah* cost of Rp 18 per kg, which is above the Rp 16 per kg floor price for "village dry" *gabah* at the mill. The cost (and value added) of reducing the moisture to "mill dry" is included as a mill activity.

input, moisture, variety, by-product rates, and so on, but the average figures shown in table 1 capture the general trend: the larger and more capital-intensive facilities have significantly higher extraction rates. Thus the hand-pounding rate is taken as 57 percent, the small mill rate as 59 percent, the large mill rate as 63 percent, and the small and large bulk facility rates as 65 percent and 67 percent, respectively. As was noted earlier, these differences are not to be taken as strictly due to different milling techniques, but capture the overall impact of the significantly different drying and storage facilities connected with each type of mill.

Apart from the sheer differences in physical output per ton of input, each facility is presumed to produce an output with varying consumer value. Thus one kg of hand-pounded rice sells for only Rp 40, while the output of the large bulk facility is valued at Rp 50 per kg; facilities between these two extremes sell at appropriate values in between, as shown in table 1. Although the different values include some allowance for better by-product retention in the larger facilities, these prices still somewhat overstate the actual market differences that consumers are willing to pay for rice quality per se, as opposed to varietal price differentials, which are substantial. Should these consumer preferences ever be developed, however (or if they were ever imposed by Bulog),[5] the smaller facilities and especially hand-pounding would be at a severe disadvantage.

The overall impact of the physical and monetary conversions is that one thousand tons of rough rice input is transformed into Rp 22.8 million in output by hand-pounding, Rp 26.6 million by small rice mills, Rp 30.2 million by large rice mills, Rp 32.2 million by small bulk facilities, and Rp 33.5 million by the large bulk facilities. That is, the large bulk facilities are able to produce 47 percent more value of output from a given input than hand-pounding and 26 percent more output than the small rice mills. The differences in value added, when Rp 18 million is subtracted from value of output as the cost of the rough rice input, are even more dramatic. The large bulk facility produces more than 200 percent more value added than hand-pounding and almost double the value added from small rice mills. At this stage of the analysis the larger facilities seem to hold a very substantial competitive edge.

The last step required in the construction of a unit isoquant is to calculate the investment cost and numbers of laborers needed to produce a given amount of value added—Rp 10 million in table 1. Since the small rice mill produced only Rp 8.6 million in value added from one thousand tons of rough rice input, it is necessary to increase the investment-cost and number-of-laborers data under that heading by 10/8.6, or 1.16. Thus to produce Rp 10 million in value added, the small rice mill needs $8,049 × 1.16 = $9,359 in investment cost and 12 × 1.16 = 13.95 operative laborers. The calculations for the other facilities are similar, and the results are shown in the last two lines of table 1.

These numbers are the "x, y coordinates" of the desired isoquant, which is drawn in figure 1. Because only five different processing techniques are considered in table 1, the isoquant in figure 1 does not look exactly like the smooth, twice-differentiable isoquants shown in neoclassical production economics textbooks. But the family resemblance is very close. In the linear-segmented world shown in figure 1 smooth tangencies of iso-cost lines to the isoquant must give way to corner tangencies. Thus it is that all three iso-cost lines shown are (corner) tangent at small rice mills. This means that small rice mills are the least-cost facilities for producing value added in rice processing, at least at the wage levels shown in figure 1.

The wage level used to calculate the iso-cost lines was $200 per year, a level used by the *RMS Report* to evaluate their recommendations. The present value of a $200 wage payment each year for fifty years was calculated using three different time rates of discount: 12 percent, 18 percent, and 24 percent. Although it is

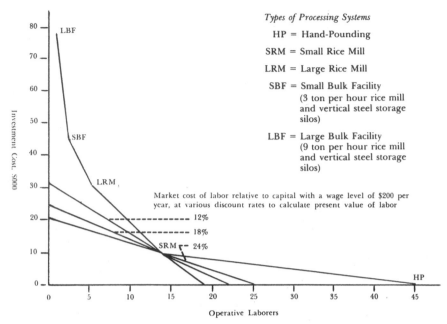

Fig.1. Isoquant Relating Investment Cost and Laborers Needed to Produce Rp 100 Million in Value Added Assuming Rough Rice Costs Rp per kg

always difficult to determine the appropriate social discount rate under any circumstances, investment calculations in rice milling on Java should use something close to the social opportunity cost of capital. Most observers would place this closer to the 24 percent end of the spectrum, with 12 percent clearly reflecting a substantial subsidy. Thus at the opportunity cost of capital—24 percent—a wage of $200 per year has a present value of $833. This means that the slope of the "24 percent" iso-cost line in figure 1 is the same as a line that connects $833 on the Investment Cost axis with one Laborer on the horizontal axis.

Table 2 presents the present values of a range of wage levels discounted at the three different discount rates. The three iso-cost lines drawn in figure 1 (all of them with corner tangencies at SRM) represent the highest assumed wage under consideration. Two other wage levels, not shown in figure 1, are also worth consideration. The $80 wage is close to an actual market wage for unskilled labor for large parts of Java. The $40 wage represents a shadow wage to take account of the high degree of surplus labor on Java, although this may actually be close to a market wage in certain heavily populated rural areas.

The striking effect of discounting to obtain the present value of wages stands out in table 2. The $200 wage for fifty years is a total wage bill of $10,000, but its present value is only $1,661 when discounted at 12 percent per year, the subsidized rate of interest for medium-/long-term investment credits in Indonesia. Using a market interest rate of 24 percent reduces the present value wage

TABLE 2
PRESENT VALUE OF ALTERNATIVE WAGE RATES
($)

Assumed Wage Levels per Year	Discounted Present Value of Wages[a]		
	12% Discount Rate	18% Discount Rate	24% Discount Rate
$200 (RMS)	$1,661	$1,111	$833
$80 (Market)	664	444	333
$40 (Shadow price)	332	222	167

[a]The present worth factor for fifty years is as follows:

Discount Rate (%)	Present Worth Factor
12	8.304
18	5.554
24	4.167

to $833. Market wages ($80) discounted at market interest rates have a present value of $333, while a shadow wage rate equal to half the market wage has a present value of less than $200. Whether one is calculating annual capital charges on a fixed investment or determining the present value of a worker's lifetime earnings, the effect of discounting, the only known way of evaluating future economic events at the present time, is dramatic indeed.

What would the optimal rice processing technique be at the lower market and shadow wage rates? And what happens if the selling price of rice is held constant (by competition or imports) while the price of rough rice paid by the milling facilities increases? Both these questions are answered in table 3, where the maximum present value wage at which each rice processing technique remains optimal for various rough rice prices is shown. Thus for a rough rice price of Rp 18 per kg (the value used to construct the isoquant in table 1 and figure 1), hand-pounding is the optimal technique until the present value wage exceeds $294; small rice mills are optimal from a present value wage of $295 to $2,335, beyond which large rice mills, small bulk facilities, and ultimately large bulk facilities become optimal.

Similarly, the maximum present value wage a facility can afford and still remain optimal declines as the rough rice price increases. At a price of Rp 18 per kg for rough rice the small rice mill can pay up to $2,335, but at Rp 20 per kg it can pay only $1,956. At a price of Rp 26 per kg the mill would have to be subsidized to remain optimal; that is, it would have to receive $260 per worker (for his lifetime services). At Rp 28 per kg the small rice mill actually produces a negative value added—its output sells for less than the cost of its rough rice input. No subsidy can make the firm optimal, although obviously a large enough subsidy would permit the small rice mill to survive (but never to produce a positive value added).

TABLE 3
MAXIMUM PRESENT VALUES OF WAGE RATES THAT YIELD CORNER TANGENCIES
TO THE ISOQUANT

	Maximum Present Value Wage at Which the Indicated Facility is Optimal for Various Rough Rice Prices Rp/kg					
Corner Solution at	18	20	22	24	26	28
Hand-pounding (HP)	294	202	70	*a*	*a*	*a*
Small rice mills (SRM)	2,335	1,956	1,457	766	−260	*a*
Large rice mills (LRM)	5,617	5,034	4,265	3,197	1,699	−728
Small bulk facilities (SBF)	22,789	21,829	20,468	18,879	16,296	12,316
Large bulk facilities (LBF)[b]	greater than the value shown for SBF					

[a]Negative value added.

[b]Just for comparison, it is worth noting that the discounted present value of $6,000 per year at 8 percent is $73,400. Thus the relative capital intensity of even the large bulk facilities (LBF) is low by U.S. standards.

The interesting comparisons are between the various present value wages of table 2 and the maximum wages that yield optimum solutions in table 3. At either $200 per year or the market wage of $80 per year, for all three discount rates, the small rice mills remain the optimal rice processing facility at normal rough rice prices. When the price reaches Rp 24 per kg, the large rice mills are optimal at the highest wage for all three discount rates. The small bulk facilities only enter the picture when the rough rice price reaches Rp 28 per kg, so high that the small rice mills yield negative value added. This situation could only come about by full "modernization" of Indonesia's entire rice processing system or a rigidly enforced price policy that used imports to control retail price and large-scale facilities (or large subsidies to smaller mills) in connection with a vigorous floor price. The general point ought to be clear, however: in a squeeze between rough rice and milled rice prices only the technically more efficient facilities can survive.

It is not hard to see, then, the reasons why few large rice mills (or bulk facilities) have been installed in recent years in Indonesia. Where market forces—low wages, high interest rates, and cheap rice prices—have been allowed to work, the overwhelming superiority of small rice mills as a generic class has been apparent to investors, and these facilities have indeed mushroomed throughout Java. Some large mills have been built, but they have been either government- or army-sponsored (where market forces are little felt in the decision making) or close to cities, where wage rates are higher than in rural areas, rough rice prices relatively higher, and when investment capital at 12 percent was available. Under these circumstances investment in the larger rice mills is understandable, though it may not be socially desirable.

At the other end of the spectrum, the economies of hand-pounding are fascinating. If market wages of about $80 per year (say Rp 100 to Rp 150 per day) must be paid, hand-pounding is not optimal unless the discount rate is greater than 24 percent or unless the *gabah* price falls below Rp 16 per kg (at the same time that the retail price is Rp 40 for the end product). So it is not hard to see why hand-pounding has virtually disappeared from Java as a cash-hire activity. And yet it is still frequently profitable for the farmer or his family to hand-pound their rice for home consumption if the perceived opportunity cost of the labor spent is not great. For example, hand-pounding is economically optimal (despite the very large losses that are assumed) if the wage rate is $40 per year and is discounted at 18 percent or higher, at least for rough rice prices less than Rp 20 per kg, as they are likely to be in many rural areas. And in fact, of course, some rural families still do hand-pound their rice.

The evidence from the countryside, which showed literally thousands of small rice mills installed on Java in the past three years, is thus strongly corroborated by the economic analysis. Only at the extremes of economic conditions existing in Indonesia could hand-pounding or large rice mills be explained. The small rice mills were shown to be socially and privately optimal over a wide range of circumstances in between. There are exceptions to be sure: exporting rice would require facilities not optimal in this analysis, and Bulog may have some special needs that are not fully met by all small rice mills. But in total this is a good example of where "getting prices right" has helped the development effort at minimal cost and effort to the scarce planning manpower in the government. Not all development problems are so easy, of course, but some are made harder by inappropriate pricing policies. Indonesia's rice processing sector still faces some difficult problems, especially with regard to drying and storage. But milling has been largely removed as a constraint.

EMPLOYMENT IN RICE MILLING

The employment potential of the entire rice economy—production, harvesting, processing, transporting, storing, selling—is enormous. Rice marketing, defined broadly, is only part of this potential, and rice processing but part of this part. Still, the total employment figures must be large indeed. No reliable survey data are available to serve as a reference here, but table 4 provides a rough point of departure for discussion.

The intent of table 4 is to work backward from the input/output micro data used to generate the isoquant to an overall estimate of the number of workers needed to process the entire 1971 rice crop, assuming only a single technique were used. This is obviously an artificial number. But somewhere within the range of the 399,000 full-time workers needed to hand-pound the crop to only 33,000 workers needed if large bulk facilities were used lies the actual full-time employment potential. (If work sharing is pervasive, the numbers actually earning a livelihood in rice processing could be much larger.) It is interesting that each technique employs roughly double the number of workers of the next most

TABLE 4
EMPLOYMENT AND INVESTMENT IN RICE PROCESSING IN 1971 USING
ALTERNATIVE MILLING TECHNIQUES

| | *Inputs* | | | |
| | Per 1,000 Tons of Rough Rice | | For 1971 Harvest[a] | |
Milling Technique	Investment Cost ($)	Operatives (Number)	Investment Cost ($m)	Operatives (Thousands)
Hand-pounding (HP)	$ 0	22.00	0	399[b]
Small rice mills (SRM)	8,049	12.00	146	217
Large rice mills (LRM)	36,204	6.40	656	116
Small bulk facilities (SBF)	62,956	3.75	1,141	68
Large bulk facilities (LBF)	120,645	1.81	2,186	33

SOURCE: Calculated from table 1.

[a]For each technique, the figure shows the investment and employment required to process the 1971 rice crop of 18.123 million tons of rough rice, assuming that particular technique is the only one utilized. Obviously this shows alternative hypothetical magnitudes only, and none of the figures should be interpreted as representing actual employment levels in rice milling.

[b]This is the full-time equivalent required for hand-pounding. More than 399,000 laborers would be needed if hand-pounding were done only part-time.

capital-intensive technique. This is simply a repeated and forceful demonstration that this particular part of the economic system does not exhibit fixed technical relationships between capital and labor. Indeed, the "wrong" choice of technique, whether by government decision directly or by private investors reacting to inappropriate price signals, can easily cost many thousands, in fact, hundreds of thousands, of jobs. The choice between small and large rice mills depended very much on the government's interest rate policy, its rice price policy, and unskilled wage levels. Given that a dramatic transformation to mechanized rice processing had been occurring at private initiative in Indonesia in the past few years, the country was fortunate indeed to have those critical policies more or less in order.

As recently as 1971 it was assumed that as much as 80 percent of Java's rice crop was hand-pounded. Although hand-pounding has certainly not been eliminated over the past few years, the evidence does suggest that it no longer accounts for more than perhaps 20 percent of the crop, at least in Java. Upwards of 100,000 jobs have probably been lost (at least jobs in the sense of an opportunity cost income—the "return" to milling is no longer captured by the family but by the miller). This loss of jobs should be kept in perspective, however. The farmer having his rice milled is frequently one of the laborers in the small rice mill, thus capturing part of the milling cost for his family. In addition, little cash income has been forgone, and the small rice mills are frequently so much more technically efficient that the farmer appears to go home with more rice than if he had hand-pounded it. (But since the farmer ate the bran if the rice were hand-pounded, whereas the miller keeps it for himself, this is probably not usually the case.) Lastly, hand-pounding is drudgery, and the people obviously welcome its demise.

SUMMARY

Two main points have been presented in this paper. The first is that economic analysis shows labor-intensive (but mechanical) rice processing facilities to dominate both hand-pounding and more capital-intensive techniques. And this is a result amply confirmed by recent evidence on actual investments in rice processing facilities in the countryside. A second, more general point is that the employment effects of the choice of technique decision are not trivial and are critically dependent on parameters directly subject to government control. "Getting prices right" is not the end of economic development. But "getting prices wrong" frequently is.

NOTES

1. Anonymous, "Report from the Agricultural Credit Specialist" (1972); "Rice Processing in Java" (Manila: Asian Development Bank, August 1972), cited hereafter as ADB, *Rice Processing Report*.

2. Weitz-Hettelsater Engineers, "Rice Storage, Handling, and Marketing Study: Economics and Engineering Aspects" (Kansas City, Mo., 1972). The final draft was submitted to the Republic of Indonesia in December 1972. This report is referred to in this article as Rice Marketing Study (RMS).

3. C. Peter Timmer, "Employment Aspects of Investment in Rice Marketing in Indonesia," *Food Research Institute Studies in Agricultural Economics, Trade, and Development* 11, no. 1 (1972); and idem, "Choice of Technique in Indonesia" (Cambridge: Harvard Center for International Affairs, Occasional Papers, 1973).

4. Ibid.

5. Bulog is the Indonesian state food logistics agency.—ED.

A Comment

WILLIAM L. COLLIER, JUSUF COLTER, SINARHADI,
AND ROBERT D'A. SHAW

Over the past few years, nothing short of a revolution has occurred in the process of rice cultivation in Java. Probably one of the most rapid and widespread changes of all has been the displacement of traditional hand-pounding techniques by rice hullers. Perhaps the most interesting and widely debated aspect of these changes is the distribution of the benefits arising from them. Dr. Timmer implied that villagers in general welcome the demise of hand-pounding, since those engaged in the activity gained little income from it. Recent information suggests that this proposition is not tenable. It appears that Dr. Timmer's estimate of the number of jobs lost is far too low. More important in terms of rural poverty, he has failed to give sufficient weight to the large number of women who, prior to the introduction of hullers, gained a sufficient share of their income from hand-pounding. Moreover, it seems that Dr. Timmer overestimated the amount of employment created by rice hullers.

These differences are very important when they are considered in the aggregate. While Dr. Timmer thinks that "upwards of 100,000 jobs" may have been destroyed, our estimate using the same assumptions is much higher. Of even greater consequence is our estimate that earnings of laborers engaged in hand-pounding of rice on Java may have been reduced by as much as $50 million annually. Most of those losing work and sources of income from hand-pounding are likely to be members of the poorest families in the rural areas, those with little or no access to land. Thus the spread of rice hullers has, in our opinion, probably worsened the distribution of income in a substantial way.

These opinions are based on surveys carried out in twelve villages in Java by the Agro-Economic Survey in August and September 1973. Approximately four hundred farmers, laborers, village leaders, and owners of rice hullers were interviewed in these surveys of rural change in rice production. The interviews included information about hand-pounding and mechanical hulling. The material is supplemented by some additional information from eight other villages in the Agro-Economic Survey sample that were surveyed earlier in 1973.

WILLIAM L. COLLIER, JUSUF COLTER, and SINARHADI are agricultural economists in Bogor, Indonesia. ROBERT D'A. SHAW is director of special programs, Aga Khan Foundation.

Even though we believe that more of the total rice crop on Java is still being hand-pounded than is indicated in Dr. Timmer's model, this factor is more than compensated for by his overestimation of the amount of rice that can be hand-pounded per day. The actual amounts hand-pounded per day and per hour by workers in our sample villages vary from 12.5 kg to 50.0 kg of *padi* per day. Much of the variation is accounted for by the number of hours worked by each woman. Usually this is five to six hours per day, but in those villages where women undertake contracts for hand-pounding it stretches up to an amazing thirteen hours per day. Thus the average weight of *padi* pounded per hour per person was 5.0 kg, with the range varying from 3.1 to 7.8 kg. This average translates into 3.9 kg of *gabah* per hour and 2.4 kg of *beras* (milled rice) per hour.

Dr. Timmer, however, used an estimate of 150 kg of *gabah* per day. If we assume that he was using a working day of eight hours, this converts to 18.7 kg of *gabah,* or nearly 12 kg of *beras* per hour. Since this is about five times the figure found in our survey, it seems clear that his estimate has little empirical basis.

However, Dr. Timmer's models have additional problems. In the first place, while the title of his article and his coefficients apply to Java alone, Timmer's employment estimates are made on the basis of the total Indonesian rice crop. Information about the rice processing situation outside Java is, in fact, conspicuously inadequate. At the same time, it is probably fair to assume that the greater availability of employment in the other islands makes this technological change less important in terms of human welfare. We will therefore limit our estimates on the impact of mechanical hulling to Java, where nearly two-thirds of the population of Indonesia live and approximately one-half of the country's rice is produced.

Moreover, within Java, Dr. Timmer's estimates for the employment and income effects of hullers would seem to be misleading in the following important ways:

(1) His estimate of the percentage still hand-pounded is probably too low—20 percent against our estimate of 40 percent.
(2) While the above mitigates the unemployment resulting from the use of hullers, this is more than offset by our findings that he used estimates of the hand-pounding capacity of women that seem to be five times too high.
(3) The importance of wage labor in hand-pounding was almost entirely neglected by Dr. Timmer. In our estimate, this may have involved half the total crop on Java.
(4) Lastly, Dr. Timmer may have exaggerated the employment created by hullers by a factor of two.

Let us now take a schematic look at these changes to give an indication of the orders of magnitude of their importance on Java. For this purpose, we shall use a figure of 12 million tons of milled (*gabah*) rice for the total Indonesian rice crop.[1] Typically, half of the total is produced in Java—a total of 6 million tons in our example. If we further assume that 50 percent of this would have been hand-pounded by wage laborers in the absence of hullers, this amounts to 3 million tons that would have created wage employment. Let us now postulate conservatively that one woman can hand-pound enough *gabah* in an hour to obtain 3 kg of *beras* (cf. our estimate of 2.4 kg). To hand-pound 3 million tons would take 1 billion woman-hours, or 125 million woman-days. At a wage of Rp 180 per day, this amounts to earnings of Rp 22.5 billion in a year, or just under $55 million.

To estimate the earnings of employees in SRM hulling this amount, if we assume that one SRM can hull 1,000 tons of *gabah* per year (or approximately 620 tons of *beras*), then to obtain 3 million tons of *beras* requires nearly 5,000 SRM. At an average wage bill of $80 per month, the annual earnings of laborers in these SRM would be just under $5 million.

Thus the total loss in laborers' earnings attributable to the introduction of hullers seems to be of the order of $50 million annually in Java, where the cash incomes of the rural poor are exceedingly low and where the possibilities of alternative employment opportunities are often slight. This represents a substantial diminution of income for large numbers of households of landless laborers and small farmers. Three million tons of rice could provide wages for one million women every day for four months each year.

The beneficiaries of the new technology are those farmers who would otherwise have hired laborers to pound their rice, the huller operators and the buyers of rice, to whom prices of milled rice may be around Rp 5 per kg lower than those that would have prevailed if hand-pounding had remained in force.[2] The losers, on the other hand, are those wives of small farmers and landless laborers who gain additional income from hand-pounding. These are the people who can least afford such a drop in income, as the number of alternative work opportunities is so limited.

The major conclusion we draw from this rough approximation of the impact of the introduction of hullers is that this redistribution of income in favor of relatively large farmers and SRM operators requires, as an urgent matter of public policy, massive programs to create additional income opportunities for the rural disadvantaged. In contrast to our estimate of 125 million woman-days of wage labor lost in Java, the *kabupaten* public works program in 1972–73 provided 43.6 million man-days of employment throughout Indonesia. This program is an excellent start but clearly inadequate to meet the needs.

NOTES

1. The actual total for 1971–72 was estimated at 12.8 million tons.
2. Whether such potential savings have in fact been passed on to rice buyers is impossible to determine because of the very rapid rise in rice prices over the last two years for other reasons.

A Reply

C. PETER TIMMER

Everyone stands in debt to Messrs. Collier, Colter, Sinarhadi, and Shaw (hence-forth acronymized in good Indonesian fashion as CCSS) for providing a substan-tial body of empirical material dealing with the impact of changing technology in rice milling. I am especially pleased to have some firm evidence on the technical coefficients for hand-pounding. This was a topic of so little concern to the Weitz-Hettelsater Rice Marketing Study[1] that hand-pounding was completely ignored in its report. The coefficient of forty workers per one thousand tons of *gabah* per year used in its final report was picked up from a draft of my first paper on this topic. Since I relied on that document for the great bulk of my technical and cost data, I am not surprised to find that the crude estimates were fairly far off the mark.

Granting this, however, it is important not to lose sight of the meaning and impact of the new numbers provided. The first issue is how they affect the economic analysis of the choice of technique; the second issue is their impact on a social analysis of the economic results. For space reasons, my article does not deal at all with the relationship between an economic analysis and a social analysis, but my earlier article on "Employment Aspects of Investment in Rice Marketing in Indonesia"[2] provided a framework for comparing these two view-points (and others). An economic analysis can be done with either market prices or shadow prices. The shadow price analysis results in the largest national income possible when all prices are taken at their social rather than their private values (and this should include distributional and employment considerations). A social analysis carries the concern for unemployment and an unfavorable dis-tribution of income into the political sphere, with the possible (but not inevitable) result that measures taken to relieve unemployment in specific situations would actually have an adverse impact on social equity for the entire economy and society. Only the economic perspective (with both market and shadow prices) is presented in this article, with the exception of the short section on employment impact. It is on this section that CCSS focus their comments, but the data have significant implications for the economic analysis as well.

Picking even the most optimistic figures about hand-pounding productivity and hours worked from the CCSS data, it is evident that the coefficient I used in the choice of technique analysis was off by a minimum of a factor of two and perhaps on average by a factor of four or five. That is, hand-pounding is at most only one-half as productive as I assumed and probably less. The bias I built into the analysis was in favor of hand-pounding entering the tableau of optimal economic activities under a realistic set of circumstances, and, of course, that was one of the striking results of the analysis. Even with the high productivity of hand-pounding that I assumed, it did not become optimal under any set of market price conditions on Java, but it still seemed to make economic sense for farm families (and harvesters) to hand-pound for their own consumption if their opportunity labor costs were below the market wage rate.

The new data provided by CCSS dash this economic rationality completely. Hand-pounding makes sense only when the opportunity wage is virtually zero and not even then if there is any significant squeeze between *padi* prices and milled rice prices. Hand-pounding quickly succumbs to negative value added in such a price squeeze (perhaps caused by a too narrow range between the floor and ceiling prices, which is defended by large-scale imports) because of its technical inefficiency. It is important that we understand this result. From an economic viewpoint, hand-pounding is shown by the CCSS data to be a completely inappropriate technique under present market conditions on Java and would make sense only if labor were shadow priced at a near zero wage (and the government paid the difference between this level and the market wage) and the shadow value of rice were well below present market prices (and the government could afford this subsidy as well).

Having just argued that the only significant effect of the CCSS data is to make hand-pounding nearly impossible to justify on economic grounds, I do agree with the major thrust of the social concern demonstrated by the authors. The distribution impact of the SRM has been higher incomes for large farmers and for operators of the SRM, but at the expense of the poor village women who have lost a source of case income and are now pressing into the harvest labor forces, with serious economic and social consequences. I fully accept the conclusions of CCSS with respect to lost cash income potential of village women. Their numbers without doubt more correctly assess the impact here than my own, based as they were on very rough estimates. But even as early as 1971 hand-pounding as a cash-hire activity was a rapidly vanishing phenomenon. My whole perspective on this particular issue was colored by this *fait accompli*. In historical terms the loss of cash wages by the poor women villagers is important, but it had little immediate bearing on the policy issue directly before the government, namely, Would Indonesia be best served by investment in large bulk facilities for drying, milling, and storing rice? We should all be very thankful to CCSS for redirecting our attention to the neglected social issue now that the immediate policy issue has been resolved. Their pleas for a vastly expanded rural works program will be met with enthusiasm by all whose consciences are moved by the plight of the rural (and urban) poor in Indonesia.

This brings us to the other side of the distributional impact of the new milling technology. Rice prices to consumers are perhaps "Rp 5 per kg lower than those that would have prevailed if hand-pounding had remained in force" (CCSS). As CCSS point out, it is hard to tell, with rice prices in such turmoil over the past few years, whether these cost reductions have actually been passed on to the consumer, but let us work with this magnitude and examine its implications. Do lower consumer prices for rice for a given farm price hurt income distribution or help it? I would argue that a Rp 5 per kg reduction in consumer rice price while farm prices are held constant has an enormous welfare impact on the lower half or two-thirds of the income distribution. The magnitudes are just as impressive as the $50 million quoted by CCSS as wage losses to the rural poor. A Rp 5 per kg cost saving to the new technology applied to a 13-million-ton rice crop gives a resulting saving to consumers of $165 million. Even if only half of this benefits the lower half of the population—a very conservative assumption—its gain exceeds $80 million.

We must also put in the balance the greater outturn of rice from a given volume of *gabah* achieved by the machine technology. The new data on extraction rates provided by CCSS raise the savings to truly important proportions. The difference between 57 percent extraction for hand-pounding and 66 percent for the SRM on average is 9 percent. For a *gabah* crop of 18 million tons a milling industry composed entirely of SRM would yield *over one and a half million tons more milled rice* than if the crop were hand-pounded. At a very conservative price of $200 per ton this is an added value to society of more than $300 million. Again, the exact distributional nature of this gain is not clear, but it is hard to see how the unemployed women are made worse off by this aspect of the technological change.

Losing the efficiency gains by banning small rice mills (thus forcing a return to hand-pounding) would be an enormously costly way of helping the displaced women whose primary source of wages during the harvest has been removed. We must set the $50 million loss to these women against a gain to society of more than $450 million, and some of that gain accrues to these very same women, although not a sufficient amount to offset their losses. But surely with the comprehensive and statistically documented picture presented by CCSS to create awareness of the problem, a mechanism can be found that would redistribute 10–15 percent of the social gain to the private losers.[3]

Lastly, I should like to enter a confession. I started this entire area of research with the intention of demonstrating in simple, clear-cut terms that both economic planners and engineering consultants would understand that the large-scale rice mills and bulk silo terminals were inappropriate in the Indonesian countryside. The battle to be fought in the planning agency was not hand-pounding versus small rice mills but large bulk facilities versus small rice mills. I was nearly laughed out of court for defending the small rice mills, but the analysis spoke for itself and still does. In terms of prevailing market prices and any imaginable modification of them (including reasonable shadow prices), facilities in the generic class "small rice mills" are the most appropriate for Indonesia.

NOTES

1. Weitz-Hettelsater Engineers, "Rice Storage, Handling, and Marketing Study: Economics and Engineering Aspects" (Kansas City, Mo., 1972).

2. Timmer, "Employment Aspects of Investment in Rice Marketing in Indonesia," *Food Research Institute Studies in Agricultural Economics, Trade, and Development* 11, no. 1 (1972).

3. Another distributional issue that neither CCSS nor I have treated is nutrition. The primary source of the B-vitamin complex for the poorer half of the population is the bran left on hand-pounded rice. A complete shift to the white rice made possible by well-operated small rice mills could easily result in serious vitamin deficiencies that could be offset only by a fairly expensive vitamin fortification program. I have no way of knowing how these costs would compare with the gains already cited nor with the wage losses cited by CCSS.

V

Lessons from Economies in Transition

Introduction

Modern development economics is now fifty years old. Looking back through the lens of history, one can conclude that much has been learned about the development process. One key lesson is the critical role of increasing the productivity of the food system, which reduces the relative size of the agricultural sector and drives down the real cost of food over time (Staatz 1994).

Despite decades of research by social and technical scientists, however, many puzzles about development remain. Douglass North recently sifted through the literature on the transition experience and concluded that "a good deal is known about the underlying characteristics of both the developed economies and rapidly developing economies. What is not known is how to get there" (North 1997, 413). He suggested that the proper study of economic history can help economists better understand "the making of economic policy in a world of dynamic change." Adelman and Morris recently concluded that the heterogeneity found among the almost two hundred nations in the world calls for policy analysts to "take full cognizance of the historical and situational relativism of the multifaceted nature of the development process" (Adelman and Morris 1997). In practice, this means striking a balance between learning from the experience of other countries and devoting attention to the uniqueness of each country when tailoring policies and institutions to a country's individual conditions and economic history.

Part V presents five case studies aimed at achieving this balance. The studies stress how policies, technologies, and institutions have interacted in specific settings around the world to affect the pattern of agricultural and economic development, particularly as countries have gone through the turbulent economic transitions of the 1980s and 1990s. In many cases, the stories told are specific to particular settings. Broader lessons also emerge, such as the importance of keeping a reasonable alignment between domestic incentives and international opportunity costs, the payoffs to investing in domestic scientific and policy analysis capacity, and the path-dependent nature of institutional change. The chapters in part V illustrate how many of the concepts discussed earlier in the book play out in specific country settings and how they interact with one another.

We begin part V with an original paper by Justin Lin (chapter 31) on China's agricultural development and reform experience since 1979. China's transition experience is of interest to agricultural development specialists for three reasons.

First, because it is the world's most populous nation, what happens in China has an enormous impact on human welfare, both within China and, through trade and investment links, in the broader world. Understanding what has been happening in China is central to understanding a major part of what is happening in economic transformation throughout the world. Second, since 1979 China has sustained very rapid agricultural and economic growth,[1] which has affected the broader world economy. This raises the question of what lessons other countries might learn from China's experience. In particular, China's incremental policy reform, begun in 1979, has been more successful than the shock therapy approach pursued in the former Soviet Union in the 1990s. Third, there is concern over whether China's rapid growth in food demand and food imports will threaten global food reserves.

Chinese agrarian reform from 1949 to 1998 can be divided into three periods: (1) the 1949–58 postindependence reform period, culminating in the introduction of communal farming in 1958 and the adoption of the heavy industry–oriented development strategy; (2) the communal farm era, which lasted twenty years, 1958–78; and (3) the period of rural reforms and liberalization since 1979. China's agricultural development experience has been dominated by rapid agricultural growth from 1979 to 1985, stagnant grain production from 1985 through 1989, and respectable agricultural growth since 1990 (Lin, Cai, and Li 1996).

In chapter 31, Lin analyzes how China has addressed three critical reform issues since 1979: evolution of the household responsibility system, experimentation with alternative land-tenure systems to achieve both food production and equity goals, and grain marketing reforms, including the movement towards a more market-driven agriculture. Lin's analysis illustrates some of the points raised earlier in this book: the limits on the ability of compulsory grain procurement to gain control over the grain supply and to meet the demand of urban residents for low-cost grain, the constraints imposed on agricultural pricing reforms when the government feels compelled to maintain a high level of consumer subsidies, the need to structure the land-tenure and marketing systems in a way that creates incentives both to produce in the short run and invest over the long run, and the impact of agriculture on other sectors through intersectoral linkages. For example, Lin points out that while the commune system was effective in mobilizing large amounts of labor for infrastructure development, it limited farmers' individual incentives to produce.

The shift to the household responsibility system in 1979 increased farmers' incentives and sharply reduced the problem of monitoring agricultural labor. In order to encourage farmers to invest in land productivity improvements, the government recently allowed land contracts to be extended by up to thirty years. Lin stresses the powerful role of institutional innovations such as the household responsibility system in increasing incentives to farmers, which contributed to a doubling of the annual rate of growth of grain production between the periods of 1953–78 and 1979–84.

Currently China is experimenting with grain policy reforms, including a re-examination of its goal of national food self-sufficiency. Lin rejects Lester Brown's pessimistic food scenario and argues that China has the potential to feed itself in the twenty-first century and that China's welfare would improve if it pulled back from a policy of grain self-sufficiency and allowed a gradual increase in food imports, especially wheat. Lin's analysis is consistent with an assessment by the International Food Policy Research Institute that "China will never empty the world grain markets nor become a major grain exporter" (Huang, Rozelle, and Rosegrant 1997, 17).

In chapter 32, Peter Timmer points out that "rapid economic growth was invented in East Asia." It took 115 years for Great Britain to double its per capita income during the first Industrial Revolution, while it only took South Korea 11 years and China a decade. But rapid economic growth in East Asia was not foreseen in the standard development textbooks some thirty years ago. For example, Gunnar Myrdal, anthropologist Clifford Geertz, and many other specialists on Asian development were uniformly pessimistic in the 1960s about Indonesia's prospects for peasant farming and economic progress. But Indonesia's economy grew, on average, more than 6 percent a year starting in 1970, and by 1995 it had achieved the status of a lower-middle-income country, with a per capita GDP of around $1,000, an adult literacy rate of 84 percent, and a life expectancy of 64 years (World Bank 1997).

When President Suharto, son of a Javanese rice farmer, assumed power in 1968, he placed investment in agriculture and rural infrastructure at the center of Indonesia's new development model. Timmer discusses how the combination of agricultural policies (financed in part through prudent reinvestment of oil revenues) and new rice varieties increased food production and the growth of the rural economy. Getting agriculture moving contributed to economic growth and reduced rural poverty. It took Indonesia sixteen years (1968–84) to move from the world's biggest rice importer to rice self-sufficiency. While Indonesia's growth from the late 1960s through the late 1990s was very impressive, the financial crisis of 1997 and 1998 illustrates how the loss of investor confidence can lead to political change in a world where capital is highly mobile. This confidence is very sensitive to the rules governing financial markets, foreign investment, and international trade.

Chapter 33 addresses the food production challenge in Africa. On the eve of independence in the mid-fifties, there were forty-five colonies and two independent nations (Ethiopia and Liberia) in sub-Saharan Africa. Political independence was launched in Africa on a grand scale in 1960 when seventeen colonies won their independence. Others followed, and by 1995 all forty-seven nations on the subcontinent were free of colonial rule. In 1960, Africa had a booming agricultural export sector and it was a modest net exporter of food. Buoyed by these favorable initial conditions and the removal of the colonial shackles, most leaders of new nations were optimistic that Africa could "catch up" with industrial nations by the year 2000.

But in Africa today the air is heavy with disappointment. Africa is the poorest part of the global economy and hostage to a chronic food bottleneck. In four decades of independence, much has been learned about the complexity and diversity of African agriculture, the motivation of farmers, weather patterns, and the use and misuse of foreign aid. There are literally thousands of evaluations of ill-fated agricultural strategies and projects, including many imported models, such as state farms from Russia, communal farms from China, and Moshav farm settlements from Israel.[2]

Bad weather and the alleged lack of economic motivation of African farmers, however, are not the causes of Africa's food crisis. Studies have shown that when African farmers have access to incentives, technology, support services, and markets, they have proven to be just as calculating money managers as farmers in Iowa or in the rice bowl of Asia (Jones 1960). Weather can be ruled out as a cause of Africa's *chronic* food gap, because annual food production grew at only half the rate of population from 1970 to 1985, proving that drought for a year or two was not the cause of the long-term agricultural stagnation.

After the failure of state farms, farm settlements, Ujamaa (communal) farms, and integrated rural development projects in the sixties and seventies, attention turned in the early eighties to poor economic policies as the cause of agrarian stagnation. A 1981 World Bank study led by Elliot Berg argued that the fundamental cause of Africa's economic stagnation was bad domestic policies, including overvalued exchange rates, heavy taxation, and money-losing state industries (World Bank 1981). Basically, the Berg report argued that internal factors were the cause of Africa's economic malaise. The African response to Berg was quick and vehement; it charged that external policies of industrial nations were the causes of Africa's development crisis (Amin 1982; Adedeji and Shaw 1985).

The Berg report provided the rationale for IMF and World Bank loans and grants to help African governments carry out structural adjustment programs by redesigning their policies, reducing the size of government bureaucracies and subsidies to industries, and correcting the bias against agriculture in price, tax, and exchange-rate policies. Despite a spate of Bank studies of the "success" of structural adjustment programs over the past fifteen years, the overall record is mixed. One fatal error of the 1981 Berg report was the promise that policy "distortions" could be corrected in a few years and that "real gains could be achieved" in both development and incomes "in the near future" (World Bank 1981, 133). But the events of history have shown that removing subsidies and redesigning economic policies are long-term and unpredictable processes, and that even if new policy regimes were put in place, policies by themselves could not quickly slay the dragons of economic stagnation and poverty.

Africa's structural adjustment experience has humbled the World Bank. The juxtaposition of the dreams of the Berg report and the reality of Africa's development experience in the 1980s and 1990s helps explain why the World Bank recently declared that effective institutions matter as much as sensible policies in development (World Bank 1997). The second round of structural adjustment lending is now being broadened to include institutional reform, rebuilding of human capital, fiscal decentralization, and broader participation of civil society in the economy. Africa's transition from a controlled to a more open and market-oriented approach to managing economies requires a new research agenda to addressing the gaps in economic research (Smith 1995; Ndulu 1997).

Today, Africa's food crisis is the most challenging problem in the world for agriculturalists. Since two-thirds of the people in Africa are dependent on agriculture and the rural economy for their livelihood, it follows that "getting agriculture moving" is high on the policy agenda. But instead of turning to Asia for lessons, increasingly Africans are looking inward for ideas on increasing agricultural productivity.

Maize has recently replaced cassava as Africa's most important food crop (Byerlee and Eicher 1997). In chapter 33, Carl Eicher and Bernard Kupfuma distill the lessons of Zimbabwe's success in increasing maize production. Zimbabwe's maize revolution was spearheaded by the release of a high-yielding hybrid maize variety in 1960, five years before the Green Revolution was launched in India in the mid-sixties. The authors analyze the key factors in Zimbabwe's qualified success story and outline four generic lessons for closing Africa's food gap.

In response to the 1982 debt crisis, many Latin American countries initiated a period of extraordinary reform and change.[3] Although some economists, such as Edwards (1995) report that the reforms have been a success in countries such as Chile, others (Morley 1997; Green 1995; Huddle 1997) have decried the high level of inequality and poverty and the "dangerous" levels of unemployment that have accompanied the policy reforms in Bolivia, Costa Rica, Argentina, and Mexico. Two economists in the Inter-American Development Bank report that the number of poor in Latin America nearly doubled during the 1980s, increasing from about 80 million to almost 150 million and that the recent economic recovery has not made a dent in Latin American poverty (Birdsall and Londoño 1997). Also, there is great inequality in Latin America in the distribution of assets, such as land, and in access to education and loans, and this inequality has worsened after the reforms (Huddle 1997, 882).

To be sure, reform optimists such as Edwards showcase Chile's achievement of a 6.1 percent average growth in GNP per capita from 1985 to 1995 as the mark of what can be achieved under the "free market—free trade" paradigm, but many Latin American specialists urge caution in generalizing about Latin America's aggregate growth rates in terms of the impact on the poor and about the ability to replicate Chile's "success story." De Janvry, Key and Sadoulet (1997) argue that while macroeconomic reforms have generated many important results, the region is plagued with market failures, institutional gaps, and pervasive rural poverty. They argue that agricultural policy is now treated as an appendage of macroeconomic policy and that "bold new initiatives" are required "to improve the production performance of agriculture, reduce rural poverty, and ensure the political sustainability of economic growth" (33).

In chapter 34, Alain de Janvry and Elisabeth Sadoulet use Colombia as a case study to illustrate the asset inequalities in agriculture in the region and examine the reasons why fifty-three years of agrarian reforms there have been unsuccessful. They argue that agricultural policy in Colombia should consist of two complementary activities. First, it should eliminate the big subsidies going to large farms. These subsidies block any hope of land redistribution, by reducing incentives of large farmers to sell their land and by raising land values above the levels that small-scale farmers or the landless could ever hope to repay. Second, a redistributive land reform needs to be accompanied by a complementary rural development strategy. That strategy should aim at increasing small-scale farmers' and rural industries' access to the financial services, information, and the input and output markets needed to make the land reform succeed.

Chapter 35 turns to the dramatic but variable speed of the move to market-oriented economies in Central and Eastern Europe.[4] Johan Swinnen examines agricultural reform in nine Central and Eastern European countries (CEECs). Poland took the lead in 1989, liberalizing most of its agricultural and food prices. Swinnen points out the variability in resource endowments and the speed of the transition.[5] High transaction costs, and the lack of stable property rights are impeding land redistribution. Most of the nine CEECs have a melange of family farms, "private" cooperative farms, joint-stock companies, and part-time farmers. Swinnen contends that it is unclear which type(s) of farm production models will survive in the long run. The liberalization process should be viewed as a work in progress. As suggested by the concept of path dependency, the choice of policy reforms and the impact of the reforms will differ substantially between countries. The experience will undoubtedly yield new insights into the relationships between institutional structure and agricultural development.

NOTES

1. Between 1980 and 1995, following the breakup of the communal farming system in 1978, tiny farms, averaging one acre in size, generated the highest rate of agricultural growth in the world. Likewise, China's annual rate of growth of per capita GDP was the second highest (8.3 percent) in the world from 1985 to 1995 (World Bank 1997, 234).

2. For an assessment of Africa's agricultural development experience since 1960, see de Wilde et al. 1967; Food and Agriculture Organization 1978; Mellor, Delgado, and Blackie 1987; Staatz and Wohl 1991; Eicher and Baker 1992; Delgado 1995; Sanders, Shapiro and Ramaswamy 1996. See Please 1996 for a review of four studies of structural adjustment.

3. See de Janvry and Sadoulet 1993, Edwards 1995, Green 1995, and Huddle 1997 for a discussion of policy changes in the 1980s and 1990s, and Schuh and Brandão 1992 for an extensive review of the literature on agricultural economics research from 1960 to 1990. See Birdsall and Jasperson 1997 for a comparison of East Asian and Latin American growth experiences.

4. For a historical record of the sixty years of Soviet agriculture from Stalin in 1929 to Gorbachev's adoption of the family farm, see Brooks 1990. For a progress report on Russia's food economy in transition, see von Braun et al. 1996.

5. Agriculture's share of the population ranges from 6 percent in the Czech Republic, the most industrialized country, to 60 percent in Albania, the most agrarian society.

REFERENCES

Adedeji, Adebayo, and Timothy Shaw, eds. 1985. *Economic Crisis in Africa: African Perspectives on Development Problems and Potentials.* London: Francis Pinter.

Adelman, Irma, and Cynthia Taft Morris. 1997. "Editorial: Development History and Its Implications for Development Theory." *World Development* 25 (6): 831–40.

Amin, Samir. 1982. "A Critique of the World Bank Report Entitled `Accelerated Development in Sub-Saharan Africa.'" *Africa Development* 7 (1–2): 23–29.

Birdsall, Nancy, and Frederick Jaspersen, eds. 1997. *Pathways to Growth: Comparing East Asia and Latin America.* Baltimore: Johns Hopkins University Press.

Birdsall, Nancy, and Juan Luis Londoño. 1997. "Asset Inequality Matters: An Assessment of the World Bank's Approach to Poverty Reduction." *American Economic Review* 87 (2): 32–37.

Brooks, Karen. 1990. "Agricultural Reform in the Soviet Union." In *Agricultural Development in the Third World,* 2nd edition, edited by Carl K. Eicher and John M. Staatz, 459–79. Baltimore: Johns Hopkins University Press.

Byerlee, Derek, and Carl K. Eicher, eds. 1997. *Africa's Emerging Maize Revolution.* Boulder, Colo.: Lynne Rienner Publishers.

de Janvry, Alain, Nigel Key, Elisabeth Sadoulet. 1997. "Agricultural and Rural Development Policy in Latin America: New Directions and New Challenges." Working Paper no. 815, Department of Agricultural and Resource Economics, University of California, Berkeley.

de Janvry, Alain, and Elisabeth Sadoulet. 1993. "Market, State and Civil Organizations in Latin America beyond the Debt Crisis: The Context for Rural Development." *World Development* 21 (4): 659–74.

Delgado, Christopher. 1995. "Agricultural Transformation: The Key to Broad-based Growth and Poverty Alleviation in Africa." In *Agenda for Africa's Economic Renewal,* edited by Benno Ndulu and Nicholas van de Walle, 151–77. Washington, D.C.: Overseas Development Council.

de Wilde, John C., Peter F. M. McLoughlin, Andrè Guinard, Thayer Scudder, and Robert Maubouché. 1967. *Experiences with Agricultural Development in Tropical Africa.* Vol. 1, *The Synthesis.* Vol. 2, *The Case Studies.* Baltimore: Johns Hopkins University Press.

Edwards, Sebastian. 1995. *Crisis and Reform in Latin America: From Despair to Hope.* New York: Oxford University Press for the World Bank.

Eicher, Carl K., and Doyle C. Baker. 1992. "Agricultural Development in Sub-Saharan Africa: A Critical Survey." In *A Survey of Agricultural Economics Literature.* Vol. 4, *Agriculture in Economic Development, 1940s to 1990s,* edited by Lee Martin, 3–328. Minneapolis: University of Minnesota Press.

Food and Agriculture Organization. 1978. "Regional Food Plan for Africa." Report of the Tenth FAO Regional Conference for Africa, September 18–29, 1978. Rome.

Green, Duncan. 1995. *Silent Revolution: The Rise of Market Economies in Latin America.* New York: Monthly Review Press.

Huang, Jikun, Scott Rozelle, and Mark W. Rosegrant. 1997. "China's Food Economy to the Twenty-first Century: Supply, Demand, and Trade." Food, Agriculture, and the Environment Discussion Paper 19, International Food Policy Research Institute, Washington, D.C.

Huddle, Donald L. 1997. "Review Article: Post-1982 Effects of Neoliberalism on Latin American Development and Poverty: Two Conflicting Views." *Economic Development and Cultural Change* 45, no. 3 (July): 881–97.

Jones, William O. 1960. *Economic Man in Africa.* Food Research Institute Studies. Stanford, Calif.: Food Research Institute.

Lin, Justin Yifu, Fang Cai, and Zhou Li. 1996. *The China Miracle: Development Strategy and Economic Reform.* Hong Kong: Chinese University Press.

Mellor, John, Christopher Delgado, and Malcolm Blackie, eds. 1987. *Accelerating Food Production in Sub-Saharan Africa.* Baltimore: Johns Hopkins University Press.

Morley, Samuel. 1997. "Review of `Crisis and Reform in Latin America.'" *Journal of Economic Literature* 35 (June): 816–18.

Ndulu, B. J. 1997. "Editorial: Capacity for Economic Research and the Changing Policy Environment in Africa." *World Development* 25 (5): 627–30.

North, Douglass C. 1997. "Cliometrics—40 Years Later." *American Economic Review* 87 (2): 412–14.

Please, Stanley. 1996. "Book Review Article: Structural Adjustment and Poverty—Blunting the Criticisms." *Development Policy Review* 14:185–202.

Sanders, John H., Barry I. Shapiro, and Sunder Ramaswamy. 1996. *The Economics of Agricultural Technology in Semiarid Sub-Saharan Africa.* Baltimore: Johns Hopkins University Press.

Schuh, G. Edward, and Antonio Salazar P. Brandâo. 1992. "The Theory, Empirical Evidence, and Debates on Agricultural Development Issues in Latin America: A Selective Survey." In *A Survey of Agricultural Economics Literature.* Vol. 4, *Agriculture in Economic Development, 1940s to 1990s,* edited by Lee R. Martin, 545–967. Minneapolis: University of Minnesota Press.

Smith, Lawrence D. 1995. "Malawi: Reforming the State's Role in Agricultural Marketing." *Food Policy* 20 (6): 561–71.

Staatz, John M. 1994. "The Strategic Role of Food and Agricultural Systems in Fighting Hunger through Fostering Sustainable Economic Growth." Staff Paper no. 94-39, Department of Agricultural Economics, Michigan State University, East Lansing.

Staatz, John M., and Jennifer B. Wohl. 1991. "The Evolution of Food Self-Sufficiency Policies in West Africa." In *National and Regional Self-Sufficiency Goals: Implications for International Agriculture,* edited by Fred Ruppel and Earl Kellogg, 65–87. Boulder, Colo.: Lynne Rienner.

von Braun, Joachim, Eugenia Serova, Harm tho Seeth, and Olga Melyukhina. 1996. "Russia's Food Economy in Transition: Current Policy Issues and the Long-Term Outlook." Discussion Paper no. 19, International Food Policy Research Institute, Washington, D.C.

World Bank. 1981. *Accelerated Development in Sub-Saharan Africa: An Agenda for Action.* Washington, D.C.: World Bank.

———. 1997. *World Development Report, 1997.* Washington, D.C.: World Bank.

31

Agricultural Development and Reform in China

JUSTIN YIFU LIN

INTRODUCTION

 China is highly acclaimed for feeding over one-fifth of the world's population with only one-fifteenth of the world's arable land. When the People's Republic of China was founded in 1949, cultivated land per capita was only 0.18 hectare. By 1978, rapid population growth had caused that figure to drop to 0.1 hectare. The government nevertheless was able to keep grain production ahead of population growth. The economy also experienced a dramatic transformation. The share of agricultural sector in total national income dropped from 57.7 percent in 1952 to 32.8 percent in 1978, while the industrial sector expanded from 19.5 percent to 46.8 percent during the same period (see table 1). The institutions that the Chinese government adopted to cope with the increasing food demand from the rapidly growing population and to obtain the necessary accumulation for the industrial expansion were a collective farming system in agriculture and a state monopolized procurement and marketing system of grain, cotton, and other major farm products. This Chinese strategy was often considered a development model for other densely populated low-income countries (Robinson 1964).

Really remarkable achievements in Chinese agriculture did not occur, however, until the beginning of more recent agricultural reform in 1979. Between 1952—the year the Chinese economy recovered from twelve years of war destruction—and 1978, the growth rate in grain production was 2.4 percent per year, which was only 0.4 percent above the population growth rate in the same period. Per capita availability of grain, therefore, increased only 10 percent over a quarter-century. The growth rates of other farm products were not much higher than the population growth rate either (see table 2). Frustrated by the country's failure to raise living standards substantially after thirty years of socialist revolution, the moderate veteran leaders, who had been purged during the Cul-

JUSTIN YIFU LIN is professor and founding director of the China Center for Economic Research at Peking University in Beijing and professor of economics at Hong Kong University of Science and Technology.

TABLE 1
SECTORAL PERCENTAGE OF NATIONAL INCOME

Year	Agriculture	Industry	Construction	Transportation	Commerce
1952	57.72	19.52	3.57	4.24	14.94
1978	32.76	49.40	4.15	3.92	9.77
1993	25.30	51.69	8.25	4.47	10.19

SOURCE: State Statistical Bureau 1994, 33.

tural Revolution and came into power again after the death of Chairman Mao Zedong in 1976, initiated in 1979 a series of sweeping reforms in agriculture. The most important reform was the emergence and eventual predominance of the household responsibility system, which by 1984 had completely restored the primacy of the individual household in place of the collective team system as the basic unit of production and management in rural China. While the population grew at 1.4 percent per year between 1978 and 1984, the net value of agricultural product and grain output, respectively, grew at 7.73 percent and 4.95 percent annually during the same period. Other agricultural products also grew at an accelerated rate in the reform period (see table 2). The success of agricultural reform, especially the success of the household responsibility system, greatly encouraged the moderate political leaders. As a result, a series of more market-oriented reforms was undertaken at the end of 1984 in both urban and rural sectors. It is fair to say that the rural reform was the driving force for the market-oriented reform in China.

Agriculture as a whole still grew at a respectable average rate of 5.8 percent per year in 1984–95. Grain production, however, stagnated after reaching a peak of 407 million tons in 1984 and did not return to that level until 1989, and in 1995 per capita grain output was 1.3 percent lower than in 1984. Population in

TABLE 2
AVERAGE ANNUAL GROWTH RATE OF POPULATION AND FARM PRODUCTS

	1952–78 (%)	1978–84 (%)	1984–95 (%)
National population	2.00	1.36	1.36
Gross value of agriculture	1.85	7.73	5.81
Grain	2.41	4.95	1.24
Cotton	1.97	19.33	−.25
Oil-bearing seeds	0.84	14.74	5.93
Sugar crops	4.49	12.31	4.72
Fruit	3.88	6.97	14.13
Pork, beef, and mutton	3.63	10.28	9.67
Aquatic products	4.03	4.85	13.63
Per capita consumption of farm population	1.73	9.29	4.97[a]

SOURCE: State Statistical Bureau 1996.
    [a]The figure is for 1984–94.

China is expected to rise continuously until 2030, and per capita income is expected to increase simultaneously. Therefore, the demand for grain is expected to rise substantially. The slow growth in grain output has aroused a worldwide concern about the question of whether China will be able to feed herself in the future. Such suspicion seems to be supported by the severe grain price spikes in 1993–95 and a large increase in grain imports in 1995.[1]

This chapter provides an analytical overview of China's experience with agricultural development and reforms. The relationship between China's development strategy and the choices of grain policy and farming institutions before the reforms are investigated first, then the farming institutional reform and its achievements. Lastly, the major changes in grain policy and China's grain future are discussed, and some lessons from China's agricultural development and reforms are drawn.

DEVELOPMENT STRATEGY AND AGRICULTURAL COLLECTIVIZATION

The farming institutions and grain policy in China prior to the 1979 reform were all shaped by the development strategy that the Chinese government adopted in the early 1950s.[2] At the founding of the People's Republic of China in 1949, the Chinese government inherited a war-torn economy in which 89.4 percent of the population resided in rural areas. Industry contributed 12.6 percent of the national income. In 1952, in order to strengthen its national power, the government adopted a Stalinist development strategy oriented towards heavy industry. The goal was to build as rapidly as possible the country's capacity to produce capital goods and military materials.

China was an underdeveloped agrarian economy in the early 1950s. Capital was extremely scarce and the voluntary saving rate was far too low to finance the high rate of investment in heavy industry sought by the development strategy. To facilitate rapid capital expansion, a policy of low wages for industrial workers evolved alongside the heavy-industry-oriented development strategy. The assumption was that through low wages, the state-owned enterprises would be able to create large profits and to reinvest the profits in infrastructure and capital construction. The practice of establishing low prices for energy, transportation, and other raw materials, such as cotton, was instituted for the same reason.

To implement low wages, the government was required to provide urban dwellers with inexpensive food and other necessities, including housing, medical care, and clothing. A restrictive food rationing system was instituted in 1953 and kept in effect until 1992.[3] Meanwhile, in order to secure the food supply for rationing, a compulsory grain procurement policy was imposed in rural areas in 1953.

The industrial development strategy also resulted in a great demand for agricultural products. First, the urban population increased dramatically, from 57.65 million in 1949 to 71.63 million in 1952 and 99.49 million in 1957. Since the industrial strategy would not permit the use of large amounts of scarce foreign reserves to import food for urban consumption, satisfying the increasing food demand in urban areas hinged on the growth of domestic grain production. Second, since the bulk of China's exports consisted of agricultural products, the country's capacity to import capital goods for industrialization depended on agriculture's growth.[4] Third, agriculture was the main source of raw materials for many industries, such as textiles and food-processing. Agriculture, therefore, was clearly viewed as the bottleneck and major point of intervention in pursuing the overall economic development strategy in China in early 1950s.

Under these conditions, agricultural stagnation and poor harvests would not only affect food supply but also have a direct and almost immediate adverse impact on industrial expansion.[5] As the government was reluctant to divert resources from industry to agriculture, a new agricultural development strategy was adopted that would permit and even foster the simultaneous development of agriculture alongside the development of industry. The core of this strategy involved mass mobilization of rural labor to work on labor-intensive investment projects, such as irrigation, flood control, and land reclamation, and to raise yields in agriculture through traditional methods and inputs, such as closer planting, more careful weeding, and the use of more organic fertilizer. Collectivization of agriculture was the institution that the government believed would perform these functions. Collectivization also was viewed as a convenient vehicle for effecting the procurement of grain and other agricultural products by which to carry out industrial development strategy.

The independent family farm had been the traditional farming institution in rural China for thousands of years prior to the founding of the People's Republic. The typical farm was not only small but also fragmented. In the wake of the socialist revolution, nearly half of the cultivated land in rural China was owned by landlords, who rented land to peasant families. Rent was often as high as 50 percent of the value of the main crops. A land reform program was implemented in areas under the Communist Party's control, starting in 1940s. Under this program, land was confiscated without compensation from the landlords and distributed to the tenants.

Experiments with various forms of cooperatives began even before the completion of the land reform in 1952. The first type of cooperative was the "mutual aid team," in which four or five neighboring households pooled their farm tools and draft animals and exchanged their labor on a temporary or permanent basis; each household's land and harvest remained its own. The mutual aid team was the predominant form of cooperative up to 1955. The second type was the "elementary cooperative," in which about twenty to thirty neighboring households pooled not only farm tools and draft animals but also land under a unified management. The net income of the cooperative was distributed in two categories: rent for land, draft animals, and farm tools; and remuneration for work performed. Land, draft animals, and farm tools were still owned by member households. The third type was the collective farm, or the "advanced cooperative," in which all means of production, including land, draft animals, and farm tools, were collectively owned. Remuneration in an advanced cooperative was based solely on the amount of work each member contributed, and took the form of work points. The income of a family in an advanced cooperative depended on the number of work points earned by the family members and on the average value of a work point. The latter, in turn, depended on the net production of the collective farm. An advanced cooperative initially consisted of about thirty households; later it evolved to include all households in a village, approximately 150–200 households.

The official approach to collectivization, initially, was cautious and gradual. Peasants were encouraged and induced to join the different forms of cooperative on a voluntary basis. However, in the summer of 1955 proponents of accelerating the pace of collectivization won the debate within the party. There were only 500 advanced cooperatives in 1955. By the winter of 1957, 753,000 advanced cooperative farms, comprising 119 million member households, had been established nationwide.

Collectivization was surprisingly successful in the initial stage. It encountered no active resistance from the peasantry and was carried out relatively smoothly. This experience greatly encouraged the leadership within the party and led them to take a bolder approach. The main rationale of collectivization was rooted in the notion that mobilizing rural surplus labor would increase rural capital formation and, hence, increase production. However, while a collective farm of 150 households provided a basis for mobilizing labor for work projects within the collective, the collective farm did not solve the problem of mobilizing labor for large-scale projects, such as digging irrigation canals, building dams, and the like. These kinds of projects would in general require the simultaneous participation of labor from several dozen collective farms. The obvious solution for the large-scale labor mobilization was to pool twenty or thirty collective farms of 150 households into a larger collective unit. In this way, the "People's Commune" came into existence in 1958. From the end of August to the beginning of November, in the space of only three months, 753,000 collective farms were transformed into 24,000 communes, which consisted of 120 million households, over 99 percent of total rural households in China in 1958. The average size of a commune was about 5,000 households, with 10,000 laborers and 10,000 acres of cultivated land. Payment in the commune was made according to subsistence needs and partly according to the work performed. Work on private plots, which existed in the other forms of cooperatives, was prohibited.

Billions of man-days were mobilized, as expected. The irrigated area increased from 18.5 percent of China's cultivated land in 1952, to 24.4 percent in 1957, and further to 29.7 percent in 1962. Most of the increase came from the expansion of large, labor-intensive, gravity irrigation systems. But a profound agricultural crisis occurred between 1959 and 1961. The gross value of agriculture measured at the constant prices of 1952 dropped 14 percent in 1959, 12 percent in 1960, and another 2.5 percent in 1961. Most importantly, grain output was reduced 15 percent in 1959, another 16 percent in 1960, remained at the same low level for another year, and did not return to the 1952 level until 1962. As compared to 1952, the population by 1959 had increased 17 percent, and the dramatic reduction in grain output had resulted in a widespread and severe famine. Thirty million people are estimated to have died of starvation and malnutrition during this crisis (Lin 1990; Becker 1997).

Communes were not abolished after the 1959–61 famine. However, starting in 1962, the agricultural operation was divided and management was delegated to a much smaller unit, the "production team," which consisted of 20–30 neighboring households. In this new system, land was jointly owned by the commune, brigade, and production team. However, the production team was treated as the basic operating and accounting unit. Income distribution, based on work points earned by each member, was undertaken within the production team. This remuneration system was similar to that in the advanced cooperative. After 1962, experiments were carried out to improve the grading of work points. The production team, nevertheless, remained the basic farming institution until the household responsibility system reform began in 1979.

After the 1959–61 crisis, greater emphasis was given to modern inputs. Although the mobilization of rural labor for public irrigation projects continued, irrigated acreage was added mostly by increasing use of irrigation pumps rather than by constructing labor-intensive canals and dams. Irrigated acreage increased gradually after 1962. The utilization of chemical fertilizer was accelerated after 1962, accompanied by the promotion of high-yield fertilizer-responsive modern varieties. Dwarf varieties of rice and wheat were introduced in early 1960s. By the end of the 1970s, about 80 percent of the traditional varieties of rice and wheat had been replaced by the modern dwarf varieties. After 1976, dwarf varieties of rice were replaced by higher-yielding hybrid rice. Modern varieties of corn, cotton, and other crops were also introduced and promoted in the 1960s and 1970s. The pace of mechanization also accelerated after 1965, especially during the 1970s.

Despite dramatic increases in modern inputs during the sixties and seventies, the performance of agriculture continued to be poor. The discouraging picture of Chinese agriculture changed in 1978 when China started a series of fundamental reforms in the rural sector. Output growth accelerated to a rate several times the long-term average in the previous period (see table 2). The dramatic output growth was a result of a package of reforms that gave priority to increasing incentives to individuals and reducing government interventions.

THE HOUSEHOLD RESPONSIBILITY SYSTEM

The main defect of the production team as an institution for agricultural development was its incentive structure. Team members, working under the supervision of a team leader, were credited with work points for the jobs they performed. At the end of the year, net team income was distributed according to the work points that each member had accumulated during the year. Work points were supposed to reflect the quality and quantity of effort that each member had contributed to the team's work. The work point system is not inherently an inefficient incentive scheme: if the monitoring of each peasant's work is perfect and complete, the incentive to work will be strong rather than weak. The return on a peasant's additional increment of effort has two components: a share of the increase in team output and a larger share of the total net team income, for if he contributes a larger share of total effort he obtains a larger share of total work points. The sum of these two components is likely to make a worker exert him- or herself beyond the point at which the value of the work expended equals that of the leisure forgone. On the other hand, if the monitoring of work effort does not exist, a peasant is not likely to obtain additional work points for additional effort. In this case, the return has only a single component, namely, a share of the increase in team output. The incentives to work then would be insufficient. The extent to which a work point share increases for an additional unit of effort depends on the degree of monitoring. Incentives to work in a production team are positively correlated with the degree of monitoring in the production process. The higher the degree of monitoring, the higher the incentives to work, and thus the more effort contributed.

However, monitoring is costly. The management of the production team has to balance the gain in productivity due to enhanced incentives with the rise in the cost of monitoring. The monitoring of agricultural operations is particularly difficult because of agricultural production's sequential nature and spatial dimension. In agricultural production, the process typically spans several months over several acres of land. Farming also requires peasants to shift from one job to another throughout the production season. In general, the quality of work provided by a peasant does not become apparent until harvest time. Furthermore, it is impossible to determine each individual's contribution by simply observing the outputs, because random effects of nature influence production. It is thus very costly to provide close monitoring of a peasant's effort in agricultural production. Consequently, the optimal degree of monitoring, even under the best circumstances, has to be very low. The increment of income for each additional unit of effort will be only a small fraction of the marginal product of effort. Therefore, peasant's incentives to work in a production team are likely to be low (Lin 1988).

The commune, brigade, and production team system of agricultural production management, with its work point system of compensation, has been challenged ever since its establishment. After the disaster of the Great Leap Forward, land was reallocated to individual families, and households were restored as the units of production in many parts of China, especially in Anhui Province. Production soon recovered in these areas. Nevertheless, this practice was prohibited and criticized as capitalistic, and those people responsible were punished. Although the reallocation of land to individual households, secretly or sometimes openly, was never totally eliminated in some areas, real change was not possible until 1978, when moderate leaders came into power again after the chaos of the Cultural Revolution and the death of Chairman Mao.[6]

At the end of 1978, the government proposed a sweeping change in rural policies.[7] In place of a lopsided stress on grain production, the new policy encouraged the development of a diversified economy. Better prices were set for the state's purchase of farm produce. Production teams were granted more freedom in making decisions about their own affairs. Private plots and the country fairs in which farm people sold their surplus products were revived and expanded. It had been recognized at that time that solving the managerial problems of agriculture within the production team system was the key to improving work incentives, yet the household-based farming system reform was considered the opposite of the socialist principle of collective farming and, therefore, was prohibited. The official position at that time maintained that the production team was to remain the basic unit of production, income distribution, and accounting. Nevertheless, a small number of production teams, first secretly and later with the blessing of local authorities, began to experiment with a system of contracting land, other resources, and output quotas to individual households towards the end of 1978. A year later, these teams brought in yields far larger than those of other teams. The central authorities later conceded the existence of these practices and named them "the household responsibility system." However, the authorities required that this practice be restricted to poor agricultural regions, such as hilly or mountainous areas, and to poorly functioning teams in which people had lost confidence in the collective. In practice, this restriction could not be put into effect at all. Rich regions welcomed the household responsibility system as enthusiastically as did poor regions. Full official recognition of the household responsibility system as universally acceptable eventually was given in late 1981. By the end of 1983, almost all households in China's rural areas had adopted this new system. Under the arrangement of the household responsibility system, land is contracted to individual households for a period of fifteen years. After fulfilling the procurement quota obligations, farmers are entitled to sell their surplus on the markets or retain it for their own use.

The government's current position on farming institutions is to maintain the stability of the household responsibility system. In 1993 the government adopted a policy that allowed the land contract to be extended another thirty years after the expiration of the existing contract. The land can be subleased to other households with compensation if a household member has a nonfarm job and gives up farming. A household can also hire temporary workers for farm work. Therefore, despite the existence of some ideological restrictions, land and labor markets have reemerged in rural China (Lin 1995a).

The shift to the household responsibility system is China's most successful reform. A careful econometric analysis, using province-level input-output data covering the period 1970 to 1987 and employing the production function approach, found that of the 42.2 percent output growth in the cropping sector in 1978–84, about 54 percent can be attributed to productivity growth due to reforms. Of the productivity growth, 97 percent is attributable to the changes in farming institutions from the production team system to the household responsibility system (Lin 1992).

The shift from the production team system to the household responsibility system also improved farmers' incentives to adopt new technology and may thus be expected to speed the diffusion of new technology (Lin 1991). Therefore, the household responsibility system is also expected to have a long-term dynamic impact on the growth of agricultural productivity.

THE GRAIN POLICY REFORMS AND CHINA'S GRAIN FUTURE

As discussed above, the basic framework of existing grain policy was set up in 1953. It was instituted to secure the government's control of grain supply, on the one hand, and to meet the demand of urban residents for low-priced grain, on the other hand. As in many other countries, grain is more than just a commodity. Once the government is involved in the distribution of grain, price becomes a political issue. To avoid possible political unrest, ration prices remained largely unchanged until late 1980s.

Compulsory grain procurement is divided into two categories: the "basic quota" and "above quota." Both categories involve obligatory grain deliveries by farm units to the state marketing agency (and later, collective traders), but above quota deliveries receive a price premium. When the quota system was introduced in 1953, procurement prices were set to give the state grain procurement and marketing agency a small profit. However, after the great agricultural crisis in 1959–61, grain procurement prices were raised an average of 25.3 percent, to improve the incentives for grain production. After 1961, four other major price adjustments were made, in 1966, 1979, 1985, and 1988. Adjustments in the ration prices lagged behind the increases in procurement prices, and the increases in ration prices were fully compensated by increases in food subsidies to the urban residents, so each rise in procurement prices resulted in an increase in the government's financial burden.

At the beginning of the 1979 reforms, political leaders in China reached an agreement that farm income was too low and grain output was barely sufficient to meet subsistence needs. In order to increase farm income and boost grain production, procurement prices for grain and other major crops were increased by a big margin, in 1979. The basic quota price of grain was raised 20 percent, and the above quota price was raised from 130 percent to 150 percent of the basic quota price.[8] Furthermore, the state monopoly on grain marketing was gradually lifted. Private as well as collective traders were allowed to handle grain marketing alongside the state marketing agency.

The household responsibility system reform, along with the marked price increase, resulted in an upsurge of grain output. The annual growth rate increased from an average of 2.41 percent annually in the period 1952–78 to 4.95 percent in the period 1978–84. Since the output growth rate was about twice as large as the growth rate of consumption in 1978–1984, China became a net grain exporter in 1985, after being a net importer for a quarter-century (see table 3). The sudden success, however, brought with it issues that the Chinese government had never addressed before. According to the regulations at that time, the government was obliged to buy all grain at the above quota price after a farmer had fulfilled his basic quota obligation. Consequently, the greater the output growth, the larger was the government's financial burden. Food subsidies (including subsidies on edible oils) increased from 5.6 billion yuan in 1978 to 32.1 billion yuan in 1984, representing 21 percent of the government's budget in that year. Furthermore, there existed a serious shortage of storage facilities. Because the government was unable to buy all the grain that farmers wanted to sell, the market price for grain dropped substantially throughout the country. In some grain surplus areas, the market price at harvest time even approached the basic quota price set by the government.

In order to reduce the government's financial burden and to increase the role of the market in the production and distribution of grain, the mandatory quota procurement system was changed to a contract procurement system at the beginning of 1985. According to the new system, the procurement quantity was to be determined by contracts based on mutual agreements between the government and individual farmers. The contract price was fixed at a price calculated as a weighted average of the original basic quota price (30 percent) and the above quota price (70 percent). This contract price was 135 percent of the original basic quota price and about equivalent to the market price at harvest time of 1984 in major grain production areas. However, it was 10 percent lower than the above quota price. As a supplement to contract procurement, the government agreed, in addition, to purchase certain amounts of grain on the market at the market prices.

The contract procurement system, however, met with a host of problems in its first year. Management costs for signing contracts with millions of agricultural households were tremendous, and the means to enforce contracts were limited. The contract price did not provide enough incentives to farmers, especially in areas where the contract price was lower than or even roughly equal to the market price in 1984. Enforcement of contracts was made difficult because of a 6.9 percent drop in grain output in 1985. The drop in output led to a 10 percent increase in 1985 grain prices. As a result, the gap between the contract price and the market price had widened, and farmers were reluctant to fulfil the contracts.

As a reaction to this experience, contract procurement by the end of 1985 had reverted to the original compulsory quota procurement system, even though the name "contract" was not abolished. The quantity of procurement was reduced and the quantity of market purchase was increased. To minimize administrative costs, procurement quotas in each region were allocated to households in proportion to the cultivated land that each household operated under the household responsibility system. The government also sharply raised the procurement prices between 1986 and 1989 and promised to provide farmers with fertilizers,

TABLE 3
CHINA'S OUTPUT, IMPORTS, AND EXPORTS
OF GRAIN, 1952–1995 (1,000 TONS)

Year	Output	Imports	Exports	Net Import
1952	163,900	0	1,530	−1,530
1953	166,850	15	1,825	−1,810
1954	169,500	30	1,710	−1,680
1955	183,950	180	2,230	−2,050
1956	192,750	150	2,650	−2,500
1957	195,050	165	2,090	−1,925
1958	200,000	225	2,885	−2,660
1959	170,000	0	4,155	−4,155
1960	143,500	65	2,720	−2,655
1961	147,500	5,810	1,355	4,455
1962	160,000	4,920	1,030	3,890
1963	170,000	5,950	1,490	4,460
1964	187,500	6,570	1,820	4,750
1965	194,550	6,405	2,415	3,990
1966	214,000	6,440	2,885	3,555
1967	217,800	4,700	2,995	1,705
1968	209,050	4,585	2,600	1,985
1969	210,950	3,785	2,235	1,550
1970	239,950	5,360	2,120	3,240
1971	250,150	3,175	2,620	555
1972	240,500	4,755	2,925	1,830
1973	264,950	8,130	3,895	4,235
1974	275,250	8,120	3,645	4,475
1975	284,500	3,735	2,805	930
1976	286,300	2,365	1,765	600
1977	282,750	7,345	1,655	5,690
1978	304,750	8,830	1,875	6,955
1979	332,100	12,355	1,650	10,705
1980	320,550	13,430	1,620	11,810
1981	325,000	14,810	1,260	13,550
1982	354,500	16,115	1,250	14,856
1983	387,300	13,530	1,150	12,380
1984	407,300	10,410	3,190	7,220
1985	379,110	6,000	9,320	−3,320
1986	391,510	7,730	9,420	−1,690
1987	402,980	16,280	7,370	8,910
1988	394,080	15,330	7,180	8,150
1989	407,550	16,580	6,560	10,020
1990	446,240	13,720	5,830	7,890
1991	435,290	13,450	10,860	2,590
1992	442,660	11,750	13,640	−1,890
1993	456,490	7,520	15,350	−7,830
1994	445,100	9,200	13,460	−4,260
1995	466,570	20,270	420	19,850

SOURCE: Data for 1952–59 from Ministry of Agriculture 1989; for 1960–91 from Food and Agriculture Organization; for 1992–95 from State Statistical Bureau, statistical yearbooks for 1993–95 and statistical survey for 1996.

diesel fuel, and credit at subsidized prices, although farmers frequently complained that these promises were never met. However, because farmers were given more autonomy in the production decisions, and the government's enforcement measures had been weakened as a result of the household responsibility system reform, farmers allocated resources to more profitable activities, such as fruits, aquatic products, and township or village enterprises. As a result, grain output stagnated after the decline in 1985. Grain output did not recover to the level of 1984 until 1989 (see table 3).

The main problem in China's grain policy in the 1980s arose from the procurement practice and sale prices. The adjustment in sale price lagged far behind the adjustment in procurement prices. Under this situation, an increase in procurement price meant an increase in the government's subsidy. Because of the gap between the government-set procurement price and the market price, the government was confronted with a dilemma. If the government tried to make the procurement price as competitive as the market price, its financial burden became unbearable. If the government, on the other hand, attempted to limit the procurement price so that the amount of food subsidies could be controlled, peasants' incentives to produce grain and to fulfill the quota obligations were impaired. Since individual households had been given more autonomy in production decisions and the government's enforcement measures had been weakened as a result of the household responsibility system reform, how to stimulate grain production became a difficult issue.

The attempt to keep the ration price at a low level was justifiable in 1950s. For example, the expenditure on grain alone represented 22.8 percent of total household expenditure for an average urban household in 1957. The share of expenditure on grain in an urban household's total expenditure declined to 7.6 percent in 1987. The government's attitude towards urban food rationing took a dramatic turn in 1990. The grain production recovered to the 1984 level in 1989 and scored a new historical record of 446.2 million tons in 1990, which represented a 10 percent increase over 1989 levels (see table 3). The output stabilized in that level in the subsequent two years. The sudden increase in output depressed the market prices; the grain price in rural market fairs declined 19.9 percent in 1990. Moreover, the consumer price index dropped from 18 percent in 1989 to 3.1 percent. Grain stocks were often used as a means of savings in rural China, so the expectation of continued deflation induced farmers to reduce their grain stocks (Song and Johnson 1995). As a result, the grain price dropped further, 19.4 percent in 1991, and stayed at the low level in 1992. The collapse of grain market prices increased farmers' incentives to sell their output to the government. In 1992, as a way to reduce its financial burden, the government raised the urban ration prices of grain to a level that did not require government subsidies. In 1993, both the procurement and sale prices of grain were decontrolled. Nevertheless, farmers were still required to meet the grain quota obligations.

The market price of grain took an unexpected turn after the market liberalization. The price increased 31 percent in 1993, 51 percent in 1994, and 36 percent in 1995. Moreover, China imported 20 million tons of grain in 1995. The price spikes and the high volume of imports caused widespread concern about the future of China's grain supply. However, the rapid increases in price and imports were not caused by failures of grain production. In 1993, China's grain output scored a historical record of 456.5 million tons. The grain output in 1994 dropped 2.5 percent, which was within the normal range of output fluctuation, as grain production is subject to the random impacts of weather. China's grain output in 1995 increased 4.5 percent and scored another record, 466.6 million tons. The main reasons for the price spikes were twofold: The first was the impact of double-digit inflation in 1992–95, which changed farmers' inflation expectation and caused farmers to increase their grain storage as a way to hedge against inflation, which reduced the marketable supply. The second was the reduction of grain cultivation in the grain-deficient coastal provinces, where cultivating grain was no longer to farmers' comparative advantage. As a result, in the coastal provinces the supply of grain fell while the demand for grain increased.

When market prices started to rise, the government again resorted to administrative intervention in the grain market. The central government's policy in 1995 required each provincial governor to be responsible for the balance of grain demand and supply in his or her province, a policy that intensifies the local governments' intervention in grain production and marketing.

Unless the government is willing to subsidize farmers heavily, any government restriction on the function of grain markets will reduce the profitability of grain production and thus grain output. The government in China is financially weak, but it gives a high priority to the goal of achieving grain self-sufficiency. Therefore, the administrative restrictions on grain markets will probably be removed gradually in order to give farmers incentives to produce grain.

Because of population growth and rapid economic growth, China's grain demand will continue to grow rapidly while the amount of land in cultivation will decline gradually as a result of the expanded demand for housing and industrial purposes, salinization of irrigated lands, and so forth. Some studies speculate that China may have to import huge quantities of grain in the future. This in turn would lead to high world prices, and many poorer importing countries would be priced out of the market (Brown 1995). Future growth of China's grain output, however, can come from higher yields through many measures, such as increases in input use and technological change, as well as effective policies to encourage their use. Grain yield potentials in China are still very large. If the Chinese government invests adequately in seed improvements and other agricultural research and allows markets to function well, China has the potential to produce enough food to feed herself in the twenty-first century (Lin 1995b).

However, grain is a land-intensive crop and China is a land-scarce economy. In the prereform period, China used imports of grain to help meet its domestic needs (see table 3). If China continues its current rate of GNP growth, China's comparative advantages will change rapidly. The welfare in China will improve if China exports labor-intensive agricultural and industrial products and imports grain (Anderson 1990). Therefore, instead of pursuing a policy of grain self-sufficiency, a more appropriate policy for China is to allow a gradual increase in imports to meet part of the future needs for domestic grain consumption, especially of wheat and feedgrain (Lin 1998).

SUMMARY AND IMPLICATIONS

China's experiences in agricultural development before and after the 1979 reform provide many valuable lessons for other developing countries. It is remarkable that China has been able to feed, at a reasonably high level, more than one-fifth of the world's population with only one-fifteenth of the world's arable land, and to quickly develop a major industrial capacity. While managing to do this, however, China carried an unnecessary burden before the 1979 reform. The collective farming system and monopolized procurement and marketing policy were so detrimental to work incentives that, despite sharp improvements in technology and increases in the use of modern inputs in the 1960s and 1970s, grain production in China barely kept up with population growth.

The individual household-based farming system reform in 1979 greatly improved peasants' work incentives. Grain production and the agricultural sector as a whole registered unprecedented growth between 1978 and 1984. The success of agricultural reform greatly encouraged the Chinese leadership to adopt a more ambitious reform in the urban sector and provided the material basis for the economy to grow outside the planned system.

The increase in work incentives resulting from the institutional reform in farming had mainly a once-and-for-all impact on agricultural productivity. While the average annual growth rate of agriculture after 1984 was still very remarkable compared to the agricultural growth rates of other developed and developing countries, grain production in China stagnated after reaching its peak in 1984 and did not recover that level until 1989. This stagnation was mainly due to the incompleteness of macro-policy reform. Individual households have been given more autonomy in production decisions, so farmers in the household system will allocate more resources to crops that command higher profits. Reforms have freed the prices and marketing of most cash crops and other products of animal husbandry and fisheries. Grain, however, is among the exceptions. Farmers are still required to meet grain quota obligations at government-set prices. Grain production in the postreform period has been held back by the artificial effects of these price distortions on the profitability of grain production.[9]

Because of the stagnation of grain production in 1984–88, the optimism about Chinese agriculture which developed during the first six years of reform was quickly replaced by pessimism. The small farm size and the fragmentation of cultivated land in the household-based farming system are often blamed for the poor performance in grain production after 1984. However, the lessons of the period before the 1979 reform demonstrate that collectivization is not a solution to the increasing demand for grain arising from population growth and industrial expansion.

Agriculture was a supporting sector in the prereform development strategy, receiving public attention only when a poor harvest became a constraint on industrial development. Under such a strategy, the contribution that agriculture made to modern economic growth was systematically undervalued, and a cyclic pattern in agricultural production was inevitable. Sustained agricultural growth will be possible only when China replaces its existing policy environment, molded under the heavy-industry-oriented development strategy of the earlier five-year plans, with one that stresses China's regional as well as international comparative advantages. To make such a transition in development strategy, further reforms will be required to improve the security of land tenure system, the functioning of outputs and inputs markets, and the role of international trade.

NOTES

Data in this paper are from the statistical yearbook of China (State Statistical Bureau), various issues from 1981 to 1995, unless otherwise noted.

1. The market price of grain increased 30 percent in 1993, 51 percent in 1994, and 36 percent in 1995. In 1995, grain imports totaled 20 million tons.

2. This section draws from Lin, Cai, and Li 1996.

3. In addition to grain, edible oils, pork, and sugar were included under rationing.

4. In 1953, raw agricultural products alone represented 55.7 percent of the total value of China's exports, with another 25.9 percent consisting of processed agricultural products. Up to the mid-1970s, agricultural and processed agricultural products represented over 70 percent of the total value of exports. See Almanac of China's Foreign Economic Relations and Trade 1986.

5. This argument is clearly supported by the fact that the heavy-industry-oriented development strategy had to give way temporarily to the "agricultural first strategy," after the harvest failures caused by the collectivization in the late 1950s.

6. A village in Guizhou Province had maintained this practice secretly for more than ten years before the recent reform. The villagers did not dare to admit it until the new policy was announced (Du 1985, 15).

7. The policy changes were proposed in the Third Plenary Session of the Eleventh Central Committee of the Communist Party of China, held in December 1978. The session adopted the "Decisions of the Central Committee of the Communist Party of China on Some Questions Concerning the Acceleration of Agricultural Development (Draft)." The draft was promulgated nine months later by the Fourth Plenary Session of the CPC Central Committee in September 1979. For the text of the decision, see Agricultural Yearbook of China 1980 (56–62).

8. The overall weighted-average price increase was 33 percent.

9. Another important exception is cotton, which is the major input for the state-owned textile industry. To reduce the textile industry's costs of production, the state controls cotton procurement and marketing and represses its price. As in the case of grain production, this policy is responsible for the decline and stagnation of cotton production in China (see table 2).

REFERENCES

Agricultural Yearbook of China Editorial Board. 1980. *Zhongguo Nongye Nianjian, 1980 (China Agriculture Yearbook, 1980)*. Beijing: Agriculture Press.

Almanac of China's Foreign Economic Relations and Trade Editorial Board. 1986. *Almanac of China's Foreign Economic Relations and Trade, 1986*. Beijing: Zhongguo Zhanwang Press.

Anderson, Kym. 1990. "Changing Comparative Advantages in China: Effects on Food, Feed and Fibre Markets." Paris: Organiztion for Economic Co-operation and Development.

Becker, Jasper 1997. *Hungry Ghosts: Mao's Secret Famine.* New York: Free Press.

Brown, Lester R. 1995. *Who Will Feed China? Wake-up Call for a Small Planet.* New York: W. W. Norton.

Du, Runsheng. 1985. *China's Rural Economic Reform.* Beijing: Social Science Press.

Lin, Justin Yifu. 1988. "The Household Responsibility System in China's Agricultural Reform: A Theoretical and Empirical Study." *Economic Development and Cultural Change* 36, no. 3 (April supplement): s199–s224.

———. 1990. "Collectivization and China's Agricultural Crisis in 1959–1961." *Journal of Political Economy* 98 (6): 1228–52.

———. 1991. "The Household Responsibility System Reform and the Adoption of Hybrid Rice in China." *Journal of Development Economics* 36:353–72.

———. 1992. "Rural Reforms and Agricultural Growth in China." *American Economic Review* 82, no. 1 (March): 34–51.

———. 1993. "Exit Rights, Exit Costs, and Shirking in Agricultural Cooperatives: A Reply." *Journal of Comparative Economics* 17 (June): 504–20.

———. 1995a. "Endowments, Technology and Factor Markets: A Natural Experiment from China's Rural Institutional Reform." *American Journal of Agricultural Economics* 77 (May).

———. 1995b. "A Study on Grain Yield Potential and Research Priority" *Zhongguo Nongcun Guancha* (Chinese Rural Observation), no.2 (March).

———. 1998. "How Did China Feed Itself in the Past? How Will China Feed Itself in the Future?" (Second Distinguished Economist Lecture.) Mexico, D.F.: CIMMYT.

Lin, Justin Yifu, Fang Cai, and Zhou Li. 1996. *The China Miracle: Development Strategy and Economic Reform.* Hong Kong: Chinese University Press.

Luo, Hanxian. 1985. *Economic Changes in Rural China.* Beijing: New World Press.

Ministry of Agriculture, Planning Bureau. 1989. *Zhongguo Nongcun jingi tongji zhiliao dachuan, 1949–1986 (Comprehensive Statistical Data of China's Rural Economy).* Beijing: Agriculture Press.

Robinson, Joan. 1964. "Chinese Agricultural Communes." *Co-Existence* (May): 1–7. Reprinted in *The Political Economy of Development and Underdevelopment,* edited by Charles K. Wilber. New York: Random House, 1973.

Song, Guoqing, and D. Gale Johnson. 1995. "Grain Storage as a Hedge against Inflation." Working Paper, Department of Economics, University of Chicago.

State Statistical Bureau. Various years. *Zhongguo Tongji Nianjian (China Statistical Yearbook).* Beijing: China Statistics Press (annually 1981–95).

———. 1996. *Tongji Zhaiyao, 1996 (A Statistical Survey of China, 1996).* Beijing: China Statistics Press.

32

The Role of Agriculture
in Indonesia's
Development

C. PETER TIMMER

 In 1967 Gunnar Myrdal wrote in *Asian Drama* that no one in the economic development profession held out any hope for Indonesia. It is impossible to understand the political economy of Indonesia's experience with rapid economic growth, or its response to the Asian financial crisis in 1997–98, without understanding that starting point.

My earliest memories of Indonesia are shaped by news clips from the mid-1960s about rampant inflation, hunger in the streets, and, ultimately, a violent spasm of political and military disorder and a society run amok. Only with the return of political order and a new government was it possible to assess just how poor the people were. Food intake between 1965 and 1969 averaged less than 1,650 kilocalories per person per day, well below minimum levels for adequate health. Many of those calories came from cassava and maize; virtually no meat or milk was being consumed by the bottom 90% of the income distribution. Nearly everyone was poor.

I remember flying into Kemayoran airport one night in April 1970. Jakarta was a city of about four million people then, but it was lit by kerosene lanterns. From the air it looked like an enormous village. The traffic jam leaving the airport was caused by the hundreds of *becaks* (pedicabs) in the streets, not the dozen or so automobiles we saw on the way to our house. I had never been in a poor country before (unless you count Scotland in 1963). It was my first experience with the sheer magnitude of the problem of poverty: tens of millions of people struggling day to day just to feed themselves and their families. I asked myself many

C. PETER TIMMER is Dean of the Graduate School of International Relations and Pacific Studies at the University of California, San Diego.

Originally titled "The Political Economy of Rapid Growth: Indonesia's New Development Model," copyright © 1995 by JAI Press, Inc., published in *Research in Domestic and International Agribusiness Management,* 1995, pp. 117–25. Published with minor editorial revisions by permission of JAI Press and the author.

times in the first few months what I was doing and whether it could make any conceivable difference in a country with such monumental problems.

As it turns out, this is precisely the question the economics profession is asking itself today: Is there anything governments can do, guided by the historical record on economic development, to speed up the rate of economic growth? That record is littered with examples of what government should not do, but is there a set of positive policies and public investments that will lead to, and sustain, rapid economic growth? Attempts to answer this question are at the top of the agenda in Eastern Europe and the former Soviet Union, where fierce academic battles are being waged over appropriate strategies for restructuring socialist economies. In East and Southeast Asia, several countries maintained a steady pace of rapid economic growth for thirty years. After 1965, Indonesia joined that club. What did it do?

It is important to understand just how unusual rapid economic growth is as a historical experience and what difference rapid growth makes to the welfare of a society. Rapid economic growth requires a country to capture the advantages of "economic backwardness," that is, the accumulation of knowledge and technology that development pioneers have left as a legacy. By its very nature, rapid economic growth is "catch-up" growth. That does not, however, make it easy. Few countries have succeeded.

According to data and calculations from the World Bank, between 1965 and 1990 only ten countries in the world (with populations larger than two million) experienced growth in per capita incomes of 4 percent per year or more, and all but two were in East or Southeast Asia.[1] Rapid economic growth was invented in East Asia. Great Britain needed 115 years for per capita incomes to double during the first industrial revolution. Japan achieved the same doubling in 34 years, from 1885 to 1919 (outpacing Germany and Russia). With vast improvements in technology and knowledge to tap after World War II, South Korea was able to double per capita incomes in just 11 years, from 1966 to 1977. China is growing at rates that will double incomes per capita every decade, and Thailand was not far behind that rate of growth until the financial crisis in 1997.

By contrast, however, developing countries outside Asia have had a difficult time increasing per capita incomes at all, despite access to the same bank of knowledge and technology. Of the low- and middle-income countries with statistics reported by the World Bank, only those in East Asia and the Pacific and South Asia recorded gains in per capita incomes in the 1980s. On average, countries in sub-Saharan Africa, the Middle East and North Africa, and Latin America and the Caribbean experienced declines in their incomes per capita during that decade.

Such declines are not necessarily just short-term aberrations. At the turn of the century, Argentina was one of the five richest countries in the world. It is now classified as a "developing country." In sub-Saharan Africa, economic declines have been long term and pervasive. In 1960, Ghana was richer than Malaysia, and Uganda was richer than Thailand, as best as official statistics can indicate.

In 1990, Malaysia and Thailand were six times richer than Ghana and Uganda. Nigeria's per capita income was higher than Indonesia's in 1960. In 1990, the Indonesian population was twice as well off as that of Nigeria, and the rate of material progress in Indonesia was probably even faster than suggested by the comparative income statistics in dollars.

As these examples suggest, rapid economic growth in one country and economic decline in another can transform their relative status as well as their absolute degrees of prosperity. If both countries start at $500 per capita, for example, 25 years of growth in per capita incomes in the successful country at 5 percent per year results in a per capita income of nearly $1,700. By contrast, a decline of 2 percent per year in per capita incomes in the unsuccessful country leaves incomes at only $300 per capita. Within just a quarter century, two countries equally poised on the threshold of middle-income status are transformed, one by rapid growth into the upper ranks of the middle-income family, the other by economic failure back into the midst of low-income countries. It is terribly important to learn what these two countries did to end up in such sharply contrasting circumstances. At a general level, this is similar to asking what East and Southeast Asia did right from 1960 to the 1990s, and what Africa did wrong. At a more specific level, the question is what Indonesia did right after the late 1960s compared with what it did wrong for the two decades before that.[2]

The Indonesian approach to development that was worked out in the late 1960s sought to achieve three objectives: growth, stability, and equity. Many of my technically oriented colleagues regard this development trilogy as little more than a political slogan. However, a development strategy that integrates all three factors, I will argue, is the key to successful achievement of sustained and rapid economic growth, not just in Indonesia, but in Asia generally. In addition to the obvious lessons from East Asia—maintaining a competitive exchange rate and an outward-oriented economy that is driven by exports—the potential importance of equity during the growth process has been stressed in analysis of rapid growth along the Pacific Rim. Development models in the 1950s were little concerned with equity or income distribution except as a factor explaining savings rates. Early models of economic development that stressed the difference between traditional and modern sectors, for example, often emphasized the need to keep increases in incomes in the hands of potential savers, usually identified as industrialists, the government, or upper-income households. If more equitable distribution of assets and incomes contributes positively to economic growth, traditional models are of little relevance.

The Indonesian case adds an additional challenge to these models: the positive role that economic and political stability can play in stimulating rapid economic growth and in spreading its benefits to the poor. When the rest of the economic environment is favorable, economic and political stability provide the confidence to make long-term investments that lead to rapid gains in productivity. Stability of the rural economy, especially protection from a sudden fall in grain prices, allows farmers to be confident about investing in new inputs and technology. At the same time, price stability protects the landless rural and urban poor from steep increases in the price of their most important expenditure item—staple foods.

East and Southeast Asia are very densely populated in relation to the amount of arable land; Java is one of the most densely settled agricultural regions in the world. In view of the large populations in relation to available agricultural land in much of Asia, economic and political stability can be provided only by governments that have solved their domestic problem of food security. Hunger and famine in rural areas and food riots in urban areas undermine any efforts to build up a modern economy. Food security for individual households in rural areas and stable food markets in urban areas are essential to beginning and maintaining the process of economic growth.

Large countries in Asia had to develop their agricultural sectors, especially their rice economies, as the first step in providing food security. When the high-yielding varieties of rice and wheat became available in the mid-1960s, the Green Revolution transformed the potential of Asian countries to solve their food problems and bring stability to their economies. The countries that used this potential successfully were then able to accelerate the pace of economic growth. And because the growth process was initially centered on the rural economy, the rate of poverty was lowered rapidly. In Indonesia, a change in government strategy in the mid-1960s marked a significant turning point in the development process, but the discovery of high-yielding rice varieties at the same time meant that prospects were brighter not only for Indonesia but for poor countries throughout Asia. The 1970s and 1980s show a close correspondence between the rate of growth in per capita food supplies and growth in per capita incomes (see figure 1).

Two points about economic growth are important: countries need to grow rapidly if they are to get rich, and they must grow rapidly for a long time. Starting from a level of $200 per capita, a country whose income per capita is growing at 2 percent per year will reach a per capita income of just $244 after a decade and only $1,450 at the end of one hundred years. By contrast, a fast-growing country—4 percent per year—will still be poor after a decade, with per capita incomes of $296. But the simple arithmetic of compound interest means incomes will reach over $10,000 in a century. The United States may have the world's highest standard of living, but it has achieved that status by growing at 2 percent per year for more than two centuries. From the same starting point, a country growing at 4 percent per year would achieve that standard in roughly half the time.

Sustaining rapid economic growth for decade after decade was the miracle of development in East Asia—Japan, Korea, and Taiwan. Several countries in Southeast Asia learned how to sustain rapid growth as well, at least during the early stages. The Indonesian development approach incorporates lessons from East Asia in all three components of its development strategy. The most important lesson is to use the agricultural sector and the rural economy to provide the

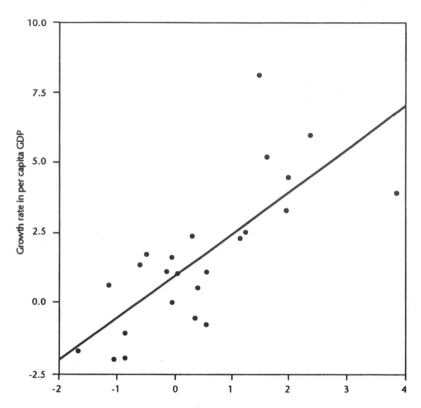

Fig. 1. Change in per Capita Food Production, Percent per Year, 1970s and 1980s

foundation that permits the development strategy to pursue growth, stability, and equity simultaneously and to pursue them in a complementary rather than a competitive fashion. When the rural sector becomes only a small part of the economy, rapid growth can no longer be sustained through this approach alone.

In the traditional model of economic development used widely in developing countries in the 1950s and 1960s—and in Africa and Latin America until the 1980s—efforts to achieve simultaneously rapid growth, stability, and equity pulled policy makers in opposite directions. The trade-offs were often posed in stark terms. A country could have rapid industrial growth with high inflation and deterioration in living standards of the rural poor. Or a country could choose slow growth with repressive stability and maintenance of traditional lives for peasants. The rural economy was never seen as a key element of growth itself.

The Indonesian approach to development, incorporating postwar experience in East Asia, rejected the idea that there was a necessary trade-off among these three objectives. By placing agriculture at the center of the development trilogy and using the rural economy as a positive contributor to growth, the Indonesian approach was able to address the problems of poverty, economic and political sta-

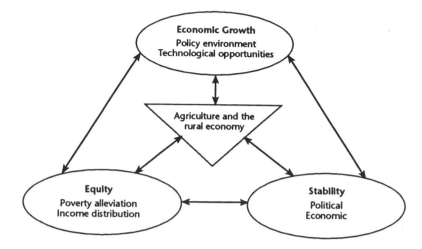

Fig. 2. The Development Trilogy in Indonesia

bility, and rapid economic growth—all at the same time. Such a strategy was limited without the potential for rapid gains in agricultural productivity that became available with the Green Revolution. These gains could be turned into an engine for rapid growth, however, only in the context of a rural-oriented development strategy—a strategy pursued during the 1970s and 1980s in Indonesia. The elements of that strategy and the mechanisms by which it was implemented seem quite obvious now to an Indonesian audience, but they were little short of revolutionary at the time. This approach is still controversial to many in the international development community.

Each component of Indonesia's development strategy has two dimensions (see figure 2). Economic growth has a policy component and a technological component. A concern for equity is multifaceted, which reflects the need first of all to raise everyone above some absolute poverty line but extends to broader issues involving the distribution of income, economic mobility, and equality before the law. Stability is both a political and an economic concept.

Economic stability comes in the form of macroeconomic policies and stability of the food economy (whenever the latter is a large part of the overall economy). Political stability ensures continuity of economic policy as well as confidence for domestic and foreign investors that basic "rules of the game" will not be changed. There is fine line between the political stability that is repressive and unresponsive to needs of the society and the political stability that reflects a vision of positive government involvement in stimulating economic development (and President Suharto and his family became progressively less responsive during the 1990s). For government involvement to be positive, its leaders must defend hard choices that recognize the scarcity of public revenues in the face of pressing needs for food subsidies, health clinics, and higher wages for public employees. There is no clear evidence that American-style democracy is essential, in the early stages of development, for this responsive form of political stability. Higher standards of living do lead to demands for greater political voice from ordinary citizens. The complexity and openness of the economies that achieve such standards of living require much greater personal freedom as well. An outward orientation is not just an economic strategy designed to increase export; it is also a state of mind—an understanding of other societies and a willingness and ability to deal with them. Looking back from the perspective of mid-1998, it is clear that the Suharto government failed badly in responding to this particular challenge.

How a government addresses the broader dimensions of equity evolves over time. Early in the development process, a government must work to alleviate absolute poverty. Later, with sheer destitution eliminated as a pressing social issue, concern should turn to other facets of equity. Very few countries have been able to grow rapidly without some skewing of the income distribution, whereby the rich get richer. The incentives needed to mobilize savings and direct them to the most productive investments, and the need to keep real wages low to stimulate choices of technologies that lead to large gains in employment, inevitably cause some widening in the share of incomes going to the top 20 percent of the distribution in relation to the share going to the bottom 20 percent. At the same time, economic mobility might be enhanced through public and private investments in health, education, and family planning. The sharply lower fertility and mortality rates achieved in Indonesia since 1970, for example, have transformed the expectations and prospects of women and children with respect to their potential economic roles.

In the early stages of development, however, the main focus should be on reducing the level of absolute poverty. This task requires raising the incomes of the rural landless, the underemployed, and the urban migrants working in the informal sector as *becak* drivers, trash pickers, household servants, and peddlars. No poor country has the resources to transfer incomes directly to these people in the form of subsidies. The economy must create enough jobs for unskilled workers that they obtain more secure and regular incomes. Typically, having a regular job is a major factor in whether an individual rises above the poverty line. When wage rates in rural areas start to rise as underemployed labor is fully absorbed into productive jobs, the poverty rate drops very quickly.

Indonesia had a remarkable record in reducing the rate of absolute poverty. When a calorie-based measure is used as a standard, the poverty rate in Indonesia declined from well over 50 percent of the population in the late 1960s to well under 20 percent in 1990. With per capita income in Indonesia in 1990 nearly $600 per year at the official exchange rate and over $2,300 in terms of purchasing power parity, there is understandable controversy about the continued relevance of a poverty measure based primarily on the cost of calories. The concern of the population is now shifting to broader measures of income distribution and the open and public displays of new wealth. This concern is a very healthy development for Indonesia so long as it does not threaten the success of policies and programs that reduce poverty and does not erode the broad support in rural areas for the political and economic strategies that have led to that success.

The basic economic policy designed to stimulate rapid growth is quite straightforward: improve the incentives for faster mobilization of both foreign and domestic capital, and promote public policies and investments that help markets function efficiently. The market-oriented growth that results from this policy approach, however, often tends to worsen the distribution of income.

Fortunately, the technological potential available to latecomers in the development process offers a way to improve income distribution. In particular, growth opportunities created by scientific revolutions in agricultural technology allow the rural economy to participate in the process of rapid development. These opportunities do not mean the agricultural sector can grow as rapidly as the manufacturing sector. No country has been able to do that for long. Eventually all countries will see their agricultural sectors shrink in relation to the industrial and service sectors. But the healthy way for this structural transformation of an economy to take place—from poor and agricultural to rich and industrial—is through rapid growth in the industrial and service sectors, not a reduction in agricultural output caused by starving the sector of infrastructure, new technology, and adequate incentives.

In the early stages of development, the role of agriculture is to stimulate economic growth through the establishment of linkages to the rest of the economy— supplying food to the cities, purchasing the output from newly established industries, and providing savings and labor to these factors. In the middle stages of development, when incomes are rising rapidly in the modern industrial and service sectors, the role of agriculture is to provide a buffer of income-earning opportunities for a large share of the work force not yet equipped with the education and skills to be productive in the modern sectors. Indonesia was in the early stage for most of the first 25-year strategic plan (from 1969 to 1994), when agriculture provided more than 40 percent of the new jobs for a rapidly expanding labor force and somewhat less than 20 percent of the increases in economic output. Aggressive investments in agricultural development paid Indonesia high dividends in economic growth, reduced poverty, and increased rice production. Each of these facilitated economic and political stability.

Most of the second 25-year strategic plan will be spent in the middle stage, where agriculture is no longer a major contributor to economic growth, although agriculture will be crucial to rapid recovery from the 1997–98 financial crisis. As a result, the economic policies needed for agriculture—policies that will buffer the pressures on the incomes and employment of the rural population— will be quite different from those appropriate at a time when the sector was a leading contributor to rising output. Rural inhabitants will feel the loss of their economic competitiveness, and they might demand the same kind of compensation that Japanese, Korean, Taiwanese, and Malaysian farmers have demanded.

They want high rice prices. Such demands will challenge the two-decades-old policy in Indonesia of maintaining domestic rice prices on the long-run trend in world prices to maximize efficiency in the agricultural sector.

These challenges from the rural sector cannot be ignored. All three objectives in the development strategy—growth, stability, and equity—must be pursued simultaneously if rapid growth is to be sustained for long periods of time. Economic growth itself depends on stability in economic policy and in political systems. Such stability, however, depends on standards of living rising fast enough to meet growing expectations, not only among well-paid urban workers and rich industrialists but also among unskilled workers and small farmers. To be achieved, each objective of the development trilogy depends on input from the other two. In turn, achievement of one objective then contributes directly to achievement of the other two. A positive developmental synergy emerges among all three elements, but only when the basic development strategy is designed to create and stimulate such effects.

Trade-offs do continue to exist, however, and choices must be made. Stability must not turn into rigidity in either economic or political affairs, as it did' in the waning days of the Suharto regime. The concern for equity in the development process must not turn into populist pressures for universal equality of incomes and immediate consumption at the expense of long-term investments. Economic growth must recognize the environmental as well as financial costs of resources. The role of political leadership in the development process is to seek a balance among these trade-offs and to articulate the role of the government in achieving this balance.

The fundamental choice for government is when to change the outcome from market forces. Much of the development process must be left to market forces, but some market failures are so serious that government intervention is required. In each element of the development trilogy, government has the potential to alter the market outcome. The right investments in education, health, infrastructure, and technological innovations can speed the rate of economic growth. Careful interventions in the rice economy can stabilize food prices around their long-run opportunity cost in world markets. Well-timed interventions by the central bank can stabilize the foreign exchange rate around its market-determined trend. Equity can be improved by spending in the social sectors, by targeting elements of the economic growth process to rural areas, and by stimulating choices of technology that create millions of jobs for unskilled workers.

But government interventions can make matters worse in each of these areas— often much worse. Most countries of the world would experience faster economic growth if the government intervened less rather than more. In many countries, instability in food prices and foreign exchange rates would be less if the government stopped trying to control them. Protection for large industrial concerns and biases against agriculture make the distribution of income much worse and the perceptions of unfairness even sharper. How is a country to know what to do? How can it do it well?

The Indonesian experience offers several lessons. First, investing to make markets work more to the benefit of economic growth is a legitimate task of government, but preventing markets from exerting competitive pressures and from sending signals to investors on how best to allocate resources will inevitably slow the rate of economic growth. With limited human and financial resources, most governments will do well to let markets lead the process of economic growth.

Second, the minimum task of governments in providing economic and political stability is to avoid worsening the inherent uncertainty about future events. The world is highly unpredictable even at the best of times. Governments often add uncertainty through erratic financial policies that create high and variable rates of inflation, arbitrary interventions into food and energy prices, and capricious manipulation of the basic rules governing the political system. When a government is highly competent and can exercise restraint in the face of potential vested interests—and several governments in East and Southeast Asia were able to meet this test for several decades—some limited interventions to bring added stability to the domestic economy may be justified through the basic calculus of improved efficiency. My own research argues strongly on behalf of stabilizing rice prices in the early stages of economic development, but only through policies that also stimulate growing participation by the private sector in rice marketing. It is hard to name other commodities for which a similar case can be made in favor of intervention. Even rice prices do not need to be stabilized when countries become rich.

Finally, I want to argue that the most important task of the government is to worry about the many dimensions of equity over time. The process of economic growth is measured not in years, but in decades and centuries. Unless the vast majority of the population participates in this process, they simply will not support the rigorous policies that are responsible for generating large savings and the directing of those resources to the most productive investment opportunities.

Redistribution of existing incomes through taxes and subsidies is a poor way to solve this problem. Redistribution is bureaucratically expensive, politically divisive, and creates negative incentives for investors. It is better to do as Indonesia did after 1967 and structure the growth process from the very beginning to help solve the problem of poverty. This approach inevitably means finding a strategy for raising productivity of rural labor. In most settings, such a strategy requires agricultural development with a focus on small farmers. Indonesia ignored this approach for the first two decades of its independence while it concentrated on the political process of nation building. But the fortuitous coincidence of a new government, oriented toward economic growth, and a new agricultural technology that opened the potential for rapid gains in rural productivity, put the country on a path that doubled per capita incomes every 15 to 20 years. With a slowdown in agricultural growth and increased diversion of resources to family enterprises, the growth strategy became vulnerable in the 1990s.

There are many challenges ahead for Indonesia. Maintaining an equitable distribution of the gains from rising incomes will be difficult as the role of agriculture in the economy declines. Urban workers, having risen from the poverty of 25 years ago, may begin to envy the wealth of the new industrial elite. Populist pressures for higher wages and lower food costs can halt the growth process, as they did in Argentina. Entrenched vested interests determined to defend their status at all costs can have an equally devastating effect on economic growth. Responses from the industrial elite in the Philippines to efforts aimed at stimulating export-led growth immobilized their economy for more than a decade. Both sets of pressures are distinct possibilities in Indonesia, and both are likely to be realized before the end of the century.

The hard times, it turns out, were not securely past. The specter of Argentina, the Philippines, and Africa hangs over all countries lined up on the runway of economic takeoff. Abundance in natural resources, an energetic people, and good economic policy from the late 1960s until the early 1990s have taxied Indonesia onto this runway. But the political economy that held these prospects in balance was fragile and dependent on the goodwill and participation of all elements of society. The failure of the development strategy to include that participation as the economy became more urban and industrial now forces the Indonesian society to restart the growth process from a badly shaken foundation.

NOTES

This article is a revised version of an address to the Indonesian Institute for Management Development at the sixteenth graduation ceremony of its MBA program, in Jakarta, December 21, 1992. The view and interpretations are those of the author and should not be attributed to the institute. I would like to thank Carol F. Timmer for her usual editorial acumen. Minor revisions were made in mid-June 1998, at the stage of page proofs, but extensive discussion of the cause and effects of the financial crisis has not been possible.

1. In order of increasing per capita incomes, the countries with growth rates in per capita incomes of 4.0% or higher are as follows (growth rates from 1965 to 1990): China (5.8), Indonesia (4.5), Egypt (4.1), Paraguay (4.6), Thailand (4.4), Malaysia (4.0), South Korea (7.1), Singapore (6.5), Hong Kong (6.2), and Japan (4.1). In addition, three countries with populations under 2 million had rapid growth rates: Lesotho (4.9%; population 1.8 million), Botswana (8.4%, population 1.3 million), and Oman (6.4%, population 1.6 million). See World Bank *World Development Report, 1992.*

2. An advantage of restricting the comparison to Indonesia before and after 1965 is that one need not consider the great differences in cultural and social factors between Africa and Southeast Asia. Important lessons are also likely to be learned by studying Indonesia pre- and post-1997.

33

Zimbabwe's Maize Revolution: Insights for Closing Africa's Food Gap

CARL K. EICHER AND BERNARD KUPFUMA

AFRICA'S FOOD CRISIS

With the population of sub-Saharan Africa (hereafter referred to as Africa) growing at 2.7 percent and food demand at 3.0 to 3.5 percent per year, Africa faces the same type of long-term food crisis that Asia faced in the early sixties (Schultz 1964). Although rising food imports (mostly food aid) have helped close Africa's food gap in the near term, there is little doubt that rapid technical change in the six major food staples—maize, cassava, sorghum, millet, wheat, and rice—represent the key to stepping up food production and closing Africa's chronic food gap (Mitchell, Ingco, and Duncan 1997). Increased productivity through technical change in food crops has the potential to feed Africa's growing population, reduce the real (inflation-adjusted) price of food to consumers and contribute to broad-based economic growth by raising rural incomes.

Three reasons explain why Zimbabwe's maize revolution is of special importance to African policy makers and donors. First, maize has recently replaced cassava as the most important food crop in Africa in terms of calories consumed (Byerlee and Eicher 1997). Hybrid maize is spreading rapidly in eastern and southern Africa and now covers roughly 40 percent of the area planted to maize. Africa's emerging maize revolution and the recent success in developing improved cassava varieties in West Africa and increased rice production in Mali,

CARL K. EICHER is University Distinguished Professor in the Department of Agricultural Economics and the African Studies Center, Michigan State University.

BERNARD KUPFUMA is an agricultural economist in the Department of Research and Specialist Services, Harare, Zimbabwe.

An earlier version, by Carl K. Eicher, entitled "Zimbabwe's Maize-based Green Revolution: Preconditions for Replication," appeared in *World Development* 23, no. 5 (1995): 805–18. Published, with omissions and editorial revisions, by permission of Elsevier Science Ltd., Oxford, England and the authors.

and sorghum production in the Sudan represent rays of hope for closing Africa's food gap over the coming ten to fifteen years.[1] Second, Zimbabwe generated a maize revolution in 1960, five years before the Green Revolution was launched in India. Third, Zimbabwe's maize revolution is an indigenous food production model rather than a prepackaged model imported from another continent. Zimbabwean scientists patiently carried out research on hybrid maize for twenty-eight years (1932–60) before they hit the jackpot, developing a maize hybrid that increased yields an average of 46 percent without fertilizer. Zimbabwe also developed a number of institutions and policies that stimulated maize production and exports and created the capacity to manage its national maize economy during periods of drought and abundance.

The purpose of this chapter is to distill the essence of Zimbabwe's maize revolution and discuss the preconditions for replicating this success story in other nations in Africa. Zimbabwe's maize revolution is defined and analyzed in terms of a sharp increase in maize production, not in terms of access to food. Although food access issues are of critical importance, they are beyond the scope of this chapter.

Over the past two decades many Asian experts have promoted the view that Asia's Green Revolution model could be implemented quickly in Africa. The Asian model has captured the attention of many African leaders because it dramatically boosted the yields of Asia's two main food staples, wheat and rice; but there are two main reasons why the Asian Green Revolution model has been unsuccessful in closing Africa's food gap. First, Asia's Green Revolution was based on two main food crops grown under irrigation. By contrast 90 to 95 percent of the food production in Africa is rainfed.[2] This explains why successful rainfed food production models such as Zimbabwe's are of broad interest throughout Africa. The ability of Zimbabwe's short season maize hybrids to out perform sorghum in many low-rainfall areas has undermined the contention that maize is a "fashionable crop" that is "vulnerable in years of low rainfall and competitive for land with safer crops" (Lipton 1989, 362). Second, unlike Asia, where two dominant food crops are grown in large homogeneous areas under irrigation, Africa has an array of food crops grown under diverse ecologies and severe weather instability. The policy implication of Africa's diversity in diets and ecologies is that developing improved technology is going to require more research and development resources and time in Africa than it did in Asia.

MAIZE IN ZIMBABWE'S ECONOMY

Zimbabwe is a nation of eleven million people with an average life expectancy of fifty-seven years, near universal primary education, and a per capita GNP of US$540 (World Bank 1997). Although the agricultural sector contributes only 15 percent of the gross domestic product, it is the major employer in the country and is responsible for around half of total export earnings.

Zimbabwe's dualistic agricultural sector has two subsectors: the large-scale commercial farming sector and the smallholder sector (Rukuni and Eicher 1994). Today there are 4,000 large-scale commercial farms, down from 5,000 when independence was achieved in 1980. The smallholder sector encompasses 1,000,000 communal farms, 8,500 small-scale commercial farms, and 56,000 recently created resettlement farms.[3] Large-scale farmers control about two-thirds of the land in Natural Region II, the region of prime agricultural land. Most smallholders are located in Natural Regions IV and V, the driest parts of the country.

Maize is the national food staple of Zimbabwe. Smallholders have historically had the largest area of maize under cultivation. From 1965 to 1994, smallholder maize accounted for 70 percent of the national maize area, but the average smallholder yield was around one-fourth of the average maize yield on large-scale farms. The average smallholder maize yield increased during the eighties, but variability also increased, because of recurring drought. The large increase in smallholder maize production in the eighties is a product of higher prices to farmers, a backlog of hybrid maize varieties, yield increases, and an increase in market collection points in the smallholder areas.

Zimbabwe has generated two maize revolutions: the first was spearheaded by large-scale commercial farmers in the 1960s and 1970s. The second was launched by smallholders after independence in 1980.

THE FIRST MAIZE REVOLUTION: LARGE-SCALE COMMERCIAL FARMERS, 1960–1980

In 1890, Cecil Rhodes dispatched European settlers living in South Africa to move north and colonize Zimbabwe, but after failing to find gold deposits on a par with those in South Africa, the settlers turned to farming.[4] The early settlers focused on growing maize, and maize exports grew at the phenomenal annual rate of 18.8 percent between 1909 and 1930, mainly to satisfy the demand for white maize in England's starch industry (Masters 1994, 228). The settler farmers subsequently gained control over prime agricultural land through the passage of a series of Land Ordinances that "guaranteed white economic dominance and black poverty during the 90-year colonial period" (Herbst 1990). The colonial strategy of confiscating land and depressing the wages of farm workers and migrant laborers and the profitability of small-scale farms created a favorable macroeconomic environment and a labor reserve for large-scale farms. The same type of agricultural development strategy was also pursued in South Africa and Kenya (Deininger and Binswanger 1995).

The political and institutional foundation for Zimbabwe's first maize revolution was laid in the early part of this century. The government established agricultural research stations between 1903 and 1919 in response to pressure from white commercial farmers. These farmers established provincial farmer associations which subsequently evolved into several powerful farm organizations, including the Zimbabwe Tobacco Association, representing the tobacco farmers, and the Commercial Farmers Union (CFU), representing the large-scale commercial farmers (Blackie 1987, 119). During World War II, the government secured the cooperation of commercial farmers in increasing food production, in exchange for the passage of the Licensing Act of 1942. This required all commercial farmers and ranchers to buy a license from the newly formed Rhodesian National Farmers Union, which was subsequently renamed the Commercial Farmers Union after independence. The passage of the Licensing Act of 1942 has been described as a "stroke of organizational brilliance," because it assured the Union a sound financial base (dues from farmers and ranchers), which allowed white farmers to finance research and lobbying exercises (Herbst 1990, 40). The CFU currently has a large salaried staff and is led by a farmer who leaves his farm to work full time at the CFU headquarters during his term of office (Bratton 1994).

The technical and institutional preconditions for the first maize revolution were developed through large public and modest private investments in the four prime movers of agricultural development from 1920 to 1950:

1. new technology that was produced by long-term public and private investments in agricultural research;
2. human capital and managerial skills that are produced by investments in schools, training programs, and on-the-job experience;
3. capital investments in infrastructure, such as dams, irrigation, telecommunications and roads; and
4. investments in farmer support institutions such as marketing, credit, fertilizer, and seed distribution systems.

Public and private investments in these prime movers provided the foundation for commercial farmers, who dramatically increased maize yields and production from 1960 to 1980.

Research on hybrid maize was initiated by H. C. Arnold at the government research station in the capital city of Harare in 1932. In 1949, after seventeen years of research, a hybrid variety, Southern Rhodesia 1 (SR1), was released to commercial farmers, but yields were unstable (Mashingaidze 1994). This explains why maize breeders continued to work on improved hybrids throughout the 1950s. In 1960, after twenty-eight years of research on maize hybrids, breeders released the highly successful SR52, a high-yielding maize variety that formed the foundation of Zimbabwe's first maize revolution. SR52 seed increased maize yields on farms by 46 percent (without fertilizer) over the yield of Southern Cross, the most common improved local open-pollinated variety (Weinmann 1975; Tattersfield 1982).

Without question, SR52 hybrid maize is the most famous improved food crop variety that has ever been developed in Africa; it is a long season (150-day) variety that was quickly adopted by commercial farmers of Zimbabwe on fertile land with high rainfall. Within eight years, (1960–68), two-thirds of the maize area of commercial farmers was planted to it (Rattray 1969, 10).

Two political developments of the 1950s and 1960s contributed to the rapid adoption of hybrid maize in Zimbabwe and in neighboring Zambia. The first was Great Britain's decision in 1953 to establish a regional political Federation of Rhodesia and Nyasaland, consisting of Northern Rhodesia (now Zambia), Southern Rhodesia (now Zimbabwe) and Nyasaland (now Malawi). The federation lasted only ten years (1953–63), but it facilitated the formation of a regional research network and an exchange of hybrid maize varieties among the three countries. The second political event that influenced hybrid maize adoption was Southern Rhodesia's illegal assumption of independence from Great Britain in 1965. This provoked international sanctions against Rhodesia's exports, including tobacco, the leading agricultural export. As a result, tobacco quotas were imposed, and commercial farmers scrambled to diversify away from tobacco to maize, cotton, wheat, soybeans, and coffee (Blackie 1987). The fall in tobacco exports encouraged researchers to develop a short-season maize hybrid that could replace tobacco on sandy soils in low-rainfall areas. After a few years of research, a new series of three-way maize hybrids (R200, R201, and R215) was released by government breeders in the early 1970s.[5] Fortuitously these new short-season hybrids met the needs of former commercial tobacco growers as well as those of a large number of smallholders. This is one of many examples of how technological spillovers from R&D activities for large-scale farms have helped Zimbabwe's smallholders.

Zimbabwe's commercial farmers were aggressive and proactive in developing efficient farmer support organizations to speed the uptake of hybrid maize. The development of the seed industry is an example of private initiative. In 1940, a small group of commercial farmers established the Zimbabwe Seed Maize Association to produce certified maize seed under the supervision of the Ministry of Agriculture (Tattersfield and Havazvidi 1994). In 1949, the association was available to distribute the newly released hybrid maize seed to commercial farmers. Today, commercial farmers produce hybrid maize seed for the Seed Co-op Company of Zimbabwe, which sells it at home and in a dozen countries throughout Africa. Zimbabwe's seed distribution system is currently providing maize seed to small, medium, and large farms. Zimbabwe's Seed Co-op is the crown jewel of seed distribution systems in Africa.

The rapid uptake of hybrid maize seed by commercial farmers in Zimbabwe in the sixties was aided by the excellent physical infrastructure in the large-scale commercial farming areas. These areas are served by a good network of paved roads and are close to the railway lines. All farms are electrified and are well served by a good telecommunication network. Input and output markets, crop intake depots, and banks are easily accessible. Such a system of institutions does not exist in the smallholder sector.

To summarize, Zimbabwe's first maize revolution, from 1960 to 1980, was spearheaded by politically active commercial farmers who lobbied for a strong national agricultural research system and complementary public investments in infrastructure, guaranteed farm prices, and aggressive export marketing schemes.

With SR52 maize as the centerpiece, maize production grew rapidly in the sixties and seventies because the government developed an integrated maize production and marketing system and a concurrent capacity to manage a national maize economy in times of scarcity and abundance. Zimbabwe's coordinated maize delivery system—research, extension, seed distribution, and marketing—effectively turned maize into a cash crop and enabled Zimbabwe to export maize for 19 of 21 years over the 1970–91 period.

THE SECOND MAIZE REVOLUTION: SMALLHOLDERS, 1980–1986

At Zimbabwe's independence in 1980, roughly 5,000 commercial farmers controlled half the arable land, and 700,000 smallholders (communal farmers) occupied the other half (Blackie 1982). The typical smallholder farmed around three to five hectares of arable land. The new government, headed by Robert Mugabe, declared its political support for a smallholder road to development and agreed to honor the terms of the independence agreement, which stipulated that commercial farm land would be sold on a "willing buyer–willing seller" basis for the first decade of independence. This political decision to postpone land reform and maintain a strong commercial farming community helped maintain national food security and bought time for the new government to restructure the basic agricultural institutions (e.g., credit, research, extension) to serve the majority of farmers—the black smallholders.

Zimbabwe's second maize revolution was spearheaded by smallholders who rapidly adopted hybrid maize varieties and fertilizer and doubled their maize production in six years, 1980–86.[6] This unexpected doubling of maize production is attributed to a combination of factors, including peace in the countryside, which enabled many smallholders to bring land abandoned during the civil war back into cultivation;[7] a backlog of short-season hybrid maize varieties; a sharp increase in guaranteed producer prices; removal of racial and institutional barriers to credit, which helped smallholders purchase seed and fertilizer; and expansion of subsidized government marketing services (e.g., grain buying points) in rural areas (Rohrbach 1989).[8] Unlike Zimbabwe's first maize revolution, by large-scale commercial farmers, the second revolution attracted considerable international press coverage in the mid-eighties because it was led by smallholders over a period during which a million people died in the Ethiopian famine (1984–85). This achievement garnered the Africa Leadership Prize for President Mugabe in 1988, because it showed that smallholder maize production could be profitable and maize cultivation was capable of increasing food production and generating broad-based benefits to tens of thousands of rural families and urban consumers.

Zimbabwe's smallholder-led maize revolution benefited from technological and institutional spillovers from the reform efforts of large-scale farmers. The national infrastructure of roads, research, and farmer support institutions that had been nurtured and developed by commercial farmers from 1930–80 helped jump-start the smallholder-led maize revolution of the 1980s (Blackie 1990). At independence, the new government inherited one of the most productive public agricultural research systems in Africa, including high-quality research programs in maize, tobacco, cotton, and livestock. Smallholders had access to a backlog of short-season hybrid maize varieties, which contributed to the rapid uptake of hybrids and the doubling of smallholder maize production in six years. The estimated annual rate of return to public investment in hybrid maize research was 43 percent from 1932 to 1990 (Kupfuma 1994).

But Zimbabwe's R&D experience since independence in 1980 includes some problems that should be carefully studied by other countries in Africa. Soon after independence, the Mugabe government directed its national agricultural research service to develop relevant technology for smallholders, especially those living in low-rainfall areas where maize, sorghum, and millet were the food staples. This shift in the research mandate was difficult to implement, however, because of a loss of experienced research officers[9] and a failure of the new government to provide adequate funds to finance the required field trials in the smallholder farming regions.

The expansion of government credit for smallholders was also a major contributor to the smallholder-led maize revolution in the early 1980s. The main government credit agency, the Agricultural Finance Corporation (AFC), has its origins in the Land Bank of 1911, which had a mandate to serve white commercial farmers. At independence, the government decided to expand credit to smallholders, especially those producing maize and cotton. The number of loans to smallholders increased from 18,000 in 1980/81 to 77,000 in 1985/86. But the number of loans was sharply reduced, to 30,000, in 1990/91 because of managerial and loan supervision problems in "scaling-up" the credit program. Also, the delinquency rate was high, partially because recurrent droughts increased risk and the rate of default and partially because of the rapid extension and inadequate supervision of the loans.[10] The AFC responded to these problems by becoming more selective and reducing the number of loans to smallholders to 30,000 in 1990 and 23,000 in 1994, which indicates that it is lending to only 2.3 percent of the one million smallholders in the country.[11]

Zimbabwe's postindependence experience illustrates how difficult it is for a new government to restructure agricultural credit, research, and extension institutions that are primarily serving commercial farmers and redirect the energy of these institutions into serving hundreds of thousands of smallholders, especially those in marginal areas with poor infrastructure and little political muscle. Over the past four decades, donors have helped many African governments design and implement farmer support projects (credit, extension, seed, fertilizer) to serve pockets of smallholders. But most ministries of agriculture have had great difficulty developing the managerial capacity and financial resources to replicate successful projects on a national level. Zimbabwe's smallholder credit program sheds light on the complex managerial task involved in scaling-up farmer support institutions to serve the rural majority, the smallholders. The "scaling up" problem has plagued the Sasakawa-Global 2000 food production project in Ghana and similar projects in other countries.[12]

Who benefited from Zimbabwe's second maize revolution? Without question, smallholders in higher rainfall areas in the heart of Zimbabwe's maize belt were major beneficiaries of the second maize revolution, because they supplied 70 percent of the total smallholder maize sales to the Grain Marketing Board in the 1980s (Stack 1994, 261).[13] But there were also large welfare gains accruing to smallholders who planted R200, R201, and R215 hybrids in lower-rainfall areas, because these high-yielding hybrids typically out-yielded local maize and sorghum varieties, enabling these farmers to release land and labor to expand oilseed production and livestock raising and to pursue rural nonfarm activities.

Fueled by higher producer prices, improvements in seed, credit, and fertilizer, and by marketing subsidies, Zimbabwe was awash with maize by the mid-eighties. This explains why an analysis of Zimbabwe's experience must go beyond production issues and examine how the government managed its national food economy during several vastly different food policy scenarios, ranging from overflowing grain silos in the mid-eighties to the catastrophic drought of 1992 and the food riots in Harare in 1998. In 1985, good rainfall and excellent growing conditions produced a record crop of three million tons of maize, an amount equivalent to three years of domestic consumption. The added cost of financing the government's maize reserve (2 million tons in 1985), however, forced a reappraisal of producer pricing policy and the level of maize reserves to carry over. The government subsequently encouraged commercial farmers to reduce the area under maize for the 1985/86 crop year and diversify into oilseeds, game ranching, and horticultural crops for export. Both commercial farmers and smallholders slowly reduced the area under maize cultivation in the late eighties, but the area under smallholder maize cultivation has increased in the nineties.

The Mugabe-led government performed brilliantly during the severe drought that blanketed Southern Africa in 1992. Zimbabwe and other countries in the region pooled rainfall information from their early warning systems and mobilized rail cars to carry 12 million tons of grain into the region, thus preventing drought from turning into famine.

But the pursuit of macroeconomic stability and policy credibility has been fraught with difficulties, especially in the 1990s. After pursuing a coherent set of macroeconomic and agricultural policies in the early eighties, the economy faltered in the late eighties under the weight of money-losing state industries and heavy food subsidies. In 1989, under pressure from donors, the government embarked on economic policy reforms, with the goal of liberalizing and privatizing the food system and opening up the market economy. But government policies have wavered in the 1990s, and in 1997 President Mugabe announced a bold program to expropriate about half of the country's private farm land, most of it owned by whites, without having the domestic or foreign aid to finance and implement the land reform. Also in 1997, the government agreed to disburse generous pensions for 50,000 ex-soldiers, even though the economy was in dire straits. These hasty political and macroeocnmic decisions created an atmosphere of economic uncertainty and in early 1998 sparked riots in Harare protesting price hikes on basic commodities. These examples illustrate how the art of managing a food economy is a subset of political and macroeconomic factors.

To summarize, Zimbabwe's second maize revolution saw smallholders double maize production between 1980 and 1986. This achievement cannot be attributed to a single factor, such as higher prices, fertilizer, greater access to credit, or an improved extension model. The second revolution was achieved by a combination of factors including raising maize producer prices, developing short-season maize varieties and modifying institutions (e.g., credit and marketing) to meet the specific needs of smallholders (Blackie 1994).

CHANGING ROLES OF THE PUBLIC AND PRIVATE SECTORS

Zimbabwe's maize revolutions shed light on the changing roles of the state, of nongovernmental organizations (NGOs), and of the private sector in increasing food production over time. Despite donor pressure on African governments to enlarge the role of the private sector and NGOs in increasing food production, it is important to remember that NGOs did not develop Zimbabwe's impressive all-weather road network. Neither did private seed companies carry out the decades-long sustained research that led to the development of the hybrid maize varieties that fueled the first and second maize revolutions. Finally, donors did not develop the politically powerful farm organizations that made the case for sustained government investments in the prime movers of agricultural development, including the development of productive public research and farmer support organizations.

Instead, the state was the organizer and risk taker in developing Zimbabwe's maize breeding program, all-weather road network, and its grain marketing and storage system. Zimbabwe's experience highlights the strategic importance of an active government role in the early stage of development—i.e., the agrarian stage—because private investors and traders were understandably reluctant to make long-term investments in agricultural research and to assume the risk involved in developing credit, seed, and fertilizer distribution systems for smallholders, especially those living in remote areas. Nevertheless, the private sector played an important role in both of Zimbabwe's maize revolutions. Commercial farmers provided leadership in developing a seed production and distribution system in the 1950s. Since independence the private sector has taken on a greater role in maize breeding, fertilizer and seed distribution, and the marketing of new high-valued export crops. In fact, private seed companies in Zimbabwe currently have a larger maize breeding program than the government in terms of scope, scale, and size. For other African nations, the critical lesson to be learned from Zimbabwe's experience is the need to avoid dogmatism about what should be done by the state or the private sector in closing the food gap. The issue for policy makers is to focus on the changing comparative advantage of the public and private sectors over time and the changes that are needed to develop a legal and incentive framework that will encourage private investment in the entire food system, including R&D, farmer support organizations, production, marketing, and processing.

Looking ahead, however, it is clear that strategic government investments are still needed to assist smallholders who lack the basic infrastructure essential for rapid agricultural growth. Since the private sector rarely invests in the development of the physical infrastructure, because of the difficulties in internalizing the benefits from such investments, the improvement of the rural infrastructure must remain the responsibility of the public sector. The use of public funds to improve the infrastructure for smallholders in the future should be seen as an investment rather than as a subsidy. The costs to the state of establishing telecommunications, roads, and other infrastructural services in smallholder areas will be high in the short to medium term, but the economic, social, and political benefits can be substantial in the long run.

CLOSING AFRICA'S FOOD GAP: INSIGHTS FROM ZIMBABWE

Despite layers and layers of skepticism among politicians and policy makers about the ability of smallholders to meet Africa's food demand in the twenty-first century, there is a large body of evidence that smallholders can be productive if they are given access to resources (e.g., land, credit), appropriate institutions, incentives, and markets. This is what happened in Asia when smallholders served as the engine of Asia's Green Revolution from 1965 to 1985.[14] China's experience in leveling the playing field for smallholders illustrates the critical influence that agricultural policies can have on smallholder production. After China abandoned collective farming in 1978 and assigned most land to families (on average one-half hectare per family) and raised producer prices, farm output grew at the highest rate in the world (6 percent per year) over the next fifteen years (see chapter 31 in this volume). The dynamism of smallholders in Indonesia, Thailand, and Vietnam adds further evidence to the global generalization that smallholders can be a reliable source of increased food production.

Nevertheless, despite the incontrovertible record of smallholders in spearheading Asia's Green Revolution, there is still an abundance of skepticism about the smallholder food production model in policy and bureaucratic circles in many countries in Africa. This skepticism is especially noticeable in South Africa (Eicher and Rukuni 1996). Zimbabwe's experience illustrates that smallholders can fulfill their productivity potential if they are supported by political leadership, macroeconomic stability, cost-effective farmer support institutions, a stream of new technology from home and abroad, and access to domestic and international markets. Many of these ingredients have been missing from hastily conceived crash food production campaigns in other countries in Africa.

PRECONDITIONS FOR REPLICATION

Zimbabwe's first and second maize revolutions were achieved by fulfilling the same basic preconditions: political support, a stream of new technology from home and abroad, institutional innovations, and favorable economic incentives and markets for farmers (Eicher 1989). This nexus of policies, institutions, technology, and incentives and markets created a *system* of national development institutions with a capacity to develop new technology, adapt it to local ecosystems, diffuse it to farmers, and manage a national food economy in times of either abundance or scarcity. The most important precondition for getting agriculture moving and increasing food production in Africa is political leadership for agriculture, the scarcest ingredient in African politics (Eicher 1982).

Political Leadership

Africa's development experience has shown that political support for agriculture cannot be imposed by foreign donors. Political support for a rapid and sustainable increase in food production may be generated from indigenous farm organizations, agribusinesses, professional agriculturalists, and political leaders who understand the political and economic importance of achieving a reliable food surplus (from home and abroad), the contribution of agricultural growth to reducing rural and urban poverty, and the importance of maintaining macroeconomic stability. Indigenous political leadership has four strategic roles to play in agricultural development. First, as Timmer points out in chapter 11, political leaders must pursue fiscal, monetary, and trade policies that create macroeconomic stability. Second, political leaders must give high priority to creating a broad-based agrarian structure that is capable of putting people to work. In countries with a dual agrarian structure, land reform, taxing unused land, and expanding the use of contract farming are needed to open up land for the landless and for farmers without enough land to support a family. There is a strong economic case for land reform in dual agrarian societies; empirical evidence from throughout the world shows that small-scale, broadly dispersed family farms can help increase agricultural productivity *and* help ensure that the benefits of increased agricultural productivity are broadly distributed through employment and agricultural growth linkages. Third, political leadership is required to take the hard decisions on mobilizing some of the agricultural surplus (taxes) and putting it back into public investments such as rural infrastructure, and agricultural research which can help achieve a higher rate of agricultural growth in the future. Fourth, political leadership is crucial in facilitating the participation of the rural majority in the political process, including the freedom to organize commodity groups, farm organizations, and cooperatives and in increasing the participation of rural people in the management of rural schools and extension programs.

In Zimbabwe, commercial farmers developed a strong national farm organization, the Commercial Farmers Union, and affiliated commodity associations that promoted the economic interests of commercial farmers in the political arena. For example, as a result of pressure from commercial farmers, the government in 1931 established the Maize Control Board, subsequently renamed the Grain Marketing Board (GMB) (Muir 1994). In 1945 the Zimbabwe National Farmers Union (ZNFU) was formed to represent the interests of small-scale (black) commercial farms. At independence in 1980, the new government made a political commitment to creating a smallholder path to development and assisted in expanding the program of work of the National Farmers Association of Zimbabwe (NFAZ).[15] The ZNFU and NFAZ were merged in 1991, and a new organization, Zimbabwe Farmers' Union (ZFU), was formed to represent the interests of both smallholders and small-scale commercial farmers. At the time of the 1991 merger about 10 percent of the smallholders in the country were paid-up members of the new farm organization (Bratton 1994).[16] Zimbabwe's experience is a sober reminder of how difficult it is to mobilize hundreds of thousands of dispersed smallholders into politically active farm organizations that can counter the urban bias of urban consumers, trade unions, the military, and the civil service (Bates 1993). (See also chapter 13 in this volume.) The challenge ahead in Africa is to open up the political system and to help smallholders and rural people develop grassroots organizations and to make the case for their economic interests in the local and national political arenas.

Economic Incentives and Markets for Farmers

The economic preconditions for a sustainable food crop revolution concern farm profitability and fiscal sustainability. The foundation for a rapid increase in food production is profitable farming on a recurring basis. In Zimbabwe it has been proven that hybrid maize can be profitable for many smallholders at low levels of fertilizer use and even in many low-rainfall areas. The challenge for policy makers is to create in farmers the expectation that it will be profitable for them to invest their resources (especially family labor) in farm and land improvements and the adoption of new technology. These accretionary types of farm capital formation (e.g., leveling land and building soil conservation terraces) are critical to improving land productivity in a land-scarce economy.

An important unresolved issue is how to finance a sustainable maize revolution. At independence, Zimbabwe's new government made a commitment to leveling the playing field for smallholders by unifying the two extension services, expanding the size of the extension staff, and dramatically increasing the number of loans to smallholders. Also, the government's Grain Marketing Board incurred large subsidies in expanding the number of seasonal grain buying points from 5 in 1980 to 148 in 1985, in order that smallholders would have improved access to the market. The GMB's overall support to the maize industry required substantial government subsidies (Masters 1994). By the mid-eighties, however, it was clear that the marketing subsidies and the interest charges on carrying over a national maize reserve of two million tons (equivalent to two years of domestic consumption) could not be sustained. As a result, farmers were urged to reduce maize production starting in 1986, and maize marketing and consumer subsidies were scaled back in the late eighties and early nineties. Also, the number of grain buying points was lowered to 42 in 1989 and 9 in 1991. The lack of fiscal sustainability of Zimbabwe's maize revolution is a critical problem that is now being addressed in Zimbabwe's economic reform programs (Jayne et al. 1997). The same problem emerged in neighboring Zambia when government subsidies in support of the maize industry reached 17 percent of the total government budget in 1988 (Howard and Mungoma 1997). Since then, the government of Zambia has carried out major reforms to reduce maize subsidies.

Technological Innovation

A continuous stream of new technology from home and abroad is a precondition for a food crop revolution and sustainable agricultural growth. The starting point in technology development is to blend improved farm practices with technology developed by local, regional, and international public and private research systems. The ability of a country to borrow scientific knowledge and technology from abroad and blend it with indigenous technology, however, requires the same type of scientific capacity that is required to invent new technology.

Zimbabwe's public agricultural research system developed a formidable capacity to borrow as well as develop new maize technology. Because inbred and hybrid maize lines from the Corn Belt of the United States were found to be ill-suited to the agroecologies of Zimbabwe, varieties from Central America and South Africa were imported and crossed with local varieties. Stable government funding for research provided the continuity of investigation that was essential for the development and release of the acclaimed SR52 maize hybrid in 1960 and the subsequent development in the 1970s of R200, R201, and R215 hybrids for low-rainfall areas where a high proportion of smallholders were living.

Zimbabwe's experience illustrates the time required to develop an improved food crop variety. A small team of maize scientists carried out breeding research on maize hybrids for 28 years before releasing the SR52 hybrid in 1960. The experience of the United States is also instructive of the long gestation period for developing new technology. The theory of hybridization dates back to 1905, U.S. public research expenditures on hybrid corn began in 1910, but hybrid corn production did not become widespread until the 1930s.

Continuity of scientific leadership also played an important role in Zimbabwe's maize success story. Small teams of highly motivated and well-paid local scientists devoted their entire careers to research on one or two commodities.[17] Zimbabwe's favorable scientific culture is illustrated by the fact that four senior maize breeders were in charge of hybrid maize research over a fifty-six-year span, 1932 to 1988 (Eicher 1990). Each senior breeder had at least five years of overlap with his predecessor (Olver 1988). In contrast to this unusual continuity of scientific leadership, there have been six directors of neighboring Malawi's Department of Agricultural Research in over just the twelve years 1985–97 (Rukuni, Blackie, and Eicher 1998).

Zimbabwe's experience also sheds light on the significance of the size of public research systems. Unlike many African countries that increased their number of agricultural scientists five- to tenfold after independence, the government of Zimbabwe decided not to significantly increase the number of agricultural scientists following independence.[18] However, the Department of Research and Specialist Services (DR&SS) is now under pressure to expand its research program for smallholders, and more researchers and higher operating budgets will be required to meet the diverse research needs of smallholders, especially those living in low-rainfall areas (Rukuni 1996).

A sobering lesson that flows from Zimbabwe's story is how quickly the technological leadership of a nation can evaporate when a government reduces its real (inflation-adjusted) outlays on research and allows incentives for scientists to deteriorate. In the early 1980s public expenditures on research and extension were roughly the same, but in course of the decade the government increased its expenditure on extension relative to research and by 1991/92, the annual extension expenditure was more than double that of research (Zimbabwe 1991, 43). Also, Zimbabwe's public agricultural research budget was cut by 33 percent in real terms from 1980/81 (Z$8.0 million) to 1993/94 (Z$5.4 million) (Zimbabwe 1995). The decline in DR&SS's real budget occurred over the same time that its research mandate was being significantly expanded to carry out more research that was relevant to smallholders. In 1997, faced with the sharp cut in its budget and a shortage of operational funds to carry out field research, DR&SS scientists and representatives of farm organizations are engaged in intensive discussion of the feasibility of increasing public and private research partnerships, private sector research, and increasing Zimbabwe's capacity to become an intelligent "borrower" of technology from neighboring countries and regional and international research networks (Maredia and Eicher 1995).

Institutional Innovations

The third precondition for a maize revolution involves the art of developing a responsive and cost-effective system of farmer support institutions (public and/or private) to diffuse improved technology to farmers and to market the increased agricultural output. Over the past decade many academics have stressed the crucial role of effective institutions in promoting development (North 1987).

One of the important institutional lessons that emerges from Zimbabwe's experience is the role of time in crafting a system of development institutions. For example, Zimbabwe's public research system was slowly and pragmatically pieced together by indigenous scientists who enjoyed fairly consistent government financial support from 1920 to 1960. During the civil war in the seventies, commercial farmers financed the acquisition of a private research station (Rattray-Arnold) in 1973 in anticipation of the shift in emphasis of the public research system to smallholders after independence. In 1982 commercial farmers launched another private venture, the Agricultural Research Trust, on a 260-hectare research farm, for the purpose of testing new technology on large-scale commercial farms. Today public and private research systems coexist, illustrating how private research has substituted for and supplemented public research over time.

Since Africa's rural landscape is littered with inefficient government seed organizations, it is timely to examine Zimbabwe's public and private practices in distributing maize seed. Because farmers must replace hybrid maize seed every year, it is critically important for an efficient seed service to be in place to ensure a timely distribution of new seed to farmers before planting season. In 1940 a group of commercial farmers organized a seed cooperative in Zimbabwe, some nine years before the first hybrid maize variety was released. The Seed Co-operative was given exclusive access to all seed varieties developed by government researchers, in exchange for storing adequate seed for replanting in case of a national crop failure. Pannar, a private South African–based seed company, entered the Zimbabwe market in 1979 and was followed by Pioneer HI-Bred International in 1985. In the early 1990s Zimbabwe's Seed Co-op signed an agreement with DeKalb Genetics Corporation (USA) to gain access to DeKalb's global germplasm base and its international marketing skills. Seed distribution in Zimbabwe has demonstrated that both cooperatives and private seed companies can be relied upon to deliver hybrid seed to farmers before planting season and at prices that are affordable to resource-poor farmers. Today virtually 100 percent of the area under maize cultivation in Zimbabwe is planted to high-yielding maize hybrids, compared with 60 percent in neighboring Zambia (Howard and Mungoma 1997) and 24 percent in Malawi (Smale and Heisey 1997).

CONCLUSIONS

When its countries were gaining independence in the late fifties and early sixties, Africa was a modest net exporter of food, while Asia was the home of the world's food crisis. It is easy to understand why the leaders of most of Africa's new nations, buoyed by a favorable food balance sheet and inspired by a fervent belief that industrialization was the engine of progress, gave priority to industry and highly visible social services and treated agriculture as a national parking lot for the poor. By the late sixties, however, famine in the Sahelian region of West Africa signaled the need to develop an indigenous capacity to address famine and other short-term food emergencies. Africa's food balance sheet changed in the early seventies, as population growth accelerated and Africa became a net importer of food. From 1970 to 1985 annual food production in Africa grew at half (1.5 percent) of population growth (3.0 percent). In the late seventies it became clear that Africa was facing a long-term food production problem. The combination of short-term food emergencies and stagnation in long-term food production reminded the world that Africa was facing the same type of a chronic food crisis that had plagued India and other Asian nations in the sixties and seventies.

Every nation in Africa needs to develop the capacity to deal simultaneously with short-term food emergencies and long-term growth in food production. Because of increasing population pressure and land constraints, future food production in many countries will have to come from raising crop yields rather than through area expansion. Although it is currently fashionable to draw for Africa lessons from Asia's Green Revolution, there are some important differences between Africa and Asia in terms of their agroecologies, crop diversities, and stages of scientific and institutional development. These differences help explain why many Asian-style Green Revolution food production campaigns have failed in Africa and why African policy makers, scientists, and donors should turn inward and examine Africa's own food production success stories, starting with those of hybrid maize in Zimbabwe, Kenya, and Zambia.

Zimbabwe's first maize revolution, from 1960–80, was spearheaded by several thousand white commercial farmers who developed a powerful farm organization that made the case in the political arena for a strong national public research system, efficient public farmer support institutions, favorable economic incentives for commercial farmers, and an export-oriented farm policy to ensure overseas markets for its maize surpluses. In 1960, after twenty-eight years of work on hybrid maize, the government research program released SR52, a high-yielding hybrid maize variety, which increased farm yields by 46 percent and served as the foundation of Zimbabwe's first maize revolution. Zimbabwe's first maize revolution, however, failed to capture the attention of Africa's new leaders in the sixties, because it was led by large-scale farms rather than smallholders.

Zimbabwe's second maize revolution was led by smallholders, who doubled their maize production from 1980 to 1986. The state played a strategic role in the second revolution. At independence in 1980, Zimbabwe's new majority-ruled government helped level the playing field for smallholders by extending access to credit and marketing, integrating the two racially divided extension services, raising the price paid to farmers for maize, and directing the national public research system to reorder priorities in favor of smallholders. Without question, some of the technology and the institutions that facilitated the first maize revolution helped jumpstart the second revolution. The rapid expansion of smallholder maize production in the 1980s provides solid evidence that smallholders will respond to new production opportunities if four interrelated preconditions are met: aggressive political leadership for a smallholder road to development, a stream of new technology, efficient public and private farmer support institutions, and economic incentives and markets for crops grown by smallholders.

Zimbabwe's smallholder-led maize revolution represents a compelling but qualified African success story. The usefulness of Zimbabwe's smallholder-led food production model to other African countries increases in direct proportion to our appreciation of its limitations. Zimbabwe's mixed record to date in reforming its farmer support institutions to assist smallholders should be studied by countries seeking to replicate Zimbabwe's smallholder-led Green Revolution. Zimbabwe's experience has shown how difficult it is to "scale-up" farmer support organizations (which have historically served large-scale white commercial [settler] farmers) to serve hundreds of thousands of dispersed smallholders. In 1995, after fifteen years of independence, only 2.1 percent (21,000) of the one million smallholders were receiving government credit. Zimbabwe's challenge now is to develop cost-effective marketing policies and institutions to finance and sustain its smallholder maize revolution.

Zimbabwe's maize revolutions demonstrate that there is no magic bullet that can boost food production and close Africa's food gap. Zimbabwe's maize revolutions were not based on a single input, such as seed or a new extension model. Rather Zimbabwe generated a reliable maize surplus through an accretionary process of developing an integrated *system* of institutions that facilitated maize production, including politically active farm organizations, a stream of new varieties, an innovative and aggressive seed cooperative, the use of subsidies, and an aggressive export marketing program. Zimbabwe's utilization of a food systems approach to increasing maize production stands in sharp contrast to the experience of many other African nations that have squandered resources on crash food production programs that focused on one or two magic bullets (improved seed or credit) and assumed that success could be achieved in a few years.

Because of the wide variability in agroecologies and stages of development in Africa, each African nation must develop its own strategy for increasing food production and a capacity to manage its national food economy in times of abundance and scarcity. Because of the immensity, diversity, and complexity of Africa, Western experts and donors should stop peddling the Asian Green Revolution model and prepackaged institutions such as the training and visit extension model in Africa. Case studies of increasing food production in other nations in Africa are needed to help deepen our understanding of the changing roles of the public and private sectors, the sequencing of institutional investments, and how to develop an indigenous capacity to become "intelligent" borrowers and adapters of technology from neighboring countries and the global research system.

NOTES

1. Improved cassava varieties have been developed for West African conditions after two decades of research by national research programs and the International Institute of Tropical Agriculture in Nigeria (Nweke 1996). See Sanders, Shapiro, and Ramaswany 1996 for a discussion of hybrid sorghum production.

2. About 5 percent of the cultivated land in Africa is under irrigation as compared with about 35 percent in India and 60 percent in Indonesia.

3. Large commercial farms cover about 2,000 hectares, smallholder farms between 3 and 5 hectares, small-scale commercial farms about 200 hectares, and resettlement farms up to 12 hectares.

4. The Southern Rhodesia Order of 1898 led to the designation of reserves for Africans. Subsequently, the Land Apportionment Act of 1930 legalized the segregation of land between European settlers and Africans.

5. These varieties were developed from in-bred lines from South Africa (Rattray 1988).

6. Although we have pinpointed 1980 as the starting date for the smallholder maize revolution, smallholders started to adopt hybrid maize seed in the early seventies, after the release of the stress-

tolerant three-way hybrids. Rohrbach (1989) reports that 20 to 30 percent of the smallholder maize area in Zimbabwe was planted to hybrids before 1980.

7. About one-third of the increase in smallholder maize production from 1980 to 1986 came from bringing idle land back into cultivation after the termination of the civil war in 1979. The remaining two-thirds was due to higher yields (Rohrbach 1989).

8. The years 1980 and 1986 were chosen for comparative purposes because they had fairly normal maize growing seasons. In 1980, a year of slightly below normal rainfall (700 mm) smallholders planted 931,000 hectares of maize, harvested 738,000 tons, and delivered 89,000 tons of maize to the Grain Marketing Board (GMB). In 1986, a year with normal rainfall and growing conditions, smallholders planted 1.1 million hectares of maize, harvested 1,338,000 tons, and sold 682,000 tons of maize to the GMB (Jayne et al. 1993).

9. After four years of independence, "nearly two-thirds of the mainly experienced cadre of European scientists left, to be replaced by inexperienced African university graduates. This has seriously weakened the capacity of DR&SS [Department of Research and Specialist Services] to respond effectively in the short term to the new set of demands placed on the Department" (International Service for National Agricultural Research 1988, 15).

10. In 1990, 80 percent of the smallholders borrowing from AFC were in arrears (Chimedza 1994, 145).

11. After a decade of independence, commercial farmers were still receiving a large share of subsidized government credit. Even though the number of AFC (government) loans to commercial farmers declined significantly in the eighties, the total value of AFC loans to 1,133 commercial farmers in 1990/91 was more than seven times the total value of AFC loans to 30,190 smallholders (Chimedza 1994, 146). This raises a fundamental political question: Why should 1,133 commercial farmers receive more subsidized government credit than 30,190 smallholders?

12. Yudelman et al. (1991, 41), report that the loan repayment rate fell sharply when the Sasakawa-Global 2000 food production program in Ghana scaled-up its credit program:

Year	Farmers Receiving Credit	Loan Repayment Rate
1987	1,644	95%
1988	15,737	77%
1989	78,218	39%

13. Three-fourths of the increase in maize production from 1980–85 occurred in 18 of the 150 smallholder areas in the country (Jayne and Rukuni 1993).

14. In the mid-1960s the government of India took a high-level political decision to launch a national wheat production campaign in seventeen favorably endowed districts (e.g., irrigation, roads) and to target seed, fertilizer, credit, and extension to farmers in these districts (Mellor 1976). Today, three of India's twenty-five states form the country's breadbasket by producing 36 percent of its national food grain production and 80 percent of its public food procurement (Lele and Bumb 1995).

15. The NFAZ predates independence. Before 1980 it was a nonpolitical master farmer organization in Fort Victoria (Masvingo) Province.

16. At the time of the merger of the two farm organizations in 1991, NFAZ had approximately 65,000 paid-up members and ZNFU had around 4,500 paid-up members.

17. From 1930 to 1964, the director and chief research officer of Zimbabwe's public agricultural research system were paid as much as the highest-ranking civil servant in the Ministry of Agriculture (Kupfuma 1994, 93).

18. DR&SS had 127 research scientists in 1992 as compared to 110 in 1982. By contrast, Nigeria increased the number of its agricultural scientists tenfold (from 100 to 1,000) from independence in 1960 to 1980 (Pardey, Roseboom, and Beintema 1997).

REFERENCES

Bates, Robert H. 1993. "'Urban Bias': A Fresh Look." *Journal of Development Studies* 29:219–28.

Blackie, Malcolm J. 1982. "A Time to Listen: A Perspective on Agricultural Policy in Zimbabwe." *Zimbabwe Agricultural Journal* 79 (5): 151–56.

———. 1987. "The Elusive Peasant: Zimbabwe's Agricultural Policy, 1965–1986." In *Food Security for Southern Africa*, edited by Mandivamba Rukuni and Carl K. Eicher, 114–44. Harare: UZ/MSU Food Security Project, University of Zimbabwe.

———. 1990. "Maize, Food Self-sufficiency and Policy in East and Southern Africa." *Food Policy* 15:383–94.

———. 1994. "Realizing Smallholder Agricultural Potential." In *Zimbabwe's Agricultural Revolution*, edited by Mandivamba Rukuni and Carl K. Eicher, 335–47. Harare: University of Zimbabwe Publications.

Bratton, Michael. 1994. "Micro Democracy? The Merger of Farmer Unions in Zimbabwe." *African Studies Review* 37:9–37.

Byerlee, Derek, and Carl K. Eicher, eds. 1997. *Africa's Emerging Maize Revolution*. Boulder, Colo.: Lynne Rienner Publishers.

Chimedza, Ruvimbo. 1994. "Rural Financial Markets." In *Zimbabwe's Agricultural Revolution*, edited by Mandivamba Rukuni and Carl K. Eicher, 139–52. Harare: University of Zimbabwe Publications.

Deininger, Klaus, and Hans P. Binswanger. 1995. "Rent Seeking and the Development of Large-Scale Agriculture in Kenya, South Africa, and Zimbabwe." *Economic Development and Cultural Change* 43 (3): 493–522.

Eicher, Carl K. 1982. "Facing Up to Africa's Food Crisis." *Foreign Affairs* 61 (1): 151–74.

———. 1989. "Sustainable Institutions for African Agricultural Development," Working Paper no. 19. The Hague: International Service for National Agricultural Research.

———. 1990. "Building African Scientific Capacity for Agricultural Development." *Agricultural Economics* 4 (2): 117–43.

———. 1995."Zimbabwe's Maize-Based Green Revolution: Preconditions for Replication." *World Development* 23 (5): 805–18.

Eicher, Carl K., and Mandivamba Rukuni. 1996. "Reflections on Agrarian Reform and Capacity Building in South Africa." Staff Paper no. 96-3, Department of Agricultural Economics, Michigan State University, East Lansing.

Herbst, Jeffrey. 1990. *State Politics in Zimbabwe*. Berkeley: University of California Press.

Howard, Julie A., and Catherine Mungoma. 1997. "Zambia's Stop-and-Go Maize Revolution." In *Africa's Emerging Maize Revolution*, edited by Derek Byerlee and Carl K. Eicher. Boulder, Colo.: Lynne Rienner Publishers.

International Service for National Agricultural Research. 1988. *A Review of the Department of Research and Specialist Services, Zimbabwe*. Report to the Government of Zimbabwe. The Hague: ISNAR.

Jayne, Thomas S., Stephen Jones, Mulinge Mukumbu, and Share Jiriyengwa. 1997. "Maize Marketing and Pricing Policy in Eastern and Southern Africa." In *Africa's Emerging Maize Revolution*, edited by Derek Byerlee and Carl K. Eicher. Boulder, Colo.: Lynne Rienner Publishers.

Jayne, Thomas S., and Mandivamba Rukuni. 1993. "Distributional Effects of Maize Self-sufficiency in Zimbabwe: Implications for Pricing and Trade Policy." *Food Policy* 18 (4): 334–41.

Jayne, Thomas S., Tobias Takavarasha, E. A. Attwood, and Bernard Kupfuma. 1993. "Postscript to Zimbabwe's Maize Success Story: Policy Lessons for Eastern and Southern Africa." Staff Paper no. 93-68, Department of Agricultural Economics, Michigan State University, East Lansing.

Kupfuma, Bernard. 1994. "The Payoff to Hybrid Maize Research and Extension in Zimbabwe: An Economic and Institutional Analysis." Master's thesis, Department of Agricultural Economics, Michigan State University, East Lansing.

Lele, Uma, and Balu Bumb. 1995. "The Food Crisis in South Asia: The Case of India." In *The Evolv-*

ing Role of the World Bank: Helping Meet the Challenge of Development, edited by K. Sarwar Lateef, 69–96. Washington, D.C.: World Bank.

Lipton, Michael, with Richard Longhurst. 1989. *New Seeds and Poor People.* Baltimore: Johns Hopkins University Press.

Maredia, Mywish K., and Carl K. Eicher. 1995. "The Economics of Wheat Research in Developing Countries: The One Hundred Million Dollar Puzzle." *World Development* 23 (3): 401–12.

Mashingaidze, Kingstone. 1994. "Maize Research and Development." In *Zimbabwe's Agricultural Revolution,* edited by Mandivamba Rukuni and Carl K. Eicher, 208–18. Harare: University of Zimbabwe Publications.

Masters, William A. 1994. *Government and Agriculture in Zimbabwe.* Westport, Conn.: Praeger.

Mellor, John. 1976. *The New Economics of Growth: A Strategy for India and the Developing World.* Ithaca, N.Y.: Cornell University Press.

Mitchell, Donald O., Merlinda D. Ingco, and Ronald C. Duncan. 1997. *The World Food Outlook.* Cambridge: Cambridge University Press.

Muir, Kay. 1994. "Agriculture in Zimbabwe." In *Zimbabwe's Agricultural Revolution,* edited by Mandivamba Rukuni and Carl K. Eicher, 40–55. Harare: University of Zimbabwe Publications.

North, Douglass. 1987. "Institutions, Transactions Costs, and Economic Growth." *Economic Inquiry* 25 (5): 419–28.

Nweke, Felix I. 1996. "Cassava as a Cash Crop in Africa." *Tropical Root and Tuber Crops Bulletin,* April 5–7.

Olver, R. C. 1988. "Zimbabwe Maize Breeding Program." In *Towards Self-Sufficiency: A Proceedings of the Second Eastern, Central, and Southern Africa Regional Maize Workshop, March 15–21, 1987,* 34–43. Harare: International Maize and Wheat Improvement Center (CIMMYT).

Pardey, Philip G., Johannes Roseboom, and Nienke M. Beintema. 1997. "Investments in African Agricultural Research." *World Development* 25 (3): 409–23.

Rattray, A. G. H. 1969. "Advances and Achievements in Crop Research." In *Proceedings of the Conference on Research and the Farmer,* 9–15. Salisbury, Rhodesia, Department of Research and Specialist Services, September 18–19.

———. 1988. "Maize Breeding and Seed Production in Zimbabwe up to 1970." In *Proceedings of the Eighth South African Maize Breeding Symposium, March 15–17,* pp. 14–16. Pretoria, South Africa: Department of Agriculture and Water Supply.

Rohrbach, David. 1989. "The Economics of Smallholder Maize Production in Zimbabwe: Implications for Food Security." MSU International Development Paper no. 11, Department of Agricultural Economics, Michigan State University, East Lansing.

Rukuni, Mandivamba. 1996. "A Framework for Crafting Demand-Driven National Agricultural Research Institutions in Southern Africa." Staff Paper no. 96-76, Department of Agricultural Economics, Michigan State University, East Lansing.

Rukuni, Mandivamba, Malcolm J. Blackie, and Carl K. Eicher, 1998. "Crafting Smallholder-Driven Agricultural Research Systems in Southern Africa." *World Development* 26 (6).

Rukuni, Mandivamba, and Carl K. Eicher, eds. 1994. *Zimbabwe's Agricultural Revolution.* Harare: University of Zimbabwe Publications.

Sanders, John H., Barry I. Shapiro, and Sunder Ramaswamy. 1996. *The Economics of Agricultural Technology in Semiarid Sub-Saharan Africa.* Baltimore: Johns Hopkins University Press.

Schultz, Theodore W. 1964. *Transforming Traditional Agriculture.* New Haven: Yale University Press.

Smale, Melinda, and Paul W. Heisey. 1997. "Maize Technology and Productivity in Malawi: A Delayed Green Revolution." In *Africa's Emerging Maize Revolution,* edited by Derek Byerlee and Carl K. Eicher. Boulder, Colo.: Lynne Rienner Publishers.

Stack, Jayne L. 1994. "The Distributional Consequences of the Smallholder Maize Revolution." In *Zimbabwe's Agricultural Revolution,* edited by Mandivamba Rukuni and Carl K. Eicher, 258–69. Harare: University of Zimbabwe Publications.

Tattersfield, Rex. 1982. "The Role of Research in Increasing Food Crop Potential in Zimbabwe." *Zimbabwe Science News* 16 (1): 6–10.

Tattersfield, Rex, and E. K. Havazvidi. 1994. "The Development of the Seed Industry." In *Zimbabwe's Agricultural Revolution,* edited by Mandivamba Rukuni and Carl K. Eicher, 114–26. Harare: University of Zimbabwe Publications.

Weinmann, H. 1975. "Agricultural Research and Development in Southern Rhodesia: 1924–1950." Series in Science, no. 2. Salisbury: University of Rhodesia.

World Bank. 1997. *World Development Report, 1997.* Washington, D.C.: World Bank.

Yudelman, M., J. Coulter, P. Goffin, D. McCune, and E. Ocloo. 1991. "An Evaluation of the Sasakawa—Global 2000 Project in Ghana." In *Africa's Agricultural Development in the 1990s: Can It Be Sustained?,* edited by Nathan C. Russell and Christopher R. Dowswell, 45–55. Mexico, D.F.: CASIN/SAA/Global 2000.

Zimbabwe, Government of. 1991. "Estimates of Expenditures for the Year Ending June 30, 1992." Harare: Government Printer.

———. 1995. "The Agricultural Sector of Zimbabwe." Ministry of Agriculture, Harare.

34

Path-dependent Policy Reforms: From Land Reform to Rural Development in Colombia

ALAIN DE JANVRY AND ELISABETH SADOULET

Even though land reform has been on the political agenda in Colombia since the 1930s, effective land redistribution has not happened. Using the theory of public choice and the concept of path dependency, we propose an interpretation of this deadlock in policy reform. Because the first phases of land reform sought to modernize large farms under the threat of expropriation, the rise in political power of the modernized landlords who adopted Green Revolution technology allowed them to block subsequent attempts at redistribution. This was done by effectively using rent-seeking to raise land values on large farms, through public subsidies, above levels at which compensation by family farms could be achieved.

A paradox of land reform in Colombia is that, while existence of an inverse relation between total social factor productivity (TSFP) and farm size has been convincingly established (Berry and Cline 1979) and while land reform has been on the policy agenda since the 1930s, no significant land redistribution has occurred. We propose an interpretation of this policy failure by looking at the particular sequence of reforms that were introduced, using the concept of path dependency. Because of the changes early reforms induced in the political economy of Colombia, this sequence blocked the possibility of capturing the efficiency gains potentially offered by redistributive land reform and it enhanced social tensions in the rural areas. Path-dependent policy reforms thus ultimately resulted in socially inefficient resource use and often explosive rural poverty. Persistence

ALAIN DE JANVRY is professor and ELISABETH SADOULET is associate professor of agricultural economics at the University of California, Berkeley.

Reprinted from *The Economics of Rural Organization: Theory, Practice, and Policy,* edited by K. Hoff, A. Braverman, and J. Stiglitz (New York: Oxford University Press for the World Bank, 1993), by permission of the publishers and the authors.

of the current highly unequal land tenure system consequently does not reflect superior social efficiency, but rather a political settlement in a context of highly unequally distributed political power that was the product of past reforms.

We first retrace the historical sequence of reforms in Colombia, from modernizing land reform under the threat of expropriation in the 1930s, to failed attempts at redistributive land reform and effective rent seeking by large farmers in the 1960s, and to abandoning land reform for rural development in the 1970s. We then explain this sequence of reforms in terms of a critical path of changes in the distribution of political power induced by the reforms themselves, technological change, and evolving international pressures. Finally, we extract implications for feasible policies to induce growth and equity in Colombian agriculture.

THE CONFLICT BETWEEN REDISTRIBUTIVE AND MODERNIZING FORCES IN LAND REFORM

To conceptualize the determinants of the sequence of agricultural reforms in Colombia, we shall draw on the framework used by Zusman (1976) and Becker (1983), in which the political economic process is endogenously determined by specification of the pressure groups with their objective functions, a set of feasible policy instruments, the influence functions of the pressure groups on the state, and the constraints imposed by the economic system. The outcome is the policy that maximizes a weighted average of the objectives of the different groups, where the weights are the marginal influences that each group has over policymakers. Extending this framework to an intertemporal problem, we keep invariant through the whole period the set of feasible policies and the groups, while focusing on the endogenous changes in their demands and on the evolution of their influence weights. A key issue is how past reforms affect the distribution of political power and hence the political feasibility of further reforms. In analyzing each period of reformism, we consequently stress how reforms have changed the configuration of the political economy for the subsequent period— that is, the demands of each group and the weights of their demands on the state.

The social actors who influenced agrarian reformism were (1) the landless and marginal or "subfamily" farmers $(L + SF)$; (2) the family farmers, initially the tenants of the haciendas who subsequently became independent households (F); (3) the large farmers, referred to as landlords (Ll); and (4) the urban interests, both consumers and employers (U). The policy instruments were all the policies that had been implemented, attempted, or advocated during that period: (1) modernizing land reform in which threats of expropriation were used if minimum productivity levels were not reached after a predetermined time lapse and where guarantees of nonexpropriation were given if modernization occurs; (2) modernizing land reform with expropriation if productivity was below that attained on family farms and where compensation was paid at the current land price if expropriation occurred; (3) public goods support to modernization (principally subsidies for the adoption of Green Revolution technology); (4) redistributive land reform whereby large farms were carved into family farms; and (5) rural development to increase the productivity of family farms.

MODERNIZATION UNDER THREAT OF EXPROPRIATION WITH GUARANTEES, 1936–57

The first decades of this century saw rising pressures on agriculture to improve its economic performance. Industry was emerging under import substitution policies and public works programs swelled employment. Both sets of policies increased the urban demands on agriculture for staple foods. Serious crises of food availability, leading to recurrent emergency food imports, made increasingly evident the bottleneck that an archaic hacienda system imposed on the economy. Pressures for social change also arose from within the agricultural sector. The sharecroppers and tenants of the haciendas, often bound by extraeconomic coercion and personal service obligations, were pressing for their transformation into pure tenants or free workers.

It is in this context that Colombia passed its first land reform law, in 1936 (Law 200). The objective was economic: to use the threat of expropriation of lands that were abandoned or insufficiently productive to induce landlords to modernize their farming practices. However, the heavy influence of the landlords on the state allowed them to set the policy agenda that agriculture was to respond to for the pressures of modernization. This allowed them to make the guarantees of nonexpropriation-if-modernization credible and to set relatively low minimum productivity standards (a requirement that productive use be made of no less than half of the farm area and a fifteen-year grace period to reach these standards before expropriation could be considered). A politically feasible response was thus possible to the multiplicity of demands for agrarian change if the landlords would satisfy the modernizing demands of both the F and U sectors.

While there were very few expropriations and minimal land redistribution, the threats of expropriation were highly effective in increasing agricultural productivity. Yet these achievements proved to be insufficient to end land reform at that stage. The modernization of agriculture could not accommodate the rapidly rising urban demands on agriculture created by post–World War II prosperity and industrial growth. This led to growing conflicts between landlords and the urban bourgeoisie that have been identified as an important cause of the (yet poorly explained) breakout of the "Violencia" period, a ten-year civil war between Liberals and Conservatives that left some 200,000 dead, principally in the countryside (Moncayo 1986).

The social impact of this process of modernization under threat was disastrous. Agricultural modernization transformed traditional social relations in the hacienda and led to widespread eviction of tenants. The regressive effects of the reform contributed to rootlessness and the social tensions of the Violencia. The civil war itself reinforced the process of social modernization initiated by the land reform: many old-style tenants fled to the cities, a new class of entrepreneurs appropriated abandoned lands, and the decline in land rents allowed entry of a group of large-farm tenants. The civil war ended in 1957 with the National Front agreement between Conservatives and Liberals to share power during a period of sixteen years, with alternation of government control every four years.

The dynamic carry-overs from this first phase of reformism into the next phase of reforms to be initiated by the National Front were (1) the emergence of a new Ll class of modern, large-scale entrepreneurs, replacing the old agrarian oligarchy, with considerable ability to exercise economic and political influence over the state and to use this influence to pursue modernization; and (2) increasing social inequities that in the aftermath of the civil war reinforced the weight of the $L + SF$ in policy making. To this was to be added, exogenously, international pressures for redistributive land reform as a response of the Alliance for Progress to the shock of the Cuban Revolution in 1959.

MODERNIZATION UNDER THREAT OF EXPROPRIATION WITH COMPENSATION, 1958–73

Under the National Front, the demands of the different social actors had changed relative to the previous period of reformism. The $L + SF$ were pressing for land redistribution. The Ll were demanding the protection of private property and full compensation in case of expropriation. And the U were requesting both a more rapid modernization of agriculture and the reduction of conflicts in the rural areas. A harmonious response to this variety of demands was not possible, because the demands of the $L + SF$ were incompatible with the Ll's demands. A political solution was, however, possible through a coalition between Ll and U to assist the Ll in sufficiently modernizing to escape expropriation, by making compensation no longer possible. The coalition had to exclude the $L + SF$ and F, thus reproducing the social problem in the next phase.

The initial policy response to rising social tensions was the enactment of a redistributive land reform (Law 135 of 1961) aimed at creating a family farm sector and thus at capturing both the equity and efficiency gains that redistribution promised. The redistributive line won politically during the Liberals' turn in power (under Presidents Camargo and Lleras Restrepo), but implementation of the law was dominated by the Ll–U alliance. It undermined Law 135 by rent-seeking that resulted in government benefits' being channeled disproportionately to large farmers, making expropriation with compensation impossible.

Modernization of large-scale farming was to a great extent achieved through institutional distortions in the delivery of public goods and services to large farms. This is the period when local adaptation of the rice varieties responsible for the Green Revolution in Asia was completed and these varieties released. Their adoption required irrigation (mainly the privilege of large farms), access to credit (subsidized institutional credit is exclusively monopolized by large farms), and market organization (Federación Nacional de Arroceros, FEDEARROZ,

TABLE 1
THE EFFECTS OF TECHNOLOGICAL CHANGE ON RICE PRODUCTION

	Upland Sector (%)	*Irrigated Sector (%)*
Average annual growth in yields		
1954–56 to 1965–67	1.8	1.5
1965–67 to 1973–75	1.8	6.7
Distribution of rice production		
1959	43	57
1970	26	74
1975	9	91
Change in the number of farms with rice as a principal crop, 1959–70		
Farms of 0–5 hectares	−55	−40
Farms of 5–50 hectares	−59	−23
Farms of more than 50 hectares	−52	19

SOURCE: Scobie and Posada 1977.

a large farmers' professional organization). While the technology itself was neutral to scale, the institutional and policy environment where it was released was not. As a result, these new varieties spread very rapidly between 1966 and 1974, concentrating production in the irrigated large-farm sector (from 57% of total production in 1959 to 91% in 1975), while small upland farms correspondingly lost ground (see table 1). A whole set of policies was also introduced to support modernization in the large-farm sector while price controls were applied to the staple foods principally produced by peasants. As the data in table 2 show, the share of land in intensive use increased by 59 percent in the large farms (above fifty hectares) while it was stagnant in the small farms. With yields and per acre incomes higher in large than in small farms, land values made expropriation with

TABLE 2
COMPARISON OF PERCENTAGE OF LAND IN INTENSIVE AND EXTENSIVE USE,
BY FARM SIZE, 1960 AND 1970

	Intensive Use						*Extensive Use (Pastures, Fallows, and Others)*		
	Temporary Crops			*Permanent Crops*					
Farm Size (hectares)	*1960*	*1970*	*Percentage Change*	*1960*	*1970*	*Percentage Change*	*1960*	*1970*	*Percentage Change*
0 to 5	35.9	29.1	−18.9	23.9	29.5	23.4	40.2	41.4	3.0
5 to 50	16.0	13.5	−15.6	14.9	18.5	24.2	69.1	68.0	−1.6
50 or more	3.1	4.2	35.5	2.0	3.9	95.0	92.7	91.9	−0.9
All farms	7.1	6.8	−4.2	5.5	7.6	38.2	87.4	87.7	0.3

SOURCE: Agricultural censuses, 1960 and 1970.

compensation impossible, thanks to the distorted institutional framework that allowed large farms to externalize part of the costs of modernization. The *Ll–U* alliance was thus able to pervert the legislative victory of the redistributive line. Instead, the *Li-U* policies induced an unprecedented boom in the production of commercial and export crops (Kalmanovitz 1978).

Census data show the extent to which the redistributive intent of the law was frustrated. Land concentration actually increased between the agricultural censuses of 1960 and 1971—the share of land in farms smaller than fifty hectares fell by 8 percent while that in farms larger than fifty hectares increased by 3 percent. Rapid expropriation of sharecroppers and tenants continued—the number of farms in fixed and share rents declined by 41 percent. The few lands expropriated were generally of inferior quality and in marginal locations. In the first year only 2,340 families received land, instead of the projected 10,000. By the end of the phase of redistributive land reform in 1972, Instituto Colombiano de Reforma Agaria (INCORA), the land reform agency, had granted 123,000 titles out of the 935,000 families that had been declared eligible in 1970 alone. Only 1.5 percent of the land in large farms had been redistributed. The social tensions created by exclusion of the $L + SF + F$ interests pushed them into open opposition to the government. This was in a sense the logical consequence of a system of power sharing between the two dominant parties that left no room for the expression of dissent except by insurgency. The peasant union created by government in 1967 to mobilize support for the land reform process, Asociación Nacional de Usarios Campesinos (ANUC), thus openly turned into opposition, and insecurity in the rural areas escalated.

The dynamic carry-overs from this second phase of reformism were consequently (1) heavy investment in large farms, many of which have the characteristic of sunk costs, thus sealing the continuation of an *Ll–U* alliance to protect the gains of agricultural modernization in large farms, and (2) frustrated expectations for the *L, SF,* and *F* households, leading to growing intensity of rural conflicts. At the same time, international influences were moving away from the redistributive philosophy of the Alliance for Progress toward use of the instrument of rural development to modernize family farming.

RURAL DEVELOPMENT AND COUNTERINSURGENCY, 1973 TO THE PRESENT

In this third period of reformism, which opened in the last years of the National Front, the demands of the $L + SF$ continued to be for redistributive land reform. The *F* were pressing for modernization specifically targeted at their type of farming, and their demands were supported by the international movement toward integrated rural development championed by the World Bank and the U.S. Agency for International Development. The *Ll* wanted to protect not only private property, as in all previous periods, but also the large investments made with public support to adopt the technologies of the Green Revolution. Finally, the *U* wanted not only to consolidate the productivity gains achieved in agriculture by modernization of the large farms but also to modernize staple food production in the family farm sector. The reason for focusing on family farming to promote food production was that price interventions on food products made their production generally unattractive to large farmers (Reinhardt 1988). There consequently existed the basis for a broad coalition that sought rural development, which included not only the *Ll* and *U,* as in period 2, but also the *F.* The *F* saw in rural development a source of welfare gains, while the *Ll* saw the possibility of reducing rural conflicts and pressure on the land, and the *U* saw both social stability and continued productivity gains in agriculture. The heavy influence of this coalition, together with the resources made available by international support, overwhelmed the political agenda and marginalized again the *L + SF* into insurgent opposition.

Policy response thus consisted of a new social accord between Liberals and Conservatives. The 1972 Chicoral Pact declared the end of redistributive land reform and thereby eliminated the threat of the land invasions that it had fomented (no fewer than 2,000 land invasions were recorded in 1972). Under Law 4 of 1973, expropriations were confined to abandoned and unproductive lands, just as they were under Law 200 of 1936. An ambitious program of integrated rural development was introduced in the 1975–78 development plan "To Close the Gap," at the same time as new laws (Law 5 of 1973, in particular) were introduced to further support the modernization of commercial and export-oriented large-farm agriculture. Rural development programs were organized by the Colombian Agricultural Institute (ICA) and the National Planning Ministry, giving priority to the areas of peasant concentration and guerrilla activity. From the outset, but gradually more so as the marginalization of *L + SF* and the radicalization of the ANUC increased guerrilla warfare, rural development was closely integrated with counterinsurgency initiatives (Bejarano 1985).

The achievements of sixteen years of integrated rural development are not insignificant. The approach allowed the reduction of some of the historical, institutional, and public goods biases against peasant agriculture. Research on peasant farming systems was promoted, credit was made available to the chosen family farms, and in some cases incomes of family farmers increased. Yet these gains applied only to a small fringe of family farms, the few with enough land and enough proximity to markets to effectively use the support provided by the state to modernize agricultural production (Valencia González 1982). For the majority of the rural poor—both *L* and *SF* who derive the bulk of their household income from off-farm activities because of lack of land—not only did a production-oriented program not have much to offer, but increased competition by modernized *F* farms eventually enhanced displacement. Evaluation of the first eight years of the rural development program thus led to a redefinition of its target clientele from "peasants" in general to "viable peasant" producers, explicitly confirming marginalization from the program of the *L* and *SF* and refusal to address their problem of access to land.

By 1984 more than five decades of agrarian reformism had failed to change the concentration of landownership. The Gini coefficient of farm distribution by size, which was 83 percent in 1960, was still 82 percent in 1984. The annual rates of growth in the number of farms and the distribution of land by farm size between 1960 and 1984 are given in table 3. The *Ll* (20 to 200 hectares) were the clear beneficiaries of this process, while the *L* + *SF* (0 to 5 hectares) were in the same situation as in 1960. While a buffer class of modernized family farms (5 to 20 hectares) had been consolidated, the social consequences of ending redistributive land reform and of fomenting rural development were disastrous. The 1980s witnessed a rapid growth of armed movements, primarily with a rural base and sometimes associated with indigenous organizations. Reported armed assaults increased from 958 in 1972, to 1,895 in 1980, and to 3,682 in 1984 (Bejarano 1985). Many of these conflicts occurred in areas of frontier colonization to which peasant households were pushed. Peasants had lost access to land and to employment opportunities in areas of traditional settlement due to a combination of labor-saving technological change and the spread of extensive livestock operations associated with the modernization of large farms.

The social failure of agricultural reforms contributed, in turn, to the undermining of agricultural modernization in the large-farm sector. After 1982 the growth rate of agriculture slowed down markedly. While the average annual growth rate of agriculture was 3.7 percent between 1970 and 1982, it fell to 1.4 percent between 1982 and 1986. There are, of course, a number of other reasons that explain this poor performance of agriculture: an appreciated real exchange rate associated with the coffee boom and the influx of foreign exchange from drugs, reduction of public expenditures in agriculture, and sharply rising real interest rates have all reduced the relative profitability of agriculture and induced a displacement of capital from agriculture to the financial and nontradables sectors. Yet widespread violence also bears negatively on agricultural investment. Many lands are again being abandoned, and the productivity of large farms is declining. It is this social climate of violence, associated with the political marginalization of the *L* + *SF*, that is the intertemporal carry-over into the future definition of agrarian reforms.

THE POLITICAL ECONOMY OF PATH-DEPENDENT REFORMISM

This historical sequence of reforms is conceptualized in figures 1, 2, and 3 with the aid of three indicators: (1) TSFP, which gives the social criterion in assessing reforms; (2) income per hectare and land value (*y*), which indicate the possibility of compensation at market prices; and (3) yield or total factor productivity at farm prices (TFP), which is the observable criterion for political debate and for the setting of modernization thresholds.

The inverse relation between TSFP and farm size (represented by curve *FT* in figure 1) before the Green Revolution in Colombia was due to the widespread existence of two market imperfections: moral hazard in the use of hired labor

TABLE 3
NUMBER OF FARMS, DISTRIBUTION, AVERAGE SIZE, AND AREA COVERED, 1960, 1970, AND 1984

	Farms	Distribution (percentage of total farms)				Average Farm Size (hectares)	Area Covered (percentage of total farm area)			
		0–5 Hectares	5–20 hectares	20–50 hectares	50–200 hectares		0–5 Hectares	5–20 hectares	20–50 hectares	50–200 hectares
1960	765,300	60.1	24.7	13.4	1.8	15.9	4.8	11.5	36.0	47.6
1970	738,900	57.1	24.9	15.8	2.1	17.4	4.0	10.3	37.4	48.4
1984	978,600	56.6	25.2	16.5	1.7	22.2	4.2	11.2	43.1	41.6

SOURCE: Lorente, Salazar, and Gallo 1985.

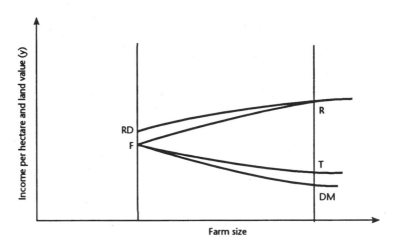

Fig. 1. Phases of Agrarian Reformism in Colombia: Feasibility of Compensation (Note: *T* = traditional large farm, *DM* = defensive modernization, *R* = rent-seeking, *F* = traditional family farm, *RD* = family farm with rural development.)

and lack of a rental market or constraints in access to credit for land rental (Eswaran and Kotwal 1986). This inverse relation underlies the expectation that both efficiency and equity gains could be achieved by a redistributive land reform.

In addition to these two market imperfections, there exists a third prevalent distortion resulting from the highly unequal distribution of credit and public goods across farm sizes. In Colombia, as a result of successful rent-seeking, institutional credit is typically monopolized by large farms, and public goods are heavily biased in their favor. Once technological change sharply increased the capital-labor ratio in agriculture, the capital market advantage of large farms eventually helped them achieve higher yields and higher per acre incomes than small farms (curve *FR* in figure 1). If landlords whose farms have been expropriated must be compensated at the prereform level of income per acre (that is, at the level *R* of land values in large farms with privileged access to credit and public goods), Pareto-optimal reform is no longer possible. Either the landlord has to lose or a grant from a third party has to be transferred to the beneficiary to make compensation feasible (Adelman and Morris 1974, Binswanger and Elgin 1989).

As the Colombian experience has shown, a state with urgent needs to increase agricultural production and under heavy influence of the agrarian oligarchy will be pressed to first induce modernization in the large-farm sector before seeking expropriation. An effective instrument for that purpose is the threat of expropriation by land reform, to coerce landlords into modernizing above some established productivity threshold. This is what we called "modernizing land reform"

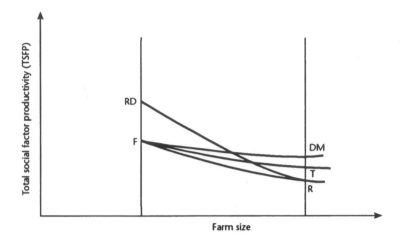

Fig. 2. Phases of Agrarian Reformism in Colombia: Social Criterion (Note: T = tradition-al large farm, DM = defensive modernization, R = rent-seeking, F = traditional family farm, RD = family farm with rural development.)

as opposed to redistributive land reform. The efficiency gains of a modernizing land reform are thus sought in the nonreform sector, while the creation of a re-form sector serves as a threat (de Janvry 1981). If the modernization thus in-duced is insufficient to exceed TSFP on small farms (as was the case in Colom-bia and as illustrated in figure 2), land reform remains justified on an efficiency basis. Other defensive strategies must then be used by landlords.

The political power that the landlord class achieves from enhanced economic power derived from modernization under threat can be applied to two strategies for blocking a potential subsequent redistributive land reform, depending on whether expropriation is announced without or with compensation. If expropria-tion occurs without compensation, the only possibility to avoid expropriation is to gain sufficient control over the state to obtain credible guarantees of nonexpropri-ation if an observable minimum productivity (TFP) standard has been achieved (*DM* in figure 3). In this latter case, the cost of avoiding expropriation is a loss in income per acre relative to T, since T was an economic optimum (see figure 1), while TFP increases to the established threshold level. While compensation of landlords would remain feasible because income per hectare at *DM* is lower than at F, expropriation of these modernized elites is no longer politically feasible. This was the outcome of phase 1 of Colombian agrarian reformism (figure 3).

If expropriation is done with compensation at the pre-expropriation level of income per acre (which sets the price of land), the defensive strategy that land-lords can follow is to use their power over the state, reinforced by the outcome of phase 1, to effectively rent-seek through collective action and to socialize part of the cost of raising TFP and land prices in large farms above the levels achieved

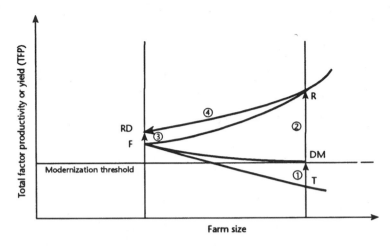

Fig. 3. Phases of Agrarian Reformism in Colombia: Historical Sequence (Note: *T* = traditional large farm, *DM* = defensive modernization, *R* = rent-seeking, *F* = traditional family farm, *RD* = family farm with rural development; *1* = modernizing land reform with guarantees, *2* = modernizing land reform with compensation, *3* = rural development, *4* = potential redistributive land reform.)

in family farming. In figure 1, this is represented by strategy *R*. As observed in many areas where capital-intensive modernization has occurred, there is today a positive relation between yields and farm size. Since the cost of modernization has been achieved by a bias in the definition and social allocation of public goods—roads, irrigation, technology, and subsidized credit—toward large farms, private modernization has been achieved at the cost of social efficiency. TSFP on large farms is, consequently, at its lowest level (figure 2). While compensation is made impossible by the level of land prices in large farms, redistribution toward family farms remains socially more desirable than ever. Yet redistributive land reform has again been effectively held in check. This was the outcome of phase 2 of Colombian agrarian history, as shown in figure 3.

With the end of land reform and the perpetuation of the social problems created by rural poverty, rural development has been used as an alternative instrument to raise the productivity and income levels of peasants (*RD* in figure 1). While the strategy leaves behind many subfamily farmers and landless workers for whom the approach has no benefits, it can raise TFP and incomes on family farms. Since rent-seeking by large farmers continues to succeed, the positive relation between TFP and farm size is likely to remain in spite of the labor cost advantage of family farms. The same is true for land values, still holding in check the possibility of land reform with compensation. Yet it is well established that family farms have been operating under strong institutional biases in the definition and access to publicly provided goods. Modernization under rural development is thus quite distinct from modernization by rent-seeking. If rural development removes some of the effective constraints on and institutional biases against peasants, TSFP is increased to *RD* on family farms in figure 3. This was the outcome of phase 3 of Colombian agrarian history. While still economically impossible with compensation, land reform becomes all the more socially desirable. It is in that sense that rural development should have been used as a complement to redistributive land reform, occurring after redistribution had occurred, and not as a substitute for the failure of redistributive land reform. This is, however, the unwritten phase 4 of potential agrarian reformism in Colombia.

THE FUTURE OF AGRICULTURAL POLICY REFORMS IN COLOMBIA

Today the demands of *L* + *SF* continue to be for redistributive land reform, while the alliance (*Ll* + *F* + *U*) seeks preservation of the status quo. Yet this status quo is increasingly difficult to maintain. While possible solutions to this conflict include stepped-up counterinsurgency and an urban-industrial solution to rural poverty, they are unlikely to succeed. Redistributive land reform consequently remains the potentially most effective approach.

What has been learned from the fifty-three years of agrarian reformism analyzed in this chapter is that economically successful and politically feasible redistributive land reform will require the following two prerequisite measures:

1. Elimination of distortions created by rent-seeking that result in extensive public subsidies to the large farms and that raise land values in these farms above the levels that permit compensation by family farmers. Removing these subsidies may be easier in a period of fiscal crisis that imposes overall fiscal austerity. A good place to start a stabilization program is thus with the elimination of subsidies to the large-farm sector. In addition, a land tax based on land values is necessary to erase residual benefits to large farms. A tax reform is consequently an essential preliminary to land reform with compensation. Its political feasibility can also be enhanced by conditionality lending in the context of stabilization.
2. Renewed support to rural development, in spite of the many failures that were denounced worldwide, to restore the productivity advantage that small farms can derive from their low labor costs, even in post–Green Revolution agriculture. Competitive access to credit, technology, information, and markets is essential for that purpose. Rural development thus remains more important than ever as a complement to redistributive land reform. Here again, depreciation of the real exchange rate associated with the necessary adjustments to the debt crisis, and the resulting possibility of import substitution in the production of staple foods, would create the economic context to make rural development with redistributive land reform an attractive strategy of economic development.

Path-dependent agricultural policy reforms have led Colombian agriculture into a course that is neither economically efficient nor socially tenable. The large farms derive their yield advantages from socially costly government subsidies, the family farms remain few in number and underprovisioned in infrastructure and services, and the potential gains from the combination of rural development and redistributive land reform with compensation have been blocked. Social tensions require the growing use of force, and extensive rural poverty is perpetuated. Since this path of reforms was endogenous to the Colombian political economy, it cannot be attributed to policy mistakes, given the information that was available to the different actors of the policy-making process. Yet it is certain that the design of agrarian reformism has not been based on a clear understanding of the nature of the transactions costs that characterize different types of farming organizations, of the politics of influence in the making of agricultural policy, and of path dependency in policy reforms. One can only hope that in the future, development of such new understanding will allow policy makers to better account for not only the direct economic effects of policy choices but also for their indirect effects through the changes they may induce in future government policies.

NOTE

The authors are indebted to Clive Bell for his useful suggestions.

REFERENCES

Adelman, Irma, and Cynthia Taft Morris. 1974. "Growth, Income Distribution, and Equity-Oriented Development Strategies." *World Development* 4:67–76.

Becker, Gary. 1983. "The Theory of Competition among Pressure Groups for Political Influence." *Quarterly Journal of Economics* 93 (August): 372–400.

Bejarano, J. A. 1985. *Economía y Poder: La SAC y el Desarrollo Agropecuario Colombiano, 1871–1984.* Bogotá: Fondo Editorial CEREC.

Berry, Albert, and William Cline. 1979. *Agrarian Structure and Productivity in Developing Countries.* Baltimore: Johns Hopkins University Press.

Binswanger, Hans, and Miranda Elgin. 1989. "What Are the Prospects for Land Reform?" In *Agriculture and Governments in an Interdependent World,* edited by Allen Maunder and Alberto Valdés. Aldershot, U.K.: Dartmouth Publishing.

de Janvry, Alain. 1981. *The Agrarian Question and Reformism in Latin America.* Baltimore: Johns Hopkins University Press.

Eswaran, Mukesh, and Ashok Kotwal. 1986. "Access to Capital and Agrarian Production Organization." *Economic Journal* 96 (June): 482–98.

Kalmanovitz, Salomon. 1978. *Desarrollo de la Agricultura en Colombia.* Bogotá: Editorial La Carreta.

Lorente, L., A. S. P. Salazar, and A. Gallo. 1985. *Distribución de la Propriedad Rural en Colombia, 1960–1984.* Bogotá: Corporación de Estudios Ganaderos y Agrícolas.

Moncayo, Victor. 1986. "Política Agraria y Desarrollo Capitalista." In *Problemas Agrarios Colombianos,* edited by A. Machado. México: Siglo XXI Editores.

Reinhardt, Nola. 1988. *Our Daily Bread: The Peasant Question and Family Farming in the Colombian Andes.* Berkeley: University of California Press.

Scobie, Grant, and Rafael Posada. 1977. *The Impact of High-Yielding Rice Varieties in Latin America, with Special Emphasis on Colombia.* Cali, Colombia: International Center for Tropical Agriculture.

Valencia González, S. 1982. "Experiencia de la Fase I del Programa DRI y Recommendaciones para la Fase II." DNP-UEA Working Paper. Bogotá: Dirección Nacional de Planeación.

Zusman, Pinhas. 1976. "The Incorporation and Measurement of Social Power in Economic Models." *International Economic Review* 17(2): 447–62.

35

Agricultural Reform in Central and Eastern Europe

JOHAN F. M. SWINNEN

INTRODUCTION

 The agro-food sector in Central and Eastern Europe has undergone dramatic changes since 1989. Poland started first, liberalizing most of its agricultural and food prices in October 1989. Other Central and Eastern European countries (CEECs) followed.[1] Since then all of them have also started privatization of collective and state farm assets and of the upstream (input) and downstream (processing and marketing) industries. Major disruptions in the agro-food sector have resulted from these reforms and from the dramatic changes in the general economic environment that occurred simultaneously.

At the same time, agricultural reforms have had important impacts on the general economy. The share of the agriculture and food sector in the economy in CEECs is large in comparison with OECD countries. The share of agriculture in total employment ranges from 6 percent in the Czech Republic, the most industrialized country, to 60 percent in Albania, the most agrarian society (see table 1). The share of food in consumption expenditures varies between 25 percent in Hungary and 60–70 percent in Romania and Albania.

This chapter analyzes the agricultural reforms in the CEECs and their impact. The first section summarizes key characteristics of the prereform agro-food sector, which influence the ongoing reforms. Then several important policy and institutional changes—land reform, privatization, and price and trade policy reform—are discussed in more detail. The last sections discuss reforms in the food system and in the credit market.

THE PRETRANSITION FOOD AND AGRICULTURAL ECONOMY

FOOD CONSUMPTION

For decades, citizens of CEECs were offered stable and subsidized food prices. Retail food prices changed little in nominal terms for several decades, despite

JOHAN F. M. SWINNEN is associate professsor of agricultural economics, Catholic University of Leuven, Belgium.

TABLE 1
IMPORTANCE OF AGRICULTURE AND FOOD IN CEECs, 1994

	Share of Agriculture in GNP (%)	Share of Agriculture in Employment (%)	Share of Food in Consumer Expenditures (%)	Agriculture and Food Trade Balance (millions US$)
Albania	56.0	60.0	72.0	−70
Bulgaria	9.0	9.0	37.8	317
Czech Republic	3.1	6.3	31.5	−268
Hungary	8.9	6.7	25.0	1,178
Poland	6.0	25.4	30.0	−302
Romania	22.0	34.0	60.0	−251
Slovakia	6.5	8.4	38.0	−213
Slovenia	4.5	11.5	28.0	−338

Source: OECD 1995.

growth in nominal incomes. The food subsidies were a heavy burden on the state budget. Despite the heavily subsidized prices, food absorbed a large share of income. A comparison of physical consumption levels between the pretransition CEECs and West European market economies indicates some important differences (Brooks et al. 1991). Caloric intake was the same as that in market economies with higher levels of income per capita. Meat and dairy product consumption was especially high in comparison with market economies of similar per capita income levels. This consumption pattern resulted from distorted prices, particularly from high subsidies for livestock and dairy products. The subsidy system benefited mostly wealthier urban groups in society, who had better access and consumed more of the most subsidized products.

However, since markets did not clear at these official prices, the actual prices that people paid were higher than official prices. As the gap between official prices and market-clearing prices grew, queues lengthened and sales on legal and illegal alternative markets increased. Excess demand was fueled by macroeconomic imbalance. The monetary overhang increased as growth in wages exceeded growth in opportunities to consume and invest.

THE ORGANIZATION OF AGRICULTURAL PRODUCTION

Pretransition Central and Eastern European agriculture was characterized by a dual production structure. A small-scale private sector based on small private gardens and plots coexisted symbiotically with very large collective and state farms. However, this production structure differed considerably from one country to another and has varied over time (see table 2). In Poland and the former Yugoslavia, collectivization largely failed, and even under the communist regime the majority of farm production came from the private sector. The other extremes were Albania and the former USSR, where private farming occupied less than 2 percent of total agricultural land. In Bulgaria, all collectivized farms were consolidated with food processing and the rest of the agroindustry into huge agro-

TABLE 2
COMPARISON OF FARM STRUCTURE IN 1987 AND 1994

	State Farms (%)		Cooperatives (%)		Companies Partnerships (%)		Individual Farms (%)	
	1987	1994	1987	1994	1987	1994	1987	1994
Albania[a]	21.1	5.0	78.4	—	—	—	0.5	95.0
Bulgaria[b]	90.0[c]	7.0	—	48.2	—	0.9	10.0	43.9
Czech Republic	38.0	2.8	61.0	47.7	—	20.8	1.0	20.4
East Germany	7.7	—	82.5	35.9	—	44.2	9.7	19.9
Hungary[d]	14.9	—	71.4	29.3	—	33.2	13.7	22.3
Romania	29.8	13.3	54.7	13.7	—	11.9	15.6	61.1
Slovakia	26.0	20.3	68.0	69.9	—	4.6	6.0	5.3
Slovenia	11.0	8.0	—	—	—	—	89.0	92.0

SOURCE: Pryor 1992, European Union Commission 1995, and Swinnen, Buckwell, and Mathijs 1997.
[a]Before reform: 1983 and based on cultivated land.
[b]After reform: based on arable land.
[c]Includes agroindustrial complexes of which an important part were previously collective farms.
[d]Companies include transformed state farms.

industrial complexes in the early 1970s. Beginning in 1986 these complexes were abolished. Countries such as Hungary and the former Czechoslovakia had a majority of cooperative farms. Hungary slowly reformed its food system over several years, giving more autonomy to the individual cooperatives than did other CEECs, especially during more liberal political periods. In Hungary, conservative crackdowns led to freezes on reform programs and recentralizations of the production system (Juhasz 1991).

Originally, farm workers in collective farms (*kolkhozes*) were remunerated at the end of the year based on the performance of the collective farm. Collective farms enjoyed somewhat more autonomy than state farms (*sovkhozes*) in their decisions. In state farms all assets, including land, were owned by the state, and farm workers were like employees in any other industrial firm, receiving fixed wages and social security benefits. Gradually, however, collective farm workers began to receive the same social benefits as state farm workers. By the 1980s, workers in both state farms and cooperatives had a high degree of job and wage security, little responsibility for the financial performance of the farm, and little incentive to improve productivity. Both types of farms were protected from bankruptcy by a soft budget constraint. While land ownership titles remained in collective farm members' possession, effective property rights were strongly in the hands of collective farm management or the state.

Farm workers were allowed to have a small garden or private plot, where they could grow vegetables and fruits for their own consumption. Private farming provided an increasing share of the fresh food supply (especially vegetables and fruits) and supplied the rural areas with food at a time when the production from large-scale farms was very low. This subsistence level of food supply reduced political pressure and, therefore, postponed fundamental changes in the agricultural system.

YIELDS, PRICES, AND WAGES

Crop and livestock production yields were between the yields of the intensive production system of Western Europe and the extensive production system of major agricultural exporters, such as the United States, Canada, and Australia (Brooks et al. 1991). These yields were obtained by high input use, resulting in high unit costs of production. In addition, widespread application of fertilizers, pesticides, mechanization, and irrigation contributed to important environmental and health problems.

Despite the lower labor productivity in agriculture, agricultural wages were approximately equal to other sectors, with income from private plots adding to an even higher total income.[2] High wages were sustained by relatively high fixed purchase prices for agricultural products plus recurrent loans and grants to farms. A peculiar feature of the centrally planned system was that government-controlled procurement organizations paid different prices to different farms for the same product. Price differentiation entered through zonal pricing and through the bonus system. The most important bonuses were quality differentials, bonuses for sales in excess of a moving average of past years sales, and premium prices for farms in financial stress. Differentiated prices and meticulous measurement of land quality were intended to capture rents the farms earned through their preferential access to land at no cost (Brooks 1991).

AGROINDUSTRY

Prereform agroindustry was highly concentrated, and food processing, distribution, and input supply were managed by several large state monopolies. Storage and distribution management were poor, and production in excess of distribution capacity was often wasted. With pervasive excess demand for food, processors had little regard for product definition and quality. Moreover, processing technology was outdated and technological constraints further reduced the efficiency and quality of processing. Modernization of food processing was dependent on direct budgetary allocations, instead of commercially based investments. The rising fiscal burden of direct food subsidies was reducing budgets available for investments in food processing. Further, food processing was considered light industry and thus given low priority by the government. Finally, central planning problems and the low level of political influence possessed by agricultural enterprises resulted in the wrong inputs often being supplied to agriculture or the most critical inputs simply being unavailable.

LAND REFORM, PRIVATIZATION, AND FARM RESTRUCTURING

Land reforms, and privatization in general, in Central and Eastern European agriculture have had important effects on efficiency and on income distribution.

Empirical evidence suggests that secure and unrestricted private property rights to land and other productive assets are essential to ensuring the most efficient form of agricultural production. Privatization and land reform also change the distribution of income and wealth. In the case of land reforms in CEECs, the distributional effects include two separate issues: the social ("equity") considerations of the reforms and the legal ("historical justice") demands of precollectivization land owners whose land was confiscated by the communist regime or who were forced to participate in the collectivization.

Productivity improvements required a reform of the large-scale collective and state farms, which were inefficient organizations because they reflected suboptimal factor allocations and incorporated poor incentive structures. Restructuring therefore has included both a reallocation of production factors (land, labor, and capital) and an organizational reform (e.g., from cooperative to family farm or to a joint stock company).

LAND REFORM AND PRIVATIZATION PROCESSES

Restitution of collective farm land to former owners and sale of state farm land are the most common forms of land privatization in CEECs (see table 3). A significant share of collective farm land has been returned to former owners in the majority of CEECs. Typically, land was returned to former owners using historical boundaries where possible. Otherwise, former owners were given property rights to a plot of land of comparable size and quality. The main exceptions to the restitution of collective farm land are (1) the sale (for compensation bonds) of two-thirds of the land used by Hungarian cooperatives, (2) the land distribution in kind to the rural population in Albania, and (3) the land distribution in

TABLE 3
LAND PRIVATIZATION METHODS

	Collective Farm Land	State Farm Land
Albania	Distribution (in kind)	Distribution (in kind)[a]
Bulgaria	Restitution	Miscellaneous
Czech Republic	Restitution	Sale (leasing[b])
East Germany	Restitution	Sale (leasing[b])
Hungary	Restitution + distribution (in kind) + sale for compensation bonds	Sale for compensation bonds + sale (leasing[b])
Latvia	Restitution	Restitution
Lithuania	Restitution	Restitution
Poland		Sale (leasing[b])
Romania	Restitution + distribution (in kind)	Undecided + restitution
Russia	Distribution in shares	Distribution (in shares)
Slovakia	Restitution	Sale (leasing[b])
Slovenia		Restitution
Ukraine	Distribution in shares	Distribution (in shares)

[a]Farm workers received vouchers in newly established joint ventures. However, as most of these joint ventures failed, farm workers received first-user rights and eventually full property rights.

[b]Land is leased to individuals or entities of sale.

shares in Russia and Ukraine. In the majority of CEECs, state farm land is being sold. The land is leased until sales are implemented. For example, in the former East Germany, nationalized land is managed by the Land Utilization and Administration Company and leased to former owners and to legal entities.

The main determinants behind these land reform choices are the postcollectivization legal ownership, ethnic factors, precollectivization land distribution, and efficiency considerations (Swinnen 1997). As a rule, land is never returned to foreigners. In addition, land that was still privately owned in 1989 has been returned to its owners. All agricultural land was nationalized by the communist regimes in the former Soviet Union and Albania. However, in all other CEECs, at least part of the land remained privately owned by individuals who joined the collectives (or by their heirs). Even in Bulgaria, where the collective farms were reorganized into huge state agroindustrial complexes, formal land ownership remained in private hands.

Land redistribution programs typically have five stages: (1) claims are submitted; (2) ownership certificates are issued, indicating the rightful claim of the person or family to an asset; (3) the precise value of the asset is calculated and/or land parcels are redrawn and the precise land parcel identified; (4) surveys are completed; and (5) land titles are issued. The uncertainty over property rights is solved only in the fifth stage.

REFORM IMPLEMENTATION

Commissions and agencies have been created in all CEECs to handle the agricultural privatization and land reform program. In the former Czechoslovakia, each cooperative and state farm has elected a transformation board to handle the privatization of the farm. The management of Bulgarian collective farms was assumed by the Liquidation Council, which is responsible for the privatization of farm assets and the management of the farms during the transition. Under the land restitution program, the claims of land ownership are handled by municipal land councils. Romania has similar commissions in each village to redraw the maps and allocate the land among claimants. In many instances the members of these councils represented collective farm interests—which were opposed to farm disruptions and land restitution. The inherent transaction costs and asymmetric information in reform implementation have allowed local agents to manipulate the reform implementation and limit the transfer of effective property rights.

In many CEECs these developments have been reenforced by additional land reform legislation—often implemented under pressure of collective farm members and supported by former communist parties—to limit the rights of new owners to use and transfer the land. For example, Slovenia has introduced the concept of "co-ownership of land" to give the former state farms security of operation during an "adjustment period" of several years, during which the state farms can continue their operation, without fear of being disrupted, on land destined for restitution.

Local opposition has slowed reform implementation, as have technical and legal complexities. For example, Hungary's reforms have been slowed considerably by the introduction of additional compensation laws after the start of the reforms. In Poland, Hungary, and the Czech Republic, the slow pace of reform has resulted in amendments to the original laws, to speed up the process and penalize opposition. On the other hand, in Romania and Albania, where reform started fairly late, a fast and widespread "spontaneous privatization" has resulted in a quick de facto large private agricultural sector.

A slow privatization process prolongs the uncertainty of property rights. As long as property rights are uncertain, decapitalization of agriculture continues through the liquidation of productive assets, including the slaughtering of livestock, and a reduction of investment and maintenance. Since land titles have not been assigned, a land market cannot emerge and producers cannot obtain credit for purchasing basic inputs. With low overall profitability in farming, the poorly developed banking system refuses to lend to agricultural producers without collateral. Under these circumstances, agricultural output declines further and incomes continue to fall.

THE EMERGING FARM STRUCTURE

The emerging farm structure is determined by the privatization and land reform process, and other economic, political, and institutional factors. The economic factors include the impact of transition risk and uncertainty, and negative terms-of-trade developments. A key political factor is the use of decollectivization and land restitution to create an anticommunist political base of small property owners in the rural areas.

Most CEECs now have a mix of "private" cooperative farms, joint-stock companies, family farms, and part-time farmers. The mix varies among CEECs (see table 2). Currently, virtually all farms in Albania are individual farms smaller than 5 hectares and virtually all farming in Slovakia is by large-scale cooperatives and farming companies of more than 100 hectares. The latter situation is more typical of the region; even in Romania, where very small farms occupy around 60 percent of the land, there is still a substantial number of large-scale farms (Organization for Economic Co-operation and Development [OECD] 1993, 1994, 1995, 1996).[3]

The break-up of the collective farms is substantially higher in CEECs where an important share of the land was distributed to farm workers (Albania and Romania) instead of being returned to former owners. In comparison with other procedures, distribution of farm land to workers reduces the transaction costs of renting or selling land and other assets for individuals wanting to leave the collective farms (Mathijs and Swinnen 1996). Further, government policies differ in the incentives or hurdles they have created for individual farming. For example, the dominance of individual farms of 5–100 hectares in Latvia is due in part to a government policy that focused explicitly on the recreation of precollectivization farm structure (OECD 1996; Swinnen 1997). By contrast, the Slova-

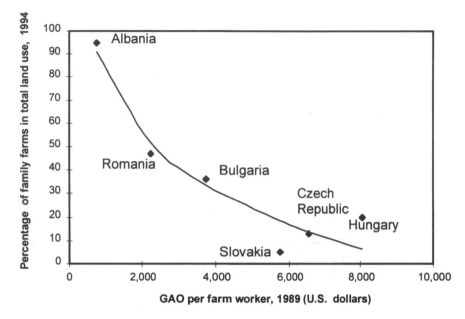

Fig. 1. Relationship between Importance of Family Farming in 1994 and Gross Agricultural Output (GAO) per Farm Worker in 1989 (Source: Mathijs and Swinnen 1996. Note: In U.S. dollars weighted by 1995 prices. Curve is based on a least squares regression after a logarithmic transformation of GAO per farm worker.)

kian government has protected the large-scale farms. Whereas in the Czech Republic a "sanction" law was approved to penalize cooperatives that did not fulfill property claims, such a law was not approved by the Slovak government, and enforcement costs therefore increased for individuals wanting to withdraw their assets. Moreover, Slovak cooperatives are allowed to issue vouchers, which will be tradable only after seven years, further restricting the property rights of Slovak former owners (Kabat and Hagedorn 1997).

Another important factor determining the emerging farm structure is the average productivity on collective farms. Individuals were more reluctant to leave the large-scale farms in countries where the collective farms were most productive and least labor intensive. This is illustrated in figure 1, which shows a negative correlation between the break-up of collective farms into family farms and the prereform average productivity of the collective farms (Mathijs and Swinnen 1996).

OUTPUT EFFECTS, EFFICIENCY, AND LONG-RUN DEVELOPMENTS

A striking observation is that the CEECs with the most dramatic disruption in the farm structure have realized the strongest growth in agricultural production. For example, Albanian agricultural output has increased sharply every year since the beginning of its reforms and Romania has had positive agricultural output growth since 1993. In contrast, gross agricultural output in Hungary continued to fall and only leveled out in 1995. In Hungary, the Czech Republic, and Slovakia, output has fallen more sharply in absolute terms, but the reduction in the farm labor force induced by farm restructuring has led to important productivity improvements.

Two questions emerge for the future. First, will extreme fragmentation become a major impediment to sustained growth in the coming years? For example, is the rapid growth in Romania and Albania merely a short-run phenomenon due to the extremely low output and productivity of collective farms in these countries before the reforms? An efficient and transparent land market, including well-defined property rights, will be required to overcome the threat of land fragmentation. In most CEECs, only an informal land market has developed so far. However, a transparent land market may be insufficient. Experience shows that market transactions may not result in sufficient land consolidation to create productivity improvements, and that major land consolidations typically arrive only through government programs (Platteau 1992).

Second, which types of farms will survive in the long run in those CEECs with a variety of emerging farms? The general opinion seems to be that on average individual farms in CEECs are too small and large farms still too large for efficient production in the long run. Most agricultural economists are skeptical about the survival chances of cooperative organizations in agricultural production activities. Some argue that it is just a matter of time until family (managed) farms will prevail, for they have major transaction costs advantages over cooperative organizations (Schmitt 1993; Hagedorn 1992).

REFORM OF TRADE, PRICE, AND TAX POLICIES

Prior to the reforms, prices, production, and trade were determined by the state, often reflecting political rather than economic (comparative advantage) objectives and resulting in distortions and inefficiencies in production, consumption, and trade patterns. Price and trade liberalizations, including subsidy cuts, are aimed at allowing prices to reflect factor scarcity, consumer preferences and comparative advantages. Market prices, in combination with decentralized decision making by independent agents and organizations, allow a more efficient distribution of information and more flexible reactions of consumers and producers to changes in the environment, thus ensuring a more efficient allocation of consumption, production, and trade.

Initially, prices and trade regimes were liberalized and subsidies abolished. Consumer prices soared, real incomes often declined, and domestic demand fell. In addition, foreign market access had been reduced, as the traditional agricultural export markets in the former Soviet Union dwindled because of lack of hard currency and because the Western countries maintained trade barriers for CEEC agricultural exports. At the same time, input prices for agriculture increased relative to producer prices. The result was a decline in the terms of trade for most agricultural producers. As this decline continued, demand for government intervention increased.

In the second phase of reform, agricultural policies to support farmers and consumers were reintroduced on an ad hoc basis, adding to the uncertainty induced by general economic reforms and privatization programs. More and more market and price interventions emerged, as dramatic declines in real incomes increased political demand for government intervention. These interventions included not only import tariffs, export subsidies, and guaranteed minimum prices, but also maximum prices and export restrictions. Since food security issues were important political concerns, governments tried to behave in a risk-averse way in setting food policies. However, the government and the administrators of the policies were inexperienced in dealing with the uncertainty of the emerging market environment. For example, measures that had been effective in the past, such as price controls and trading restraints (import and export licences, quotas, or outright bans), generated some unanticipated policy effects in the new environment. Some CEEC governments reacted by introducing more restrictions and ad hoc regulations. As a result, agricultural policy making acquired the characteristics of a fire brigade (OECD 1993, 1994, 1995, 1996).[4]

In the third stage, as the CEEC governments gained familiarity with the characteristics of the market economy and its reactions to government interventions, they moved from ad hoc policy interventions to formulating a comprehensive set of agricultural policies for the future. Several CEECs have installed policies that resemble those of the European Union's Common Agricultural Policy (CAP) prior to the MacSharry reforms. Such CAP-style agricultural policy packages include guaranteed prices, production quotas, (variable) export subsidies, and import levies.

The introduction of CAP-style policies does not necessarily imply heavy producer protection. Between 1992 and 1993, price and trade interventions increased the average real protection rate (RPR)[5] from 3 percent to around 20 percent (for six CEECs and nine products). The RPR has since decreased slightly but varies widely across countries (Bojnec and Swinnen 1995). Slovenia is subsidizing agriculture heavily (70–80 percent), followed by Hungary, which protects those sectors which face competition from imports. Average RPRs in the Czech Republic and Slovakia vary between -4 percent and +11 percent, somewhat less than in Poland, where they average 15 percent. In contrast, Bulgaria is heavily taxing its agricultural sector, primarily through export constraints on its grain sector.

The reemergence of these protectionist policy regimes in CEECs has been explained by some as being driven by the CEECs' strategy to gain EU membership by creating an agricultural policy that is consistent with the EU's CAP. But the reemergence of interventionist policies in the Central and Eastern European agro-food sector is primarily driven by domestic political economy factors (Swinnen 1993, 1996a). This analysis suggests that future policy changes will be further affected by domestic political economy factors, which in turn depend on structural changes in the economies. As the CEEC economies grow and reforms continue, a number of structural effects will occur simultaneously, such as a decline in the comparative advantage of agriculture, a decline in the share of food in consumer expenditures and in total GDP, improvement of processing, an increase in the capital-labor ratio in agriculture, and the importance of family farms. Some of these effects have opposite impacts on agricultural protection. However, on aggregate, the incentives for politicians to increase agricultural protection are expected to increase in the medium-to-long run (Swinnen 1994, 1996a).

Since domestic political economy factors will provide incentives for governments to increase price and trade distortions, international agreements will become more important as constraints on trade and price interventions. They reduce the government's policy choice set and alter its incentives in decision making. In particular, the GATT Uruguay Round Agreement (URA) limits future CEEC trade and price interventions. For several of the CEECs, the URA commitments may become binding constraints on their policies.

Another international agreement with a potentially important impact on CEEC agricultural price and trade policies is the recent proposal to extend the Central European Free Trade Agreement (CEFTA) to agricultural trade. If free trade regulations will be applied to agriculture, they will impose constraints on policy options of the CEECs that are involved (Poland, Hungary, Slovakia, and the Czech Republic) and those that want to join this trade agreement (Slovenia).

A third factor is the EU-integration strategy: as it becomes more likely that EU integration will occur in the medium term, one should expect that EU-CEEC agricultural policy alignment will become more important in future CEEC agricultural policy making. Of course, much will depend on the EU's proposed strategy for integration. According to many studies (e.g., Buckwell et al. 1995 and Tangermann and Josling 1995), further CAP reform will be unavoidable, in the light of CEEC accession and GATT commitments. But there remains much uncertainty about what the CAP will look like at the time of accession and how it will therefore influence policy alignment. Before this information is available, CEEC policy makers, even if they want to base their policy strategy on minimizing adjustment costs of integration with the future CAP, can only try to hit a moving target.

REFORM OF THE FOOD SYSTEM

Privatization and de-monopolization in the input supply and processing industry are a *conditio sine qua non* for an effective reform of the agricultural and food sector. Without a more efficient allocation of inputs and a competitive, more efficient, and more quality-oriented processing and distribution sector, reforms in the farm-level production sphere will not be reflected at the retail level. The lack of improvement also prohibits exports to Western markets. Furthermore, the transition restructuring still leaves room for rent extraction due to remaining marketing imperfections and collusive vertical integration. While there is much ad hoc discussion of these practices, data are unavailable to measure this. An exception is the study by Ivanova et al. (1995) on transfers in the Bulgarian agrofood chain. They show that while farmers are taxed to keep grain prices low, consumers benefit little from this. Most of the rents are collected by the processing and trading enterprises, because of the continuing market power of the now-privatized former state monopolies and because of collusive practices that occur between enterprise managers and potential investors during privatization (Swinnen 1996b).

In Bulgaria, privatization of up- and downstream industries is part of the mass privatization program, which started in 1995. Only a small minority (around 20 percent) of food-processing enterprises have been privatized, and the core upstream and downstream enterprises are still state owned. In the Czech Republic, the second wave of voucher privatization almost completed the privatization. Strong competition between enterprises in specific food-processing sectors is the principal factor promoting structural changes. In Hungary, the state still owns nearly one-third of the capital of the food-processing companies, but no sector remains under majority state control. Almost all upstream state-owned companies have been privatized; most were sold to management and employee groups. In the Slovak Republic, 80 percent of state-owned food-processing enterprises have been privatized (OECD 1996).

Trading activities are essentially being privatized through the entry of new firms. State trading monopolies were disbanded early on in the Czech and Slovak Republics, Hungary, and Poland, so that private individuals could engage in trade with relatively few restrictions. Also, in Romania and Bulgaria, trade restrictions have been eased, but state trading monopolies continue to play a very important role in some of the key food sectors. The privatization of the state grain trading monopolies is politically very sensitive and conceptually difficult because of the mixture of functions these companies were fulfilling under the central planning system: contracting, purchasing, storing grain, selling grains and oilseeds, as well as storing national reserves, exporting, importing and providing services. Some of these functions can be performed better by private enterprises in a market economy, but some activities are typically considered roles for the government in market economies, complicating the privatization of these enterprises.

In general, reform of the food-processing industry has progressed faster than that of the input industries. One reason is that low profitability in agricultural production reduces the attractiveness of investment in the upstream sector. A second factor is the size of the industry: downstream activities on average can (in the short and medium run) be performed well by relatively small-scale firms. Overall, privatization of small(er) companies has taken place earlier than privatization of large-scale enterprises in most countries, and a large share of the early privatized small(er) scale enterprises were involved in food distribution and processing. At the beginning of the transition, the growth in private sector food-processing activities was due less to the privatization of state-owned food companies than to the emergence of many small and medium-sized private firms.

Also within the food industry there are important differences between subsectors. In general, sectors producing high-value finished products, such as vegetable oils, confectionery, tobacco, and beer, were privatized quickly, often with foreign and multinational participation. Other product areas, such as meats and dairy products, have proven more difficult (OECD 1996). Another factor affecting foreign direct investment is the competitive environment. Boeckenhoff and Moeller (1993) found that in Hungary markets with low competition due to high market concentration and high barriers to entry were more likely to attract foreign direct investment.

AGRICULTURAL CREDIT

Agricultural production activities and investments in productivity improvements require access to credit for financing working capital and investments, especially when the applicant's own resources for financing are limited. CEEC agricultural producers faced important credit constraints during transition, which had negative effects on both production and farm restructuring.

Credit and risk markets in the most advanced countries work imperfectly, largely because of the imperfection and high cost of information, which are particularly important in agriculture. In addition to "normal" imperfections, a series of specific, transition-related problems have constrained the financing of the Central and Eastern European agricultural economy since 1989. First, the nature and role of credit is different in a planned economy than in a market economy. In centrally planned economies, the main monetary policy instrument was credit allocation. Second, the banking sector is also undergoing a major transformation, so credit markets are underdeveloped. The lack of experience and skills of banking officials in dealing in a market economy pose serious problems, as loan evaluation procedures are very different than in a planned economy. Third, credit supply in the system is further limited because of the decline of the CEEC economies during the transition. The CEECs cannot generate enough of the capital needed for development of their economies. Fourth, accumulated bad debts during the centrally planned economies create problems in two directions: they ration the supply of credit and hamper the speed of privatization and land restitution. Fifth, lack of collateral due to uncertain property rights, low profitability, and macroeconomic uncertainty make banks view the agricultural sector as a high-risk investment (Swinnen 1995).

The credit constraints during agricultural transition impose high costs in terms of rural unemployment and poverty, distortion of production, and liquidation of assets (Brooks et al. 1991). A costly transition is more likely to be interrupted or reversed politically, a danger which is evident from the heated political debates in all CEECs. Consequently, governments have attempted to overcome the problem by subsidizing credit and setting up credit guarantee funds. Some programs, such as credit subsidies, have not been very successful, as they do not overcome the key transition problems. Also, there is a high probability that programs intended to improve access to credit during transition will become a permanent feature of agricultural policy. Subsidized credit has been used in many countries to overcome actual or perceived failures in financial markets and discrimination against agriculture. The record of subsidized credit programs and the institutions created to deliver it in developing countries is poor (Calomiris 1993).

Some of the financing problems of the agricultural sector are specific to the transition process (e.g., the collateral problems). However, high nominal interest rates and the lack of liquidity and financial infrastructure are likely to remain important impediments in the medium run. To the extent that current government programs, such as credit subsidies and high-risk government-backed loan guarantees, will add to the budget deficit and will increase government's debts, they will drive up interest rates in the future and will turn out to be counterproductive in the longer run.

CONCLUSION

Agricultural reform has caused dramatic changes in the agro-food sector in Central and Eastern Europe. Price and trade liberalization has caused dramatic price, consumption, and output adjustments. Privatization and land reform reinstated private property rights and induced a restructuring of the collective and state farms. All this has importantly affected the general economy and the political debates, because the agro-food sector occupies a large share in employment, output, and consumption in Central and Eastern European economies.

The choice of the reform policies and the impact of the reforms differ substantially among the countries of Central and Eastern Europe. While Slovenia is heavily subsidizing farmers, Bulgaria is focusing on trying to keep consumer prices low and in the process is taxing producers, e.g., through export restrictions. While most CEECs have chosen to return collective farm land to former owners, some CEECs have distributed land to farm workers. The emerging farm structure differs sharply between CEECs, from a complete fragmentation of land and break-up of the collective and state farms in Albania, to a strong consolidation of the large-scale structures in Slovakia. Furthermore, the output responses to liberalization and property rights reform differ strongly as well.

The completion of the remaining privatization and restructuring in the food system is necessary in order to reduce the legal and institutional uncertainties in the market. Uncertainty and the lack of clear and legal property rights is the major impediment for the development of the land market and a major reason for the continued decapitalization of agriculture. Furthermore, any improvement in the financing of agricultural production and any investment in new technology are contingent on the establishment of clear property rights.

Both political and economic forces are determining the reform policies and their effects. Political considerations (reflecting historical and distributional factors) have been the primary determinants of the choice of land reform policies (Swinnen 1997). On the other hand, the main determinants of the break-up of the collective and state farms and the emergence of individual farming seems to be economic: the break-up of the collective farms is strongest where collective farm productivity was lowest, and where the opportunity costs of leaving the farms were lowest. Government policies have primarily affected this process indirectly, that is, through their impact on the access of potential farmers to land and other assets and by changing the costs of leaving the collective farm.

Price and trade policy developments have also been determined by a combination of liberalizations within the general economic reforms and by the reintroduction of price and trade interventions induced by political considerations following pressures from various interest groups in society, reflecting the policies' income-distributional effects. These political economy factors have increasingly dominated price and trade policy choices and suggest that international agreements such as GATT, CEFTA, and the integration of the EU will provide important and credible constraints on the response of CEEC governments to domestic pressures for redistributive market interventions.

NOTES

1. The analysis in this chapter is based largely on information from Albania, Bulgaria, the Czech Republic, Slovakia, Hungary, Poland, Latvia, Lithuania, and Slovenia.

2. There is always a measurement problem. In most CEECs, "workers" in agriculture included many old persons and part-time workers. However, wages were usually quoted as being for "full-time" workers.

3. Farms in the 5–100 hectare range have been recreated in Lithuania and Latvia during the reform process.

4. For example, Ivanova, Mishev, and Tzenova 1995 reports that from 1991 to 1995 more than twenty changes occurred in government policies and decrees regulating the Bulgarian grain market.

5. Real protection rates measure the difference between domestic prices and so-called reference prices, adjusted for divergences between nominal and equilibrium exchange rates.

REFERENCES

Boeckenhoff, G., and K. Moeller. 1993. "Foreign Direct Investment into Hungarian Industries." Paper presented at the Seventh EAAE Congress, Stresa, Italy, September 6–10.

Bojnec, S., and J. Swinnen. 1995. "The Pattern of Agricultural Protection in Central Europe." Working Paper, Leuven Institute for Central and East European Studies, Leuven, Belgium.

Brooks, K. 1991. "Price Adjustment and Land Valuation in the Soviet Agricultural Reform: A View Using Lithuanian Farm Data." *European Review of Agricultural Economics* 18 (1): 19–34.

Brooks, K. M., J. L. Guasch, A. Braverman, and C. Csaki. 1991. "Agriculture and the Transition to the Market." *Journal of Economic Perspectives* 5 (4): 149–61.

Buckwell, A., J. Haynes, S. Davidova, and A. Kwiecinski. 1995. *Feasibility of an Agricultural Strategy to Prepare the Countries of Central and Eastern Europe for EU Accession,* Final Report to DG-I, Brussels: European Union Commission.

Calomiris, C. W. 1993. "Agricultural Capital Markets." In *The Agricultural Transition in Central and*

Eastern Europe and the Former U.S.S.R., edited by A. Braverman, K. M. Brooks, and C. Csaki. Washington D.C.: World Bank.

European Union Commission. 1995. *Agricultural Situation and Prospects in the Central and Eastern European Countries.* DG-IV, Brussels.

Hagedorn, K. 1992. "Transformation of Socialist Agricultural Systems." *Journal of International and Comparative Economics* 1:103–24.

Ivanova, N., J. Lingard, A. Buckwell, and A. Burrell. 1995. "Impact of Changes in Agricultural Policy on the Agro-Food Chain in Bulgaria" *European Review of Agricultural Economics* 22 (1995): 354–71.

Juhasz, J. 1991. "Hungarian Agriculture: Present Situation and Future Prospects." *European Review of Agricultural Economics* 18 (3): 399–416.

Kabat, L., and K. Hagedorn. 1997. "Privatization and Decollectivization Policies and Resulting Structural Changes of Agriculture in Slovakia." In *Agricultural Privatization, Land Reform and Farm Restructuring in Central and Eastern Europe,* edited by J. Swinnen, A. Buckwell, and E. Mathijs, 229–79. Aldershot, U.K.: Avebury Publishers.

Mathijs, E., and J. Swinnen. 1996. "The Economics of Agricultural Decollectivization in Central and Eastern Europe." Working Paper 3/1 of the FAIR Project Agricultural Implications of CEEC Accession to the EU, Department of Agricultural Economics, Catholic University of Leuven.

Organization for Economic Co-operation and Development (OECD). 1993, 1994, 1995, 1996. *Agricultural Policies, Markets and Trade in the Central and East European Countries (CEECs), The New Independent States (NIS) and China: Monitoring and Outlook.* Paris: OECD.

Platteau, J. P. 1992. *Land Reform and Structural Adjustment in Sub-Saharan Africa: Controversies and Guidelines.* Food and Agriculture Organization Economic and Social Development Paper 107, Rome: FAO.

Pryor, F. L. 1992. *The Red and the Green: The Rise and Fall of Collectivised Agriculture in Marxist Regimes.* Princeton: Princeton University Press.

Schmitt, G. 1993. "Why Collectivization of Agriculture in Socialist Countries Really Has Failed: A Transaction Cost Approach." In *Agricultural Cooperatives in Transition,* edited by C. Csaki and Y. Kislev, 143–60. Boulder, Colo.: Westview Press.

Swinnen, J. 1993. "The Development of Agricultural Policies in Eastern Europe: An Endogenous Policy Theory Perspective." *Food Policy.* June: 187–91.

———. 1994. "A Positive Theory of Agricultural Protection. " *American Journal of Agricultural Economics* 76 (February): 1–14.

———. 1995. "Agricultural Credit Problems during the Transition to a Market Economy in Central and Eastern Europe." In *Agro-Food Sector Policy in OECD Countries and the Russian Federation,* 50–62. Paris: OECD Centre for Co-operation with the Economies in Transition.

———. 1996a. "Endogenous Price and Trade Policies in Central European Agriculture." *European Review of Agricultural Economics* 23 (2): 133–60.

———. 1996b. "On Policy Induced Transfers in the Bulgarian Agro-Food Chain: The Case of the Wheat-Flour-Bread Chain," Working Paper 3/3 of the FAIR Project, "Agricultural Implications of CEEC Accession to the EU," Department of Agricultural Economics, Catholic University of Leuven.

———, ed. 1997. *Political Economy of Agrarian Reform in Central and Eastern Europe.* Aldershot, U.K.: Avebury Publishers.

Swinnen J., A. Buckwell, and E. Mathijs, eds. 1997. *Agricultural Privatization, Land Reform and Farm Restructuring in Central and Eastern Europe.* Aldershot, U.K.: Avebury Publishers.

Tangermann, S., and T. Josling. 1995. *Pre-accession Policies for Central Europe and the EU,* Final Report to DG-I, Brussels: EU Commission.

Name Index

603

Subject Index

Library of Congress Cataloging-in-Publication Data

International agricultural development / edited by
Carl K. Eicher and John M. Staatz. — 3rd ed.
p.   cm. — (Johns Hopkins studies in development)
Updated ed. of: Agricultural development in the Third World. 2nd ed. c1990.
Includes bibliographical references and index.
ISBN 0-8018-5878-X (alk. paper). — ISBN 0-8018-5879-8
(pbk. : alk. paper)
1. Agriculture—Economic aspects—Developing countries.
2. Agriculture and state—Developing countries.
3. Rural development—Government Policy—Developing countries.
4. Agriculture—Economic aspects—Europe, Eastern.   5. Agriculture
and state—Europe, Eastern.   6. Rural development—
Government policy—Europe, Eastern.   I. Eicher, Carl K.
II. Staatz, John M.   III. Agricultural development
in the Third World.   IV. Series.
HD1417.A4483   1998
338.1′09172′4—dc21   98-3472   CIP